Colonial America

RICHARD MIDDLETON
AND ANNE LOMBARD

Colonial America

A History to 1763

FOURTH EDITION

WILEY-BLACKWELL

A John Wiley & Sons, Ltd., Publication

This fourth edition first published 2011
© 2011 Richard Middleton and Anne Lombard

Edition history: Blackwell Publishing (1e, 1992; 2e, 2001; 3e, 2002)

Blackwell Publishing was acquired by John Wiley & Sons in February 2007. Blackwell's publishing program has been merged with Wiley's global Scientific, Technical, and Medical business to form Wiley-Blackwell

Registered Office
John Wiley & Sons Ltd, The Atrium, Southern Gate, Chichester, West Sussex, PO19 8SQ, United Kingdom

Editorial Offices
350 Main Street, Malden, MA 02148-5020, USA
9600 Garsington Road, Oxford, OX4 2DQ, UK
The Atrium, Southern Gate, Chichester, West Sussex, PO19 8SQ, UK

For details of our global editorial offices, for customer services, and for information about how to apply for permission to reuse the copyright material in this book please see our website at www.wiley.com/wiley-blackwell.

Library of Congress Cataloging-in-Publication Data

Middleton, Richard, 1941–
  Colonial America : a history to 1763 / Richard Middleton and Anne Lombard. – 4th ed.
    p. cm.
  Includes bibliographical references and index.
  ISBN 978-1-4051-9004-6 (pbk. : alk. paper)
  1. United States–History–Colonial period, ca. 1600-1775. I. Lombard, Anne S. II. Title.
  E188.M52 2012
  973.2–dc22

                                                                          2010047220

A catalogue record for this book is available from the British Library.

This book is published in the following electronic formats: ePDFs [ISBN 9781444396270]; ePub [ISBN 9781444396287]

Set in 10/12.5pt Galliard by Thomson Digital, Noida, India
Printed and bound in Singapore by Fabulous Printers Pte Ltd

1 2011

Contents

Figures

Maps

Documents

Preface to the Fourth Edition ⸺

This book tells the story of the British North American colonies, from the initial encounters between Europeans and the Native Americans who lived here in the sixteenth century to the end of the Seven Years War in 1763, when Great Britain won political control over most of the territory in North America east of the Mississippi and north of the Gulf of Mexico.

Since the first edition of this book appeared in 1992, historical scholarship about this story has been substantially revised. History is always a work in progress, and the need to understand America's origins has been a compelling one for each generation of scholars. Not long ago the main objective of historians studying the colonial period was to understand the political and economic institutions created by British North Americans and their place in the development of democratic capitalist societies. Historians' focus, therefore, was mostly upon the Englishmen who settled in North America between 1607 and 1776 and the societies that they created.

Over time the scope of historians' questions about early British American history broadened. Scholars began to look not only at the roots of political democracy and social mobility but also at the origins of institutions such as slavery and indentured servitude. Assumptions about the impact of individuals on the historical process began to be questioned as historians realized that historical change is often shaped more by the unintentional consequences of interactions between many actors than by the intentional actions of a few. Rather than implicitly assuming that the only European colonists to influence North American history were men, researchers began to focus upon the impacts of European women on colonial development. Scholars became increasingly interested in the millions of Africans who were transported to the Americas during the seventeenth and eighteenth centuries, asking how their presence and their actions shaped the societies of which they became a part. Perhaps the most fruitful new questions concerned the millions of indigenous Americans who were killed, displaced, or assimilated into European-American societies as the colonies developed.

But these have not been the only changes. Since the ending of the Cold War in the early 1990s, scholarship on British colonial North America has experienced something of a paradigm shift as historians began to consider their findings in the light of globalization. Rather than focusing on the internal dynamics of particular societies, scholars have increasingly begun to consider the ways in which cross-border interactions have shaped the historical process. New questions have been raised about the contest between the English colonizers and indigenous American peoples for control of the land. More attention has also been paid to the efforts of competing European powers to gain ascendancy in North America. How did British competition with the Spanish, French, and Dutch for control of the population, territory, trade, commodity production, and naval dominance shape the growth of the English-speaking colonies? Another result of this paradigm shift has been the greater scrutiny of the transoceanic flow of commodities, pathogens, crops, livestock, and migrants. What were their impact on the economies, societies, and political institutions of communities on both sides of the Atlantic?

These changing trends in historical scholarship have inevitably been reflected in the evolution of this book. The first edition explained the political and institutional development of the early American colonies while also describing the lives of European-American women and families, African-Americans, and indigenous North American peoples during the colonial period. The second edition, in 1996, added newer scholarship about the history of indigenous peoples before the colonies began. The third edition, in 2002, provided more background on the transnational competition of England, France, and Spain for control over North America in the eighteenth century.

This new, fourth edition broadens the topic still further, incorporating a multiplicity of perspectives on colonial America. While we have retained much of the book's original focus on the origins and development of the British colonies in North America, we show that their creation was the product of interactions between a variety of peoples and nations with distinct histories, interests, and objectives. The story told here is not so much about the planting of English seeds in North American soil and their growth into American institutions, as about the many different groups of Europeans, Africans, and indigenous North Americans who competed as well as cooperated to gain control of North American resources. Their interactions transformed traditional legal, political, and social institutions and created a dynamic New World unlike the worlds in which any of these peoples, or their ancestors, had lived.

To make it easier for students to understand the implications of the new scholarship on colonial America, we have made some changes to the structure of the book. In Part I, to help students understand how transatlantic interactions between western Europeans, West Africans, and indigenous North Americans contributed to the creation of new societies in colonial America, we take a brief look at western European, African, and Native American societies *before* the fifteenth century Atlantic seagoing voyages that brought these three continents into sustained contact with one another. In Part II, we have sought to incorporate new findings about how Native American peoples influenced and responded to the colonizing process from the beginning. We chronicle their roles in shaping the earliest colonies, explore the origins and outcomes of major Indian wars and rebellions, and explain their roles in the various imperial wars fought on the continent before 1713. In addition, consistent with the broader geographical focus of recent scholarship, we have added new sections on the development of slavery in the British West Indies and the founding and expansion of New France.

Part III provides a topical rather than a chronological account of the economic, social, cultural, and political changes that took place within (and on the borders of)

British North America during the eighteenth century. Our own respective backgrounds, one as a scholar of political and military history and the other as a scholar of the history of gender and society, have informed our reframing of sections on Anglo-American women and families, and the section on the Seven Years War and the Indian wars that grew out of it. These chapters suggest that families' childbearing and economic decisions contributed to the growing North American demand for British goods that in turn helped convince the British government to invest in the defense of its North American possessions during the 1750s. We have extensively updated and rearranged chapters on Native Americans and the borderlands so as to highlight the roles played by Native Americans along with their French and Spanish allies in shaping the imperial contest for control over North America during the eighteenth century. We end the book not with the beginning of the American Revolution, but with the Seven Years War and the culmination of that long imperial contest in 1763.

This edition, like previous ones, provides a number of pedagogical tools designed to help students understand history as an interpretive process. To show how historical inquiry evolves, chapters feature brief discussions not only of the kinds of interpretive questions historians have asked about the period or a topic but also of how approaches to these questions have changed. Footnotes have also been provided in order to highlight new research questions and explain the evolution of particular historical debates. To encourage students to consider the relationship between primary sources and historical interpretation, we have included 28 primary source excerpts, along with questions to provoke discussion and analysis. We include a timeline at the beginning of each chapter so as to reinforce students' understanding of relationships between events across time, illustrations to give students a visual sense of the world they are learning about, and a total of 26 maps to help students place the peoples of colonial North America into a geographical context. Finally, we have compiled a selected bibliography to provide students with suggestions for further reading on topics of current historical interest.

Acknowledgments ―――――――――

We would like to acknowledge the help of Peter Arnade, Jessie Cammack, and the anonymous reviewers of this book for their comments and suggestions on various drafts of this new edition, or portions thereof, and thank Paul Mapp for generously sharing his unpublished manuscript. We are also grateful to all the students who offered suggestions regarding the book's contents, particularly Patricia Manley and Craig Frame. The editorial staff at Wiley-Blackwell was immensely helpful and professional. We would especially like to thank Peter Coveney, Galen Smith, and Jacqueline Harvey.

The authors and publisher gratefully acknowledge the permission granted to reproduce the copyright material in this book:

Document 2: From Karen Ordahl Kupperman, ed., *Major Problems in American Colonial History: Documents and Essays* (Lexington, Mass., 1993), 13. Paper, 1E © 1993 Wadsworth, a part of Cengage Learning, Inc. Reproduced by permission.

Document 5: From Warren M. Billings, *The Old Dominion in the Seventeenth Century: A Documentary History of Virginia, 1606–1689* (Chapel Hill, 1975), 216–19. Published for the Omohundro Institute of Early American History and Culture © 1975 by the University of North Carolina Press. Used by permission of the publisher.

Document 8: From Thomas Hutchinson, *The History of the Colony and Province of Massachusetts-Bay*, edited by Lawrence Shaw Mayo (Cambridge, Mass., 1936), Vol. 2, 368, 370, 383–4. Copyright © 1936 by the President and Fellows of Harvard College. Copyright © 1964 by Lawrence Shaw Mayo. Reprinted by permission of the publisher.

Document 9: From Karen Ordahl Kupperman, ed., *Major Problems in American Colonial History: Documents and Essays* (Lexington, Mass., 1993), 135. Paper, 1E © 1993 Wadsworth, a part of Cengage Learning, Inc. Reproduced by permission.

Document 14: From Thomas Hutchinson, *The History of the Colony and Province of Massachusetts-Bay*, edited by Lawrence Shaw Mayo (Cambridge, Mass., 1936), Vol. 2, 31–2, 34. Copyright ©1936 by the President and Fellows of Harvard College. Copyright © 1964 by Lawrence Shaw Mayo. Reprinted by permission of the publisher.

Document 16: From *The Papers of Benjamin Franklin*, edited by Leonard W. Labaree et al. (New Haven: Yale University Press, 1961), Vol. 4, 225–34.

Document 19: From *The Adams Papers: Diary and Autobiography of John Adams, Diary 1755–1770*, edited by L. H. Butterfield, Leonard C. Faber, and Wendell D. Garrett (Cambridge, Mass.: Belknap Press of Harvard University Press), Vol. 1, 54–5. Copyright © 1961 by the Massachusetts Historical Society. Reprinted by permission of the publisher.

Document 20: From Karen Ordahl Kupperman, ed., *Major Problems in American Colonial History: Documents and Essays* (Lexington, Mass., 1993), 454. Paper, 1E © 1993 Wadsworth, a part of Cengage Learning, Inc. Reproduced by permission.

Document 22: From Warren M. Billings, *The Old Dominion in the Seventeenth Century: A Documentary History of Virginia, 1606–1689* (Chapel Hill, 1975), 160. Published for the Omohundro Institute of Early American History and Culture © 1975 by the University of North Carolina Press. Used by permission of the publisher.

Document 23: From Karen Ordahl Kupperman, ed., *Major Problems in American Colonial History: Documents and Essays* (Lexington, Mass., 1993), 489. Paper, 1E © 1993 Wadsworth, a part of Cengage Learning, Inc. Reproduced by permission.

Every effort has been made to trace copyright holders and to obtain their permission for the use of copyright material. The publisher apologizes for any errors or omissions in the above list and would be grateful if notified of any corrections that should be incorporated in future reprints or editions of this book.

Part I

Old and New Worlds Meet

1

The Peoples of Eastern North America

Societies in Transition

30,000–11,000 BCE	Indian peoples migrate to North America from Asia via the Bering Strait.
11,000 BCE	The land bridge disappears as the climate warms.
5000 BCE	Agriculture begins to develop in Tehuacan Valley, Mexico.
1200 BCE	The first Mesoamerican civilization, the Olmecs, emerges.
500 BCE	Mayan civilization flourishes.
500 BCE–**400** CE	Adena and Hopewell cultures develop in the Ohio Valley.
600 CE	The Mississippi mound builders emerge.
1000 CE	Eastern Woodlands societies adopt agriculture.
1200 CE	The city of Cahokia's population numbers around 30,000.
1300 CE	The "Little Ice Age" begins.
1400 CE	The Mississippi mound builders disappear. Warfare becomes common among the Eastern Woodlands peoples.
1450 CE	The Iroquois form the League of Five Nations.

Colonial America: A History to 1763, Fourth Edition. Richard Middleton and Anne Lombard.
© 2011 Richard Middleton and Anne Lombard. Published 2011 by Blackwell Publishing Ltd.

1 AMERICA BEFORE COLUMBUS AND THE PROBLEM OF HISTORY

T HE STORY OF the North American British colonies begins in America. For well over 12,000 years before Columbus made his accidental landfall in the Bahamas, people had been living on the North and South American continents, where they had created agricultural societies and complex cultures, developed political systems, fought wars, and formed alliances. When Europeans began to arrive, first in 1492 and then with increasing frequency during the sixteenth and seventeenth centuries, it was these indigenous American people who decided whether the newcomers would be welcomed to stay or forced to flee for their lives. Native Americans would make key decisions that shaped diplomatic relationships, influenced the kinds of colonial societies that could be built in North America, and changed the course of empires. To understand how they influenced the colonial process – to understand why they behaved as they did – we need to begin with their story.

The problem for historians is *how* to tell that story. Unlike peoples who had developed a written language, the original Americans left no written records. Although surviving oral traditions can tell us a great deal about Native American origin stories and collective memories, they are far removed in time from the events they describe. Of course Europeans, once they arrived and began observing Native American peoples, produced all sorts of written records: descriptions, memoirs, pictures, maps, and other kinds of documents. All of these have provided historians with additional sources about Native American societies. But the testimony of fifteenth- and sixteenth-century Europeans about their encounters with indigenous Americans is deeply problematic as a source for twenty-first-century historians. Fifteenth-century Europeans had never imagined that the American continents existed, much less that there were people who had lived here for over 11,000 years. Thus when European observers like Christopher Columbus, Hernando de Soto, Jacques Cartier, and John White tried to understand who these people were and why they acted as they did, they were unable to comprehend this new world except in the context of their own experiences. The lens through which they viewed the Americas produced thousands of distortions and mistakes. Indeed the very term "Indian" was applied because Columbus was mistakenly convinced that he had arrived in Asia.[1]

The inaccuracies that crept into the earliest European records of encounters with Native Americans in North America have persisted in shaping the way we imagine the past. For example, one of the most commonly asserted misrepresentations of Native American peoples in the early modern era was that they were simple primitives, people who had not yet been caught up in the historical processes that were transforming the rest of the world by the end of the fifteenth century.[2] In the past many historians

---

[1]   The authors will employ the terms "Indian" and "Native American" interchangeably to refer to indigenous American peoples, since the use of both are generally accepted in the United States. A plurality of Americans of indigenous descent identify themselves as Indians or American Indians, but many use the term "Native Americans" instead.

[2]   The influence of America on the development of English historical thought from the sixteenth to the eighteenth centuries, is discussed in David Armitage, "The New World and British Historical Thought: From Richard Hakluyt to William Robertson," in Karen Ordahl Kupperman, ed., *America in European Consciousness, 1493–1750* (Chapel Hill, 1995), 52–75.

unwittingly contributed to this distortion by portraying the Indians as the helpless victims of European colonizers who had superior technology, broader worldly experience, and more lethal diseases.

More recently, however, historians have used a range of sources that go beyond conventional written records to reconstruct the histories of indigenous American peoples in North America *before* the arrival of Europeans. Evidence about climate change has allowed historians to estimate the dates of various changes in the North American environment, while archaeological evidence has provided information about the kinds of societies indigenous peoples developed as they adapted to these changes. Evidence about the behavior of Native Americans after the arrival of Europeans has been re-examined alongside the oral traditions of contemporary Native American peoples and the findings of ethnographers so as to understand that behavior in the context of their own cultural traditions and experiences. These sources have enabled historians to understand that the economies, cultures, and political relationships of Native Americans on the eastern seaboard of North America had already undergone a wrenching historical transformation over the 500 years between approximately 1000 and 1500 CE. Well before Columbus arrived on American shores, millions of Native American peoples had been swept up by a saga of war, diaspora, relocation, and rebirth, decades before any contemporary European even dreamed that they existed.[3]

2 THE AMERICAS IN ANCIENT TIMES

Scholars generally agree that the first Indian peoples came to North America from Siberia by way of the Bering Strait between 30,000 and 11,000 BCE when the Ice Age lowered sea levels, creating a huge land bridge between Asia and North America. Bands of nomadic hunters followed game from eastern Siberia to Alaska, eventually penetrating both North and South America.

These first Paleo-Indian peoples were essentially hunter-gatherers, their largest quarry being mammoths, large-horned bison, musk ox, large antelope, caribou, and, ironically, horses. The rest of their diet consisted of berries, nuts, fruits, fish, birds, and wildfowl. Their material culture was simple but effective. Animals provided skins for clothing; crude shelters were found in caves, rock overhangs, or made from the branches and bark of trees; while simple canoes or even logs provided the means for crossing rivers. Flint knives and scrapers enabled food and other materials to be prepared, while fire was used for keeping warm and cooking.

---

[3]   Until 1945 the study of precontact Indian peoples was left to archaeologists. Postcontact eras were the province of anthropologists and ethnologists. American history proper was considered to begin only with the arrival of Europeans, the Indians thereafter constituting passive and disappearing bystanders. After about 1970 historians began to combine these approaches, as described in Bruce Trigger, *Natives and Newcomers: Canada's "Heroic Age" Reconsidered* (Montreal, 1985), 1–49, 164–72; and James Axtell, "The Ethnohistory of Early America: A Review Essay," *William and Mary Quarterly*, 35 (1978), 110–44. More recently they have incorporated the insights of environmental history. One important account that shows the centrality of climate change and other environmental factors to precontact Native American history is James Rice, *Nature and History in the Potomac Country: From Hunter-Gatherers to the Age of Jefferson* (Baltimore, 2009).

With the gradual warming of the earth's climate around 9000 BCE and the extinction of the larger mammals, the peoples of North and Central America were forced to adapt. First the mammoth disappeared, then the large-horned bison, followed by the horse. Although the people continued to live as hunter-gatherers, they became less migratory, confining their activities to smaller areas. Since the earth's warming had produced a rise in water levels which covered the original land bridge, people in the Americas were essentially cut off from further contact with Asia. Purely indigenous cultures developed. Different language groups became established, with a wide range of individual tongues within each group. By the time that Europeans began to arrive more than 10,000 years later, there were still more than 2,000 languages being spoken in the Americas.[4]

The most momentous phase in the early development of North American societies was the horticultural revolution. The peoples of the Tehuacan Valley of central Mexico, with its warm climate and varied plant species, including a wild ancestor of maize, were the first to develop agriculture around 5000 BCE. Elsewhere, horticulture began with the growing of beans, squash, or gourds; but invariably maize or corn was added at some point. Initially all these crops were cultivated from wild plants, but in time selection of the best seeds or hybridization through cross-pollination produced better strains, giving higher yields. In contrast to Africa, Europe, and Asia, however, no animals except dogs and turkeys (and llamas in South America) could be domesticated, since most of the large mammals that had migrated to the continent had disappeared along with the game. In many ways the lack of livestock did not matter, since the cultivation of beans and maize ensured a high-protein diet, especially when supplemented by meat from hunting.

Once a group of people began to rely on horticulture for their food, profound consequences followed. Cultures were radically altered as communities became more settled to allow the planting, harvesting, and protection of their crops. Horticulture also allowed the support of larger populations, which in turn permitted greater diversification and specialization. It is no coincidence that the beginnings of agriculture corresponded with the appearance of ceramics and the first advances in metallurgy. Specialized skills encouraged trade and the growth of towns. These in turn required more complex administrative systems, which led to the emergence of temporal and religious elites.

The eventual results in Central America and the Andean highlands were the highly complex, densely populated civilizations of the Olmecs, Mayas, Toltecs, Aztecs, and Incas. Each of them could lay claim to impressive technological achievements. In North America the Olmecs, who were active between 1200 and 500 BCE, built large temple mounds faced with stone. They also devised irrigation systems and carved huge heads from blocks of basalt, suggesting not only craftsmanship but sophisticated beliefs and organizational ability. The Mayas, who thrived from 500 BCE to 700 CE, wove elaborate cotton textiles, used gold and silver to fashion intricate jewelry, and constructed large stone buildings incorporating the corbeled vault. Equally impressive was their development of hieroglyphic writing carved in stone or painted on paper, invention of an elaborate calendar based on detailed observation of the solar system, and knowledge of

---

[4]   The main North American language groups were Wakashan, Salishan, Penutian, Siouan, Iroquoian, Algonquian, Muskogean, Caddoan, Hokaltecan, Azteco-Tanoan, Athapascan, and Eskimo Aleut.

mathematics. The Aztecs, recent arrivals to central Mexico from further north, managed by the fifteenth century to create an empire of six million people. At its height their capital city of Tenochtitlan had a population of more than 100,000. Built on an artificial island in the middle of a lake and joined to the mainland by stone causeways, Tenochtitlan contained numerous squares, paved streets, stone temples, and other buildings that astounded the Spanish on their arrival in 1519.

North of the Rio Grande the pace of technological, social, and political development was slower, partly as a result of climatic conditions in the aftermath of the Ice Age and partly because it took time before plants bred for cultivation in southern latitudes could be adapted for cultivation much further north. In the Southwest, among the Hohokam and Anasazi pueblo peoples, new varieties of corn, squash, and beans, all originally Mesoamerican plants, began to be cultivated around 2000 BCE. Over time the Hohokam and Anasazi developed complex systems of irrigation to bring water to their crops in the arid climate of the Southwest. They built permanent towns in which they lived in structures made of adobe or stone, grew cotton which they wove into cloth, and developed extensive trade ties with people in Mesoamerica as well as further north by about 700 CE.

In the lower Mississippi Valley and adjacent areas, horticulture first began to emerge after 1500 BCE. Evidence suggests that peoples in these regions may have cultivated edible plants like gourds, sunflowers, goosefoot, and marsh elder, independent of the plant domestication taking place in Mesoamerica around the same time. Eventually the people here acquired the ability to grow maize as well. But just as in the Southwest, the adoption of full-time horticulture was slow; people in the Mississippi Valley region grew plants only to supplement what they could reap from hunting and gathering of wild foods for some time.

Gradually, beginning around 500 BCE, societies organized around part-time or full-time farming emerged in the Midwest and the Southeast. The people in these societies all developed certain cultural practices in common: all built mounds for burial and other religious purposes; all developed urban settlements; all practiced some form of horticulture; all possessed pottery; and all were familiar with copper for making ornaments and tools. Peoples who were part of the Adena cultural complex, in the Ohio Valley, were still largely hunter-gatherers but practiced some horticulture, notably cultivation of gourds and other squashes. As the Adena peoples shifted to agriculture they became more territorial, building burial mounds to commemorate the dead and filling them with numerous practical and ornamental objects to support the deceased in the afterlife. Then came the Hopewell peoples, whose culture flourished not only in the Ohio Valley but in adjacent areas along the Illinois and Miami rivers, from about 100 BCE to 400 CE. Like the Adena peoples, the people of the Hopewell culture built mounds to honor the dead and for other religious purposes, but their mounds comprised concentric circles and other geometric patterns instead of simple squares. Others were grouped together inside an enclosure to elevate houses or other secular structures, suggesting that the Hopewell people lived in sizable towns. Their burial mounds contained material originating from great distances, such as obsidian from the Rockies, copper from Lake Michigan, and conch shells from Florida, evidence that the Hopewell were engaged in widespread trade and commerce.

The Mississippian cultures, emerging around 600 CE, initiated the largest and most complex phase of mound-building activity. Mississippian peoples' mounds comprised large platform edifices grouped around a central plaza. The size and complexity of these sites indicate towns and cities of thousands of inhabitants, suggesting that the Mississippian cultures by now depended primarily on agriculture for their subsistence. The greatest of the Mississippian cities was Cahokia, near present-day St. Louis. Cahokia had an enclosed area of several square miles, containing over 100 earthworks. Thirty thousand people may have lived there at the city's height around 1200 CE. Archaeologists working in Cahokia have uncovered copper chisels, awls, and punches (for piercing leather), needles, harpoons, spear points, and knives, showing that the Mississippian people had developed technologies for working in metal. A small percentage of the dead appear to have been buried with copper brooches, bracelets, gorgets, and clasps for decorative purposes, evidence that Mississippians had developed hierarchical societies, in which members of a high-status group possessed considerably more wealth than the majority of the population. Non-elite Mississippians, in contrast, still used arrowheads, scrapers, knives, hoes, and axes made of bone, shell, or stone.

The advantage of agriculture for a population is its ability to produce more food per acre than hunting and gathering, so that populations can grow and societies become more complex. The disadvantage of agriculture is that it makes a population dependent on particular patterns of rainfall and sunshine. In the event of climate change, hunting and gathering societies in the ancient world would generally move on and adapt, but fully agricultural societies could be devastated. This seems to be what happened to

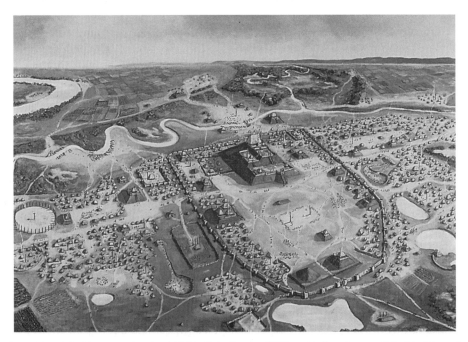

Figure 1   Cahokia mounds, circa 1150. Painting by William R. Iseminger. Cahokia Mounds State Historic Site.

people of the Hohokam and the Anasazi cultures. Between 1100 and 1350 a shift in rainfall patterns led to food shortages, and the Hohokam and Anasazi people abandoned their settlements and migrated to other parts of the Southwest, reorganizing new communities and becoming integrated with other groups in their new locations. Similarly, a cooling of the climate after about 1300 in the Mississippi Valley made farming less productive and created food shortages. The Mississippian mound builders abandoned their cities and towns and migrated south and east, where they reorganized themselves into smaller communities.

In addition to forcing communities to split up and move, climate change commonly produced stresses that increased conflict. Forensic evidence from sites across the continent suggests that rates of violent death increased between 1000 and 1500, most likely caused by increased competition for scarce resources. In the large societies of the Southwest and the Mississippi Valley, internal discord apparently contributed to societal collapse. These societies reorganized themselves into much smaller tribes and chiefdoms, whereupon they were often beset by intense rivalries and shifting coalitions. The main legacy of these peoples' shared past was often a set of enduring rivalries between their new communities.

3 THE EASTERN WOODLANDS, 1000–1300

By 1000 CE the horticultural revolution had spread eastwards, and most Indian peoples in the Eastern Woodlands region, along the Atlantic coast of North America between Florida and southern Canada, began to adopt horticulture for at least part of their diets. A minority of Indian peoples, especially those who lived in cold climates with very short growing seasons such as in northern Canada, spurned farming as a way of life, most likely because they had little incentive to engage in the tedious labor required to grow crops where the land would yield so little and game was still abundant. (Conversely, North American people in temperate regions with rich resources and a low population density, like California, refused to adopt horticulture too, probably because they had no need to give up hunting and gathering.) However, most Eastern Woodlands Indians began farming for at least part of their subsistence, and once they did, particular social and cultural patterns tended to follow.

First, peoples who adopted farming became more sedentary. Instead of living together in small bands whose members moved from one place to another depending on the time of year, Eastern Woodlands peoples began increasingly to live in permanent or semi-permanent villages of 100 or 200 inhabitants near the land they farmed. Farming produced considerably more food than hunting and gathering alone, and populations grew to a substantially greater density than in the past. Estimating the population of the region has been fraught with controversy, as early estimates were based on the observations of Europeans who wanted to convince their sponsors that the land was thinly inhabited. Another problem is that by the time most European observers came to eastern North America, diseases brought by the Spanish may have already caused dramatic depopulation. Current estimates based on the best evidence suggest that before 1492, as many as five million people lived north of the Rio Grande in what would later become the United States. Of these some 30,000 lived in the vicinity

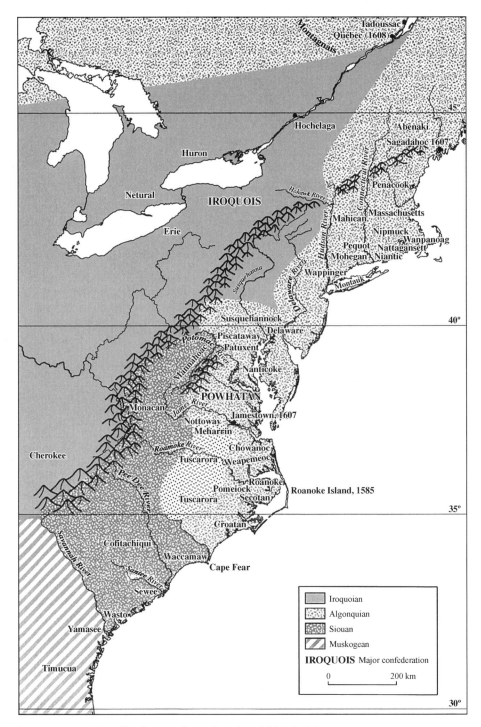

Map 1   Eastern Woodlands coastal peoples, circa 1530–1608.

of the lower Chesapeake Bay and 150,000 in what would become New England, the two regions which Englishmen would first attempt to colonize.[5]

These were linguistically diverse peoples, representing four main linguistic groups by the fifteenth century. Algonquian-speaking peoples occupied the coastal regions from New-foundland to northern Carolina, though a number also resided around the Great Lakes. Siouan peoples inhabited the coastal areas of the Carolinas. Muskogeans lived in Georgia and the Floridas, and Iroquoian peoples lived almost entirely inland from the St. Lawrence Valley and the area southwards to the piedmont of Virginia and the Carolinas. Within each of these language groups there were distinct dialects and some people spoke multiple languages. Common linguistic roots did not necessarily mean close political or cultural ties. Still, many Indian peoples appear to have been receptive to alliances and cooperation with others with whom they shared linguistic similarities. It was relatively common for part or all of a tribe to migrate, particularly if its members had suffered significant population losses, and become integrated into another tribe with a similar language.

Farming techniques were adapted to the environment of the particular region. Because there were no domesticable animal species in North America, the use of animal-drawn plows was of course impossible. Trees were abundant, so clearing the land was a major problem. Trees could be killed by girdling the bark from the trunk and burning the undergrowth, but this did not remove the stumps. Hence planting was done by digging holes between the stumps and then heaping soil around the plants as they grew. Eventually stumps were removed by scorching the roots, though by then the soil had lost much of its fertility. As a result, every 10 or 20 years the inhabitants typically moved to another site. The restricted ability to practice intensive agriculture to some extent limited the density of the population. Most people lived in villages rather than cities.

Despite these constraints, the Indians' farming techniques were efficient and highly productive. Women did all of the farming, using wooden hoes tipped with flint or shell to cultivate tobacco, maize, beans, and squash, which were sown together in the same plot. This method allowed the beans and squash to use the maize for support and also

---

[5] Debates about the size of indigenous American populations before Columbus are longstanding. It suited nineteenth- and many early twentieth-century historians to believe that the Indians were few in number to justify their displacement, and early twentieth-century demographers estimated a precontact population of only around one million people north of the Rio Grande and about 10 million throughout the rest of the Americas. The first widespread attempt to reassess the population of the indigenous inhabitants occurred only in the 1960s, when there was greater readiness to acknowledge America's ethnic diversity. Historical anthropologist Henry Dobyns estimated in 1966 that before European contact, as many as 12 million people may have lived north of the Rio Grande and another 80 to 90 million in Central and South America. Although more recent estimates are somewhat lower, it is clear that the subsequent impact of European diseases reduced this population dramatically during the first 300 years of contact with Europeans. The early view is well represented by the work of James Mooney, "Population," in *Handbook of American Indians North of Mexico* (Washington, 1910), and A. L. Kroeber, *Cultural and Natural Areas of Native North America* (Berkeley, 1939). For more recent estimates and analyses, see Henry F. Dobyns, "Estimating Aboriginal American Population: An Appraisal of Techniques with a New Hemisphere Estimate," *Current Anthropology*, 7, 395–416; William M. Denevan, ed., *The Native Population of the Americas in 1492* (Madison, 1976; rev. edn, 1992); Henry F. Dobyns, *Their Number Become Thinned: Native American Population Dynamics in Eastern North America* (Knoxville, 1983); and Russell Thornton, *American Indian Holocaust and Survival: A Population History Since 1492* (Norman, 1987). For an account of the historical debate, see John D. Daniels, "The Indian Population of North America in 1492," *William and Mary Quarterly*, 49 (1992), 298–320.

helped fertilize the soil, since the beans replaced the nitrogen taken by the maize. During the 1580s, the English observer John White in Roanoke, Virginia, noted that a first sowing of corn was made in April, with further sowings in May and June, so that successive crops could be harvested from midsummer until the fall. His companion Thomas Harriot elaborated, commenting that an acre of corn yielded "at least two hundred London Bushelles," whereas in England 40 bushels of wheat per acre was considered a good yield. On the other hand, Englishmen William Strachey and Henry

Figure 2   The Indian town of Secotan, by John White. Library of Congress, Washington, DC.

Spelman described the fields at Jamestown as small, while White's drawing of the town of Secotan near Roanoke in 1585 shows trees close to the settlement and only small cultivated plots in between. These observations suggest that a village of 20 or 30 dwellings would typically have about 200 to 300 acres under cultivation.[6]

Horticulture provided between 30 and 70 percent of food requirements, depending on the time of the year and location. Peoples like the Timucuas in Florida enjoyed a long growing season and probably secured two-thirds of their subsistence from horticulture. The Abenakis, on the other hand, who lived just south of the St. Lawrence River in Canada, probably secured less than 50 percent of their food by such means. In any case, other food sources besides domesticated plants were still abundant, and people continued to rely on game, fish, and wildfowl to supplement the food supplies produced in the fields. The particular mix depended what was available and whether a settlement was near the coast, by a river, or on high ground inland. Meanwhile the combination of farming, hunting, and fishing largely determined patterns of work and social life.

Since the women of a village did the majority of the farming, they generally stayed in or near the village for most of the year so they could be close to their fields to cultivate and harvest the crops. During the colder months women had other work to keep them occupied. They built the houses and made baskets, mats, and cooking implements, pounded the corn, processed meat and animal skins, and did all the other things necessary in the village itself. Women also nursed infants and were expected to rear both girls and boys while they were young, although the training of boys usually fell to their uncles (generally considered to be boys' closest adult male kin) as they grew older.

Meanwhile, the men of a village hunted and fished, meaning they spent much of their time away. The principal hunting seasons were fall and early winter when animals were at their prime weight. Deer constituted the most readily available source of meat; bear, fox, raccoon, and beaver were also caught. Since the habitats for these large animals were often at some distance from the village, most adult men left their villages and traveled during the winter hunt, sometimes for weeks at a time. Most animals were either snared or hunted with bows and arrows. However, over time Indian men had also developed ingenious techniques to make hunting easier and more productive. Deer were often caught with the help of fire, being driven by the flames into an ambush. The large trees were not normally affected by such conflagrations, which typically destroyed only the saplings and other undergrowth. Such fires thus not only cleared the woodlands but encouraged the growth of grasses that attracted the deer to return. Fire also helped rid an area of insects and made travel to and from the hunting grounds easier. In addition, clearing the brushwood around a village made it more difficult for an enemy to approach unseen. The undergrowth was often fired twice a year, which accounted for the "parklike" appearance of many woods to the early Europeans.

Before the spring the men generally returned to the village to remain through the summer. For the rest of the year they hunted or fished close to home, sometimes moving to a temporary camp close to the village. One source of meat that could often be

---

[6]   As suggested above, the observations of European artists and writers necessarily have to be treated with caution. John White's figures tend to have European rather than Indian faces, and he may have emphasized the beauty and orderliness of many aspects of Native American life in order to appeal to potential investors in colonial ventures. But the sketches and memoirs of early European observers still provide valuable eyewitness evidence about the culture of the eastern Indian peoples, when used critically.

Figure 3   Indian hunter, by John White. From *Collectiones peregrinationum in Indiam orientalem et Indiam occidentalen* (Francof., 1590). The Bodleian Library, Oxford.

found close at hand was wildfowl, abundant during spring and fall when migratory birds such as passenger pigeons, Canada geese, and other species passed by. John Smith, one of the leaders at Jamestown, noted in 1608 as winter approached, the "rivers became so covered with swans, geese, ducks, and cranes, that we daily feasted."[7] Another prolific wildfowl in most regions was turkey, which providentially did not migrate and was available in large numbers. The availability of fish varied from one region to another. Along the coast men fished in shallow waters using dugout tree logs or wood-framed birch bark canoes. On the rivers they could fish either in boats or from the bank, using nets made from vegetable fibers or weirs constructed with poles or rocks, which channeled the fish into a confined area where they were either speared or caught by hand. They also used lines tipped with bone hooks. Fish were abundant. The Chesapeake and Delaware bays offered shad, bass, sturgeon, and eels; the rivers of New England were equally stocked in spring with spawning runs of alewives, salmon, and eels; and the coastal waters proliferated with clams and other shellfish.

In general the Indian peoples of eastern North America enjoyed a relatively balanced and healthy diet; Europeans were continually struck by their well-proportioned limbs and physical agility. So prolific were their food sources that the production or accumulation of surpluses for resale was rarely considered. Only corn was stored year-round, though dried fish and meat were kept for a time. In general the Indians knew that they could survive each season until the next part of the food cycle arrived.

---

[7]   Smith may have been exaggerating here so far as he and his companions were concerned, since it was one thing to describe the game, but another to catch it (see Chapter 3, section 1).

Figure 4 Indians fishing, by John White. From *Collectiones peregrinationum in Indiam orientalem et Indiam occidentalen* (Francof., 1590). The Bodleian Library, Oxford.

This philosophy led many Europeans to condemn them for their want of foresight and lack of work ethic. The Indians seemingly ignored the biblical command to have "dominion" over the earth and every living creature in it. But in reality the Indians had developed a different system than the Europeans for supporting their societies, taking advantage of an abundant variety of food sources to feed their populations, in addition to what they could support through farming. Their system allowed their societies to thrive.

Relationships between men and women were considerably more egalitarian among the Eastern Woodlands peoples than in Europe, where patriarchy was the norm.

DOCUMENT 1

The upbringing of children, Father Gabriel Sagard, 1632, reprinted in James Axtell, ed., *The Indian Peoples of Eastern America: A Documentary History of the Sexes* (New York, 1995)

The following is a description by a French Franciscan monk of the parenting styles of Hurons he encountered in present-day Canada. Father Sagard's description reflects his European upbringing, and shows a failure to appreciate that the Huron used other mechanisms, including example, encouragement, public shaming and social ostracism, to teach their children to become self-disciplined. Questions to consider: *What kinds of assumptions does Father Sagard make about children? What kinds of assumptions do you think the Huron made about children?*

Nevertheless they love their children dearly, in spite of . . . the fact that they are very naughty children, paying them little respect, and hardly more obedience; for unhappily in these lands the young have no respect for the old, nor are children obedient to their parents, and moreover there is no [corporal] punishment for any fault. For this reason everybody lives in complete freedom and does what he thinks fit; and parents, for failure to punish their children, are often compelled to suffer wrongdoing at their hands, sometimes being beaten and flouted to their face. This is conduct too shocking and smacks of nothing less than the brute beast. Bad example, and bad bringing up, without punishment or correction, are the causes of all this lack of decency.

As farmers, women typically produced at least half of the food, a contribution that probably enhanced their importance within their societies. Most Native American groups were matrilineal and often matrilocal (meaning the couple lived with the wife's kin, and the house belonged to the wife). Thus children took their mother's name and looked to her relatives for protection and support. Women had considerable sexual freedom, at least before marriage. And in most societies, divorce was easily available, merely requiring an agreement by the two parties. A woman who was dissatisfied with her husband could leave him and marry a different partner instead. Since the house belonged to her, of course it was the man who left the household once a marriage ended. The absence of patriarchy was also apparent in the Indians' lenient attitude towards children, who were rarely punished and often indulged. Children were teased as a way of getting them to accept society's norms, but were not struck or physically threatened.[8]

---

[8] These practices caused considerable confusion for Europeans who were accustomed to children taking the name of their father and receiving their inheritance from him. To Europeans, a matrilineal society implied a society without male control or proper order. Ann Plane, *Colonial Intimacies: Indian Marriage in Early New England* (Ithaca, 2000), provides a comparison between Native American and English marriage practices, and shows how English colonizers in early New England forced the Indians to change their practices.

Figure 5 Indian man and woman preparing a meal, by John White. From *Collectiones peregrinationum in Indiam orientalem et Indiam occidentalen* (Francof., 1590). The Bodleian Library, Oxford.

The basic social unit in most Indian nations was the clan, a kinship group which was usually organized around matrilineal lines. A man belonged to the clan of his mother, and his primary obligations were to that clan. Although a man did apparently have a kinship relationship with his father, members of his father's clan were generally not considered to be kin. Kinship obligations within the clan were the most important bonds a person had. As one recent historian has commented, "Kin taught children the ways of the world, from the secrets of making pots or arrows to the enemies of their people, from proper behavior toward one's fellow villagers to the mysterious forces controlling the universe ... Kin met to celebrate a young hunter's first kill or decide on the propriety of a marriage offer. Kin avenged one when one was harmed, took care of one in sickness, and mourned one after death."[9] Clans also offered a means of minimizing conflict and increasing the political and economic effectiveness of families. In due course they facilitated a number of complementary objectives. Hospitality could be sought from someone of the same clan, no matter how distant, which was especially useful in a society where men spent so much time away from home hunting or making war.

While clans served as a force for social cohesion, they could also provide the impetus for their members to go to war. The purpose of warfare in Eastern Woodlands societies was not to conquer territory, as in European societies, but to restore harmony and balance to a clan whose members had somehow been injured or aggrieved. Its underlying logic was related to concepts of law and crime. If a clan member was killed, the most important legal

[9] James H. Merrell, *The Indians' New World: Catawbas and Their Neighbors from European Contact through the Era of Removal* (Chapel Hill, 1989), 20.

consequence was not really punishment of the guilty party (the emphasis in English law) but providing compensation for the grieving relatives. The clan had a collective obligation to avenge the death of their kinsman by taking a life for the life that had been lost. In theory the taking of the second life evened the score and ended further killing.

War was typically, at least in part, an extension of this principle of retaliation. Native American cultures in North America usually incorporated the belief that the spirits of those who had been killed in battle could not rest until they had been avenged. Unlike soldiers in wars fought in European state-based societies, whose object was to kill as many enemies as possible and take control of territory, the task of an Indian warrior was to capture a member of an enemy tribe and bring the captive back to his clan. Particularly among Iroquoian-speaking peoples, clan members would then decide whether to adopt or enslave the captives to serve as symbolic substitutes for their lost family members (usually the fate of women and children), or to exact revenge through a ritualized execution. Executions were carried out by the entire clan, with the victim often being maimed (scalps removed, fingers cut off) before being slowly burned alive. All the while the victim was expected to prove his courage and his manhood by singing bravely and showing no fear of death. The process, as anthropologists and ethnohistorians have suggested, relieved feelings of anger and grief and restored the clan to an emotional balance so that they could return to normalcy. Wars conducted in this manner have been called "mourning wars."

The logic of mourning wars inhibited the scope of war making, since the point was to bring back captives to restore the dead, rather than to kill as many of the enemy as possible. War parties were usually small, while arrows and tomahawks tipped with flint or horn were only moderately lethal. Battle tactics often involved stealth and surprise attacks instead of frontal attacks or mass charges. On the other hand, war making served other functions for Indian societies besides the taking of captives, so they could result in killing for other purposes. Performing courageously in battle was an important way for young men to prove their manhood and to earn prestige and status within their clans. Taking scalps as trophies of one's success in battle was a practice in some Indian cultures (much as taking the heads or ears of defeated enemies was a practice in parts of Europe), long before Europeans began offering bounties for scalps. Moreover, war could also be a means of controlling territory to ensure game and food supplies, although Native Americans did not need to control territory in the European manner; simply depopulating an area was enough to assert their claim. Warfare to occupy territory would have resulted in needless killing on a larger scale.[10]

---

[10]   Although such practices may seem barbarous or cruel, they were no more so than European practices like drawing and quartering people found guilty of crimes, pillaging the villages of enemies, and enslaving prisoners of war, practices which in European state-based societies took place on a much larger scale. Ethnohistorians who have considered the differences between European and Indian warfare include Francis Jennings, *The Invasion of America: Indians, Colonialism, and the Cant of Conquest* (New York, 1975), ch. 9; James Axtell, *The European and the Indian: Essays in the Ethnohistory of Colonial America* (New York, 1981); Daniel K. Richter, "War and Culture: The Iroquois Experience," *William and Mary Quarterly*, 40 (1983), 529–37; Trigger, *Natives and Newcomers*; and Colin G. Calloway, *New Worlds for All: Indians, Europeans, and the Remaking of Early America* (Baltimore, 1997), ch. 5. An analysis of the importance of war for Iroquoian, Algonquian, English, and Anglo-American manhood may be found in Ann M. Little, *Abraham in Arms: War and Gender in Colonial New England* (Philadelphia, 2007).

DOCUMENT 2

The Indian method of warfare, Thomas Harriot, 1588, reprinted in Karen Ordahl Kupperman, ed., *Major Problems in American Colonial History: Documents and Essays* (Lexington, Mass., 1993), 13

This document by a sixteenth-century English naturalist is based on his observations of coastal Algonquian Indians around Roanoke, Virginia. Questions to consider: *What methods of fighting does he describe? What assumptions does he make about the Indians' fighting methods and their effectiveness?*

Their manner of wars amongst themselves is either by sudden surprising one another, most commonly about the dawning of the day, or moonlight, or else by ambushes or some subtle devices. Set battles are very rare, except it fall where there are many trees, where either part may have some hope of defence, after the delivery of every arrow, in leaping behind some or other.

   If there fall out any wars between us and them, what their fight is likely to be, we having advantages against them so many manner of ways, as by our discipline, our strange weapons and devices else, especially by ordinance great and small, it may easily be imagined; by the experience we have had in some places, the turning up of their heels against us in running away was their best defence.

Another key aspect of Eastern Woodlands societies that had began to develop by 1300 was a highly participatory and egalitarian type of political organization, quite unlike the hierarchical political organizations of European monarchies. Decisions about war, peace, and diplomatic alliances provided the main subject of political deliberation among Eastern Woodlands people, whose decisions were mostly made at a local level within each individual village or town. A village was usually led by a chief or head man, who had generally inherited the position, though leadership ability was also essential. Succession among the Algonquian peoples was largely through the female line, passing from a woman's eldest son through the younger brothers to the sisters and then the heirs of the eldest sister. Other peoples allowed women an expanded role in the selection process. For example, among the Iroquois it was village women who chose the chief (though he was always a male.) While chiefs periodically deliberated together in a tribal council with other village chiefs, it was understood that each clan or village made its own decisions and was not bound by the will of the others. Indeed, a chief's authority within his own village was quite limited. Decision making was highly democratic and chiefs led by persuasion rather than by command. Essentially the only way to make a binding political decision (such as a treaty) was to ensure that the men involved had all agreed to it. Although women did not generally participate in deliberations about war and peace, among many peoples the older women in a clan could call upon the young male warriors to avenge a death and thus could exercise considerable influence in war-making councils.

4   EASTERN WOODLANDS SOCIETIES IN TRANSITION, 1300–1500

These patterns of social life had become fairly well established in Eastern Woodlands societies when they were disrupted by the same phenomenon that was transforming the societies of the Mississippi Valley: climate change. The Little Ice Age, beginning around 1300 CE, was a period of global cooling that would last through the eighteenth century. Temperatures dropped: spring arrived later, and winter frosts came earlier, shortening the growing season and making harvests unpredictable. For people who had become dependent on agriculture, even a small change in the climate could be devastating. The consequences were especially severe in the north, where growing seasons became shorter than were needed to produce enough food to sustain a village.

To survive, people in the Eastern Woodlands began to migrate, usually to more fertile land at lower altitudes and lower latitudes where they could continue to support themselves through farming. As they moved, clans invariably crossed boundaries and encroached on the claims of other clans. People became more territorial; increased competition for the best land resulted in more frequent warfare between peoples. War, of course, caused death and grieving, and given the logic of the mourning war these new deaths produced pressure for still more warfare. Occasional skirmishes gave way to frequent raids, which then required retaliation, in a destructive cycle that had the potential to destroy entire societies. The increased frequency of warfare became a new challenge to which people would be forced to adapt.

One way in which Indian peoples coped was by developing more intricate trading relationships with other clans or tribes. Trade meant something different for Native Americans than it did for Europeans. The exchange of goods was part of a gift culture rather than the operation of a commercial market; it provided an important mechanism for building trust and friendship, in addition to acquiring goods. Among Native Americans status was measured by the ability to give rather than to possess. In this context, trade was actually a form of mutual gift-giving, which had the effect of raising the status of each of the givers and allowing each of them to feel magnanimous. Gift-giving ceremonies played an important role when an alliance was being formed or a treaty agreed to because they helped to bolster mutual feelings of goodwill. Gifts were also important when treaties were renewed or reconfirmed; good feelings made it likely that an amicable relationship would continue.[11]

As trade and alliances became more important, people's work priorities may have changed somewhat, as they spent more of their time producing objects that were highly prized in trade, like ceramics or ornaments made from copper and shell beads. Some

---

[11]   The argument that trade was an essential aspect of American Indian life before European contact is made by Helen C. Rountree, ed., *Powhatan Foreign Relations, 1500–1722* (Charlottesville, 1993). Several others argue that it was less important before the arrival of Europeans. See Daniel K. Richter, *The Ordeal of the Longhouse: The Peoples of the Iroquois League in the Era of European Colonization* (Chapel Hill, 1992), 28, and Trigger, *Natives and Newcomers*), 104, 183. For the suggestion that increased migration, warfare, trade, and political consolidation all began well before the arrival of Europeans and resulted from climate change see Rice, *Nature and History in the Potomac Country.*

Figure 6   The Algonquian Indian village of Pomeiock, Gibbs Creek, North Carolina, with protective stockade. Sketch from observations made by English expedition under John White in 1585. Archaeologists have found that stockaded villages became more common in the fifteenth and sixteenth centuries, presumably in response to the increased likelihood of enemy raids. © World History Archive/Alamy.

people may have stepped up their production of food so as to have a valuable commodity to trade for other goods. For example, according to the Franciscan monk Pierre Sagard, who visited the Great Lakes in the 1630s, the Huron sowed enough corn for two or three years, "either for fear that some bad season may visit them or else in order to trade it to other nations for furs and other things."

Another adaptation for many clans in the Eastern Woodlands was to develop more consolidated forms of political authority. The best example – and quite probably the first – was the Iroquois Great League of Peace, or the Iroquois Five Nations. After having made war upon one another for many years, village and tribal leaders in five separate Iroquoian-speaking tribes (also called nations) reached an agreement in approximately 1450 to stop the bloodshed. After reaching this accord the warriors of the Mohawk, Onondaga, Cayuga, Oneida, and Seneca nations regarded one another as members of the same people, and stopped waging war against each other. Members of the Iroquois League now held annual meetings to renew their bonds of friendship, and killing between members effectively ceased. However, the League did not end Iroquois war-making against other groups. The culture of warfare had become too entrenched, and young men continued to feel pressure to go to war in order to prove their manhood. Having agreed to avoid war with one another, the members of the League instead turned their aggressions against neighboring peoples. In time the confederacy became a powerful alliance that allowed its members to call upon other members to help them against their enemies.

Facing increased aggression from the Iroquois Five Nations, other tribes were now forced to adapt. The Iroquoian-speaking Susquehannocks, for example, migrated south from the upper Susquehannock River in modern Pennsylvania and into southern Pennsylvania or Maryland in order to escape Iroquois raiders. Meanwhile, the Hurons, another group of Iroquoian speakers, formed their own confederacy so as to be able to defend themselves more effectively against the Five Nations. Many Eastern Woodlands villages came together to form chiefdoms led by a single ruler who could coordinate diplomatic policy for the entire group. The effect of these kinds of changes was in many cases to create more hierarchical political structures, with chiefs being able to demand tribute from subordinate group members. The most prominent such chief along the eastern seaboard was Wahunsonacock, chief of the Powhatan Confederacy, who at some time during the late sixteenth century extended his authority over 31 tribes in the Chesapeake region. A similar consolidation was taking place among the Piscataway and Patuxent peoples higher up the coast. These confederacies in turn often dominated smaller tribes in their respective regions, causing new tensions. The specific rivalries varied from place to place, but they existed in each region, as part of the continual competition for resources in a changing environment.

The peoples who lived north of the Rio Grande would have no contact at all with Europeans until the sixteenth century, and sustained contact would begin only in the 1560s. Already, though, they had undergone profound historical changes. The largest civilization centers, in the Southwest and the Midwest, had collapsed. New patterns of collective life had developed. New rivalries had formed. Trade ties and alliances had been forged, governed by long-established, commonly understood norms. It was these rivalries and alliances into which Europeans would be swept when they first began to arrive on North American shores.

5   EARLIEST CONTACTS WITH EUROPEANS

During the sixteenth century, Native Americans in North America would begin to have sporadic contacts with small groups of Europeans, as we shall see in Chapter 2. Their reactions to Europeans would be shaped by the cultural practices they had developed over the previous centuries. Native American people were generally receptive to trade if it was offered, since trade goods could be used to consolidate friendships and build alliances. An alliance with a group of Europeans could consolidate a chief's leadership position within a newly organized confederacy, or provide a much needed shield for a smaller tribe that was struggling to retain its autonomy in the face of threats from a larger group. As individuals faced the choice of trading with a group of strangers or trying to drive them away, they would make decisions to promote the interests of their clans and tribes in a competitive political environment. The sum of their choices could well determine the fate of a party of European explorers or a group of colonists.

When Europeans began to arrive in North America during the sixteenth century, they would in turn shape the societies of the Native Americans they encountered, although often without understanding what they were doing. Probably the Europeans' most significant impact on Native Americans during the early years was to expose them to new diseases. Native Americans had their share of diseases before contact with Europeans, including syphilis, hepatitis, encephalitis, polio, and dental caries. How-ever, various contagious diseases including smallpox, whooping cough, chicken pox, diphtheria, influenza, scarlet fever, typhus, dysentery, cholera, measles, and yellow fever were unknown in the Western Hemisphere before 1492. For thousands of years the peoples of Africa, Asia, and Europe had exchanged pathogens – sometimes with devastating results, such as the outbreak of bubonic plague in fourteenth-century England. The long-term effect of these exchanges was constant reimmunization of the inhabitants of the Old World against a huge array of diseases. People with a natural immunity to a disease survived, reproduced, and passed on their immunity to at least some of their children. No matter how devastating the epidemic, the population always recovered. But this microbiological exchange did not take place among the Native American peoples, who had been cut off from the rest of the world since 11,000 BCE.[12] As a result Native American populations had no immunities to Old World pathogens.

When Old World diseases reached the Americas, they caused what are known as "virgin soil epidemics" and devastated huge proportions of the population. The problem for the Indian peoples was that, as soon as one epidemic passed, the survivors were often afflicted by another. Even a single pathogen could devastate a community, leaving crops unattended, the game not hunted, and survivors so emotionally devas-tated that they sometimes even lost their will to fight against the next outbreak. After an illness, communities sometimes lost the skills and resources to remain economically viable, let alone defend themselves from external attack.

Calculating the effects of these diseases on the peoples living north of the Rio Grande before the arrival of permanent European colonists is difficult given the paucity of the evidence. When early European explorers traveled through the Southeast they found deserted towns, devastated by what the inhabitants called a "pest." Had they been killed by European diseases, or something else? Nobody knows. More than a century later,

---

[12] The concept of virgin soil epidemics is explained in Alfred W. Crosby, "Virgin Soil Epidemics as a Factor in the Aboriginal Depopulation in America," *William and Mary Quarterly*, 33 (1976), 289–99. Some scholars have argued that the Americas were not totally isolated after the submerging of the land bridge. For a discussion of possible transoceanic contacts before 1492 with Australasia, China, Japan, India, Africa, and the ancient Mediterranean world, see Jesse D. Jennings, ed., *Ancient North Americans* (San Francisco, 1978), 557–613. Recently epidemiologist David S. Jones has criticized historians for oversimplifying the idea of virgin soil epidemics in "Virgin Soils Revisited," *William and Mary Quarterly*, 60 (2003), 703–42, observing that resistance to disease is a complex phenomenon not reducible to simple genetic immunity. Very large numbers of Indians eventually died from Old World diseases carried to North America by Europeans. However, the process was more complex than historians once believed.

when English colonizers reached the Southeast, the great towns and temples once observed by the earliest Spanish explorers were gone. Had these civilizations been devastated by European diseases after the Spanish left? Again, nobody knows. Among the Eastern Woodlands peoples, historians are sure that some Indians were exposed to new diseases by the traders and occasional slavers who came sporadically to their shores before the arrival of European colonizers. For example, a devastating epidemic struck the Plymouth Bay region in the early 1600s, a few years before the arrival of the Pilgrims, which killed as much as 75 percent of the population. But historians now believe that diseases spread intermittently, affecting local populations at different times. Thus people further inland may not have been touched.

Where epidemics did occur, they increased the intensity of other processes that were already underway. Depopulation caused by disease heightened existing rivalries and increased warfare between tribes, as some peoples went to war with their neighbors in order to gain captives and restore their numbers. Population movements probably also increased. For example, historians know that the Huron people responded to population losses by migrating north and west into what is now Ontario in order to join together with kin. Was this population loss spurred by Old World epidemics or by climate change? Historians remain divided, but both forces were probably influential.[13]

When European ships began to arrive on North American shores during the sixteenth century they also brought trade goods, which they typically traded for fish or furs. As we have seen, gift-giving and trade had long played an important part in Native American cultures, and the Indians themselves understood their establishment of trade ties with Europeans in traditional terms as a mechanism for building friendships with strangers. However the Indians' cultures were not static; they would continue to adapt after Europeans arrived just as they had adapted to other changes in the past. Those Indians who lived along the Canadian coast and took part most frequently in exchanges with Europeans were already, by the end of the sixteenth century, changing their views of trade. While gifts had traditionally been valued for their beauty, some Canadian peoples had come to value certain European goods for their utility instead. Steel could be used to fashion knives and arrowheads that were sharper than similar implements made of flint or bone; brass cooking pots were lighter and often more durable than cooking pots made of clay. Demand for useful goods like these was rising, although gifts of beautiful objects like colorful glass beads were still welcomed.

Thus the impact of contacts between Native Americans and Europeans was beginning to be apparent by the late sixteenth century among a few of the peoples of North America. Epidemics had occurred, leaving some villages weakened and others untouched. Some Native Americans had learned that the newcomers were dangerous and untrustworthy. Others had gained valuable trading partners, thereby elevating their own status within their regions. What is important for us to understand, as we look at the consequences of the increasingly frequent contacts between Native Americans and

---

[13]   On the contributions of disease as opposed to other factors to intertribal conflict before 1607, see James H. Merrell, *The Indians' New World: Catawbas and Their Neighbors from European Contact through the Era of Removal* (New York, 1989); Neal Salisbury, "The Indians' Old World: Native Americans and the Coming of Europeans," *William and Mary Quarterly*, 53 (1996), 435–58; and Daniel K. Richter, *Facing East from Indian Country: A Native History of Early America* (Cambridge, Mass., 2001).

DOCUMENT 3

A first meeting with Europeans, printed in Colin G. Calloway, ed., *The World Turned Upside Down: Indian Voices from Early America* (Boston 1994), 35–8

This account of Henry Hudson's arrival in 1609 was written down in the mid eighteenth century by a Protestant missionary, John Heckewelder, after talking to some Delaware Indians whose ancestors had inhabited the area of Manhattan. Questions to consider: *How and why might the Delaware storytellers have reframed this story for the benefit of their European listener? According to the storytellers, what were the first reactions by the Indians to the arrival of this European ship? Would you characterize them as open or hostile to the Europeans? What might explain their responses?*

A long time ago, when there was no such thing known to the Indians as people with a white skin [their expression], some Indians who had been out fishing, and where the sea widens, espied at a great distance something remarkably large swimming, or floating on the water, and such as they had never seen before. They immediately returning to the shore, apprised their countrymen of what they had seen, and pressed them to go out with them and discover what it might be. These together hurried out, and saw to their great surprise the phenomenon, but could not agree what it might be; some concluding it either to be an uncommon large fish, or other animal, while others were of the opinion it must be some very large house. It was at length agreed among those who were spectators, that as this phenomenon moved towards the land, whether or not it was an animal, or anything that had life in it, it would be well to inform all the Indians on the inhabited islands of what they had seen, and put them on their guard. Accordingly, they sent runners and watermen off to carry the news to their scattered chiefs, that these might send off in every direction for the warriors to come in. These arriving in numbers, and themselves viewing the strange appearance, and that it was actually moving towards them (the entrance of the river or bay), concluded it to be a large canoe or house, in which the great Mannitto (great or Supreme Being) himself was, and that he probably was coming to visit them. By this time the chiefs of the different tribes were assembled on York island, and were counselling (or deliberating) on the manner they should receive their Mannitto on his arrival. Every step had been taken to be well provided with plenty of meat for a sacrifice; the women were required to prepare the best victuals; idols or images were examined and put in order; and a grand dance was supposed not only to be an agreeable entertainment for the Mannitto, but it might, with the addition of a sacrifice, contribute towards appeasing him, in case he was angry with them. The conjurers were also set to work, to determine what the meaning of this phenomenon was, and what the result would be. Both to these, and to the chiefs and wise men of the nation, men, women and children were looking up for advice and protection. Between hope and fear, and in confusion, a dance commenced. While in this situation fresh runners arrive declaring it a house of various colours, crowded with living creatures. It now appears to be certain that it is the great Mannitto bringing them some kind of game such as they had not before; but other runners soon after arriving, declare it a large house of various colours, full of people yet of quite a different colour than they [the Indians] are of; that they also dressed in a different manner from them, and one in particular appeared altogether red, which must be the Mannitto himself . . . Many are for running off into the woods, but are pressed to stay, in order not to give offense to their visitors.

Europeans during the seventeenth century, is that native peoples dealt with them in ways that made sense within the context of their own experiences and cultures. As we shall see, their decisions would shape the story of the North American colonies from beginning to end.

2

The Age of European Exploration

1420	The Portuguese discover and settle Madeira.
1440	The Portuguese settle the Azores.
1464	The Songhay empire emerges in West Africa.
1471	Portuguese mariners reach the Gold Coast.
1487	Bartholomew Díaz rounds the Cape of Good Hope.
1492	Columbus reaches the Americas.
1494	The Treaty of Tordesillas divides the Atlantic between Spain and Portugal.
1497	John Cabot initiates English exploration by searching for a northwest passage around America.
1498	Vasco da Gama reaches India.
circa 1500	The first African slaves are brought to Hispaniola.
1519	Hernando Cortés marches against the Aztec empire.
1531–3	Francisco de Pizarro overthrows the Inca empire.
1539–42	Hernando de Soto explores North America from the Gulf of Mexico to the Ozarks.
1558	Elizabeth I becomes queen of England.
1565	St. Augustine is founded by Spain in Florida.
1576	Martin Frobisher resumes the English search for a northwest passage.
1585	The first English colony is founded at Roanoke Island.
1588	The Spanish Armada is defeated by England.
1605	Sir George Weymouth explores the New England coast.
1606	The London and Plymouth companies are chartered.

Colonial America: A History to 1763, Fourth Edition. Richard Middleton and Anne Lombard.
© 2011 Richard Middleton and Anne Lombard. Published 2011 by Blackwell Publishing Ltd.

1   WESTERN EUROPE, 1300–1450

T HE NEXT CHAPTER in the story of colonial North America begins in western Europe, the home of the earliest European colonizers and conquerors. This story is easier for historians to piece together than the history of Native Americans, since the Europeans left behind so many traditional sources of historical evidence like first-person memoirs and chronicles of wars. Yet historians explaining the western European antecedents of colonization still face several challenges. Existing records create a misleading impression that the European encounter with the peoples of Africa and the Americas was foreordained. The truth is that the "discovery" of the Americas by western Europeans at the end of the fifteenth century was an accident, far from inevitable. Another problem is that European record keepers often disingenuously suggested that they controlled the terms of their encounter with Africans and Native Americans. In reality all participants played a role in negotiating these encounters. Though Europeans had considerable power, their colonial ventures in the Atlantic world remained contingent and uncertain from the moment that colonies began to be contemplated until those colonies gained their independence.

At the beginning of the fifteenth century, western Europe was a backwater on the margins of the world, residing on the periphery of the commercial networks that had integrated the economies and linked together the cultures of the Mediterranean, eastern Europe, the Middle East, and Asia for 1,000 years. The great trade routes of the world, including the overland trans-Saharan routes from northern to western and central Africa, the Mediterranean, the Red Sea, and the Indian Ocean, were dominated by Islamic traders, including merchants from the rising Ottoman empire. True, eastern Europeans still had access to the Silk Roads, Italians plied the Mediterranean, and Swedish and Danish merchants thrived along the Baltic corridor. However, western Europeans remained culturally and economically provincial, situated far from the main water corridors to Asia and northern Africa. No one could have foreseen in 1400 that western Europeans in Portugal and Spain were on the verge of crossing the Atlantic and initiating a new set of connections that would link together the Americas, Africa, and Europe and change the direction of world history. The vast Atlantic Ocean, with its difficult, mostly non-navigable currents and winds, remained the "Sea of Darkness," usable only for local commerce and far too vast to contemplate crossing.[1]

Western Europeans' hopes and expectations about their world had been shaped by a shared past. Although they were diverse peoples, their similarities were strong enough to

---

[1]   At one time historians saw the colonial history of the Americas as a product of the inevitable advance of European cultures across the Atlantic and onto North and South American shores. Today, historians tend to emphasize the contingency and unpredictability of historical change. Moreover historians are now less inclined to look at history primarily in terms of the development or advance of any single group, emphasizing instead the ways in which history results from interactions between diverse groups of people, often across a wide geographical area. One important recent school in the historical analysis of colonial North and South American history is known as Atlantic world history. It focuses on the ways in which exchanges, interactions, and links between Europe, Africa, and the Americas would produce changes in each of these regions, as well as shaping the history of the entire Atlantic basin. A recent assessment of the vast literature on Atlantic history is Jack P. Greene and Philip D. Morgan, eds, *Atlantic History: A Critical Appraisal* (New York, 2009). This chapter draws extensively from the findings of Atlantic historians.

allow us to describe the common features of fifteenth-century European economies, family arrangements, war-making practices, and political systems, all of which contrasted in important respects with those of indigenous North Americans during the same period. Understanding these common features helps us to explain how and why they behaved as they did, both in Europe and also in Africa and the Americas. On the other hand, it is important too to understand how western European societies were changing, since those changes help to explain changes in the behavior of European colonizers over time.

By 1400, western European peoples had lived in fully sedentary agricultural societies for several millennia. Most people engaged in farming, raising wheat, oats, and barley, along with some livestock and poultry. Men and women divided the tasks of farming: men plowed the fields and herded cattle or sheep, while women were responsible for vegetable gardens, dairies, and food processing. Although the division of labor in European societies was more or less evenly shared by members of each gender, legal and political power was not. Western European family relations were invariably patriarchal, that is dominated by men, rather than complementary as in Native American families. When families owned property, men generally controlled it. Another important difference was that western European societies were markedly more hierarchical than Native American societies. Everywhere farmers were less likely to own the land they farmed than to be tenants or serfs on property owned by a manor lord. Social hierarchy was thought to be natural, and thus inevitable. Manor lords and members of the nobility typically had the power to govern those who lived on their land, and enjoyed significantly greater power and wealth than the rest of the population.

Much like indigenous North Americans, western Europeans by the end of the fourteenth century were in the midst of their own historical transformation. European peoples too had recently been forced to adapt to the effects of the Little Ice Age, the cooling trend that during the fourteenth century shortened growing seasons through-out much of the world. One major difference from North America was that human societies in Europe had by 1300 become overpopulated, relative to people's capacity to produce food. Europeans were therefore chronically malnourished. Thus when climate change shortened growing seasons, the impact in Europe may have been even more devastating than in North America. Food shortages produced famines, which were followed in the middle of the fourteenth century by devastating plagues. The population fell dramatically, sometimes by as much as 40 to 50 percent. The resulting instability slowed economic activity and trade.

Paradoxically, one long-term result of the population decline in western Europe was to raise the wages paid for work, giving some ordinary people new opportunities to make money. Eventually farm production stabilized and the population recovered. In England, the lives of many tenant farmers became less stable, as landlords took advantage of new opportunities for profit and forced their tenants off parts of their land. On the other hand some tenant farmers became more productive and were able to negotiate more rights to the land on which they farmed. Meanwhile trade and commercial ties, which had declined during the crisis, gradually began to revive. During the fifteenth century European merchants in urban centers once again began looking for new trading opportunities. To some extent they were being forced by political changes to adapt, for by the middle of the century the Ottoman empire had gained control over many of the older trade routes to Asia. European merchants had to look beyond the Mediterranean for commercial prospects.

Like North Americans, most ordinary Europeans did not identify with a government or a state, but with their villages and local communities. No empire had arisen to control western Europe since the fall of Rome, though most western Europeans in 1400 were at least nominally Roman Catholics, governed in religious matters by the pope. For centuries monarchs and nobles had competed with one another for power and authority. By the fifteenth century, this competition had grown very expensive. Armies were growing larger, and keeping them supplied with arms cost money. In order to wage war effectively, monarchs in Spain, France, Portugal, and England developed government institutions such as courts, tax collection systems, and mechanisms for the impressment of soldiers so that they could raise funds and amass armies. These institutions laid the foundations for the modern nation-state. Thus, just as in North America, the trend in western Europe was towards the consolidation and centralization of political power. However the war-making powers of European princes and kings were vastly different than those of Native American chiefs, since they did not have to obtain the consent of their warriors every time they went to war, and could raise and support large armies to fight wars over extended periods of time.

2   THE PORTUGUESE IN AFRICA

During the fifteenth century, two related developments began to push western Europeans to begin to look beyond their borders towards the rest of the known world – not across the Atlantic, but south towards Africa and, eventually, east towards Asia. First was a series of incremental advances in sailing techniques and technologies which made possible longer commercial expeditions down the Atlantic coast. Portuguese and Catalan merchants and sailors had been engaged in slave raiding and in trade with the Canary Islands for about a century. As these Iberian seamen gradually learned to utilize technological advances in ship construction and navigational instruments, they gained the ability to explore further and further south along Africa's Atlantic coast. Expeditions sponsored by Portugal's Prince Henry reached the Senegal region in 1444, Sierra Leone around 1460. Later expeditions explored the Gold Coast, the site of modern Ghana, in 1471, and Benin in 1472. Each of these destinations provided opportunities to raid trading caravans for gold and, occasionally, slaves, or to establish ties with local traders. Eventually, Portuguese sailors and their sponsors broadened their objectives to seek a new passage to the Indian Ocean so as to avoid the Ottoman Turks, who controlled the eastern Mediterranean. In 1487 Bartholomew Díaz rounded the Cape of Good Hope, and in 1498 Vasco da Gama reached India by the same route.

The second development was the effort by European kings and queens to centralize their political power, which enabled them to sponsor foreign conquests and enforce their claims to territorial sovereignty. By conquering non-Christian territories in northern Africa, European rulers could enhance their claims to be defenders of Christendom, while acquiring gold and other commodities could help them strengthen their military power. Portuguese rulers captured the Muslim city of Ceuta in 1415, and sponsored the creation of colonies in Madeira, Cape Verde, the Azores, and São Tomé, all islands in the Atlantic Ocean off the African coast, between 1420 and 1485. Some of these colonies became bases for trading and raiding. Others were turned into agricultural colonies, producing such commodities as sugar, wheat, and pepper. The Iberian monarchs Ferdinand and Isabella, whose kingdoms of Aragon and Castile had been unified through their dynastic marriage in 1469, turned much of their own expansionist energy towards the Mediterranean rather than towards Africa. Eventually they conquered the Islamic kingdom of Granada in 1492. But much like the Portuguese, they too looked towards the Atlantic islands for conquests and captured the Canary Islands between 1478 and 1496.

One result of both colonial expeditions and territorial conquests was to create closer and more sustained contacts between western European and West African peoples during the second half of the fifteenth century. Western Africa south of the Sahara was a diverse region politically and culturally. By 1400 West Africa proper, that is the region which today extends from Senegal in the West to Niger and Nigeria in the east, was a densely populated area whose people sustained themselves by farming. Its inhabitants communicated with the larger world to the east through a system of trade conducted along the Niger and Senegal rivers, as well as by overland routes. Islamic travelers had been coming here since the eighth century, and had converted some West Africans to Islam, though many still preserved their traditional religions. Rulers in the northern portion of West Africa controlled large and well-developed states with considerable resources. The empire of Mali became known for its wealth after one of its rulers, Mansa Musa I, made a pilgrimage to Mecca between 1324 and 1326, spending so much gold along the way that the price of gold on the world market became depreciated for years afterwards. By the middle of the fifteenth century Mali had been eclipsed by the Songhay empire, whose territories in extended from the Atlantic in the west to far beyond Timbuktu and Gao in the east, an area considerably larger than modern-day Spain and France combined. It was through these empires that caravans of traders carried gold, silver, iron, cloth, spices, and other commodities to Egypt and beyond. Further to the south, on the other hand, the population remained more isolated. People in western central Africa, south of modern-day Cameroon, lived in largely self-sufficient, tribal communities, mostly unaffected by world commerce.

When Portuguese merchants began traveling to West Africa in the 1430s and 1440s, their primary interest was gold. However, they might also buy other commodities, such as pepper, ivory, and slaves. Slaves could be exchanged with other traders for gold or sold in the Iberian peninsula as domestic servants, for slavery was legally permitted in the Mediterranean region. Islamic merchants had been bringing slaves along with other commodities to markets in ports like Valencia and Tunis and Alexandria since the eighth and ninth centuries. Indeed slavery remained a significant institution in the Mediterranean region, though it had declined in much of northern Europe by the Middle Ages with the rise of other forms of labor exploitation such as serfdom.

Slavery was common during the fifteenth century in much of Africa as well. Frequent wars among competing states in sub-Saharan Africa produced large numbers of captives who could be kept by the victors or sold to traders and exported. African elites wanted laborers so as to build their own wealth and prestige, especially important to their status since their legal systems generally did not recognize property in land. Most slaves were non-Muslims, since converts to Islam could not legally be enslaved. Their status varied. Most slaves during this period were employed as domestic servants rather than for commercial purposes, generally living in families and often becoming assimilated into the cultures into which they had been placed. The institution of slavery was sufficiently fluid that the children and grandchildren of slaves could often acquire greater rights and a higher social rank than the enslaved parents. However, such fluidity was not an invariable feature of African slavery. Some slaves, including many in the Songhay empire, were put to work on plantations growing wheat or rice. Here they had little hope of achieving a better life for themselves or their children.

Portuguese traders found that any African slaves they purchased could easily be resold to Portuguese planters, who wanted agricultural laborers for plantations in Madeira, the Azores, and the Cape Verde Islands. By the 1480s, African slaves carried on Portuguese vessels were increasingly being shipped to the Portuguese islands (and to the Canaries, which had been conquered by the Castilians) to grow and process sugar, a coveted luxury product for rich Europeans. Over the next few hundred years, this new demand for African slaves would produce a diaspora of tragic proportions, as slaves were transported by the millions from Africa to the Americas. But such a future was still inconceivable, since none of these Old World people had yet imagined that the Americas existed.

3 SPAIN ENCOUNTERS THE NEW WORLD

Christopher Columbus was well situated to take advantage of the technical advances pioneered by the Portuguese in navigating the Atlantic. Born in Genoa in 1451, Columbus spent much of his adult life as a sailor and merchant in Portugal and Madeira. He had extensive experience navigating the Mediterranean and along the Atlantic coast, traveling as far north as Iceland and as far south as the Portuguese colony of Sao Jorge da Mina. Columbus's travels aroused his curiosity and his ambition, and by the 1480s he had begun working out a set of theories about the size of the earth and the amount of time it would take to reach China by sailing westward across the Atlantic. Educated Europeans had long understood that the world was round, not flat, and that by sailing westward a mariner would, in theory, eventually reach the east. However, most geographers believed (with good reason) that the prospect of sailing all the way around the world was impractical. No ship yet built could possibly carry enough water and supplies for a voyage that was sure to take at least five months to complete. Nevertheless Columbus, unlike most geographers, was an unusually poor mathematician, who had managed to convince himself that the earth was smaller in circumference than most scholars believed.

In 1485, Columbus approached King John of Portugal to seek funding for an exploratory voyage from the Canary Islands to China across the Atlantic. He argued that the distance of the voyage would be less than 5,000 miles, instead of the 10,000–12,000 miles estimated by most mathematicians and geographers. The king refused, advised (correctly) by experts that Columbus's calculations were wrong and he would never make it to Asia. Advisers to the Spanish monarchs Ferdinand and Isabella reached the same conclusions. However, the Spanish king and queen proved more susceptible to persuasion and in 1492, after years of stalling, approved funding for a voyage. The Spaniards were fresh from the conquest of Granada: they were probably more fired up with missionary zeal than the Portuguese. Certainly they were aware that without some new discovery for Spain, their kingdoms would soon be eclipsed by the Portuguese in the race for profits from the seaborne trade. Columbus accordingly sailed from the Canaries on September 6, 1492. Luckily for him, he had made a mistake in assuming that there was no major landmass in the Atlantic between Europe and Asia. He reached land after five weeks – not Asia, as he had predicted, but the Bahama Islands.

Columbus returned in March of 1493 to Spain, where Ferdinand and Isabella greeted him as a hero. The monarchs understood his voyage in the context of the Reconquista, the seven-decade-long struggle to defeat Islam throughout the Iberian peninsula, and saw it as a glorious opportunity for Christendom. They showered him with titles and promised him a tenth of all profits he could make by founding a colony in Hispaniola, one of the islands he had found in the West Indies. Additionally, they charged him to convert the indigenous peoples he had found in these new islands to Christianity.

We now know that Columbus was *not* the first mariner from the Old World to have reached the Americas. There is good evidence showing that Leif Erickson, Thorfinn Karlsefni, and other Vikings explored the northern coasts of North America and even established a temporary colony on the tip of Newfoundland at L'Anse aux Meadows around 1000 CE. Some speculative evidence has been offered to suggest that Chinese ships from the treasure fleets of Zheng He may have reached the shores of California around 1421. Nevertheless Columbus's voyage was unquestionably the most significant of all these journeys for the history of the world. It was Columbus's accidental "discovery" of the Americas that set in motion the dramatic reorientation of the relationships between peoples in four continents on both sides of the Atlantic that would transform the world between 1500 and 1800. It would produce what scholars call the Columbian Exchange, an exchange of plants, animals, and pathogens from one side of the world to the other that would cause the deaths of untold numbers of indigenous Americans (perhaps as much as 80 percent of the population) and transform the diets of Old World peoples through the introduction of American fruits and vegetables like corn, potatoes, tomatoes, and manioc. It would initiate massive migrations of peoples and shipments of goods, transforming economies, populations, and nations on both side of the Atlantic. It was these transformations that helped to bring into being the societies we now call American societies.[2]

Reports of Columbus's voyage were published and widely disseminated, and inevitably other Europeans sought to emulate his transatlantic voyage and explore further. Within five years of Columbus's first voyage, John Cabot, a Venetian seaman with a patent from Henry VII of England, sailed from Bristol to find a route to China via the northwest, which the Spanish conquest had disappointingly failed to do. The French made similar efforts. The Portuguese followed suit, with even greater success. Like the Spanish, they were technologically and geographically well placed for exploring the Atlantic, since Portugal had been engaged in long-distance Atlantic voyages since the 1420s, considerably longer than Spain.

Initially it seemed that the Portuguese and Spanish would dispute control over their discoveries. However, under the auspices of Pope Alexander VI in 1494, the two crowns signed the Treaty of Tordesillas, which divided their claims with an imaginary line 370 leagues (about 1,000 miles) west of the Cape Verde Islands. Spain was to have

---

[2] The phenomenon of the Columbian Exchange was described in Alfred W. Crosby, *The Columbian Exchange: The Biological and Cultural Consequences of 1492* (Westport, 1972), a book that broke new ground in suggesting that biological exchanges of plants, animals, and diseases across the Atlantic had a greater impact on the history of the early modern world than did human decisions. Crosby's work is an early example of Atlantic world history.

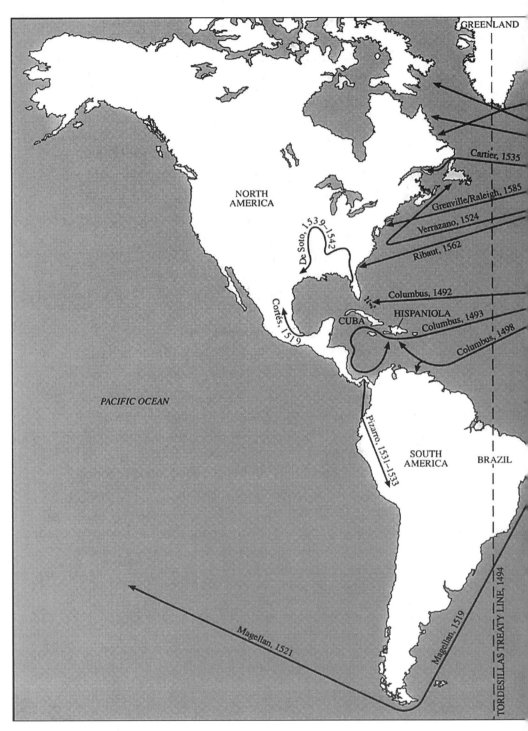

Map 2   The age of exploration.

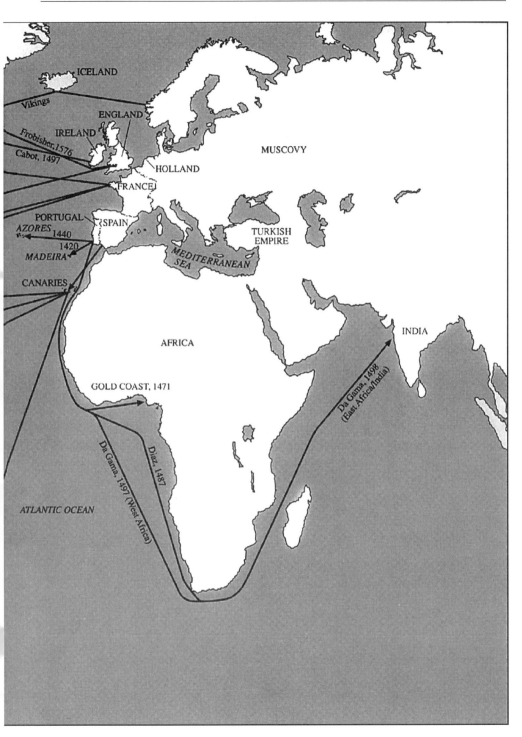

Map 2 (*Continued*)

DOCUMENT 4

License granted by Henry VII to John Cabot, reprinted in W. Keith Kavenagh, *Foundations of Colonial America: A Documentary History* (New York, 1973), Vol. 1, 18–19

This document shows the desire of England's King Henry VII to emulate Spain's example by sending an expedition to conquer non-Christian territories. Ironically, like the Spanish, Henry VII had to employ an Italian mariner to undertake the exploration for him. Question to consider: *What kinds of assumptions does the author make about the kinds of people the English will find, and the kind of relationships they will create?*

Be it known that we have given and granted . . . to our well beloved John Cabot, citizen of Venice [and his sons] full and free authority, leave and power to sail to all parts, countries, and seas of the East, of the West, and of the North under our banners and ensigns . . . to seek out, discover and find whatsoever isles, countries, regions or provinces of the heathen and infidels whatsoever they be, and in what part of the world soever they be which before this time have been unknown to all Christians. We have granted to them . . . license to set up our banner and ensigns in every village, town, castle, isle or mainland newly found by them which they can subdue, occupy, and possess as our vassals and lieutenants, getting unto us the rule, title and jurisdiction of the same villages, towns, castles and firm land so found.

---

exclusive rights to all new territories west of the line, while Portugal was to enjoy similar advantages to the east. Neither had any qualms about annexing such lands, since Christian doctrine had granted the right to the persons and property of heathens and infidels since the time of the Crusades. Even Cabot had been given full authority to "subdue, occupy, and possess" native habitations.

Despite high expectations, the new territories were initially a disappointment, since they seemed to present a new barrier to the east while offering little in return. Traces of gold were found in the possession of the native inhabitants, but there was little else of interest. The first settlement of any promise was on Hispaniola, where some gold was found, while after 1500 tobacco, ranching, and sugar – which the Spanish already had experience of growing on the Mediterranean coast and Canary Islands – proved moderately profitable.

The pace of the Spanish invasion increased with the subjugation of the islands of Puerto Rico, Jamaica, and Cuba from 1509 to 1511. Trading posts were established soon after in Venezuela and Colombia at Santa Marta and Cartagena. Then in 1519 the economic potential of what Europeans were now calling the New World began to be realized at last with the expedition of Hernando Cortés to Mexico to conquer the Aztec empire of Montezuma. Cortés discovered significant Indian cultures with advanced agriculture, sophisticated building techniques, and enormous deposits of gold and other precious metals. Twelve years later Francisco de Pizarro overthrew the Inca empire in Peru and discovered wealth beyond his wildest expectations.

Before Spain could reap the benefits of its newfound riches it had to find sufficient labor to exploit the new territories. Initially the Spanish adventurers who had conquered the new territories enslaved indigenous peoples and forced them to work on plantations and in gold mines. In Hispaniola and Cuba this was a disastrous policy. The people sickened and died from diseases brought by the Europeans, their numbers being reduced in some areas by almost 90 percent. After 1510 an alternative supply of labor began to be found when the Spanish king authorized the first shipment of African slaves to Hispaniola, brought there from Lisbon by Portuguese traders.[3] In Mexico and Peru, the exploitation of indigenous labor was more successful, since the local populations were so vast. Although many died from European diseases, the surviving populations were often large enough to meet Spanish demands for labor in mines and on ranches. Where there were not enough indigenous workers, Spaniards imported enslaved Africans. During the early years most of these had previously been slaves in Spain or the Canary Islands, spoke Spanish, and were Christian converts.

Thanks to their heavy reliance on Indians and Africans for labor, the Spanish American colonies developed racially diverse and racially integrated societies. The colonizers themselves were mostly Spanish men, while domestic labor and conjugal companionship were usually provided by Indian women. The Spanish Crown and church alike encouraged Spanish men and Indian women to formalize their unions in Christian marriages, and allowed their mixed race (*mestizo*) children to become educated and assimilated into Spanish colonial societies. Spanish policy also encouraged the Christianization of the Indians, even catechizing them in their indigenous languages, thereby encouraging indigenous languages to survive and flourish. Meanwhile, because Indian workers often worked alongside enslaved Africans in Spanish American mines, plantations, ranches, and artisan workshops, intermarriage between Indians and Africans was common as well. All of these marriages were recognized by Spanish legal codes, which had for many years recognized slavery and tried to mitigate its worst abuses. By the end of the sixteenth century, therefore, the Spanish American colonies had developed significant populations of *mestizos* and other mixed race peoples, many of whom had achieved a middling social status and assumed responsible positions in Spanish American societies.

Having founded colonies in the regions of Central and South America, which offered the greatest opportunities for profit, the Spaniards continued to explore much of the region north of the Rio Grande and the Gulf of Mexico before 1542, looking either for comparable sources of wealth or a route to the Pacific. In 1513 Juan Ponce de León of Spain explored the coast of Florida, and in 1521 he tried to establish a settlement there but failed after antagonizing the Calusa Indians in the region. In 1526 Lucas de Ayllón made another attempt farther north in what is now Georgia, but this effort foundered too after most of the settlers died from starvation and disease. Another party led by Panfilo de Narvaez in 1528 alienated the Apalachee Indians while blundering through northern Florida, then became lost after sailing to modern-day Texas, where the survivors were enslaved by Karankawas Indians. Eventually three of the Spaniards and one African slave made it back to Mexico, after an eight-year ordeal.

The survivors' reports fuelled more rumors about the possible existence of rich kingdoms in North America, inspiring further expeditions. Spain's Hernando De Soto

---

[3] Robin Blackburn, *The Making of New World Slavery: From the Baroque to the Modern, 1492–1800* (London, 1997), 135.

arrived with nine ships in Florida in 1539 and proceeded to storm through the Southeast between 1539 and 1543. Along the way the Spaniards encountered a densely populated region of peoples descended from the Mississippians, living in large towns with elaborate ceremonial centers and burial mounds, surrounded by rich farmland. Although the Indians were open to forming an alliance, the Spanish were interested only in conquest and pillage. They forced local inhabitants to cooperate with them by using terrorist tactics including hostage taking, torture, and bloody executions. Before long the word spread that the Spaniards were not to be trusted, and the Indians began to launch surprise attacks against De Soto and his men. Eventually, having failed to find wealth comparable to that of the Aztec empire in Mexico, the Spaniards left. Unfortunately they left behind a legacy of destruction as well as exposure to Old World diseases.

Other Spaniards explored the West, both overland and along the Pacific coast. Between 1540 and 1542, Coronado's expedition in the Southwest encountered Pueblo peoples descended from the Anasazi. Accompanied by 300 Spaniards and 1,000 Indians from Mexico, Coronado ranged through the countryside seizing pueblos and taking their food supplies. Finally during the winter of 1540–1, a group of Pueblo Indians who were suffering from food shortages attempted to rebel against their Spanish occupiers. The Spaniards destroyed 13 Indian villages in the course of putting down the rebellion, in one place burning all of the inhabitants alive in order to set an example for other would-be rebels. However in 1542 Coronado finally abandoned his conquests and returned to Mexico, having failed to find any gold. Here, just as in the Southeast, the Indians would remember Europeans as violent, untrustworthy people who brought death and destruction. Another Spanish expedition led by Juan Rodríguez Cabrillo sailed up the California coast with three ships in 1542 and 1543, reaching what is now the southern boundary of Oregon. Along the way the local Indians repeatedly shot at Cabrillo and his men. Having heard stories about Coronado's exploits further inland, they were taking no chances.[4]

From the Spanish point of view, these voyages of exploration yielded nothing, despite many rumors and hopeful promises. Even at the end of these expeditions, Spanish mapmakers had acquired only a sketchy understanding of North American geography north of the Rio Grande. Speculation about the possible existence of a water route through North America to the Pacific continued for centuries to come. As one historian has recently pointed out, it is surprising that Spain failed adequately to map North American terrain during the sixteenth century, since Spanish explorers had mastered equally difficult terrain in Central and South America. Why did Spaniards not persist in their explorations of North America? The most likely explanation is that North America had too little to offer. The Spanish had found riches beyond their wildest dreams further south, and it was not worth their time to finance continued exploration of a region that seemed to have so little wealth. The hostility of the Indians (who could see no reason to tolerate the Spaniards' heavy-handed tactics) was an additional disincentive.[5]

---

[4] For information on Spanish incursions into North America, see David J. Weber, *The Spanish Frontier in North America* (New Haven, 1992).

[5] Paul W. Mapp, *The Elusive West and the Contest for Empire, 1713–1763* (Chapel Hill, 2011), demonstrates that the lack of geographical knowledge would play an important role in future imperial contests for North America as Spain, France, and Great Britain all sought control over the North American West during the seventeenth and eighteenth centuries in hopes that a water route to the Pacific might still be discovered.

4 SIXTEENTH-CENTURY EUROPEAN COMPETITORS

Even before 1546, with the opening of the Potosí silver mines in colonial Peru, the silver that Spanish ships had begun to transport annually back to Seville was transforming Spain and, with it, the balance of political power in western Europe. Spain's American wealth made it a center for trade and finance, and the Spanish monarchy was able to create the most powerful navy in Europe. A dynastic union with the Habsburg empire along with an expansionist military policy gave Spain's rulers effective control over territory across much of continental Europe.

Spain's chief political rival at this time was King Francis I of France. With a long history of military conflict with Spain, France became the first European state to seek out ways to compete with Spain by exploiting American wealth and resources. Francis authorized several exploratory expeditions for France, including the 1524 voyage of Giovanni de Verrazzano, who found the Hudson River and sailed as far north as present-day Nova Scotia, and the 1535 expedition of Jacques Cartier, who sailed up the St. Lawrence to the future site of Montréal. In addition to sponsoring voyages of exploration, he encouraged French sea captains to siphon off a share of Spanish silver and gold through piracy. From 1521 to 1559, a period of ongoing warfare with Spain, French kings authorized privateers to raid Spanish galleons and Spanish colonial cities in the Caribbean, which they did with great frequency.

Meanwhile the French government also had the idea to create a permanent American base for privateering raids, which could help it to compete militarily with Spain. A Crown-sponsored settlement in Canada in 1541 was tried, but collapsed. Jean Ribaut and a group of French Protestants founded a settlement at Charlesfort in what is now South Carolina in 1562, hoping to create a refuge for use in case of persecution by French Catholics and a base from which to attack Spanish ships sailing up the coast to catch return currents across the Atlantic. This settlement also failed. Two years later Ribaut led a second expedition, this time to build a fort and settlement at Fort Caroline on the St. Johns River in Florida. Unfortunately for the French, this second, more substantial expedition merely induced the Spanish to make a new effort to establish themselves in that area. In the summer of 1565, a force of 1,500 men under Pedro Menéndez de Avilés first founded the town of St. Augustine and then tracked down and destroyed Ribaut's settlement. The Spanish then placed various missions along the coast to convert the local inhabitants and to prevent any further intrusion by the subjects of a rival power.

Though French colonizing efforts had little initial success, a number of French adventurers did begin to succeed as fishermen and traders in the second half of the sixteenth century. French fishermen had long journeyed west in the summers, traveling as far as Greenland in search of cod, haddock, and other fish from the north Atlantic. After Cartier's voyage to Canada in 1535, French fishermen began to travel further west to Newfoundland and Acadia (Nova Scotia). By the 1560s and 1570s, fishermen in temporary French fishing camps had begun to make sustained contacts with local Iroquoian and Algonquian-speaking Indians along the coasts of Québec, the Maritime Islands, and even northern New England. The Indians' tradition of trade with other peoples predisposed them to offer gifts of food and beaver skins to the newcomers; their hope was to build trade ties and alliances with the Europeans in order to strengthen the own political standing of their own clans and tribes within the region. The Frenchmen, seeing an opportunity for profit, offered glass beads and metal tools in exchange for the beaver skins, which they brought back to Europe to sell along with the fish. Since many fur-bearing mammals had become extinct in overpopulated Europe, beaver and other furs were highly prized in France and could fetch good prices.

Portugal, the other main legal claimant to American territory under the Treaty of Tordesillas, initially held back from colonizing the Americas, even though Portuguese sailors had discovered Brazil in 1500. A territorial empire seemed unnecessary for a nation that was already reaping untold profits from its African and Asian trades. Portuguese merchants did use Brazilian harbors in its trading activities, purchasing brazil wood, a source of red dye, from the local Indians in exchange for cloth, metal tools, and ornamental beads, occasionally transporting a shipment of African slaves to Spanish buyers in the Caribbean or on the mainland. However, when French merchants became interested in Brazil in the 1540s, and especially in 1557, after a group of French adventurers and settlers established a short-lived colony in the Rio de Janeiro bay, the Portuguese government changed its priorities. Portugal sent a military expedition to destroy the French fort and then founded its own colony at Rio de Janeiro. Portugal would also now begin to promote the development of a sugar industry in Brazil.

The rise of Brazilian sugar would be an important milestone in the history of the Americas, for it marked the beginning of the large-scale importation of African slaves into the colonies. The local Indian population, with its susceptibility to European diseases, had dwindled to small numbers and could not be used for labor. Instead, Brazilian planters began to import slaves directly from West Africa, supplied by Portuguese merchants. Spain's takeover of Portugal at the end of the 1570s soon made it possible for Spanish colonizers, too, to purchase African slaves from Portuguese suppliers. Before 1550 Portuguese and Spanish merchants had brought only about 10,000 African slaves into the Americas, but over the next 50 years as many as 200,000 Africans arrived in Brazil and Spanish America. These numbers would continue to grow exponentially. By the time the African slave trade to the Americas ended in 1880, a total of 11 million Africans had been transported to the Americas by Portuguese, Dutch, English, French, and Spanish merchants.[6]

The arrival of millions of African slaves would have a profound impact not only on the American societies to which they were being transported, but also on the African societies they had left behind. The enormous forced diaspora devastated West African villages and disrupted local economies. Warfare became endemic, destabilizing entire societies. Meanwhile West African slave traders profited handsomely as their business expanded. Historians once believed that African traders were unable to resist European demands to expand the slave trade because they had become dependent on Europeans for supplies of guns, iron tools, and textiles. Recent research shows, however, that African traders largely controlled the terms of the slave trade that they conducted with Europeans. Local traders actively worked to expand the slave trade because they stood

---

[6] For the changing volume of the slave trade, see David Eltis, "The Volume and Structure of the Transatlantic Slave Trade: A Reassessment," *William and Mary Quarterly*, 58 (2001), 17–46.

to benefit both economically and politically. In order to increase the number of slaves they could supply, they provoked raids on villages across an ever widening expanse of territory, in the process setting off a cycle of retaliation and warfare that would devastate the populations of western and central Africa for the next three centuries. Meanwhile the slaves they sold across the Atlantic would increasingly face a new kind of slavery. Instead of working as household servants, they would work on commercial plantations producing crops like sugar, first in Brazil and later in the Caribbean, under increasingly exploitative and brutal conditions, for planters whose demand for more slaves grew by the year. The institution of slavery now beginning to be created in the Americas would have a profound influence on the types of societies that would develop there.[7]

In 1580, with the rapid growth of silver exports from Spanish mines and slave imports from Portuguese traders, it may have appeared that Iberian hegemony in the Americas would last forever. Spain had found an unparalleled source of wealth in Mexico and Peru. Sugar exports from Brazil were growing, and thousands of African slaves were being transported to the Americas to produce it. France had been unable to establish a permanent base, although by the 1570s French fishermen were traveling every summer to Canada's Atlantic shores, where Spanish ships never ventured. A few English privateers had succeeded in marauding Spanish and Portuguese vessels, but England was too weak politically to contemplate a permanent settlement. Other European nations, meanwhile, seemed unable to make any impression. Holland, although well situated to become a commercial power, remained a province of Spain until 1579; Germany was divided into small states; and Sweden and the other Scandinavian countries were remote and impoverished. In addition the trauma of the Reformation was still sweeping through most of northern Europe, channeling the region's energies away from exploring the New World.

5 ENGLAND: THE ELIZABETHAN PRELUDE

The Reformation in Europe began in 1517 when Martin Luther protested against what he considered to be the corrupt practices of the Roman Catholic Church under the pope. Luther and others believed that faith alone, not good works, could secure salvation. They also felt that the church contained too much ceremony, pomp, and superstition to be compatible with the Christian message contained in the Bible. Ultimately most of northern Europe, including England, denounced the pope and separated from Catholicism. However, the process of reforming the English church proved tortuous. Many years of conflict between Catholics and Protestants in England produced lasting bitterness, and it was not until 1559 that Elizabeth I effected even a partial settlement.

England had begun to emerge from its poverty and isolation in the early 1500s, spurred by the growth of cloth manufacturing for export to Europe. However,

---

[7] This newer argument was proposed by John Thornton, *Africa and Africans in the Making of the Atlantic World* (Cambridge, 1993; 2nd edn 1998). Thornton's book provides another example of Atlantic world history in that he shows how both the Atlantic slave trade and American slavery were shaped by the interactions of African peoples and Europeans, rather than being created primarily by Europeans.

England's economic rise was halting. After 1550, the flood of Spanish silver into Europe's economy caused an inflationary spiral that indirectly provoked a collapse in the market for English cloth in western Europe. English merchants began turning their attention towards new ventures, trading with Russian and Turkish merchants, exchanging English textiles for gold and sugar in Morocco, even attempting to buy and sell African slaves in Guinea. The English public became vaguely aware of successful raids by the mariner John Hawkins on Portuguese slave ships in the Caribbean in the 1560s, and by Francis Drake on Panama in 1573. Interest in the New World picked up in 1576, when Martin Frobisher set off on a series of journeys to seek a northwest passage, and in 1577, when Francis Drake set out on a privateering voyage bound for the Pacific side of South America. To investors, the idea of a colony to serve as a base for privateers became increasingly appealing. In 1578 the English adventurer Sir Humphrey Gilbert obtained a patent from Queen Elizabeth for the discovery and colonization of the northern continent (though he unfortunately drowned off the Newfoundland coast in September 1583 before he could accomplish anything).

To the chagrin of English merchants, however, the queen had little enthusiasm for a colony in North America. At the outset of her reign in 1558, Elizabeth was more interested in strengthening English control within the British Isles through the recolonization of Ireland and a political alliance with Scotland than in becoming involved with European rivalries on the continent or in America. However the transnational religious and political conflicts set off by the Reformation in continental Europe inevitably drew her attention outward. Dutch Protestants rebelled against Catholic Spain in 1568 and Spanish troops were sent to suppress the rebellion, just across the water from England. Spain annexed Portugal in 1580, disrupting a longstanding alliance between Portugal and England. Many English Protestants, recalling the religious strife that had divided England during the reign of Elizabeth's predecessor, Mary, believed Spain was conspiring with Rome to re-establish Catholic rule throughout Europe. A more assertive foreign policy towards Spain began to seem desirable, and English privateering bases in the Americas might be useful for such a policy.

However, any efforts to establish colonies would have to be financed by private investors, not the Crown. While Spain, Portugal, and France had provided some financial sponsorship for voyages of exploration and colonization efforts, Elizabeth refused to do so, pleading a lack of funds. Instead she would license private ventures and allow private investors to take the initiative. After Gilbert died in 1583, his half-brother Sir Walter Raleigh took up Gilbert's patent, and managed to interest a number of influential courtiers and seafaring men like Sir Francis Drake and Richard Grenville in financing a venture. As a result an expedition comprising two small vessels was dispatched in April 1584 under Philip Amadas and Arthur Barlowe to explore the coast of North America. They duly made their way via the West Indies and early in July reached the outer banks of North Carolina, where they made contact with the inhabitants of Roanoke Island and the surrounding area. Before leaving they persuaded (or forced) two inhabitants, Manteo and Wanchese, to accompany them back to England, to provide more information, not least knowledge of their language.

Amadas and Barlowe were sufficiently encouraging about trading prospects and the defensive advantages of Roanoke to persuade Raleigh and his friends to dispatch a major expedition the following year, this time to establish a permanent base. Raleigh put considerable thought into planning the expedition. Not only were Manteo and Wanchese to return as interpreters but Thomas Harriot, a young Oxford graduate and scientist, and John White, an artist, were hired to assess the resources and draw the flora and fauna of the region, now called Virginia, in honor of the celibate queen.

Raleigh's expedition, comprising five large and two small vessels under the command of Grenville, left England in early April 1585 and arrived off the outer banks early in July. Here the English began to encounter the native inhabitants, and the Indians to get a close look at the English. Not surprisingly, some of the English were fearful and suspicious. As the English force explored the interior, a silver cup went missing. Grenville's decision to avenge this incident by burning an Indian village was hardly calculated to maintain good relations. Yet despite English blundering, not all relations between the English and the Indians were hostile. After Grenville departed for the Caribbean towards the end of August, Captain Ralph Lane remained behind with approximately 100 men to complete a fort and other dwellings. The Roanoke Indians and their chief, Wingina, sought out an alliance with the English, and Lane was able to explore the surrounding area, even dispatching a party under White to winter among the Chesapeake Indians. Harriot and White gathered considerable quantities of information for their report.

In the end, however, the Englishmen's suspicions got the better of them and poisoned the relationship between Lane and the local inhabitants. When supplies began to run low towards the spring, Lane became convinced that the Indians were plotting an attack and carried out a pre-emptive strike, murdering Wingina and a number of his people. The other Indian communities now refused to continue trading with the white men, thus intensifying the food shortage. Not surprisingly, when Drake called unexpectedly in June 1586 after a buccaneering expedition in the West Indies, Lane and his men insisted on returning home. When Grenville arrived a few weeks later with fresh supplies and men, the original party was gone, though Grenville left 15 men to hold the fort until a further group of colonists could arrive the following year.

Meanwhile, in England, White and a number of others remained optimistic about colonization. One major question that had to be answered before an English colony could succeed was whether the English should plan to subdue the native inhabitants by force, as the Spanish had. Several promoters argued that the English would have an advantage against the Spanish if they could win the Indians over as allies and friends, since the Indians would then ally with them to overthrow the Spanish Catholics. As White and Harriott began working on their *Briefe and True Report of the New Found Land of Virginia*, they sought to portray the Indians as sympathetic and fully human, if ignorant and in need of civilization. An illustrated version of the report which appeared in print a few years later would emphasize not only the Indians' apparent simplicity and backwardness, but also their attractiveness, their ingenuity, their apparent interest in European technology, and the orderly arrangements of their villages. The report's overwhelming message was that the Indians were capable of being civilized, and ready to be taught.[8]

---

[8] Historians have been divided on the question when and whether early European encounters with Native Americans were shaped by ideologies of race. Recent literature suggests that the concept of racial difference (as opposed to difference based on degree of civilization) did not originate in Europe, but emerged after years of interaction and struggle between Europeans, Native Americans, and Africans.

Figure 7   Roanoke and its vicinity, 1585, by John White. Colored engraving by Theodore de Bry. From *Admiranda Narratio* ... (1585–1588). Service Historique de la Marine, Vincennes, France/Giraudon/The Bridgeman Art Library.

White suggested a new plan to settle the Chesapeake area, which he believed would provide better harbor facilities and a more friendly population. Under White's prompting the scheme this time was less martial and more agricultural, being aimed primarily at establishing a colony of predominantly families and freeholders as opposed to soldiers and servants. It was to be called the City of Raleigh.

Accordingly in April 1587 some 85 men, 17 women, and 11 children set sail, this time for the Chesapeake. Unfortunately the two vessels were late in departing, and the captain insisted on leaving the settlers at the old site on Roanoke. White may have agreed to this, for the Englishmen Grenville had left behind would be present to welcome the newcomers. Unfortunately, it turned out the men were no longer there. Not surprisingly, after the murder of Wingina local people had turned against the Englishmen and driven them away. This meant that no crops had been sown, nor habitable accommodation maintained. In this critical situation it was decided that White should return to England for additional help.

Unluckily for the settlers, war broke out between England and Spain before White could return with fresh supplies. Philip II had been increasingly angered by Elizabeth I and her policies. England had begun covertly supporting the Dutch revolt against Spain, and the activities of Drake and Grenville clearly challenged Spain's legal claims in the Americas. Having previously been married to Elizabeth's half-sister and predecessor, Queen Mary, Philip still had pretensions to the English throne. His religious belief – he was a devout Catholic and received the title of "most Catholic monarch" from the pope – also led him to oppose Protestant England, much as many English leaders opposed Catholic Spain. By 1588 he had decided on a course of action. With the support of Pope Sixtus V, he resolved to invade England, claim its throne for himself, and rid the world of a dangerous heretic.

Thanks to the war all communication with Roanoke was severed until after the Spanish Armada had been defeated. Finally in August 1590 a relief vessel got through, but all trace of the settlers had vanished. White had left instructions that the colonists were to move to a neighboring location in the event of trouble, providing a message as to their whereabouts. The only message was the word "Croatan" carved on a doorpost, an apparent reference to a neighboring island on which Manteo's people lived. But no other clue to the settlers' fate could be found, and diminishing supplies and poor weather prevented a visit to Croatan itself.

The fate of the Roanoke settlers has never been determined. Possibly they died of starvation, were killed by hostile Indians, or drowned at sea while trying to make their escape. However, some scholars believe it likely that some of the settlers survived. Local indigenous people in the Chesapeake region many years later told stories that survivors had intermarried with the local people and migrated into the interior of the continent or had gone north to join the Chesapeake Indians. These stories would shape relationships between these peoples and English explorers and settlers in the region during the early 1600s, though they could never be definitely confirmed.[9]

There were several reasons for the English failure to sustain a permanent presence on the continent at this time. The first was poor timing. Had the Armada not sailed, the Roanoke settlers would probably have been rescued by White's relief expedition. The second was the poor nature of the site, which was swampy, not readily accessible, and disease-ridden. A third and even more important factor was the project's poor organization, which stemmed mainly from Raleigh's limited funds. Mounting an expedition so far from home in such uncertain conditions required either huge resources, or considerable cooperation from the local inhabitants. Since the English had offered the local Indians no real reason to work together with them, such cooperation was unlikely.

Another cause of England's early failures was the expectations of both the investors and the would-be colonists. The Roanoke colony was really an adjunct to English privateering, that is government-licensed attacks on foreign ships by privately owned merchant vessels. English investors in Roanoke were interested mainly in seizing existing wealth, either from newly discovered empires or from Spanish treasure fleets. Indeed the lure of such conquests remained strong until the next century, despite the diminishing returns that even successful buccaneers like Drake and Grenville experienced. As late as 1617, Raleigh was still proposing another expedition to discover a new El Dorado, reputed to be a fabulously rich Indian empire in the interior of Guiana. But privateering bases were unstable, impermanent places. The settlers who came to them

---

[9] For the argument that the colonists joined the Chesapeake Indians see Karen Ordahl Kupperman, *Roanoke: The Abandoned Colony* (Totowa, 1984), and David B. Quinn, *Set Fair for Roanoke: Voyages and Colonies, 1584–1606* (Chapel Hill, 1985). For a recent reassessment of how news of the lost colonists influenced English actions in early Virginia, see James Horn, *A Land as God Made It: Jamestown and the Birth of America* (New York, 2005).

lacked the motivation and practical skills to get a settlement started, and had little incentive to establish the kinds of trade ties with the Indians that allowed French traders to thrive in Canada during the same period.

Although the last decade of the sixteenth century witnessed no fresh attempt at settlement by the English, promoters continued to advocate the colonization of North America. Yet their vision for colonies was beginning to change, if subtly. Increasingly, it was not only the prospect of carrying away silver and gold that made the Americas attractive. Atlantic commerce was becoming more diversified. By the 1580s there was growing awareness of the wealth being produced by Spanish and Portuguese American plantations. Thanks to the French example in Newfoundland and Acadia, it was now appreciated that even the northern coastline of North America offered potential opportunities for profit. Thus, promoters argued that precious metals and jewelry were not the only commodities to bring wealth. Increasingly sugar, cotton, cacao, coffee, tobacco, furs, and even fish were being recognized as having equal value. Indeed, as the Dutch were beginning to demonstrate by 1600, shipping these goods alone could be a highly profitable undertaking.

This realization in turn led some to conclude that a different kind of operation was required to profit fully from the New World. Buccaneering might result in the interception of a treasure fleet; it could hardly enable a crop to be harvested. To grow marketable crops, a more sober type of colonist was needed. Richard Hakluyt, Jr. advocated this and other ideas in his book *The Principal Navigations, Voyages, Traffiques and Discoveries of the English Nation*, which appeared in 1589. In various chapters Hakluyt listed the advantages which would result from plantations, as he called them. The new settlements could provide naval stores like pitch, tar, and hemp. Ships would be required to supply them, thus increasing the pool of seamen and naval resources of the nation. It was not that Hakluyt's vision was necessarily realistic in all respects, for he (and others) clearly misunderstood the North American climate. He assumed that since the region around the Chesapeake shared approximately the latitude of Spain, commodities like olives, vines, and citrus fruit could be grown, thus ending both dependence on foreign producers and the drain on bullion. But the idea of colonies was changing. Instead of bases for pirates' raids on Spain, North American settlements, he predicted, would "yield unto us all the commodities of Europe, Africa and Asia ... and supply the wants of all our decayed trades."[10]

Promoters further argued that colonies could solve England's growing problems of overpopulation and unemployment. England's population was soaring, even as its economy was undergoing a wrenching transformation that was turning farms into commercial ventures and forcing tenant farmers from their homes to wander from town to town in search of work. As Sir George Popham, one of the first architects of English settlement in Virginia argued, a colony in America could employ not only the ex-soldiers and "poor artisans" but also "the idle vagrants" and many others who could not find work at home. The poor need no longer burden the rest of the community, while the power of the state would greatly increase, as would the profit of the individual.

---

[10]   Extracts of Hakluyt's writings are to be found in David B. Quinn, ed., *New American World: A Documentary History of North America to 1612* (London, 1979), Vol. 3, 71–123.

Investors who might consider risking their capital in a North American colony were given an important boost around this time by the rise of the joint stock company, a new institution which promised to overcome the limitations of exploration by individuals such as Raleigh. By selling shares in an enterprise, such companies could harness the resources of many individuals, making possible a larger and more sustained effort. The first such ventures were the Russia and Eastland companies, formed in 1553 and 1572 respectively to trade with Muscovy, followed in 1592 by the Levant Company, set up to trade in the eastern Mediterranean. The most famous was the East India Company, established in 1600 to trade with India and the Far East. The development of these companies reflected not only the growing concentration of monied wealth, especially in London, but also the increasing opportunities for commerce. Indeed, historians have regarded European expansion in the sixteenth century as proof that the continent was emerging from its feudal, theocratic, and communal past into a more aggressive, individualistic, and capitalistic era.

Opportunities for English colonization and trade were greatly increased in 1604 by the formal signing of peace with Spain. Although Spain did not recognize the right of the English to contravene the Treaty of Tordesillas, the agreement did promise a new era in which their colonial ventures stood a better chance of success. The Spanish implicitly accepted that they had enough difficulty controlling their existing possessions without attempting to police the activities of other nations farther to the north. Moreover the treaty ended England's privateering war with Spain, cutting off English opportunities lawfully to profit by raiding Spanish galleons and forcing investors to find other ways to make a profit in the Americas.

A final contributing factor may have been English success in the colonization of Ireland. Since the beginning of her reign Elizabeth I had made determined efforts to anglicize Ireland by imposing English law, customs, and officials to bind the country more securely to the Crown. In the process a number of settlers had also been sent, and military force had been successfully employed to subdue the local population and remove rebellious natives from their lands. Of course colonizing Ireland was very different from settling North America. Ireland was nearby. It had a large population with a highly developed agriculture. Many of its people spoke English.[11] North America was 3,000 miles distant. The main challenge there was to tame a totally different environment, whose inhabitants the English knew little about. The English colonization of Ireland was nevertheless an important precedent, if only for the experience it provided. Significantly, it provided several important English promoters with the experience of having subdued the Irish, whom many Englishmen viewed as wild and uncivilized. If the indigenous peoples in North America proved similarly savage, presumably they too could be tamed.

There would be reasons, too, for certain Englishmen to consider emigrating to a North American colony themselves. One of these was religious conflict. Although Elizabeth I had tried to devise a religious settlement that permitted theological diversity, many groups were still dissatisfied. The Puritans in particular yearned for

---

[11] The argument that Ireland provided a model for the English colonization of America is put forward by Nicholas P. Canny in "The Ideology of English Colonization: From Ireland to America," *William and Mary Quarterly*, 30 (1973), 575–98.

greater cleansing of the national church. They believed that there were still too many corrupt Roman Catholic elements in the Episcopalian settlement, and their discontent increasingly brought them into conflict with the authorities. As a result, some Puritan dissenters had begun to think of leaving England to establish communities elsewhere where they could be free from such corruption. Another reason for emigration was unstable economic conditions, not only for the poor but also for weavers whose livelihoods depended on the ups and downs of the cloth trade.

By the turn of the seventeenth century, then, incentives for English merchants to invest in colonies in the New World had grown. Spain's political control in the Atlantic had been weakened, and investors had realized they might have new opportunities to profit in the Americas. Potential competition from French as well as Dutch merchants loomed. When English investors learned in 1603 that the French were sending out various expeditions under Samuel Champlain to explore the area of the St. Lawrence, they renewed their voyages of exploration. Sir George Weymouth visited the coast of Nantucket and Maine in 1605 and returned with five Abenaki Indians and a highly optimistic account of the possibilities for trade and settlement. The English public was intrigued.

Towards the end of 1605, a group of merchants and their friends, including the younger Hakluyt, petitioned the Crown for a charter incorporating two companies, one from the City of London, called the London Company, the other from the ports of Bristol, Exeter, and Plymouth, called the Plymouth Company, to establish two colonies in that part of America "commonly called Virginia." This area was defined as lying between latitudes 34 and 45 degrees north, which James I, Elizabeth's successor, affirmed was outside the dominion of either Spain or France, since neither nation had established any effective settlement there.

The plea was accordingly successful and a charter duly issued on April 10, 1606. The London Company, or South Virginia group, was granted the area between 34 and 41 degrees north: the Plymouth Company, or North Virginia group, could settle any-where between 38 and 43 degrees north, though neither company was to come within 100 miles of the other. No difficulties were anticipated in this respect, since the South Virginia group intended to concentrate on the Chesapeake area, which White and others had explored in the winter of 1585. The North Virginia group, in contrast, intended to devote itself to the area to the north reconnoitered by Weymouth.

The two ventures would be governed in part by the adventurers, overseen by a royal council chosen by the king. The normal joint stock model was not adhered to in this case because the two companies were not simple trading organizations. That they were rather aiming to develop commerce by peopling new lands with subjects of the Crown led James I to believe that his Privy Council should oversee all important aspects of the new venture. Both groups were in any case represented on the new royal council, the northern company by Sir Fernando Gorges and the southern company by Sir Thomas Smith.

Initially few objections were voiced, for the prospects still looked promising. The charter granted the companies "all the Lands, Woods, Soil, Grounds, Havens, Ports, Rivers, Mines, Minerals, Marshes, Waters, Fishings, Commodities, and Hered-itaments" within their jurisdiction. In addition they could mine for gold and other precious metals, though one-fifth of any such discoveries would belong to the Crown.

They could also mint money, a rare privilege, but could not trade with foreign nations, meaning Europeans. Finally, the companies had the right to expel any interlopers, which effectively gave each an absolute monopoly in its respective area.

The charter also had to address the status of those now going across the sea. It was clearly not intended that they should cease to be subjects of the king. On the other hand, neither should their position be disadvantaged as a result of leaving their homeland. Consequently it was agreed that the colonists and their children should be guaranteed all the "liberties, franchises, and immunities" which Englishmen then enjoyed. These were not defined, although recognized as among the most important was the right to own and inherit property. Nevertheless, all lands in North America were to be held as part of the king's demesne in free and common socage, not fee simple.[12] Except in New England, seventeenth-century property rights were never to be as absolute as they later became in the United States.[13]

What of the people who already inhabited these lands? The charter provided that the settlements might "tend to the Glory of his Divine Majesty" by spreading "the christian Religion to such People, as yet live in Darkness and miserable Ignorance." The hope was that such missionary work would "in time bring the Infidels and Savages, living in those parts, to human Civility, and to a settled and quiet Government." Perhaps the Indians could be civilized and brought to Christianity, and would not have to be conquered. And surely the Indians could be induced to trade and provide the English colonizers with food. The colonizers had every reason to be optimistic.

In the initial stages of colonization, the northern group (the Plymouth Company) proved the more speedy. By August 1606 it had a ship ready to reconnoiter its designated area. Unfortunately, the vessel was blown off course and then seized by the Spanish. A second attempt at reconnoitering the New England coast was more successful, but by the time the crew returned, the London Company had already dispatched three ships – *Sarah Constant*, *Godspeed*, and *Discovery* – with a new group of colonists on board.

---

[12] The term "socage" meant that the possessor had to pay a small annual fee, known as quitrent, to the king, as opposed to enjoying an absolute fee simple, which would have been equivalent to owning the land outright. Modern English property law uses the term "leasehold" for socage and "freehold" for fee simple. These latter terms are generally used hereafter to describe such property arrangements.

[13] This was true of all "rights" at this time, which basically fell into three categories: privileges granted by the Crown, privileges established by custom, and rights laid down by statute. Crown privileges varied according to the residence and circumstance of the individual. The same was true of custom. Only rights established by statute, notably trial by jury, were common to all. Even these were not absolute in the sense of the later state and federal constitutions of America, since what one parliament had granted another could take away.

Part II

The Seventeenth-Century Settlements

3

The English Conquer Virginia, 1607–1660

1570–1600	Rise of the Powhatan Confederacy.
1607	Jamestown and Sagadahoc are established.
1609–10	Jamestown endures "the starving time."
1611–16	Gates and Dale are governors.
1614	Peace is concluded with the Powhatan Confederacy. John Rolfe marries Pocahontas. The first shipment of tobacco is exported to England.
1618	The Virginia Charter of Liberties is granted.
1619	The first meeting of the Virginia House of Burgesses takes place. The first Africans arrive in Virginia.
1622	The Powhatan Confederacy attacks the Jamestown settlements.
1624	The Virginia Company lapses.
1625	Charles I accedes to the throne.
1639	The Crown formally recognizes the Virginia assembly.
1644–6	A second war breaks out against the Powhatan Confederacy.
1651	Virginia acknowledges the authority of Parliament.

Colonial America: A History to 1763, Fourth Edition. Richard Middleton and Anne Lombard.
© 2011 Richard Middleton and Anne Lombard. Published 2011 by Blackwell Publishing Ltd.

1 VIRGINIA BEFORE THE ENGLISH

A LTHOUGH THEY DID not know it, the Algonquian-speaking Indians who lived around the Chesapeake Bay in 1607 were about to encounter a group of prospective English colonists sent by the London Company to found a colony on their land. These were not the first Europeans they had met. In the 1560s a group of Spanish Jesuits had established a mission somewhere in the region between the James and the York rivers. In 1570 and 1571 the Jesuits' heavy-handed methods provoked a series of attacks that resulted in the violent deaths of most of the missionaries and at least 23 Indians. The erience of this massacre would be one of the factors that shaped their subsequent interactions with the English.

The early encounter with the Spanish Jesuits may also have influenced political relationships among local Indians around the Chesapeake Bay in the years after 1571. Sometime between 1571 and 1607, a number of small local tribes became part of a confederacy led by a paramount chieftain called Wahunsonacock, or, as he would be known by the English, Powhatan. By the early 1600s, the Powhatan Confederacy included about 30 tribes with over 600 fighting men, along with numerous additional allies upon whom they could call if needed. Powhatan governed not as an absolute ruler, but as the chief of a number of lesser district chiefs, called *werowances*, who owed him a loose allegiance. The tribes who joined Powhatan may have wanted his protection against the possibility of future violent attacks by the Spanish. Or they may have been concerned about local threats, since there were other powerful tribes and confederacies around them, including the Iroquoian-speaking Susquehannocks to their north and Tuscaroras to their south. In any case Powhatan had become a powerful chief who wanted to maintain or expand his power, and had confidence in his ability to do so. This political reality, too, would shape the Indians' encounter with the English.

The leaders of the Powhatan people had at least rudimentary knowledge about Europeans before 1607. Certainly some local Indians remembered the Spaniards' massacre of their relatives in 1571. They also knew that after the Spaniards had been driven out of the region, they had not returned. One local man, named Paquiquineo, had actually lived in Spain for nine years after being kidnapped by Spanish sailors before returning to his home at Paspahegh, the future site of Jamestown. Paquiquineo would have been an important source of cultural knowledge about Europeans, able to warn his kin and their allies about the dangers Europeans posed, and to point out their vulnerabilities. The Indians knew that Europeans had muskets and gunpowder that could inflict a more lethal wound than a bow and arrow. But they also knew that not all Europeans were good shots, and that they bled and died like other men. All of this knowledge would affect their behavior towards the English who were about to arrive, and would in turn affect the fate of the colony the English were about to establish.[1]

---

[1] James Horn proposes the connection between Paquiquineo and the people of the Chesapeake Bay region in *A Land as God Made It: Jamestown and the Birth of America* (New York, 2005).

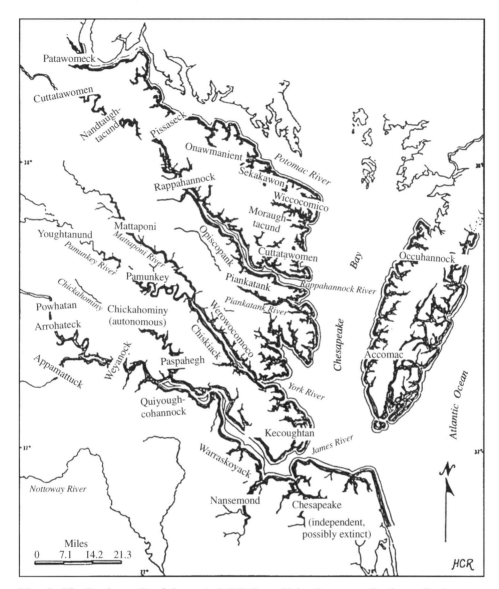

Map 3 The Powhatan Confederacy in 1607. From Helen Rountree, *Powhatan Foreign Relations* (Charlottesville, 1993).

2 THE VIRGINIA COMPANY: EARLY SETTLEMENT

The expedition organized by the London Company (also called the Virginia Company of London) set sail for Virginia on December 20, 1606, with a total of 144 colonists and crew members on three ships. The 105 prospective settlers, all of whom were male, were a mixed lot. About a third were gentlemen, including an Anglican minister, a doctor, and several ex-privateers. Forty were soldiers or ex-soldiers, and the rest included a variety of artisans and laborers. The journey took them via the Azores to the West Indies – the means of determining longitude were still unknown – and they arrived off the Chesapeake only in late April 1607. The instructions given to Captain Newport, the senior naval officer, were to find a site which was secure from Spanish attack but had access to the sea. Here Newport was to build a fort, erect a town, and explore the surrounding countryside.

The Virginia venture was envisioned from the outset as something different from previous experiments, neither a trading post nor a base for pirates but rather a permanent settlement. The investors expected the colonists to devote their energies to numerous profitable activities. In addition to building a fort, they were to try to find lucrative commodities like precious metals and to look for a water route leading west. They were also expected to trade with the Indians if possible. There was a demand in England for products things like dyewoods, medicinal plants, and spices. Also, the colonists should begin to produce crops and manufactures suitable to the climate. The hope was to develop a diverse group of exports whose profits would finance further development.

In pursuit of his instructions, Captain Newport sailed up the James River for about 50 miles. After declaring that the territory belonged to James I, he disembarked on a piece of land joined to the shore by a thin natural causeway, which made it more defensible against an enemy. The site had the additional advantage of being close to the deep-water channel, which allowed the ships to anchor nearby. The new settlement was to be called Jamestown.

Initially everything went well. A sealed box was opened to discover the names of the councillors. The Indians had at first seemed hostile, but within a few days Powhatan was offering food and hospitality, a welcome addition to the colonists' supplies. The colonists began clearing some land to build a fortified palisade with a number of simple dwellings inside. The remaining land was to be devoted to planting crops. As Newport explored upriver, he heard stories that there might be copper or gold in the mountains. He met several chiefs, including Opechancanough, the brother of Powhatan, who commanded almost 300 men. Opechancanough seemed to possess great riches in copper and pearls, a promising sign that there might be more wealth to be found in the region. At the end of June, Newport would sail back to England carrying news of the colony's early successes and samples for the company's shareholders of potentially profitable local products, including clapboard, sassafras, and some likely looking metallic ore.

Even so, there were early signs of trouble. The day before Newport's return, the English settlers were attacked. Historians speculate that the attack was instigated by Powhatan himself, in order to test the settlers' military abilities.[2] Another problem was the settlers' health. During the summer and autumn an alarming number of the colonists began to sicken and die, owing to the unhealthy location of Jamestown, on the edge of a swamp. Unknowingly the colonists had brought with them malaria, typhoid, and dysentery or the "bloody flux," which they now spread through ignorance of

---

[2]   James Horn, *A Land as God Made It*, 52.

Figure 8 English colonists landing on the Potomac River in Virginia, 1634. Engraving after John White. Getty Images.

hygienic practices. Furthermore, the water on this stretch of the river became contaminated in summer by sea water, so that those who drank it suffered salt poisoning.[3]

By the onset of autumn the colonists found that not only were they dying of disease but they did not have enough food. Although they had planted some crops, their arrival relatively late in the spring had given them insufficient time to clear as much land as they needed for a winter supply of provisions. Also, though the colonists did not know it, the region was suffering from a severe drought. The men in charge of the governing council could not agree on a strategy for solving the colony's food problems. Bitter arguments took place between the councillors and their nominal president, an ineffectual aristocrat named Edward Wingfield. Conflicts became so heated that one member of the council was actually executed for mutiny.

---

[3] The argument about salt poisoning is advanced by Carville V. Earle, "Environment, Disease, and Mortality in Early Virginia," in Thad W. Tate and David L. Ammerman, eds, *The Chesapeake in the Seventeenth Century: Essays on Anglo-American Society* (Chapel Hill, 1979), 96–122. Malaria struck periodically in the early years, and by the 1650s became endemic, which meant that some settlers lived with recurring outbreaks of the disease throughout their lives. See Darrett B. Rutman and Anita H. Rutman, "Of Agues and Fevers: Malaria in the Early Chesapeake," *William and Mary Quarterly*, 33 (1976), 31–60, and James Rice, *Nature and History in the Potomac: From Hunter-Gatherers to the Age of Jefferson* (Baltimore, 2009), 130–4.

The main reason why the colony survived its first winter was a decision by Powhatan to enter into a trading and diplomatic relationship with the colony's most energetic leader, Captain John Smith, a soldier of fortune who had been appointed as one of the councillors for the colony. Although historians have sometimes struggled to understand why Powhatan made this decision, clues to its meaning can be found in the famous story of the two men's first encounter.

During the fall of 1607, Smith embarked on a series of exploratory voyages to trade with some of the smaller local tribes for food. When trade failed, Smith and his men took what they wanted by force. In November, while Smith was out on one of these early forays, Powhatan sent a war party to take Smith prisoner. Powhatan's warriors killed Smith's companions, then held him as a hostage for several weeks before bringing him to Powhatan's camp. Here, they paid Smith much terrifying attention, dancing around him by day and tying him to a stake at night. On the third day they brought him before the great chief himself, the first Englishman to be allowed into Powhatan's presence. Several men laid Smith on the ground with his head on a rock and stood over him with clubs, evidently preparing to beat his brains out. Suddenly, Powhatan's 11-year-old daughter, Pocahontas, came running forward "got his head in her armes, and laid her owne upon his to save him from death." Two days later, Powhatan summoned Smith, told him they were now friends and promised to treat Smith like a son. Thereafter Powahatan periodically sent Pocahontas to the fort with gifts of food, which kept them alive through the winter.

Making sense of this episode has long been a puzzle for historians. Smith believed that Pocahontas had saved his life, and nineteenth-century American historians presented the story as a romance. But historians now believe that Smith had actually been subjected to an elaborately staged ritual involving his symbolic death and adoption into the Powhatan Confederacy. For Powhatan, the objective of the ceremony was to overawe Smith with his power, then offer Smith an alliance, which he would gratefully accept.[4] Understanding the reasons for Powhatan's behavior has further complicated the puzzle. Why did the Indians agree to provide the English with life-saving food supplies when a permanent European invasion was not in their long-term interest? Put another way, why did Powhatan not destroy the floundering English settlements when he had the chance? Although Smith later convinced himself that the English had managed to overawe the Indians with their superior technology, it makes little sense to think the Indians were overawed, since it was clear to them that the English were starving and dying.

Understanding what the Indians already knew about Europeans helps us to solve the puzzle. The Powhatans understood that Europeans were both potentially dangerous *and* potentially valuable allies who had valuable goods to offer in trade, including powerful weapons. Powhatan wanted allies. As the leader of the region's most powerful confederacy, he had enemies and competitors. Previous encounters between the Indians and Spaniards, while sometimes deadly, had always been limited and brief. Although Powhatan may well have understood that the Jamestown settlers planned to stay, he failed to realize that these few men would soon be followed by thousands of

---

[4] J. Leo Lemay, *Did Pocahontas Save Captain John Smith?* (Athens, Ga., 1992); Frederic W. Gleach, *Powhatan's World and Colonial Virginia: A Conflict of Cultures* (Lincoln, 1997).

others. Moreover, the previous encounter between local Indians and the English settlers at Roanoke had shown that if the Europeans could be kept off guard, they were relatively easy to control. Powhatan's behavior, which alternated between hostility and friendliness, seems to have been deliberately calculated to keep the English off balance so as to make them easier to manipulate.[5]

Just as Powhatan tried to set the terms of his relationship with the English, the English were trying on their side to control the terms of their relationship with him. When Newport returned with a supply ship in January, he brought with him instructions from the investors back in England that Powhatan was to be crowned king to secure his allegiance to the colony.[6] It is perhaps unsurprising that Powhatan's coronation was a failure; the chief refused to kneel for his crown or to make any acknowledgment of his fealty, merely offering Captain Newport his old moccasins and fur cloak in return. Although Powhatan was still prepared to trade for food, his terms were increasingly high: he now wanted an English-style house and a supply of cannons, hatchets, and swords, which the colony's leaders still refused to supply.

Though he gave it for his own purposes, Powhatan's help enabled the colony to persist. Only 38 of the original 105 settlers were still alive when Newport returned, but more recruits arrived in the spring and fall of 1608 to swell the ranks, including a few women. Smith's energetic leadership helped the situation. After Newport left again at the beginning of April, Smith compelled his fellow colonists to go to work clearing more land, planting corn, strengthening their defenses, and building dwellings for the colonists and their goods. Some of the new migrants were skilled artisans who were set to work producing glass, pitch, and potash, and forging copper. Smith arranged for the shipment of some timber and had another 30 acres of land cleared. Meanwhile, orders to search for gold and to look for a northwest passage continued in effect. Despite the venture's growing cost, the investors seemed determined to keep trying.

By 1609 the Virginia Company of London was receiving news of similar misfortunes to its sister company. Following a preliminary reconnoiter, the Plymouth Company had sent two ships in May 1607 with 120 men on board. A settlement had been established at Sagadahoc on the coast of Maine at or near the Kennebec River. Here, as in Virginia, the settlers built a fort, a church, a storehouse, and 15 dwellings. But here, unlike Virginia, the local Indians refused to supply the settlers with food. Disputes soon broke out among the council. Supplies of food ran low, and the remaining settlers experienced the full severity of a Maine winter. Although a relief ship arrived in spring 1608, the survivors refused to stay and with their departure sank the hopes of any settlement.

The Virginia Company believed that the failings of both companies were the result of the 1606 charter, which gave the Crown the power to make decisions but left the adventurers with the responsibility and the expense of implementing them. Consequently, in February 1609 an application was made to turn the company into a proper joint stock corporation. The Crown, now less sanguine of an immediate profit, was

---

[5] Gleach, *Powhatan's World and Colonial Virginia*; Camilla Townsend, *Pocahontas and Powhatan's Dilemma* (New York, 2004).

[6] Historians have been dependent for information on this period on Smith himself, who often exaggerated his exploits. For an analysis of his claims, see Philip L. Barbour, ed., *The Complete Works of Captain John Smith, 1580–1631*, 3 vols (Chapel Hill, 1986).

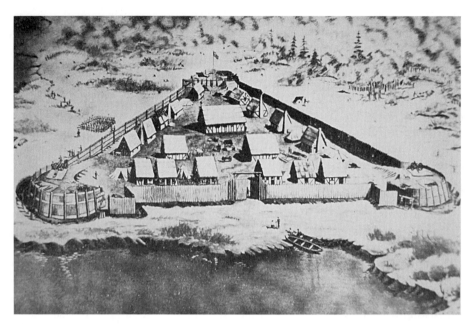

Figure 9 An artist's impression of Jamestown, Virginia, 1607. Private Collection/Peter Newark American Pictures/The Bridgeman Art Library.

happy to see its role diminished. A new charter was thus granted in May 1609, including an enlarged territory extending 200 miles north and south of Point Comfort and stretching from the Atlantic to the Pacific. The royal council was to be abolished and replaced by one elected annually by the stockholders. In the future the company could make its own laws and regulations, provided that they were to be as closely as possible "agreeable to the laws, statutes, government, and policy of this our realm."

Armed with the new charter, the company took immediate steps to put itself on a sounder footing. Even though Newport's ore had turned out to be worthless, more investors bought shares, hoping that the colony's expanded territory could yield precious minerals or other sources of profit. Stock was sold in lots of £12. 10s., £25, and £50, with the promise of a dividend from whatever gold or other valuable commodities, including land, were accumulated after seven years. To avoid further disputes in Virginia itself, the company decided to concentrate authority in the hands of a governor with full powers, including that of exercising "martial law in cases of rebellion or mutiny."

This reorganization happened just in time, for events in Virginia had taken a turn for the worse. The rapid growth of the English settlement appears to have convinced Powhatan that the newcomers threatened his authority. Powhatan therefore repudiated his former alliance with the English and turned openly hostile. Members of the Confederacy began attacking the settlers, taking some of them prisoner, killing their livestock, and burning their crops. Ominously, as the colonists had learned from Indian informants, it appeared that Powhatan had located the survivors of the lost Roanoke colony living in a village in what is now the Carolinas. Here they had been murdered, most likely on Powahatan's orders to prevent them from forming an alliance with the new settlers in Jamestown and threatening his control over the region.[7]

All of this put the Jamestown colonists in an especially precarious position. Smith had lost his ability to rally the settlers and would shortly be leaving the colony. Meanwhile the colonists were still not self-sufficient. When ships from a large relief fleet were wrecked in Bermuda after a violent storm in October 1609 and failed to arrive in Virginia, the outcome was little short of catastrophic. Powhatan's warriors, well aware that the colonists were struggling, killed the settlers' livestock and laid siege to the fort to prevent them from leaving to search for food in the surrounding woods. During the bitter winter that followed, known as "the starving time," most of the settlers in the fort perished either from malnutrition or in attacks from outside. Many were reduced to eating the flesh of their dead companions or local inhabitants, disguising the taste with herbs and roots. One man even murdered (and ate) his wife. The situation was so bad that in June 1610 the 60 survivors were on the point of quitting, as at Sagadahoc, when Lord De La Warr, the new governor, arrived with 375 new settlers, provisions, and news of the company's new charter and future plans.

Powhatan's war against the English would continue until 1614, but the English had by now decided to abandon their attempts to trade with the Indians. The colony's leaders devoted their energies to making the colony self-sufficient, and forcing the settlers to work. De La Warr ordered buildings to be repaired and fields brought back into cultivation. He divided the settlers into groups of 15, so that they could work safely and ward off the hostile native inhabitants. At the same time he launched a policy of search and destroy in a series of raids against the Indians, with resulting atrocities on both sides. During one such operation the children of the queen of the Paspaheghs were thrown into the water and shot before she herself was led into the woods to be put to death. De La Warr also ordered the settlers to seize or destroy Indian food supplies, which provoked the Indians to step up their attacks.

Although De La Warr himself succumbed to sickness and had to leave to save his health, the Virginia Company remained determined to persevere with its investment and sent out a fresh batch of ships in 1611. An advance guard sailed under Deputy Governor Sir Thomas Dale, who had seen extensive military service in the Netherlands. Dale used the more direct route to Virginia via Bermuda which had been pioneered five years earlier by Captain Argall. By the time Sir Thomas Gates, the new governor, arrived, Dale had provided men for three additional forts, and moved a good part of Jamestown's growing population to a new settlement, Henrico, at a more healthful spot 50 miles upriver. The new settlement gave the English a new base of operations from which to launch raids against the Indians, with whom hostilities continued.

For the next two years the colony was governed first by Gates (1611–13) and then by Dale (1614–16). The problems of earlier years – a contentious, undisciplined settler population and Indian antagonism – continued. For Gates, an upper-class English gentleman with views typical of men of his station, the colony's disastrous early

---

[7] The most thorough analysis to date of evidence about the killing of the lost colonists and reasons for it is James Horn, *A Kingdom Strange: The Brief and Tragic History of the Lost Colony of Roanoke* (New York, 2010).

experiences confirmed his assumption that common sorts of people were prone to lawlessness and savagery unless subjected to strong external controls. To manage the colony, Gates enacted a code of laws "Divine, Morall, and Martial," which imposed rigorous controls upon the settlers' behavior. The laws required daily attendance at divine service, imposed stiff penalties for blasphemy and other crimes against the church, and prohibited criticism of company officials. The code stipulated that work hours be from six o'clock till ten o'clock in the morning and again from two till four in the afternoon, the rest of the day being devoted to the personal repair of cottages and the cultivation of garden plots. Among the offenses carrying the death penalty were sodomy, adultery, theft, desertion, mutiny, and running away to the Indians. While Gates appears to have used the laws mostly as a threat, Dale's administration enforced them to their fullest extent, in effect imposing order through terror. Men were executed for these offenses in a manner that shocked many of the colonists, not only by being hanged but also by being burned to death, broken on the wheel, or tied to stakes and starved to death. The order imposed upon Virginia was to be an order much harsher than the one familiar to contemporaries in England.

In 1612, with bad news continuing to emanate from the colony, yet another charter was sought as a way to solve the venture's financial problems. This time the charter allowed the company to run a lottery, a popular form of speculation in the seventeenth century, from which profits could be used to finance other operations. The company also asked to have its domain extended to include Bermuda, which appeared to be suitable both for the production of cash crops and as a protective base against the Spanish. Finally, the new charter provided for more meetings of the general court to facilitate the better government of the company, and greater responsiveness to the interests of the ordinary investors, or adventurers, as they were called. With this second reconstruction of authority it was hoped that the company would finally begin to turn a profit.

Fortuitously, two new developments now helped to improve the colony's prospects. The first of these was the discovery of a potentially profitable commercial crop. Although the various staples first favored by the company had not materialized, tobacco was emerging as a promising alternative. The local plant, *nicotiana rustica*, was extremely bitter; but in 1612 John Rolfe, who had arrived in 1609, began experimenting with a West Indian variety, *nicotiana tabaccum*, which was sweet like the Spanish product. When the drought which had plagued the region in 1607 finally ended around 1613, this new crop offered the prospect of a profitable export trade to England; for although James I equated smoking with the fires of hell, his kingdom was a growing market for tobacco. Rolfe's first consignment of four hogsheads – about 2,600 pounds – was shipped in 1614. Three years later 20,000 pounds were dispatched.

The second development that would help the colony to prosper was a truce with the Indians. During a raid in 1613, Samuel Argall, a member of the council, kidnapped Pocahontas and demanded the return of English prisoners and English weapons along with a new supply of corn in exchange for her release. Pocahontas, now aged 17, lived at Henrico, learned English, and befriended some of the Englishmen, who were determined to try to convert her to Christianity. Apparently the old dream of civilizing the Indians remained alive in the minds of some of the colonists. Powhatan now agreed to a

DOCUMENT 5

John Rolfe's request for permission from Governor Sir Thomas Dale to marry Pocahontas, 1614, reprinted in Warren M. Billings, *The Old Dominion in the Seventeenth Century: A Documentary History of Virginia, 1606–1689* (Chapel Hill, 1975), 216–19

Since the colonists' lives were still strictly controlled by the Virginia Company, Rolfe needed permission from the governor's council to marry Pocahontas. Among others, he had to win over Dale, the chief enforcer of the Laws Divine, Morall and Martiall. Questions to consider: *What concerns about his marriage to a Native American woman is Rolfe trying to overcome? How does he seek to persuade his readers to allow the marriage? What kinds of assumptions about Native Americans and their relationships with the English does Rolfe communicate in this passage?*

Let therefore this [constitute] my well advised protestation . . . if my chiefest intent and purpose be not to strive with all my power of body and mind, in the undertaking of so mighty a matter, no way led (so far forth as man's weakness may permit) with the unbridled desire of carnal affection: but for the good of this plantation, for the honour of our country, for the glory of God, for my own salvation, and for the converting to the true knowledge of God and Jesus Christ, an unbelieving creature, namely Pokahuntas, to whom my hearty and best thoughts are, and have a long time been so intangled . . .

I have not only examined but thoroughly tried and pared my thoughts . . . I forgot not to set before my own eyes the frailty of mankind . . . Nor was I ignorant of the heavy displeasure which Almighty God conceived against the sons of Levie [*sic*] and Israel for marrying strange wives, nor of the inconveniences which may thereby arise . . . which made me look about warily and with good circumspection, into the grounds and principal agitations, which thus should provoke me to be in love with one whose education hath been so rude, her manners barbarous, her generation accursed, and so discrepant in all from my self, that often times with fear and trembling, I have ended my private controversy with this: surely these are wicked instigations . . .

Now if the vulgar sort, who square all men's actions by the base rule of their own filthiness, shall tax or taunt me in this my godly labor: let them know, it is not any hungry appetite, to gorge my self with incontinency . . . Nor am I so desperate in estate, that I regard not what becometh of me; nor am I out of hope but one day to see my Country, nor so devoid of friends, nor mean in birth, but there to obtain a match to my great content; nor have I ignorantly passed over my hopes there, or regardlessly seek to lose the love of my friends, by taking this course.

truce with the English, but not before the intelligent and culturally adaptable young woman had decided to stay with the English, convert to Christianity, and marry John Rolfe. Pocahontas may have taken this course because she believed it would help to cement a long-term alliance between the English and the Powhatans on the favorable terms that her father had sought.[8] Much romanticizing has surrounded this event, not least for its implication that the two races might have lived in harmony. Yet the record shows that this was the only formal marriage between an Englishman and a Native American in the English colonies at this time, in stark contrast with the Spanish colonies, where interracial marriages were common.

The marriage, along with the truce it seemed to symbolize, marked an important milestone for the colony. John Rolfe and Pocahontas, now known as Lady Rebecca Rolfe, traveled to London in the spring of 1616 with their newborn son, Thomas. Pocahontas's visit caused a sensation. A portrait of her wearing expensive English clothing was painted and widely reproduced; she was invited to parties and social events all over London and received by the king and queen in December. Everywhere, she was seen as proof that the North American Indians could be successfully civilized and turned into English subjects. Tragically, she died in London before returning to America, but the Virginia Company could not have asked for better publicity for their venture. With Pocahontas as its symbol, the colony had finally been able to present an appearance of peace and stability.

3 THE CHARTER OF LIBERTIES

Historians face another puzzle in trying to understand why it was so difficult for the Virginia Company to succeed. The Spanish had managed to establish colonies that fulfilled their investors' wildest dreams of wealth. Why was it so difficult for the English to do so? A comparison with the Spanish colonization experience offers a way to answer the question. The Spanish arrived early in the Americas, which allowed them to conquer and then colonize the most densely populated regions with the greatest surplus wealth. For them, colonization amounted to installing themselves at the head of functioning social systems and forcing fully sedentary local populations to provide them with labor and tribute. In order to manage both their newfound wealth along with their new subject populations, the Spanish Crown created bureaucratic and highly centralized systems of colonial administration to implement and enforce Crown policies. It was expensive to send Spanish officials to govern the colonies, but the wealth flowing out of colonial silver mines into the Crown's coffers made the expense worthwhile.

The English, by contrast, came late to the Americas. By the seventeenth century the only regions left for them to colonize were in far less densely populated areas, mostly along the North American coast north of Florida. The Indian populations here had

---

[8] Townsend, *Pocahontas and Powhatan's Dilemma.*

Figure 10 Pocahontas in London. From John Smith, *The Generall Historie of Virginia* (1624). Courtesy of the John Carter Brown Library at Brown University.

little surplus wealth for the English to seize. In addition they were highly mobile and difficult to conquer, as the experience with Powhatan showed. When people in an Eastern Woodlands village were threatened, they could pack up their village and move to a new location out of harm's way, a strategy that was usually unavailable to peoples in Mesoamerica. It would be far more difficult for the English to survive along the Atlantic coast using Indian labor than it had been for the Spanish further south. Also, the absence of wealth meant the English Crown had little to gain by creating an expensive governing structure here, so instead it allowed the investors considerable leeway in administering their colonial ventures themselves as they saw fit. Thanks to that freedom, colonial investors sometimes floundered for years before finding ways to create workable economic and governing systems for their colonies.[9]

Notwithstanding their early missteps, there were signs by 1616 that the Virginia Company was inching towards a workable model for organizing the venture. One thing the investors had realized was that they could not succeed with a population of temporary adventurers. Instead they would need to find ways to attract a self-sufficient, stable, growing settler population. Up until this point the population had remained obstinately static; in 1616 there were a mere 324 inhabitants, mostly men, at the company's six settlements, as against 450 in 1611. Clearly, few were tempted to endure the harsh rule of Gates and Dale when the rewards were so small. The colony had begun to deal with the problem of retention in 1614, when the surviving servants of the original settlement were due to be released from their obligation to serve the company. Dale realized that unless they were given some inducement to stay, the company's population would be quickly depleted, and the venture would fail. Accordingly, in 1614 he allotted to all those who had settled in the colony prior to 1612 three acres of land to farm for their own use, exempt from all payments except one month's service to the colony and 12 bushels of corn in rent. Still unsolved was the problem of the company's shareholders, who were supposed to receive a dividend of 100 acres of cleared land in 1616. The company had no means of honoring these terms; it could offer the adventurers no more than 50 acres of land, and that only if they subscribed another £12. 10s. in stock.

By 1619, the investors had begun to understand that the key to a successful colony was to ensure that the settlers themselves had a stake in the venture's survival. Sir Edwin Sandys, who became the head of the company in 1619, began sending large numbers of new colonists to ensure a self-sustaining population. Next he sent groups of respectable, unmarried young women so as to encourage the formation of families. He recruited more artisans to establish the long hoped for silk, glass, brick, iron, salt, naval stores, and shipbuilding enterprises. To encourage investors to emigrate permanently to America, Sandys granted subpatents to groups of subscribers or wealthy individuals in return for special administrative and judicial privileges. Subscribers' lands were now to be held in free and common socage, subject to only a nominal quitrent. The first grant was made to John Martin in 1617, but Sandys now extended the practice. Although many of the subsequent 44 patents were not taken up, including that to the Pilgrims (see Chapter 4), enough were established to accelerate the shift from company to private property.

Placing property in private hands was a key element of the company's emerging new approach.[10] While making arrangements to increase the future profitability of the colony, Sandys sought to keep shareholders committed to the company by announcing that all adventurers would be given 100 acres of land as their lawful dividend.

---

[9]   Reasons for the different development of English and Spanish systems of colonial government are analyzed in J. H. Elliott, *Empires of the Atlantic World: Britain and Spain in America, 1492–1830* (New Haven, 2006).

[10]   Karen Kupperman has observed that the key to successful colonization for each of the English colonies, beginning with Virginia, was the institutionalization of private property in land, control of taxation by a representative assembly, and civilian control of the colony's military (*Providence Island, 1630–1641: The Other Puritan Colony* (New York, 1993), 19). Kupperman further explores the evolution of English colonial efforts in *Roanoke: The Abandoned Colony*, 2nd edn (Lanham, 2007), and *The Jamestown Project* (Cambridge, Mass., 2007).

Furthermore, all those who had arrived at their own expense since 1616 would receive 50 acres, plus a similar amount for every dependent who accompanied them. This provision came to be known as the Virginia headright. Lastly, lands were set aside to support the ministry, to build a school for the native peoples in order to encourage their conversion to Christianity, and, more distantly, to establish a university for the settlers.

Sandys by no means envisioned the creation of a society of independent farmers; like his contemporaries, he envisioned the ideal society as a hierarchical one in which the best sorts of men controlled most of the property, and the poor remained dependent. Accordingly, servants who were recruited to cultivate company lands were expected after seven years of service to become tenants, not landowners, surrendering half their produce to the company so that it could pay a dividend back home. Sandys encouraged the City of London and other towns to finance the departure of some of their surplus poor and orphaned children, in effect helping to create a system of temporary servitude in Virginia that was considerably more coercive than the system then in place in England. While English young people had the option of changing masters yearly, indentured servants in Virginia sold themselves (or were sold) into servitude for a full term of four to seven years. Nevertheless, poor boys and young men continued to sell themselves into service and arrive in Virginia despite the limited freedom they would enjoy once they arrived. A contract of service provided a viable mechanism for paying one's passage across the Atlantic, and with poverty growing in England, many young men believed they had a better chance to prosper in the New World. During the next four years nearly 4,000 persons were dispatched to the colony.

As part of its administrative reorganization of the colony, the company divided up the existing settled areas into four boroughs: Charles City, Jamestown, Henrico, and Kiccowtan. The company was to retain 3,000 acres in each of these boroughs for its own servants and tenants. Ever mindful of the need to induce investors to emigrate to Virginia, Sandys decided that the settlement needed a different form of government. Gates's code of laws had already been abandoned, but further changes were necessary. Sandys hit on the device of convening an assembly in America. The scheme may have been devised partly to accommodate those adventurers who had gone to claim their land and were in consequence unable to attend the quarterly meetings in London. It had the effect of giving investors and free settlers alike a stake in the colony's future.

The new governing body was to be composed of the governor, his council, and two burgesses from every hundred or parish elected by the inhabitants. It was to meet once a year and have full power to enact measures on all matters for the colony's good government. Naturally all acts would have to conform where practical to English law and would also be subject to the veto of both the governor and the company in London. Notably, though, laws would not be handed down by the Crown, as they were in the Spanish colonies. The government of Virginia would take place locally, within the colony.

The new measure was originally intended strictly as a privilege. It was not intended to confer any rights on the settlers as Englishmen, among whom voting was the prerogative of the few. The only right was that of the adventurers to attend company meetings. However, to widen the appeal of the measure, Sandys wisely opened the vote to all free male inhabitants.[11] It was a remarkably generous gesture, and one which has

---

[11] Servants, who were not free, were not included.

DOCUMENT 6

Formal constitution for a council and assembly in Virginia, July 24, 1621, reprinted in W. Keith Kavenagh, *Foundations of Colonial America: A Documentary History* (New York, 1973), Vol. 3, 1889

Although Governor Yeardley called the first meeting of the colonists' representatives in July 1619, the company defined the new body only two years later. One interesting feature was that the company intended to make ratification of its own decrees subject to reciprocal approval by the assembly. Question to consider: *Why would the creation of an assembly have helped to induce settlers and investors to come to Virginia?*

Know that we, the said Treasurer, Council and Company, taking into our careful consideration the present state of the said colony in Virginia and intending, by divine assistance, to settle such a form of government there as may be to the greatest benefit and comfort of the people, whereby all injustice, grievance, and oppression may be prevented . . .

We therefore . . . do hereby order and declare that from hence forward there be two supreme councils in Virginia for the better government of the said colony aforesaid. The one of which councils, to be called the Council of State, whose office shall be chiefly assisting with their care and advice and circumspection to the said Governor, shall be chosen, nominated, placed, and displaced from time to time by us, the said Treasurer, Council and Company . . .

The other Council, more general, to be called by the Governor, and yearly . . . and no oftener but for very extraordinary and important occasions, shall consist for the present of the said Council of State and two Burgesses out of every town, hundred and other particular plantation to be respectfully chosen by the inhabitants. Which Council shall be called the General Assembly, wherein, as also in the said Council of State, all matters shall be decided, determined and ordered by the greater part of the voices then present, reserving always to the Governor a negative voice. And this general assembly shall have full power to . . . make, ordain, and enact such general laws and orders for the behalf of the said colony and good government thereof as shall from time to time appear necessary or requisite. Wherein, as in all things, we require the general Assembly, as also the Council of State, to imitate and follow the policy of the form of government, laws, custom, manners and administration of justice used in the realm of England, as near as may be . . . provided that no laws or ordinance made in the General Assembly shall be in force and valid unless the same shall be solemnly ratified and confirmed . . . here in England . . .

rightly been seen as a crucial episode in the development of representative institutions in British North America.

The news of these momentous changes was brought by a new governor, George Yeardley, who convened the first assembly late in July 1619 at Jamestown in the church.

Sitting in the choir stalls were representatives from the four boroughs and eight plantations. A number of laws were passed, many based on previous company ordinances. The first stated that no injury was to be done to the Indians "whereby the present peace might be disturbed and ancient quarrels revived." Then followed a series of decrees against drunkenness, idleness, gaming, and the wearing of ostentatious clothing; these were not dissimilar to Dale's laws, except for the severity of the punishment to be incurred. Trade with the Indians was permitted, though only with the consent of the governor, but constant care was to be taken since the native inhabitants were in general "a most treacherous people." Accordingly, no guns were to be sold, and all settlers were to attend church on Sunday bringing their weapons with them.

Other laws sought to create a more predictable economic environment. The company's future profit was to be limited annually to 25 percent, while private landowners were excused having to sell their produce to the company storehouse. The assembly also addressed the curing of tobacco, demonstrating the crop's importance to the colony, along with the need for the proper regulation of relations between master and servant. Finally, every household was to have one spare barrel of corn, plant six mulberry bushes, and cultivate vines. The lessons of "the starving time" had finally been learned.

4 THE MASSACRE OF 1622 AND FALL OF THE COMPANY

It seemed that the colony was now set for a period of growth. One visitor, John Pory, noted in 1619 that, although sickness was still prevalent, the colonists also enjoyed the prospect of growing wheat and excellent grapes; he commented that "a few years may bring this colony to perfection," if the English plow was introduced to improve the preparation of the soil. The only cause for concern was the obsession with tobacco, where one or two planters had made a profit of £1,000. Not surprisingly, John Rolfe reported unqualified contentment the following year. The planters, freed from the company's restrictions, "strive and are prepared to build houses and to clear their ground."

Nevertheless the growth expected by Sandys did not take place. One reason was the appalling mortality rate. Barely one-quarter of the 4,000 settlers shipped out between 1618 and 1622 survived. Another was that the company, still harboring the delusion that it could develop manufactures in the colony, sent over hundreds of craftsmen who were quite unsuited to the wilderness conditions. Other colonists were simply physically weak, for no medical examination was ever given, so that even if they survived the voyage, they succumbed during the seasoning period which all newcomers had to undergo. Pory advised that people should be dispatched only in the fall, when the weather was reasonably benign. They could then acclimatize during the winter before planting their first crops. His advice, however, was all too often ignored, and Yeardley's resources were severely strained caring for the sick and destitute.

Also, the company faced increasing competition for investors' funds. The colony in Bermuda, which had by now separated from the Virginia Company, was prospering. English companies had been organized to trade in West Africa and to explore for gold in

Guiana. Then in March 1621 James I revoked the company's right to hold a lottery, a serious blow, since it ended what had been the company's best source of revenue. The likelihood that investors would put more money into the venture after such wretched returns over the past 15 years was minimal.

As money was still required to meet the operating costs and pay the adventurers' dividends, the company's thoughts turned to the exploitation of tobacco. Although the company had not initially welcomed Rolfe's experiments, attempts to reduce the crop had been to little avail, especially after 1616 when most colonists could do what they wanted with their land. Production soared, reaching nearly 50,000 pounds in 1618, and almost 200,000 pounds by 1622.

In these circumstances the company reluctantly recognized that it had no alternative but to exploit this unexpectedly profitable commodity. Unfortunately, under the 1609 charter company products were liable to a customs levy. The Crown now proposed a duty of one shilling a pound, twice the anticipated rate. Even worse, the duties were to be collected by tax farmers, who would thus control the crop's distribution. Sandys was not happy at this loss of patronage and proposed that the company itself should import and distribute the tobacco, allowing the Crown in return one-third of the crop. To this James I consented. Many shareholders, however, were appalled at the extravagant fees proposed for those administering the scheme when so few dividends had been paid. Pamphlets were written attacking Sandys, while his opponents, led by the earl of Warwick and Sir Thomas Smith, appealed to the king to intervene. In response the Privy Council ordered the tobacco contract to be suspended while it investigated the company's affairs.

While this dispute was taking place between the investors and their critics in the government, another crisis suddenly devastated the colony, one that illustrated how deeply the company's new policies were transforming the relationship between the English and the local Indians. One result of Sandys's liberal land policy was that the settlements had become dispersed along the James River for almost 100 miles. Their farms encroached much further into Indian territory than the Powhatan people could ever have anticipated. English land uses had devastated Indian food supplies. English hogs were allowed to forage in the woods where they trampled and ate Indian corn and consumed the wild plants needed to sustain the local population of deer. Meanwhile, the political leadership of the confederacy had changed, passing from Powhatan (who died in 1618) to Opechancanough. The Powhatans' new leader had come to understand clearly what the continued presence of the English would mean: more plantations, the felling of the forests, the extinction of the game, and the destruction of his people's way of life. Tobacco, not trade, was now the main interest of the settlers. The settlers had become increasingly hostile to the Indians; as one officer of the company noted, "There is scarce any man amongst us that doth so much as afford them a good thought in his heart." Also troubling to the Indians were English attempts to convert Indian children to Christianity under the guise of educating them.

Finally, when an Englishman murdered one of the *werowances* early in 1622, and the company failed to provide redress, members of the Confederacy resolved to end the settlers' presence through a series of coordinated assaults. Since their attack on Friday, March 22, 1622, was not preceded by any overt hostility, local Indians were able to gain access to the settlement on seemingly innocuous business before revealing their true intent. Some even breakfasted with their victims. Jamestown was saved only by a last-minute warning from a native convert to Christianity. In the subsequent attacks some 350 colonists – men, women, and children – were struck down before the rest of the population could respond.

At a stroke many of the colonists' gains since 1616 were swept away. Nearly a quarter of the colony's total population of 1,500 people had been killed. Several major plantations were destroyed, notably Martin's Hundred and Charles City, with its precious iron works. War with the Indians now resumed in earnest, and would continue for another decade, with bloody reprisals on both sides. The delicate balance between self-sufficiency and starvation was upset, and lethal epidemics swept through the population. The image of the colony as a death trap was once more raised in the minds of potential settlers back home.

The attack placed the final nail in the coffin of the Virginia Company, and a reorganization of its government was now inevitable. In April 1623 the Privy Council appointed a seven-man commission under Sir William Jones to inquire into the state of the colony, and at the same time ordered the company to send help. Being bankrupt, it declined to do so, and thus stood in breach of its obligations under the charter of 1612. The Privy Council ordered the attorney general to begin legal proceedings to annul the charter. By May 1624 the Virginia Company was no more.[12] The demise of the company coincided with the death of James I and a year passed before his successor had time to decide how to reorganize the colony. Eventually Charles I simply affirmed by proclamation through the Privy Council the original intent that the colony had been established "for the propagation of Christian Religion, the increase of trade, and the enlarging of his Royal empire." Virginia would henceforth be administered by a governor and royal council answerable to the king.

Although Virginia now became a royal colony, Charles's proclamation neither disrupted its economic development nor ended the Crown's essentially hands-off policy towards its empire. The proclamation assured the colonists that the annulment of the charter was "not intended to take away or impeach the particular interest of any private planter or adventurer." Their property rights would be protected. Moreover the declaration made no mention of the assembly, whose existence the Privy Council most likely overlooked. No ban was placed on its meeting, indicating that the king's main

---

[12] It used to be thought that the demise of the company, and by implication, that of the assembly, was part of the Stuart kings' design to impose a more absolutist form of government. This interpretation was popular with nineteenth-century Whig nationalist historians, who were keen to affirm that the destiny of America was an inevitable progression to liberty and democracy. The most famous work in this mold is George Bancroft, *History of the United States*, 10 vols (Boston, 1834–74). The reality is that the disputes over the company had only tenuous links with those between the king and Parliament. The real reason for the demise of the company was its failure to make a profit, which exasperated the shareholders, enough for them first to take their cause to the general court and then to raise it in Parliament, the Privy Council, and anywhere else where they could get a hearing. The latter interpretation was first put forward by Wesley Frank Craven in *Dissolution of the Virginia Company* (New York, 1932), and by Charles M. Andrews in *The Colonial Period of American History*, 4 vols (New Haven, 1934–8{1964 in the biblio.}). Both were members of the imperial school who were keen to emphasize the benefits of the English connection, partly as a result of the greater impartiality that time brings, and partly because they felt that the Anglo-Saxon nations ought to stand together.

concern was to end the bitter altercations within the company and perhaps in time to produce some revenue. Beyond that aim he had no plans.

5   GROWTH AND CONSOLIDATION, 1625–1660

The imposition of royal government in 1625 was hardly a cause for celebration, since the colonists were uncertain what it would mean. It might merely lead to the re-establishment of the company, for during the next few years Sandys made several attempts to regain the charter. But in retrospect the removal of the company was seen to have been a blessing. The imposition of royal control actually sped the development of the kinds of policies already begun by 1619, policies which gave immigrants a stake in the colony's future by enabling them to acquire land, earn profits, form families to some extent, and participate in their own self-government. These policies, in the long run, helped to spur continued rapid migration from England and the development of a profitable tobacco export economy. England's colony in Virginia would endure and gradually become more stable (though in the future these same policies would also generate destructive forces with tragic human costs).

In 1625, the colonists themselves had two main political concerns: one was to avoid the imposition of a contract for the marketing of their tobacco; the other was to prevent the reimposition of martial law and to keep their assembly. To this end they sent various petitions and passed an ordinance declaring that "the governor shall not lay any taxes or impositions upon the colony, their lands or commodities other than by the authority of the general assembly." On the matter of an assembly, the Crown remained obstinately quiet.

As a practical matter, though, both Sir Francis Wyatt, the first royal governor, and his successor regularly summoned meetings to sound out colonists' opinions on matters of special importance. Although the governors had plenipotentiary powers, once in Virginia they found their authority limited by the absence of soldiers or a bureaucracy. Ultimately they were able to govern only with the consent of the colonists. Although for many years Charles I did not grant the assembly formal recognition, in 1639 he conceded the crucial point that the assembly "together with the governor and council shall have power to make acts and laws for the government of that plantation, correspondent as near as may be to the laws of England." Governor Wyatt was authorized to summon the burgesses "as formerly once a year or oftener, if urgent occasion shall require."

Regarding the tobacco contract, Charles I eventually settled for a customs duty of one shilling, leaving the colonists to market it themselves. Such a policy ultimately facilitated the growth of tobacco production and exports, and the creation of a commercial agricultural economy and society. Also, the removal of the company further opened the settlement of the land to private individuals. Although the Crown retained some interest, it was only too happy to encourage such settlement in return for a small quitrent. The colony was still an unhealthy destination for immigrants, many of whom perished during their first year or two in the colony, a period known as the "seasoning." Still, they continued to arrive in large numbers, lured by the prospect of making money growing tobacco. Indeed the potential profits to be gained from growing tobacco allowed even tenant farmers to earn enough to buy land of their own. Freed servants could likewise earn high enough wages during these early decades that they could buy land of their own within a few years of finishing their indentures.

As Virginia became a settler society devoted to commercial agriculture, the old effort to assimilate the Indians into English society by converting them to Christianity was abandoned and a new policy towards the Indians began to emerge instead. After the massacre of 1622, the colony's leaders struck out furiously, hoping to destroy all the Native American settlements in the vicinity of Jamestown and the lower peninsula in order to claim the land for themselves. "Our first work is the expulsion of the Salvages to gain the free range of the country for increase of cattle, swine &c," wrote Governor Wyatt. "It is infinitely better to have no heathen among us, who at best were but thorns in our sides, than to be at peace and league with them." For the next decade expeditions were sent out three times a year to kill the enemy, seize their crops, and prevent their return. No tactics were too cruel. One detachment talked with the Potomac Indians in 1623 as a ruse to poison 200 of them, including their chief. Peace was achieved only in the early 1630s, when the two sides agreed to maintain a strict separation by a line across the Jamestown peninsula, with only limited contacts for trade.[13] Unlike the Spanish, who made extraordinary efforts to assimilate and "civilize" the Indians, the English in Virginia would henceforth work to exclude the Indians altogether.

The agreement reached in 1632 was at best an uneasy truce, and another major conflict was almost unavoidable. That conflict came in 1644–6 in a war that was fought for the same reasons as before. This time the colonists were more numerous than the Indians, even though Opechancanough began hostilities with another surprise attack, in which 500 settlers were killed. The settlers no longer needed the Indians, except for a handful of fur traders. What they wanted was the Indians' land, and the war provided a convenient excuse for ridding the area of its native inhabitants. After two years of fighting, Opechancanough was captured and brought to Jamestown, where he was murdered by his guards. The result was the final destruction of the Powhatan Confederacy. Under the terms of the peace treaty of 1646 the Indians were banned from the Jamestown peninsula under pain of death, and had to acknowledge the king of England as their sovereign. Even their remaining lands on the north side of the York River were not exempt from colonization.

This gruesome turn in Anglo-Indian relations would often be repeated elsewhere over the next two and a half centuries. The initial pattern was for local Indians to form trading relationships with their vastly outnumbered new English neighbors. Over time, as the settlers' numbers increased and they became more confident, their eyes turned to the Indians' land. Conflicts over incompatible land uses resulted in intermittent

---

[13]   Various historians have concluded that English abandoned a policy of trade and assimilation and adopted a policy of expulsion after 1622. See, for example, Alden T. Vaughan, "'Expulsion of the Salvages': English Policy and the Virginia Massacre of 1622," *William and Mary Quarterly*, 35 (1978), 57–84; Bernard Sheehan, *Savagism and Civility: Indians and Englishmen in Colonial Virginia* (Cambridge, 1980), and Karen Kupperman, *Settling with the Indians: The Meeting of English and Indian Cultures in America, 1580–1640* (Totowa, 1980), 175–80. However, peaceful contacts did occur after 1622, especially in the fur trade; see Frederick J. Fausz, "Merging and Emerging Worlds: Anglo-Indian Interest Groups and the Development of the Seventeenth-Century Chesapeake," in Lois Green Carr, Philip D. Morgan, and Jean B. Russo, eds, *Colonial Chesapeake Society* (Chapel Hill, 1989).

warfare. Once a sufficient number of local Indians had left the region so that the remainder were outnumbered, the settlers launched full-scale attacks. In the end the remnants of the indigenous inhabitants were either enslaved or confined to reservations, where they could be controlled for the convenience of the colonists. Even then Indian peoples were not safe, for although sporadic attempts were made to protect them from the excesses of their white neighbors, these were rarely effective.

As new land was opened for the colonists to exploit, the cultivation of tobacco became increasingly widespread. Admittedly the Crown, like the Virginia Company before it, continued to cherish delusions of a more diversified economy. On his arrival in 1641, Governor Sir William Berkeley was ordered "to cause the people there to apply themselves to the raising of more Staple Comodities as Hemp and Flax, Rape Seed, Pitch and Tarr, for the Tanning of Hydes and leather." To no avail. Although the price of tobacco plunged more than 90 percent, from three shillings to threepence a pound, in the 1630s, the crop still produced a good profit for most planters. Equally fruitless were Berkeley's attempts to induce the inhabitants to live in towns so as to make the settlements more defensible. All planters wanted a riverside jetty where they could load their produce. Towns simply did not suit a plantation system, and Chesapeake society would remain predominantly rural. The assembly created eight English-style counties in 1635, each with justices, a recorder, a sheriff, constables, and a coroner.

Now that the basic requirements of settlement had been learned, the population at last began to grow. A steady stream of persons continued to come to Virginia, encouraged by the demand for tobacco. By 1640 the population had reached 8,000. Those who brought enough capital to set up on their own purchased land so they could grow tobacco. Tobacco was a labor-intensive crop, meaning that a planter who wished to expand his production had to find a way to purchase extra hands. Slaves from overseas were hard to come by and prohibitively expensive, while the indigenous inhabitants made poor workers, since they tended either to escape or to die in captivity. Impoverished English teenagers ready to try their fortunes in the New World, on the other hand, were plentiful and cheap, providing an abundant supply of indentured servants. They were the prime reason for the steady growth in both the population and the economy, with the production of tobacco reaching one million pounds by 1640.

The system of indentured labor shaped the development of the society. Planters' preferences for young male servants, who could produce more tobacco than young women, produced a society that was overwhelmingly male. The lack of a traditional family life meant that early Virginian society would produce few children, and could sustain its population only if it attracted a constant supply of immigrants. Most planters, accordingly, had to console themselves with the thought that, once they had made their fortune, they could go home for a wife to England. For most, Virginia was only a temporary residence.

English planters in Virginia did not object to purchasing African slaves, although the Africans brought here before 1660 were small in number. In 1634 there were perhaps 200, at a time when the settlers numbered 7,500. Meanwhile the status of these Africans was relatively fluid. In part this was due to the lack of a legal definition for African servants, for slavery had disappeared as an institution in England before the Norman Conquest and English colonizers had no reason to codify a law of slavery when they first arrived in Virginia. As a result of their ambiguous legal status, African servants were not sharply differentiated from European servants before 1660. Many lived together, not infrequently absconded together, and even intermarried. A number of Africans were provided for in wills. In cases of sexual misconduct, Africans were not necessarily punished more severely than European offenders, for racial attitudes had not yet hardened.[14] Virginia was still a "society with slaves" rather than a fully developed "slave society."[15]

The fluidity of slavery in early Virginia was a product of the experiences and choices not only of the English settlers but of enslaved Africans themselves. Many Africans who were brought to Virginia before 1660 or so were "Atlantic creoles" who had high levels of sophistication and exposure to European cultures before they arrived. For example, the first known group of 20 Africans to be brought to Virginia on a board a passing Dutch ship in 1619 had been seized from a Portuguese vessel supplying slaves from the Portuguese colony of Angola to the Spanish port of Vera Cruz in Mexico.[16] A number of these Africans were Christians with Portuguese surnames, suggesting that they were coastal people who had worked closely with the Portuguese in slave trading enclaves along the African Atlantic coast before being enslaved. The knowledge and cultural savvy they had acquired while living with Europeans enabled some of these individuals to better their situations once they arrived in Virginia.

The most famous of these "Atlantic Creoles" was an African man named Anthony Johnson, who arrived in Virginia around 1621. First known by the English as "Antonio a Negro," he had probably lived and worked with Portuguese traders in Brazil or West Africa, and knew how to work the system. Antonio made with an agreement with his master that in return for a period of diligent service he would be freed like an indentured servant. Having secured his own freedom, he anglicized his name to Anthony Johnson,

---

[14] Writers who have stressed the fluidity of the situation in the early period include Oscar Handlin and Mary Handlin, "Origins of the Southern Labor System," *William and Mary Quarterly*, 7 (1950), 199–222; Edmund S. Morgan, *American Slavery, American Freedom: The Ordeal of Colonial Virginia* (New York, 1975); and T. H. Breen and Stephen Innes, *"Myne Owne Ground": Race and Freedom on Virginia's Eastern Shore, 1640–1676* (New York, 1980). Other historians who have argued that pre-existing English racial attitudes made the development of African slavery in North America more likely include Carl N. Degler, *Out of Our Past: The Forces that Shaped Modern America* (New York, 1959); Alden T. Vaughan, "Blacks in Virginia: A Note on the First Decade," *William and Mary Quarterly*, 29 (1972), 469–78; Winthrop D. Jordan, *White over Black: American Attitudes toward the Negro, 1550–1812* (Chapel Hill, 1968), and J. Douglas Deal, *Race and Class in Colonial Virginia: Indians, Englishmen and Africans on the Eastern Shore during the Seventeenth Century* (New York, 1993). More recently, historians have argued that race is a matter of social construction rather than biology; that racial attitudes are the product of unequal relationships and misguided ideology. Such writers have been influenced by modern genetics, which indicate that there are no significant biological differences between the different races. For an interpretation arguing that race was a matter of social construction, see Ira Berlin, *Many Thousands Gone: The First Two Centuries of Slavery in North America* (Cambridge, Mass., 1998). The two approaches are discussed in Michael McGiffert, ed., "Constructing Race: Differentiating Peoples in the Early Modern World," *William and Mary Quarterly*, 54 (1997), 1–252.

[15] Historians currently make this distinction, based on the ratio between free and enslaved persons, on the grounds that "societies with slaves," where the majority of the population was free, were more likely to be humane and less racist than "slave societies," where the dominant slave population seemingly posed a threat to the white inhabitants.

[16] For the origin of these Africans, see Engel Sluiter, "New Light on the '20 Odd Negroes' Arriving in Virginia, August 1619," *William and Mary Quarterly*, 54 (1997), 396–8.

then purchased the freedom of his family before acquiring several slaves himself, together with a substantial farm. On at least one occasion he successfully sued a white neighbor for the recovery of a slave, receiving damages in the process. His son John had even more success than Anthony, acquiring an estate of at least 450 acres later in the century.[17]

Anthony Johnson was probably more the exception than the rule, since Africans typically remained firmly at the bottom of the colonial social and economic order. If they were indentured, their period of service might last up to 28 years, and unlike white servants they were rarely given formal contracts. In wills, Africans were usually placed after other servants, next to the livestock, and were recorded only by their first names. Nonetheless some Africans achieved their freedom during these early years, created families, and began building communities and ascending the social ladder. The system of slavery had not yet solidified, nor was there any reason to believe it would take root in North American soil.

For persons of European descent, the path to success was more straightforward. Extra labor would result in more crops, which could then finance the purchase of more land and servants in a growing spiral of production and wealth. In this spiral, men who began with larger amounts of capital had an advantage, for they were able to amass more land and more servants than ordinary men or ex-servants. The possibilities had been demonstrated in the late 1620s by Yeardley himself, as well as George Sandys and Abraham Piercy, all of whom had a mixed labor force of nearly 40 servants cultivating several hundred acres. Others like Yeardley, Sandys, and Piercy arrived during subsequent decades. They were minor gentry or substantial yeoman families like the Washingtons, who brought some capital and were keen to profit from the tobacco boom. Often they were younger sons of gentlemen, or members of families who first came to Virginia as traders and stayed to become planters. They had the advantage of being able to learn from the mistakes of the first generation. It was no coincidence that the history of Virginia was to be dominated by the progeny of this second generation, whose names included Washington, Carter, Harrison, Lee, Beverley, and Byrd.

By the 1640s, then, Virginia was on its way to becoming a functioning, prosperous society. The suspicion and antagonism of the Powhatan people had placed the survival of the colony in question for more than 15 years after the founding of Jamestown. In the face of Indian hostility the English were forced to raise their own food and to import their own laborers instead of relying on the Indian traders to supply them with corn. Eventually the Virginia colony was able to stabilize itself and begin to prosper because it developed mechanisms for recruiting large numbers of English settlers to occupy the land and servants to work it. Though the Virginia Company had been disappointed in its expectations of finding gold, precious metals, and a route to the Pacific, the colony was growing and had the potential to develop into a substantial exporter of tobacco, a profitable commercial commodity. It was a colonial model worth emulating elsewhere. Indeed, another group of Englishmen further to the north, in New England, was already having considerable success building several new colonies organized along similar lines.

---

[17]   The story of Anthony Johnson is detailed most fully in Breen and Innes, *"Myne Owne Ground,"* which includes information on Johnson's son John at pp. 92–3.

In the end, Virginia's success as a commercial farming colony doomed the Virginia colonizers' original hopes of living peacefully with the Indians. The mechansms that enabled the colony to prosper depended on clearing and cultivating thousands of acres of land owned by the Indians, a type of land use that was incompatible with the Indians' mixed hunting and farming economy. It remained to be seen whether the conflicts which had emerged between English settlers and Native Americans in Virginia would inevitably emerge in other colonies, as well.

4

The Conquest Continues

New England, 1620–1660

1607	The Sagadahoc settlement fails.
1616–18	An epidemic decimates population in the Cape Cod region.
1620	The Plymouth colony is founded by the Pilgrims.
1626	The settlement of Naumkeag (later Salem) is founded.
1629	The Massachusetts Bay Company is formed.
1630	The Puritans found Boston and 10 other settlements.
1632	Watertown's inhabitants protest over arbitrary taxation.
1634	Council members demand to see the Massachusetts charter.
1634–6	The first English settlements in the Connecticut River valley are founded.
1636	Roger Williams founds Providence in Rhode Island after being expelled from Massachusetts (1635).
1637	The Pequots are defeated in the Pequot War. New Haven is founded. Anne Hutchinson is banished from Massachusetts.
1642	The English Civil War begins.
1643	The United Colonies of New England are formed. Miantonomo is executed.
1644	Rhode Island is granted a charter by Parliament.
1646	Dr Robert Child protests about church membership.
1648	Book of General Laws: the Cambridge Platform is published.
1649	Charles I is executed. John Winthrop dies.
1656	The first Quakers arrive.
1660	Charles II is restored to the English throne. Mary Dyer is executed.

Colonial America: A History to 1763, Fourth Edition. Richard Middleton and Anne Lombard.
© 2011 Richard Middleton and Anne Lombard. Published 2011 by Blackwell Publishing Ltd.

1 NEW ENGLAND BEFORE THE ENGLISH

MUCH LIKE PEOPLES further to the south, the Algonquian-speaking Indians who lived in what would become New England had already encountered European traders and explorers before the first English settlers arrived in 1620. Just as in Virginia, these early encounters would influence their behavior towards the English newcomers, and would in turn shape the future direction of the English colonies they established.

Native Americans in New England probably met their first Europeans when Verrazano explored their coasts in 1524. By the late sixteenth century Indians in northern New England were experiencing yearly visits from European fishermen, who came by the hundreds every summer to the coasts of northern New England to fill their nets with cod. By 1600 the Micmacs and the Abenakis in what would later become Maine and New Hampshire had established relationships with French fur traders. Members of the Wampanoag, Massachusett, and Narragansett peoples had encountered English explorers Bartholomew Gosnold in 1603 and John Smith in 1614 (among others) along the coast of what would become Massachusetts. And the Pequots and the Mahicans had regular dealings with Dutch merchants beginning about 1608, along New England's southern coast as well as further inland.

Unlike the experience in the Chesapeake, however, early European–Indian interactions in New England had left the Indians weaker and more divided, instead of stronger and more unified. Here, just as further south, Europeans had shown themselves to be potentially untrustworthy. An English ship led by a Captain Edward Harlow had kidnapped five or six Indians and carried them back to London in 1611. One of John Smith's commanders, Thomas Hunt, kidnapped some 20 local Indians to be sold as slaves in Spain in 1614. However, unlike the Indians who lived in Virginia, the Indians in eastern New England had not become unified in a confederacy in order to protect themselves. The most significant outcome of their early contacts with Europeans seems instead to have been heightened rivalries (caused in part by competition over access to the trade goods which French and Dutch traders were supplying to their trading partners in exchange for furs) and a devastating epidemic of European origin which had swept across the region around Plymouth Bay between 1616 and 1618, killing as many as three-quarters of the local population. The death toll from this epidemic changed the balance of power within the region: the Pequots and the Narragansetts, who had not been much affected by the sickness, now had a numerical advantage over their newly weakened neighbors, the Wampanoags and the Massachusetts. The Pequots and Narragansetts, moreover, controlled much of the local supply of wampum, beads made of shells that were used as a medium of exchange between tribes, giving them an advantage in trade with the Dutch. Thus, instead of coming from a position of strength like the Powhatans in 1607, members of the smaller groups who inhabited southeastern New England were by 1620 feeling very vulnerable indeed.

The epidemic may have heightened rivalries even among former allies. In 1619 the Plymouth Company repatriated an Indian named Squanto, one of the men who had been kidnapped by Hunt in 1614. Before being dragged away from his homeland, Squanto had been a member of a small Wampanoag band called the Patuxet. Tragically, when he reached his village in 1619 after his long absence, it had been abandoned. All of his people were gone. Hoping for news of them, Squanto approached his former neighbors, the Pokanoket. Although both the Patuxet and the Pokanoket were Wampanoags, the Pokanoket greeted Squanto with suspicion rather than embracing him as a kinsman. They agreed to let him stay, but only as a subordinate (with the same status, essentially, as a captive) and not as a full member of their village. Devastation had left the peoples of southern New England uncertain and beset by rivalries. This was the changing and divided political world that the first permanent English settlers in New England were about to enter.

2   THE PILGRIMS

In the wake of the Virginia Company's successful promotional tour in 1617, a group of would-be emigrants had approached the company to express their interest in moving to North America. However, unlike the adventurers who had gone to Virginia in the early years, the members of this group were motivated more by their ideology than by a desire for easy riches. Calling themselves Pilgrims, they were members of a dissenting sect who wanted to separate completely from the Church of England believing that the established church was so corrupt it was beyond reform. Inevitably, their separatist views had brought them into conflict with the authorities, for whom uniformity was essential for the maintenance of national harmony. The Pilgrims now lived in Holland but were eager to move. Accordingly, they sought and obtained a patent from the Virginia Company to settle in Virginia. When a group of London merchants headed by Thomas Weston offered them financial help, they instead entered into negotiations with the Plymouth Company, which was in the process of reorganizing itself after the disastrous failure at Sagadahoc as the Council for New England. The Pilgrims agreed to bear a considerable share of the financial risks of the venture, promising to work for the merchants for seven years before they would begin to take a portion of the colony's profits. Under these terms the Pilgrims knew they were unlikely to grow rich in North America.

At this point the Pilgrims technically had a patent only from the Virginia Company, but they determined to set out despite the legal uncertainties. When one of their ships developed leaks, as many Pilgrims as possible along with their co-adventurers piled into the remaining ship, the *Mayflower*, and set sail on September 6, 1620. They totaled 101 persons plus crew. In contrast to the early shipments to Virginia, a number of women and children were on board in family groups, making them a relatively stable group.

Even so, the group became riven by conflict before the ship reached its destination. About half of the passengers belonged to the Pilgrims' congregation, while the rest were so-called "Strangers" with no connection to the church. When the ship came in sight of land near Cape Cod on November 11, 1620, it was well to the north of its planned destination at the mouth of the Hudson River. The captain's decision to stay in Cape Cod rather than sail south through dangerous coastal waters provoked a near mutiny by the Strangers. In order to minimize conflict, 41 of the male passengers drew up an agreement for the framing of "such just and equal laws, . . . as shall be thought

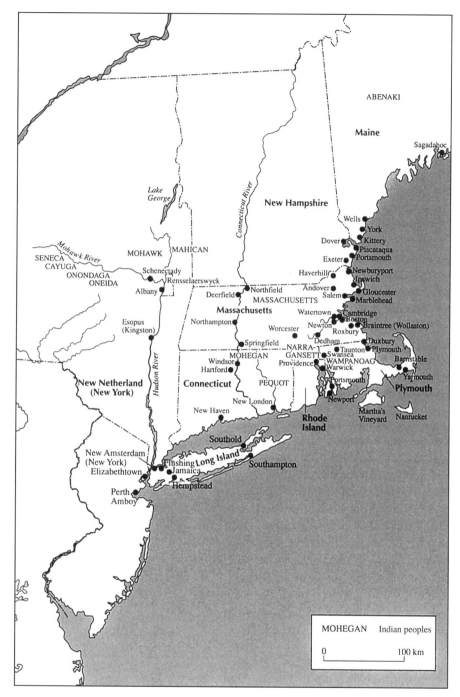

Map 4 Seventeenth-century New England and New York.

DOCUMENT 7

The Mayflower Compact, November 1620, reprinted in W. Keith Kavenagh, *Foundations of Colonial America: A Documentary History* (New York, 1973), Vol. 1, 246

The compact was only a declaration of intent and said nothing about the actual institutions of government or the exercise of power. No women were among the 41 signatories. Questions to consider: *How would this agreement have worked to prevent disagreements among the settlers? Why do you think that 11 of the signatories merited the title of "Mr" while the rest did not? What does the use of such a title tell you about these colonists' assumptions about social class differences?*

In the name of God, Amen. We whose names are underwritten, the loyal subjects of our dread sovereign lord King James, by the Grace of God, of Great Britain . . . and Ireland, King, Defender of the Faith, having undertaken, for the glory of God, and advancement of the Christian faith, and the honour of our King and country, a voyage to plant the first colony in the northern parts of Virginia, do, by these presents, covenant and combine ourselves together into a civil body politic for our better ordering and preservation and furtherance of the ends aforesaid; and by virtue hereof do enact, constitute, and frame such just and equal laws, ordinances, acts, constitutions, and officers, from time to time, as shall be thought most meet and convenient for the general good of the colony, to which we promise all due submission and obedience. In witness thereof, we have hereunto subscribed our names at Cape Cod, the eleventh of November 1620.

most meet and convenient for the general good of the colony." This agreement formed the famous Mayflower Compact. Traditional accounts have glorified the compact as the beginning of American democracy, but its true intent was simply to minimize the kind of dissension that had nearly destroyed the Jamestown colony in its early years.

By mid-December, the Pilgrims had decided upon a site for their settlement, which they were to call New Plymouth. On December 25, 1620, they began to erect their first dwellings around a crude palisade. After erecting a common store, each family labored on its own shelter; again, it was thought that this method would encourage greater endeavor and avoid the kind of disputes that had afflicted Jamestown and Sagadahoc. They were short of food, but survived in part by stealing dried corn which they found in a concealed storage bin belonging to local Indians. The Indians, still weakened by the recent epidemic, made little effort to avenge the theft, instead watching the newcomers warily throughout the winter. By spring, nearly half the settlers had died, weakened by the long voyage, poor nutrition, and the difficulties of adapting to a new environment.

Despite their losses, the Pilgrims remained guardedly optimistic. Land near the settlement was clear enough that they would be able to plant their Indian corn relatively easily, and to hope for a successful harvest. Failing to understand that they were located next to recently abandoned Indian farmland, they merely considered their good fortune to be a sign of God's providence. As they began to sow their first crop of Indian corn they were completely astonished when an Indian named Samoset walked into the settlement, uttering a few words of English. Samoset then returned with another, more fluent speaker, Squanto, the Indian who was being held captive by the Wampanoags at Pokanoket. Squanto showed the settlers how to employ the Indians' complementary farming techniques, planting squashes between the rows of corn and fertilizing the land with fish offal. Serving as an intermediary, Squanto helped to negotiate a treaty of friendship and cooperation between the English and the Wampanoag chief, Massasoit. That treaty lasted unbroken until 1675.

While the Pilgrims understood these events as providential signs of God's favor towards them, historians have now given us a way to understand them from the Indians' point of view. Unlike the Indians in the vicinity of Jamestown, who could afford to antagonize the English, the native inhabitants near Plymouth were in a precarious position. The Wampanoags had been decimated by disease and were threatened by the neighboring Narragansett and Massachusetts peoples. Their political situation was so unstable that they regarded a friendly relationship with the English as their best hope to regain control over their own lives. Massasoit and his people could use trade goods from the English to gain prestige and bargaining power among other local Indian peoples, and the English might even offer them military assistance. Indeed, within two years Massasoit had talked the Pilgrims into making an unprovoked assault on the Massachusetts tribe, in which several were murdered after being invited to a feast. Squanto, for his part, apparently hoped that a friendship with the English would give him some much needed autonomy from Massasoit (and perhaps a chance to reunite his few surviving kinsmen from the village of Patuxet). As at Jamestown, the local Indians behaved in ways that furthered their local political interests, interests that varied from one place to another.[1]

Thanks to the assistance of the Wampanoags, the Pilgrims' settlement became fairly stable within its first year of existence. The treaty allowed them to harvest their first crops in safety, and in recognition of this divine providence they declared a day of thanksgiving, one of the first to be celebrated by Europeans on American soil.[2] They continued to struggle financially, however. As of 1624 there were just 134 inhabitants, and they were still not generating the profits that English investors expected. Though some attempts were made to build fishing vessels, most Pilgrims devoted themselves to farming, since this was what they were accustomed to do. Unfortunately, farming in the area offered subsistence at best, even when carried out communally. A further problem was that most settlers wanted to farm their own land. For the first few years only personal gardens of up to one acre had been allowed. By November 1626, most of the adventurers in England were disillusioned with the project and agreed to sell their shares.

---

[1] For this interpretation of the motives of both Squanto and Massasoit, see Neal Salisbury, "Squanto: Last of the Patuxets," in David G. Sweet and Gary B. Nash, eds, *Struggle and Survival in Colonial America* (Berkeley, 1981), 228–46.

[2] Thanksgiving days were observed sporadically thereafter in Plymouth and other New England colonies. Thanksgiving became a national holiday only in 1863, following a proclamation by President Lincoln.

This agreement made it possible to distribute the settlement's collective wealth to the individual shareholders, each of whom was allotted 20 acres and a proportion of the sheep, goats, cattle, and poultry. To find the money to buy out the English adventurers, Bradford and the other leaders had to form a trading monopoly of all the colony's commercial enterprises. The most promising commodities remained fish and furs, since the latter could be traded for corn with the Abenaki peoples to the north. Sadly, the London end of the business was not well managed, and the debt was extinguished only in 1648 after much vexation and expense.

Although a few other small English colonies appeared in Massachusetts in the 1620s, in the short term they were more of a drain on the Pilgrims' resources than a help. Thomas Weston's 1622 settlement at Wessagusset survived for only a year. A small colony of fishermen was established in 1623 on Cape Ann and abandoned in 1626. Though some of the inhabitants moved to Naumkeag, later called Salem, they were too few to have much impact on Plymouth. The inhabitants of Thomas Morton's 1625 trading settlement at Mount Wollaston, later Braintree, shocked the Pilgrims' religious sensibilities with their revelries, and the Pilgrims drove them away in 1628.

Fortunately, the Pilgrims' general economic situation brightened in the 1630s with the arrival of thousands of new settlers brought by the much larger and wealthier Massachusetts Bay Company to a new colony northwest of Plymouth, on the Massachusetts Bay. With the sudden new demand for its livestock and grain, Plymouth at last attracted new settlers and its population began to rise. According to William Bradford, now the governor and historian of the colony, the number of inhabitants rose to 300 by 1630, and with continued expansion, the population had reached 550 by 1637. The Council for New England granted the Pilgrims a new patent confirming their right to frame laws and settle the area in 1630, and the colonists in 1636 adopted a formal constitution providing for a governor and court of seven assistants to be elected by the freemen, or shareholders, of the colony.

Plymouth would remain a small, politically insignificant colony, isolated from mainstream Puritanism and thus denied recruitment from a wider population. However, it was important in providing additional lessons for English investors in how to create a successful colonial venture. The negotiation of peaceful relationships with the local Indians had been shown to be possible. Bringing families to settle a farming colony had proven a viable option for creating a stable society, far preferable to a population of young, single men. And the fact that the settlers had a strong sense of common religious purpose had also helped them to persist. The much larger colony of Massachusetts was soon to build upon these lessons.

3   MASSACHUSETTS: A CITY ON THE HILL

The Massachusetts Bay Colony formally began in 1629, when a joint stock company created by a group of English merchants obtained a charter from the king giving it title to all the lands between the Merrimack River and the tip of Massachusetts Bay, as well as the right to any minerals, subject to the usual percentage for the Crown. The charter replaced a 1628 charter of doubtful validity for the same territory from the Council for New England. The new entity, to be known as "The Company of Massachusetts Bay," was to hold its lands from the king in free and common socage.[3] It was to be managed by a governor and council of 18 assistants, elected annually by the ordinary freemen (that is, shareholders), otherwise known as the general court. It would have the power "to make, ordain, and establish all manner of wholesome and reasonable Orders, Lawes, Statutes, and Ordinances," providing these were consistent with the laws of England. As in Virginia, those emigrating were to "enjoy all Liberties and Immunities of free and natural Subjects … as if born within the Realm of England." Its shareholders were much like the shareholders of other English investment companies, and included merchants and prominent gentlemen well known to the king. But in another respect, they were less typical of investors in English trading ventures, in that they were all participants in the Puritan movement.

The Puritans were part of a broad religious reform movement within the Church of England which had begun during the reign of Elizabeth I and grown during the reign of the Stuarts, James I and Charles I. Like the Pilgrims who settled at Plymouth, the Puritans shared a general concern that the doctrines and ceremonies of the Church of England had remained too similar to those of Roman Catholicism, as well as a suspicion that many members of the church were not truly committed to doing God's will. Unlike the Pilgrims, however, they were not separatists. Puritans were reformers, determined to reform the Church of England but not abandon it. Moreover, they were not a tiny oppressed minority. They constituted a significant group within the church, and many of their members held positions of influence and authority.

The Puritans' denial of separatism was important, since it enabled them to claim descent and hence legitimacy from the early Christian church. What they objected to in the Anglican Church was government by bishops, for whom they could find no biblical justification. In their view authority lay with the congregation as it had, they believed, after the death of Christ. They also quarreled with much of the liturgy in the Book of Common Prayer, believing the Bible to be the only source of Christian authority. In addition, they detested what they regarded as the many traces of popery, for example, in the vestments and altar cloths still lavishly used in Anglican churches. The same reasoning led them to abandon feast days, including Christmas, as pagan or popish relics, preferring instead simple acts of thanksgiving in accordance with the Scriptures. In this sense they were true radicals who wanted to transform English culture.

Theologically, the Puritans were disciples of John Calvin, the Genevan reformer, and herein lay their greatest criticism of the Church of England. Calvin stated that, because of original sin, the world was irrevocably corrupt. Only a few whom God had chosen through his divine grace would be saved. Although the Church of England formally acknowledged this doctrine, the thrust of its theology lay elsewhere. Luther had preached that all men could be saved if they repented of their sins. Most Anglicans went one step further, accepting the arguments of the Dutch theologian Arminius that good works were themselves a necessary demonstration of that faith. To the followers of Calvin this view was abhorrent, since it threatened to lead to all the old abuses of people trying to buy their way to heaven with good works and minimal faith, which they

---

[3] Land held in free and common socage could be bought and sold by the owner. In England, some forms of land tenure prohibited the transfer of land outside the owner's family.

associated with the Catholic Church. In their eyes such behavior spelled total depravity, for God was not to be bargained with.

The Puritans' Calvinist beliefs were coupled with religious practices that made them distinctive within the Church of England. Although they believed it was necessary to have an educated ministry in order to help them understand the word of God, they also took considerable responsibility for understanding the Bible themselves. They read the Gospels on their own and formed study and prayer groups to encourage individual engagement with Scripture. Even though they believed that God's grace was offered only to God's freely chosen elect, their goal was to prepare themselves fully for the reception of grace if it should be offered to them, by intensely scrutinizing their own souls and leading a life true to God's word. They favored ministers who could help them to understand God's word by giving biblically based sermons, and believed individual congregations should control the selection of those ministers. These practices put them at odds with some of the bishops in the Church of England, who favored more traditional forms of worship.

The ecclesiastical reforms which the Puritans wanted to put into practice would also encourage a sense of religious exclusivity. In England, everyone could take communion after confirmation by a bishop. The Puritans believed, however, that church membership should be limited to those who were truly among God's elect. Allowing the unregenerate to take communion was an affront to God. Given the structure of church governance within the Church of England, however, it was difficult to put this reform into practice in England. A few English churches had experimented with a congregational form of government, but most had only a hazy notion of what it required.

The Puritans' religious views also made them feel in some sense responsible for the moral behavior of their neighbors, a responsibility that would shape the kinds of governments they created in North America. Puritan ministers preached that every nation was bound by a covenant with God, and this covenant obligated them to enforce biblical laws on earth. A nation that fulfilled the terms of its covenant would prosper; a nation that failed to root out corruption and wickedness would be punished. Many Puritans during the 1620s worried that England had failed to fulfill its covenant, making God angry with their nation. Charles I, who had ascended to the throne in 1625, seemed determined to maintain an unreformed church by promoting high Anglicans like William Laud and sponsoring a return towards Anglican orthodoxy with the church. He had also married a Roman Catholic, Henrietta-Marie of France. These acts infuriated the Puritans.

Signs of God's apparent displeasure with England for its failure to live up to its covenant were not difficult to find. Widespread unemployment and economic distress in England's southeastern counties (caused by a depression in the textile industry during the 1620s) had made people behave in ways the Puritans considered ungodly and unchristian. The Protestant forces with whom the English had allied themselves suffered a number of severe defeats in Europe during the opening phases of the Thirty Years War. And although an assertive Puritan faction in Parliament had in the past been able to check the king's policies, in March 1629 Charles I dissolved Parliament, apparently determined to rule as an absolute monarch.

These apparent signs of God's displeasure provoked considerable debate within the newly formed Massachusetts Bay Company about what should be done. Although some

Figure 11 Miniature portrait of John Winthrop (1588–1649). Unidentified artist, circa 1630. Courtesy of Massachusetts Historical Society.

of the shareholders wanted the company to be a normal trading venture, many others had a more spiritual end in view. Among the latter was a Suffolk squire from the village of Groton, John Winthrop. A justice of the peace and graduate of Trinity College, Cambridge, Winthrop was typical of many Puritan gentry who were alarmed at the direction of events in England. Some early twentieth-century historians suggested that Winthrop was motivated by financial inducements to emigrate at this point, since not long before buying into the company he had been deprived of an attorneyship in the Court of Wards and Liveries.[4] But the evidence makes such an interpretation implausible. By 1629, it was clear that colonization was a risky business. Raleigh had reputedly spent upwards of £40,000 on his various enterprises, and Winthrop would not have undertaken

---

[4]   The view that Winthrop and other Puritan leaders went to America for economic reasons was popular in the early decades of the twentieth century with Progressive historians like James Truslow Adams, *The Founding of New England* (Boston, 1921). The Progressives were anxious to show that American democracy had always been threatened by wealthy business elites. More sympathetic is Edmund S. Morgan, *The Puritan Dilemma: The Story of John Winthrop* (Boston, 1958). This account was written during the Cold War when it was fashionable to reaffirm traditional views about America, especially the contribution of Puritan New England. For the most recent view, see note 8.

such a risky venture when he still had so much to lose at Groton. Religious belief clearly inspired his departure from England. Winthrop and the others believed that Armageddon was not far away and that all true believers must remove themselves before God visited his wrath upon the land. From a twenty-first-century perspective it is hard to appreciate the intensity of religious feeling among the population at large in this period, coupled with the prevailing sense that God was all-powerful and man merely a weak mortal. Religion helped to explain a harsh and rapidly changing world over which individuals had little control.

The religious faction formed a plan to take over the company and to emigrate to New England with the charter, where the company could avoid the prying eyes of the king's officials, notably the Anglican bishops. It was hoped that the company could slip away unnoticed, given the distance of America from England and the distractions of the Crown back home; it was not intended to disavow the English church or state but to make interference impossible. In pursuit of this dubious idea, they were aided by a remarkable oversight in the charter, which failed to specify that the company had to retain its headquarters in England. An agreement to buy out the non-Puritan elements was accordingly concluded at Cambridge, England, on August 26, 1629. Three days later the plan was accepted at a hastily convened meeting of the general court in London attended by just 27 freemen out of 125. Not long afterward Winthrop himself was elected governor.

Meanwhile, the process of launching the colony had already commenced. On the first formation of the company in 1628, a ship had been sent out to take possession of the remnants of the fishing settlement at Salem. The following April, the company had sent a further five ships carrying 200 additional settlers. Thus when the main group of the Puritans left in March 1630 in a fleet of 11 ships, they already had a substantial base on which to build. Unlike the Pilgrims, the Puritans had considerable financial resources; and, unlike the Virginia Company, they had realistic expectations, having learned from the experiences of their predecessors in Virginia and Plymouth.

The *Arabella*, with Winthrop on board, reached Salem in June, but since the location did not please the group's leaders, the main fleet went on to another site near the Charles River. It was here that they noticed a thin neck of land protruding into the bay and decided to make this site the focus of their new enterprise, not least because of its central position and defensive capabilities. They called it Boston after the town in Lincolnshire from which some of the emigrants had come. Before they landed Winthrop reminded the settlers on board the *Arabella* of their mission, which was to renew their collective covenant with God, restore the true church, and live according to God's laws. The new settlements were to "be as a city upon a hill," an example to all the world.

As at Plymouth, the local Indians around Massachusetts Bay were fragmented and weak, predisposing them to welcome an alliance and trade with the English. Since the Puritans were far better financed and supplied than the first group of Pilgrims (and could rely on the support of Plymouth), they did not depend on local inhabitants for their very survival. However, they did need a way to pay off the creditors who had financed their voyage. The Puritans' two most populous neighbors, the Narragansetts and the Pequots, were eager to trade for the coveted European goods that their inland neighbors could obtain from the Dutch. Puritan leaders therefore established trading relations with both Indian nations. The Narragansetts and the Pequots could offer few furs but they could provide wampum, an ornament made in large quantities by the native inhabitants around the Long Island and southern Connecticut coasts from the abundant supply of oyster shells that could be found there. Wampum belts had two colors: white represented peace and health; purple implied war and death. Highly valued by the northeastern tribes because of their fine workmanship and symbolic significance, wampum belts could be exchanged with northern peoples like the Abenakis for furs.

Since they planned to create a colony of settlement rather than a trading colony, the Puritans also needed land, which appeared to be conveniently available. Unaware that the Indians had been decimated by disease, Massachusetts leaders managed to convince themselves that the Indians who lived there had left the land empty and barren. They cited the international legal doctrine of *vacuum domicilium*, which provided that men who used land productively had a greater right to it than those who simply occupied it. "As the ancient patriarchs therefore removed from straiter places into more roomy where the land lay idle, and none use it, though there dwelt inhabitants by them . . . so it is lawful now to take a land which none useth, and make use of it." Indians, the Puritans argued, did not "use" the land productively, and so had no right to keep it from those who would.[5]

Despite such beliefs, the Puritans generally purchased the Indians' land since they wanted no legal complications in the settling of their commonwealth. It would not do for Puritan leaders to cause an uprising among the Indians, or to reveal an inability to control them. However, these purchases meant something different to each of the parties. The English assumed on the basis of English law that their purchases of Indian land included exclusive rights to use the land and everything on it, including game and fish in perpetuity. The Indians for their part assumed that in selling land they were merely sealing friendships and sharing the land with their allies. Their different conceptions of property would later cause bitter disputes, but for the time being relations proceeded smoothly.

Land was initially distributed not to individuals but to towns. A group of people (usually a congregation) pooled their resources and applied to the council for a grant of land. This was given in freehold or fee simple without the payment of a quitrent as specified in the royal charter, an extraordinarily secure form of land tenure that few English farmers possessed. The group members then repaired to their site, made a covenant to create a godly community, and began to build a church and clear enough land to support themselves. Once enough land had been cleared, they distributed plots of one to four acres and in 1635 began the permanent division of much larger areas, according to the amount invested by each family. Hence major contributors to the initial capital of the company, like Winthrop, were given 200 acres, the lesser settlers from 30 to 100 acres.[6] One result of these policies was that settlers in New England inhabited towns instead of isolated farms, as in the Chesapeake. Another was that

---

[5] Indian trade and land policies in Massachusetts are described in Neal Salisbury, *Manitou and Providence: Indians, Europeans, and the Making of New England, 1500–1643* (New York, 1982).

[6] For the financial aspects of Puritan town building, see John Frederick Martin, *Profits in the Wilderness: Entrepreneurship and the Founding of New England Towns in the Seventeenth Century* (Chapel Hill, 1991).

settlers here would devote considerable energy to their town governments and develop strong local commitments.[7]

This method of distributing land combined with other factors enabled the settlers to thrive. English people generally emigrated to Massachusetts for material as well as spiritual reasons. Large numbers of Puritan settlers had been spinners, weavers, and small farmers before they left England. Their occupations placed them in the middling ranks of English society, unlike the vast majority of settlers in Virginia who were members of the landless poor. However, the downturn in the English textile industry and the prolonged economic depression that accompanied it were painful reminders to these artisans and small farmers of their vulnerability to the ups and downs of England's increasingly commercial economy. What most ordinary Puritan settlers desired was a "competency," or a comfortable independence, thereby avoiding the dilemma of too much wealth, which would lead them into sin, and too little sustenance, which would inhibit the leading of a godly life.[8] The abundant land available in North America offered them a source of economic security that could not be equaled at home.

The lure of a competency combined with a strong sense of religious mission brought more than 14,000 English Puritans to New England between 1629 and 1642. The total number of immigrants was actually smaller than the total number of emigrants to either the Chesapeake or the West Indies (see Chapter 5, part 4) during the same period. However, Englishmen emigrating to New England were much more likely to survive and have children once they arrived, so the population grew rapidly. New England's demographic stability and success was so striking in comparison with the disastrous experience in Virginia that historians often describe the two colonial ventures as fundamentally different enterprises. Indeed, the New England colonies did represent something new: the transplantation of entire communities of English people seeking a religious environment where they could control their own mode of worship.

While the motivation and drive of the settlers thus helped their colony to succeed, other historical contexts contributed as well to New England's viability. The Indians in New England were much more deeply divided than the Indians in Virginia, making them much more eager to build peaceful relationships with the English. The English companies which settled New England were able to imitate models being developed by the Virginia Company for spreading the financial risk of colonial ventures and inducing permanent settlement. By recruiting settlers in family groups, Massachusetts was able to create stable, cohesive societies in short order, since

---

[7]   Historians have long recognized the importance of town governments in shaping New England politics and society. See for example John Fairfield Sly, *Town Government in Massachusetts* (Cambridge, Mass., 1930); Sumner Chilton Powell, *Puritan Village: The Formation of a New England Town* (Middleton, Conn., 1963), and Kenneth Lockridge and Alan Kreider, "The Evolution of Massachusetts Town Government, 1640–1740," *William and Mary Quarterly*, 23 (1966), 529–74.

[8]   For many years historians disagreed about whether economic or religious motivations were paramount in the minds of Puritan migrants during the 1630s. Today, historians concur that the two motives were inseparable. See Virginia DeJohn Anderson, *New England's Generation: The Great Migration and the Formation of Society and Culture in the Seventeenth Century* (Cambridge, 1991), and Daniel Vickers, *Farmers and Fishermen: Two Centuries of Work in Essex County, Massachusetts, 1630–1850* (Chapel Hill, 1994).

families provided vital sources of support in a difficult environment. Also working in the new colonists' favor was the climate, which, though harsh, was healthy, resulting in fewer diseases than in Virginia. A final advantage was that settlers themselves learned from the experiences of earlier English colonies. As a result, the Puritans had come well equipped with livestock and every kind of tool. They could also rely on the support of Plymouth.

4 ESTABLISHING AND DEFENDING ORDER

In creating a government and a legal system, the Puritans who founded Massachusetts were more committed than most colonizers to creating a new order consistent with the word of God, as they perceived it. Since they were religious reformers this was of course a problem of church government as much as civil government. Thus they immediately put into place various desired reforms, such as limiting church membership and communion to those who were truly part of God's elect. The problem, of course, was how to determine just who belonged to the elect. Now that the Puritan ministers were effectively independent from the oversight of the bishops, they developed a special process to decide who qualified for church membership. The process entailed a public examination before the congregation and consisted of four main stages. First, the intending saint had to acknowledge humanity's innate depravity – God alone could save. Next the individual had to show true repentance and a desire to be saved. Then followed the hardest part of the examination, justification, whereby the examinee had to convince the interrogators that the Holy Spirit had entered their soul and that they were open to God's covenant of grace. If the answers were satisfactory the fourth stage, sanctification, followed, indicating that the person was of the elect. Even then no relaxation was possible, for sin could quickly lead to a loss of grace. Godliness had to be worked at constantly until the saint was called to a higher place.

Having worked out the problem of identifying the saints, as they came to be called, Puritan leaders next confronted the problem of how to maintain God's laws in a commonwealth that included both saints and sinners. Among those who had crossed the Atlantic were servants who had not come by choice, and settlers who had come primarily for economic reasons. Consequently, in 1631 the general court ruled that none but the saints could participate in public affairs or vote. The godly must not be put at risk. Winthrop and the assistants also began issuing various edicts for the better government of the colony. All gaming, blasphemy, sexual misconduct, excessive drinking, and lascivious entertainment like the theater were to be severely punished, while church attendance was compulsory. Restrictions were also placed on commerce to ensure that prices were just and that profiteering and hoarding were avoided. Although many of the same restrictions had been imposed in Virginia, the difference in Massachusetts was that the majority of the population wanted to abide by them so that they might join the elect.

Massachusetts has often been accused of being a theocracy in its early years, as proudly affirmed by one of its leading ministers, John Cotton; but most writers today dispute this charge, since the clergy in the settlement were not granted temporal authority, and were indeed specifically forbidden from wielding such power. Nevertheless, in these early years the dividing line between minister and magistrate was thin. The minister was essentially the most learned member of the congregation; his sacerdotal authority was limited. Second, many magistrates, not least Winthrop himself, had pretensions to theological expertise; if there was no actual priestly caste, the saints were close to being one. Third, punishments for breaches of the moral code were imposed according to biblical, not common, law. Lastly, the settlement's whole ethos was religious, its purpose to establish a godly community. Church and state were thus inextricably intertwined. The church existed to enunciate the moral law, the state to enforce it. Those who deviated from the accepted path could expect to be punished.

Puritan leaders in the general court were convinced that they needed to rule with a firm hand in order to control the reprobate, and therefore in October 1630 they changed the colony's governing structure so as to increase the governor's control over the venture. From now on the freemen would elect the assistants, as provided under the charter, but the assistants alone would elect the governor and deputy governor. The governor and the assistants would henceforth "have the power of making laws and choosing officers to execute the same," a change which represented a huge increase in their power. During the next 18 months, Winthrop and the magistrates directed the settlement themselves, confident that the meeting of October 1630 had given them a complete mandate including the right to levy taxes on the towns.

The settlers, however, were not persuaded that a godly commonwealth should be run autocratically. They challenged the council's assumption of power, being determined from the beginning to assert a right to participate in the government of the venture. The first challenge came from the town of Watertown whose inhabitants argued in 1632 that under the charter the magistrates had no power to levy taxes. Winthrop and his colleagues grudgingly restored the freemen's right to elect the governor and deputy governor and allowed every town to send two representatives to the general court each year to confer about the assessment of taxes. Next, critics within the colony called for more frequent meetings of the general court and greater participation by the freemen in the government of the colony. At the annual meeting of the general court in May 1634, Winthrop's critics demanded that he produce the charter, which confirmed the right of the general court to raise money, make laws, and dispose of lands. Dissatisfaction was so widespread that Winthrop was defeated for the governorship in 1635 and 1636, although he maintained his seat on the council and was re-elected as governor in 1637. As settlements became too dispersed for most freemen to attend the general court, settlers further demanded that in the future each town would be represented by two deputies on all matters, not just taxation.

The result was that Massachusetts, like Virginia, now had a representative system of government. The political system was in no real sense democratic, for the franchise was still limited to freemen who not only owned property but were full church members. In a town like Dedham 70 percent of the adult males may have been communicants; in Boston the figure was about 50 percent. Thus up to half the adult males – and all females – remained disenfranchised. Nevertheless, the percentage of men who had won the right to vote was considerably higher here than in England. The colonists in Massachusetts had further reinforced the principle first established in Virginia: English settlers in the North American colonies could expect not only the opportunity to obtain property of their own, but also the right to a significant voice in the government of the ventures in which they were taking part.

Other challenges to the authority of Puritan leaders concerned their attempts to enforce religious orthodoxy. Since the Puritans taught that every believer was responsible for identifying hypocrisy and calling for reform, such challenges were perhaps inevitable. The English Puritan minister Roger Williams, who had come to Massachusetts in 1631, believed that outward conformity did not mean salvation. His quest for religious purity led him into separatism and a two-year stay at Plymouth and then to Salem, where a number of the original settlers had similar leanings. Between 1633 and 1635 Williams began calling for the complete separation of his church from the other New England congregations, which had not disavowed the Church of England. He also publicly tore the English flag because it contained the cross of St. George, a popish symbol. The general court responded by expelling Salem's deputies until they saw the error of their ways.

At this point Williams revealed his radical tendencies by denying both the religious and political authority of the Puritan establishment. He denied that the general court had any authority at all in spiritual matters, arguing that church and state should be totally separate. Furthermore he challenged the court's power to sequestrate Indian lands merely because of a charter from the king. Winthrop and his council refused to tolerate such schismatic behavior, and in October 1635 they banished Williams from the colony. The episode underlined a major difficulty for the Puritan church. How could orthodoxy be preserved without compromising the rights of the congregation? One solution was the formation of a ministerial synod similar to that of the Presbyterian church, but the congregationally minded Puritans loathed the idea of undermining the authority of the laity in favor of the ministry. The matter was a perplexing one.

While the threat posed by Williams was being successfully contained, another, more difficult challenge emerged in Boston, in the person of Mrs Anne Hutchinson, who had arrived in 1634 with her family. Hutchinson had joined the church where John Cotton was minister and as of 1636, the new governor Sir Henry Vane was a member of the congregation. Her formidable intellect and love of argument soon made her influential, not least with Cotton and Vane, whom she met at private gatherings.

Hutchinson's views veered towards an antinomian form of predestination, which affirmed that God had decided from the beginning of time who would be saved; nothing the individual did could change this, not even the strictest observance of the moral law. Hutchinson, like many Puritans, believed that the church still contained many unregenerate persons even among the clergy, who disguised their lack of belief by a veneer of good works and outward conformity to the moral law. She therefore denounced some ministers for preaching a covenant of deeds rather than one of grace.

Hutchinson's antinomian views posed a number of challenges. First, her argument that God revealed directly to the elect whether they were saved in effect denied the need for a minister's spiritual guidance. No established church could allow such bypassing of its authority, as the Pharisees had demonstrated when confronted by Christ. Second, she challenged the authority of the Scriptures as the revealed word of God on which the whole religious polity of the Puritans was based. Lastly, Hutchinson's beliefs implied that if salvation were predetermined, then logically no one need bother even to demonstrate the possession of faith. This view completely contradicted the Puritan emphasis on the need to live by God's law and to prepare for the gift of his grace. Although it was not Hutchinson's intention to do so, her arguments could equally justify the life of a libertine, which posed a threat to society itself.

Hutchinson had powerful supporters and for a time was permitted to express her views. In 1637, though, Winthrop was re-elected governor, convened the general court, and purged two of its errant deputies from Boston. Then a meeting of the church elders and magistrates was held to reaffirm the view that grace was a state that had to be constantly sought and prepared for by living in accordance with moral laws. Following these proceedings, the general court began to take action against the antinomians for heresy. First, Anne Hutchinson's brother-in-law, the Reverend John Wheelwright, was banished, along with one of the errant deputies. Then Cotton was persuaded to retract. Finally, in November 1637 Hutchinson herself was called to face her accusers before the general court. When she claimed that her views had been revealed by God, basically admitting that she had no need for the ministry, she was duly condemned and banished.

To some extent, Hutchinson appears to have received this treatment because she was a woman and encouraged other women to discuss religion independently of their husbands. While in Boston she had presided over a weekly gathering of some 60 women. Although the Puritans went further than most churches in admitting women to full membership, women were still barred from the ministry; a woman could not become a freeman, vote, or be elected a deputy or magistrate. The Puritans' patriarchal model of authority conceived the female role as strictly subordinate, and even in religious matters a woman was supposed to derive her "ideas of God from the contemplation of her husband's excellencies." The assumption of male superiority was expressed most bluntly by Winthrop himself when he told Anne Hutchinson, "We do not mean to discourse with your sex." She had offended against not only God's laws but those of men, preferring, as one minister commented, to be "a husband than a wife, a preacher than a hearer, and a magistrate than a subject." Her fate was sealed.[9]

---

[9] See Lyle Koehler, "The Case of the American Jezebels: Anne Hutchinson and Female Agitation during the Years of Antinomian Turmoil, 1636–1640," *William and Mary Quarterly*, 31 (1974), 55–78, and *A Search for Power: The "Weaker Sex" in Seventeenth-Century New England* (Urbana, 1980). Other historians have revealed a more nuanced picture of women's status in Puritan colonial societies, finding that in some respects women enjoyed more rights in seventeenth-century New England than their counterparts in England. For example, Cornelia Hughes Dayton, *Women Before the Bar: Gender, Law, and Society in Connecticut, 1639–1789* (Chapel Hill, 1995), argues that Puritan women enjoyed greater access to the courts because procedures were less legalistic. In addition, Puritan magistrates, concerned with morality rather than legality, were more disposed to listen to women of good repute. For more information on the subject see Chapter 12.

DOCUMENT 8

The examination of Mrs Hutchinson, November 1637, reprinted in Thomas Hutchinson, *The History of the Colony and Province of Massachusetts-Bay*, edited by Lawrence Shaw Mayo (Cambridge, Mass., 1936), Vol. 2, 366–91

Mrs Hutchinson gave a spirited and able defense until her confession that she had been directly instructed by God. Questions to consider: *Which of Hutchinson's ideas was the most troubling to the magistrates? To what extent were the magistrates concerned that their authority was being challenged by a woman?*

GOVERNOR WINTHROP: "Mrs Hutchinson, you are called here as one of those that have troubled the peace of the commonwealth and the churches here; you are known to be a woman that hath had a great share in the promoting and divulging of those [antinomian] opinions that are the causes of this trouble, and to be nearly joined not only in affinity and affection with some of those the court had taken notice of and passed censure upon, but you have spoken divers things as we have been informed very prejudicial to the honour of the churches and ministers thereof, and you have maintained a meeting and assembly in your house that hath been condemned by the general assembly as a thing not tolerable nor comely in the sight of God nor fitting for your sex, and notwithstanding that was cried down you have continued the same, therefore we have thought good to send for you to understand how things are, that if you be in an erroneous way we may reduce you so you may become a profitable member here among us, otherwise if you be obstinate in your course that then the court may take such course that you may trouble us no further ... "

MRS HUTCHINSON: "I am called here to answer before you but I hear no things laid to my charge."

WINTHROP: "I have told you some already and more I can tell you."

MRS HUTCHINSON: "Name one Sir ... What have I done?"

WINTHROP: "Why for your doings, this you did harbour and countenance those that are parties in this faction [the antinomians]."

MRS HUTCHINSON: "That's a matter of conscience, Sir ... "

WINTHROP: "Your conscience you must keep or it must be kept for you."

MRS HUTCHINSON: "Must not I then entertain the saints [church members] because I must keep my conscience?"

[THOMAS DUDLEY] DEPUTY GOVERNOR: "I would go a little higher with Mrs Hutchinson ... it appears by this woman's meeting that Mrs Hutchinson hath so forestalled the minds of many ... that she now hath a potent party in the country. Now if all these things have endangered us ... and if she in particular hath disparaged all our ministers in the land that they have preached a covenant of works and only Mr Cotton a covenant of grace, why this is not to be suffered ... "

MRS HUTCHINSON: "I pray Sir prove it that I said they preached nothing but a covenant of works."

DEPUTY GOVERNOR: "Nothing but a covenant of works, why a Jesuit may preach truth sometimes."

MRS HUTCHINSON: "Did I ever say they preached a covenant of works then?"

DEPUTY GOVERNOR: "If they did not preach a covenant of grace clearly, then they preach a covenant of works."

MRS HUTCHINSON: "No Sir, one may preach a covenant of grace more clearly than another, so I said … "

[*The next morning, after further questioning*]

MRS HUTCHINSON: "If you please to give me leave I shall give you the ground of what I know to be true. Being much troubled to see the falseness of the constitution of the church of England, I had like to have turned separatist; whereupon I kept a day of solemn humiliation and pondering of the thing … the Lord was pleased to bring this scripture out of the Hebrews. 'He that denies the testament denies the testator,' and in this did open unto me and give me to see that those which did not teach the new covenant had the spirit of antichrist, and upon this he did discover the ministry unto me and ever since, I bless the Lord, he hath let me see which was the clear ministry and which the wrong … "

MR NOWEL [A MAGISTRATE]:   "How do you know that that was the spirit?"

MRS HUTCHINSON: "How did Abraham know that it was God that bid him offer his son, being a breach of the sixth commandment?"

DEPUTY GOVERNOR: "By an immediate voice."

MRS HUTCHINSON: "So to me by an immediate revelation."

Not only did religious schisms fuel challenges to Puritan authority in Massachusetts; they also impelled the dissenters to spread around New England, establishing new colonies in the process. Rhode Island would begin in the aftermath of Roger Williams's expulsion from Massachusetts in 1635, when he led some of his followers to land purchased from the Narragansetts south of Massachusetts and established the settlement of Providence, Rhode Island. Likewise, Anne Hutchinson along with William Coddington, who had been implicated but not charged in the antinomian controversy, established the town of Portsmouth on the island of Aquidneck in Narragansett Bay a few years later. By March 1641, Coddington and Williams had joined together again in what they described as "a democracy or popular government," based on the right of the freemen to make "just laws." Members of a third sect led by the religious radical Samuel Gorton would arrive in 1643, before Roger Williams went to England and obtained from Parliament a patent in 1644, effectively giving Rhode Island corporate status with the right of local self-government. Its form of government would be similar to that of Massachusetts, with its strong emphasis on local autonomy and its representative assembly. The one difference was that, instead of insisting upon religious orthodoxy, the colony insisted on religious toleration.

The Connecticut River Valley attracted several groups of Puritans from both Plymouth and Massachusetts. Of these the largest was the congregation of Thomas Hooker of Newtown. Though Hooker and his congregation had no sympathy with either Hutchinson or Williams, they appear to have disliked the arbitrary actions of the general court, as well as the restrictive nature of church membership and the problem of determining who was saved. In May 1635 they migrated to Hartford. Title to their land was quickly disputed, being claimed by Massachusetts, New Netherland, and Plymouth, as well as by a group of English investors who obtained a patent to the land from the Council for New England.

Hooker's presence also provoked a disruption of relations with the local Pequot Indians. For several years the Pequots had been trading with both the English and the Dutch, but the arrival of English settlers on their land appears to have triggered new tensions. Pequots killed two English traders, Captain Stone in 1634 and John Oldham in 1636. When Massachusetts authorities insisted on trying the Pequot offenders under English law, the Pequots refused to surrender them. The Indians considered themselves to be equal partners in their relationships with the Europeans, and acknowledging the jurisdiction of the Massachusetts government would have amounted to a concession that they were its subjects rather than its equals. However, Massachusetts authorities had little incentive to compromise; provoking a war offered them the best means of securing the Pequots' land. Once the Pequots realized that war was imminent, they sought an alliance with the Narragansetts against the colony of Massachusetts. However the Narragansetts, having come to depend on their own trade ties with Rhode Island and Massachusetts, turned the Pequots down and allied themselves with the English. Meanwhile, Massachusetts received military assistance from neighboring Plymouth and from Rhode Island, as well as the colonists in Connecticut.

Once these alliances were settled, there could be little doubt as to the outcome of the conflict. In April 1637, Pequots raided the town of Wethersfield, Connecticut, killing several settlers. Leaders in Massachusetts and Connecticut seized the opportunity to make an example of the Pequot people. A Connecticut force under Captain John Mason, assisted by a number of Narragansett allies, was dispatched to surround a Pequot village on the Mystic River. Most of the village's fighting men had gone away, leaving the village inhabited by approximately 500 women, children, and old men. In the early hours of the morning, the English surrounded the village, set it on fire, and then proceeded to shoot and kill every Indian who managed to escape from the flames and tried to run away. Five hundred Pequots perished in the attack despite protests by the Narragansetts, who realized that they were witnessing a new and more destructive kind of conflict than traditional Native American forms of warfare. When an even larger group of Pequots was trapped in a swamp, the Puritans did not hesitate to kill the fighting men and sell the rest into slavery, believing that their opponents, like the Philistines in the Old Testament, had rightly been put to the sword.

After the Pequots' defeat, relationships between the English and the other peoples in the region changed markedly. English leaders began demanding tribute from their Indian allies instead of treating them as equal trading partners. The Narragansetts and Mohegans had to agree not to go to war without English permission. The Narragansett leader Miantonomo attempted to create an alliance among local sachems to drive out the English, but in 1643, English authorities had Miantonomo arrested, tried, and

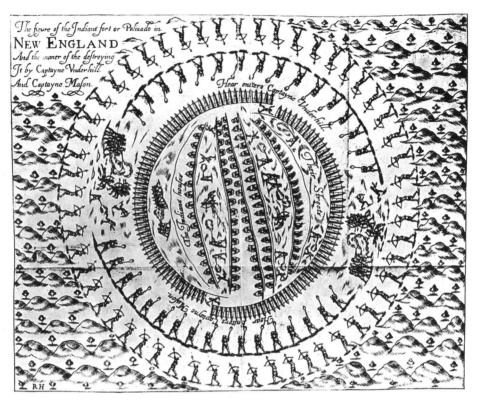

Figure 12 "Underhill's Diagram of the Pequot Fight." From John Fiske, *The Beginnings of New England, or, The Puritan Theocracy in Its Relations to Civil and Religious Liberty* (Boston: Houghton Mifflin, 1898).

executed by one of his rivals, the Mohegan leader Uncas. The English had effectively transformed their relationship with the local Indians from an alliance born of mutual necessity to a relationship of rulers and subjects.

The creation of additional colonies in New England continued as it had begun. Connecticut created its own general court, and in January 1639 agreed on a frame of government for the colony known as the Fundamental Orders. Like the government of Massachusetts, Connecticut's government was committed "to maintain and preserve the liberty and purity of the gospel of our lord Jesus as . . . is now practised." Its general court would consist of a governor and six assistants, to be elected by the freemen, for whom church membership was implicitly required. However, Hooker widened membership in the church by offering communion to all who professed the faith, so that citizenship was less restrictive. Other patterns established in Massachusetts were followed here as well. Significant local control was ensured by a provision that each town would have four deputies at the general court, to be elected "by all that are admitted inhabitants in the several towns." The Fundamental Orders recognized that the deputies had different functions from the magistrates and should meet separately, a significant gain for the assembly which Massachusetts adopted only in 1644. The

DOCUMENT 9

A call for Indian unity by Chief Miantonomo, 1642, reprinted in Karen Ordahl Kupperman, ed., *Major Problems in American Colonial History: Documents and Essays* (Lexington, Mass., 1993), 135

Miantonomo, like Opechancanough in Virginia, having tried coexistence with the colonists, could see no alternative to all-out war with them if the native peoples were not to be exterminated. Questions to consider: *What grievances did Miantonomo express towards the English? If Miantonomo's strategy had been followed, would it have been more effective than individual tribal arrangements as a way to resist the English?*

A while after this came Miantenomie from Block Island to Mantacut with a troop of men . . . instead of receiving presents, which they used to do in their progress, he gave them gifts, calling them brethren and friends, for so are we all Indians as they English are, and say brother to one another; so must we be one as they are, otherwise we shall be all gone shortly, for you know our fathers had plenty of deer and skins, our plains were full of deer, as also our woods, and of turkies, and our coves full of fish and fowl. But these English having gotten our land, they with scythes cut down the grass, and with axes fell the trees; their cows and horses eat the grass, and their hogs spoil our clam banks, and we shall all be starved; therefore it is best for you to do as we, for we are all the Sachems from east to west, both Moquakues and Mohauks joining with us, and we are all resolved to fall upon them all, at one appointed day; and therefore I am come to you privately first, because you can persuade the Indians and Sachem to what you will . . . and when you see the three fires that will be made forty days hence, in a clear night, then do as we, and the next day fall on and kill men, women, and children, but no cows, for they will serve to eat til our deer be increased again.

deputies could also convene the general court should the governor and assistants fail to do so, for an all-powerful magistracy such as had originally existed in Massachusetts was not to be allowed. The colony obtained a royal charter in 1662 that confirmed the provisions of the Fundamental Orders.

New Hampshire, too, began as an offshoot of Massachusetts. Though a few settlers had been sent there by the Council for New England[10] in the 1620s, the population began to grow when followers of the antinomian Reverend John Wheelwright moved to the town of Exeter in the 1630s. During the early 1640s additional settlements were established at Dover and Portsmouth in New Hampshire and at York and Kittery in Maine. All settled on land subject to claims by the Council for New England, and when Massachusetts sought control over the new settlements, the heirs of the company's major investors, Fernando Gorges and John Mason, sued. Eventually the dispute was

---

[10] Formerly called the Plymouth Company.

settled in 1680 when New Hampshire became a royal colony. Maine on the other hand was annexed to Massachusetts on the grounds that it was part of Massachusetts' original grant. The Maine settlements protested, but to no avail. Kittery was organized as a town with the right to send a deputy to the general court. Since it had no covenanted church, all the male inhabitants were made freemen and allowed to vote.

The last New England colony was New Haven, which began in June 1637, after the Reverend John Davenport purchased a tract of land from the local inhabitants there and led his congregants to settle on it. The Davenport group in New Haven would adopt a frame of government in 1639 similar to that of Massachusetts, restricting the franchise to church members and adopting biblical law instead of the English common law. The similarity was not surprising, since Davenport was a friend of Cotton.

Despite their theological and political differences, the New England colonies shared substantial similarities in their political structures and religious cultures which helped bring them together. The Pequot War had also had a unifying effect. Puritan leaders compared the destruction of the Pequots to the Israelites' eviction of the Canaanites from the Promised Land, and used their victory over the Indians to promote the idea that all of the various contending groups of Puritans throughout New England shared the common goal of subduing the Indians and winning their land for God's purposes. Accordingly in 1643, Massachusetts, Plymouth, Connecticut, and New Haven entered into a formal alliance, styled the Confederation of the United Colonies of New England.[11] Rhode Island, however, remained the outcast of the group; it was deliberately left out.

Dissenting religious groups would continue to challenge Puritan orthodoxy for as long as the Puritans remained in control of Massachusetts. These challenges were liveliest during the English Civil War and its aftermath, when control over religious practice in England encouraged the creation of new radical religious movements. In the early 1640s, the Gortonists appeared, followed by the Baptists, or Anabaptists, who insisted on adult immersion because the Bible did not authorize infant baptism. Most troublesome were the Quakers, who first arrived in 1656. They wished to dispense with almost all traditional Christian practice, including use of the Bible, for they believed that everyone could experience God's grace through prayer and the "inner light." The Puritan magistrates responded to all of these groups with a heavy hand, imposing fines, whippings, banishment, and (in the case of four Quakers) execution to suppress these heresies.[12] Such harsh punishments, however, often proved counterproductive, since they merely encouraged others to proclaim their faith by defying the magistrates. One concession to the dissenters was that they might hold private meetings, providing "it be without just offense." But formal congregations could be established only with the consent of the local magistrates and elders by such persons as "be orthodox in judgement." There were to be no rival establishments in the Puritan commonwealth.[13]

---

[11]   Various historians have emphasized the connection between challenges to the Puritans' authority and the ideological uses of Indian wars. On the Pequot War, see Salisbury, *Manitou and Providence.*

[12]   Among those executed was Mary Dyer, a former associate of Anne Hutchinson. For further information on the Quakers, see Chapter 7, section 3.

[13]   The Baptists managed to establish a meeting house in 1679 in Boston, but for a long time it was the sole one. The Anglicans established their first formal place of worship in Boston only in 1689, a wooden structure known as King's Chapel. This was superseded in 1723 by a handsome brick building, known as the old North Church or Christ Church; see Chapter 13, section 1.

5 CHALLENGES FROM ENGLAND

Even as the magistrates faced challenges from within Massachusetts, other challenges were being leveled at them from without. In its attempt to create a biblical common-wealth Massachusetts had enacted laws that were clearly inconsistent with English law. Challenges to the colony's leaders therefore began almost immediately.

The first threat came from Gorges and the Council for New England, who were angry that the king had issued a patent to another group in an area claimed by the council. Gorges was not opposed to the Puritan emigration; he merely wanted the Puritans to acknowledge his company's authority and accept its plan of government. Several others joined the clamor to have the affairs of Massachusetts investigated. Accordingly, in 1634 a special committee of the Privy Council was set up under Archbishop Laud to look into the affairs of the Massachusetts Bay Company. On discovering that the charter was no longer in England, the committee began legal proceedings to have the company terminated. These were slow, and it was not until the summer of 1637 that a verdict was given in favor of the king. Charles I then announced that he would govern Massachusetts, as he did Virginia, through a governor and council, with Gorges as his first representative. Fortunately for Massachusetts, the king's gesture proved hollow; his attempts during the 1630s to govern without Parliament had been a disaster, since his Scottish subjects were in rebellion and he could not wage war against them effectively without Parliament's cooperation. Any attempt to suppress the Puritans in Massachusetts would have to wait.

The beginning of the English Civil War in 1642 gave Massachusetts a respite from most legal challenges, since English officials were too occupied with political conflicts at home to interfere much with their colonies in North America. A principal aim of the majority in Parliament was the reform of the Church of England, and some New Englanders advocated going back to England to help. Among those who returned were several ministers, along with others who were simply homesick, having been unable to adapt to a strange environment. The vast majority stayed put, however, being firmly attached to their new country.

Despite their general preoccupation with matters in England, Parliament did take some interest in the conduct of church government in the colonies. The Massachusetts Puritans still possessed a congregational system but were incorporating one element of a Presbyterian one, in which ministers were subject to the authority of an assembly of the clergy, called a synod. Initially, Parliament in England was dominated by Presbyterians, with whom the Puritans had a number of disagreements, not least concerning the relationship of a congregation to its minister. Indeed, a Presbyterian, Dr Robert Child, mounted an important challenge to the common-wealth in 1646. Child moved to Massachusetts in 1645 following Parliament's triumph in the Civil War. Recognizing the disabilities under which he labored in Massachusetts, he wrote *A Remonstrance and Humble Petition* in which he made a number of charges: that his rights as an Englishman were being infringed; that the charter was being used beyond its intended purpose, being merely equivalent to an English corporation; that the laws of Massachusetts did not conform to those of England; and that the church lacked proper regulation, since it excluded most inhabitants from the sacrament and their children from baptism. Only a genuinely Presbyterian system, Child argued, would correct these faults.

Though fearing that members of Parliament might be sympathetic towards Child's legal attack, the Puritan leadership was not disposed to admit any of his charges. Child was charged with writing "divers false and scandalous passages . . . against the Churches of Christ and the civil government here established." The general court asserted that a proper body of laws had been enacted and that their only obligation under the charter was to ensure that these laws were not contrary to those of England. As to the charge that Massachusetts constituted no more than an English corporation, the court asserted that the position of a foreign plantation was necessarily different. The court determined to impose a stiff fine. When Child and his coauthors implied that they would appeal to Parliament, the general court imprisoned them while dispatching its own courier to London. Fortunately the army, dominated by the Independents, as the congregational Puritans were known in England, shortly took control as it gained the upper hand in England's Civil War. Child's complaint, therefore, was not well received when he finally reached London. From 1648 Massachusetts was seemingly safe for the first time in the affections of an English government.

Still, the Child episode had important consequences. The general court was aware that Massachusetts still had no proper legal code. Many settlers had from the beginning been worried by the arbitrary nature of the justice dispensed by the court of assistants, with its unsystematic use of the Bible, common law, and individual whim. In 1636 John Cotton had drawn up a code which Winthrop called "a model of Moses" because of its biblical references. This code had been modified in 1639 by the Reverend Nathaniel Ward, though the intent was still "to compose a model of the judicial laws of Moses." It was this draft which had finally been issued in 1641 as the Body of Liberties. Many deputies, however, felt that it still left too much to the arbitrary judgment of the magistrates and quirks of the Mosaic law. Accordingly, in 1648 a further revision was undertaken, during which a number of legal volumes were imported from England. The result, published as *The Book of General Lawes and Libertyes*, defined more precisely the powers and functions of the magistracy, the "liberties" of the individual, and the due process of the law. Another important step had been taken in the evolution of Massachusetts from a semitheocratic state to a constitutional polity.

Another result of the Child affair was the need to address the charge that non-members of the church were being discriminated against. In addition, there was a wider need for a definitive statement of the congregational church's theology and procedures. Accordingly, the Cambridge Platform of August 1648 attempted to do for the church what the *Book of General Lawes and Libertyes* had done for the state. On relations between the two it asserted, "As it is unlawful for church officers to meddle with the sword of the magistrate, so it is unlawful for the Magistrate to meddle with the work proper to church officers." The days when Winthrop could dominate both were over. The dividing lines were now clear. The church pronounced on matters of doctrine, the magistrates enforced them. As to doctrine, the ministers decided to adopt the 1648 Westminster Confession, bringing them into line with their colleagues in England. The Platform, however, made no concession on church membership, arguing that the issue of "saints by calling" was a matter for the congregations to decide. There must be no lowering of standards, whatever the civil disabilities for the rest of the community.

6 STABLE SOCIETIES

Despite religious and political challenges to the authority of the Puritan magistrates, the Puritans who immigrated to New England between 1630 and 1642 had managed to create remarkably stable societies by 1650. A model which had begun to be worked in Virginia was being more fully developed here, producing settler societies in New England that could not have been more different from Virginia's.

New Englanders were, first of all, more actively committed to the church, and this commitment translated into high rates of civic participation. Among the smaller towns in Massachusetts and Connecticut church membership was as high as 60 percent, though by 1650 Boston had only 625 saints out of a total populace of 3,000. The 1648 code had laid down that male church members who failed to qualify as freemen might still serve as constables, jurors, selectmen, and highway surveyors. An additional law permitted nonfreemen to vote for selectmen and serve as jurors. Unlike the individualistic society developing in Virginia, New England was developing a society full of active citizens.

Because of the characteristics of New England's immigrant population, its society would from the outset be exceptionally stable and family-oriented. Unlike the young, predominantly male settlers in early Virginia, a large proportion of the settlers who flocked to New England before 1642 were in their thirties and came with their spouses and a few children. They were used to working, having left behind established trades or farms. They continued to have children once they arrived in New England, largely because those children gave them their best chance for success as family farmers. Working together, a family could clear their land, improve it, and then rely upon it for their economic subsistence, insulated from the ups and downs of a commercial economy. An additional attraction of family farming was that it allowed the Puritans to raise their children in a godly manner, free from the temptations of England's increasingly commercial society and safe from the danger of slipping into the ranks of the landless poor.[14]

A third difference from Virginia was that New England's population was growing steadily. Because the healthy climate reduced childhood mortality, New England settler families grew larger than average families in England, with six to eight children typically surviving to adulthood. The settlers' fertility led to New England's remarkable expansion throughout the seventeenth century and made up for a dramatic decline in new immigration after the beginning of the English Civil War. Though almost no new immigrants arrived during the period, the number of towns in Massachusetts rose from 21 in 1641 to 33 by 1647.

Unlike the Virginians, New Englanders did not get rich during these early decades, for the region never developed a profitable staple crop. For the first 10 years, Massachusetts prospered because a continuous stream of immigrants arrived bringing cash to buy livestock and other supplies with which to establish themselves. However, most farming was of a subsistence nature, the main produce being hogs and corn.

---

[14] On the connections between competency and family patterns, see Anderson, *New England's Generation*, and Daniel Vickers, *Farmers and Fishermen*.

Those with servants could diversify into cattle and wheat, but in the absence of a profitable staple crop few families produced enough wealth to bring more servants from England. The absence of a staple crop also meant that the distribution of wealth remained fairly consistent. Although the wealthiest investors had larger landholdings than the rest, most settlers here were middling people with small farms. Unlike England, New England had no significant group of impoverished, landless laborers during the seventeenth century.

As colonial ventures, the New England colonies never fit the model of profitable, export-producing outposts that early promoters like Hakluyt had envisioned. Yet the investors in New England could be satisfied in what they had accomplished. By 1650 their economy was growing more diversified, with a fishery that managed to compete with Spain and Portugal in supplying fish for European markets. The fishery in turn encouraged a nascent boat- and later shipbuilding industry in towns like Boston and New Haven. And eventually new markets for New England farmers would appear in the West Indies, where planters were happy to exchange sugar for other provisions, primarily fish, beef, pork, and corn. Lumber and fish from Maine were also products which could be marketed in England, and some trade with the local Indians was still taking place. Not all experiments had succeeded, of course. An attempt in Massachusetts to establish an ironworks near Lynn on the Saugus River folded because of a lack of skilled labor. However small-scale smelting and the fashioning of items like nails and simple tools did continue at a number of sites.

New England's churches, too, appeared to be flourishing. The churches had become less dependent on England for qualified clergy since 1636, with the founding of Harvard College. Its first graduates were ordained as ministers in 1641, by which time over 20 scholars were in residence. In addition, basic education was being provided to the population at large, at least in Massachusetts. Since knowledge of the Scriptures was essential for salvation, all Massachusetts towns with 50 households were required after 1647 to appoint someone to teach their children to read and write, and larger towns were expected to provide grammar schools for teaching Latin, the language of university instruction.

Serious attempts had been made as well to convert the Indians. The earliest missionary activity was undertaken by Thomas Mayhew at Martha's Vineyard, partly in response to criticism by Williams and others of the Puritans' failure in this matter. As time went on many southern New England Indians became more ready to embrace Christianity, following the breakdown of their own societies under the impact of war and disease. Accordingly, in 1646 the Reverend John Eliot, the minister at Roxbury, established a mission for the surviving Pequot and Massachusetts peoples. They were herded into four settlements known euphemistically as the "praying towns," the chief one being at Natick. Eliot provided a written liturgy in 1654, when he published a translated version of the catechism, followed in 1660 by a translation of the New Testament. Plans were also made for the training of an Indian ministry at Harvard. About the same time, the Natick congregation was even admitted to the Roxbury Church, despite some reluctance on the part of the white community.

The pattern of Indian relations developing in New England by the 1650s could not, on the face of it, have been more different than the pattern established by this time in Virginia. Instead of being separated into distinct English and Indian societies, English and Indian villages in New England often coexisted side by side. New England leaders had sought to place Indian communities under the umbrella of their own authority rather than driving them out, as in Virginia. In this they had largely succeeded. Especially in the longest settled region around Plymouth, whites lived in close proximity with their Native American neighbors, interacting with them on what was sometimes a daily basis. Many local Indians had become bilingual, and some had even learned to read English and to negotiate the expectations and unwritten rules of English society.

Still, life was not improving for the Native Americans in New England, especially around the most heavily populated settler communities in the south. English livestock was driving out the game in their hunting grounds, forcing many of the Indians in Massachusetts to become fully sedentary farmers. Meanwhile English hogs were wreaking havoc on Indian cornfields, and the Indians had become dependent for many of their supplies on trade with the English.[15] Moreover it was clear by this time that the Indians had become a subordinate group within New England society. In southern New England the Indians were by now largely subject to colonial laws that restricted their purchases of arms, alcohol, and trade goods, and placed them under the jurisdiction of colonial courts. Whether or not they liked to admit it, New England's Indians had become a colonized people, living among their colonizers. It was a new and uncomfortable role.

---

[15] For the environmental changes produced by English colonization and their effect on New England Indians, see William Cronon, *Changes in the Land: Indians, Colonists, and the Ecology of New England* (New York, 1983). Virginia DeJohn Anderson explains the impact of English livestock on the Indians' livelihoods in *Creatures of Empire: How Domestic Animals Transformed Early America* (New York, 2004). Discussions of the relationships which had developed between New England Indians and English settlers by 1660 may be found in Jenny Hale Pulsipher, *Subjects unto the Same King: Indians, English, and the Contest for Authority in Colonial New England* (Philadelphia, 2005), James D. Drake. *King Philip's War: Civil War in New England, 1675–1676* (Amherst, 1999), and Joshua Micah Marshall, "Melancholy People: Anglo-Indian Relations in Early Warwick, Rhode Island, 1642–1675," *New England Quarterly* (1995), 402–29.

5

Diverse Colonies

New France, New Netherland, Maryland, and the West Indies

1608	French merchants establish Québec.
1609	Henry Hudson explores the Hudson River.
1624	The Dutch West India Company establishes New Netherland. English colonists found St. Kitts.
1624–8	The Mohawks triumph over the Mahicans.
1626	Manhattan is purchased for 60 guilders.
1629	Kiliaen Van Rensselaer establishes the first patroonship in New Netherland.
1634	The colony of Maryland is established by the second Lord Baltimore.
1635	The first assembly of freemen in Maryland takes place.
1638	The first Swedish settlement is founded on the Delaware.
1643–5	War breaks out between the Dutch and Indians near New Amsterdam.
1644–6	Maryland endures "the plundering time."
1646	The Dutch West India Company begins selling slaves in Barbados. Peter Stuyvesant is appointed director general of New Netherland.
1648	Maryland grants headrights to servants.
1648–9	The Dutch-allied Iroquois defeat the French-allied Huron.
1649	Maryland passes an act for religious toleration.
1655	The Dutch take control of New Sweden. Wappinger Indians attack New Amsterdam in the Peach War. The English seize Jamaica from Spain.
1657	Jews are permitted to become burghers of New Amsterdam.

Colonial America: A History to 1763, Fourth Edition. Richard Middleton and Anne Lombard.
© 2011 Richard Middleton and Anne Lombard. Published 2011 by Blackwell Publishing Ltd.

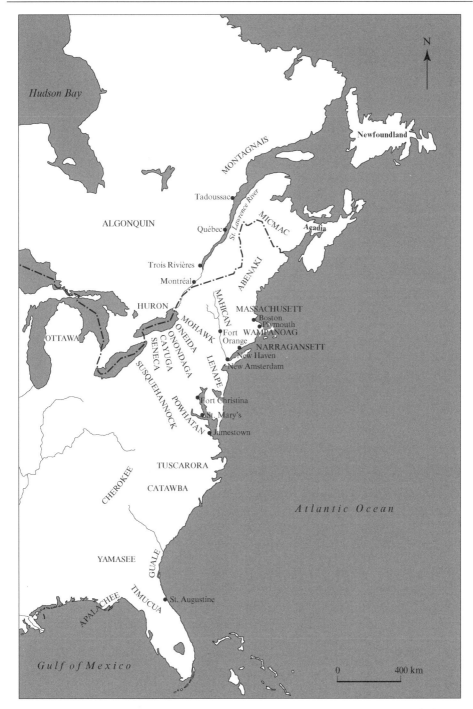

Map 5 Locations of major Indian peoples and European settlements in eastern North America, circa 1640.

1 NEW FRANCE

T HE ENGLISH WERE not the only Europeans to establish permanent colonies in North America in the seventeenth century. Merchants from France and the Netherlands would found colonies early in the century, encouraged by their respective governments who hoped to compete with Spain and profit from an American trade. The French colonies in particular would leave an indelible legacy, still obvious in parts of Canada today. Adventurers and priests from Spain would continue to develop their colony in Florida and establish a new one in New Mexico to help protect and consolidate Spanish holdings in New Spain. Other French and Spanish colonies would later follow. The full story of colonial North America involved a diverse array of Europeans, each interacting in different ways with groups of Native Americans and (usually) Africans as well.

Since the focus of our story is mainly on the 13 mainland British colonies that would form the United States in 1776, we do not attempt to provide the full details of this multifaceted story. Still, the mainland British North American colonies took shape in an era of globalization, and historians today concur that their history cannot be understood without considerable attention to the other European colonies that coexisted in North America along with them. Some of these colonies would produce economic competitors to English traders, merchants, and planters. Others would pose serious military threats that would limit the territorial expansion and the demographic development of British North America for more than a century and a half. To understand the history of the British colonies, then, we need to understand something about the other colonial North American societies with which they interacted. Since the French were their most direct competitors for much of the seventeenth century, we will begin with them.[1]

Despite the destruction of the French Huguenot colonies in South Carolina and Florida in the 1560s, French fishermen and traders had continued their yearly voyages to North America, becoming increasingly enmeshed in trading relationships with the various Algonquian- and Iroquoian-speaking peoples who lived along the Atlantic coastline and around the Gulf of St. Lawrence. Near the mouth of the St. Lawrence lived Algonquians and Montagnais, with the Huron further upriver east of the Great Lakes. The dominant group in Acadia was the Micmacs, while the Abenaki peoples lived further south near the coast. Over the many decades during which their relationships developed, French traders learned to operate within the terms demanded by their Native American trading partners. For the Indians, as we have seen, trade implied more than a simple commercial relationship. It created a bond of something like kinship, imposing various reciprocal obligations beyond providing goods at a desirable price. In order to display the generosity and trustworthiness that their Indian trading partners expected of them, the French learned to proffer elaborate gifts, to participate in ceremonial rituals, and to refrain from sharp bargaining practices. They also learned, far better than their English competitors to the south, that their trading partners

---

[1] The Spanish colonies in Florida, New Mexico, and Texas, and the French colonies in the Midwest and Louisiana, will be discussed in Chapter 15.

expected them to provide not only trade goods but also military assistance and protection against enemies.

Facing increasing pressure from English competitors, French merchants established trading posts in Acadia in 1598 and at Tadoussac, on the St. Lawrence River, in 1600. In 1603, partly to counter English attempts to encroach on the French fur trade, the French government granted charters to a merchant company led by Pierre Du Gua de Monts to establish a permanent settlement. The company hired the explorer and cartographer Samuel de Champlain to find an appropriate site for such a settlement. After several false starts, Champlain and a few dozen male settlers established a tiny fortified village at Québec, on the St. Lawrence River, in 1608.

The small size of Champlain's colony as well as the settlers' reliance on the Indian trade would shape the colony's destiny, though it did so in ways its leaders could not have anticipated. Ironically, their miniscule numbers probably helped to ensure French survival, for the local Indians perceived this tiny new settlement to pose no threat to their own way of life. Indeed, they viewed the French as desirable trading partners and allies to be welcomed. For the first few decades after the French colonies were established, the French greatly strengthened the Hurons' role as mediators of trade throughout the northern region. The effect of a permanent French presence was to bring many more native peoples into the fur trade, giving them access to coveted European trade goods. Items made from brass and iron were particularly sought after because of their utility, both as cooking implements and for use in making arrowheads that could penetrate wooden armor. But ornamental objects were also prized for the prestige they could confer when given away as gifts. In turn the Frenchmen depended heavily on their Indian trading partners for food and essential supplies, and were willing to accommodate their allies' expectations in order to preserve their relationship.

To Montagnais and Huron peoples, the new alliance with the French had a profound political significance in addition to its economic effects. The peoples in the St. Lawrence region faced powerful enemies: the members of the Iroquois League, inland and just south of the St. Lawrence River as far west as the Great Lakes. By 1600, the members of the Iroquois Five Nations– the Mohawks, Oneidas, Onondagas, Cayugas, and Senecas – numbered perhaps 25,000 people.[2] Their confederacy was by now well established, and every year some 50 sachems representing each of the various clans in the Iroquois League met at the great long house of the Onondagas to exchange presents and renew their vows of peace and friendship. The alliance gave the Iroquois advantages that other tribal groups did not have. It created a mechanism for limiting unnecessary bloodshed, enabling the Iroquois to develop greater stability and cohesiveness than other peoples. It also made the members of the Five Nations a more formidable enemy when they made war upon neighbors from outside the confederacy, including the Susquehannocks to the south and the Algonquians, Montagnais, and Hurons to the north and east.

French presence in the region would change the balance of power between the Iroquois and their neighbors, for the St. Lawrence Indians expected the French to

---

[2] For more information on the Iroquois Great League of Peace or Iroquois Five Nations, see Chapter 1, section 4.

provide them not only with trade goods but also with military assistance against their foes. Indeed in July 1609, Champlain and his men lived up to expectations when their Montagnais and Huron trading partners launched a war party against the Mohawks. Though Mohawk warriors apparently outnumbered the French and Indian war party, they fled after suffering unexpectedly heavy casualties from the assault by French guns. Now, with French backing, the St. Lawrence Indians had suddenly gained the upper hand.

Very much like the English colonizers of New England, the French sought to convert their Native American trading partners and allies to Christianity, though in their case it was Catholic and not Protestant missions that were to be created. Missionaries were present in Acadia as early as 1611 and in Québec in 1625, and members of the Jesuit order embarked on a serious missionary effort during the 1630s. In the long run, French missionaries converted members of the Huron people in far larger numbers than English missionaries were able to achieve among the various tribal groups in southern New England. The question for historians has been why French Jesuits were so successful. One factor certainly was the support they received from the French Crown, encouraging the work of the Roman Catholic Church by providing it with large grants of land in New France, land which could then be leased to settlers. During the 1630s the French government in Québec also insisted that the Hurons allow Jesuit missionaries to live in their villages as a condition of trade. Another factor was the attractiveness of Catholic religious practices. Catholic missionaries invariably presented Christianity to the Indians as a source of spiritual power, and in that context Catholic rituals, saints, and material objects could be more plausibly presented as sources of powerful magic. Protestants, with their plain services and rejection of ritual, had less to offer.[3]

Some historians have argued that French Jesuit missionaries succeeded because they were more culturally flexible than English Puritans, but other scholarship suggests a more complicated story, having to do with the indirect effects of sustained interactions between Frenchmen and native peoples. The French, just like the English further south, brought diseases which devastated local Indian populations – particularly among the Huron people, whose contacts with French traders and missionaries were both early and constant. During the 1630s and early 1640s, a small number of Hurons – mostly traders – converted to Catholicism. However, most Hurons resisted conversion, fearing that Christianity might actually be a malevolent force that was causing disease and death. It was only by the late 1640s, after a series of epidemics, famines, and stepped-up attacks by their Iroquois enemies that a large percentage of the Huron population finally gave in and decided to be baptized. In the end the surviving Hurons became deeply integrated into French Canada, living in Christian villages (called *reserves*) interspersed among French settlements. Other northern Indians would eventually convert to Catholicism as well, finding a close relationship with the French missionaries to be a helpful source of stability after their communities had been ravaged by disease or attacks from the Iroquois. The *reserves* became multicultural communities that

---

[3] For a discussion of the assimilation of Catholic rituals into Potawatomie traditions, see Susan Sleeper-Smith, *Indian Women and French Men: Rethinking Cultural Encounter in the Western Great Lakes* (Amherst, 2001).

included Algonquians, Mahicans, Ottawas, Hurons, and others, all of whose warriors were more or less explicitly allied with the French.

The French population in Acadia and Québec remained small for many years, numbering fewer than 200 for at least two decades. Champlain encouraged young male fur traders to live among the Indians rather than remaining inside the settlements, a policy which had the effect of strengthening French trading relationships with distant nations. The policy also extended French influence far inland into what became known as the *pays d'en haut*, territories which the French claimed as their own but never settled. In 1627, a trading company known as the Compagnie des Cent-Associés obtained from the French Crown a trading monopoly and land grant which included Québec and Acadia, extended northeast to Newfoundland and south through the Mississippi Valley. The company received the grant on the condition that it create a farming settlement. France's aim was to consolidate French control over Canadian territory – a goal whose importance was reinforced in 1629, when English privateers captured Québec, took Champlain prisoner, and held the city until it was restored by treaty negotiations in 1632.

Once Champlain and the French investors regained control over New France, they became responsible for administering justice on the king's behalf and distributing the land through a seigneurial system. Seigneurs, often French military officers or the Catholic Church, received large grants of land, laid out in strips perpendicular to the St. Lawrence River, which they held on the king's behalf on condition that they ensure its improvement and development. The seigneurs then divided their lands among tenants, called *habitants*, who cleared and farmed the land in exchange for annual rents paid to the seigneurs. The seigneurs never became really wealthy, for rents remained small throughout the colonial period and farmers mostly grew food for their own subsistence rather than developing a cash crop. But the social structure did remain markedly different from that found in the English colonies. New France developed a sizable nobility, while most of its farmers remained permanent tenants. This gave it a distinctive character in contrast to New England, which never developed a nobility and where ordinary farming families typically owned their own land or paid only nominal rents.

Despite its obligation to do so, the company failed to bring settlers to New France in significant numbers, concentrating instead on further developing the fur trade. In consequence its trading monopoly was suspended in 1641, and the company was dissolved in 1662. Thereafter the colony was restructured as a royal province. Governing duties were carried out by a royal council consisting of a governor responsible for diplomacy and defense, an *intendant* who was in charge of finance and administering law and order, a bishop in charge of religious matters, and a five-person advisory council. The Crown filled each of these positions. Eventually the Crown also sent a permanent military force of French soldiers, called the *troupes de marine*, to the colony to man its garrisons and protect its settlements. The presence of professional soldiers also distinguished New France from the English colonies to its south, for the English colonies had no consistent military support from the home government until the eighteenth century.

Although migration to New France picked up after the reorganization of the government, French settlers arrived at a fraction of the rate achieved in the English colonies further south. During the early years of the colony, official French policy had limited migration to Catholics, although in reality the French government did little to hinder migration by Protestants. Between 1662 and 1671 the Crown actively encouraged immigrants by sending prospective settlers on royal transports as well as ships commissioned from merchants for the purpose. And yet the immigrants failed to come, for reasons that historians have struggled to understand. Peasants in seventeenth-century France, where famines were common and economic conditions grim, might have been expected to migrate in large numbers to a place with cheap, plentiful farmland and a low rate of mortality. In fact, however, few Frenchmen moved to New France voluntarily, and Frenchmen sent to the colony as soldiers or indentured servants were twice as likely to return to France as to stay in the colonies. Part of the reason for this reluctance was a widespread exaggeration among the French of the severity of Canadian winters. An even more important factor, historians have suggested, was the nature of French society and culture. Even when they were poor, French families were more likely than English families to provide patronage and material support for unemployed young people and to discourage their children from sailing away to an unknown land. As a result, French peasants (unlike their English, Scottish, and German contemporaries) simply refused to move away from home.

A census showed the presence of 3,215 European settlers in New France in 1666. Of these, about two-thirds were male, having arrived in the colony as either soldiers or indentured servants. In order to encourage marriage, the royal government in New France sponsored emigration by poor and unmarried Frenchwomen, much as the Virginia Company had done earlier in the century. About 770 *filles du roi*, as they were called, had arrived in the colony by 1673, whereupon they were encouraged to marry and begin new lives as the wives of French farmers. The importation of young women combined with a cold and healthy climate achieved, in the end, what earlier attempts to encourage immigration had not. Frenchwomen in the colony married young, experienced many pregnancies, and lived long lives, and the population at last began to grow at a rapid rate through natural increase. By the 1680s the population had grown to about 10,000 French-Canadians, more than doubling in less than 20 years.

The French government in New France also continued to encourage exploration and the expansion of the fur trade. A mission established at Ville-Marie in 1642 to convert the Indians became a major fur-trading center by the 1660s, attracting Indian traders from the north as well as west along the St. Lawrence River corridor as far as the Great Lakes. After the English Hudson's Bay Company founded a colony north of New France in 1670 and began to compete with the French for the northern fur trade, the French government became an enthusiastic promoter of further exploration so that the French could expand their share of the trade. In 1682, Robert de La Salle explored the Mississippi and Ohio valleys on behalf of the French government, and laid claim for France to the surrounding territory. It was named Louisiana, and became part of New France.[4]

---

[4] See Chapter 15 for a fuller discussion of these developments.

2 NEW NETHERLAND AND DELAWARE: THE DUTCH AND SWEDISH BEGINNINGS

Although the French colonies being established in New France would ultimately pose a greater threat to English interests, England's main concern by the mid seventeenth century was another colony which had been created by the Dutch at several points along the Hudson River, south and west of New England. The first European to explore this area was an Englishman, Henry Hudson, operating on behalf of the Dutch East India Company. Hudson's mission in 1609 was to find the elusive northwest passage, in pursuit of which he proceeded as far as present-day Albany. Since the Dutch interest was originally trade rather than settlement, the company began shortly after this mission to send traders upriver annually to trade with the local inhabitants for furs. Among the Indians they encountered here were the Mahicans, Algonquian speakers who lived in the Hudson Valley region, and the Mohawks, the most powerful tribe within the Iroquois League, who lived a little further west. The Dutch established an outpost in the area in 1613 and remained there until 1618.

When it appeared in 1620 that war was about to break out again between Spain and Holland, Dutch interest in the area revived, in part because a base might be required for operations across the Atlantic. The Dutch East India Company was preoccupied elsewhere so a new corporation was formed to establish a base and exploit the area's commercial potential. Initially, the Dutch West India Company devoted its attention to Bahia in the Caribbean, until a small group of settlers was finally dispatched to the mainland of North America to consolidate Dutch claims to the region in 1624. Most of the party went to the site of the earlier post, now called Fort Orange, to resume the fur trade. A smaller group settled on Governor's Island at the mouth of the Hudson, while a further detachment went to the Delaware Valley, establishing Fort Nassau near the future city of Philadelphia. To guard against the possibility of attack by competing European powers, additional settlers were sent in 1625 to a fortified post on Manhattan Island called New Amsterdam.

In some respects the Dutch company resembled that of Virginia in its early stages. Governmental authority lay primarily with the director general and his officials, though they were supposed to seek the occasional advice of a council drawn from the inhabitants. Most settlers arrived as servants of the company, usually for a period of six years. After this they could take up tenancies, as in Virginia. In other respects, the Dutch company's policies were quite different from those of the Virginia Company. Dutch colonists were required only to grow food, and to sell their produce to the company. The company offered few incentives to encourage immigration. Thus, though the settlement never experienced the tribulations of Virginia, since it was self-sufficient from the outset, it grew very slowly, like the colony of New France. By 1630 it contained only 300 inhabitants.

Historians have sometimes portrayed the Dutch failure to encourage immigration into New Netherland as evidence of Dutch short-sightedness, a failure to envision the profit-making potential of an expanding agricultural colony. But recent research suggests the Dutch West India Company made a conscious, even principled decision to focus primarily on trade rather than on settlement. According to this view, the Dutch sought a colony that remained "alongshore," on the margins of Native American society, rather than one that pressed into the interior.[5] Their rights to inhabit the land would be based on contractual relationships with the native inhabitants rather than on conquest or the grants of a distant monarch. Consistent with these principles, the company initially developed policies to help it build amicable trading relationships and to avoid hostilities with the local Indians. Policy dictated that land should be purchased from the Indians, not taken by force. When Willem Verhulst and his successor Peter Minuit negotiated an alliance and purchased the island from the Manhattan Indians[6] for 60 guilders in 1626, they were following this policy. The Dutch made little or no attempt to Christianize the Indians, seeking as they did to trade rather than subdue. And the Dutch traded with all comers. Before long they were conducting a thriving fur trade at Fort Orange, north of New Amsterdam on the Hudson River, with both the local Mahicans and with the powerful Mohawks from the west.

The Mohawks, for their part, also made a conscious and considered decision to pursue a trading relationship with the Dutch as fully as they could. Ever since the arrival of the French in the St. Lawrence valley, the Mohawks' once powerful position in the diplomatic and trading relationships of their region had eroded. As we have seen, access to trade goods was vital to creating political and social alliances among Native American societies. European trade goods were especially valued because of their rarity and high prestige, which translated into political power. In addition, European goods were valued for their utility. But the Mohawks' main supplier of European trade goods for nearly two decades had been their long-time adversaries, the Hurons, who obtained them from the French. The Mohawks deeply resented their dependence on the Hurons. The arrival of the Dutch offered a unique political opportunity, for the Mohawks could regain their old autonomy and political power by entering an exclusive trading relationship with the Dutch. Accordingly the Mohawks went to war, finally driving the Mahicans out of the Fort Orange region in 1628 in order to keep the Dutch trade for themselves.

The creation of a Dutch–Mohawk trading alliance unleashed a torrent of unintended consequences that would shape European and Native American relations in the region for decades. First, the Dutch supplied the Indians with guns. These were so effective in hunting for beaver that the Mohawks' beaver supply was rapidly depleted. Second, regular trade with the Dutch meant increased exposure to European epidemic diseases, the effects of which caused the population of the Mohawks as well as other Iroquois peoples to decline dramatically by about 1640. In response to these twin disasters, the Iroquois became much more aggressive in making war upon their neighbors. The purpose of these wars was multifaceted. In part the Mohawks wanted to drive competitors out of their hunting grounds so that they could establish themselves as the dominant fur traders in the region, thereby restoring their former claim as the most powerful political entity in the northeastern region. In part, the Mohawks went to war

---

[5] The older view may be found in Thomas Condon, *New York Beginnings: The Commercial Origins of New Netherland* (New York, 1968). An example of the newer approach is Donna Merwick, *The Shame and the Sorrow: Dutch–Amerindian Encounters in New Netherland* (Philadelphia, 2006).

[6] The Manhattan Indians were Algonquian speakers who appear to have had some links to the Mahicans further north.

so as to gain captives who could substitute for lost clan members, the traditional purpose of the mourning war. Both motivations contributed to an increased number of war parties, since every death caused by smallpox could inspire a raid so that the grieving relatives could avenge their loss or acquire a replacement.

If these wars were traditional in their motivation, they soon became anything but traditional in their execution. In a conventional mourning war, cultural taboos limited both the scope of attacks and the casualties they produced, since risking the loss of warriors defeated the purpose of a war whose object was to replenish the population. During the 1640s these taboos dissolved, as Iroquois warriors developed the ability to conduct sustained and large-scale wars against their neighbors and to coordinate their attacks with other members of the Five Nations. Having turned themselves into something of a war-making juggernaut, the Iroquois proceeded to drive the Huron people from their tribal villages in 1648 and 1649 so as to eliminate their competition in the fur trade. The Iroquois then turned on the peoples who had sheltered fleeing Huron refugees, plundering trade goods and furs from every village they destroyed. In a vicious cycle, casualties suffered in these wars in turn created pressure for more wars to avenge the dead. For decades these wars, called the Beaver Wars, produced conflict and instability for any northern tribe that allied itself with the French or the English. The European colonies on the other hand benefitted from the stepped-up warfare, since it had the effect of motivating neighboring Indians to seek alliances with the colonists rather than to turn against them. Constant warfare also forced many of the native peoples to leave their ancestral homelands, opening up large areas of land around the new English and French colonies to potential settlement by Europeans.

Meanwhile, Dutch exports of furs grew slowly but steadily. To obtain the coveted beaver pelts, the Dutch offered not only European manufactured goods but also wampum belts, which originated in Long Island.[7] Dutch traders' ties with the tribes in eastern Long Island who produced this wampum gave them important competitive advantages over French traders to the north.

After a few years, divisions developed between the investors about the future direction of the Dutch company. In 1629, one group within the company pressed the directors to make a decision which they hoped would attract more settlers as well as provide another source of profit for themselves. Any investor bringing over 50 able-bodied persons would be offered a large tract of land with manorial rights, called a patroonship. Each patroon was to receive a four-mile stretch of the Hudson River extending back east or west as far as the land went. As with the previous company-sponsored settlements, the patroons had first to secure title by purchasing the land from the local inhabitants. The company agreed also to relinquish its monopoly on trading rights and to allow patroons to trade along the coast, subject to a five percent duty payable at New Amsterdam.

Although several patents were issued, the patroonship system did not succeed in attracting many colonists. Only Kiliaen Van Rensselaer, one of the investors in the company, made any real attempt to establish a patroonship, securing a large tract of land

---

[7] The commerce in wampum was relatively new, since the iron tools necessary for its mass production had been available only since the arrival of the Dutch.

in the vicinity of Fort Orange and eventually sending out some 200 tenants to cultivate his patrimony. In time, the number of immigrants flowing into the colony increased as smaller grants were made to those who paid their passage and had money to invest. But at least in the short run, the more important consequence of the grant to Van Rensselaer was to begin eroding the company's monopoly on the fur trade. Increasingly, settlers in the colony engaged illegally in private trading, which the company was unable to control. In 1638, the company decided to relinquish its monopoly and open the fur trade to all colonists, while recouping some of its lost revenues by taxing the profits of the new traders. Inevitably, the new competitiveness in the fur trade destabilized the relationship between the Dutch and the Indians.

Another source of strife by the late 1630s was the growth of the settler population in Manhattan and the lower Hudson valley. The indigenous Algonquian-speaking inhabitants resented encroachments by settlers who were now increasingly engaged in farming around New Amsterdam. Attempting to recoup some of the lost trade revenues now going to the company's competitors, Director General Willem Kieft began levying a tax on wampum in 1639. Some of the local Algonquians refused to pay and murdered several colonists. In 1643, Kieft resolved to retaliate, enlisting the Mohawks to assist the Dutch in their assault on the Algonquians. The hostilities began on February 25, 1643 with a bloody massacre, reminiscent of the destruction of the Pequots, when a contingent of Dutch soldiers surrounded the village of Pavonia and set it on fire. All those trying to escape, including women and children, were brutally cut down. The attack was especially shocking to the Algonquians because most of the victims were refugees who had fled the Mohawks to seek asylum with the Dutch. This assault in turn provoked reprisals. Among the victims was Anne Hutchinson, who had by now moved with her family from their exile in Rhode Island to eastern Long Island. Peace was re-established only in 1645, by which time much of the province had been devastated and 1,000 Indians killed.

As noted previously, the government of New Netherland was initially autocratic, reflecting an ownership concentrated in the hands of a few wealthy investors. There was no general assembly of stockholders as in Virginia and Massachusetts through which power could be diffused to the settlers. New Netherland was ruled for much of its history by the director general and a few officials who implemented company policy, dispensed justice, and levied the company's dues. When trouble with the native inhabitants was brewing in 1641, Kieft did order the heads of households to choose 12 men to represent them, though when they demanded a more responsive administration, they were promptly dismissed. Two years later Kieft arranged another meeting, this time summoning eight representatives, who immediately repeated their predecessors' protests against the company's arbitrary taxation. Even more boldly, they wrote home demanding a new director general.

This action led to a partial reorganization of the colony in 1645. Authority in future was to be concentrated in the hands of three officials: a director general, his deputy, and a fiscal. Together they were to make up a council, though they were to continue the concession of allowing "one or two persons to inform the director and council, at least every twelve months, of the state and condition" of their settlements. To help the economic development of the colony, permission was given to private individuals to import Africans, which pleased the larger merchants and landowners since it eased the labor shortage, while another concession granted the right to trade overseas on payment of a customs duty.

These changes were inaugurated by Peter Stuyvesant, who was appointed to be the colony's new director general in July 1646. Stuyvesant duly allowed the election of nine inhabitants to consult about the levying of taxes but soon terminated the experiment. Indeed, within two years the inhabitants were writing to the States-General in Holland complaining about the autocratic manner of the director general, who browbeat everyone "in foul language better fitting the fishmarket than the council board." They charged Stuyvesant with openly breaking the contraband laws by selling arms to the Indians, even when others were hanged for doing so. They also asserted that he had arbitrarily confiscated property for the nonpayment of taxes, ignoring the fact that many people were late in paying because they had suffered heavily in the recent war. New Netherland's bad reputation was affecting trade, the petitioners urged.

Following recommendations made by the States-General in 1650, more concessions were made. Stuyvesant turned New Amsterdam into a municipality in 1652, and established local courts of justice to resolve disputes. Consistent with Dutch practice, these courts were subordinate to the director general and his council. Stuyvesant also summoned representatives from the various settlements when war threatened with England, and created two new classes of burgher in 1657; the purpose was to raise enough money to complete the city's defenses by selling full or half memberships.

Challenges to Stuyvesant's authority were meanwhile emerging from another quarter. During the 1640s a number of New Englanders began settling on Long Island. Accustomed to different types of governing institutions, and in particular to participatory town meetings, the New Englanders soon began to demand a local government. In due course this was granted, but it was hardly what the New Englanders wanted, since the officials were chosen by the director general. The one concession was that the appointees be residents, but this was as far as local participation could go.

Historians disagree as to the import of these changes. In the past, some have argued that Stuyvesant's changes were designed merely to protect Dutch profits from the fur trade, and were essentially unprincipled. These historians assert that the Dutch failed to build effective institutions in New Netherland before 1664. More recently, other scholars have argued that Stuyvesant sought to create a government that conformed to Dutch ideas of efficiency and fairness. The administration of New Netherland in the early years closely resembled the administration of other Dutch trading posts. As the colony gradually developed into a settler colony, however, its governing institutions became more and more like local institutions within the Dutch Republic. Though they differed from English institutions, they were effective. Just as important is that they were generally welcomed by the Dutch settlers in New Netherland.[8]

Another important difference between the government of New Netherland and those of most of the early English colonies was its de facto policy of religious toleration. Jews were permitted to settle here, and from 1657 became burghers, as in Holland.

---

[8] For the older view, see Condon, *New York Beginnings*, as well as Michael Kammen, *Colonial New York: A History* (New York, 1975), chs 1–3. Recent work emphasizes the Dutch origins of New Netherland institutions. See especially Jaap Jacobs, *New Netherland: A Dutch Colony in Seventeenth-Century America* (Leiden, 2005).

Though only a handful did so, their status was testimony to the tolerant nature of the Dutch back home, in contrast to other European nations.[9] The arrival of the Quakers, however, prompted the director general to issue an edict in 1656 banning all Christian services which were not held according to the Calvinist Synod of Dort. Given the heterogeneous nature of the population, the edict proved unworkable, and it was relaxed in 1663.

The policy of religious toleration was largely responsible for turning New Netherland into what, for its time, was the most ethnically and religiously pluralistic colony on the continent. With low rates of unemployment at home, relatively small numbers of Dutch people wished to immigrate to the colony. But New Netherland attracted Germans from Westphalia, Huguenots from France, and Puritans from New England, in addition to Belgians, Scandinavians, and Dutch. A French Jesuit who visited New Amsterdam in 1643 commented on the town's "confusion of tongues," although historians have also found that most immigrants became assimilated to Dutch customs and learned the Dutch language once they arrived.

Dutch success in New Netherland coincided with growing Dutch dominance in the Atlantic slave trade, and this too would have an impact on the colony's ethnic and racial makeup. By the 1630s as many as 10 percent of the people being brought to the colony were enslaved Africans. Slavery in New Netherland resembled slavery in early Virginia in the sense that both systems were relatively fluid. Elderly slaves who belonged to the Dutch West Indian Company were eligible for a status called "half-freedom," which manumitted them late in life (but did not enable them to pass on their status to their children). Nevertheless, many enslaved Africans in New Netherland had enough experience with Europeans to be able to find ways to expand their rights and become incorporated into Dutch society. Slaves successfully petitioned the company to be allowed to work for wages with the object of purchasing their freedom. They learned Dutch, adopted Dutch surnames, had their marriages blessed and infants baptized in the Dutch Reformed Church, brought successful lawsuits in the courts, and participated in the militia. By 1664, one in five Africans was free, and some freed people had been able to acquire land and create independent communities. Making up perhaps 20 percent of the total population of New Amsterdam, Africans were a highly visible part of its ethnic patchwork. Even so, there is evidence that the economic position of Africans in New Netherland began to erode as the Dutch increased their commitment to slavery. By 1660 two out of every five households in New York City had an African slave, and manumission was becoming less common.

By 1660, the colony's total population had grown to perhaps 7,000. The fur trade brought in a steady income, and the colony was more than self-sufficient. In the late 1650s, however, a scarcity of beaver depressed the value of wampum, so that Stuyvesant had to issue a proclamation to stabilize prices and prevent profiteering. Also, further disputes with local Algonquian peoples began when an Indian woman was killed as she took fruit from an orchard; before hostilities ended a considerable number of both Dutch and Algonquian people had been killed.

---

[9] For the rise of the Jewish community in the Americas, see Jacob R. Marcus, *The Colonial American Jew, 1492–1776*, 3 vols (Detroit, 1970). The number of Jews throughout the colonial period was small.

Meanwhile, competitive pressure for the fur trade was increasing because of the creation of a new settlement west and south of New Netherland. Dutch claims to the Delaware or South River were challenged by Sweden beginning in 1636, when King Augustus Adolphus chartered a general trading company and secured a new charter specifically for the Delaware region. Ironically the first group of Swedes was taken there late in 1637 by the former director general of New Netherland, Peter Minuit, who established Fort Christina near present-day Wilmington.

New Sweden was always a struggling entity. Sweden was remote, and the company rarely sent supplies to the colonists. Without trade goods from Europe, the New Swedish settlers could not take part in the fur trade in a conventional sense. Yet because the Delaware Valley was centrally located at the convergence of various Indian and European trade networks, the Swedes were able to serve as brokers in arranging trade between various European and Indian groups. They bought trade goods, mostly from English merchants in New England, exchanged them for furs, and then resold the furs in New Amsterdam, New England, or Virginia. A steady supply of furs came from their main Indian trading partners, the powerful Susquehannocks, who themselves ranged far inland to arrange purchases from other Indians. To safeguard their favored trading relationship, the Swedes armed the Susquehannocks with guns, just as the Dutch occasionally did with the Mohawk. The Swedes also traded with the local Lenape Indians (later renamed the Delaware), who supplied them with food.[10]

The venture on the Delaware always posed a threat to the Dutch West India Company's aspirations to control the Indian trade in the region. From the time he had first heard the news of Minuit's settlement, Director General Kieft had warned that New Netherland would preserve its sovereignty. And when the English began the first of its trade wars against the Dutch in 1652, the Dutch became fearful of a Swedish–English alliance. So in 1655 the Dutch captured Fort Casimir, ending Swedish control in the region. Under the terms negotiated between Stuyvesant and the Swedish director, all the inhabitants were allowed to depart with their possessions. Those who stayed were to swear loyalty to the Dutch States-General. Stuyvesant then appointed a deputy director general to govern the area as a province of New Netherland.

Even more threatening to the Dutch than Swedish encroachments was the spread of the English settlements on Long Island and along the coast. During the 1643 hostilities with the Indians the Dutch and English had cooperated, but once that danger receded the tension between them returned. The Dutch still occupied Fort Hope on the Connecticut River but were becoming increasingly isolated by the presence of English colonists in that area.

The Dutch recognized that they could not treat the English as they would treat the tiny colony of New Sweden. Consequently, Stuyvesant decided to negotiate, and in September 1650 he met with representatives of the New England confederacy and

---

[10] Scholarly considerations of New Swedish roles in the fur trade include Karen Ordahl Kupperman, "Scandinavian Colonists Confront the New World," and Lorraine E. Williams, "Indians and Europeans in the Delaware Valley, 1620–1655," both in Carol Hoffecker, Richard Waldron, et al., eds, *New Sweden in America* (Newark, 1995), 89–111 and 112–120, respectively.

agreed to a boundary line dividing Long Island in the vicinity of Oyster Bay. Two sources of potential conflict remained, however: the Dutch were to keep their post at Hartford, and the English settlements of Flushing and Hempstead remained on the Dutch side of the border. Although this treaty was not recognized by Oliver Cromwell, the effective leader of the English Commonwealth after the execution of Charles I, Massachusetts insisted on honoring it when war broke out between England and Holland in 1654, being reluctant to fight a Protestant neighbor merely for the sake of England's commerce. Connecticut, however, took a different view and unilaterally seized Fort Hope. With the remaining English settlements in New Netherland still expressing discontent, it was clear that further conflict was yet to come.

3 MARYLAND: A CATHOLIC PROPRIETARY

Unlike the French and the Dutch, whose seventeenth-century North American colonies were initially organized around the fur trade, new English colonies on the mainland continued to be planned as agricultural settlements, like their predecessors in Virginia and New England. Unlike those predecessors, though, the next English colony, Maryland, was intended as a haven for English members of the Roman Catholic Church who were being persecuted because of their religion.

The Catholics had of course opposed England's break with Rome and the changes to the liturgy in the Book of Common Prayer, and insisted that the pope, not the monarch, be head of the church. For these views they were bitterly persecuted by the English government and reviled by England's Protestant majority. Their position worsened following the excommunication of Elizabeth I in 1570, which seemingly condoned the subsequent attempt by Guy Fawkes to kill James I on the opening of Parliament in November 1605 in what came to be known as the Gunpowder Plot. In addition English paranoia against Catholicism had increased with the war against Spain, in which the most Catholic state in Europe had seemingly committed its vast wealth to a crusade against the Protestant nations. A series of progressively harsher penal laws against Catholics was therefore introduced in England from 1571. Graduated fines were imposed for anyone attending mass and severe punishment was inflicted on priests who were caught officiating, while generous rewards were offered to informers.

Despite these difficulties many Catholics persisted in their faith, including some members of the aristocracy who sought to balance their attachment to Rome with loyalty to the Crown. Although they refused to take the oath of supremacy acknowledging the monarch as head of the church, they denounced regicide. Fortunately, the accession of Charles I in 1625 promised a more relaxed regime, for his queen, Henrietta Maria, was a Catholic herself.

It was inevitable in an age of colonization that the idea of Catholic emigration would surface. The Catholics, like the Puritans, felt an obligation to protect their religion and believed that ultimately the true faith would be restored. In their view Protestantism was merely an aberration in the Catholic Church's 1,600-year history. North America, in the meantime, might provide a refuge.

Among those interested in such a scheme was George Calvert, the first Lord Baltimore. For most of his life Baltimore had not been a Catholic. Indeed, for two decades he was a prominent courtier, holding the position of secretary of state. His conversion in 1625 was, however, not unexpected, for both his parents were Catholics, while his son had recently married into a recusant (i.e., Roman Catholic) family.

Calvert's interest in the New World was first stimulated by one of his Protestant relatives, the earl of Warwick, who persuaded him to invest in the Virginia Company. Later Calvert joined Warwick on the reconstituted Council for New England and started a small settlement of his own in Newfoundland to exploit the fishery, undisturbed by the French fishermen who lived nearby. Unfortunately, when he visited the site at Avalon in 1627 he found the winters too harsh and the soil too barren for any hope of a successful farming colony.

Like most other sponsors of colonial ventures, Calvert was motivated mainly by profit; and even after his conversion his actions were not entirely altruistic. Like his colleagues on the Council for New England, he hoped to increase his fortune by settling a plantation in America. But Baltimore's aspirations were shaped as well by his social class. As befitted a member of the nobility, his ambition was also to increase his estates, for more land would bring not only more income but also greater power and honor. So while the merchants saw Virginia in terms of expanding their trade, Baltimore and the nobility saw the New World primarily as a way of enlarging their estates.

After his experiences in Newfoundland, Baltimore went in search of somewhere warmer, setting sail in the summer of 1629 to explore Virginia. Once the Virginians knew he was a Catholic, however, they refused him entry and sought to prevent him obtaining a patent at all. Baltimore persevered, and only his death prevented him from seeing a charter issued on June 20, 1632, for a grant of territory in the upper Chesapeake, to be called Maryland in honor of the queen.

Baltimore had sought a patent different from those issued to Virginia and Massachusetts; his primary aim was the advancement of his family rather than of a group of shareholders, whom he believed had ruined the Virginia Company. Earlier he had discovered an old patent issued in the fourteenth century to the Bishop of Durham, giving that prelate extensive powers on the frontier between England and Scotland in the form of a palatinate. Baltimore persuaded Charles I to issue him a grant using this palatinate model of princely authority. His charter, customarily called a proprietary charter, was an essentially feudal grant of property and governing authority. Baltimore and his heirs were to be "absolute Lords and Proprietors," with the right to all minerals, except for the usual 20 percent of any precious metals reserved for the Crown. He could create his own titles and grant lands with manorial rights. This provision may have appealed to Baltimore as a way to induce members of the aristocracy and gentry to purchase land, thus eliminating the need for shareholders. Baltimore could also incorporate towns, license all trade, raise revenues, and license churches "according to the Ecclesiastical Laws" of the kingdom. Most remarkably, he was to be excused all duties to the Crown, delivering only a symbolic two arrows every year in acknowledgment of his fealty.

In addition, the charter gave Baltimore "full, and absolute Power ... to ordain, Make, and Enact Laws" subject to "the Advice, Assent, and Approbation of the Free Men of the same Province ... or of their Delegates or Deputies." The reason Baltimore gave the freemen the power to veto his legislation is uncertain, though most likely he recognized that some such concession was necessary if he was to compete with Virginia for settlers. In any case an exemption clause was included which allowed the proprietor to make laws unilaterally in an emergency, including martial law. The only restriction was that both kinds of law were to be "agreeable to the Laws, Statutes, Customs and Rights" of England. Those emigrating were otherwise entitled to the same "Privileges, Franchises and Liberties" as at home. It was a remarkable grant, conferring authoritarian powers that were already anomalous in England and were likely to prove so in America as well.

A final difference between this new patent and the charters granted to earlier investors was that it mentioned the native inhabitants only as savages who might have to be repelled. There would be no pretense here that the English were coming to North America to convert the Indians to Christianity.

Despite its intended purpose as a refuge for Catholics, the colony would be shaped from the beginning by tensions between the proprietor's plan for a Catholic haven and the fact that it was mostly Protestants who wished to emigrate to North America. An initial expedition to the colony was delayed, largely because wealthy Protestant gentry were not attracted by the prospect of investing in a colony with a Catholic proprietor. Meanwhile most Catholics had given up the idea of emigrating now that persecution had subsided. Nevertheless, some 25 gentlemen, mostly Catholics, did depart and contribute to the cost. The rest of the passengers were servants, artisans, or yeoman farmers, many of whom were Protestants. Baltimore's heir, Lord Cecilius, emphasized that all Christian denominations would be welcome. He realized there were unlikely to be enough Catholics to make the scheme a success, and seems genuinely to have believed that coexistence was the best policy to ensure that his coreligionists would not remain an isolated and distrusted minority.

Cecilius's two ships finally left Portsmouth in November 1633, reaching the upper Chesapeake by way of the West Indies in March 1634. The first mass was celebrated on the Potomac near Blakiston. The local inhabitants were mostly Piscataways and Yacomicos, small groups of Algonquian speakers who were threatened by the much larger Iroquoian-speaking Susquehannocks to the north. Apparently eager for a trading relationship and an alliance with the English to protect them against the Susquehannocks, the Indians agreed to trade with Calvert and sold him a site which had already previously been cleared for farming. A fort was built at St. Mary's with several cannon mounted on top, followed by a storehouse and chapel. With the ability to plant on land that the Indians had already cleared, the Englishmen quickly produced a crop of corn.

Baltimore himself was not one of the passengers. Instead it was his younger brother, Leonard Calvert, who began the task of organizing the colony according to the charter. The first Catholic gentry to arrive with their servants were given manors, with grants of 2,000 acres for every five servants they brought with them. Those who arrived thereafter would receive a grant of 1,000 acres for the same number of retainers, while anyone bringing over a male servant would receive 100 acres, or 50 acres for a maid. In return there was to be a sliding scale of rents, though all grants of over 1,000 acres would qualify for manorial status, each with its own court in which the owner dispensed justice for petty misdemeanors, collected fees, and enjoyed other administrative privileges. Initially some 25 manors were patented with plans for a total of 60, ranging in size from 1,000 to 6,000 acres.

Baltimore experienced challenges to his authority from the beginning. In May 1631 one of the Virginians, William Claiborne, had obtained a commission from the Crown to develop Kent Island as an independent trading post, which he had used to establish a trading relationship with the Susquehannocks. Apart from wishing to preserve control himself, Claiborne did not want to be the tenant of a Catholic landlord. The main conflict concerned Claiborne's right to trade, which according to Baltimore's charter had to be licensed from him. Shots were fired several times between vessels representing the rival elements. Fortunately for Baltimore, Claiborne was then disowned by his merchant associates in England; and the dispute ended in 1635 with Baltimore's men taking possession of the island by force.

Apparently hoping to gain greater support for his government, Baltimore ordered the issuance of a summons for a representative assembly on January 25, 1638. Leonard Calvert had called all the freemen together once before, but Baltimore nullified their acts, insisting that only he had the right of proposing laws. This time the assembly was determined to assert its authority to make laws for the colony. Its members passed an act prescribing an oath of loyalty to Charles I promising to defend him "against all conspiracies," a gesture necessary to reassure the authorities that Maryland was not going to be a haven for Catholic regicides like Guy Fawkes. It defined the future nature of the legislature, which was to comprise the governor, council, lords of the manor, and one or two freemen elected from every hundred.[11] And it passed a third act requiring an assembly to be summoned at least once every three years, with "the like power, privileges, authority, and jurisdiction ... as in the House of Commons." Clearly the assembly was seeking to acquire the characteristics of a parliament.

Because the assembly had no legal right to initiate this legislation, Baltimore nullified these acts as he had previously, declaring that the charter had given the assembly no right to initiate legislation. The following year, however, he permitted Leonard to be more flexible. As a result most of the laws were passed, though still not in the language demanded by the proprietor, being full of expressions about the rights of Parliament and the individual reminiscent of Magna Carta and other such precedents.

By 1640 Maryland contained perhaps 500 inhabitants in three main clusters: St. Mary's, St. Clements, and St. George's, all organized as hundreds on the English model. They in turn contained 16 manors, occupying over 80 percent of the patented land. Even at this stage, however, Baltimore's hopes for a European-style aristocracy were fading; only a handful of the original gentry remained, though several others had arrived to take their place.

Economically, though, the colony had established itself quickly, mainly because the requirements of settlement in the Chesapeake were now well known. The settlers sought (at least initially) to avoid conflict with the local inhabitants by paying for their land and supplies. The settlers learned from the Indians how to cultivate and use local

---

[11] A "hundred" was an administrative district within an English shire. The word originated during the medieval period, when each hundred contained approximately 100 families.

Figure 13   First Maryland State House, 1634–1694 (reconstructed). St. Mary's City. Photo by Acroterion.

plants and how to employ the slash and burn method to clear the land. They initially concentrated on making themselves self-sufficient in food by raising corn, cattle, hogs, and other livestock which flourished in the region. Corn was fenced rather than the livestock, in contrast to European practice. Cattle and hogs were left to fend for themselves because it was more profitable to use cleared land for crops. Only cows in milk were temporarily fenced. There were risks to this method of husbandry from wolves and other hazards, but the savings in labor more than offset the dangers. During the early years most farmers also planted an orchard for cider. Once these initial tasks were completed, farmers typically devoted their attention to tobacco-growing. Although tobacco prices were only a fraction of what they had been 10 years earlier, the market now was much wider. Consequently the settlers could sell all that they grew.

The 1640s were tumultuous years in England. The ascendancy of Parliament, with its anti-Catholic majority after 1640, was fraught with danger for the new settlement. Furthermore, the outbreak of hostilities in England meant that Baltimore was cut off from his province, a situation which worsened in 1642 when Leonard Calvert came to England to consult with his brother, leaving a political vacuum in America. Soon Claiborne reappeared to seize Kent Island. Meanwhile a London tobacco trader named Richard Ingle, masquerading as the protector of Protestantism, succeeded in capturing St. Mary's. Thus when Leonard returned to Maryland in the autumn of 1644 he was compelled to flee to Virginia. For two years Maryland, without any government, endured "the plundering time," which continued until Leonard returned with aid from

Governor Berkeley of Virginia. Ingle hurried off to England to accuse Baltimore and Leonard of harboring treasonous recusants but did not prove his case, and Baltimore managed to keep his charter. Parliament still had many aristocrats anxious to show that proprietary rights were not incompatible with the parliamentary cause.

The execution of Charles I in England in 1649 provoked a virtual civil war in Maryland, as neighbor turned against neighbor in a climate of suspicion and fear. To calm the situation Baltimore appointed a Protestant, William Stone, as governor, and presented the Maryland assembly with a bill for religious toleration. Baltimore's hope for such a bill was to pacify the authorities in England and induce a predominantly Protestant assembly to acknowledge his proprietary authority. Another reason was that the Catholics themselves now needed protection. The Protestant population had greatly increased with the arrival in 1643 of Richard Bennett and some 400 Puritans from Virginia, following the expulsion of their ministers by Governor Berkeley and the Anglican Church. Indeed, the Act Concerning Religion can be seen as the first attempt to protect a minority group, an unusual phenomenon in the seventeenth century, when the reverse was usually the motivation behind religious legislation.

Baltimore was undoubtedly sincere in wanting to calm the religious passions in Maryland. He may have been inspired by the new climate in England itself, where the belief was growing that Christian unity was unobtainable and that toleration was the only course. Certainly Cecilius's own measure was influenced by such reasoning. The act did not positively affirm toleration, but it made intolerance a crime, at least among Christians. Non-Christians, of course, were not included.

Unfortunately, the measure served to exacerbate the tension, since the Puritan newcomers were virulently anti-Catholic and interested in toleration only for themselves. They were soon aided by events in England, where in 1650 Parliament decided to dispatch a commission to seize several of the colonies on behalf of the Commonwealth. Baltimore's old enemy Claiborne was on the commission, as was the Puritans' leader Bennett. In 1651 these two seized effective control over Maryland's government.

The conflict continued for another six years with bloodshed on both sides. Baltimore's proprietary faction, which had a solid following in the lower counties of St. Mary's and St. George's, was pitted against the Puritan faction, which controlled Anne Arundel and Kent counties. The Puritans wanted a commonwealth like Massachusetts from which Catholics and even Anglicans were barred. When Governor Stone's advance towards the Severn River in March 1655 resulted in a complete victory for the Puritans, four of the invading proprietary party were executed, while many of the rest had to pay heavy fines or flee for their lives. Ultimately, however, the outcome of the conflict was decided in London. Here Baltimore's contacts and diplomatic skills gave him an advantage. Oliver Cromwell now ruled England as lord protector, and he had little sympathy for the extreme demands of the Maryland Puritans. In consequence the two parties had to compromise. At the end of 1657 Baltimore was reinstated as proprietor, in return for which he pardoned his opponents, who then accepted the Act Concerning Religion. For the time being, the colony's Catholic proprietor and its mostly Protestant inhabitants had achieved a truce.

DOCUMENT 10

An Act Concerning Religion, reprinted in W. Keith Kavenagh, *Foundations of Colonial America: A Documentary History* (New York, 1973), Vol. 2, 1322–4

This unique act anticipated George Mason's Virginia Bill of Rights by 130 years in its provisions for religious toleration. Unlike Mason and the later federal Bill of Rights, Baltimore's act extended only to Christians, excluding adherents of other religious faiths. Questions to consider: *What is the purpose of this act? What kinds of behavior or speech are prohibited in section 2? How are these prohibitions similar or different from modern prohibitions of "hate speech"?*

Be it therefore ordered and enacted that ...

(2) whatsoever person or persons shall, from henceforth upon any occasion of offense or otherwise, in reproachful manner or way declare, call or denominate any person or persons whatsoever inhabiting, residing, trading, or commercing within this province an Heretic, Schismatic, Idolator, Puritan, Independent, Presbyterian, Popish Priest, Jesuit, Jesuited Papist, Lutheran, Calvinist, Anabaptist, Brownist, Antinomian, Barrowist, Roundhead, Separatist, or any other name or term in a reproachful manner relating to matters of religion, shall, for every such offense forfeit and lose the sum of ten shillings sterling [half to the victim, the other half to the Proprietor].

(4) And whereas the enforcing of conscience in matters of religion has frequently [proved] of dangerous consequence in those commonwealths where it has been practised; and for the more quiet and peacable government of this province and the better to preserve mutual love and amity amongst the inhabitants thereof. Be it therefore also by the Lord Proprietary, with the advice and consent of this Assembly, ordained and enacted ... that no person or persons whatsoever within this province ... professing to believe in Jesus Christ, shall, from henceforth, be any ways troubled, molested, or discountenanced for or in respect of his or her religion, nor in the free exercise thereof within this province or the islands thereunto belonging, nor any way compelled to the belief or exercise of any other religion against his or her consent ... [Offenders to pay treble damages to the wronged party or suffer a severe whipping and imprisonment at the discretion of the Proprietor.]

During the mid-1640s Maryland's population had fallen to under 400. Thereafter it grew, as immigrants attracted by Baltimore's liberal land policy flowed in from Virginia as well as from England. In 1640 the legislature provided that on completion of their service, all male servants were to receive three barrels of corn, a new outfit of clothes, some tools, and 50 acres of land. This headright was later confirmed by Baltimore in 1648. Land remained more readily available here than in Virginia, but Maryland society was to develop along similar lines.

Maryland was no paradise for servants. Both males and females were expected to work long hours in the field, on the farm, or in the household, being constantly at the call of their masters and mistresses, whose main aim was the extraction of productive labor. Those who ran away could expect to do extra time, as could women servants who became pregnant. Despite various laws, beatings were common, diet was rarely sufficient, clothing and housing were frequently inadequate, and medical attention was negligible. A wasting sickness like malaria was often mistaken for laziness; and because sickness meant that someone else had to do that person's job, bullying by fellow servants, overseers, and masters was common. Not surprisingly, 40 percent did not survive their four- to five-year indentures. Those who did, who wished to become planters, still had to pay the surveyor's fees and register their land, as well as buy essential items to get their farms established. Such an outlay being initially beyond the means of most servants, the usual options were to continue as laborers or to lease some land, possibly on a sharecropping basis. But wages were high, as the price of tobacco rose during the 1650s, so many servants, perhaps as many as half of those attaining their freedom, did acquire their own farms in time, though some took as long as 12 years to become freeholders. In one respect the 1650s was a golden period for servants, there being no elite other than the proprietor and a few gentry. Never again were social classes to be so fluid.[12]

Like Virginia, Maryland had an overwhelmingly male social structure, the ratio in the earliest years being perhaps six males to every female. Male servants were preferred, since they were generally physically more capable of performing the exhausting tasks of clearing the land, working the soil, and erecting houses and barns. The social consequences of this imbalance between the sexes were enormous. For men it meant a late marriage and little family life. As late as the 1680s, perhaps 30 percent of men never married. Immigrant women, too, married relatively late, after serving their indentures, although they generally had a choice of suitors. Remarriage was also much easier if a partner died. Some women, blessed with exceptional health, married three or four times. Still, the relatively low marriage rate combined with the late age of marriage contributed to low fertility rates, and Maryland's population was able to grow only by means of constant immigration.

Another factor inhibiting family life was the high mortality rate among both men and women. Only one-third of marriages lasted more than 10 years. As a consequence, 20 percent of all children were orphaned by age 12, and most experienced the death of one parent before their majority. This led to the establishment of special orphan courts, something quite unknown in England. Thus stable family life was virtually impossible, and few enjoyed the kinship patterns which prevailed in New England. One compensation was that children came into their inheritances early and could marry without parental constraint. Women, too, benefited, as their scarcity allowed them to insist on

---

[12]   The traditional view was to see America as a land of opportunity for all emigrants. This view was especially popular in the nineteenth century when the examples of Andrew Carnegie and others were regularly cited. More recently the tendency has been to emphasize that only the lucky few made such progress, even in the earliest years when the social and economic structures were fluid. See Lois Green Carr and Russell R. Menard, "Immigration and Opportunity: The Freedman in Early Colonial Maryland," in Thad W. Tate and David L. Ammerman, eds, *The Chesapeake in the Seventeenth Century: Essays on Anglo-American Society* (Chapel Hill, 1979), 206–42.

better marriages.[13] Of course families of a kind did exist. Surviving parents usually remarried, creating a new type of family, comprising half-brothers and half-sisters, stepfathers and stepchildren. Although such unions created problems of inheritance and emotional adjustment, they often fostered a sense of community, love, and affection.

Much as the settlers moving into Maryland had dashed Baltimore's hopes for a Catholic colony, so too did they thwart his plans to create a stable society of manor lords and tenants. Once they could save enough money, freed servants left the manors to buy their own land. Only one manor, St. Clements, owned by Thomas Gerard, was still functioning in 1660, with 16 tenants and nine freeholders. Before long, the powers which had been given to manor lords were instead transferred to county courts and local parishes on the English model, although one or two manors continued to function.

Indeed Maryland was increasingly adopting the appearance of its neighbor to the south in many other respects, having the same pyramidal social structure of newly rich gentry planters (who dominated the assembly and ran the county courts), along with yeoman farmers, dependent tenants, and indentured servants. As in Virginia, the attraction for immigrants was the possibility of one day owning one's own land, a virtually unimaginable prospect for poor men who stayed in England.

As in Virginia, the presence of Indians within the English settler community was rare, for though the government maintained amicable relationships with their native neighbors, Indian towns were located well outside the boundaries of the English settlements. Another similarity between Virginia and Maryland was the presence of a small number of Africans – around 100, mostly coming from Virginia. As in Virginia, their status was unclear until after 1660. Thus, whatever the initial differences, the two Chesapeake societies were rapidly converging in their economic and social, if not their political, structures.

4   ENGLISH COLONIES IN THE WEST INDIES

While Maryland was struggling to establish itself on a stable footing, English investors had already begun to achieve considerable success with another series of colonial ventures in the Atlantic, this time not in mainland North America but in the West Indies (also called the Caribbean). The earliest English colonies here had been a series of semipermanent privateering bases established between 1604 and 1619, strategically

---

[13]   Until 40 years ago the structure of the population in the Chesapeake was totally overlooked because historians limited their investigations to evidence from the small, literate part of the population. Since the late 1960s, the availability of computers and new statistical methods have allowed early colonial society to be reconstituted using hitherto ignored parish registers, tax lists, wills, conveyances, and account books. See Russell R. Menard, "Immigrants and Their Increase: The Process of Population Growth in Early Colonial Maryland," in Aubrey C. Land, Lois Green Carr, and Edward C. Papenfuse, eds, *Law, Society, and Politics in Early Maryland* (Baltimore, 1977); Lorena S. Walsh, "'Till Death Us Do Part': Marriage and Family in Seventeenth-Century Maryland," in Thad W. Tate and David L. Ammerman, eds, *The Chesapeake in the Seventeenth Century: Essays on Anglo-American Society* (Chapel Hill, 1979); Gloria L. Main, *Tobacco Colony: Life in Early Maryland, 1650–1720* (Princeton, 1982); and Russell R. Menard, *Economy and Society in Early Maryland* (New York, 1985). Similar problems were experienced in Virginia: see Chapter 7, section 1.

located in Guiana and the islands of the Lesser Antilles where they were close enough to shipping routes for occasional raids on Spanish treasure ships. These were unstable, violent places, subject to attacks by Spanish, Portuguese, and sometimes Dutch vessels, and riven by conflicts with local Indians. By 1624, though, it was becoming clear to English investors that agricultural colonies held greater long-term promise for producing returns on colonial ventures than did bases for privateers. In that year a small group of English colonists brought by the English promoter Sir Thomas Warner to the thinly populated island of St. Christopher (later called St. Kitts) managed to create a permanent colony. It would soon be followed by colonies in Barbados (1627), Nevis (1628), Antigua (1632), and Montserrat (1632).

The most successful of these West Indian colonies before 1660 was Barbados, located far enough away from the Spanish to make it relatively safe from attack. Here, the local Carib Indian population had mostly died out by the time the colony was founded in 1627, simplifying the promoters' efforts to establish an agricultural settlement. Investors in the Barbados venture offered settlers grants of land in exchange for quitrents, which the settlers cleared and farmed using indentured laborers, mostly from England, Scotland, and Ireland. During the colony's earliest years, producing tobacco was profitable enough to attract thousands of young, single, mostly male servants who hoped to earn enough to buy small plots of land and become yeoman farmers once they had finished their terms of service. The lure of becoming a tobacco planter in the English West Indies was great. Once they arrived, however, young men soon learned that the reality of life in Barbados was not what they had expected. Survival rates were even lower here than on the mainland, and the settler population grew only because of the constant inflow of new immigrants. Nevertheless, immigration continued. More young English settlers went to the Caribbean islands during the seventeenth century than all of the English settlers to the North American mainland combined.[14]

English planters in Barbados, like settlers in all of the other English agricultural colonies, seem to have regarded the right to an assembly as a key privilege of property ownership, and engaged in the same kinds of struggles to control political authority in Barbados as did landowners in the other English American colonies. From 1629 onward the colony was organized, like Maryland, as a proprietary colony. The Crown granted land and governing authority to a favored courtier, the earl of Carlisle, who then appointed a governor to administer the colony and collect quitrents from the settlers. In 1639 the planters insisted that the governor convene an assembly to represent them. And just as in other English colonies, the assembly won the right to control local taxes and allocate revenues, while the governor and his council retained the power to veto their decisions.

During the 1640s the introduction of a new cash crop began to transform the lives and economic fortunes of Barbadian planters. A fall in the price of tobacco had made its

---

[14] It is estimated that 378,000 emigrants went from the British Isles to America before 1700, of which 223,000 went to the Caribbean. Henry A. Gemery, "Emigration from the British Isles to the New World," *Research in Economic History*, 5 (1980), 179–231, and "Markets for Migrants: English Indentured Servitude and Emigration in the Seventeenth and Eighteenth Centuries," in P. C. Emmer, ed., *Colonialism and Migration: Indentured Labour Before and After Slavery* (Dordrecht, 1986).

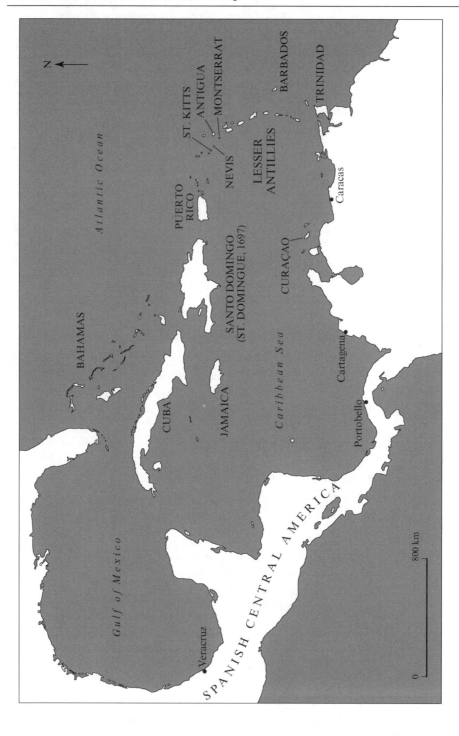

Map 6   The English West Indies, 1660.

production considerably less profitable in the late 1630s. Barbadian planters began to experiment with cotton, without much success, until Dutch merchants visiting the island provided technological assistance as well as loans for the planters to begin shifting their land to sugar cane production.[15] Continental Europeans had become regular consumers of sugar, but a disruption in the supply of Brazilian sugar caused by political instability allowed Dutch merchants to sell as much sugar as the Barbados planters were able to produce. Meanwhile English consumers seemed eager to try the sweet crystals and use them for baking, brewing, and making confections. The growing demand for sugar generated a sugar planting frenzy on the island in the mid-1640s. Yet the profits of sugar were not equally shared. In order to be profitable, sugar production required fairly large plantations as well as capital investments in refining equipment and labor. Absentee investors and more prosperous planters who could afford the investment reaped huge rewards from sugar production. Meanwhile, the price of land on the island boomed, and indentured servants found themselves unable to purchase land once they had been freed from their terms of service.

Planters needed a large supply of labor to produce the profits that sugar cultivation promised. As Barbados became a less attractive destination for servants, planters found the supply of voluntary settlers drying up, and instead looked for sources of coerced labor to meet their demands. Thousands of transported convicts as well as prisoners taken during various rebellions were shipped to Barbados during the early years of the English Civil War. But when critics at home began to express misgivings about selling white Englishmen into servitude, planters again sought new sources of coerced labor. Once again, Dutch merchants provided a solution that served both their interests and those of the planters.

By the 1640s Dutch traders were competing with great success against Portuguese traders in carrying slaves from Africa to Brazil. In 1646, during a period of political instability in Brazil, Dutch traders began offering their slave cargos to Barbadian planters on credit and at low prices. English planters turned eagerly to African slaves, whose foreignness made them easier to exploit than poor Englishmen. By 1655, there were more than 20,000 enslaved Africans on the island, along with about 23,000 white settlers.

The growth of sugar production transformed the economy and society of Barbados. Over time the planter class grew smaller and wealthier, buying up the best land. Poor planters were largely squeezed out. In time, the flow of poor white servants into Barbados shrank to a trickle. Meanwhile, African slaves were imported so rapidly that the tiny island soon became the most heavily populated English colony in the Americas – as well as the first majority black society in the English empire. By 1673, the colony's population stood at 33,000 enslaved Africans and 21,000 whites. Instead of a society in which slavery was just one form of labor, Barbados had developed into a "slave society," in which slavery was the main source of labor.

By the mid-1650s, the promise of colonies in the West Indies had become clear. Barbados was now the most profitable of England's colonies, with an output rivalling

---

[15] Historians have traditionally thought Dutch merchants supplied the capital for developing sugar plantations. For the argument that most capital in fact came from English sources, see Larry Gragg, *Englishmen Transplanted: The English Colonization of Barbados, 1627–1660* (Oxford, 2003).

that of Brazil, the world's largest sugar producer at the time. More sugar colonies would follow. During a naval campaign against the Spanish in 1655, the English navy seized control of the much larger West Indian island of Jamaica and opened the island to English investment. Although investments were initially diversified (including cattle ranching and piracy), the promise of sugar loomed in the island's future. By the eighteenth century Jamaica had overtaken Barbados to become England's pre-eminent sugar producer. Together, the two colonies were extraordinarily profitable.

The slave system being developed by English planters in Barbados (and simultaneously by French planters in the West Indian islands of Martinique and Guadeloupe) was as cruel and exploitative as any system of labor the world had yet seen. The potential of sugar production to produce enormous profits created incentives for planters to demand maximum labor from their workers, with little concern for their health or safety. Techniques to force slaves to work more rapidly and for longer hours had been initiated in Brazil, which had a mixed labor force of slaves, Indians, and salaried white workers. These techniques were now refined in the Caribbean, where planters relied mostly on imported African slave laborers towards whom they had little sense of moral obligation.[16] Slaves in the West Indies were worked in gangs, clearing, tilling, planting, hoeing, and harvesting the cane. Once the cane was harvested, it had to be processed in sugar mills that operated 24 hours a day during the six- to seven-month harvest season. Inside the mills workers faced the constant danger of losing hands or arms in the rolling machinery, or being burned by boiling liquid sugar. Slaves were kept at work for shifts as long as 18 hours a day. Because the profits to be made from sugar were so great, planters devoted few resources to food production, and slaves were chronically malnourished. Enslaved women were not allowed enough time to nurse their infants. Slaves who resisted their owners' demands were brutally punished with floggings and various other forms of physical degradation, including rape.

As Barbadian planters became increasingly dependent on African slaves, they began to pass laws to secure their rights to slave property, as well as to control the Africans who were coming to outnumber them. In 1661 the Barbados Assembly passed its first slave code, offering extensive legal protections to the owners of slaves. Among other provisions, they obtained a guarantee that a planter or overseer who mutilated or killed his slave in the course of punishment was exempt from legal sanction for his actions. Over time the local government developed other mechanisms for controlling the enslaved population, including the deployment of militias to police slaves' activities, a system requiring passes for slaves to leave their home plantations, the use of capital punishment in case of rebellion, and new legal rules which had the effect of turning slaves into commodities, with virtually no legal rights. Barbados was quickly developing a social system quite different from those of early Virginia or New Netherland. Its legal rules would effectively prevent enslaved Africans from becoming integrated into the European community by asserting their rights through the courts, being baptized, or earning their freedom. They would be slaves for life, subjected to greater exploitation,

---

[16] For the comparison between Brazilian and English and French West Indian plantation regimes, see Robin Blackburn, *The Making of New World Slavery: From the Baroque to the Modern, 1492–1800* (London, 1997), ch. 8.

harsher discipline, and more vicious degradation than workers in any of the English, Dutch, or French colonies in North America thus far.

Not surprisingly, living under these conditions without any institutions to protect them, African slaves in Barbados died at a horrific rate. Malnourished, they fell victim to diseases. Birth rates remained chronically low, for although African women survived at a high enough rate to create an even sex ratio by the end of the seventeenth century, their poor nutrition and punishing work routines inhibited fertility. Far more adult slaves were dying than babies were being born.

The profits being generated by this system were enormous. Sugar went to Europe where it was sold at a high price to eager consumers. Planters needed a constant supply of new slaves from Africa to keep their plantations and sugar mills in operation. And yet much of the profits being produced by the trade in sugar and slaves were going to Dutch merchants, whose ships carried most of the sugar from the West Indies to Europe, and slaves from Africa to the West Indies. This fact escaped the attention of neither English merchants, nor the English government.

6

The Restoration Era

1658	Oliver Cromwell dies.
1660	The English monarchy is restored under Charles II. The first Navigation Act enumerates exports from the colonies.
1662	Charters are confirmed for Rhode Island and Connecticut.
1663	The second Navigation Act regulates exports to the colonies. A proprietary grant is issued to the Carolinas.
1664	A royal commission investigates New England. New Netherland is captured by the English in the Second Dutch War.
1665	The Duke's Laws are issued for New York.
1666	Much of London is destroyed in the Great Fire.
1669	The Fundamental Constitutions are drawn up for the Carolinas.
1670	Old Charles Town is founded. Charter granted to Hudson's Bay Company for trade north of Québec.
1672–4	Third Dutch War
1673	The third Navigation Act regulates intercolonial trade.
1676	Kahnawake reserve established for Catholic Mohawks near Montréal.
1677	Culpepper's rising takes place in North Carolina. Governor Andros negotiates the Covenant Chain with the Iroquois.
1680	The Westo Indians in South Carolina are defeated. Charleston is moved to the junction of the Cooper and Ashley rivers.
1683	New York holds its first assembly and issues the Charter of Liberties.

Colonial America: A History to 1763, Fourth Edition. Richard Middleton and Anne Lombard.
© 2011 Richard Middleton and Anne Lombard. Published 2011 by Blackwell Publishing Ltd.

1 THE RETURN OF CHARLES II

T HE ENGLISH CIVIL WAR turned the English political world upside down from
1642 to 1651, as supporters of the cause of Parliament waged war against
supporters of the Stuart king Charles I. At stake were not only issues of church
governance and religious orthodoxy but also the division of powers in the English
Constitution, for Charles I had believed that the monarch had the personal power to
rule and raise revenues for government operations without consulting Parliament. His
opponents in Parliament insisted that they had the right to convene regardless of the
King's wishes, as well as the right to approve all taxes. Parliament prevailed; Charles I
was executed in 1649 and the country was ruled as a Commonwealth, with Oliver
Cromwell as lord protector, from 1651 until his death in September 1658. Cromwell's
son Richard succeeded him but soon proved unequal to the task of controlling the army
and within 18 months it was clear that only the recall of the Stuart dynasty could save the
country from anarchy. In the end the monarchy was restored and Charles II crowned as
England's new king.

Charles II has traditionally been portrayed as the "merry monarch" of the Stuart
dynasty. In contrast to his inflexible and haughty father, Charles I, he had a great sense
of fun and a love of life, not to mention his mistresses, of whom Nell Gwyn was the best
known. Easygoing and relaxed, the new king wanted above all to enjoy a quiet life
politically after his 11 years as a refugee. His priorities at the outset of his reign would be
to regain his authority, summon a new Parliament, and determine the religious
settlement of England. The affairs of the North American colonies, whose population
was still less than 80,000, were not paramount.

Nevertheless, the Civil War had raised numerous issues that would have to be
resolved before the relationship between the colonies and the English government
could be stabilized. First was the question of whether the colonial governments would
recognize the new regime. Virginia and Maryland were generally favorable. Virginia
had been strongly loyal to the Stuarts until the dispatch of the Claiborne–Bennett
commission. The Maryland settlers were more divided, but the colony's affiliations
were determined by its proprietor, who was firmly for the Crown. In the northern
colonies the Restoration received a much cooler reception. Only Rhode Island, which
was in need of friends, acted expeditiously, proclaiming Charles II king in October
1660. Elsewhere the various settlements delayed, weighing the dubious advantages of
recognition against the likelihood of punishment should they fail to do so. The possible
ramifications were enormous, as all acts passed by the English Commonwealth were
likely to be overturned. It was not yet certain, however, that the monarchy's restoration
would be permanent, and the penalties for a premature declaration might be severe.
Thus Connecticut did not proclaim for the new monarch until March 1661; New
Haven followed in June 1661. In August 1661, Massachusetts became the last
settlement to recognize Charles II, though a loyal address had been sent privately the
previous November.

A second issue would be the impact of England's religious settlement in the
colonies. In England, the Church of England had been restored to its former position,
complete with bishops and other symbols inimical to the Puritans, and it was soon clear

that those who dissented would be penalized. The Corporation Act of 1661 prohibited all dissenters from holding office and the Act of Uniformity required all services to be conducted according to the Book of Common Prayer. In addition, the Conventicle Act fined dissenters for holding meetings, while the Five Mile Act effectively prohibited their ministers from entering any town. In New England, however, the applicability of these laws remained unclear. Charles II himself preferred a more tolerant stance towards dissenters, and in general it was the Crown, not Parliament, which regulated colonial affairs. Hence the only immediate effect of the Restoration on the relationship between government and church in the colonies was the royal instruction of September 1661 to cease the prosecution of Quakers. In the future Quaker offenders were to be sent to England for trial.

Most New England colonies, including Massachusetts, sent emissaries to England to express their loyalty. Rhode Island and Connecticut in addition took the opportunity to have their charters confirmed. It proved an expedient move, for in his formal response on colonial matters in April 1662 Charles II made only four relatively lenient demands. The first was that, while regicides were to be prosecuted, all other infractions of the laws were to be pardoned. Second, everyone was required to take an oath of allegiance and all laws derogatory to the royal authority were to be annulled. Third, anyone conforming to the Book of Common Prayer was to receive the sacrament. Lastly, "all freemen, of competent estates, not vicious in conversation, and orthodox in religion" were to have the vote.

Rhode Island, Connecticut, and Plymouth quickly accepted these conditions. They harbored no participants involved in the execution of Charles I and were glad to take the oath of allegiance, since it merely reinforced the temporal authority of the king. Admission to the communion concerned only Anglicans, of whom there were very few, and there was nothing else in the royal instructions which undermined their existing religious arrangements.

Connecticut and Rhode Island were duly rewarded. Rhode Island had its grant of 1644 confirmed under the great seal; Connecticut was similarly granted a charter which conformed closely to its existing Fundamental Orders. Especially pleasing to the Connecticut government was the incorporation of New Haven as part of its grant, notwithstanding bitter protests from New Haven itself. New Haven may have been punished because it had concealed two of the regicide judges, William Goffe and Edward Whalley, and was slow to recognize Charles II.

The king made a similar offer to confirm Massachusetts' charter, but to no avail. The Massachusetts general court held the view that its existing grant endowed sufficient authority. Allegiance to the king merely meant not conspiring against him, nor aiding any foreign prince, nor harboring any fugitives from justice. Nothing more was required.

The slow response of Massachusetts and some other New England settlements led Charles II to renew his four demands in April 1664. This time he dispatched four commissioners to back them up. Compliance was urgent, since war with Holland was threatening. Indeed, the commissioners were to travel as part of a force for the capture of New Netherland. The tone of their instructions was conciliatory, since Charles II wanted New England's help against the Dutch. The commissioners, therefore, were to reassure the colonists that their various churches would be respected and, indeed, were told privately not to listen to self-appointed friends of the Church of England, who might stir up animosity. Their main objective was merely to secure the "obedience and loyalty" of the New England colonies, which could best be done if the Crown had a say in the nomination of their governors and militia officers.

The commissioners, led by Colonel Richard Nicholls, duly visited the several settlements. All except Massachusetts were anxious to show that they had conformed to the king's four points of April 1662. When the commissioners arrived at Plymouth, its leaders raised the question of a new charter, explaining that the colony had been too poor to send a special mission to London. They then produced their old grant from the Council of New England. The commissioners agreed to forward this and then suggested that Plymouth name three men from whom the king might select a governor. This offer was politely declined, though with great protestations of loyalty.

The commissioners' hope that the conduct of the other New England colonies would make Massachusetts more compliant was dashed in October 1664, when the general court actually petitioned the king to recall the commission. The Puritan leaders reiterated that the existing charter had given them permission to go into the wilderness at their own expense to govern themselves and practice their religion. If this freedom of worship was not respected, they might have to move to another jurisdiction, by which they meant that of Holland. The Massachusetts Puritans' only concession was to enact a new franchise law in August 1664. From now on, property with a rental value of 10 shillings would qualify an individual for freemanship and thus the right to vote, provided a certificate from their minister confirmed that the person was "orthodox in religion." While the royal intention was to allow Anglicans to participate in affairs, this new law was clearly designed to do the exact opposite by keeping the saints in control.

Thus Massachusetts remained obdurate on all the points specified by Charles II. The commissioners had been authorized to hear appeals from the local courts, but the magistrates refused to acknowledge their authority, affirming that "the general court was the supremest judicatory." Another cause for disquiet was the Massachusetts *Book of General Lawes and Libertyes* which contained not a single reference to the king. The commissioners recommended that the king's name be substituted for "commonwealth" and similar titles. The commissioners also recognized that the new freemanship law was a sham, since only three persons in a hundred had ratable property of 10 shillings; church membership was still the real criterion for participation in the colony's affairs.

Earlier the general court had ordered the New Hampshire settlements not to cooperate with the commissioners during their visit there. The commissioners were further angered by the knowledge that Whalley and Goffe had passed through Boston with much feasting, even though they had been declared traitors. Clearly, they felt, unless a firm stand was taken the province would continue to produce radical dissenters and rebels.

The commissioners noted that the general court set much store by the possibility that the Dutch war might produce political upheaval in England, and that the court was quite likely to adopt the tactic of writing letters and doing nothing.

The commissioners were proved right. First, they themselves were captured on the voyage home by a Dutch warship, so were unable to make their report until December 1665. When Charles II then offered the colony one last chance to explain itself, Massachusetts simply stalled. Such defiance might have seemed foolhardy, but although the Dutch war had not produced the hoped-for political deliverance, Charles II had too many other concerns to enforce his demands. London was devastated first by the plague and a year later by the Great Fire, while in Europe the ambitions of Louis

XIV of France were of increasing concern. For the moment Massachusetts was able to do as it pleased, even annexing Maine, though the commissioners had arranged for that area's settlements to be administered independently.

In reality the Crown still lacked the machinery of government to enforce its decisions. At the start of his reign Charles II had created a council of trade, but its members invariably had other responsibilities, and the body received little money for bureaucratic support. Provided the New England colonists acknowledged Charles II, recognized the laws of trade, and did not harbor regicides, they could still expect to remain self-governing.

2   MERCANTILISM: THE NAVIGATION LAWS

Although the regulation of the colonies was not an initial priority for the new government, it was becoming increasingly clear by 1660 that England's role in the world was changing, and the concerns of its government were changing along with it.

The material benefits of owning colonies had been a prime reason for chartering the first trading companies. Attention had initially been fixed on the discovery of precious metals, a phase usually associated with bullionism, an economic theory that defined a nation's wealth in terms of the amount of precious metals it possessed. But with England's growing involvement in global trade, theories about the purposes of empire began to be reframed. By the 1620s it was being argued that the key to wealth and national power was a favorable balance of trade, which could best be achieved by monopolizing the production and export of staple commodities like sugar and tobacco. Exports of these commodities would generate profits for the planters and the English merchants who re-exported them, and then taxes on their profits would generate revenues for the government.

Before the Civil War trade between the colonies and the mother country had been regulated on an ad hoc basis, mostly through the imposition of duties on profit-making commodities like tobacco. The only colonies being administered by the English government (through governors appointed by the Crown) were Virginia, Barbados, the Leeward Islands, and Jamaica, and the regulation even of these colonies had been unsystematic. By 1650 more thought began to be given to the question of how to make this system of administration rational and systematic. Part of the answer was a set of legal rules later known as the mercantilist system.[1]

---

[1]   The term "mercantilism" was first used by Adam Smith in his book, *The Wealth of Nations*, published, ironically, in 1776. Before this, contemporaries referred either to the navigation laws, plantation duties, or acts of trade. Historians, following Smith, have traditionally seen mercantilism as a monolithic system with a coherent philosophy. However, as Joyce Oldham Appleby shows in *Economic Thought and Ideology in Seventeenth-Century England* (Princeton, 1978), English economic thought was anything but coherent during the seventeenth century. Arguments favoring free trade were common before the 1670s and it was only at the end of the century that theorists began to advocate restrictions on the outflow of gold and silver. Heretofore, regulation was largely the result of uncoordinated pressure, often from competing interest groups. Among these were a group of new merchants who pressed for trade regulations to promote their interests against the Dutch, and government officials who sought new sources of revenue. Robert Brenner, *Merchants and Revolution: Commercial Change, Political Conflict, and London's Overseas Traders, 1550–1653* (Cambridge, 1993), and Michael Braddick, *Nerves of State: Taxation and the Financing of the English State, 1558–1714* (Manchester, 1996).

In the turbulent era of the English Civil War, as we have seen, the Dutch had steadily appropriated much of the trade from the colonies. Dutch shipping rates were cheaper and their masters more adept at finding markets for their cargoes. The Dutch could supply not only herring from the North Sea but also slaves from Africa as well as products shipped from around the globe, from cotton cloth and coffee to the tobacco and sugar that English merchants had hoped to control for themselves. By 1648 England had lost much of its colonial trade, while it seemed that the Dutch would not be content until they had an absolute monopoly. Meanwhile the English government had begun to recognize that it would benefit from promoting English trading interests and regulating the trade.

Accordingly, in 1651 Parliament passed the first Navigation Act, which laid down two basic principles. The first was that all goods imported into England from any plantation in America, Africa, or Asia must be shipped in vessels owned and manned by Englishmen or English colonists. The second was that all European goods destined for the colonies had to be carried in English vessels or vessels belonging to their country of origin. The act's aims were twofold, first to exclude the Dutch from the carrying trade and, second, to encourage the growth of English enterprise. The Crown stood to benefit because the expansion of English trade would increase its customs revenues.

The success of the act has been disputed. The Dutch, however, considered it sufficiently damaging to fight the first of its three wars against England in the period 1652–74.

The 1651 act lapsed following the Restoration, because the Crown refused to recognize any laws passed during the interregnum. However, the exclusion of the Dutch from the carrying trade had now become a cardinal aim of the merchant community, and some alternative measure was essential if Charles II was to retain their support in Parliament. Many believed that the 1651 act had not gone far enough because it did not prevent the shipment of colonial goods to Holland or elsewhere in foreign vessels. As a result, a considerable proportion of the colonies' trade was not directly benefiting the mother country, particularly with respect to customs revenue. In October 1660, therefore, Parliament passed a new act which excluded foreign traders altogether by permitting only vessels owned and built in England or its American colonies and three-quarters manned by Englishmen to enter English colonial ports. Second, this act enumerated a list of colonial goods which had to be exported to England before being shipped elsewhere: sugar, tobacco, cotton, indigo, and other dyes. All those trading in such goods had to give bonds of up to £2,000 to the governors to ensure that they brought their cargoes to England.

The act of 1660 by no means completed the economic regulation of the colonies, for it was recognized that the provinces were not simply producers of raw commodities but also an increasing market for English goods. Consequently, in 1663 a further measure was passed, this time requiring all foreign goods going to the plantations to be shipped via England, where they could be taxed and thus denied any competitive advantage.

Finally, in 1673 an act was passed requiring the colonists to pay the same enumerated duties as their compatriots at home. In the future all enumerated goods shipped from one colony to another were to be treated as though they were destined for England. To ensure that these "plantation duties" were properly collected, the Crown arranged for customs commissioners to be appointed in every colony.

These measures promised to secure the commerce of England for the sole benefit of England. Parliament was of course only copying the example of Spain, Portugal, and France, for as the 1663 act averred, "It was the usage of other nations to keep their plantation trade to themselves." As already noted, however, it was not simply the commodities but the method of commerce itself which was now important. The new government measures would promote the development of the English shipbuilding industry by requiring that commodities be carried on English vessels, and encourage additional ships' voyages between the colonies and England by requiring that goods exported from the colonies be shipped through English ports. The expanded carrying trade helped sustain a large mercantile marine, giving employment to thousands of seamen. That in turn provided the sinews of naval power, which was increasing in importance as the century progressed. If the king's navy was to match its rivals, it must have a ready reserve of seamen, which its growing merchant fleet promised to supply.

3 NEW YORK BECOMES AN ENGLISH COLONY

English government efforts to force the Dutch out of the colonial trade were not limited to trade regulations. England had already employed its growing navy in attempting to force Dutch merchants out of the North American trade during the first Anglo-Dutch war from 1652 to 1654. In 1663, rivalry between the English and the Dutch spilled over into Africa after Charles II chartered the Royal Africa Company to monopolize the supply of slaves to the English West Indies, thus threatening the long-established Dutch slave trade. Another Anglo-Dutch war began in 1664.

In connection with its competition against the Dutch, the English had begun to focus new attention on the colony of New Netherland, sandwiched between two fast-growing areas of English settlement, the Chesapeake and New England. In English eyes the Dutch colony was a serious impediment. Much coastal trade was calling there to evade the newly passed navigation laws. If the new regulations were to be effective, this loophole would have to be closed. In addition, English settlers on western Long Island were still complaining about their arbitrary treatment at the hands of the Dutch. James, duke of York, Charles II's younger brother, was anxious to extend his patrimony: where better than in the New World at the expense of the Dutch?

The interests of Charles II and his brother coincided. Accordingly on March 12, 1664, Charles granted James a charter to the area between the Connecticut and Delaware rivers, giving him an essentially feudal grant with powers similar to those granted to Lord Baltimore in Maryland. The duke acquired possession of all the lands within the grant along with the right to make laws and appoint such officers as he wished, providing the former were "as conveniently may be, agreeable to the laws, statutes and government of this our realm of England . . . " Like Baltimore, James owed a nominal tribute, 40 beaver skins a year, to the king, though Charles II retained the right to hear appeals. There was no mention of an assembly in the duke's charter.

James quickly organized an expedition under the command of Richard Nicholls, one of the commissioners who were to investigate the condition of New England. Accompanying him were 400 troops, several frigates, and a bomb vessel. This force was more than enough for the intended target, for help was also expected from New England. Nicholls arrived off New Amsterdam on August 18, 1664, where he linked up with a force from Connecticut under John Winthrop, Jr. New Amsterdam's governor, Stuyvesant, with the fortifications of the town still incomplete, found himself hopelessly outnumbered. He had only 150 troops, and even the Dutch population, at least the commercial class, was lukewarm about resisting. Stuyvesant accordingly surrendered on August 27 after Winthrop had acted as intermediary. Generous terms were granted: the property of the Dutch inhabitants, including that of free blacks, was to be protected; those who wished to leave were given a year to do so, while new settlers from Holland would be admitted; liberty of conscience was guaranteed; and Dutch inheritance laws were to be respected.

Nicholls decided to call his conquest New York in honor of the duke. He then dispatched Sir Robert Carr, another of the commissioners, to seize the settlements on the Delaware. Victory was relatively easy here too, with the Swedish population welcoming deliverance from the Dutch.

The territory now had to be reorganized to ensure the loyalty of its ethnically diverse population. Although the Dutch and English had been accustomed to living together as refugees and coreligionists for the past 100 years, their interests were potentially at odds. James simplified the task of governing by selling the lands between the Hudson and Delaware to two friends, John Lord Berkeley and Sir George Carteret, who had helped plan the expedition. However, the task of creating a viable government was complicated both by the reluctance of the Dutch majority to live under an English legal system, and by the need to appease the towns of eastern Long Island, which were now to become part of the duke's province. In the aftermath of the campaign, Winthrop had ceded Connecticut's claims to the island in exchange for a more favorable boundary on the mainland.

Nicholls generally sought to adapt the institutions of government in New York to reflect those of England more closely. At the beginning of March 1665 he issued what came to be known as the Duke's Laws. These laws attempted to integrate English practice with those Dutch customs protected under the recent treaty and were heavily influenced by the laws of New England. Twelve crimes were to merit the death penalty, among them the denial of God, murder for gain, sodomy, conspiracy to overthrow the government, treason, and resistance to the king's lawful authority. Rules were laid down for the conduct of the magistrates, sheriffs, and constables, with justice to be administered through annual courts of session, as in New England. English common law rules were to apply in the courts, although the Dutch were permitted to follow Dutch inheritance law and keep their property. Local government, too, reflected New England practice. The freeholders of each town would elect overseers, who were to have the same functions as selectmen and the same powers as petty magistrates. Later a county structure was added, consisting of a panel of justices who were also to be appointed by the duke or his representative.

New Amsterdam, now renamed New York, was also remodeled politically. The Dutch municipal officials were replaced by a "mayor, aldermen and sheriff, according to the custom of England." However, these officials were to be appointed by the duke, rather than nominated from among themselves. The Dutch burghers protested at what they considered a breach of the surrender terms, but to no avail.

Figure 14   The Stadthuys of New York in 1679, corner of Pearl Street and Coentijs Slip.
Lithograph by G. Hayward & Co. From *Journal of Jasper Danckaerts, 1679–1680*
(New York, 1867), plate 8. Collection of the New York Historical Society,
New York City.

Although the peace treaty guaranteed liberty of conscience to the Dutch, it was not intended to open the floodgates to other religious denominations. Ministers of religion had to show that they had been properly ordained. Nevertheless, no congregations were to "be disturbed in their private meetings" nor anyone "molested, fined, or imprisoned for differing in judgement in matters of religion who profess Christianity." Although tithes were to be levied, it was left to the overseers in each town to decide which church to support. This liberality was similar in many respects to Baltimore's Act Concerning Religion. Perhaps it was no coincidence that James, like Baltimore, was a Catholic.

The Duke's Laws made concessions to both the English and the Dutch populations; yet neither group was completely satisfied. The principal weakness from the English settlers' point of view was the absence of any assembly to make laws and levy taxes, partly because such a body would have had a Dutch majority. Nevertheless, by 1665 all of England's other American colonies had an assembly, and the lack of one in New York was to be a source of much grievance, especially among the towns in eastern Long Island which had formerly been represented in the Connecticut general assembly.

DOCUMENT 11

The Duke's Laws, April 2, 1664, reprinted in W. Keith Kavenagh, *Foundations of Colonial America: A Documentary History* (New York, 1973), Vol. 2, 1037–45

The influence of New England can be seen in the laws concerning children and sexual misconduct. Punishment for same-sex sexual intimacy was especially harsh. Question to consider: *Do these laws reveal anything about the problems that the English colonial government faced in trying to govern a colony full of Dutch inhabitants?*

1 If any person within this government shall, by direct expressed impious or presumptuous ways, deny the true God and his attributes, he shall be put to death.
2 If any person shall commit any willful and premeditated murder, he shall be put to death.
3 If any person slays another with sword or dagger who has no weapon to defend himself, he shall be put to death.
4 If any man shall slay or cause another to be slain by lying in wait privately for him or by poisoning or any such wicked conspiracy, he shall be put to death.
5 If any man or woman shall lie with any beast or brute creature by carnal copulation, they shall be put to death and the beast shall be burned.
6 If any man lies with mankind as he lies with woman, they shall be put to death, unless the one part were forced or be under fourteen years of age; in which case he shall be punished at the discretion of the Court of Assizes.
7 If any person forcibly steals or carries away any mankind, he shall be put to death.
8 If any person shall bear false witness maliciously and on purpose to take away a man's life, he shall be put to death.
9 If any man shall traitorously deny his Majesty's right and titles to his crown and dominions or shall raise arms to resist his authority, he shall be put to death.
10 If any man shall treacherously conspire or publicly attempt to invade or surprise any town or towns, fort or forts, within this government, he shall be put to death.
11 If any child or children above sixteen years of age and of sufficient understanding shall smite their natural father or mother, unless thereunto provoked and forced for their self-preservation from death or maiming, at the complaint of the said father and mother, and not otherwise . . . shall be put to death.
12 Every married person or persons who shall be found or proved . . . to have committed adultery with a married man or woman, shall be put to death.
13 Every single person or persons who shall be found or proved . . . to have committed carnal copulation with a married man or woman, they both shall be grievously fined and punished as the Governor and Council or the Court of Assizes shall think meet, not extending to life or limb.

These towns led a protest against Nicholls's plan in 1665 to register all land titles as the prelude to collecting a quitrent. The same towns led the refusals in 1669 and 1670 to pay their rates, on the grounds that they were "inslaved under an Arbitrary Power" and denied the "Liberty of Englishmen." In 1672 several of them requested to be returned to Connecticut's jurisdiction.

The new English governors similarly failed to appease the Dutch. Nicholls initially refused to have any of them on his council, although in 1668 his successor, Governor Lovelace, did promote two Dutchmen and appointed a third to be mayor of New York City. In time, a group of the most successful Dutch merchants accommodated themselves to English rule and became part of New York's ruling elite. For many Dutch New Yorkers, however, the imposition of an English legal system produced a traumatic loss of economic security and prestige. The loss was particularly acute for Dutch women. The Dutch community property system had given married women significant economic autonomy and control over their property, but this control disappeared with the introduction of English law, which insisted on married women's strict legal subordination to their husbands.[2]

Dutch New Yorkers found their opportunity to protest English rule in 1672, when news arrived that England and Holland were at war again. This third conflict was mainly the result of the 1670 secret Treaty of Dover in which Charles II had promised to assist Louis XIV in any conflict with the Dutch. This time it was the Dutch government which took advantage of the hostilities to change the status of New York. After assembling a force in the West Indies, they first visited the Chesapeake, destroyed the English tobacco fleet, and then arrived off New York. Here they met little opposition, as the Dutch population greeted the fleet with open arms. The English towns refused to resist either; the Dutch ruler, William of Orange, was a fellow Protestant with close ties to the English royal family, and many Englishmen disapproved of England's aggression towards Holland on behalf of the Catholic king of France. The Dutch expedition enjoyed similar success in retaking the settlements on the Delaware.

This respite from the duke's rule was to be short-lived, however, for by the 1674 Treaty of Westminster New York was returned to English control. The duke accordingly reissued his code of laws, though he now allowed the governor and council to amend them if necessary. He also appointed a new governor, Major Edmund Andros, who had served in the West Indies and had also fought in the Dutch service. It was the confident and authoritative Andros's first civil appointment.

Andros's tenure as the governor of New York marked the beginning of a shift in the structure of England's relationship with its North American colonies, for Andros would soon begin an attempt to consolidate imperial control not only over New York but over the other northern colonies as well. His actions appear to have been the product not of a predetermined philosophy but of his efforts to deal with the challenges of governing

---

[2] On the decline in Dutch women's legal status under English law, see David E. Narrett, *Inheritance and Family Life in Colonial New York City* (Ithaca, 1992) and Deborah Rosen, "Women and Property across Colonial America: A Comparison of Legal Systems in New Mexico and New York," *William and Mary Quarterly*, 60 (2003), 355–82.

New York as they arose. The first problem he faced as governor was the same problem which had perennially faced his predecessors, namely the lack of money. Andros's attempts to raise revenue soon provoked the English towns to renew their clamor for an assembly. The episode convinced the governor that James must take over either all of New England or at least western Connecticut and New Jersey if New York was to be a viable settlement. Andros subsequently undertook an exploratory visit to Connecticut but was warned off by the local militia. He also tried to give instructions to the authorities in New Jersey but had limited success. The only other way of raising money, he suggested to the duke, might be the summoning of an assembly.

James quickly responded that such notions must be discouraged. As he told Andros in January 1676, an assembly "would be of dangerous consequence, nothing being more known than the aptness of such bodies to assume to themselves many privileges which prove destructive to ... the peace of the government." The colonists had been guaranteed their rights and property under the laws. If they had a grievance they could appeal to him through the courts. However, he confided to Andros that he would be "ready to consider of any proposals you shall send to that purpose," thereby suggesting that he was less inflexible on the matter than is commonly supposed.[3]

Andros also had problems when the burghers of New York refused to take an oath of allegiance. Believing that firmness was the best policy, he eventually imprisoned seven of the resistance leaders, including Nicholas Bayard, forcing them to forfeit one-third of their estates. In this situation there could be no question of having any Dutch in positions of authority. But from 1677 Andros gradually relaxed his stance, admitting several leading merchants to the council, most notable among them Frederick Philipse and Stephanus Van Cortlandt. The first signs of integration among the elite were beginning to take place.

A related concern for Andros was the high cost of maintaining security in a colony where Native Americans controlled most of the territory. In 1665 New York's settler population was only about 5,000. The population of the Iroquois League alone was at least twice as high, thanks to their success in replacing losses through the adoption of captives taken in wars. Moreover, the Indians' relations with the English were becoming dangerously unstable. The Iroquois had lost a vital ally and trading partner with the departure of the Dutch at the same time as their own supply of furs was being depleted, and they had already engaged in a seemingly endless series of wars with other tribes to seize their furs and drive them out of the trade. The Iroquois had destroyed the Hurons in the 1640s, the Erie, Petun, and Neutral nations in the 1650s, and the Ottawas in the early 1660s. The native inhabitants of the Ohio Valley were fleeing Iroquois attacks, some (like the Shawnees) migrating east even as others migrated to the western Great Lakes. New wars were now erupting between the Iroquois and Abenaki peoples on the northern borders of New England, as well as with the Susquehannock and Mahican peoples on the western borders of Virginia and Maryland. The Iroquois were determined to establish their political and diplomatic dominance throughout the

---

[3] The correspondence is published in Michael G. Hall, Lawrence H. Leder, and Michael G. Kammen, eds, *The Glorious Revolution in America: Documents on the Colonial Crisis of 1689* (Chapel Hill, 1964).

region. However the Iroquois at this point lacked a stable European ally and trading partner. In order to obtain the necessary supplies of guns and other trade goods, many of the western Iroquois had begun to pursue trading relationships and potentially an alliance with the French.

Andros was committed to winning the members of the Iroquois League over to the side of New York instead of New France. Accordingly, at his instigation, English and various pro-English Iroquois leaders began during the early 1670s to negotiate a series of alliances that became known as the Covenant Chain of Friendship. New York agreed to supply the Iroquois with arms and other trade goods on favorable terms. Meanwhile Andros brokered treaties between the Iroquois, the Mahicans, and the Susquehannocks so as to stabilize New York's borders. Susquehannock refugees were invited to resettle within New York's boundaries, where they were to be protected by the Iroquois in exchange for their allegiance.

The English appear to have understood the Covenant Chain as an acknowledgment by the Iroquois of their subordination to the English, and a guarantee that the Iroquois would provide military assistance against the French and their Indian allies. For Andros, such a guarantee was highly desirable since the Crown had never been willing (or able) to provide an army to protect the colonies from attacks by hostile Indians or by the French. Andros expected the Iroquois to provide the colony with its main line of defense.

Members of the Iroquois League, on the other hand, seem to have understood the Covenant Chain differently. First, the Covenant Chain was actually a series of agreements between the English and numerous other Native American tribes and kinship groups south and west of New York. In each of these agreements the Iroquois would enjoy a privileged position as the representative of the other Indians. These agreements allowed the Iroquois to claim that they had established dominance over these other peoples, who were now their tributaries. Second, the Iroquois as a group never saw the Covenant Chain as an exclusive partnership with the English. The Iroquois League was not a unified nation, like a European nation-state, but rather a confederacy with a decentralized decision-making structure. A significant faction within the confederacy continued to support an alliance with the French. In fact a number of Iroquois, mostly Mohawks, had already converted to Catholicism and begun to move to New France. The village of Kahnawake, established in 1676 as a *reserve* for Catholic Iroquois continued to attract new immigrants at a steady pace. By 1700 it had some 800 inhabitants.

However, the English guarantee of military assistance for the time being had boosted the prestige of the pro-English faction with the majority of the Iroquois. Pro-English leaders could now promise their people greater success in war and greater prosperity from the fur trade. The English would provide them with a considerably more reliable supply of the consumer goods they had come to covet, the trade goods that would enhance their political prestige, and the new guns and supplies they needed for campaigns against their enemies. Over the next few decades the alliance with the English produced more wars, not fewer, as Iroquois warriors proceeded to invade the Illinois country and attack other groups on the western borders of South Carolina. However, the favored targets were tribes to the west of the English colonies, so the English did not see these wars as their concern.

A final piece of Andros's program to consolidate control over New York was his attempt to increase revenue, using the traditional Stuart devices of arbitrary taxation and the sale of monopolies. In particular, the decision in 1678 that all overseas trade must pass through New York City effectively gave its merchants a stranglehold on the colony's trade, for which they paid handsomely. The agreement also helped facilitate the collection of customs by eliminating Southampton and Southold on Long Island as ports of entry. Andros's alliance with the city merchants was further consolidated two years later when he gave them a monopoly over the milling of flour for export.

These monopolies and trading privileges were immensely unpopular in the colony as a whole. The Long Island towns were especially bitter at the loss of their customs privileges, which threatened their trade with New England. Equally hurt were the merchants of Albany, who had previously enjoyed a significant share of the flour trade. Although they retained their monopoly of the fur trade, they were clearly disadvantaged by the need to channel everything through their rivals. The discontent quickly boiled over in 1680 when Andros neglected to renew the customs duties while on a visit to England. Many merchants not only refused to pay the levies but also took William Dyer, the collector, to court. A grand jury demanded that James place the province "upon equal ground with our fellow Bretheren and subjects of the realm of England," by which it meant the granting of an assembly.

These disturbances finally led James to the conclusion that the colonists were themselves perhaps best qualified to extract money. He therefore resolved to make a fresh start. First he appointed a new governor, Thomas Dongan, to replace the unpopular Andros. Then he decreed an assembly and gave its deputies full "liberty to consult and debate among themselves all matters" for the drafting of "laws for the good government of the said colony." Public revenues were to be levied in the duke's name, however, and Dongan was privately told to raise sufficient revenue to make further meetings of the assembly unnecessary.

The first assembly in the history of New York met in October 1683. A majority of the deputies were from the Dutch towns, but the English deputies from Long Island took the lead, being more familiar with such institutions. They began by drafting a charter of liberties or frame of government similar to that of Connecticut. The supreme legislative authority under the proprietor was to lie with the governor, council, and "the people in general assembly," who were to meet at least once every three years "according to the usage, custom and practice of the realm of England." All freeholders or freemen were to have the vote. New York City was to return four deputies, and the other counties two each, except Schenectady, which was to have one. Members were to have all the privileges of a parliament: freedom from arrest, free speech, and the right to adjourn. Together with the governor and council, the deputies were to impose all taxes.

What followed effectively constituted a bill of rights for New York's inhabitants, based mainly, though not entirely, on English precedents. Trial was to be by jury, due process of the law was to be observed, and punishment was to fit the crime. In accordance with an act of 1679, no soldiers were to be quartered on any settlers against their will except in wartime, and martial law was to be restricted to the military. Lands were to be an "estate of inheritance, not chattel or personal" which could be seized on some technical fault, and they were to be free of feudal dues as in England. The charter also addressed the question of religion. All peaceably behaved Christians were guaranteed freedom of conscience, though they still had to support a minister chosen by a majority of the local inhabitants. Widows were to be protected and women with property were to have the right to affirm in open court that it was their wish to sell.

Unlike other fundamental orders in America, which had been designed to protect the position of a dominant group, this document sought to consolidate the loyalties of all of its diverse groups by establishing the rights of all settlers. The document has a modern ring to it, being comparable to the 1776 Virginia Bill of Rights, which was similarly designed for a society which was no longer homogeneous.[4] The action of the assembly was more than Dongan or James had anticipated, but it was not specifically against the ducal instructions. Dongan had in any case secured a substantial revenue as the *sine qua non* for convening the assembly. Consequently, he accepted its measures pending approval from England.

New York, like Virginia in 1619, at last seemed set on a course towards political stability and economic success. The population and resources of the colony were growing slowly but steadily. By 1685 the number of colonists had risen to 15,000. Of these, 3,000 were in New York City, 1,500 in Albany, and 6,000 on Long Island, where Southampton was the largest settlement with 700 people. Yet despite this continuing growth, integration of the two main ethnic groups had made little progress. Albany and Esopus remained almost exclusively Dutch, while Long Island was divided between five Dutch and 12 English settlements. Only in New York City did the two nations come close together, and even there assimilation was limited.

4 THE CAROLINAS: EARLY SETTLEMENT

Although trade was the main reason for the conquest of New York, it was not the only motivation for colonial ventures after 1660. Land, too, was increasingly important. Although Lord Baltimore's venture giving him the personal right to govern the colony of Maryland had not increased his fortunes dramatically, feudal land grants like his still seemed to have much to offer. As has been mentioned, the noble families of England were anxious to enlarge their estates, and North American colonies seemed to promise a way for them to do so. The Crown itself had few objections to proprietary grants such as the grant Charles I had given to Baltimore, for Charles II had no definite policy regarding the internal administration of the colonies. As long as a venture was successful, the Crown stood to benefit. And proprietary grants allowed the king to pay off financial obligations which he had incurred in exile.

Interest in the area south of Virginia had been growing for some time. Indeed, settlers had already begun moving from Virginia into the area around Albemarle Sound, though settlement further south had so far been inhibited by the threat of

---

[4] While past historians have tended to emphasize the expansion of individual rights and liberties created by these political reforms, recent studies, often benefiting from their authors' ability to use sources written in Dutch, have shown that the imposition of English law created losses as well as gains. On the trauma of the English takeover for an ordinary Dutchman, see Donna Merwick, *Death of a Notary: Conquest and Change in Colonial New York* (Ithaca, 1999). Studies emphasizing the declining status of Dutch women are cited above, in n. 2.

Spanish retaliation and the presence of numerous Indian nations. England's capture of Jamaica in 1655 indicated that Spanish power was on the decline; the local Indians, however, remained a concern. Many of the Native Americans in the area were descended from members of the Mississippian cultures, who by the seventeenth century had reorganized themselves into smaller political units. The peoples here included members of the Muskogean-speaking Yamasee and Creek nations, the Iroquoian-speaking Cherokees, and the Siouan-speaking Catawbas. All were relatively numerous, lived in well-defined territories, and were powerful enough to have prevented the English from colonizing the region, had they chosen to do so. However, traders and settlers from Virginia had begun to discover that the Indians were more apt to trade with Europeans than to fight with them, so there was increasing optimism that a colony here could be successful.

The chief promoter of English colonization at this time was a Barbadian planter, Sir John Colleton. Barbados, like other West Indian islands, was by 1660 experiencing a crisis, all of its land being either exhausted or claimed. Sugar was an expensive crop to grow, and its production was becoming concentrated in the hands of a wealthy few, which left an increasingly discontented mass of poor planters or younger sons no longer able to compete. An opportunity to settle elsewhere was thus likely to be well received. Colleton was on good terms with Sir William Berkeley of Virginia, his brother John Lord Berkeley, and an ambitious young politician, Anthony Ashley Cooper, who had once owned a plantation in Barbados. Lacking sufficient resources to launch a new colony, the four men entered an arrangement with four of the most powerful figures in the kingdom: Edward Hyde, earl of Clarendon, the king's chief minister; George Monck, duke of Albemarle, whose march from Coldstream had made possible Charles II's restoration; and the earl of Craven and Sir George Carteret, two prominent friends of the duke of York. Together, the eight men agreed to approach the king for a palatinate grant, like Lord Baltimore's grant in Maryland.

The king's grant, issued on March 24, 1663, gave the eight proprietors lands extending from Luck Island on the thirty-sixth parallel to the St. Matthias River on the borders of Florida. They were to be "absolute Proprietors of the Country," paying a nominal rent for lands which they could sell or lease. They could also create titles and manors, make war in defense of their territories, and declare martial law for the suppression of any rebellion. They were empowered to make all laws and raise taxes. As in Maryland, they could issue emergency decrees which would have the same force as acts of the assembly. Thus the proprietors had enormous powers to rule over the colony, though they were subject to several legal restrictions. Laws made by the proprietors or their agents could not contravene the settlers' "liberties, franchises and privileges" as Englishmen. Taxes were subject to "the advice, assent and approbation of the freemen of the said province." And the settlers were also to be allowed liberty of conscience, provided they periodically affirmed their loyalty to the throne.

To avoid the problems of acclimatization and the expenses of an Atlantic crossing, the proprietors planned to recruit settlers already in America, particularly from Barbados. The proprietors believed that the lack of available land in Barbados would be sufficient inducement to get the enterprise started. They expected settlers to be lured by the rich alluvial lands along the many rivers, which would, they hoped, support the cultivation of silk, vines, ginger, waxes, almonds, and olives.

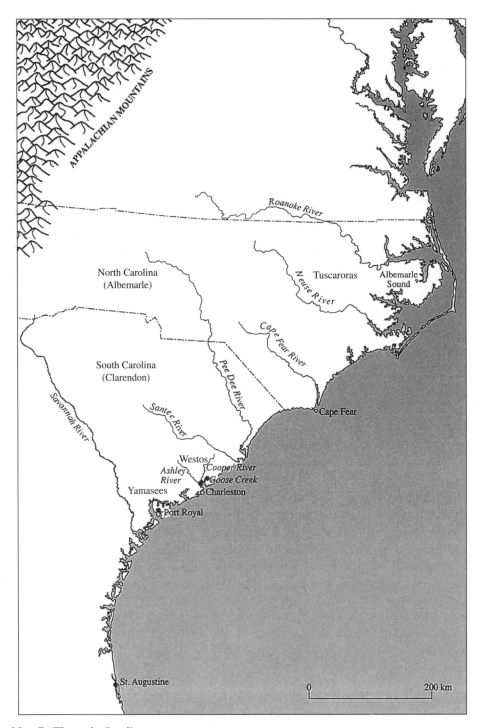

Map 7   The early Carolinas.

Between 1663 and 1665, Colleton and the governor of Barbados, Sir John Yeamans, organized a number of exploratory voyages, which proved sufficiently encouraging for a substantial group of Barbadians to offer themselves as colonists. But the enterprise did not last long. The newcomers disliked the demand for quitrents and found the Cape Fear region relatively infertile, so that within two years the settlement had broken up. Some colonists went on to Virginia; the rest returned to Barbados.

Nevertheless, the proprietors, notably Cooper, now earl of Shaftesbury, determined to persist, not least because the Privy Council had announced that in future such grants would lapse unless settlement was effected within a reasonable period. Another incentive to continue was that a peace treaty had been concluded in 1667 with Spain, reducing the fears of a Spanish attack.[5]

The proprietors put into place a system of government which reveals a great deal about their vision of an ideal society. The chief architects of this system, called the Fundamental Constitutions of Carolina, were Lord Shaftesbury and his secretary, John Locke. The constitutions were designed to create a society led by great landlords who, it was assumed, would promote order and stability more effectively than merchants and traders.[6] The province was to be administered by a palatinate court, which could call the provincial "parliament," prepare legislation, appoint officers, and dispose of public money. The parliament itself was to consist of the proprietors and other nobility, together with deputies representing the freeholders of every precinct. Each representative had to possess 500 acres and each voter 50, thus ensuring that laws would be made by landed gentlemen and not by social upstarts. The parliament was to sit every other November, and its first action would be to reaffirm the Fundamental Constitutions.

Although the Church of England was to be supported from public funds, other Christian sects would be tolerated. The Indians, too, would be shown forbearance as their "idolatory, ignorance, or mistake gives us no right to expel or use them ill." The proprietors hoped a policy of toleration would attract settlers and would simultaneously bring Indians into their society, first as peaceful trading partners and then as farmers. The Fundamental Constitutions also stipulated, however, that African slaves who converted to Christianity would *not* be freed, thus closing off potential legal challenges to the enslavement of Christians. The proprietors clearly anticipated that Carolina's plantations would be developed using the labor of African slaves, who by now provided the main source of labor in Barbados.

To ensure that aristocrats and landed gentlemen could exert sufficient influence to guarantee social stability, the Fundamental Constitutions created a pyramidal land-holding structure. Carolina was to be divided into two provinces, Albemarle and Clarendon, each comprising a number of counties. Each proprietor would own 12,000 acres in every county. Next in rank would be a landgrave, who would possess four baronies of 12,000 acres each, followed by two caciques, holding two baronies apiece. The landgraves and caciques would constitute the nobility. After them would come the

---

[5] For further information on Anglo-Spanish relations at this time, see Chapter 15, section 1.

[6] For this emphasis on the proprietors' idealized vision of a stable, rural society, see S. Max Edelson, *Plantation Enterprise in Colonial South Carolina* (Cambridge, Mass., 2006).

lords of the manor, each with 3,000 to 12,000 acres, followed by the rest of the freeholders, who collectively would own three-fifths of the land.

Shaftesbury and Locke were seemingly influenced here by the writings of James Harrington, who argued that the English Civil War had occurred because of an imbalance between the landed classes, though Harrington favored the gentry and yeomanry over the aristocracy or monarchy as bulwarks of stability. Shaftesbury and Locke apparently believed that their pyramidal structure would achieve the same effect, creating a gentry along with a large yeoman class whose members would share a commitment to upholding property rights.[7]

The authors realized that the Fundamental Constitutions could not be implemented immediately in an infant colony. Accordingly they issued a set of temporary laws, restricting the initial size of the baronies until enough settlers had arrived to make the scheme workable. The expectation was that each barony would contain between 15 and 30 persons within seven years.

The first batch of settlers left England in August 1669 in three ships, financed by a contribution of £500 from each proprietor. They arrived off the Ashley River in April 1670, after journeying by way of Barbados where additional settlers were recruited. An immediate start was made clearing a site on the south bank for the building of a stockade around the principal settlement of Charles Town. Two years later the settlement had 271 men and 69 women, but this number was not nearly enough to implement the Fundamental Constitutions, since there were as yet no caciques or lords of the manor and only one landgrave – Sir John Yeamans, the governor. Nevertheless, Yeamans summoned the first parliament in July 1671 and began implementing a survey. Squares of 12,000 acres were marked along the Ashley River: six for the people, two for the proprietors, and two for the nobility.

From the start, the plan was unworkable. A number of landgraves and caciques were created, but most grantees lacked sufficient labor or capital to develop agricultural enterprises on a large scale. In 1682 all free inhabitants were promised a headright of 50 acres, including servants on the expiry of their service. The only charge would be a quitrent of one penny an acre. Yet most settlers resented paying even this, given that the proprietors were absentee landlords, and responded by refusing to take the oath acknowledging the Fundamental Constitutions.[8]

Finding a profitable commodity around which to build the colony was a major challenge. Silk, olives, oranges, wine, and cotton all were tried without success. A few individuals prospered raising cattle and hogs, which they could sell to planters and pirates in the Caribbean. Corn, peas, lumber, tar, and pitch could also be profitably sold. The Barbadians had brought some African slaves with them, assuming from the outset that slave labor would be their primary labor source. However, without a profitable commodity to justify their purchase and transportation costs, Africans were not imported in large numbers. Those who lived in the colony generally worked as cowboys

---

[7] For the full text of the Fundamental Constitutions, see Kavenagh, *Documentary History*, Vol. 3, 1761–74. Harrington's book *Oceana* was first published in 1656.

[8] The settlers' attitude stymied the whole scheme, since the proprietors had accepted that their system of government could be considered lawful only after it had been ratified by the people as part of an original compact. This provision foreshadowed Locke's *Second Treatise of Government* (1690) in which he argued that government must be based on a contract reflecting the consent of the people.

or farmhands, and had considerable freedom compared to slaves in the Caribbean. The proprietors' hopes of a stable society of planters growing exotic export commodities appeared to have stalled.

To sustain their economy, the settlers instead took advantage of the local Indians' willingness to trade. The area was rich in game, especially deer. Some local Indians had already begun trading with settlers from Virginia, obtaining European trade goods in exchange for deerskins – and more ominously, captives from other tribes whom they sold as slaves, either to Caribbean planters or to other colonists on the mainland. The proprietors sought to prohibit settlers from engaging in trade, arguing that an unlicensed trade would alienate the Westos, a small tribe living in the area whose friendship was essential to the colony. The proprietors also ordered the governor and parliament to ban the enslavement of Indians.

The proprietors' edicts went unheeded. The governor and parliament objected that the proprietors were trying to engross the one profitable activity in Clarendon province. For their part, the governor and parliament prohibited ordinary settlers from engaging in trade with the Indians, but indulged in it themselves, especially in the sale of Indian captives as slaves. The result of this conflict between the proprietors and the officials they had appointed to govern on their behalf was to encourage wild, unregulated competition in the Indian trade, with tragic consequences for the Indians. The parliamentary faction initially encouraged members of a small local tribe called the Cusabos to make war on the more powerful Westos. But after achieving a settlement in that conflict, they encouraged the Westos to capture and enslave the Cusabos, as well as other tribes in the region. Meanwhile settlers excluded from the slave trade simply began trading with other nations hostile to the Westos. After the Westos' defeat in 1680, the parliamentary faction began trading with the Savannah people (over the objection of the proprietors).

Parliamentary opposition to the will of the proprietors came mostly from Barbadians, men who had come to Carolina not to advance some utopian vision but to get rich. Yeamans himself was typical of their kind – aggressive, resourceful, and determined to make his fortune. The proprietors lacked the political will to stop them. Significantly, instead of persisting in their efforts to ban the Indian slave trade, in 1683 the proprietors called for the creation of a licensing system to verify that captives being sold as slaves had been taken lawfully, in wars the English considered to be just. The result of the licensing system, in the long run, was not to curtail the trade, but rather to encourage settlers to pay Indians to start wars so they could obtain more slaves.[9]

In 1680 the main settlement – hereafter referred to as Charleston – was moved to the junction of the Ashley and Cooper rivers, a much healthier site open to the Atlantic breezes. The population of Charleston at this time was about 300. It remained a small struggling outpost. The colony's settlers experimented with different types of food production, raising corn as well as other crops, along with hogs and cattle. Hogs and

---

[9] Historians once treated the Indian slave trade as tragic but incidental to the long-term development of Carolina's economy. Recent work, however, suggests it played a central role in ensuring Carolina's eventual success, providing the main source of capital necessary to develop a plantation economy. On the slave trade and its importance, see Allan Gallay, *The Indian Slave Trade: The Rise of the English Empire in the American South, 1670–1717* (New Haven, 2002).

cattle did particularly well, since they did not have to be killed in winter, and planters from Clarendon County could export them to the West Indies, where the Barbadians exchanged their provisions for sugar. With so much to be gained from the Indian trade in deerskins and slaves, the search for a staple crop was not urgent.

Nevertheless, investors continued to look for alternative ways to make money. Exports of lumber and naval stores were clearly growing by 1690. In addition, between 1690 and 1700 they began to develop a new staple crop: rice. Sometime in the 1670s, a few individuals had apparently experimented with cultivating rice, and by the 1690s planters were beginning to grow the crop for export. Historians disagree about who was most responsible for this development. Some argue that the first cultivators of rice were probably West African slaves growing the grain for their own consumption, after it had been brought on an African slave ship. People from certain regions of West Africa had a great deal of experience with rice cultivation in swampy lowlands. Other historians believe it more likely that white South Carolinian planters experimented with rice cultivation first, then ordered African slaves to begin growing the plant on a regular basis. Given the nature of the evidence it may never be possible to pinpoint the precise origins of rice in the Carolina low country, but it is clear that by 1699 South Carolina planters had begun to export a substantial quantity of rice, using African slave labor. Over the next few decades, South Carolina's economy would increasingly rely on imported African slaves to grow and process rice for export. By 1720 rice had become its main staple commodity.[10]

If the province of Clarendon took some time to develop a stable economy and become profitable to the proprietors, Albemarle to the north took even longer. Beginning in 1664, Governor Berkeley of Virginia had sought to control the area, and issued a number of permits guaranteeing the holders their lands on the same terms as in Virginia. Other settlers simply bought titles from the local inhabitants without regard to the proprietors' rights. To prevent further chaos, in 1667 the Carolina proprietors nominated a governor with instructions to appoint a surveyor to sell lands, reserving to the proprietors a quitrent of one halfpenny an acre and 50 percent of all precious metals. Freedom of conscience was guaranteed and an assembly was to be created, with the sole right to raise taxes and to make laws, provided they were consistent with the laws of England and did not contravene the interests of the proprietors. Although the

---

[10]   The theory that African slaves played a major role in the introduction of rice cultivation was advanced by Peter Wood, *Black Majority: Negroes in Colonial South Carolina from 1670 through the Stono Rebellion* (New York, 1974), and further developed by Daniel C. Littlefield, *Rice and Slaves: Ethnicity and the Slave Trade in Colonial South Carolina* (Baton Rouge, 1981), and Judith A. Carney, *Black Rice: The African Origin of Rice Cultivation in the Americas* (Cambridge, Mass., 2001). Some historians have recently challenged the "black rice" thesis, arguing on the basis of demographic evidence about the origins of slaves that it was unlikely for a group of skilled rice-growing slaves to have arrived in South Carolina from the main rice-cultivating regions of West Africa between 1671 and 1700. See David Eltis, Philip Morgan, and David Richardson, "Agency and Diaspora in Atlantic History: Reassessing the African Contribution to Rice Cultivation in the Americas," *American Historical Review*, 112 (2007), 1329–58. This argument is challenged by Gwendolyn Hall, "Africa and Africans in the African Diaspora: The Uses of Relational Databases," *American Historical Review*, 115 (2010), 136–50. S. Max Edelson, "Beyond Black Rice: Reconstructing Material and Cultural Contexts for Early Plantation Agriculture," *American Historical Review*, 115 (2010), 125–35, argues that the introduction of rice may be best understood as the product of informal exchanges between Africans and Englishmen in an undeveloped frontier economy.

proprietors expected Albemarle to conform to the Fundamental Constitution, it soon became clear that Albemarle was too remote to offer much profit and the proprietors concentrated their limited resources on Clarendon instead.

Since most of Albemarle's settlers were from Virginia, it quickly took on the appearance of that colony. The settlement's main activity was subsistence farming, supplemented by the production of a little surplus tobacco and corn, which were sold to passing New England traders. Albemarle itself had little institutional cohesion, since it contained no towns and few churches. The governor on Roanoke Island had to shift for himself with the aid of a motley council. The one institution which did thrive was the assembly, because the inhabitants were familiar with Virginia's House of Burgesses.

The settlers in general quite failed to comprehend the proprietary system, except to recognize that it was incompatible with their existing land titles. They also resented the demand for quitrents and were further irritated by the passage of the 1673 Navigation Act, which threatened to stifle the province's small trade. The result was a climate of instability.

The governor in 1673 was John Jenkins, one of the early settlers from Virginia. He and other leading planters, notably John Culpepper and George Durant, were especially unhappy about the new trade laws. This group was opposed by another faction, led by Thomas Miller and Thomas Eastchurch, which succeeded in persuading the proprietors to transfer authority to them by appointing them governor and collector of customs. Miller's faction then began confiscating his opponents' property as punishment for contravening the 1673 act, provoking an uprising by Culpepper's faction in December 1677. Miller was seized, while Culpepper, with the support of the assembly, established his own government before going to England to defend his actions.

Since Culpepper and his followers had not overtly challenged the authority of the king or the proprietors, they were exonerated, and calm returned to the province. But the incident underlined the weakness of proprietary government. It was the proprietors' poor judgment in appointing Jenkins and Miller which had sparked off the trouble in the first place. Then they had passively watched as the struggle unfolded. Mercifully, bloodshed had been avoided, a remarkable achievement in light of the fact that Virginia to the north had just emerged from a bloody civil war.

7

The Later Years of Charles II

1660	Sir William Berkeley is restored as governor of Virginia.
1662	The Congregational Church agrees to the Half-Way Covenant.
1673	Virginia land rights are awarded to Lords Culpepper and Arlington. The Lawne's Creek protest takes place.
1675	King Philip's (Metacom's) War breaks out in New England; Northfield is abandoned. The Privy Council sets up a committee for supervising the colonies. Englishmen attack Doegs and Susquehannocks in the Chesapeake.
1676	Bacon's Rebellion is quashed. King Philip is defeated. William Penn and other Quakers purchase West New Jersey.
1679–81	In the Exclusion crisis in England the Whigs attempt to bar James, duke of York from the succession.
1680	New Hampshire becomes a royal colony.
1681	Penn is granted a charter to establish Pennsylvania. Edward Randolph is appointed customs collector for New England.
1682	Philadelphia is founded. Plant cutter riots break out in Gloucester County, Virginia.
1686	The first German Pietists arrive in Pennsylvania.
1689	The Keithian Schism divides Quakers in Pennsylvania.

Colonial America: A History to 1763, Fourth Edition. Richard Middleton and Anne Lombard.
© 2011 Richard Middleton and Anne Lombard. Published 2011 by Blackwell Publishing Ltd.

1 VIRGINIA: BACON'S REBELLION AND ITS AFTERMATH

Thanks to their achievement of economic self-sufficiency, guarantees of voting rights to freemen, and (after 1646) the defeat of the Powhatan Indians, English settler societies in the Chesapeake had survived and begun at last to generate revenue for the English Crown. Yet these successes did not yet mean that social and political stability had been achieved. Tensions continued to erupt during much of the seventeenth century between the settlers and the native peoples upon whose lands they had encroached. Meanwhile new conflicts developed between ordinary settlers and governing elites, and structural problems with colonial governing systems often prevented those conflicts from being resolved. In 1676 these sources of tension came together to produce one of the most dramatic uprisings in the colonies in England's oldest, most valuable, and loyal colony, Virginia.

Settler societies in the Chesapeake by 1660 were obsessed by the search for wealth, and had become ruthlessly exploitative. Servants were worked to the limit, their existence made doubly hard by the lack of prospects once their service was completed. Mortality rates, though not as terrible as in the period before 1624, remained high. Although land itself was relatively cheap, former servants still had to pay the surveyor's fees and then find enough capital to buy livestock and other essential equipment, for which their freedom dues were totally inadequate. Another problem was that by the 1660s all the best land had been claimed. A freed servant might find a plot of land to rent, but distance from shipping routes could add so much to his production costs that he would be unable to save enough money ever to buy land of his own. Thus only 6 percent of all servants actually became successful enough to purchase their own labor force. Fully 25 percent failed to become landowners at all, continuing to work as tenant farmers, foremen, or laborers.

A related problem, for immigrant men, was the shortage of women. After Virginia's reorganization as a royal colony in 1625, the population had grown steadily, reaching nearly 30,000 by 1670. But unlike the rapidly growing settler population in New England, the settlers of Virginia and Maryland were still predominantly male. Among new immigrants entering Virginia after 1625, men generally outnumbered women by a ratio of at least four to one. Even after men were freed from servitude, large numbers of them were unable to marry and for many decades the settler population remained dominated by bachelors. This had important consequences for Cheseapeake society, since early modern English people treated bachelors as outsiders, granting men full social respect and membership in the community only if they married and owned land. Many unmarried men in the Chesapeake therefore felt less than fully committed to maintaining Virginia's social order, and disorderly behavior was common.[1]

---

[1] Historians have a long-standing debate about the social origins of immigrants to the Chesapeake. Abbot Emerson Smith, *Colonists in Bondage: White Servitude and Convict Labor in America, 1607–1776* (Chapel Hill, 1947), 82–3, categorized most servants as "Rogues, Whores and Vagabonds." This view was challenged by Mildred Campbell in "Social Origins of Some Early Americans," in James Morton Smith, ed., *Seventeenth-Century America: Essays in Colonial History* (Chapel Hill, 1959), 63–89. Campbell found that most

As Virginia's governor himself complained of the potentially explosive situation, "Six parts of seven at least are Poore, Indebted, Discontented and Armed."

Another source of dissatisfaction was Virginia's government, which had become more oligarchical after the colony was placed under royal control. Following the Restoration, Sir William Berkeley had returned to Virginia as its royal governor without resistance. Berkeley's previous period in office had been widely approved because of his handling of the Indian war of 1644–6 and his readiness to work with the assembly. Yet by 1670 this esteem was beginning to erode. Berkeley had found his allies in the 1662 house so amenable to his desires that he determined to retain them, and refused to call any new elections for the House of Burgesses. Meanwhile, the colony was growing rapidly, with many new counties being added and fortunes being made.

The sense of exclusivity was reinforced by the Franchise Act of 1670 which for the first time since 1619 significantly curtailed freemen's voting rights. In the future only freehold landowners and householders were to have the vote, to prevent propertyless and disorderly men from disrupting elections. Parish councils were similarly ceasing to be elective, their membership being instead coopted. Thus at both a provincial and a local level, Virginians had a growing sense that government was becoming the preserve of a small clique of colonists who owed their position to Berkeley. Their inequitable system of taxation became an additional grievance. Virginia's government obtained most of its revenues from a poll tax, levied on each person in a household. The burden of poll taxes fell more heavily on poor farmers than on rich ones because paying them required a larger percentage of poor men's annual incomes. The House of Burgesses refused to pass a land tax, which would have alleviated inequity by taxing large landowners more heavily than small ones. Moreover, the governor and members of his council were exempt from taxes of any kind.

The effects of the navigation laws on the local economy were a further cause for concern. The legislation passed in 1660 and 1663 had been, in Berkeley's words, "mighty and destructive" of Virginia's economy, having reduced the market for tobacco while excluding the cheaper goods and services of the Dutch. Virginia was seemingly being sacrificed for the benefit of a few English merchants. The economy had already become depressed because of a slump in tobacco prices caused by overproduction; annual output was now running at between seven million and nine million pounds for the Chesapeake as a whole. Falling tobacco prices reduced planters' profits,

---

immigrants were respectable maids and skilled artisans. Her view was qualified by David W. Galenson in "'Middling People' or 'Common Sort'? The Social Origins of Some Early Americans Re-examined," to which there is a rebuttal by Campbell, *William and Mary Quarterly*, 35 (1978), 499–524. More recently, Russell R. Menard has concluded that the truth lies somewhere in between. See "British Migration to the Chesapeake Colonies in the Seventeenth Century," in Lois Green Carr, Philip D. Morgan, and Jean B. Russo, eds, *Colonial Chesapeake Society* (Chapel Hill, 1988), 99–132. The distorted sex ratio of Virginian society was first noted by Wesley Frank Craven in *White, Red, and Black: The Seventeenth-Century Virginian* (Charlottesville, 1971). The subject is explored in greater detail by Edmund S. Morgan, *American Slavery, American Freedom: The Ordeal of Colonial Virginia* (New York, 1975); and by Darrett B. Rutman and Anita H. Rutman, *A Place in Time: Middlesex County, Virginia, 1650–1750* (New York, 1984). The implications of the imbalanced sex ratio for men's achievement of manhood status and as a cause of conflict is explored in Kathleen Brown, *Good Wives, Nasty Wenches, and Anxious Patriarchs: Gender, Race, and Power in Colonial Virginia* (Chapel Hill, 1996). Immigrant gender ratios were similar in Maryland (see Chapter 5, section 3).

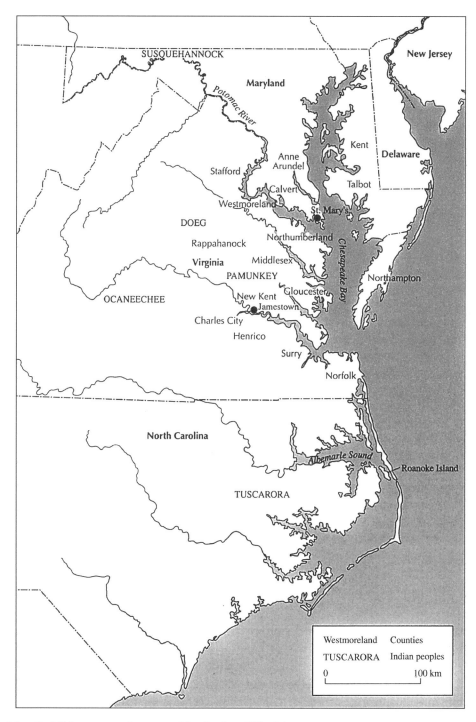

Map 8 Mid-seventeenth-century Maryland and Virginia.

causing particular hardship for newly freed servants and tenant farmers, for whom growing indebtedness made it increasingly difficult to purchase land. Resentment increased after the enactment of an even more comprehensive Navigation Act in 1673 and the creation of an oversight board, the Lords of Trade and Plantations, to ensure the enforcement of the navigation laws.

Wars with the Dutch also worsened economic hardships for colonial tobacco planters. In 1667 18 tobacco vessels were seized at the end of the second war with the Dutch. Two years later the province had to contend not only with another Navigation Act but also with a third Dutch war, during which 11 tobacco vessels were captured by the fleet heading for New York. This was despite the construction of several forts near the entrance to Chesapeake Bay. Coming as it did on top of reduced markets and poor prices, this misfortune was a body blow. Many planters, especially bitter that so much money had been spent on the defense of the Chesapeake to so little effect, protested at Lawne's Creek in Surry County in an attempt not to pay any taxes.

The Crown's propensity to use colonial land claims as a way to raise money did not help matters either. In 1673 news arrived that Charles II had consigned his land rights in Virginia to Lord Arlington and Lord Culpepper for 31 years. They could create new counties, appoint sheriffs, and dispose of all unsettled lands. More alarming, they were empowered to collect quitrents throughout Virginia and to control the Anglican Church. Charles II had acted to pay off yet another debt, but his measure was singularly ill-considered, threatening as it did existing institutions. Berkeley himself was quick to express "the people's grief" at an act which undermined all confidence in the future. A delegation was immediately sent to England to try to overturn the grant and, so as to prevent the recurrence of such an action, to seek a formal charter, which Virginia had lacked since 1624. Though the grant to Culpepper and Arlington was eventually reduced, the damage had been done. Nothing disturbed the settlers more than the questioning of their land titles and the diminishing of their assemblies.

While many of the small planters' grievances were about the structure of government and imperial policies, what finally brought them into open conflict with Virginia's governing elite was an ongoing dispute about relations with the Indians. Some of the colony's settlers (particularly recent immigrants, newly freed servants hoping to acquire land, and land speculators) wanted the colony to expand into new territory. Such expansion was likely, of course, to antagonize Virginia's Native American neighbors, for whom the clearing of forests meant shrinking food supplies. Therefore the long-established landowners who dominated the House of Burgesses favored restricting new settlement. Since 1646, Governor Berkeley had tried to contain white settlement behind a defensive perimeter of forts so as to avoid conflict with the Indians. Recent settlers resented having to pay taxes to support these forts, which they saw as designed to impede their opportunities rather than to protect them.

Tensions between the settlers and Native Americans increased in the early 1670s as the Iroquois expanded their control over the fur trade between the Chesapeake and the Ohio River, forcing several new groups of Indians, including the Doegs and the Susquehannocks, to move east into the Chesapeake region. A major source of conflict between settlers and the Indians concerned the settlers' livestock. Instead of keeping their animals fenced in, as was common in England, settlers in North America commonly allowed them to range freely in search of food. This made sense for the settlers since they were perennially short of labor. However, for the Indians this practice had disastrous results. Herds of swine and cattle wandered into Indian cornfields and hunting grounds where they devoured the plants that normally sustained deer and other game. Frustrated by the destruction of their meadows and forests, Indians from time to time responded by confiscating and killing the animals.[2]

In the spring of 1675 a settler vigilante group attacked and murdered several Doeg Indians in a dispute over some missing hogs. The Indians retaliated by killing the ringleader's son and two of his servants. Local settler leaders George Mason and John Brent gathered up the Stafford County militia and pursued the Indians. Coming upon two cabins, they began shooting the inmates; only after killing 14 of them did Mason discover that he had shot friendly Susquehannocks by mistake.

Although Governor Berkeley favored an investigation, his deputies decided instead to escalate the fighting. This time Colonel John Washington commanded the militia of all the Rappahannock counties. Washington's orders were to inflict "such Execution upon the said Indians as shall be found necessary." In due course the force joined a party of Marylanders and surrounded a Susquehannock fort. Indicating a desire to treat, five chiefs came out to parley, denying any knowledge of the recent killings and blaming a Seneca war party from the north. Their answer did not satisfy the Virginians, since several Susquehannocks had been found near the scene of recent incidents with the clothing of murdered whites. The chiefs were accordingly executed, though on whose orders it is not clear, since the Virginians subsequently tried to exculpate themselves by blaming the Marylanders.

The Susquehannocks quickly launched a series of retaliatory attacks on the Virginian backcountry as far south as Surry County. Berkeley's first response was to propose a new militia expedition, but fearing an escalation of the troubles and recognizing that the Indians were not entirely to blame, he ordered the expedition to return. Aware that a ferocious war had broken out with the Indians in New England and fearing a united Indian uprising, Berkeley ordered the Virginians to remain inside their perimeter forts. The frontier settlers argued such forts were inadequate; soon Berkeley was accused of pursuing this policy simply to protect his fur trade interests.

Planters on the frontier in Charles and Henrico counties, who were isolated and seemingly ignored by the governor and his clique at Jamestown, found a leader in a wealthy and well-connected young man who had recently come from England to establish a plantation out on the western frontier. Nathaniel Bacon had an uncle on the council and had himself been invited to join because, as Berkeley commented, "Gentlemen of your quality come very rarely into this country." Bacon, whose own overseer had just been killed in an attack, convinced his followers to launch an expedition against the Susquehannocks in defiance of Berkeley. Bacon and his men solicited help from a group of Ocaneechee Indians, tracked down a party of the Susquehannocks, and butchered most of them in a surprise attack. After the attack,

[2] Recent historians have increasingly sought to understand the origins of Indian–European conflicts from Indian and not only European points of view. For example, Michael Leroy Oberg discusses changes in Indian settlement patterns in the Chesapeake between 1646 and 1675 in *Dominion and Civility: English Imperialism and Native America, 1585–1685* (Ithaca, 1999), while Virginia DeJohn Anderson explores the reasons for disputes about livestock in *Creatures of Empire: How Domestic Animals Transformed Early America* (New York, 2004).

Bacon and his men claimed the spoils. Their native allies objected, having expected reciprocity from the Englishmen. Bacon and his men therefore turned on the Ocaneechee men, women, and children, burning them to death in their cabins and shooting them as they attempted to flee. Bacon proudly boasted, "In the heat of the Fight we . . . destroyed them all," and he gloated that his forces had "left all nations of Indians . . . ingaged in a civil war amongst themselves [to] their utter ruin and destruction." Later he justified his action to Berkeley by declaring that the Indians were "all our enemies."

News of these events infuriated Berkeley, who concluded the attacks had jeopardized all hopes of peaceful relations with the Indians and represented a direct challenge to his own authority. He therefore declared Bacon a traitor. Berkeley, however, was aware of his own unpopularity, and not simply with the frontiersmen. The tidewater counties, too, were alienated from the Green Spring clique which controlled the assembly, local government, and the granting of land. Accordingly, in May 1676 Berkeley attempted to placate Bacon instead of challenging him directly. He ordered fresh elections for the first time in 14 years, inviting all those with grievances to state them openly and defending his long association with the province.

Initially, this ploy seemed to work. Bacon himself was elected for Henrico County and requested the governor's pardon for his late escapade. Berkeley agreed, though by now both men distrusted each other, as Bacon demonstrated by keeping a considerable guard about him. Berkeley even agreed to grant Bacon a commission to march against the Indians with a force raised from all the inhabitants. In addition, Berkeley asked the assembly to pass a measure prohibiting all trade except with "friendly Indians," while any deserted land was to revert to the colony. And finally, at Bacon's request, the assembly passed several reforms to appease the small planters, most significantly annulling the Franchise Act of 1670 and restoring the vote to all freemen rather than just freeholders.

Unfortunately Berkeley's attempts to placate the small planters were not enough to quell the frontier uprising. On June 23, 1676, Bacon arrived in Jamestown with 400 armed men. The plan to levy a force from the whole population apparently did not please him or his associates – Giles Bland, William Drummond, and William Lawrence – who wanted to recruit men from Henrico and New Kent, believing that they would be more effective and doubtless more amenable. Bacon also desired his commission immediately, not in three months' time when the necessary taxes had been raised. A confrontation ensued on the steps of the general assembly, with the timorous representatives beseeching Berkeley to give in and Bacon threatening fire and the sword if his demand was refused. Although Berkeley finally gave way, Bacon and his comrades would not depart until they had compelled the assembly to pass an act of indemnity in compensation for their proceedings.

This humiliation was too much for the governor. As soon as Bacon had marched off to attack the Indians, Berkeley declared him a traitor again and summoned the militia to his aid. Now Berkeley experienced the full effects of his alienation from the tidewater counties. Though a few Berkeley loyalists tried to muster the Gloucester and Middlesex levies, the militia simply melted away when Bacon reappeared in July 1676. This time Berkeley had to flee to the eastern shore, while Bacon issued a manifesto "in the Name of the People of Virginia," accusing Berkeley of graft and corruption, of levying huge taxes for personal profit, and of condoning murder by the native inhabitants to preserve his illegal trading

DOCUMENT 12

Declaration of Nathaniel Bacon in the name of the people of Virginia, July 30, 1676, reprinted in W. Keith Kavenagh, *Foundations of Colonial America: A Documentary History* (New York, 1973), Vol. 3, 1783–4

Bacon's declaration was calculated to appeal both *to the tidewater areas about high taxes and the monopolization of office by the clique that surrounded Berkeley, and the backcountry, which wanted a more aggressive policy towards the Indians.* Questions to consider: *How does Bacon characterize the Indians? How does he characterize the backcountry settlers? Do you think that Bacon was a champion of democratic values?*

Charges against Sir William Berkeley

1 For having, upon specious pretenses of public works, raised great unjust taxes upon the commonalty for the advancement of private favorites and other sinister ends …
2 For having abused and rendered contemptible the magistrates of justice by advancing to places of judicature scandalous and ignorant favorites.
3 For having wronged his Majesty's prerogative and interest by assuming monopoly of the beaver trade and having for unjust gain, betrayed and sold his Majesty's country and the lives of his loyal subjects to the barbarous heathen.
4 For having protected, favored, and emboldened the Indians against his Majesty's loyal subjects, never contriving, requiring, or appointing any due or proper means of satisfaction for their many invasions, robberies, and murders committed upon us.
5 For having … when we might with ease have destroyed them … sent back our army by passing his word for the peaceable demeanor of the said Indians, who immediately prosecuted their evil intentions …
6 And lately, when upon the loud outcries of blood, the assembly had, with all care raised and framed an army for the preventing of further mischief … for having, with only the privacy of some few favorites without acquainting the people … forged a commission, by we know not what hand, not only without but even against the consent of the people, for the raising and effecting civil war and destruction.

Of this and the aforesaid articles we accuse Sir William Berkeley as guilty of each and every one the same.

---

monopoly. Bacon's intention was "to represent our sad and heavy grievances to his most sacred majesty." In the meantime, being "general by Consent of the people," he issued a list of Berkeley's "wicked and pernicious councillors" who were to surrender immediately. Any colonists giving them aid would have their property confiscated.

Having secured his position, Bacon marched inland once more. His target this time was the English-allied Pamunkey people, who had to flee into a swamp for safety. Berkeley meanwhile returned to Jamestown, only to be attacked by Bacon once more. During the assault on September 18 the town was burned, and Berkeley for a second time had to take refuge on the eastern shore. In the aftermath armed servants and slaves took advantage of the general lawlessness to exact revenge on those who had used them ill. Among the sacked plantations was Berkeley's at Green Spring.

It is difficult to predict quite how long these events might have lasted had not Bacon fallen ill and died in October. Deprived of his charismatic influence, the movement soon disintegrated. Bacon's confederates were steadily rounded up and brought before the embittered Berkeley. Twenty-three were summarily hanged, despite a royal proclamation pardoning everyone except Bacon.

Ultimately the Crown reasserted its control, sending Colonel Herbert Jeffreys, who arrived in February with 1,000 troops to quell the disorders. Berkeley was forced to surrender his governorship, and the executions stopped. In the course of an inquiry conducted by Colonel Jeffreys into the causes of the rebellion, the inhabitants of Gloucester County emphasized the hardships caused by the various taxes, the fear that the Arlington–Culpepper patent would lead "to the enslaving" of the inhabitants, and the terror created by conflicts with the Indians, all of which had given Bacon the opportunity to exploit the situation. The commissioners themselves blamed Bacon's ability to exploit the "giddy headed multitude," most of whom "had but lately crept out of the condition of servants." However, they conceded that high taxes had been a factor.

In the early twentieth century this episode was portrayed as a bid for independence, with Bacon playing the role of a George Washington, but this interpretation no longer holds credence. Bacon had been in Virginia less than two years, and had no program or philosophy. He was certainly not fighting against the English government. Today, historians are less interested in Bacon's goals than in the motivations of the many planters who participated in the rebellion. Most have concluded this was a populist rebellion fuelled by the resentments of poor and disfranchised planters and servants against the colony's wealthy elite. Berkeley himself described the conflict as pitting the "Rabble" against "the better sort of people." Indeed, many contemporaries commented on the presence of many blacks among Bacon's followers, suggesting that poverty and lack of opportunity were major sources of shared grievance. Another important shared grievance, it has been suggested, was the frontier settlers' hatred of the Indians, whose land they wanted and had been prevented from taking by the colony's governing elite.[3]

---

[3] The view that Bacon was an early George Washington can be found in Thomas J. Wertenbaker, *Torch-Bearer of the Rebellion: The Story of Bacon's Rebellion and Its Leader* (Princeton, 1940). For a contrary view, see Wilcomb E. Washburn, *The Governor and the Rebel: A History of Bacon's Rebellion in Virginia* (Chapel Hill, 1957). A more recent version of the old interpretation is Stephen Saunders Webb, *1676: The End of American Independence* (New York, 1984). Modern historians who emphasize the rebels' class-based grievances include Edmund Morgan, *American Slavery, American Freedom*, and Kathleen Brown, *Good Wives, Nasty Wenches*. Recently it has been argued that conflicts over Indian policy were at the root of the political dispute between frontiersmen and Berkeley's faction (Oberg, *Dominion and Civility*, ch. 5).

As a populist uprising, Bacon's Rebellion was not successful, since Virginia's government became even less responsive to the concerns of ordinary farmers after the rebellion ended. The political reforms passed by Bacon's assembly were lost, notably that relating to the franchise, while several others were amended. The Crown issued a charter which failed to give the assembly any overt recognition. Indeed the next royal governor, Lord Culpepper, had specific instructions not to allow the burgesses the right to initiate legislation. In addition he was to seek a permanent revenue to strengthen royal control. The planters were sufficiently cowed to grant him a two-shilling duty on each hogshead of tobacco exported.

Though Bacon's Rebellion failed to democratize Virginia's political system, it did reduce some sources of social conflict within the colony. The uprising greatly diminished the number of Native Americans in the region, particularly weakening the Susquehannocks. Divisions over Indian policy became less explosive. The small planters' economic grievances continued, and indeed in 1682 serious riots in Gloucester County were provoked by the low price of tobacco. Nevertheless, Bacon's Rebellion did constitute a watershed, for in the years that followed Virginian society underwent a significant transformation. The planters began to decrease their reliance on white indentured servants for labor and turned instead to African slaves. The consequence of this substitution in the long run was to lessen tensions between poor white planters and Virginia's planter elite.

The shift from indentured servitude to slavery resulted from a confluence of factors. England's population had declined after 1650, driving up wages. English youths now faced better prospects if they remained in England or (after 1682) emigrated to Pennsylvania, rather than moving to the Chesapeake. Meanwhile African slaves were becoming cheaper. The ending of the Royal African Company's monopoly in 1698 encouraged more traders to enter the slave business. At the same time a decline in the demand for slaves in the Caribbean, where the production of sugar had temporarily peaked, forced many slave traders to look for other markets, dropping their prices at the same time.

Although these demographic and economic changes were independent of Bacon's Rebellion, memories of the recent uprising made planters particularly interested in purchasing African slaves instead of English servants. African slaves had the advantage of being easier to control. Africans could not claim the rights of English subjects, so they could be prohibited from associating with one another, from bearing arms, and even from being freed. Africans could be exploited more thoroughly than English servants, and they could be isolated on the basis of their nationality and the color of their skin. Finally, unlike indentured servitude, slavery could become self-perpetuating. The children of African slaves could be automatically designated as slaves, so that slaves would reproduce themselves in perpetuity. A series of laws passed in Virginia beginning in 1661 had already begun to regulate the status of African slaves in the same ways as slaves were regulated in Barbados. These rules made it more difficult for them to move upward in Virginia society and closed off the kinds of options once available to men and women like Anthony and Mary Johnson.

A final reason for the increased trade in Africans was the changing attitude of the planters towards Virginia itself. Until the 1680s most planters aimed to make their fortune quickly so that they could retire to England. It did not make sense to pay the extra cost of a slave whose labor the owner might not live to enjoy. Short-term white indentures were far more cost-effective even if it meant replacing the workforce every four or five years and knowing that some ex-servants would buy plantations and become competitors. Now profound demographic changes in the colony were encouraging more planters to think in the long term. Until 1680 Virginia had been overwhelmingly a land of immigrants with short life spans. Now a growing percentage of the population was native-born, with greater immunity to disease than their parents and a longer life expectancy. The gender ratio gradually became more even, and the new Creole generation were also able to marry earlier and raise larger families.[4]

In consequence a white native population evolved which could see not only the advantages of a permanent slave labor force, especially one that reproduced itself, but also the attractions of their environment. Virginia was their home, not a temporary refuge, and as a result they now built for the future. At last, after nearly 100 years, the crude wattle-and-daub structures inhabited by even the richest planters in the colony's early years now began to give way to grander houses, often of brick, or at least with brick chimneys and foundations. The wealthier inhabitants began to enjoy English standards of comfort.[5] Political and social horizons also changed. Even the most successful no longer thought of returning to England, instead aspiring to become local grandees who served on the council or assembly and developed institutions like the College of William and Mary, which received its charter in 1692. Local pride was also behind the writing of Robert Beverley, Jr.'s *History of Virginia*, in which he described the province as the "best poor man's country." Unknowingly the colony had changed from a crude frontier society to the more sophisticated type of province which was to be so conspicuous a feature during the eighteenth century.

There was one other important, though unanticipated, development which resulted from these changes, including the new restrictions being placed on African slaves. This was the different relationship between the elite and the rest of the white population. No longer was it one of exploiter and exploited; the position of the exploited had been taken over by the African Americans. Tidewater Virginia was no longer a "society with slaves," in which slaves were only one among several groups of exploited workers. It had become a "slave society," in which the fundamental social division was now the division between masters and slaves. Herein lay the reason for the new amity among whites. The small planters constituted the bulk of the militia and would be responsible for suppressing any uprising by the slaves. Almost subconsciously the grandees began to cooperate more with their less affluent neighbors, helping them market their crops, giving them credit, and

---

[4] The view that Africans were substituted for servants because they were easier to control than Englishmen is put forward by Morgan in *American Slavery, American Freedom*, though he believes that the decision was more subconscious than rational. The argument that the switch occurred primarily because of a decline in the supply of servants is presented in Russell R. Menard, "From Servants to Slaves: The Transformation of the Chesapeake Labor System," *Southern Studies*, 16 (1977), 355–90. The effects of greater life expectancy and the creation of a white native class are discussed by Allan Kulikoff in *Tobacco and Slaves: The Development of Southern Cultures in the Chesapeake, 1689–1800* (Chapel Hill, 1986). For a useful summary, see Warren M. Billings, John E. Selby, and Thad W. Tate, *Colonial Virginia: A History* (New York, 1986).

[5] See James Horn's *Adapting to a New World: English Society in the Seventeenth-Century Chesapeake* (Chapel Hill, 1994), in which the author argues that most people suffered a drop in their standard of housing before 1700 compared with what they would have enjoyed in England.

assisting them in numerous other ways. They were encouraged to do so because this attitude complemented the new image they had of themselves as leaders of a civilized provincial society. The effect of their behavior was to make poor whites feel like they too were part of the privileged class, who had a stake in maintaining the social order.

2 MASSACHUSETTS: THE STRUGGLE TO REMAIN SELF-GOVERNING

Massachusetts, like the other New England colonies, had achieved remarkable social stability during its early decades. Even so, in Massachusetts just as in Virginia, internal social stresses, tensions between English settlers and native populations, and an ongoing conflict over political authority within the colony gave rise to a bitter war in 1675.

The English settler population in Massachusetts had continued to grow since the colony's founding and to expand the amount of land under cultivation with each new generation. Most settlers were family farmers who produced food for their own use and employed their children, particularly teenaged and adult sons, as their main labor force. Sons spent years working to cultivate and improve their fathers' farms. Typically, they were rewarded at some point around their late twenties either with a share of the family land or with help in purchasing a new plot of land in a more remote and less settled location.

Though subsistence farming remained the norm, more commercial opportunities were emerging in and around Massachusetts. As Dutch merchants were forced out of the carrying trade to the West Indies, merchants and entrepreneurs in Boston and Salem began building ships to engage in the carrying trade for themselves. Indeed, Massachusetts shipbuilders soon found they had competitive advantages over ship-builders in England, with cheap lumber readily available to them from suppliers in New Hampshire and Maine. As trade increased, New England farmers also began to prosper. West Indian planters were shifting out of food production and into sugar, creating opportunities for farmers in southern New England to earn modest amounts of cash by raising extra cattle and hogs to ship to Barbados and (after 1655) Jamaica.

Their increasing prosperity was undeniable, but in this profoundly religious society, commercial growth could be a source of anxiety as much as optimism. Massachusetts magistrates and clerics worried that along with the growth of commerce had come a decline in religious zeal. The second generation appeared forgetful of why the first had come to Massachusetts and displayed a distinct preference for acquiring material wealth – particularly land. As one leading minister commented, "Land hath been the idol of New England ... they that profess themselves Christians, have foresaken Churches, and Ordinances, and all for land."

Typical of this new hunger for wealth was the example of Winthrop's own son, John. From an early stage he was involved in the settling of the Connecticut Valley, driven by speculative rather than spiritual considerations. Then in 1644 he tried to establish a blast furnace and iron foundry on the Saugus River and also to exploit other metals like lead, tin, and copper. His later involvement in the capture of New York was similarly rooted in commercial motives, as was his participation in the activities of the Atherton Company, which sought to secure the Narragansett country from its native owners. Winthrop also helped found several Massachusetts towns, notably Ipswich, even though he resided there for only a few months. New settlements were always anxious to attract the support of wealthy sponsors, offering them in return a share of the land.

The Pynchon family of Springfield presented a similar example. John Pynchon followed his father, William, in establishing a virtual monopoly of wealth in this frontier community. Thirty percent of the population were Pynchon's tenants, and few escaped that status, unless they were foreclosed. Pynchon helped too in the establishment of several new towns. Such activities made Winthrop and Pynchon, in effect, professional town promoters.

It was not only the wealthy who were acting in an entrepreneurial fashion. Sometimes entire towns speculated in land. The proprietors of Dedham, anticipating the day when land might no longer be available for their descendants, obtained a grant from the general court for the establishment of Deerfield in western Massachusetts. Few actually left Dedham, and only those with capital to invest stood to benefit. Similar ventures were undertaken by other long-established towns.

Some historians have argued that what was taking place was a fundamental transition from a community-based society, dedicated to the observance of God's covenant, to one which was aggressively capitalistic and individualistic. The concept of the just price, once cherished by the Puritan founders, had given way to the more competitive values of the marketplace. Usury, or lending money for interest, was no longer considered extortion. In consequence, capital was triumphing over labor. The Puritan was being replaced by the Yankee.

In fact, such materialism was not incompatible with the Puritans' religious zeal, and in some ways was actually the product of it. The early Puritans had never ignored the economic benefits of their new commonwealth. They had always encouraged capital investment to develop public works, trade, and the shipping industry. And their religiously motivated work ethic had helped to spur the slow, steady economic expansion of the economy, despite an inhospitable climate.[6] Thus most historians have now rejected the view that religious commitment in New England was in decline.

Still, Puritan leaders worried constantly that their holy experiment was failing. Why they should have felt such anxiety in the face of success has been a persistent problem for

---

[6] For the changing values of seventeenth-century New England, see Richard S. Dunn, *Puritans and Yankees: The Winthrop Dynasty of New England, 1630–1717* (Princeton, 1962); Darrett B. Rutman, *Winthrop's Boston: Portrait of a Puritan Town, 1630–1649* (Chapel Hill, 1965); Frederick Martin, *Profits in the Wilderness: Entrepreneurship and the Founding of New England Towns in the Seventeenth Century* (Chapel Hill, 1991); Stephen Innes, *Creating the Commonwealth: The Economic Culture of Puritan New England* (New York, 1995); Mark Valeri, "Religious Discipline and the Market: Puritans and the Issue of Usury," *William and Mary Quarterly*, 54 (1997), 746–68; and Margaret Ellen Newell, *From Dependency to Independence: Economic Revolution in Colonial New England* (Ithaca, 1998). The continued predominance of the community over the individual is argued by Helena M. Wall, *Fierce Communion: Family and Community in Early America* (Cambridge, Mass., 1990). For the entrepreneurial Pynchon family, see Stephen Innes, *Labor in a New Land: Economy and Society in Seventeenth-Century Springfield* (Princeton, 1983). Historians are unable to agree on when the market became predominant. Gary B. Nash finds traces of the old communal values as late as the 1730s, notably in Boston when there was a dispute over the building of a new market house: see *The Urban Crucible: Social Change, Political Consciousness, and the Origins of the American Revolution* (Cambridge, Mass., 1979). In contrast, James Henretta, *The Origins of American Capitalism: Collected Essays* (Boston, 1991), and Allan Kulikoff, *The Agrarian Origins of American Capitalism* (Charlottesville, 1992), believe that the era of the American Revolution and federal Constitution was the time when capitalism, wage labor, and free markets first triumphed. Other writers push the origins of the market further into the past (see Chapter 10, section 2).

historians to explain. Several factors were undoubtedly at work. One is that the Puritan movement had become less cohesive and less influential in England after the Restoration, and the Puritans in Massachusetts were under growing pressure to reform their political system. The Crown's commission had in 1665 issued a report recommending legal changes in Massachusetts (such as imposing limited religious toleration). If implemented, such changes would threaten the colony's distinctive religious culture. Another factor was the growing visibility of religious and political dissent as the Puritans' political authority grew less secure. For example, Boston's Baptists, who in the past had been fined repeatedly for failing to attend worship services in a Congregational church, openly proclaimed their status as a church in 1665. Even the elect appeared to be growing more litigious. Such a development was not surprising in a society that was becoming more complex and more commercial. However, for the Puritans it sent a distressing signal that the people's commitment to building a godly commonwealth had waned. With their providential view of history, Puritan ministers were inclined to see these events as evidence of God's judgment against them. Their frustration increasingly resulted in jeremiads, or sermons forecasting damnation and hell for their flock unless they returned to the way of the Lord.

The Puritans' concerns about their society's political future were bound up as well with their concerns about the religious welfare of the next generation. The number of young people seeking full church membership had been declining for at least a decade. As a result the number of full church members was shrinking relative to the total settler population. The children of the unregenerate (that is, nonmembers) could not be baptized and therefore could not become saints, thus further decreasing the church's eligible membership. Although many parents accepted their own exclusion from full membership, they were distressed that their children must always be denied the chance of salvation. Colonial leaders were as concerned as the parents. Declining church membership meant fewer men would qualify to vote or serve in office. If the Puritans became a minority in Massachusetts, how could they shoulder the burden of creating a godly society whose members lived according to divine law?

In an attempt to resolve this dilemma, in 1662 the ministers agreed to the Half-Way Covenant, permitting the baptism of children even though the parents were not of the elect. The hope was that the offspring might succeed where the parents had failed. Since the Puritans were congregational, however, it was left to the individual churches to implement the new covenant. Ironically many refused, on the grounds that the Half-Way Covenant undermined the fundamental standards of Puritanism. This stance has led many historians to conclude that the colonists continued to be as committed to Puritan ideals as ever.[7]

---

[7] The view that Puritanism was in decline was popular with Progressive historians during the two world wars. See James Truslow Adams, *The Founding of New England* (Boston, 1927), and William W. Sweet, *Religion in Colonial America* (New York, 1942). It was to counter such views that Perry Miller wrote *Orthodoxy in Massachusetts, 1630–1650: A Genetic Study* (Cambridge, Mass., 1933) and *The New England Mind*, 2 vols (New York, 1939), though Miller argued that Puritanism was in decline by the end of the seventeenth century. The declension thesis was challenged subsequently by, among others, Robert G. Pope, *The Half-Way Covenant: Church Membership in Puritan New England* (Princeton, 1969), and Gerald F. Moran and Maris A. Vinovskis, "The Puritan Family and Religion: A Critical Reappraisal," *William and Mary Quarterly*, 39 (1982), 29–63. The argument that concerns about youth were central to the Half-Way Covenant is found in Jenny Hale Pulsipher, *Subjects unto the Same King: Indians, English, and the Contest for Authority in Colonial New England* (Philadelphia, 2005). The debate about declension has more recently shifted to the eighteenth century (see Chapter 13, section 1).

Massachusetts leaders became ever more anxious as the Crown continued to intrude into the colony's affairs. The 1673 Navigation Act had empowered the governor of each colony to appoint a naval officer to monitor its implementation within that colony, but the Massachusetts governor had failed to appoint one. In 1675 the newly appointed Lords of Trade issued a stern warning requiring all the navigation laws to be observed, and soon sent a special envoy, Edward Randolph, to check on Massachusetts' compliance. The Massachusetts general court was determined to remain self-governing. The members believed that since Massachusetts was not represented in Parliament, Parliament's laws were not valid in the colonies. As Governor John Leverett bluntly told Randolph on his first visit in 1676, "The Laws made by your Majesty and your parliament obligeth them in nothing but what consists with the interest" of the colony, for "the legislative power abides in them solely" by virtue of the charter. The most that the commonwealth would do was to pass duplicate legislation as a gesture of goodwill.

By 1675, the English government was not the Puritans' only problem, for their Indian allies had begun to resist the authority of the colonial governments as well. Massachusetts had effectively subordinated its Native American allies since 1643, following Miantonimo's execution. After 1660, however, the Indians became emboldened to question their subordinate status as they realized that the authority of the Massachusetts officials was under threat. The Narragansetts successfully petitioned the royal commissioners in 1664 to remove their land from the control of Massachusetts and place them under the direct protection of the king. Similarly King Philip,[8] Massassoit's successor as the tribal leader of the Wampanoags, had gone to the king's commissioners to obtain confirmation of his own people's rights to their land. The effect of these actions was to undermine local political power over the Indians by removing colonial governments from the chain of authority. Colonial officials had good reason to worry that they were losing control.[9]

As time went on, many New England Indians, notably the Wampanoags, Narragansetts, Mohegans, Poducks, and Nipmucks, became divided among themselves over their continuing alliance with the English. For some time relations with the settlers had been deteriorating. The settlers' population expansion placed tremendous pressure on the livelihoods of the native peoples, which were particularly compromised when the white settlers' hogs and cattle strayed into their fields. Their game had been driven away and the fur trade ceased. The demise of the fur trade undermined ties that had helped the New England Indians to maintain friendly relations with the Iroquois, making them vulnerable to devastating attacks from the north. Significant numbers of Indians had become utterly dependent on the English for their livelihoods, working as casual laborers on English farms and converting to Christianity. Some Indian sachems, meanwhile, resented the activities of missionaries like John Eliot, since the Christianization of their people undermined the authority of the chiefs and shamans. They also

---

[8] Scholars have disagreed about how to refer to the Wampanoag leader. Some describe him as Metacomet or Metacom, others as King Philip. However, Jill Lepore, *The Name of War: King Philip's War and the Origins of American Identity* (New York, 1998), xix–xxi, argues for keeping the traditional name of Philip, a name which he himself had adopted. Recent scholarship follows this convention.

[9] Although tensions between settlers and local Indians have traditionally been seen as stemming from purely local causes, it has recently been shown that the Indians were able to use the colony's political problems with the Crown to bolster their own political position (Pulsipher, *Subjects unto the Same King*).

resented the periodic attempts by Massachusetts and Plymouth officials to reassert their dominance over indigenous peoples.

These various tensions erupted into hostilities in 1675. In January of that year a Christian Indian was murdered, supposedly at the instigation of Philip, who suspected him of spying for the English. Three of Philip's men were tried and executed for the crime. Angered by this clear attempt by Plymouth to assert political authority over his people, Philip and the non-Christianized faction of the Wampanoags prepared for war, beginning their campaign with an assault on the English settlement at Swansea. At this point a general uprising by the native peoples does not seem to have been planned; however, once Massachusetts went to the aid of Plymouth, a wider conflict developed. After Philip persuaded the Nipmucks to enter the war, fighting spread to the upper Connecticut Valley and the town of Northfield had to be abandoned in September 1675. Up to this point the Narragansetts had remained neutral, but the colonists themselves precipitated their entry into the war. When information was received in November that some Narragansetts were harboring some of Philip's women and children in an area of Rhode Island known as the Great Swamp, the United Colonies sent a combined force under Josiah Winslow against them. Winslow's force killed 300 men, women, and children. As at the Pequot fort in 1637, most of the victims were burned to death, for the first thing Winslow did was to surround the Narragansett fort with a ring of fire. This savage assault promptly increased support for Philip, since considerable numbers of the Indians now realized that they were fighting for their lives. Plymouth and Providence came under fire, as did Weymouth and Sudbury, only 20 miles from Boston. Most notable was the routing of a force under Captain Lathrop in the Connecticut Valley, in which 60 of Lathrop's men were killed. Philip achieved another success near Providence when 60 men under Captain Pierce died.

Well into the winter of 1675, the war seemed to favor Philip and his allies, whose daring raids had proved too much for the slow-footed colonists. The English were internally divided. Many towns resisted the colony's attempt to impress young men from established families into the militia, drafting poor men and outsiders instead. The draftees understandably made poor soldiers, since they were committed neither to the towns that had impressed then, nor to the war itself.[10] Philip himself had significant support not only from local tribes but also from various Abenaki peoples to the north. However, one critical Native American group failed to back him: the members of the Iroquois League. Even as the war was being fought the Iroquois had begun the negotiations with New York's Governor Andros that would eventually lead to the Covenant Chain alliance. In early 1676, urged on by New York's Governor Andros, the Mohawks agreed to enter the war on the side of the English. When Philip sought the assistance of the Mahican nation, he was attacked by the Mohawks and forced to

---

[10] Historians once believed that the early English colonists were committed to universal military service, especially in New England. See, for example, John Shy, "A New Look at the Colonial Militia," in *A People Numerous and Armed: Reflections on the Military Struggle for American Independence* (New York, 1976), and Robert Gross, *The Minutemen and Their World* (New York, 1976). This conclusion has been challenged by Kyle Zelner, *A Rabble in Arms: Massachusetts Towns and Militiamen during King Philip's War* (New York, 2009), which shows that town militia committees avoided drafting fathers of families or the sons of established farmers and church members, instead drafting men considered part of the "rabble," including poor men and those formerly convicted of crimes.

withdraw with heavy losses. The setback proved especially calamitous because the winter fighting had depleted the Wampanoags' reserves of food, ammunition, and shelter.

In the end, Philip and his allies were defeated because the United Colonies with their population of 70,000, their reserves of food and ammunition, and their significant numbers of Indian allies were better equipped to fight a sustained total war. Native American societies, with their delicate balance between humans and nature, were far too easily disrupted by prolonged warfare. Women and children were especially vulnerable if their crops and habitations were destroyed prior to the onset of winter. In addition, Philip had to contend with the colonists' Indian allies, though ironically the Massachusetts government had not initially appreciated their help. This failure by Massachusetts in particular proved significant, for it was not until Indian allies were enlisted that the war finally changed in the colonists' favor. As John Eliot readily confessed: "In our first war with the Indians, God pleased to show us the vanity of our military skill, in managing our arms after the European mode. Now we are glad to learn the skulking way of war."

As a result many members of the various tribal groups were steadily tracked down, killed, or sold into slavery in the West Indies, as indeed were Philip's own family, after he had been cornered and shot in a swamp. Others fled to the north, taking refuge among the Abenakis in northern New England or creating new villages in New France. Fighting ended in southern New England by the summer of 1676, though it continued on the Maine frontier until 1678. The Indians of southern New England were effectively reduced to remnant communities cooped up in special villages, their way of life and environment destroyed forever. Among the casualties were Eliot's praying towns, most of whose inhabitants, though firmly loyal to the English, had been interned on Deer Island near Boston in conditions of great hardship. Indeed, in the confusion some were shipped to the West Indies, despite the protests of Eliot and Samuel Gookin that this contravened the Puritan obligation to convert the native peoples. Afterwards only four praying towns remained, while Eliot's seminary at Harvard produced only one Indian minister before it closed in 1692.[11] The prospects for interethnic harmony even among the converted had been hopelessly compromised.

As in Virginia, the net result of the war was the clearing of the coastal areas for exclusive white settlement. The war had been fought at a terrible price. Twelve towns had been destroyed, almost half the rest had suffered some damage, one out of every 15 men of military age had been killed, and all of the United Colonies had incurred large debts. Moreover, damage of another kind had been inflicted, that to the New Englanders' sense of identity and purpose. During the war they had committed as many atrocities as the enemy, disemboweling their dead and placing their heads on poles as trophies. The conundrum of living in a wilderness while attempting to remain a civilized and godly people was profoundly unsettling.[12] The scars of the war were to remain for a long time.

---

[11]   The four surviving towns were Natick, Punkapaug, Hassanamesit, and Wamesit.

[12]   The publication in 1682 of Mary Rowlandson's account of her capture by the Nipmuck Indians at Lancaster also highlighted the dilemma. Not only was Rowlandson's life spared, but she was treated with something akin to respect in contrast to the New Englanders' treatment of their captives.

It was to address such doubts that the general court of Massachusetts agreed to a new congregational synod in 1679. At the top of the agenda was the perceived declension in New England's religiosity. The ministers, however, were unable to suggest anything other than the old shibboleths of a more rigorous observance of the sabbath, stricter parental control of unruly children, a closer regulation of taverns, and a turning away from material goods. The last, they believed, could be achieved by new sumptuary laws regulating the clothing which people were permitted to wear.

Meanwhile the threat of further English intervention remained omnipresent, though Massachusetts continued doggedly to resist the Crown's authority. Massachusetts continued to mint the 1652 pine tree shilling, an abuse of one of the Crown's most cherished privileges. The province had also unilaterally reasserted control over New Hampshire and Maine, despite the recommendations of the commissioners in 1665. New Hampshire was finally declared a royal province in 1680, but Massachusetts kept its grasp on Maine, angering the Crown further by buying out the heirs of Sir Fernando Gorges in an attempt to make good its claim. Royal officials once more ordered Massachusetts to send envoys to England to answer Randolph's charges that it was flouting English laws.

Massachusetts still hoped that the government of Charles II would either lack the means to implement its plans or be overthrown by a *coup d'état*. During 1680 England was convulsed by a Whig opposition attempt in Parliament to curb the Crown. God had saved Massachusetts from the ravages of King Philip; a similar miracle might also save it from Charles II. Holding onto this vain hope, the general court continued to drag its feet. The court obstructed Randolph when he returned in 1681 with a permanent commission as collector of the customs by appointing its own naval officer. Of the 34 vessels prosecuted by Randolph, colonial judges released every one and made Randolph pay the costs. Meanwhile the collector catalogued so many colonial misdemeanors that even the lackadaisical Charles II could not but take action eventually. Apart from their infractions of the trade laws, Randolph noted that the Puritans continued to persecute Quakers, failed to take the oath of allegiance, and omitted the king's name in their official proceedings. The day of reckoning could not be far off.

3 NEW JERSEY AND PENNSYLVANIA: THE BEGINNINGS

Randolph's concern for the Quakers was judicial rather than religious, for like most English people he did not believe in toleration. Religious persecution was rife in England too. The Test Acts of 1673 and 1678, for example, imposed religious tests for public office by specifically excluding Catholics from holding office and sitting in Parliament. In the colonies, however, few suffered so severely as the Society of Friends, or Quakers, as they were commonly called because they allegedly trembled or quaked at the name of the Lord.

The Quakers were followers of George Fox, an itinerant preacher who wanted to restore Christianity to its original simplicity. Fox and his followers were part of the Protestant Reformation, and like other dissenters, they criticized religious ritual and hierarchy within the church. But quite unlike the Puritans, they believed that everyone could be saved, since all were the children of God and could experience his inner light. They therefore had no need of a formal priesthood or liturgy like the Bible and Book of Common Prayer. Even the Holy Trinity was of little importance. They relied solely on the innate goodness of the individual and the power of communal prayer to produce an environment in which they could live in "holy conversation."

These views were naturally abhorrent to the other churches, which considered them a denial of everything they believed necessary for salvation. Unfortunately the Quakers exacerbated their persecution by further deviations from accepted community standards. One problem was their refusal to swear oaths on the Bible, an act which, they argued, would imply that they were not telling the truth on other occasions. Another was their view that the taking of life could never be justified. This belief led them to refuse to perform militia service or to pay taxes even for self-defense. Finally they insisted upon wearing plain black garments which visibly set them apart from the rest of the population. They suffered cruelly both in England and in America.

The Quakers, however, did not lack support. Many of them did well in commerce, because of their truthfulness and penchant for hard work. They also made an exceptional convert in a well-connected young gentleman with considerable wealth, William Penn. Penn's father, who had been a senior naval commander during the first and second Dutch wars, subsequently introduced his son to both Charles II and James, duke of York. This personal connection was to be of immense value, for it enabled Penn, like Maryland's Lord Baltimore, to use his influence to secure a refuge for his coreligionists. Penn's motives were not totally altruistic; like all New World proprietors he was anxious to increase his own wealth by acquiring land and participating in the fur trade.

Penn first attempted to establish a settlement in America in 1676, when he and several other Quakers became trustees for a Quaker investor in the colony of West New Jersey. New Jersey had been part of New Netherland until the duke of York granted it in 1664 to Sir George Carteret and John Lord Berkeley, noblemen who had supported him during the English Civil War. At this point the settler population did not exceed 200 (mainly Dutch) settlers living in Bergen County, though the number grew following the sale by New York's new governor of 400,000 acres to some Long Island Puritans, who created the townships of Elizabeth and Newark (hereafter referred to as the Elizabeth and Newark associates). Later on, Scottish Presbyterian and English Quaker settlers would settle the western portion of the territory. The two Jersey proprietors, who were also involved in the Carolinas, did little to advance their new possessions and subsequently divided the territory into two smaller colonies, East and West Jersey. In 1674, Berkeley sold his holdings in West Jersey to two Quaker investors, Edward Byllinge and John Fenwick.

It was when these two men quarreled over their purchase that Penn became involved. The area's current legal status was unsatisfactory from his point of view, as the Jersey grant gave title to the land but did not officially grant governmental authority to pass laws protecting the Quaker religion. Once the duke of York finally confirmed the investors' right to establish a government, Penn and 11 other prominent Quakers jointly purchased East New Jersey for themselves in 1682. In that very transaction lay another problem: with so many proprietors, confusion was inevitable.

Penn decided to seek his own, more substantial, grant elsewhere. Knowing from his current investment that the lands west of the Delaware were still unclaimed, he sought

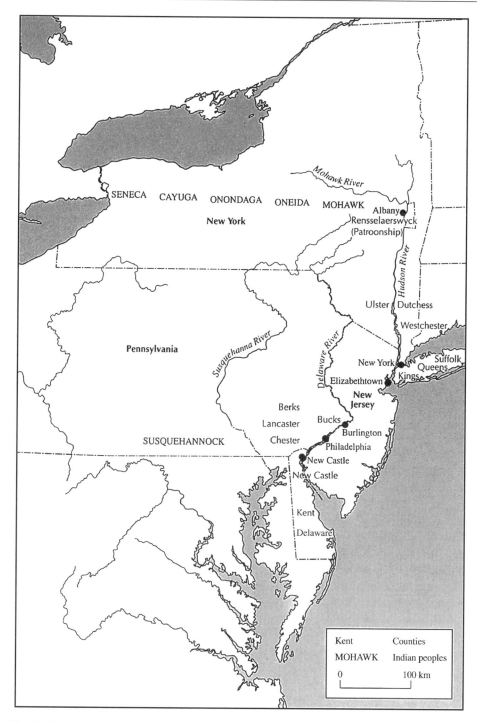

Map 9 The middle colonies in the later seventeenth century.

a formal charter for them. Charles II, who had borrowed heavily from his father, the admiral, owed Penn a considerable sum. Once again the king used his claims to land in North America to pay off his debts to a friend.

Penn's charter for the colony of Pennsylvania, awarded in February 1681, was another proprietary grant like those conveyed in Maryland, New York, and Carolina. Penn's lands were to extend from 12 miles north of Newcastle along the Delaware River until the forty-third parallel. He received extensive powers to distribute his lands on such terms as he chose, create manors, and make all laws and raise taxes, subject to "the advice, assent, and approbation of the Freemen of the said Country." In an emergency he could issue ordinances without the assembly. Yet his power was not absolute, for all laws were to be forwarded within five years for inspection by the Privy Council, which could disallow those found to be inconsistent with English law. Furthermore, all commerce was to be "according to the lawes made or to be made within our Kingdom of England" and Penn was obliged to admit any officers sent for their enforcement. In return the king promised to levy no taxes except with "the consent of the Proprietary, or chief governor, or assembly, or by act of Parliament in England."

As was evident from the terms of Penn's charter, colonial administration was beginning to change. Now proprietary grants were coming to be conceived less like feudal palatines and more like grants of power to operate a division within an empire ultimately controlled by the Crown. Also, this charter mentioned Parliament for the first time, reflecting its new role in the administration of the colonies following the passage of the Navigation Acts. Ironically, at this very moment Charles II was trying to reduce Parliament's influence at home.

These restrictions did not worry Penn unduly. No mention was made of religion beyond the right of 20 inhabitants to petition the bishop of London for a minister. Penn's own intention was that there should be no established church but that toleration would be the norm, resulting in a society where all Christians lived in harmony bound by mutual respect. Penn called this his "holy experiment," although the kind of holy experiment he sought was very different from the one envisaged earlier by John Winthrop. Penn, like all Quakers, believed that people were intrinsically good and needed only marginal direction. This view was the exact opposite of the Puritan concept of human depravity. Hence the kind of autocratic, repressive government which Winthrop regarded as necessary had no place in Penn's scheme of things. To him persecution, not dissent, was the real crime.

Like the Puritans, though, Penn's motives combined religious idealism with a desire to expand his own fortunes. This meant he had to attract investors and sell land to settlers, who would pay him modest quitrents. For investment capital, he turned to a group of wealthy Quakers, called the Free Society of Traders, who arranged for the purchase of various holdings of 10,000 acres each and also negotiated special privileges, including the choice of the best waterfront sites in the new city which Penn was planning. To attract settlers, Penn publicized his intention to offer them land on generous terms. In the spring of 1681, after appointing a council with himself as governor, Penn issued a document called "Concessions to the Province of Pennsylvania." Its terms were remarkably generous: 50 acres were to be granted to every male servant on completion of his service, and all lands were to be subject to only a small quitrent of one shilling per 100 acres. No limit was placed on the size of holdings, though a certain proportion had to be settled within three years. Strict instructions were also issued concerning disputes with the Native Americans which were to be arbitrated between six whites and six Indians, with everyone treated equally before the law.[13] Next Penn circulated a pamphlet in England, Wales, and parts of Holland and Germany, where the Society of Friends was also well established, describing the proposed settlement. Several English and Welsh groups, not all of them Quaker, immediately expressed interest, encouraged by Penn's offer that anyone participating in the purchase of the first 500,000 acres would receive a free lot in the new city. Some 600 people took advantage of this offer to become "First Purchasers."

As the first settlers began to arrive on the Delaware, a pleasing prospect awaited them. Penn had fortuitously obtained the best real estate on the east coast of America. The land along the river was extremely fertile, and a favorable site was quickly found on the banks of the Delaware and Schuylkill rivers for the principal town and port of Philadelphia, so called after the Greek word for brotherly love. The town was soon laid out in neat rectangular blocks as Penn desired, anticipating the later American gridiron style of urban planning. Houses were to be a certain distance apart to contain fires and to prevent the spread of disease. In the countryside, as well, Penn envisioned the orderly development of compact towns where settlers would work together to promote the common welfare.

A key part of Penn's strategy for establishing a stable settler colony was to negotiate peaceful relationships with the local Indians from the outset, agreeing to purchase the land needed for his settlement and promising that the Indians would be left undisturbed on their own lands in the future. The main Indians living in eastern Pennsylvania by the early 1680s were the Algonquian-speaking Lenapes (or Delawares). A decentralized group whose members been long engaged in fur trading with Dutch and Swedish merchants in the region, the Lenapes had by this time suffered population declines caused by exposure to European diseases, and were relatively weak. They had good reasons for pursuing an alliance with the English, who could provide trade goods and military assistance. Moreover, their experience with the tiny, dispersed settlements of the Dutch and the Swedes gave them no reason to think the influx of European settlers would eventually lead to their own dispossession.

Pennsylvania's early success in maintaining peaceful relations with the Indians was also partly the product of the colony's late establishment. Penn founded the colony after New York's Governor Andros had negotiated the Covenant Chain with the members of the Iroquois League. Thus the Iroquois were not only friendly to Pennsylvania's early settlers, they also helped to maintain control over less powerful groups living in the region. The Susquehannocks, for example, migrated into this area after being driven out of the Chesapeake by Bacon's forces. The Iroquois helped to ensure that the Susquehannocks' hostility towards the new settlers would remain muted.[14]

---

[13] The full text is printed in Kavenagh, *Documentary History*, Vol. 2, 1131–4. The right of servants to a headright of 50 acres was abandoned after a few years.

[14] The Lenapes' perspective on their famous treaty with William Penn is explored in Thomas Sugrue, "The Peopling and Depeopling of Early Pennysylvania: Indians and Colonists, 1680–1720," *Pennsylvania Magazine of History and Biography*, 116 (1992), 3–31.

Figure 15 *William Penn's Treaty with the Indians.* Detail after original painting by Benjamin West, 1771. Engraving by Robert Delaunay, Paris, circa 1772. William Penn and settlers are shown trading with Native Indians, with buildings under construction in the background. Library of Congress, Washington, DC.

Other factors, too, aided the establishment of Pennsylvania. One was the fact that Pennsylvania faced no immediate external threats, being protected by New York to the north, Maryland to the south, and the mountains to the west. Unlike earlier colonies, Pennsylvania had older, settled English colonies nearby with whom to engage in trade. Pennsylvania's fertile soil and relatively long growing season (at least compared to New England's) made it a good place for farmers to grow grain, which by the 1680s had a ready market in the Caribbean. And even the humbler Quakers were fired with a sense of mission to make the most of God's bounty. Like the Puritans, they were firm believers in the Protestant ethic.

The settlement around Philadelphia thus experienced rapid growth. Some 50 ships filled with settlers, organized by the Free Society of Traders, arrived between 1682 and 1683. Within a year crops were being harvested and the surplus shipped for export. When Penn himself arrived late in 1682 to take up the governorship, he was well pleased to see that the settlement already had some 4,000 inhabitants and contained 80 dwellings in Philadelphia alone. Among the early arrivals were several groups of Welsh and Irish Quakers, together with some African slaves whom Penn bought to work on his farm. Soon Penn announced that the duke of York had sold him the three counties of Delaware, Newcastle, Kent, and Sussex, which were then annexed to Pennsylvania subject to the new colony's laws and privileges.

Before his departure for Pennsylvania, Penn had drafted a frame of government and charter of liberties, asserting that government was a divine institution whose purpose was to "terrify evil doers" and "cherish those that do well." He agreed with virtually all seventeenth-century political thinkers that some institutional framework was necessary to maintain social order. His philosophy of government, however, expressed little of the pessimism about human nature so characteristic of other colonial founders. His philosophy, "Let men be good and the government cannot be bad," was to demonstrate that people of varying religious persuasions could live in peace and harmony. To that end, he decreed that power was to be vested in him as governor, together with the freemen of the province, meeting as a provincial council and general assembly, "by whom all laws shall be made, officers chosen and public affairs transacted." Freemanship was accorded to any male who owned 50 acres of partially cultivated land or who paid the local taxes. Some Quakers wanted to deny the vote to non-Quakers to maintain their control, but Penn insisted on a broad franchise, believing that so benign a regime would not be challenged, even by outsiders.

In many respects, Penn's document was remarkably liberal, in keeping with the egalitarian nature of the Quaker religion. At the same time, however, Penn believed (like most political thinkers of his time) that government ought to be left to "men of wisdom and virtue," though he was quick to deny that by this he meant wealth. The council was to comprise 72 persons (later reduced to 18) "of most note for their wisdom, virtue and ability," who were to serve on a rotating basis for three years, helping the governor to prepare all legislation. The assembly's role, in contrast, was to be restricted to accepting or rejecting bills, though its members could propose amendments. Penn's frame of government also included a list of privileges and liberties. Trial was to be by jury, fees were to be moderate, and punishment was to fit the crime. Servants were to be protected, while everyone who acknowledged "the one almighty and eternal God ... [would] in no ways be molested or prejudiced in their religious persuasion." This protection included exemption from tithes, as there was to be no established church.

The legislature initially played its expected role by passing a series of laws imbued with the Quaker spirit. Anyone settling a dispute by violence was to be sentenced to three months in the house of correction; 10 days was the punishment for riotous behavior or cruel sports. Provision was made for the destitute. There was, too, a heavy emphasis on honesty between the inhabitants, and meticulous attention was given to weights and measures. Finally, in December 1682 a bill was passed confirming religious tolerance. All freemen who declared "Jesus Christ to be the son of God" and "saviour of the world" could hold office and participate in the affairs of the province. As a legal code it was a model of reasonableness and humanity.

Yet the harmony was short-lived, for various factions began jockeying for greater control within the first decade after settlement began. The non-Quaker counties of

Delaware constituted one discordant factor, since they resented their inclusion in the new colony. Most of the inhabitants were Swedish or Dutch, while even those of English descent were Presbyterians or Anglicans. Also, the initial grant of special privileges to the Free Society of Traders now became an issue. Their claims to the choicest lands along the Delaware and best plots in Philadelphia rankled with the poorer Quakers, most of whom owned small farms. The result was a split in their ranks. The wealthy Friends led by Thomas Lloyd dominated the council, while the poorer inhabitants looked to the assembly for protection. Each group vied with the other and generally ignored the orders of Penn's lieutenant governor, especially after Penn returned to England in 1684 to fight the territorial claims of Maryland.

In truth Penn was less than brilliant as an administrator. Though genuinely concerned for his coreligionists, he was too full of his own importance to appreciate their point of view, believing instead that he deserved their gratitude and deference. Like many others, he failed to see that the pursuit of his own material advantage conflicted with his professed altruism. Before he died he was to be sadly disillusioned.

Communal divisions were soon compounded by religious schism, following the arrival in 1689 of George Keith from New Jersey. Keith basically believed that the Friends were losing their purity, but his proposed remedy was not a return to the simple ways of the movement in its early years but rather a purification of the Quaker religion through stricter discipline. Unfortunately such discipline threatened the religion's spontaneity as well as the principle of freedom of conscience. In the resulting split in the Quaker ranks, perhaps a quarter of the Society took Keith's position. His followers were drawn mainly from the poorer Quakers, many of them Scots like himself, and the dispute began to have political ramifications when Keith took issue with Lloyd and his wealthy supporters in Philadelphia's main meeting house.

The new colony nevertheless continued to take shape, aided by the influx of capital and willing hands. Philadelphia was well established and three counties – Bucks, Philadelphia, and Chester – had been founded. Already the population had reached 10,000, with more settlers on their way. In 1686 some Pietists from Frankfurt and Quakers from Kreveld, led by Francis Pastorius, purchased a tract of 25,000 acres and established a settlement which in 1691 became Germantown. Even this development was not free from controversy, however, for the Welsh settlers then argued that they should have been similarly privileged with a county of their own. Pennsylvania was already set to become a society of many ethnic groups and religions, just like the later United States.

8

James II and the Glorious Revolution

1683	*Quo warranto* proceedings are instituted against Massachusetts.
1685	James, duke of York becomes King James II. Articles of Misdemeanour are drawn up against Rhode Island and Connecticut. The Dominion of New England is created.
1686	Sir Edmund Andros is named governor-general of the new dominion. New York's assembly and Charter of Liberties are revoked by James II.
1687	The New England towns protest against arbitrary taxes.
1688	New York is included in the Dominion of New England. William III invades England and initiates the Glorious Revolution.
1689	(April) The Dominion of New England is overthrown in Boston. (June) Jacob Leisler takes control in New York. (July) The proprietary government in Maryland is overthrown. War breaks out with France.
1690	Schenectady is devastated by the French and their Indian allies.
1691	Jacob Leisler is executed in New York. A new charter is issued for Massachusetts.
1695	An act of Parliament overturns the verdicts against Leisler and Milborne.
1702	Nicholas Bayard is tried for treason.

Colonial America: A History to 1763, Fourth Edition. Richard Middleton and Anne Lombard.
© 2011 Richard Middleton and Anne Lombard. Published 2011 by Blackwell Publishing Ltd.

1   THE DOMINION OF NEW ENGLAND

C HARLES II DIED in February 1685. For most of his reign his administration had been neither wise nor consistent. Except for the Navigation Acts, which were the work of Parliament, his policy had lacked direction, at least until 1680, for his main concern was to avoid the mistakes which had led to his father's execution. Expediency was therefore his guiding principle, laziness his natural bent. He preferred to put off today what could be done tomorrow.

His successor, his brother James, duke of York, was a very different character, being a man of strong convictions. A staunch Catholic and a keen administrator, James II sought to centralize the management of his government and strengthen the power of the English Crown. It is important to note here that James was greatly influenced in this respect by Louis XIV, under whom France had replaced Spain as the most powerful state in Europe. Louis XIV's power stemmed not least from the bureaucratic abilities of his chief minister, Jean Colbert, who had centralized many branches of French government. Discordant groups, notably the aristocracy and Huguenots, as the French Protestants were known, had been brought to heel, while the army and navy had been placed on a professional footing. France was now the envy of Europe.

In 1685 England's status was still minor compared to the grandeur of France under Louis XIV. To James, there seemed to be two roads which the English state could now take. It could remain dominated by special interest groups concerned only with their own rights and privileges. Alternatively, it could become a modern, centralized monarchy which was powerful at home and abroad, an option seemingly justified by the political theory of divine right of kings. Propounded by Sir Robert Filmer and other royal apologists, this theory held that the English monarchs were descended from Adam and were divinely appointed. Hence all rights were merely privileges which the monarch could summarily take away. Monarchs received their powers from God and were answerable only to him.[1] James was committed to this theory, and no fear of exile or upsurge of militant republicanism ever made him consider moderating his beliefs.

Members of the Whig party in Parliament on the other hand opposed Filmer's theories, arguing instead that government originated with the consent of the people. While the Whigs had no quarrel with monarchy per se, they believed that constitutional monarchy was just as efficient and more conducive to prosperity than absolute rule. The Whigs also tended to be anti-Catholic, believing that a supposedly tyrannical Catholic Church was trying to impose both tyranny and popery on the English population. In 1680 Shaftesbury and the Whigs in Parliament attempted to have James excluded from the succession because he was a Catholic. Charles realized that to preserve the succession and the English Crown, Parliament must be tamed. Accordingly, Charles dissolved Parliament and began to remodel the borough charters by writ of *quo warranto*. This step was necessary because these charters determined the method by

---

[1]   Sir Robert Filmer, *Patriarcha, or, The Natural Power of Kings* (London, 1680).

Figure 16 Portrait of King James II, by Sir Godfrey Kneller, 1684. The National Portrait Gallery, London.

which each town chose its member of Parliament. By changing the rules governing the election of members, he hoped to ensure the return of a more friendly House of Commons. The first borough to suffer such proceedings was the City of London in 1681.[2]

Since many colonial institutions were based on similar charters, it was always likely that these centralizing processes would also be applied to them. The North American colonies by 1681 were a mosaic of small units, vulnerable to attack and difficult to administer. For 20 years Massachusetts had defiantly claimed that its charter placed it outside royal control while collector Randolph reported numerous breaches in the trade laws and loss of revenue to the king.

Then in 1682 Massachusetts was ordered to send envoys to London to discuss the revision of its charter. Among the powers sought by the Crown were the appointment of governors and the hearing of appeals. The general court rejected both as undermining the political and religious purposes of the colony. The magistrates still believed that it was better to defy the king than to sin against God. They also noted that those English corporations which had already surrendered their charters had gained nothing by doing so. The magistrates were encouraged to resist by the prominent Boston minister Increase Mather, who argued that God would deliver them, as he had in 1637 and 1664, if they remained true to the covenant. Thus although envoys were finally sent, they were given no instructions to negotiate.

The Crown's law officers accordingly commenced *quo warranto* proceedings against Massachusetts in June 1683. The list of infractions presented by Randolph was extremely damaging. Although Massachusetts sent its attorney general, he unfortunately did not contest the suit to indicate the province's disavowal of the action. The tortuous methods of the English legal system were extremely slow not least because the actual charter was still in America. Indeed, the Crown was reduced to seeking an alternative procedure, a warrant known as *scire facias*, to complete its case. Nevertheless, the inevitable verdict of the Court of King's Bench in October 1684 was that the charter was invalid.[3]

---

[2] A writ of *quo warranto* required a person or entity to show proof of his authority to act. The Crown demanded the documents granting Massachusetts its governing authority so that it could rescind them or show them to be inadequate.

[3] A writ of *scire facias* required the defendant to produce documents or records. In this case the Crown sought to force Massachusetts to bring its original charter to England, where it could be rescinded.

The dissolution of the Massachusetts charter opened the door for the administration of James II to radically reorganize England's other North American possessions beginning in 1685. The hope was to create a vice-regal model of government, under which the Crown would appoint a governor to serve as its representative over a large territory, uniformly enforcing policies formulated by the Crown's advisors rather than by local governments. Spain had long used such a vice-regal system to govern its colonies in New Spain and Peru. The Crown already controlled New Hampshire, while Plymouth had no charter other than that issued by the defunct Council of New England. It was therefore decided to combine these with Massachusetts and Maine into one colony called the Dominion of New England. Not yet satisfied, the bureaucrats turned their attention to Connecticut and Rhode Island. In July 1685, Randolph charged their governments with misusing judicial power, failing to administer the required oaths, and persecuting Anglicans. Proceedings were also to be undertaken against the Jerseys and New York, on the grounds that these struggling entities were prejudicial to the king's authority and the collection of his revenue.

If the members of the Massachusetts general court thought they could still maintain their independence, they were mistaken, for James II was a far more energetic absolutist than his brother Charles. His administration was determined to make its views prevail. James II had met his first Parliament in the spring of 1685 and secured a large revenue, a sign that the remodeling of the borough charters was working. His enemies were either in hiding or in sanctuary abroad and, unlike his predecessor, he had a professional army of 20,000 men and an efficient navy. Although the house of deputies in Massachusetts still talked of resistance, the magistrates knew that the end had come. To some extent the old leadership had lost confidence in the wake of the disasters of the past few years. In May 1686 the final meeting of the general court concluded with a short prayer amid tears.

Initially, James II appointed Joseph Dudley, a political moderate, along with the Puritans' long-time nemesis, Edward Randolph, to run the colony, assisted by a council made up of members of the Massachusetts merchant elite. No formal charter was issued to replace the old; the king's commission was considered sufficient authority. Power was to be vested in the governor and council, who could try cases, convene the militia, appoint all officers, and make other arrangements for the defense of the dominion. Liberty of conscience was to be allowed, especially to such people "as shall be conformable to the rites of the Church of England." No mention was made of an assembly or the passing of laws. For the time being the council would levy the existing taxes.

Despite this radical challenge to the old Puritan-led system of government, many distinguished Massachusetts inhabitants remained willing to serve on Dudley's council, including Wait Winthrop and Fitz-John Winthrop, grandsons of the colony's founder. Some historians have argued that these men recognized the need to compromise in a world of commercial and imperial expansion, being more forward-looking in their outlook than the old Puritan leadership, with its community and precapitalist values. Self-interest was also a factor, since Dudley obliged members of his council with generous land grants. It was not long before Randolph was criticizing the new order for its lack of commitment to the Anglican Church and failure to observe the navigation laws.

Within months, in June 1686, James II nominated Sir Edmund Andros as governor in chief.[4] Andros's commission specifically gave him and the council power to make all laws and raise taxes, without input from any local assembly. To ensure that the former were conformable to English practice, laws and taxes were to be sent for approval by the government in Whitehall within three months.

The imposition of the dominion was a bitter blow to all the colonies, and to none more so than Massachusetts. The general court was replaced by a nonelective council nominated by a royal governor. The Congregational Church was ousted from its special position. It seemed likely that Anglicanism would become the established religion, especially after Andros took over the Old South Meeting House and kept the regular congregation waiting while the Anglican minister celebrated morning service. These moves seemed especially threatening given widespread popular fears of a Roman Catholic conspiracy, to which New Englanders had always been particularly prone. It did not help matters when Andros introduced various new customs into public life. Massachusetts Puritans were horrified by a new requirement that litigants take an oath on the Bible before testifying in court, which they regarded as a violation of their covenant with God. They were even more appalled when authorities of the Andros government reintroduced the celebration of saints' days, considered a clear sign of popish idolatry. Puritans were especially fearful that Andros would require religious toleration of Catholics.

Taxes were another grievous matter. Although Andros adopted the assembly's 1680 book of rates, there was nothing to prevent him from raising these later when it suited him. In 1687 several towns, notably Ipswich in Essex County, protested that the taxes were illegal, not having received the consent of the inhabitants according to the fundamental right of Englishmen. Andros quickly arrested the leading protesters and crushed the opposition. Indeed, one of the remarkable aspects of the period was the speed with which the commonwealth collapsed. It seemed the Puritans' confidence in their claim to be a covenanted people had been profoundly shaken.

Other shocks lay in store. The courts of justice were streamlined; juries were to be appointed by the sheriffs rather than the local justices so as to better serve the purposes of the king. All lands purchased from the native inhabitants henceforth had to be validated by new deeds and were subject to quitrents. Such purchases had been widespread and, although most titles were confirmed, the expense and uncertainty involved left New Englanders deeply anxious, especially as certain holdings were challenged. This step suggested that all freehold titles would be terminated and quitrents imposed, thereby erasing the economic security which the settlers believed they had attained by immigrating to North America. The merchants, too, were shocked

---

[4] Historian Stephen Saunders Webb has argued that Andros's appointment was part of a plan to create a garrison or military style of government throughout the American colonies, in *The Governors-General: The English Army and the Definition of Empire, 1569–1681* (Chapel Hill, 1979). Others argue that Andros was selected for the much more mundane reason that he had already served James II in New York 10 years earlier, was familiar with America, and had a claim on James II's patronage. In any case, Andros had no orders to impose martial law. For this view, see Richard R. Johnson, "The Imperial Webb: The Thesis of Garrison Government in Early America Reconsidered," *William and Mary Quarterly*, 43 (1986), 408–30; and Ian Steele, "Governors or Generals? A Note on Martial Law and the Revolution of 1689," *William and Mary Quarterly*, 46 (1989), 304–14.

when the number of ports available for customs clearance was reduced to five. Equally disturbing was the decision that all infractions of the trade laws were to be determined in an admiralty court with no jury, only a presiding judge.

In March 1688 curbs were imposed on the towns to prevent a repetition of the events at Ipswich. In the future meetings were to be held only once a year for the election of officials and no selectman could serve more than two consecutive terms, making it difficult for local leaders to establish themselves.

Lastly, Andros's troops created a disturbing presence. Although he had arrived with only one company of redcoats and a frigate, the sight of these raised apprehensions about arbitrary rule, not least because Andros was given full power to declare martial law should an insurrection occur. Such fears were greatly increased by the general belief that James II's grand design was to impose popery on the people of America. Although no Catholics had yet arrived in New England, New York had an Irish Catholic governor, Thomas Dongan, and other Catholic officials. It was even feared that James II might ally with the French and their Indian allies to achieve his purpose.

An outbreak of violence on the frontiers of Maine in 1688 thus did nothing to allay the New Englanders' apprehensions. Andros antagonized the population by impressing 300 young Massachusetts men into the militia, to be commanded by English officers as they marched northwards to attack the Abenaki. Confronted with strange officers and unfamiliar ideas of discipline, the men revived concerns about a popish plot and threatened to desert. For his part, Andros inadvertently repeated the mistake of Virginia's ex-governor Berkeley 15 years earlier, by appearing too lenient in attempting to negotiate with rather than fight the Indians.

Although Andros had few friends even among the councillors appointed by Dudley, the inhabitants of New England were seemingly powerless to prevent events from taking their course. In December 1686 *quo warranto* proceedings were completed against Rhode Island. A year later it was the turn of Connecticut to join the dominion, after its inhabitants had indicated a preference for union with Massachusetts rather than New York. Their compliance meant that the legal surrender of their charter was never completed. In spring 1688 New York was included in the dominion, though it retained a deputy governor and council.

The situation looked hopeless, although the Puritans had sent Increase Mather to London to plead their cause. They prayed that God might move the king to look more favorably on his dissenting subjects in North America. After all, God moved in mysterious ways; perhaps a direct appeal might have some effect.

2 MASSACHUSETTS RECLAIMS CONTROL

Unknown to the troubled New Englanders, deliverance was actually at hand. James II's plans to create an absolute monarchy were rapidly alienating the English too. Nevertheless, he would probably have succeeded but for his simultaneous attempt to return England to Catholicism. It was one revolution too many.

Although James never published his plans, it is clear that he hoped to reverse the Reformation in the manner in which it had begun, by royal example and decree. The first steps in this scheme had been to suspend the Test and Corporation Acts in 1687 and thus permit Catholics to serve in the army and hold public office. At the same time pressure was put on members of the nobility to convert to Rome. In so hierarchical a society the nobles were likely to be followed by their followers and dependants, thus beginning the great work of returning England to Catholicism.

It was a monumental miscalculation on the king's part. There were enough Tories to help James II curb Parliament, but they were deeply upset by his open encouragement of Catholicism and lack of support for the established Anglican Church. It was by no means simply a question of religion; the Reformation had seen a change in the ownership of land following the dissolution of the monasteries and reorganization of the church. These titles were implicitly threatened should the religious settlement be undone.

Until 1688 the nation was sustained by the knowledge that James II was old and apparently infertile, and that his daughter Mary, the heir, was a Protestant. In spring 1688, however, James's second wife, Mary of Modena, gave birth to a son, raising the prospect of a Catholic succession and the continuation of James II's policies in both church and state. This was too much. The Whigs were already alienated by the persecution of their leaders following the Exclusion crisis. Now even prominent Tories began to look for an alternative. One beckoned: William of Orange, Stadholder of Holland and husband of James's daughter, Mary. William had not only married a princess in the line of succession to the throne, he was also known throughout Europe as a symbol of Protestant resistance against Catholicism. In June 1688, seven prominent Whigs and Tories wrote to William to come and rescue the people of England.

William was more than happy to oblige. Holland was again threatened by Louis XIV, and the possibility of enlisting England in the struggle against France was reason enough to forge an alliance. In addition, William did have claims to the English throne, both through his own family and that of his wife, should the allegations that James II's son was illegitimate prove true. In the fall of 1688 William swiftly assembled an army and fleet, landing in the West Country at Torbay. Everywhere he was greeted as a savior, while James II's army melted away or joined the invader. By the middle of November the king found it expedient to flee to France, first throwing the Great Seal into the Thames.

Rumors of William's landing began to reach America in early spring 1689. They had been preceded by a warning from James II himself about the imminent danger of a Dutch invasion. Hence some discussion had already taken place in Massachusetts among the former elite as to whether they ought to take control should the news prove true. It was not until April 1689 that William's success was confirmed and the New Englanders realized that the English had secured what they still sought: the right to an assembly, the supremacy of the laws, protection from Catholicism, and protection against external foes.

During these critical weeks Andros was handicapped by lack of orders from London, for which Mather was to blame. The minister had persuaded William that Andros ought not to be entrusted with his command, even though non-Catholic officials were being confirmed in their posts. In this vacuum rumors abounded, including one that Andros was about to join the French and their Indian allies in an attack on the English! In this situation it needed only a trivial incident to bring Massachusetts and the other New England provinces to arms. When some militia seized the captain of the *Rose* man-of-war near Boston harbor on the morning of April 18, the city's whole population spontaneously came out onto the streets and went to the town house, where Randolph was seized and put in jail. Andros himself took refuge in Fort Hill, where he was surrounded and eventually persuaded to surrender without bloodshed. Most of his troops were in New Hampshire, and the rest were mutinous for want of pay.

In this crisis the old Puritan leadership came forward, led by Increase Mather's son, Cotton, and Simon Bradstreet, the last of the old governors. They quickly formed a "Council for the Safety and Conservation of the Peace," similar to the former court of assistants, with Bradstreet as president. Though many wanted to resume the old charter immediately by holding elections for the house of deputies, others realized that such action would be illegal because the old frame of government was invalid. In the end it was agreed to convene an interim general court pending further directions from England. The council issued a public declaration supporting the new King William III and Queen Mary II and sent a denunciation of Andros, along with a plea that the old charter be restored, to be handled by Mather in London.

Elsewhere in New England events were similarly bloodless. In Rhode Island Dudley was seized while acting as a circuit court judge and sent to Boston. An impromptu assembly then acknowledged the new regime in England and reactivated the charter until more specific instructions arrived. Connecticut, too, sent early congratulations to William and Mary and a plea that its charter be reconfirmed, as it had technically never been surrendered. Later that May an unofficial meeting of the general court voted to "reestablish the government as it was before ... until there shall be a legal establishment."

The action of the New Englanders, especially in Massachusetts, was a calculated risk. There was no guarantee that William III would remain on the throne or that he would be sympathetic to the pleas now being put forward. He certainly had not come to dismantle the powers of the Crown; indeed he was surrounded by many of the men who had assisted James II in building them up. The liberties that William had been invited to protect were somewhat different from those to which the colonists aspired; their rebellions were unwelcome and even dangerous.

Mather nevertheless had some advantages as he walked the corridors of power in London. Massachusetts had promptly proclaimed William and Mary king and queen, and the coup had been bloodless. Since the dominion itself was no more, it would have to be replaced by something. Moreover, William was immersed in other, more urgent matters. By 1690 James had invaded Ireland, and William's presence was also required in Flanders to oppose the French. It would obviously be advantageous if the North American colonies could be pacified quickly. With considerable skill, Mather lobbied both the Whig and Tory factions to win their cooperation.

A compromise was arranged in October 1691 with the issue of a new charter, for there could be no going back to the original 1629 version. The Massachusetts government would now be subject to considerable oversight by the Crown. In the future there would be a royal governor, with the right to veto all legislation, which was also to be submitted to England for approval. Liberty of conscience was to be granted, except for Catholics. And the right to vote would now be based on property-holding instead of church membership.

Massachusetts leaders had meanwhile won several important concessions. The lower house regained control over taxation as well as the right to approve all spending by the governor. The lower house also gained the right to select the council, provided that its candidates were acceptable to the governor. The rights of the towns were to be restored. Land titles, too, were confirmed in freehold and no quitrents levied. And although the Congregational Church was no longer technically established, liberty of conscience would in practice amount to indulging the governor and his entourage. Outside Boston the towns could do as they pleased in levying tithes to support their churches, as long as they did not prevent other Protestants from holding services. And finally, Massachusetts was not only to keep Maine but also to incorporate Plymouth.

New Hampshire would also become a royal colony with a governor, nominated council, and elected assembly, just as before the Dominion. In fact, the settlement created by the Glorious Revolution in both Massachusetts and New Hampshire established a pattern of colonial government that would soon become the norm in most of English North America. In the future, colonies would be more integrated into the empire, with royal governors to assert the interests of the Crown. Meanwhile the settlers would continue to be represented by a locally elected assembly, which often had considerable control over taxation and spending, while the local elite would exercise significant influence over the governor as members of his council.

In New England, the only exceptions to this pattern of increased royal control were Rhode Island and Connecticut. Since neither province had Massachusetts' reputation for defying the English government, their charters were restored intact, and they were allowed to retain the autonomy they had enjoyed since their founding in the early seventeenth century.

3 NEW YORK: LEISLER'S REBELLION

While New England's settlers presented a generally unified opposition to the Andros regime, the population of New York was to go in a different direction. New York society in the seventeenth century was divided and unstable. This made it difficult to govern, but would also prove an obstacle to political action against any government which the people opposed.

The roots of New York's instability were complex. One was a structural problem: the province did not have a tradition of government by elective assembly. The original Dutch population had little interest in creating an assembly; as long as their government guaranteed religious toleration, they felt their liberties were secure. However, the English settlers in the colony were deeply aggrieved by their lack of representation. Though the towns on Long Island in 1683 had seemingly won their case for an assembly and secured a Charter of Liberties to guarantee it, James II had in 1686 revoked the assembly and disavowed the Charter.

Another challenge for New York was its ethnic diversity: English, Scots, Dutch, Germans, French Huguenots, and Africans were all present in substantial numbers. Despite their diverse origins the earliest settlers had mostly become assimilated to Dutch customs, but after 1664 this process of assimilation slowed. The various populations formed distinct ethnic communities, organized around their distinct languages and religions. Among the Dutch, who formed the largest share of the population, only a few wealthy families showed any enthusiasm for learning the English language or adopting English religions or customs. In addition there were geographic divisions. Long Island was separate from Manhattan and the Hudson Valley. Most important, however, was the rivalry between New York and Albany, especially over the control of the flour and fur trades. New York's disparate groups were united only by their hatred of Catholicism.

Governing New York was a challenge not only because of its disunity, but also because it was difficult to defend. New York was particularly exposed to attacks and invasion from the north via Lake Champlain and the Mohawk River by Algonquian allies of the French. Though for some years New York had been protected by the members of the Iroquois League, it was clear by the end of the 1680s that the French and their allies were regaining their ability to destabilize the region. In 1684 the Iroquois had humiliated a French invasion force under Governor Barre, after it had been devastated by sickness. The French had responded by reinforcing their colony under Governor Denonville, and encouraging their allies to become linked into a military alliance. The members of this alliance then launched a devastating attack on the Senecas (of the Iroquois Five Nations) in 1687. The inhabitants of New York were terrified that the French would use the Jesuits to stir up the native inhabitants even more, giving rise to the prospect of a quasi-religious war in which the divided New Yorkers would be pitted against a united foe using the Hudson River as an invasion route.

James II, though aware of these problems, continued to govern by imposing the same kinds of measures used in New England. The governor he had appointed in 1681, Thomas Dongan, was an Irish Catholic. After revoking the Charter of Liberties in 1686, James ordered Governor Dongan to raise additional revenue to shore up New York's defenses. Dongan's means, however, soon stirred up discontent, for by confirming New York as the sole port of entry in 1687, he inevitably aroused further protests from merchants in competing ports. Next, Dongan tried to levy quitrents on all land grants issued since the time of Andros, forcing most communities to seek new patents and therefore causing much unease, for those who failed to do so were prosecuted in a new court of exchequer. Lastly, he affirmed that he would continue the taxes voted by the ill-fated assembly, even though these had been part of the bargain for its right to meet. Further protest predictably ensued, this time from Staten Island and the town of Jamaica. A final blow, for the Dutch community at least, was the announcement in 1688 that New York was to be annexed to the Dominion of New England. A lieutenant governor and subcouncil would run New York separately, but this provision offered little consolation, since the officials would be answerable to Andros in Boston.

To bring the situation under control James chose Colonel Francis Nicholson as the colony's new lieutenant governor in 1688. Nicholson had the advantage of not being a Catholic, unlike Dongan, but the presence of several Catholics on his council, including the customs collector, Matthew Ploughman, made Nicholson suspect. When rumors began to arrive of James's abdication, Nicholson initially tried to conceal the news. Like Andros in New England, he faced a cruel dilemma. To announce William's invasion too soon would be tantamount to treason, while to do nothing would only increase tension among the population. All kinds of rumors were circulating, the most insidious being that Andros was plotting to help the French destroy the Five Nations. To calm popular fears, Nicholson agreed at the end of April 1689 to garrison the main fort with units of the militia.

Once news of the rising in Boston became widespread, however, an explosion was almost unavoidable. Resistance began, not surprisingly, among the inhabitants of Suffolk County on eastern Long Island who followed Boston's example early in May by ousting their royal officials. The predominantly Dutch population of Queens and Westchester counties then followed suit. They were especially eager for a declaration supporting William, since his arrival in England might presage a return to Dutch rule. In the middle of May many of them marched to Jamaica, not far from New York City. About the same time some of the merchants refused to pay the customs to a Catholic collector. In response Nicholson declared that all such levies would be devoted solely to defending the city from a possible invasion by France.

The final provocation came on May 30 when Nicholson, in an altercation concerning the placing of a sentry in Fort James, told a militia officer that he would rather burn New York than put up with any more insubordination. The next day the city militia repudiated the authority of its commander, Nicholas Bayard, and took over the fort, though without bloodshed.

Prominent among those participating in these events was Jacob Leisler, one of the militia captains, who had originally come to New York in 1660 as a soldier of the Dutch West India Company. He had subsequently prospered as a merchant and married a rich widow, ranking among the colony's seven richest men by 1676. Leisler, however, was not part of the anglicizing Dutch elite that had governed the colony, and unlike them was unwilling to compromise with Catholic officeholders. Leisler was the son of a Huguenot exile and deeply sympathized with the Huguenots who had been forced to flee from Louis XIV's France. He hated Catholics for their persecution of Protestants. Although no real violence had yet occurred, the council deemed it prudent for Nicholson to leave immediately for England to seek assistance. Leisler and the other militia captains quickly filled the vacuum by forming a committee of safety similar to that in Massachusetts, on which there were two representatives from each of New York's southern counties, as well as one from Ulster County. The committee proclaimed William and Mary king and queen on June 3, 1689.

As in Massachusetts, events had so far gone relatively smoothly, with no bloodshed or apparent support for the ousted council. Here the similarities ended. Nicholson had powerful connections to plead his cause in England. Leisler subsequently sent envoys to London, but they had no standing or experience. Ploughman, the customs collector, was dismissed and the revenues collected on the grounds that they had been authorized by the last assembly under the Charter of Liberties. This action caused dissension among some of the English settlers, who saw it as a violation of their right to elect a new assembly for the raising of taxes.

In December 1689 a letter from William III arrived addressed to Nicholson or "such as for the time being do take care for the preservation of their Majesties' Peace." Leisler interpreted this message as giving him the authority to do as he pleased, even though it had been written before Nicholson got to England. He replaced the aldermen of the city and imprisoned his most implacable opponents, Nicholas Bayard and William Nichols. The committee of safety was then superseded by a mostly Dutch council with Leisler as lieutenant governor.

Leisler's lack of support among the non-Dutch groups was amply demonstrated in August 1689 when he tried to summon a representative meeting of the counties. No deputies arrived from Suffolk or Ulster counties. Even Albany, which did have a heavy concentration of Dutch people, sent none, its inhabitants being still fearful that the New Yorkers had designs on the fur trade.

Another element in the struggle now taking place was class conflict. The wealthy Anglo-Dutch families resented the intrusion of mere traders like Leisler and Milborne into the affairs of the colony. As a memorial of Nicholas Bayard later emphasized, the leaders of the uprising were "all men of mean birth, sordid Education, and desperate Fortunes," who sought to consolidate their power "by inflaming the people." In contrast, they were opposed by "all the men of best repute for Religion, Estates and Integrity of the Dutch nation." Leisler's support was thus confined to the largely Dutch lesser tradesmen and farmers in the vicinity of New York, a limitation which proved a crucial handicap.[5]

Leisler did try to widen his support, especially in Ulster and Albany counties, dispatching a force to protect the exposed northern frontier. Unfortunately, this expedition arrived too late to save Schenectady, where some 60 inhabitants were killed on the night of February 9, 1690, by a combined French and Algonquian force. Leisler was blamed because he had not secured the cooperation of Albany's principal residents, Philip Schuyler and Robert Livingston, representatives of the Anglo-Dutch elite in the colony's northern counties.

In spring 1690 Leisler decided that the best means of protecting the northern frontier was to join Massachusetts and Connecticut in an invasion of Canada. The New Englanders were to attack by sea while the New Yorkers advanced overland via Lake Champlain. Reluctantly the burghers of Albany opened their gates after Livingston had retired to Connecticut. In the event both attacks proved abortive, whereupon Leisler tried to imprison the commander of the land force, Fitz-John Winthrop, a member of the Connecticut Provincial Council, thus antagonizing the leaders of that province.

Leisler made a second effort to widen his support by calling an assembly in April 1690, partly to defuse an earlier clash with the English inhabitants of Queens County, who had protested against the high taxes and oppression of the Leislerians. Also on the agenda was a bill to terminate New York City's flour-milling monopoly, which had so

---

[5] Historians have inevitably differed in their reasons for the rebellion. Thomas Archdeacon, *New York City, 1664–1710: Conquest and Change* (Ithaca, 1976), stresses the threat posed to the Dutch community by the imposition of English culture. Robert C. Ritchie, *The Duke's Province: A Study of New York Politics and Society, 1664–1691* (Chapel Hill, 1977), emphasizes the frustration of the population in general and fears of a Catholic plot in particular. He asserts that the leadership was mainly middle-class. The view that the rebellion was a class struggle between rich and poor was argued most strongly by Jerome R. Reich in *Leisler's Rebellion: A Study of Democracy in New York, 1664–1720* (Chicago, 1953). The anti-Catholic dimension of Leisler's motives is explored in John M. Murrin, "The Menacing Shadow of Louis XIV and the Rage of Jacob Leisler: The Constitutional Ordeal of Seventeenth-Century New York," in Stephen L. Schechter and Richard B. Bernstein, eds, *New York and the Union: Contributions to the American Constitutional Experience* (Albany, 1990), 29–71.

angered Albany. Not surprisingly, this proposal in turn further alienated the powerful Anglo-Dutch New York merchant families, who were already upset over Leisler's arbitrary proceedings.

Meanwhile England's response continued to be slow, for New York was no more a priority for William III than Massachusetts. Not until December 1689 was Colonel Henry Sloughter appointed governor of the province, Nicholson being sent to Virginia instead. Sloughter had other military duties and did not leave until the end of 1690, accompanied by Major Richard Ingoldsby and several hundred troops. Nothing in Sloughter's commission required him to treat Leisler harshly. New York was to be on the same footing as Virginia, with a governor and council appointed by the Crown and an assembly chosen by the freeholders "according to the usage of our other plantations in America." The commission enjoined all civil and military personnel to be "obedient, aiding and assisting" unto Sloughter, but said nothing to suggest that Leisler be treated as a traitor.

Unfortunately Sloughter's vessel was separated in a storm, so that Ingoldsby and the troops arrived before him in February 1691. Leisler offered them accommodation but refused Ingoldsby's demand to be quartered in the fort, uncertain that the soldiers under his command really represented William, as claimed. Three times Ingoldsby issued his demand and three times Leisler refused. The confrontation proved fatal, resulting in some sporadic firing and several deaths which allowed Leisler to be branded as a traitor. Even when Sloughter finally appeared six weeks later, Leisler still delayed handing over the fort, attempting to conduct negotiations through emissaries. This behavior outraged Sloughter and convinced him that Leisler was a rebel who should stand trial for his crimes. Leisler, along with his chief lieutenant, Jacob Milborne, were accused of treason, tried, convicted, and hanged, much to the delight of the oligarchy.

The rebellion had been a divisive affair, reflecting tensions among the province's diverse political and religious groups. It bore some similarity to Bacon's Rebellion. Like Bacon, Leisler was supported mainly by the poorer sections of the population who opposed the ascension to power of an aristocratic elite. However Leisler seems to have overestimated the extent of his political support. Unwilling to compromise his anti-Catholic principles, he assumed without justification that a Dutch king would be generous to his own compatriots. In addition, ranged against him were the great Anglo-Dutch families of New York, who were able to plead their cause more effectively in England. They particularly emphasized Leisler's lack of gentlemanly accomplishments, especially his inability to speak or write proper English, which reinforced the impression that he and his followers were a dangerous rabble.

Like the rebellion in Massachusetts, Leisler's Rebellion failed to accomplish its goals but forced a political compromise. The rebellion ended the Dominion of New England and ensured that New York could no longer be denied an assembly. From 1691 the colony's government conformed to the standard pattern of royal governor, appointed council, and elected assembly. Nevertheless, New York lacked the tradition of government by elective assembly, and its colonial leaders remained unable to effectively counter the power of royal governors, as their counterparts did in other colonies. Moreover, the rebellion and its aftermath had permanently embittered relationships between the Anglo-Dutch elite and the Leislerians. As a result, governors of New York for many years after 1691 were able to manipulate political divisions within the assembly to thereby consolidate their own power and strengthen royal influence over the colony's political affairs.

4 MARYLAND

The last colony to experience a serious uprising during the Glorious Revolution was Maryland. Just as in Massachusetts and New York, the seeds of the disturbance were to be found in the previous decades. And just as in those colonies, anti-Catholic fervor was a central factor – indeed it played an even larger role in the uprising in Maryland.

By the 1680s, Protestants comprised four-fifths of Maryland's population but had few places on the council, a state of affairs which was especially disturbing since the governor and council made all land awards and inevitably favored Catholics. The Protestants also felt that the Act Concerning Religion discriminated against them. Although no church was officially established, a number of generous grants were made to Catholic chapels and their priests, while Protestant ministers, in contrast, had difficulty supporting themselves. A further point of conflict was the distribution of patronage. Since most offices went to Catholics, and in particular to relatives of the proprietor, ambitious Protestant newcomers had no chance of advancing themselves. The one institution in which rising planters could express themselves was the assembly.

Adding to popular discontent in the years following the Restoration were depressed tobacco prices, as already noted in regard to Virginia. Despite the poor economic situation, the proprietor, Cecilius Calvert, the second Lord Baltimore, still expected his duty on every hogshead of tobacco exported to England. Nor did he make any concessions after the 1673 Navigation Act imposed additional burdens on the colony's trade.

The first serious confrontation between the proprietor and the lower house occurred in 1669, after a Protestant minister had urged the deputies to model themselves on the House of Commons. In response, the assembly drew up a document listing its "Grievances," complaining that the proprietor disallowed acts of the assembly, levied taxes without consent, acted arbitrarily, and demanded exorbitant fees. The response of the proprietor was to charge the assembly with mutiny and sedition, and restrict the franchise to freeholders rather than allowing all free males to vote. Too many discontented persons seemed to be using the elections to disturb the peace, for by now Maryland, like Virginia, contained a large number of discontented servants and tenant farmers. Voters now had to have landed property worth £50 or a personal estate worth £40. Baltimore also reduced the number of representatives from each county, most likely to copy the Virginia House of Burgesses.

Like Virginia, the colony had experienced conflicts during Bacon's Rebellion in 1676. The issues were partly economic and political. Sixty armed men gathered in August 1676 in Calvert County to protest the high poll tax of 300 pounds of tobacco. Fortunately for Charles Calvert, the third Lord Baltimore, few others from the population of 15,000 joined them; the rebels were easily hunted down and the two ringleaders, William Davis and John Pate, were executed. For the settler population, political resentment often merged with religious tensions. During 1676 rumors spread of a conspiracy ostensibly involving Lord Baltimore, Virginia's Governor Berkeley, the Susquehannock Indians and a group of Catholic priests to take over England. Once again, anti-Indian and anti-Catholic hostility merged to fuel paranoid fears.

When news arrived in 1680 that Whig leaders in Parliament were attempting to exclude James, duke of York from the succession, rumors flew that the Catholic proprietary government in Maryland too would fall. Baltimore responded by having two of his leading opponents, Josiah Fendall, the former governor, and John Coode, a militia officer, arrested on charges of mutiny and sedition. In the end Coode was acquitted, though Fendall was fined and banished, having offended once too often. The incident prompted the Lords of Trade to recommend that Baltimore appoint more Protestant officials, but to no avail.

These events coincided with another slump in tobacco prices, causing plant-cutting riots in Virginia. Baltimore rightly feared these would spread to Maryland but refused to make any concessions when the assembly met in 1682. The representatives began by insisting on their rights as Englishmen, including the right to conduct their affairs as the House of Commons did. Baltimore replied by reaffirming his position as absolute proprietor, arguing that the colonists could enjoy only what he was graciously pleased to give them, for their status was that of inhabitants in a conquered territory. To demonstrate his authority, the following year he unilaterally abolished the headright system on the ground that it had been abused.

Baltimore was soon to face not only political dissension at home but new challenges from the king's ministry in England. By 1684 he had to deal with a border dispute with Pennsylvania and was then accused of defrauding the royal customs. The situation was made worse when Baltimore's nephew, the acting governor, George Talbot, killed the chief revenue collector, Christopher Rousby. The incident gave James II, who was now king, every justification to begin *quo warranto* proceedings.

Yet despite these setbacks, Baltimore continued to act as though his authority was unquestioned. His last choice of governor was William Joseph, an Irish Catholic who began by addressing the assembly on the doctrine of divine right: "The Power by which we are assembled here is undoubtedly derived from God to the King and from the King to his Excellency the Lord Proprietary." A new oath of fidelity incorporating this doctrine was required. Worse, Joseph brought an order from the Crown that in the future only high-quality cask tobacco was to be exported, to exclude the inferior bulk product. This measure threatened the smaller producers with ruin, especially when Joseph also served notice that in the future the proprietor expected all dues to be paid in specie, not tobacco, since the depressed market price was diminishing his income.

At this point news arrived of James II's warning about an invasion from Holland. The council responded by ordering all public arms to be brought in for inspection by the local gunsmiths, ostensibly to be put in order, but in reality to be distributed among the proprietor's own supporters. To the majority this appeared simply to be a device to disarm them as the prelude to a combined Catholic and Indian attack. During March 1689 wild rumors circulated of an impending assault by the Senecas, causing a panic among the militia of Calvert County.

Because conditions in Maryland were so volatile, the proprietary government decided in April 1689 not to call an assembly. By now news had arrived that Virginia and the provinces to the north had declared for William and Mary. The response of Coode and others was to organize "an Association in arms for the defense of the Protestant Religion." Still Baltimore did nothing to declare William and Mary king and queen. When no action had been taken by mid-July, Coode and his association marched on St. Mary's.

Little resistance was offered and no bloodshed. Some attempt was made to rally the proprietary forces at Baltimore's mansion on the Patuxent River, but to little effect. An assembly was summoned and a declaration issued which affirmed Maryland's commitment to William and Mary, as well as expressing the belief that the colonists' cause was the same as England's: to stop "Slavery and Popery." Once the assembly met, Coode wisely surrendered the "supreme power" which he had momentarily exercised. A committee was appointed to investigate the Indian–Catholic conspiracy, after which the assembly was dissolved pending approval from England, leaving an interim council under Coode to protect what had been won.

Later in 1690 a further meeting was held to draw up charges against Baltimore, which Coode and another deputy then took to London. The charges were a compilation of all the previous grievances: the monopoly that Catholics enjoyed in the council, the support enjoyed by their religious establishments, the disallowance of the assembly's acts, the excessive fees demanded by the proprietary officials, the conspiracy with the French and Indians, and the failure to declare for William III and Mary II.

Coode's reception in London was generally favorable, since the charges against Baltimore confirmed the current prejudice against proprietary government. The decision was made in August 1691 to strip Baltimore of his governmental rights, leaving him only his property interests. In future there was to be a royal governor with similar powers and instructions as in New York. Thus the principal objectives of the Maryland majority had been obtained: proprietary government had been overthrown, the Protestant religion saved, and the place of the assembly assured.

5 AFTERMATH

Elsewhere in America the changes of 1689 were relatively peaceful. Pennsylvania and the Carolinas were too recently settled and remote for there to be much reaction.[6] More surprising was the lack of violence in Virginia. One explanation may be that the colony remained cowed in the aftermath of Bacon's Rebellion. The governor, Lord Effingham, a strong supporter of James II, was in England when William invaded and the acting governor, Nicholas Spencer, sensibly proclaimed the new order towards the end of April 1689. Some unrest occurred in the northern counties of Stafford and Rappahannock, but it was due mainly to fears of an attack by Indians rather than a rejection of the authorities in Jamestown.

The disturbances in New England, New York, and Maryland have certain similarities. All were inspired by a fear of Catholicism and the dread of an Indian attack; all occurred in frontier societies which felt vulnerable to such attack; and everywhere was heard the demand for the rights of Englishmen, even in Massachusetts, where the charter was equated with that end.[7]

---

[6] The governor of North Carolina had to flee, but for reasons unconnected with events elsewhere. See Chapter 9, section 4.

[7] Traditional accounts of 1689 have stressed the participants' American aims. That the colonists were seeking the rights of Englishmen is the theme of David S. Lovejoy, *The Glorious Revolution in America* (New York, 1972).

The similarities are significant, for the three rebellions mark the beginning of a new political language or rhetoric which would provide a unifying vision in times of political crisis. One aspect of this rhetoric was the settlers' justification of their right as Englishmen to resist a tyrannical monarch. The invoked their rights as Englishmen, citing the English Bill of Rights in their support. The language of English rights would become increasingly important in colonial political life during the eighteenth century. An equally (or more) important aspect of this rhetoric, as several historians have recently argued, was its consistent invocation of Protestantism. In the past each of these colonies, except in New England, had seen themselves as acting in isolation from others. The Glorious Revolution was a different matter. This time the participants, whether they were Dutch or German or English, each imagined their rebellions as part of a larger struggle to defend Protestantism against popery. In other words, they articulated their grievances in terms of a shared religious vision. This shared vision had the potential for the first time to unify the diverse settler populations in the English colonies across ethnic lines.[8]

As the colonists rejoiced in the overthrow of the Catholic James II and his replacement by the Protestant William II, they may have failed to appreciate that the events which had occurred represented less a declaration of individual rights than an expression of parliamentary authority. One form of absolute sovereignty, divine kingship, had been replaced by a new one, that of the king in Parliament, which institution was eventually to display as exalted an opinion of its authority as any Stuart monarch.

All these developments lay in the future. For the moment, the overthrow of James II and the granting of new charters or governments were sufficient to satisfy colonial aspirations. Even Cotton Mather declared, "It is no little Blessing of God that we are part of the English nation."

The Revolution of 1689 was a crucial turning point in the political and constitutional life of the English North American colonies. After the Restoration but prior to 1689, it seemed they were subject to the whim of Stuart monarchs who believed themselves above the ordinary law, unlike their subjects, who must meekly submit. After 1689 this situation changed significantly. Just as William and Mary had to abide by the laws of England, so their agents in America increasingly had to observe a similar code of conduct. In 1700 Parliament passed an act permitting the prosecution of governors who "oppressed their provinces." In 1703 the Privy Council ordered that, to prevent corruption, officials must not accept presents from their assemblies. More extensive instructions were formulated for them to follow; for example, all expenditure was to be monitored and the details sent to the Treasury.

[8] For recent scholarship emphasizing the shared anti-Catholic dimensions of the revolutions, not only in the colonies but also in England and Wales, see Brendan McConville, *The King's Three Faces: The Rise and Fall of Royal America, 1688–1776* (Chapel Hill, 2006); Owen Stanwood, "The Protestant Moment: Antipopery, the Revolution of 1688–1689, and the Making of an Anglo-American Empire," *Journal of British Studies*, 46 (2007), 481–508; and Carla Gardina Pestana, *Protestant Empire: Religion and the Making of the British Atlantic World* (Philadelphia, 2009).

DOCUMENT 13

The Bill of Rights, 1689, *The Statutes at Large*, 1 William and Mary, Session 2, Chapter 2

Unlike the 1683 New York Charter of Liberties or later American Bill of Rights, the English version was concerned mainly with the rights of Parliament rather than those of the individual. Only articles 5, 7, 10, 11, and 12 are aimed at protecting the ordinary person. Question to consider: *Why do you think the right to bear arms (item 7) is limited to "subjects which are Protestants"?*

1 That the pretended power of suspending of laws or the execution of laws by regal authority without consent of Parliament is illegal.
2 That the pretended power of dispensing with laws or the execution of laws by regal authority, as it has been assumed and exercised of late, is illegal.
3 That the commission for erecting the late Court for Ecclesiastical Causes, and all other commissions and courts of like nature [i.e., prerogative courts], are illegal and pernicious.
4 That levying money for or to the use of the Crown by pretence of prerogative without grant of Parliament, for longer time or in other manner than the same is or shall be granted, is illegal.
5 That it is the right of the subjects to petition the King, and all commitments and prosecutions for such petitioning are illegal.
6 That the raising or keeping a standing army within the kingdom in time of peace, unless it be with consent of Parliament, is against the law.
7 That the subjects which are Protestants may have arms for their defense suitable to their conditions and as allowed by law.
8 That the election of members of Parliament ought to be free [from interference by the Crown].
9 That the freedom of speech and debates or proceedings in Parliament ought not to be impeached or questioned in any court or place out of Parliament.
10 That excessive bail ought not to be required, nor excessive fines imposed, nor cruel and unusual punishments inflicted.
11 That jurors ought to be duly empanelled and returned, and jurors which pass upon men in trials for high treason ought to be freeholders.
12 That all grants and promises of fines and forfeitures of particular persons before conviction are illegal and void.
13 And that for redress of all grievances and for the amending, strengthening, and preserving of the laws, Parliaments ought to be held frequently.

Of course the scions of noble families still came to America to serve as royal governors so they could make money, but they could do so only in well-regulated ways. Those who stepped beyond the line were punished, as Lord Cornbury shortly discovered while governor of New York (see Chapter 18, section 3). Above all, the Glorious Revolution guaranteed the sanctity of property. In this respect the colonists benefited as much as their English compatriots. A new era of constitutionalism had arrived, in which the provincial assemblies were given a key role. Whatever the ultimate disagreements about colonial rights, the events of 1689 and the regranting of the charters gave the colonists lawful protection against the worst abuses of arbitrary government. For the colonists, that was a great step forward.

9

The Eras of William and Mary, and Queen Anne

1689	The League of Augsburg is formed; war begins in Europe.
1690	Sir William Phips attempts to invade Canada.
1692	The French and Abenaki Indians attack villages in Maine. Witchcraft trials take place in Salem.
1696	The Board of Trade is established.
1697	The Peace of Ryswick is signed.
1699	Captain Kidd is arrested in Boston.
1701	The Iroquois conclude a treaty of neutrality with the French. William Penn issues his last frame of government. Delaware is granted a separate charter.
1702	East and West New Jersey become a royal province. War in Europe is renewed. South Carolina and Yamasee Indians attack St. Augustine.
1704	The French and Abenaki Indians attack Deerfield.
1707	Colonel Benjamin Church's assault on Port Royal fails.
1710	Francis Nicholson captures Port Royal.
1711	The British fail to take Québec.
1711–12	The Tuscarora War takes place in North Carolina.
1713	The Treaty of Utrecht is signed.
1715	The Yamasee War takes place in South Carolina.
1718	William Teach (Blackbeard) is killed by Virginian naval forces.
1719	South Carolina ousts its proprietary officials.
1729	Proprietary rights to North and South Carolina are formally surrendered.

Colonial America: A History to 1763, Fourth Edition. Richard Middleton and Anne Lombard.
© 2011 Richard Middleton and Anne Lombard. Published 2011 by Blackwell Publishing Ltd.

1 WILLIAM AND MARY'S COLONIAL POLICY

T HE ACCESSION OF William and Mary is often described by historians as a counter-revolution, in that they overturned the centralizing and innovative policies of James II. However, as Massachusetts had already discovered, the clock could not be turned back completely; the colonies had become too important to the Crown's ambitions for it to revert to the old Elizabethan strategy of chartering investment companies to finance and administer colonies as private enterprises. As Sir Robert Southwell, a leading bureaucrat, emphasized to one of the king's principal ministers in March 1689, North America's 250,000 inhabitants furnished "a full third part of the whole Trade and Navigation of England ... a great nursery of Our Sea Men and the King's Customs depend mightily thereon." The customs duties they generated would become, if anything, more essential after William's accession than before.

Although William was no absolutist, he was like his predecessor in being a modernizer, determined to transform the capacities of England's government so that it could begin to assume a new role in European politics. Under William's leadership England was now an ally of the Dutch, part of a Europe-wide coalition determined to check the expansion of French power. Its new diplomatic commitments propelled the English nation into a prolonged war with France and its Catholic allies, called the Nine Years War, or the War of the League of Augsburg, beginning in 1689. This war would require large military expenditures to defend English control in Ireland, to protect Dutch allies from French aggression in the Low Countries, and to guard English colonial possessions in North America and the Caribbean from French attacks. The task of raising money to meet these new expenditures would transform the English state, since more extensive taxation and a corresponding expansion of the powers of Parliament would be required. In addition the Bank of England and other bureaucratic structures would be created to manage the massive new borrowing needed to finance a modern military.

Meanwhile the powers of the Crown's imperial bureaucracy increased as well. Since their founding the colonies had been haphazardly supervised by various committees of the Privy Council. However, as the war progressed, it became evident that some more permanent body was required for the sake of cohesion. In 1696, under pressure from members of the House of Commons to enforce the navigation laws more effectively, William III created a new department to manage colonial affairs, the Board of Trade, consisting of a president and seven other salaried members, plus clerks. Apart from enforcing the navigation laws, these "knowing and fit persons" were to sift through the colonial laws and governors' reports before forwarding them to the Privy Council for action. A huge backlog of business awaited them, including the vetting of over 100 provincial laws.

That same year Parliament extended to the colonies an act that gave revenue officers greater powers of search by means of writs of assistance, allowing entry to any premises where smuggling was suspected. In addition the Privy Council ordered the governors of Massachusetts, New York, Pennsylvania, Maryland, and Virginia to establish vice-admiralty courts, which had no jury, only a presiding judge, to facilitate convictions for breaches of the trade laws.

At home in England, the imperatives of war-making shaped politics and imperial policy for nearly a quarter of a century. Although the Nine Years War ended in 1697, England was drawn into a second European war from 1702 to 1713. The War of the Spanish Succession was prosecuted mainly by William and Mary's successor, Queen Anne, who assumed the throne in 1702. For 11 years, England fought alongside the Dutch Republic and other allies to prevent the unification of France and Spain under a single crown.

Although the most important battles of both wars were fought in Europe, people in the English and French colonies in North America as well as in the Native American communities that surrounded them became enmeshed in both conflicts. In the colonies, the wars acquired distinct names: King William's War and Queen Anne's War. Heightened tensions between English and French settlers and their Indian allies had already led to hostility and skirmishes in 1688; thereafter the bloodshed only intensified as serious fighting was instigated by both English and French colonial governments on the frontiers between Canada and New England and New York. The English, with their far larger settler population, might have been expected to possess the advantage. To the settlers' great frustration, however, their forces achieved little success. An attempt by New York and the New England colonies to launch a joint expedition against Québec and Montréal in May 1690 failed disastrously, as did a smaller assault the following year. Meanwhile attacks by the French and their Indian allies ravaged settler communities in northern New York and New England. The English could seemingly do little except to launch retaliatory attacks on French settler communities, with the help of members of the Iroquois League.

King William's War and Queen Anne's War and the political upheavals that accompanied them would have profound impacts on both settler and Native American societies in North America. Several communities in northern New England became so traumatized that they nearly tore themselves apart in a series of witchcraft trials, in a crisis that ended only after over 100 people had been accused of selling their souls to Satan. Native American peoples near the northern and southern frontiers were drawn into local and regional conflicts which devastated their populations and transformed their societies. In Carolina the long-term result of these conflicts was to bring down the proprietary government. Even colonies where there was little or no fighting were turned upside down politically in the aftermath of the Glorious Revolution and the accession of William and Mary.

The extended period of political turmoil brought antagonisms between the British, French, and Spanish North American colonies to the surface. When the wars ended, after the Treaty of Utrecht in 1713, conflicts between these three colonial powers in North America would be driven underground again for some time, re-emerging once again only in the 1740s and the 1750s. However, by this time the affected communities had been irrevocably changed. This chapter will examine the various ordeals which they endured from 1688 to 1713, and the political changes that resulted.

2   THE SALEM WITCHCRAFT TRIALS

The imperial wars affected English settlers in the northern colonies in diverse ways. Some of the colonists fought in battles, while others were the victims of raids on villages that left death and economic losses in their wake. Many more became caught up in a general mood of fear, even panic. Periodic attacks by French-allied Indians had taken place since King Philip's War, particularly in northern New England, where the war continued into the late 1670s. Now during King William's War, the attacks resumed. French-allied Algonquians killed dozens of settlers in the village of Schenectady, New York, in February 1690. Abenaki Indians killed another 100 and captured 80 settlers from the town of York, Maine, in late January 1692. Other attacks followed: on the town of Wells, Maine, during the summer of 1692; on Durham, New Hampshire, in June 1694; and on Haverhill, Massachusetts, in March 1697.

English settlers were terrified at the prospect of such attacks, and understandably so. The main objective of French-allied Indian raids on English villages was the traditional one of obtaining captives, although during the imperial wars these captives would sometimes be traded with the French instead of being kept for adoption. From the point of view of the people being raided, the ultimate aims of the raid mattered little, for to Europeans the tactics that Native American warriors used to achieve their objectives were shocking and incomprehensible. Warriors preferred to launch a coordinated surprise attack on an enemy village while its inhabitants were all asleep, since this was a highly effective way for them to get the enemy to surrender quickly while minimizing their own casualties. If a raid worked perfectly, nearly all the inhabitants of a village could be captured alive. However, when perfect coordination was impossible, the attackers used their tomahawks and war clubs to kill resisters. Terror, like surprise, was an effective technique for inducing people to surrender in a hurry. Settlers who survived an attack often fled their homes in panic, and no doubt carried the psychological scars of their experiences for years.

Although most New England settlers never witnessed an Indian attack, many worried about them, especially in northern Massachusetts, where people fleeing from the Maine frontier often took refuge. Massachusetts religious leaders explained Indian attacks in the same religious terms that had shaped their understanding of declining church membership, threats of Catholic tyranny, and the loss of the Massachusetts charter. Comprehending all events in history as direct manifestations of a holy struggle between God and Satan, they suggested that Satan was luring the Puritans away from their covenant with God. Years of being warned of Satan's presence in their midst had begun to take a psychic toll on the settlers. One visible manifestation of their distress, historians have suggested, were the dramatic occurrences in Massachusetts during 1692 known collectively as the Salem witchcraft trials.

Prosecutions for witchcraft were not a new phenomenon. They had been a feature of Christianity since its foundation, though their incidence had increased with the Reformation. The Protestant churches, in their search for purity, were less tolerant of any deviation that could be linked to Satan, including many popular superstitions. Nevertheless, popular culture on both sides of the Atlantic incorporated beliefs in magic and witchcraft. Early modern people lived in an intensely insecure and unpredictable world, without the modern confidence that nature can be predicted and controlled.

Ordinary people resorted to many occult practices associated with alchemy, astrology, and chiromancy in their attempts to understand and influence the natural world, without having any sense that their beliefs contradicted Protestant doctrine.

During the sixteenth and early seventeenth centuries, witchcraft scares had periodically swept various communities in Europe, although by the late seventeenth century they were quite rare. In Massachusetts charges of witchcraft had been relatively infrequent as well as limited in scope. Between 1630 and 1690 there were only 24 indictments, seven convictions, and five executions. The first capital offenses occurred in 1647 and 1648 when two women were executed; further executions took place in 1651 and 1656. Cases were relatively more prevalent in the Connecticut Valley, where serious outbreaks occurred at Wethersfield and Springfield in the late 1640s and in Hartford in the early 1660s. Typically those accused were charged with malefic magic, of doing someone harm, rather than with heresy. Cases often arose out of indictments for slander, in which the defendant tried to prove the truth of a defamatory statement by bringing a charge of witchcraft. Another cause for indictment after 1656 was association with the Quakers, whose strange clothing and beliefs made them suspect.

Charges of witchcraft thereafter steadily declined in both Massachusetts and Connecticut. A small upsurge occurred in the 1680s, but nothing presaged the deluge of more than 100 accusations, along with dozens of indictments and convictions, that was to sweep Salem and the neighboring communities of Massachusetts in 1692. One question that must be addressed is why such an outbreak occurred at a time when witchcraft accusations were generally in decline, and why the scope of the crisis was so massive, The general atmosphere of fear and paranoia created by King William's War as well as the loss of the charter help to explain the particular timing and some of the hysteria associated with this event.

The first signs that something was amiss occurred in February 1692, when Betty Parris and Abigail Williams, the nine-year-old daughter and 11-year-old niece of Samuel Parris, the local minister of Salem village, a suburb of Salem town, began experiencing fits which the local physicians diagnosed as bewitchment after failing to find any physical cause.[1] Parris discovered that his Caribbean Indian slave Tituba had used an old English folklore remedy, or species of white magic, to find out the cause of the girls' distress. A cake made of rye meal and the girls' urine had been fed to a dog in the belief that this would reveal the names of their tormentors. To Parris this was tantamount to witchcraft itself. After further questioning, Abigail and Betty named two women, Sarah Good and Sarah Osborne, as the cause of their affliction, adding Tituba for good measure. They were supported in their accusations by two other girls, Ann Putnam, the 12-year-old daughter of a prominent local farmer, Thomas Putnam, and Elizabeth Hubbard, a 17-year-old servant girl.

All three accused were interrogated by the local magistrates at the end of February 1692. Though Good and Osborne stoutly maintained their innocence, the magistrates were quickly convinced of their guilt because of Tituba's confession that she was

---

[1]   Although secondary accounts of the Salem episode often assert that the afflicted girls engaged as a group in fortune-telling, a recent examination of the primary sources shows that only one unnamed girl tried fortune-telling, an event which contemporaries thought to have no bearing on the girls' subsequent afflictions. Mary Beth Norton, *In the Devil's Snare: The Salem Witchcraft Crisis of 1692* (New York, 2002), 23.

familiar with Caribbean occult practices and had been helped by the other two women. If further proof were needed, it was supplied by the children themselves, who began writhing in agony, claiming they were being tortured by the specters of Good and Osborne. The magistrates accordingly ordered the three to be sent to jail in Boston pending a formal trial before an assize court.[2]

Despite the drama surrounding the girls, the proceedings so far had not been particularly different from other witchcraft episodes in New England. What changed now was that several more young women and even a few older ones began experiencing fits, blaming not only Tituba, Osborne, and Good, but also three relatively prominent members of the community, Martha Corey, Rebecca Nurse, and Elizabeth Proctor. Nor did the charges stop there: by May more than two dozen people had been accused, including several men who had sought to defend their wives and a minister from Wells, Maine, George Burroughs. Unlike previous witchcraft investigations, which had led rapidly to trials, in this episode the accused languished in jails after being questioned. In early 1692 the Massachusetts government still had no charter, so its authority to try the suspects was uncertain. The delays encouraged public anxiety to grow unchecked, and accusations multiplied.

In May 1692 the governor, Sir William Phips, arrived with the new charter and decided to appoint a special court of *oyer* and *terminer* to try the cases.[3] The court proceedings here also encouraged accusations to multiply. During its proceedings the accusers frequently fainted or screamed when confronting the defendants, accusing them of having appeared as specters weeks or even years before. The accused in turn were subjected to minute inspection to check whether they had any marks of the devil on their body, the most important of which was a teat for suckling Satan's young. They were also required to recite the Lord's Prayer fluently, which it was believed no one possessed by the devil could do. The problem for the accused was that such evidence was hard to disprove; specters could be summoned up at any time of the day or night, while the absence of marks could be attributed to the cunning of the devil. Even recitation of the Lord's Prayer was difficult in the tension of a crowded courtroom. Lastly, the accused were denied any form of counsel to ensure that their defense was conducted properly.

In these circumstances the normal judicial processes were completely overturned, as was demonstrated in the case of Rebecca Nurse. Although she was initially acquitted, her accusers set up such a clamor that the magistrates ordered the jury to reconsider their verdict, which they dutifully did. Given the prevailing mood, many of those accused preferred to confess, since a confession normally entitled a person to leniency. Unfortunately, those like Tituba who took this course had to name their accomplices in order to be convincing, so that even children denounced their parents in the general hue and cry.

Until May 1692 the charges were confined to the vicinity of Salem village and town. In June, however, accusations began to be made at Andover, Haverhill, Topsfield, and Gloucester. By October over 140 people had been indicted, of whom 50 had confessed, 26 had been convicted, and 20 executed, 19 of them by hanging. The exception among

[2] For Tituba's role in the early stages of the event, see Elaine G. Breslaw, *Tituba, Reluctant Witch of Salem: Devilish Indians and Puritan Fantasies* (New York, 1996). An assize court met periodically to hear serious criminal cases that could not be handled by the regular quarterly county court sessions.
[3] Courts of *oyer* and *terminer* were convened specially for extraordinary or unusually serious criminal prosecutions.

Figure 17   The Salem witch trial (artist's reconstruction). Library of Congress, Washington, DC.

DOCUMENT 14

Recantation of the women of Andover, 1692, reprinted in Thomas Hutchinson, *The History of the Colony and Province of Massachusetts-Bay*, edited by Lawrence Shaw Mayo (Cambridge, Mass., 1936), Vol. 2, 31–2

The following document summarizes the testimony of several women who confessed to witchcraft and then recanted. Bear in mind that in this society women were thought to be more likely to sin than men. Questions to consider: *What does this testimony reveal about why people might confess falsely to a crime they had not in fact committed? In this society, might pressure to make a false confession be especially heavy for women?*

[When] . . . at Mr Parris's house, several young persons, being seemingly afflicted, did accuse several persons for afflicting them . . . we [were] informed that if a person was sick, the afflicted person could tell what or who was the cause of that sickness. Joseph Ballard of Andover, his wife being sick at the same time, he, either from himself or by the advice of others, fetched two of the persons, called the afflicted persons, from Salem Village to Andover, which was the beginning of that dreadful calamity that befell us in Andover . . . After [the Reverend] Mr Barnard had been at prayer, we were blindfolded, and our hands were laid upon the afflicted persons, they being in their fits and falling into their fits at our coming into their presence, as they said; and some led us and laid our hands upon them, and then they said they were well, and that we were guilty of afflicting them. Whereupon, we were all seized, as prisoners, by a warrant from the Justice of the Peace and forthwith carried to Salem. And, by reason of that sudden surprizal, we knowing ourselves altogether innocent of that crime, we were all exceedingly astonished and amazed, and consternated and affrighted even out of our reason; and our nearest and dearest relations, seeing us in that dreadful condition and knowing our great danger, apprehended there was no other way to save our lives, as the case was then circumstanced, but by our confessing . . . [I]ndeed that confession, that it is said we made, was no other than what was suggested to us by some gentlemen, they telling us that we were witches, and they knew it, and we knew it, which made us think that it was so; and our understandings, our reason, our faculties, almost gone, as we were not capable of judging of our condition; as also the hard measures they used with us rendered us incapable of making our defence, but said anything and everything which they desired, and most of what we said was but, in effect, a consenting to what they said. Some time after, when we were better composed, they telling us what we had confessed, we did profess that we were innocent and ignorant of such things; and we hearing that Samuel Wardwell had renounced his confession, and quickly after condemned and executed, some of us were told we were going after Wardwell.

Confession of Sarah Carrier, aged seven, August 11, 1692, reprinted in Thomas Hutchinson, *The History of the Colony and Province of Massachusetts-Bay*, edited by Lawrence Shaw Mayo (Cambridge, Mass., 1936), Vol. 2, 34

The following is a portion of the examination of Sarah Carrier, whose mother had already been condemned to death. Questions to consider: *Would we consider this testimony to be reliable evidence of the truth? Why, or why not?*

It was asked Sarah Carrier by the Magistrates or Justices . . . : How long hast thou been a witch. Answer: Ever since I was six years old. Question: How old are you now? Answer: Near eight years old, brother Richard says, I shall be eight years old in November next. Question: Who made you a witch? Answer: My mother, she made me set my hand to a book [of the devil]. Question: How did you set your hand to it? Answer: I touched it with my fingers and the book was red, the paper of it was white ... Being asked who was there beside, she answered her Aunt Toothaker and her cousin. Being asked when it was, she said, when she was baptized. Question: What did they promise to give you? Answer: A black dog. Question: Did the dog ever come to you? Answer: No. Question: But you said you saw a cat once. What did that say to you? Answer: It said it would tear me in pieces if I would not set my hand to the book. She said her mother baptized her, and the devil or black man was not there, as she saw, and mother said when she baptized her, thou art mine for ever and ever and amen. Question: How did you afflict folks? Answer: I pinched them . . . Being asked whether she went in her body or her spirit, she said in her spirit. And she said her mother carried her thither to afflict. Question: How did your mother carry you when she was in prison? Answer: She came like a black cat. Question: How did you know that it was your mother? Answer: The cat told me so that she was my mother.

those executed was Giles Corey, whose wife had already been condemned because she had protested her innocence, the presumption being that she would not give up the devil. Corey refused to implicate himself or his wife any further by pleading before the court, since a confession would probably have led to the forfeiture of all his lands. His ploy did him no good; he was ordered to be crushed under a pile of stones. Many prominent persons now went into hiding or fled to neighboring provinces.

By this time ministers like Increase and Cotton Mather were becoming uneasy at the court's excessive reliance on spectral evidence. They were also alarmed at the contradiction of sparing confessing witches while executing those who asserted their innocence. Equally disturbing was the correlation between confessions and new accusations: the more people who confessed, the greater the number of accused. Indeed, the net was being cast so wide that even members of the civil and clerical establishment were being mentioned. Among those incriminated were the wives of Governor Phips, the Reverend John Hale, Parson Samuel Willard, and Dudley Bradstreet, a leading magistrate in Andover, all of whom had voiced their opposition to further prosecutions. Although the courts refused to take these latter charges seriously, their refusal to do so further undermined the legitimacy of their proceeding against others. At this point the credibility of the accusers themselves finally came into question, especially when early in October Increase Mather delivered a sermon suggesting that it was better that 10 suspects went free than that one innocent person was hanged. Even Parris, who had been most zealous in pursuit of those who had afflicted his children, began to recoil. A week later the governor, Sir William Phips, ordered the special court of *oyer* and *terminer* to be dissolved. By early 1693 the Superior Court of Judicature, which had replaced the previous tribunal, refused to hear further charges based solely on spectral evidence, in an implicit acknowledgment that wrong had been done. Several of the accused, however, remained in jail, unable to pay their jailers' fees. The first public apology came only in 1697 from Samuel Sewall, one of the judges, but not until 1711 was compensation paid to the surviving victims whose lives and those of their families had been ruined. Even then most people preferred to believe that the devil was to blame, even if innocent blood had been shed. For this reason no action was taken against either the accusers or the prosecuting justices. Most of the accusers drifted into obscurity, but the magistrates, like William Stoughton, the lieutenant governor and presiding judge, remained in high office.

Though this extraordinary episode had many complex causes, historians have often argued that its most basic source was the stresses of the times. Ministers had spent decades preaching that God was angry with the colonists for their backsliding and warning that the colonists must guard vigilantly against Satan's assaults. Every crisis from King Philip's War to the loss of the charter had been presented as a chastisement from God. War then had broken out. All of these events helped to create an atmosphere of panic among ordinary people. The idea that Satan was causing their troubles, assisted by people within their midst, was entirely plausible. Massachusetts leaders, in turn, seem to have taken the accusations seriously because they too feared that Satan was trying to destroy their holy experiment.[4] As Cotton Mather argued, "Where will the Devil show the most malice but where he is hated ... most?"

The dynamics of the relationship between ordinary people and Puritan leaders encouraged the process to spiral out of control. The clergy encouraged the accusers. Magistrates then allowed the accusations to multiply by permitting those with spectral visions to behave as they liked. The Putnam family, for example, intervened in support of witnesses and made statements about the defendants in blatant disregard of all due process.[5] As the accusers were encouraged to describe their nightmarish fears and fantasies, the accusations grew in scope. Among the accusers were several young women who had fled their villages in Maine after Indian attacks in which their families' homes had been destroyed and family members killed. As time went on, these young women and others accused not only the kinds of vulnerable women ordinarily suspected of witchcraft, but also prominent political leaders, clergymen, and merchants, many of whom had ties to Maine. These later accusations are the most puzzling, until we remember that these prominent people were the kinds of people whom ordinary men and women expected to protect them from the devastation of war. The terrible violence on the frontier had to be explained, and the notion that powerful men had conspired with the Abenakis, the French, and Satan to attack the people provided a plausible explanation.

---

[4] For the emphasis on the Indian wars, see Mary Beth Norton, *In the Devil's Snare* (2002), as well as Richard Godbeer, *The Devil's Dominion: Magic and Religion in Early New England* (New York, 1992).

[5] The emphasis on the stresses of the times, particularly the loss of the charter and the revolt against Andros, was most famously offered by Perry Miller, *The New England Mind: From Colony to* Province (Cambridge, Mass., 1953). For the failure of the judiciary, see Peter Charles Hoffer, *The Salem Witchcraft Trials: A Legal History* (Lawrence, 1997).

Dozens of studies have explored the many complex dimensions of the Salem outbreak. Some historians have suggested that the afflicted children, brought up in a repressive manner, used the trials to attract attention and turn the tables on their parents. Others have argued that the initial accusations came from young girls who were approaching puberty, a time when psychological and physical stresses are acute. It was easy for them to become hysterical, making wild accusations to disarm their parents' anger and avoid blame for possible misdeeds. These hypotheses present the accusations as essentially fraudulent.[6]

Other historians posit that the girls really believed they were bewitched, and (encouraged by adults) directed the blame towards individuals whom they feared or resented. Religious divisions may have contributed to such resentments. Parris was a stern opponent of the Half-Way Covenant and used this to exclude members of his congregation from taking communion. George Burroughs was distrusted in part because he appeared to have Baptist leanings. Finally, the Proctor and Nurse families had relatives who belonged to the Quakers, still an object of suspicion in the minds of many country people.

Many of those initially accused were vulnerable women. Some historians have argued they became suspects because of their age, misfortune, or refusal to conform to social norms. For example, Good had a reputation for being a quarrelsome beggar, while Bridget Bishop, the first to be executed, had been accused of witchcraft a decade earlier. But such an interpretation does not explain the inclusion of persons like Elizabeth Carey, the wife of a wealthy Charlestown merchant, and Martha Corey, who were neither old, poor, widowed, nor social outcasts, though one common factor seems to have been that most of the women were beyond their childbearing years. Women beyond the menopause were thought to resent those who could still have children, which made them vulnerable to satanic influences. But that does not explain the inclusion of Elizabeth Proctor, who was pregnant at the time of her indictment.

A more comprehensive interpretation is that the witchcraft accusations reflected patterns of gender repression and gendered power. Virtually all of the accusers were young, unmarried girls, who were among the least powerful members of their patriarchal society. Under ordinary circumstances young girls had little control over their lives, being governed by their fathers or their masters. Some of these girls would surely have resented their lack of power. Possession gave them a voice, made them momentarily important to their communities, and allowed them to express their resentments without being punished. In this interpretation, possession provided a temporary release from socially imposed repression.

---

[6]   The charge of fraud was first hinted at by Thomas Brattle, a Boston merchant, in an open letter on October 8, 1692. It was later taken up by Thomas Hutchinson in his *History of the Colony and Province of Massachusetts-Bay*, Vol. 2 (Boston, 1768). For a similar, more recent interpretation, see Bernard Rosenthal, *Salem Story: Reading the Witch Trials of 1692* (Cambridge, 1993). Apart from hysteria, there are two other medical interpretations. One is that the accusers had contracted ergot poisoning after eating contaminated rye bread, which caused them to hallucinate. Another is that the accusers were suffering from encephalitis, or inflammation of the brain, caused by a virus. However, the ergot interpretation fails to explain why the afflicted were the only sufferers, not the population at large. For this interpretation, see Linda Caporeal, "Ergotism: Satan Loosed in Salem," *Science*, 192 (1976), 21–6. It was promptly rebutted by Nicholas P. Spanos and Jack Gottlieb, "Ergotism and the Salem Village Witch Trials," *Science*, 194 (1976), 1390–4. The possibility of encephalitis is advanced by Laurie Winn Carlson, *A Fever in Salem* (Chicago, 2000).

Women's lack of power also helps to explain why it was mostly women who were accused. This was a society whose members believed property should be controlled by men, and whose male members often felt resentful towards women who owned property in their own right, as a few did. Historian Carol Karlsen has found that a disproportionate number of those accused of witchcraft in Salem were women who owned or stood to inherit property, either as childless widows or as daughters in families without sons. Male witnesses feeling covert hostility towards such women may have encouraged charges of witchcraft against these women, while the women had little power to defend themselves. Ironically, the accusers were often aided by the accused women themselves, who frequently confessed. Like everyone else, the accused women subscribed to the view that women were the morally weaker sex, since it was Eve who had succumbed to the temptations of the serpent and caused the Fall. Perhaps they too were in some way to blame for their plight.[7]

A different line of inquiry has suggested that the trials originated in the tensions between Salem town and Salem village. There is evidence to suggest the town was modern, commercial, and prosperous, while the village, especially its western half, was largely agrarian, steeped in more medieval and communitarian values. Tax lists have been interpreted to show that the accusers came from a part of Salem village where most inhabitants were subsistence farmers while most of those initially accused lived close to the town, where the greatest wealth lay. This hypothesis may explain why John Proctor was among the accused, for he ran a thriving tavern for travelers on the main road running north from Boston to the east of the village. The same entrepreneurial activity was also true of Israel Porter and his family, who also had considerable wealth, not only in land but also in milling enterprises. Recent historical analysis has challenged the evidence for some of these conclusions, but historians concur that economic tensions played some part in shaping events.[8]

Certainly Salem had a long history of contention. Roger Williams had been one of its first pastors. Notable disputes had included a quarrel with George Burroughs over his salary as minister of Salem village before he left for Maine in 1683. Parris, the next minister, had been involved in a similar dispute. Among his supporters were the Putnam family, who favored a tax to fund the minister's stipend. Opposed to this faction were the Porters, Proctors, and others who were subsequently victimized. One of the factors behind the salary dispute was that many living on the eastern side of the village disputed the need for a separate church at all, since it was convenient for them to worship in Salem town. They were also angry that the village parsonage had been surreptitiously given to Parris, rather than leased, as required under the original bequest granting the land.

---

[7] For an interpretation of the trials based on gender, see Carol F. Karlsen, *The Devil in the Shape of a Woman: Witchcraft in Colonial New England* (New York, 1987). The seventeenth-century belief that women were morally weaker is discussed by Elizabeth Reis, *Damned Women: Sinners and Witches in Puritan New England* (Ithaca, 1997).

[8] For the thesis concerning the location of the accusers and accused, see Paul Boyer and Stephen Nissenbaum, *Salem Possessed: The Social Origins of Witchcraft* (Cambridge, Mass., 1974). Recent questions about the evidence are explored in Richard Latner, "Salem Witchcraft, Factionalism, and Social Change Reconsidered: Were Salem's Witch-Hunters Modernization's Failures?" *William and Mary Quarterly*, 65 (2008), 423–48, and Benjamin Ray, "The Geography of Witchcraft Accusations in 1692 Salem Village," *William and Mary Quarterly*, 65 (2008), 449–78.

They accordingly used their influence in Salem to block the demands for the tax to fund Parris's salary. In response, the Putnam group decided to seek town status for the village so that they could have a fully covenanted church and run their affairs without interference from Salem. However, in October 1691 they were thwarted once more when the Porter group gained control of the village committee. Within six months the first charges of witchcraft were being made, fanned by Parris's sermons about the dangers facing the community and the need to destroy the ungodly.

These facts suggest that the trials may have been partly the result of personal grudges. In the past, charges of witchcraft had sometimes been brought by those who had a grievance against an individual. The Putnam family apparently had designs on some woods owned by the Nurse family, while several of those accused in neighboring Topsfield had pursued litigation against the Putnams over land. Vengeance might also explain the spread of witchcraft charges to other towns, as former neighbors caught up with their longtime adversaries. Lastly, vengeance might account for the charges made by servants against their master. John Proctor and George Jacobs both became suspect when Mary Warren and Sarah Churchill accused them of witchcraft, following unsympathetic treatment at their hands. George Burroughs was another person to fall foul of a former servant, Mercy Lewis.

All of these various explanations provide insight into the kinds of resentments and social tensions that contributed to witchcraft accusations in Salem and elsewhere. They do not, however, explain why a small number of accusations in Salem Village grew into an epidemic that convulsed the entire colony. It seems clear that an outbreak this large would not have occurred without the perception among the colony's Puritan leaders that their society was in crisis. Massachusetts leaders not only believed in but in some cases were demonstrably anxious about the presence of witches, which they feared might be partly responsible for God's seeming abandonment of their colony. Their fears were exacerbated by previously published accounts of two witch trials in England, while the eminent Massachusetts minister Cotton Mather had written an essay on the subject in 1689. From the beginning the Puritans had been obsessed about preserving the purity of their commonwealth. By the 1690s the Puritans had developed something like a siege mentality with their constant warnings that the Satan was trying to destroy their godly experiment. The war, and the Indian attacks that it provoked, seemed to confirm their fears that God had forsaken them. Certainly many ministers were disposed to see the Salem trials as justification for their jeremiads. In such a climate the subsequent excesses become understandable.

Ultimately the explanation of the Salem witchcraft trials depends on a fusion of a variety of factors. The political instability created by the loss of the charter, the trauma of war, fear of the Indians, the obsession with sin, belief in satanic forces, social turmoil, personal vendettas, and the prejudices of a patriarchal society all created a climate conducive to witchcraft accusations, which were then encouraged to get out of hand. The episode in some respects constituted the death throes of a passing era. Though belief in the supernatural remained widespread, the church and magistracy found it safer to distance themselves from Satan and his agents, leaving God to decide on the punishment of deviants. After 1700 no further charges of witchcraft were entertained by the courts in Massachusetts or elsewhere in the colonies.

3 WAR ON THE NORTHERN FRONTIER, 1689–1713

The North Americans who suffered most as a result of the imperial wars were not European settlers but Native Americans, especially those who lived north and west of New York and New England and on the border with New France. A larger proportion of the Native American population than of Europeans was drawn into the fighting, and Indian villages were raided and destroyed at least as often as the villages of the English and the French. At the same time the northern Indians were not simply war's victims, for many groups took advantage of wartime conditions to promote their own interests. The Iroquois in particular, thanks to their strategic location and their ability to coordinate with one another, were able to forge a central role for themselves in both wars as they developed strategies to maximize their own chances for survival in a colonial world.

Indians were vital to North American warfare during the seventeenth and early eighteenth centuries, as we have seen. Neither English nor French colonial governments had sufficient resources to defend their territories alone, so they relied on their Native American allies to provide considerable military support. For their part, the Indians understood that they were indispensable to the colonists. They expected that their participation in the colonizers' conflicts would benefit them in the long run, both economically and politically. However in the end, especially for the English-allied members of the Iroquois League, those expectations would be disappointed.

By the 1680s, the French had long since established a successful fur-trading economy in Canada, along with a small but growing population of farmers, merchants, and clerics. By this time, French trade with various Indian groups extended west to the Great Lakes and south through much of the Mississippi Valley. New France had towns or villages at Québec, Montréal, and Trois-Rivières on the St. Lawrence, as well as Port Royal and a number of smaller settlements in Acadia. Yet the French colonies still had a far smaller population than their English neighbors to the south, with only about 12,000 settlers in 1690. The French government provided only a few hundred soldiers to man its Canadian garrisons. Meanwhile, English competition for the fur trade was growing both in northern Canada and on New York's northern and western frontiers. That economic competition, along with the ever present threat of invasion from the south, created a need for a system of defense.

Because of the numerical weakness of its population, New France depended heavily for its own survival on military alliances with Hurons, Algonquians, and Montagnais in the St. Lawrence region, the Abenakis in northern New England, a number of western tribes around the Great Lakes, and the Catholic Iroquois. Canadian militias developed strategies that were compatible with those of their Native American allies, who generally fought alongside them. They used surprise attacks, and made effective use of cover whenever possible before beginning to fire on their enemies. They limited engagements in order to keep their casualties low. The royal government in New France worked to preserve their alliances by inviting allies to settle in the *reserves*.

Although it might seem anomalous from a Western point of view, French-allied Iroquois did not forfeit their membership in the Iroquois League by moving to New France or by siding with the French. They were always in the minority, for most League Iroquois favored the continuation of the Covenant Chain alliance with the English. Nevertheless, by the late 1680s, members of that pro-French minority had begun to argue at League councils that a peace agreement with the French would better serve Iroquois interests in the long run than the alliance with the English. After all, the English had asked the Iroquois to fight for them in several needless wars. Now the Iroquois were increasingly being drawn into conflicts with the French for which they risked much but gained little. The arguments of the pro-French groups gained considerable force after 1687, when the French governor Denonville made his devastating raid on Seneca settlements.

Conflicts escalated considerably with the beginning of King William's War. In May 1690, Massachusetts determined to organize an expedition under William Phips to attack Port Royal in Nova Scotia and thus secure its eastern frontier. Jacob Leisler suggested that New York take part in a joint offensive against Québec and Montréal.[9] Assured by officials in Albany that the English were going to use their great military might to defeat the French, approximately 1,000 Mohawks and other Iroquois warriors joined the New York forces for the assaults on their long-term foes. To their chagrin, Massachusetts bungled the plan. Instead of bringing their forces immediately to join the combined assault on Canada, Massachusetts insisted on carrying out the Port Royal expedition first. As a result, Phips and his men did not reach Québec until October 15, far too late to begin a siege. In any case Phips's force of 2,300 militia was insufficiently equipped and had to retreat. Fitz-John Winthrop, commanding the forces marching by way of Lake George, made even less progress. His forces were too small, lacked supplies, and were then beset by smallpox. After reaching Wood Creek he determined to withdraw, although he dispatched a raiding party towards Montréal.

This failure was a costly one for the Iroquois, who probably had no more than 2,000 warriors in total at this point. Not only did they have to reckon the costs of this loss, but they were still reeling from the combined effects of continuing attacks by the French. Meanwhile the Iroquois had for the past decade been engaged in conflicts on their western frontiers with Miamis, Ojibwas, Illinois, Shawnees, Fox, and Ottawas.

Moreover the English continued to ask them for more assistance. After Henry Sloughter assumed the governorship in New York, his officials urged the Iroquois to provide still more warriors for another raid into Canada alongside English forces led by Peter Schuyler. This effort, too, was a disaster. English-allied Iroquois ended up exchanging fire with French-allied Iroquois, threatening the very existence of their confederacy. Iroquois warriors at League councils increasingly questioned the benefits of the alliance with the English.

English colonial governments possessed a limited capacity to defeat the French in North America, as these failed military operations revealed. The home government was unwilling to supply military resources, while the colonial governments themselves lacked unity. For these reasons the initiative passed to the French and their Indian allies, who meted out retaliation against English settlements in Maine and New Hampshire in

---

[9] See Chapter 8, part 3.

attacks that came nearly every winter between 1692 and 1697. Not only the English settlers suffered; the French also attacked the English-allied Iroquois. The Mohawks lost 300 of their people in 1693. Then in 1696 it was the turn of the Onondagas and Oneidas to have their villages razed, in retaliation for an Iroquois raid in 1689 on the French settlement at Lachine.

Slowly the fighting died out. The provincials on both sides did not have the resources for sustained warfare, while their respective mother countries were much too engrossed in Europe to send assistance. Hostilities formally ended with the signing of the Peace of Ryswick in September 1697, and the prewar status quo was restored. Meanwhile the Iroquois were becoming increasingly reluctant to support the English, who by the end of the war had come to seem less like powerful military allies and more like bunglers. The Iroquois were still being attacked from the west and many tribal leaders believed they should husband their resources and avoid further bloodshed. The French-allied Iroquois group based near Montréal gained considerable support within the League by the mid-1690s for its arguments in favor of Iroquois neutrality and peace with the French.

The government in England made another attempt to organize colonial governments and their Iroquois allies for military purposes in 1698, when the Board of Trade appointed Richard Lord Bellomont not only governor of New York, Massachusetts, and New Hampshire but also commander of the Connecticut, Rhode Island, and New Jersey militias. In 1700 Bellomont invited the governors of Virginia, Maryland, Pennsylvania, and New Jersey to New York for a conference with members of the Iroquois League, the first time that so many officials had gathered together. Although Bellomont was a capable leader, the task of coordinating all these governments was too great. Colonial distrust of anything that smacked of the Dominion of New England remained strong, and the Iroquois representatives remained noncommittal. The French meanwhile increased their presence along the upper Mississippi and began the construction of a series of forts, among them Detroit, to exclude the English from the western fur trade. At the same time French Jesuits used their influence among the Indians of the St. Lawrence Valley and Great Lakes to secure support for the French cause.[10]

Finally the members of the Iroquois League decided to take action on their own. A drastic reduction in their numbers – from 2,550 to 1,230 braves – had at last convinced a majority of Iroquois leaders that peace was essential. In 1700 Iroquois leaders entered simultaneous negotiations with both the French and the English, and in 1701 signed a separate treaty with each. The treaty with the French promised that the Iroquois would remain neutral in wars between England and France. The treaty with the English gave up Iroquois claims to a huge tract of land in the west (land which the Iroquois did not in fact control) in exchange for a promise of English military protection there. The second treaty's effect was mostly symbolic, in that it gave the impression that the Iroquois were still firmly bound to the English. In reality, of course, the Iroquois had just agreed to peace with the French. Meanwhile the Iroquois made peace with their enemies to the west as well.

When war broke out once more in Europe in 1702, the English and the French renewed their hostilities. This time, however, the Iroquois mostly stayed out of the conflict. Instead of being drawn into costly battles, they avoided conflicts with the French even when urged to engage in them by the English.

---

[10] For further information on French policies towards their allies, see Chapter 15, sections 3 and 4.

For their part the French aggressively pursued hostilities against the English, taking advantage of the fragmentation and lack of unity among the various English colonies, along with the English government's lack of commitment to the colonial war effort. The French-allied Abenaki, in retaliation for encroachments on their land and various attacks on their own people, first raided several Maine settlements in August 1703. Then in February 1704 they attacked Deerfield in Massachusetts. Coming in the depths of winter, the attack was a surprise. Forty-seven colonists were killed and over 100 captured, among them the local minister, the Reverend John Williams. All attempts to convert him to Catholicism failed, but his daughter Eunice married an Indian and became a Catholic convert.[11]

Massachusetts attempted to regain the initiative by countering with another attack on Port Royal in Acadia, destroying several French villages but failing in its main objective. In 1707 Massachusetts made another unsuccessful attempt on Port Royal. The fiasco finally led to the realization by the English government that its colonies needed help. Accordingly plans were made in 1709 for the dispatch of a force from across the Atlantic to sail up the St. Lawrence. They were to be supported by 1,200 Massachusetts men, while another 1,500 recruits from New York, Connecticut, New Jersey, and Pennsylvania advanced overland under Nicholson. In one of the few exceptions to the new Iroquois policy of neutrality, the English force was accompanied by a small contingent of Mohawks led by a chief named Theyanoguin, who was anxious to demonstrate his attachment to the English despite the recent agreement of other tribal leaders with the French. Again, the expedition failed when at the last minute the troops in England were diverted to Portugal.

Finally, Massachusetts sent Nicholson to England early in 1710 to argue the case for a further renewal of the assault on Port Royal. He returned the following June with several frigates and 400 marines. This time Nicholson was able to put his military training to good effect. Port Royal fell in October 1710.

His achievement duly impressed the government in London, as did the dispatch of four Indian "Kings," led by Theyanoguin, who was introduced as "Emperor" of the Iroquois; his presence was used to convince the English government that the Iroquois remained loyal to their colonies.[12] The Tory administration in London agreed to another expedition up the St. Lawrence in conjunction with a colonial advance by way of Lake George. The amphibious force was to comprise 15 warships and seven regular regiments under the overall command of Admiral Walker. The colonists were to be led

---

[11]   Accounts of the attack on Deerfield include Richard I. Melvoin, *New England Outpost: War and Society in Colonial Deerfield* (New York, 1989), John Demos, *The Unredeemed Captive: A Family Story from Early America* (New York, 1994), and Evan Haefeli and Kevin Sweeney, *Captors and Captives: The 1704 French and Indian Raid on Deerfield* (Amherst, 2003). Demos describes the attempts of the Williams family to reclaim Eunice over a period of almost 70 years. Although contemporary whites were astonished by the readiness of European captives and sometimes runaways to accept the Indian way of life, historians have shown that the Indians' more egalitarian way of life could be very attractive to escaped servants, army deserters, and young women. Haefeli and Sweeney explain the reasons for and meaning of the raid for its varied Indian, French, and English participants.

[12]   In reality, only one of the Indians was a sachem, let alone a king or emperor in the European sense. See Eric Hinderaker, "The 'Four Indian Kings' and the Imaginative Construction of the First British Empire," *William and Mary Quarterly*, 53 (1996), 487–526.

by Nicholson advancing north from Albany. Once more, Massachusetts voted £40,000 for the project, while all the other northern colonies contributed either men or money – including £2,000 from Quaker Pennsylvania "for the Queen's use."

As it turned out, this operation was even less successful than that of Winthrop and Phips in 1690. Admiral Walker's fleet with 7,000 troops on board arrived in Boston in June 1711, but received a lukewarm reception from colonists offended by the visiting army's airs of superiority. Although the required supplies and shipping were assembled, and the expedition proceeded for the St. Lawrence in good time, the navy had no charts of the river. On the night of August 23, Walker lost eight ships and 700 men. This misfortune unnerved him and he sailed back across the Atlantic. Nicholson was left waiting to advance at Lake George until news of Walker's departure finally reached him in October, by which time it was too late to do anything except throw his hat on the ground in frustration, shouting "rascals, damned rascals."

When the European conflict finally ended with the signing of the Treaty of Utrecht in April 1713, the French retained control over most of Canada, although they had been forced to make some important concessions. The English gained jurisdiction over Acadia, renamed Nova Scotia, along with its French and Indian inhabitants. The English also gained Newfoundland, previously claimed by both the English and the French, as well as French recognition of their claims to Hudson Bay. Finally, the English gained the right to trade with tribes in the west who had previously had ties to the French. In fact, however, most of these concessions meant little. England could not effectively exercise power over these new territories without occupying them, and they lacked the manpower to do so. And though a new English fort at Oswego would begin to open up trade between the English and western tribes, any real English dominion over the West remained elusive.

Meanwhile the Iroquois League had emerged from the war in a stronger diplomatic position than they had begun. Having made peace with the French, League members no longer had to worry about attacks from French-allied western peoples. In fact they could now lawfully act as intermediaries in the western fur trade without fear of reprisals. They had simultaneously preserved the friendship of the English. The result was the maintenance of their freedom from either European empire, which gave them space to rebuild their own empire and replenish their populations without interference.

4 WAR AND POLITICAL CHANGE IN THE CAROLINAS

King William's War had relatively little impact on the southern colonies, since the French had minimal power in the region during the 1690s and the Spanish, with their colony in Florida, were allied with the English. However, after Spain and France became allies in Queen Anne's War in 1702, the entire region between Florida and Carolina would become a center of conflict. Already one of the least politically stable of the English colonies, Carolina would come under increasing scrutiny by royal authorities as its leaders demonstrated their seeming incapacity to govern during wartime. Meanwhile the Indians in the region would begin to learn about the perils of allying themselves with Europeans. Just like the Iroquois, by the end of an extended period of warfare they would begin to develop new strategies for their own survival.

The Spanish had established missions among the Timucuans, Guales, Apalachees, and Apalachicolas in Florida by about 1635. By the time English settlers began to arrive in Carolina during the 1670s, the Spanish missions were dwindling, but many Spanish-allied people still lived in the region. Then French traders arrived along the Gulf Coast. Eventually the French would found their own colony near the mouth of the Mississippi in 1699 and create their own alliances and trading partnerships with Native American peoples west of Florida. The simultaneous presence of three rival European powers, each with its own Indian allies and trading partners, was a recipe for conflict.

Carolina would have been an unstable colony even without its troubled relationships with its neighbors. Although the colony's proprietors had attracted several thousand white settlers to the southern part of the colony by 1690, they had done little to establish a stable government. The proprietors clashed continually with the faction known as the Goose Creek men, which controlled the assembly, in disputes about the proper regulation of the Indian slave trade. Piracy was another divisive issue: by the late 1680s, Carolinians were conducting a substantial trade with pirates operating out of the Bahamas and the Caribbean.[13] Most aspects of the Fundamental Constitutions had not been achieved. Indeed, after several failures to win the assembly's consent to implement the Fundamental Constitutions, the proprietors declared the document invalid, and abandoned it after 1698.

Settlers in the Albemarle Sound and Cape Fear regions to the north also resisted the proprietors' attempts to govern. In 1689 they ousted the proprietary governor there, Seth Southel, for corruption and malfeasance. Southel's administration had been a catalogue of misdemeanors, for he took the view that his recent purchase of a proprietorship gave him a license to do whatever he pleased. (After his ouster Southel went to Charleston, claimed the governorship in the south, and for the next 18 months arbitrarily imprisoned and fined both the inhabitants and the proprietary officials until he was recalled by the palatine court.) In 1691 the proprietors attempted to systematize governing authority by empowering a governor for the southern portion of the colony to appoint a deputy governor for the north. Yet despite their efforts, conflicts between the northern settlers and the proprietors continued.

Religious conflict created further dissension. Although numerous Baptists, Puritans, Huguenots, and Quakers had settled in the southern portion of the colony over the past few decades, the outbreak of war with France gave the Goose Creek faction a pretext to expel the Huguenots from the assembly as a danger to the province's security. In May 1704 they passed a bill requiring all members of the assembly to be members of the Church of England. A second bill in November 1704 divided Clarendon province into six Anglican parishes, each with its own church to be supported with local taxes. The proprietors accepted both of these acts despite the objections of the religious dissenters, who made up nearly half of the population. Though the dissenters briefly managed to get the two acts disallowed, they were overruled again when another bill to establish the Anglican Church was passed in 1706. The settlers and their government were deeply at odds.

Yet, of all of its varied problems, the proprietary regime's ultimate weakness would be the incompatibility between its Indian policies and the objectives of the empire. The

---

[13] The centrality of these issues to Carolina politics in the 1680s and 1690s is covered in Alan Gallay, *The Indian Slave Trade: The Rise of the English Empire in the American South, 1670–1717* (New Haven, 2002).

Carolina proprietors had for years encouraged their Native American neighbors to make war upon each other in order to obtain captives to sell as slaves. One consequence of this policy of constant warfare was to decimate the local Indian population. Another consequence was to antagonize the Spanish and the French in the region. The English encouraged their Yamasee allies to attack the Spanish-allied Timucuas in Florida as early as 1684, provoking retaliation by the Spanish against a community of Scottish settlers south of Charleston, in Stuart town, in 1686. By 1699, the English were encouraging the Chickasaws to go on slaving expeditions along the Mississippi River against French-allied Arkansas, Tunicas, and Taensas. The French countered by offering to arm their allies against the Chickasaws, hoping through a combination of threats and diplomacy to unite all of the Mississippi Valley Indians into an alliance with France.

When war broke out in Europe in 1702, unifying France and Spain under the house of Bourbon, the Carolinians realized that the chickens of their previous policies were coming home to roost, thereby threatening the destruction of Carolina itself. Accordingly, to avert this danger they attempted a pre-emptive strike. Carolina's Governor James Moore decided to invade Florida, organizing a joint expedition of 50 Carolinians and 1,300 Yamasees for the purpose. The expedition found the stone walls of the Castillo de San Marcos at St. Augustine impenetrable. The Spanish missions, on the other hand, provided an easy target. Over the course of the war the English in Carolina encouraged first the Yamasees and then the Creeks to raid the Spanish missions on multiple occasions. Some 10,000 Timucuas, Apalachees, and Guales were captured and sold as slaves over the course of the war.

These raids in turn helped to convince the Spanish and French governments that the English were bent on conquering the entire region. The French therefore organized a joint expedition with Spain to attack Charleston in 1706. The invasion failed miserably. However, officials within the imperial bureaucracy in England took note of the rising cost of defending Charleston and began raising questions about Carolina's policy of encouraging slave raids. The policy increased the likelihood of attacks by the Spanish and French, which might threaten English possessions in the Caribbean with their lucrative plantations. Although slave-raiding might produce short-term profits for the settlers and the proprietors, it conflicted with the long-term interests of the empire.

Over the next few years the South Carolina assembly made real strides towards reforming the Indian trading system, even if conflicts within the government frustrated their enforcement. The Anglican Church began to make an effort to send missionaries to the Indians. However, despite these efforts to begin to stabilize English–Native American relations, the long simmering tensions in the region could no longer be defused.

One set of problems arose in the relationship between the Europeans and the Tuscaroras, an Iroquoian-speaking people in what is now North Carolina. For years the Tuscaroras had been the victims of periodic raids by English-allied Indians from the area around Charleston. In 1710 their problems were made worse by the migration of 400 Swiss and German immigrants into their territory without their permission. In 1711 a group of Tuscaroras captured two of the settlers while they were exploring the area around the Neuse River, killing one of them. The Tuscaroras next proceeded to attack and kill more than 130 of the settlers. South Carolina quickly came to the settlers' defense, sending hundreds of volunteers (the vast majority of whom were Native Americans) to launch a series of successful attacks on the Tuscaroras. The South

Carolina allied forces slaughtered several hundred male Tuscarora captives and burned their villages. Then, following long tradition, the allies sold hundreds of their captives into slavery, either locally or to planters in the West Indies. Some 2,000 Tuscaroras escaped and fled north, where they were eventually taken under the wing of their kinfolk in the Iroquois League.

Having quelled the Tuscarora uprising, the Carolina government was soon faced with another, even more serious, Indian conflict. Before 1702 the most important Indian nation in Carolina was that of the Yamasees, who inhabited the coastal plain to the south of Charleston. During the first 40 years of the settlement, they had been loyal allies of the Carolinians, especially after they had supplanted the Westos as the principal channel for the deerskin and Indian slave trades. They not only provided the bulk of the forces for Governor Moore in his expedition to St. Augustine in 1702 but also gave him help when he decided to attack the Spanish missions in western Florida at the end of 1703. In due course, however, the initial harmony declined, reflecting the increasing scarcity of game in the area through overhunting, a disruption in the European market for furs caused by the war, and constant competition for new captives. Many English traders had begun dealing with the Cherokees and other peoples to the west, bypassing the Yamasees altogether.

The relationship between the Yamasees and the English was showing signs of tension as early as 1711. Then by 1714 a clear diplomatic breakdown occurred, convincing a number of other Indian peoples in the region, notably the Savannahs, Lower Creeks, and the Euchees, to join an alliance with the Yamasees against the English. War finally broke out in 1715. When it did so the Yamasees gained additional allies among some of the Upper Creeks, Choctaws, Cherokees, and Catawbas.[14] The conflict was as serious for Carolina as King Philip's assault had been for New England. The Yamasees and their many allies carried hostilities to the very gates of Charleston, killing over 400 settlers. Once more the colonists appealed to the proprietors for aid, again to no effect. Virginia offered help, but only if the Carolinians sent a large number of slaves in compensation, and the few volunteers who did arrive were described as useless. So desperate was the situation that even slaves had to be armed. Ironically, the war eventually turned in favor of the English thanks to the same dynamic that had shaped similar conflicts in the past. The Cherokees decided that their dependence on English trade required them to side with the English and turn against fellow Native Americans, in this case by helping to destroy the Yamasees. After defeating the Yamasees, the Cherokees sold most of their captives into slavery.[15]

The Yamasee War raises an interpretive question for historians, as do previous conflicts between Europeans and North American native peoples. Why did the Indian nations not unite to drive the English out of their region entirely? The answer, as the Yamasee War shows, is that Native Americans made widely varying decisions about their relationships with European nations, mainly because their interests differed. Native American peoples in the early eighteenth century thought of themselves as members of

---

[14] Accounts of the war's causes have varied. Recently discovered evidence shows that the Yamasees themselves went to war because they were convinced the English planned to attack them. See William L. Ramsay, "'Something Cloudy in Their Looks': The Origins of the Yamasee War Reconsidered," *Journal of American History*, 90 (2003), 44–75.

[15] This was the last time that Indians were enslaved in any significant numbers.

discrete groups defined by shared kinship, culture, and language, not as "Indians" with a common racial identity or a universal set of interests. In this respect they were no different than English, Spanish, French, or Dutch people, all of whom were far more likely to think of themselves as members of distinct groups defined by religion and language than as "Europeans" with the same racial identity or the same interests. At the same time, the experience of fighting this war on such a large scale changed some groups' assessment of how best to promote their tribal interests. The Creeks, who had long been part of an affiliated confederacy, realized after the Yamasee War that they were best served by avoiding an alliance with any single European power. During the decades that followed the war the Creeks made diplomatic overtures to both English Carolinians and Spanish Floridians and in effect maintained their neutrality in conflicts between the two, just as the Iroquois had been able to do further north. The Cherokees adopted a similar strategy, making occasional overtures to the French and insisting on hard bargains with the English. The Yamasee War had proved their indispensability as English allies, so the English generally did what they asked.

The proprietors' failure to defend the colony during the Yamasee War led to further pleas for Carolina to be placed under royal protection, especially as the colony was by now on the verge of bankruptcy. Another war with Spain threatened, and in November 1719 the assembly took control by electing its own governor, James Moore. The colonists, however, were careful to send a full explanation of their actions to the king, accompanied by yet another denunciation of the proprietors. The ploy was successful since the officials in Whitehall had long been hostile to the concept of proprietary government, especially its ability to enforce the laws of trade. Accordingly, in August 1720 the veteran Francis Nicholson was appointed royal governor with power to appoint a council, summon an assembly, and take all measures for the administration of the colony. The Board of Trade bought out the proprietors' land claims and rights to govern, finally completing the process in 1729 with an act of Parliament that rewarded them with payments of £2,500 each.[16]

The demise of proprietary government, the expulsion of the Yamasees, and the ending of the war in Europe all helped foster some important economic and social changes. For its first 45 years the colony had survived largely on the deerskin and Indian slave trades. Depopulation among native peoples had by the 1710s opened the colony to wider settlement and a more diversified economy. Rice had been introduced in the 1690s, its cultivation aided by the importation of African slaves whose familiarity with the crop as well as their labor helped to make successful cultivation possible. Soon a plantation system developed along the main rivers and their tributaries, while at the same time Charleston became a center of commerce and administration to which the planters gravitated during the fall and winter months when the assembly was sitting. South Carolina was finally changing from a frontier to a provincial society. It had also become a "slave society" rather than a "society with slaves."

The agreement between the Crown and the proprietors in 1729 also covered North Carolina, which had come under scrutiny for similar reasons. As in South Carolina, attempts by the assembly to establish the Anglican Church in 1701 and again in 1704 had created much antagonism among religious dissenters, particularly the Quakers.

---

[16] The exception was Lord Carteret who gave up his governmental but not his property rights.

The Quakers were backed by a faction within the Anglican majority, and disputes between this faction and the ruling Anglican faction became so bitter that the supporters of the dissenters even attempted to overthrow the government. In the end the Anglican majority prevailed and managed in 1715 to impose an Anglican establishment, supported by local tax revenues. However, the episode illustrated to the imperial bureaucracy the general ineffectiveness of the proprietary government.

This ineffectiveness was further evidenced by the inability of the proprietors to defend the province, as demonstrated by the Tuscarora War. Although the North Carolinians had been able to obtain help from both Virginia and South Carolina, they had (as usual) received no assistance from the proprietors, and this failure did not go unnoticed in London.

A final cause of royal displeasure was the suspicion that North Carolina was providing a haven for pirates, once again illustrating the corruption and incompetence of the proprietary government. The ending of the war in Europe led many licensed privateers to become pirates, perhaps the most notable of whom was Captain Teach, or Blackbeard, who found the waters of Albemarle Sound a most convenient haven. Tobias Knight, the provincial secretary, and possibly Charles Eden, one of the proprietors, were suspected of complicity in providing Teach with harbor facilities and help in the sale of his booty. An expedition from Virginia, organized by Nicholson, was required to bring the scourge to an end. In 1718 Teach was finally cornered and killed on the Albemarle outer banks near Ocracoke Inlet.

After 1718 North Carolina was effectively a royal province, since the Crown insisted on vetting the next nominee for governor, but formal surrender was achieved only through the same act of Parliament which ended the proprietors' title to South Carolina.

Traditional accounts have tended to view proprietary experiments like those in the Carolinas as doomed to failure, incompatible with the seeds of liberty already planted in North American soil.[17] Proprietary colonies, however, were established successfully by the French in Canada, the Spanish in Central America, and to some extent the Dutch in New York. The system failed in the Carolinas for other reasons. The proprietors failed to establish an effective government over the white settlers, and were too short-sighted to create a viable long-term policy for dealing with their Indian neighbors; instead their pursuit of short-term gain caused terrible instability and conflict. The paradox is that a pyramidal society was eventually established in the Carolinas, though not in the way envisaged by Locke and Shaftesbury, the authors of the Fundamental Constitutions. By the middle of the eighteenth century a local aristocracy had emerged, though it owed nothing to the proprietors and placed little reliance on a yeomanry. This aristocracy had come to depend instead on African slavery for its labor requirements. Thus were the projects of the Old World turned upside down in the New.

5 PROPRIETARY PROBLEMS IN PENNSYLVANIA AND NEW JERSEY

Although Pennsylvania was relatively untouched by violence during the imperial wars, it experienced plenty of political strife following the accession of William and Mary.

---

[17] See, for example, Louis Hartz, *The Liberal Tradition in America* (New York, 1955).

By the time Queen Anne's War ended in 1713, Penn's proprietorship had survived, although the government of Pennsylvania had assumed a form vastly different from the one he originally envisioned. Meanwhile, Delaware became separated from Pennsylvania, while the Jerseys were united into a single royal colony called New Jersey.

After the Glorious Revolution, Penn's close ties to James II and his policy of religious toleration brought him under intense scrutiny by the new regime, and in July 1690 he was accused of high treason. Although Penn made his peace with William III, his proprietary rights were suspended in October 1692 when William III appointed Benjamin Fletcher to be joint governor of Pennsylvania and New York. Fletcher's appointment was justified "by reason of the great neglects and miscarriages" which had occurred in Pennsylvania during Penn's absence. An unstated reason was the desire to create a more effective system of defense now that the Dominion of New England had been disbanded. But if Fletcher imagined that he would have more authority as the king's representative than Penn had enjoyed, he was soon disabused of this notion. The assembly challenged Fletcher just as it had earlier challenged Penn, demanding the right to initiate legislation. It also insisted on auditing all public monies, out of concern that funds might be siphoned off for military purposes. On that matter the Quakers were adamant; war was unlawful no matter how perilous the situation might be.

Fletcher's difficulties led to Penn's being restored to his proprietorship in August 1694, despite the opposition of the royal bureaucracy. William III could hardly claim to be the savior of English rights if he abolished one of its most distinctive species, proprietary government. In any case a Quaker proprietor might be more effective in securing the supplies the government so desperately wanted.

Penn had to guarantee a number of conditions to get his title back, the most important of which was his return in person to secure Pennsylvania's defense. While awaiting his arrival the colony would be governed by his lieutenant governor, William Markham. The lower house by no means welcomed the restoration of proprietary government. There would again be an elective council with a rival claim to represent the people. To placate the assembly, in November 1696 Markham issued a new frame of government, giving the lower house the right to initiate legislation. However, Markham's frame still allowed the governor and council considerable powers, including the same right to initiate legislation as the assembly. The assembly could not accept this measure, and claimed the sole right to initiation. Furthermore, the deputies now demanded the authority to audit the public accounts, which was presently reserved to the council. The majority in the lower house now had a new leader, David Lloyd, a cousin of the former anti-proprietary leader. Trained as a lawyer in England, Lloyd was well versed in constitutional procedures. Under his leadership the acrimony between the assembly and the council continued unabated.

In 1699 Penn finally left England, still believing that Quaker principles founded on reason could produce calm. After two years, however, he recognized that further concessions were necessary, not least because his proprietorship was under attack once more in England. Accordingly, in 1701 Penn issued a new frame of government. It was remarkably short, making no mention of the council and declaring that all laws were to be made "By the Governor with the consent and approbation of the freemen in general assembly met." Pennsylvania was to have a unicameral legislature, a unique phenomenon in England's American colonies. The only check on the assembly was that all bills were still subject to the veto of the proprietor and, ultimately, of the Privy Council.[18]

The assembly quickly accepted Penn's concessions, though the pattern of Pennsylvanian politics did not change. The proprietary family still controlled the executive branch and the granting of all land, which were the issues behind the next dispute with the assembly.

In a separate proviso Penn indicated that the three Delaware counties could separate from Pennsylvania. They would keep the same governor and privileges, the only difference being that their representatives would meet at Newcastle to frame their own laws. Delaware's inhabitants quickly seized this option, since most of them disliked the Quakers. Nor was their departure in November 1702 opposed, since they had been overrepresented in the assembly. One element of contention was thus removed, though Delaware itself remained in an anomalous position, since its separation was never formally recognized by the Crown.

Penn's legacy for his colony included continued peaceful relations with the native inhabitants. Indeed, Pennsylvania (along with its neighbors, Delaware and New Jersey) was unusual among the English colonies in that before the mid-1700s it was spared the violent confrontations between settlers and Native American inhabitants that nearly tore so many of the other colonies apart. This was due in part to the Quakers' good luck in having arrived relatively late in the process of colonizing North America.

Penn also contributed to the colony's good relations with the Indians by consistently following his policy of purchasing land before claiming it for the colony. In this he undoubtedly learned from the experience of other colonizers that it was prudent to do so. During the 1690s Penn once again tried to purchase land for trade reasons, this time from the Iroquois in the Susquehanna River region. New York claimed it had already acquired the land as a gift from the Iroquois. However, Penn persisted, and in 1701, after the Iroquois had become disenchanted with their two-and-a-half-decade-long relationship with New York, they agreed to sell the Susquehanna Valley land to Penn.

It would be misleading to suggest that Penn's policies towards the Indians were purely benevolent. The Lenapes (Delawares), interpreted the sale of their land differently than the English, and expected continuing payments in exchange for allowing settlers to build farms along the Delaware River. Penn's decision to invite refugees from other tribes, including the Nanticokes and the Conoys from Maryland and the Shawnees from South Carolina, to resettle in the region did not necessarily benefit the Lenapes. However, the evidence makes clear that Penn and the original Quaker leaders of the colony were sincerely committed to maintaining peaceful relationships with the local Indians. These relationships persisted for as long as Penn was alive.

Historians have extolled the Quakers for their commitment to principles that we now admire. First, they alone believed in religious toleration at this time, as a consequence of which they welcomed other groups, making Pennsylvania the first province to offer refuge to the oppressed. The Quakers also believed in simplicity of manners and in human equality, holding that God created all human beings in his image. Only the Quakers attempted to treat the Indians as equals, while this same

---

[18] For the full text see W. Keith Kavenagh, *Foundations of Colonial America: A Documentary History* (New York, 1973), Vol. 2, 1160–4.

egalitarianism was leading them to denounce slavery as well. It also led them to be more equitable than any contemporary English society in their treatment of women. Moreover, only in Pennsylvania was charity distributed without the recipient being expected to acknowledge shame. Finally their pragmatism made the Quakers exponents of technology, helping to launch the technologically innovative society that Americans would later develop.[19]

With so much that is praiseworthy about the Quakers, it has sometimes seemed incongruous that they were unable to conduct their political affairs in the spirit of friendship and peace for which they are so well known. But their very contentiousness, produced in part by the anti-authoritarian spirit of the Quaker religion, helped to produce a political system that was in many ways the most democratic in all of the English colonies. With the 1701 Charter of Liberties, Penn gave up his ideal of a benign, deferential society and pragmatically agreed to a model of government in which ordinary people would have considerable power. The unicameral legislature discouraged the creation of a political elite based on wealth. The assembly also had substantial powers to operate without interference from either the proprietor or the Crown. Pennsylvania's political system, in its early years, was unusually responsive to popular pressure.

While Penn was making his final dispositions for Pennsylvania, another province in which he had once had an interest was also undergoing change. The situation in East and West New Jersey was becoming increasingly confused as one group of proprietors sold its interest to another. Because these changes made the titles to their land uncertain, in 1700 some 200 inhabitants of East New Jersey appealed to the Crown for redress and charged the proprietors with failing to defend the colonies. The Board of Trade took note of their petition, not least because the old suspicion resurfaced that the acts of trade were being ignored. Edward Randolph, the old nemesis of Massachusetts, compiled a long list of misdemeanors that became the basis for recommendations that all the proprietary colonies be taken over by the Crown. After a series of negotiations, the proprietors agreed to surrender their governmental powers to both East and West New Jersey in return for keeping their land rights in 1702.

To help unify the province, Queen Anne, William III's successor, ordered that the council should comprise six men from the east and six from the west, with the assembly alternating between Perth Amboy and Burlington. Freeholders who held 100 acres of land would qualify for the vote. Although New Jersey was to have the same governor as New York until 1738, it was now a full-fledged royal colony.

---

[19]   Daniel J. Boorstin in *The Americans: The Colonial Experience* (New York, 1958) argues that the Quakers were inflexible doctrinaires. For a more sympathetic account, see Frederick B. Tolles, *Quakers and the Atlantic Culture* (New York, 1960). For a more recent, generally neutral analysis, see Richard S. Dunn and Mary Maples Dunn, eds, *The World of William Penn* (Philadelphia, 1986). For a summary of the consensus view on the Quakers in Pennsylvania, see Ned C. Landsman, "The Middle Colonies: New Opportunities for Settlement, 1660–1700," in Nicholas Canny, ed., *The Origins of Empire: British Overseas Enterprise to the Close of the Seventeenth Century* (New York, 1998), 351–74.

Part III

The Eighteenth-Century Provinces in a Changing Continent

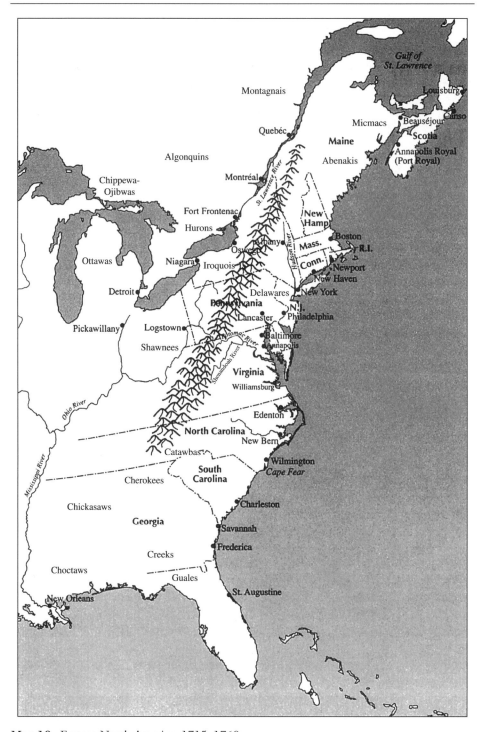

Map 10   Eastern North America, 1715–1760.

10

The Economy and Labor System in British North America

1690	Paper money is first issued in the colonies by Massachusetts.
1693	Rice culture is introduced into South Carolina.
1699	Parliament bans the export of colonial woolens.
1704	Parliament grants bounties for the production of naval stores.
1707	Parliament regulates the silver content of colonial coinage.
1718	Parliament passes the Transportation of Convicts Act.
1720	The South Sea Bubble causes financial panic in Britain.
1723	The Pennsylvania loan office issues its first notes.
1725	Pennsylvania passes the Flour Inspection Act.
1730	Virginia passes the Tobacco Inspection Act.
1732	Parliament passes the Hat Act.
1733	Parliament passes the Molasses Act.
1735	The first poorhouse is established in Boston.
1740	The Land and Silver banks are established in Massachusetts. Commercial wheat cultivation begins in the Chesapeake.
1741	Indigo cultivation is introduced into South Carolina.
1748	Maryland passes the Tobacco Inspection Act.
1750	The Iron Act prohibits rolling and slitting mills.
1751	The New England Currency Act is passed.
1755	Paper money is first issued in Virginia.

Colonial America: A History to 1763, Fourth Edition. Richard Middleton and Anne Lombard.
© 2011 Richard Middleton and Anne Lombard. Published 2011 by Blackwell Publishing Ltd.

1 THE BRITISH ATLANTIC ECONOMY

Money makes the world go round, it is popularly said. This aphorism was certainly true of the British North American colonial world, which was dominated by the need to make a living. The possession, creation, and spending of wealth determined people's goals, tastes, and living standards, as well as shaping their identities. For this reason the colonial economy is considered before the family, gender identity, religion, and culture.

In order to understand the economic development of particular regions in the British North American colonies, it is first necessary to understand the broader transatlantic commercial system of which they and (after 1707) Great Britain[1] were a part. As colonial promoters like Hakluyt had predicted, the creation of colonies in the seventeenth century had provided a destination for England's poor and unemployed and produced revenues for the Crown. Moreover the colonies had become inextricably linked to the mother country through trade, though this trading system had developed in ways that Hakluyt could not have foreseen.

Over the course of the seventeenth century, between 300,000 and 400,000 Englishmen left England to settle in North America and the Caribbean.[2] The vast majority of them were poor, as Hakluyt had suggested they would be. They were also primarily young and male. This large exodus of marriageable young men had a predictable impact on the fertility rate in England. The shortage of young men combined with poor economic conditions contributed to a decline in marriages and a decline in English population growth after 1650.[3] This demographic shift helped to solve the terrible crisis of unemployment which had fuelled out-migration in the first place. Thus by 1700 poor, unskilled English youths were less likely to move to the colonies since they could find paid work at home. In turn the relative scarcity of labor in England drove up real wages (wages measured by their purchasing power), so that by the 1680s ordinary people had small amounts of disposable income for the first time in English history.

Economic historians have suggested that even though the extent of people's new purchasing power was not great, it made a difference to England's economy. Wages rose at a time when new products from the colonies were becoming available for sale in England, and ordinary Englishmen and -women responded by changing their buying habits and becoming consumers of colonial staple commodities. The development of a market for tobacco offers an example. When English merchants first began to import tobacco early in the seventeenth century, smoking tobacco became a fashionable activity among English gentlemen and merchants. Because tobacco commanded a high price, though, it was only a luxury commodity. Ordinary people could not afford it. Then over the course of the seventeenth century, as the spread of tobacco production caused the price to fall, ordinary English laborers discovered for themselves the joys of

---

[1] The 1707 Act of Union between England and Scotland created the United Kingdom of Great Britain. When discussing the period after that date, the noun "Britain" or adjective "British" is used in place of "England" or "English." Too many writers use "England" when they mean Britain, to the annoyance of most Scots and Welsh.

[2] An additional 100,000 people from England and Wales migrated to Ireland during the period.

[3] The English population is estimated to have shrunk from 5.3 million to 5 million between 1650 and 1700.

nicotine addiction and demand for tobacco grew exponentially. In response to the new demand, imports of tobacco from the American colonies into England expanded from one million pounds in 1640 to 28 million pounds in 1700.[4]

The development of a market for sugar followed a similar trajectory. When first introduced into English markets, sugar was a luxury consumed only by the rich. As production became more efficient and the price of sugar fell, the English population developed a new taste for sweetness. Sugar exports from the West Indian colonies (mostly Barbados and Jamaica) rose from 8,000 tons in 1663 to 25,000 tons in 1700. During the eighteenth century, demand for sugar rose even faster as British consumers developed a taste for imported tea (and to a lesser extent coffee and chocolate) sweetened with sugar from the West Indies, and consumed as much of it as could be produced.[5]

Historians see this change in consumption patterns as part of a larger phenomenon called the "consumer revolution," which represented a new type of human behavior not seen in peasant societies. In the past, consumption of non-necessities had been limited to the rich. However around the end of the seventeenth century ordinary English people began to aspire to enjoy novel or exotic products that could make their lives more comfortable (or at least more stimulating). Widespread desire for novelty fuelled demand for tobacco, sugar, tea, calicoes from India, and tableware from China, producing new patterns of spending, especially among the middling sort but even among poor laborers.[6]

English consumers' new ability and willingness to spend money on colonial products in turn spurred other kinds of trade, much of it channeled in particular ways by the English navigation laws, or the mercantilist system. Indeed the navigation laws would encourage additional commercial connections and economic activity which the original theorists of mercantilism could hardly have foreseen. English traders who carried tobacco from the Chesapeake to London then re-exported it to continental Europe. Merchants who brought sugar from the West Indies to England then carried English manufactured goods to sell to planters on their return voyages. By 1700 English merchants had replaced the Dutch as the world's premier slave-traders, carrying slaves by the thousands from West Africa to the West Indies (and increasingly to the North American mainland).[7] Products not covered by the Navigation Acts, such as fish and

---

[4] Figures may be found in Anthony McFarlane, *The British in the Americas, 1480–1815* (London, 1994), 117, citing Russell R. Menard, "The Tobacco Industry in the Chesapeake Colonies, 1617–1730: An Interpretation," *Research in Economic History*, 5 (1980), 109–77.

[5] See Nuala Zahedieh, "Economy," in David Armitage and Michael J. Braddick, eds, *The British Atlantic World, 1500–1800* (London, 2002), 57, citing Noel Deerr, *The History of Sugar*, 2 vols (London, 1949–50).

[6] The consumer revolution has been a relatively new topic for economic historians, who in trying to explain the rise of capitalism have more commonly focused on the production and distribution of goods rather than on consumer demand. For efforts to explain the rise of consumer demand in seventeenth- and eighteenth-century Europe, see, e.g., Neil McKendrick, John Brewer, and J. H. Plumb, eds, *The Birth of a Consumer Society: The Commercialization of Eighteenth-Century England* (Bloomington, 1982); Simon Schama, *The Embarrassment of Riches: An Interpretation of Dutch Culture in the Golden Age* (New York, 1987); John Brewer and Roy Porter, eds, *Consumption and the World of Goods* (London, 1993).

[7] It is estimated that from the introduction of sugar and slavery to Barbados in the 1630s until 1700, some 450,000 African slaves were imported into the English and French sugar colonies in the West Indies, while about 30,000 African slaves were taken to the North American mainland. Herbert S. Klein, *The Atlantic Slave Trade* (Cambridge, 1999), 31–2.

furs from Newfoundland or Maine, could be taken straight to European ports, where they could be traded for commodities like wine. Lumber and livestock from New England and grain from Pennsylvania could be shipped to both the British and the French West Indies, and exchanged for sugar, which could be distilled into rum and sold within the colonies. Because the navigation laws had provided incentives for English investors to build more ships, the number of ships available for global trading voyages more than doubled between 1650 and 1700. This reduced the cost of shipping goods (and lowered their prices). The increase in the size of the merchant marine expanded the number of vessels available to the king's navy, making it possible for the English government to drive out its competitors in the global trade. By the end of the seventeenth century, Britain had displaced Holland as the financial and commercial leader of Europe and was also experiencing the beginnings of the phenomenon known as the Industrial Revolution.

By 1713, British North American colonial economies had, with a few exceptions, embarked on paths of development shaped by the British Atlantic economic system, with its flows of people and its patterns of consumer demand. Most colonists were increasingly becoming part of a wider market economy, devoting much of their productive energy to produce goods or services to sell to others. The ways in which they took part in that economy – the types of production in which they engaged and the labor systems that they developed in order to produce goods for the market – varied greatly, particularly between the South and the North. It is these variations we will now examine.

2   THE SOUTHERN PLANTATION SYSTEM

Historians have disagreed as to whether economic growth in British North America during the eighteenth century occurred because colonial economies developed a greater capacity to produce goods, or because of the growing demand in Europe for American-produced staples. A related question is whether the domestic market was more important than the export market in the southern economy.[8]

To some extent the first distinction is artificial, since supply and demand are two sides of the same coin. However, both factors played some part in expanding exports from the South. Making the second determination has also proved difficult. Exports were certainly important to the South, because the region was geared to the production of cash crops. On the other hand, the majority of its population were owners of small farms who produced primarily for their own needs. Since the export of staples is usually considered the most dynamic element in the southern economy, it will be considered first.

The most important staple in mainland British North America was tobacco. Even by 1700 production had reached 28 million pounds and it continued to climb, reaching 80 million pounds by 1760. By this time tobacco comprised almost

---

[8]   The debate is surveyed in John J. McCusker and Russell R. Menard, *The Economy of British North America, 1607–1789* (Chapel Hill, 1985). See also David W. Galenson and Russell R. Menard, "Approaches to the Analysis of Economic Growth in Colonial British America," *Historical Methods*, 13 (1980), 3–18.

45 percent of mainland colonial exports. The total value of the exported crop was some £700,000. Seventy percent of it was grown in Virginia.

This increase had been achieved as a result of both supply and demand factors. Among the more important supply elements was the growth in the labor force. In 1660 the population of Virginia had been 25,000, Maryland had 10,000 settlers, while North Carolina had only a few hundred. By 1760 Virginia had almost 350,000 inhabitants, Maryland 160,000, and North Carolina 120,000.

Another supply factor was improved efficiency. By the eighteenth century, the average tobacco worker was able to attend between two and three acres or up to 10,000 plants, producing between 700 and 1,000 pounds of tobacco. The seventeenth-century average attendance had been only 3,000 plants.

Also on the supply side was the availability of land. Without this, extra hands would have been to no avail. Land and people were two advantages enjoyed by the Chesapeake colonies in particular.

But demand factors were also very important. During the eighteenth century European purchases of tobacco continued to grow steadily. After the 1707 Act of Union between England and Scotland exports of tobacco were further stimulated by the advent of an aggressive Scottish merchant community to market the crop. This was especially beneficial to smaller producers who until then had to rely on the intermediary services of the larger growers. As we have seen, even the decline in price was advantageous, as it widened the market. By the middle of the eighteenth century, tobacco was no longer a luxury for most of Europe's population.

Two kinds of tobacco were cultivated during the eighteenth century, one the sweet-scented variety originally introduced by John Rolfe, the other the Orinoco from South America. The type planted was partly a matter of climate. The Orinoco was a hardier plant and better able to thrive in the shorter summers of the upper Chesapeake and less fertile soils of the Piedmont. Much of this was exported to continental Europe. However, most tidewater planters continued to grow the more traditional sweet-scented variety, since this was most popular in Britain.

Despite the growth in production, the cultivation of tobacco was not without its problems. Late frosts posed a serious hazard in the early stages, while too much rain was similarly disastrous before harvesting. In between, pests like the tobacco fly and hornworm could ruin a crop. The owner then had the difficult decision of when to cut his tobacco, since a mistake would leave him with an inferior product. Curing and packing were also delicate operations that required great care if the tobacco was to get to market in good condition.

To protect its industry, Virginia developed a system of inspection. For almost a century various attempts to control the quality of the tobacco had met with fierce opposition from the small-scale planters, who feared that their inferior bulk product would be excluded. An act passed in 1712 was subsequently disallowed by the Privy Council, but an amended version, passed in 1730, required all tobacco to be brought to a public warehouse for inspection to ensure that it was properly cured. One unanticipated benefit was that the receipts provided a useful circulating medium. The system of inspection was sufficiently successful to be copied by Maryland in 1748.

A common criticism of the tobacco industry in the eighteenth century was its extravagant use of land. Tobacco made heavy demands on the soil, wearing it out in three or four years, after which the planter had to move on to fresh acreage. While land was so abundant, however, this practice made economic sense, for as Jefferson later noted, it was cheaper for British North Americans to buy a new acre than to manure an old one. Such reasoning was not generally appreciated by European visitors, who forgot they were looking at agriculture from a different perspective when making derogatory remarks. In Europe labor was plentiful and land scarce; moreover, the countryside had been under intensive cultivation for many centuries. Hence behavior in North America that seemed slovenly and wasteful was often the result of attempts to avoid the high cost of labor. Best practice on the two continents necessarily differed at times.

Like all industries, tobacco suffered cyclical movements in its prosperity. Prices were highest – around two and a half pence a pound – in the periods 1700–4, 1714–20, 1735–43, and 1747–53, which generally coincided with peace in Europe. In between, prices often fell below one penny a pound.

The uncertainty concerning prices and the difficulties of production led many Chesapeake planters to turn to wheat after the outbreak of war in the 1740s. Wheat could be grown in fields left fallow after tobacco, often as a winter crop. Over a 20-year period 12 crops of wheat might be grown to three of tobacco, though the value of tobacco was approximately six times greater. George Washington was one of those who switched to wheat after the French and Indian War ended in 1763. Wheat permitted the use of ox-drawn plows, making it less labor-intensive and therefore allowing more time for building and other improvements. Production climbed steadily throughout the later colonial period, though its export value, around £150,000 by 1760, was still less than one-fifth that of tobacco. Most wheat was shipped to southern Europe or to the West Indies.

By comparison, South Carolina's economy was still in transition in 1713. The deerskin and Indian slave trades had been its lifeline during the seventeenth century. These would soon decrease with the end of the Yamasee War and the decline in the supply of game.[9] A profitable market for rice, however, was beginning to develop in both the Mediterranean and northern Europe. Production, which rose from 10,000 to 100,000 barrels between 1720 and 1760, was boosted by the expansion of cultivation to the adjacent areas of North Carolina and Georgia. Other factors also helped production. One was the partial removal of rice from the enumeration list in 1730, which allowed its direct export to Spain, Portugal, and the Mediterranean. Production was also aided towards the end of the colonial period by the use of wind-powered fans for winnowing the rice and of draft animals for pounding it, which made processing easier and more efficient. By 1760 rice accounted for about 20 percent of colonial commodity exports, bringing in about £300,000. This made it the second most valuable export after tobacco. However, like tobacco, it was susceptible to market fluctuations. This was especially true during the War of Jenkins' Ear, when the price plummeted from nine to two shillings a hundredweight.

Rice, unlike tobacco, was a relatively hardy plant to grow. The main requirement (and difficulty) was the need to immerse the crop in water at various stages during the growing season. This meant the construction of special fields protected by embankments, with

---

[9]   For the economics of the southern fur trade, see Kathryn E. Holland Braund, *Deerskins and Duffels: Creek Indian Trade with Anglo-America, 1685–1815* (Lincoln, Nebr., 1993).

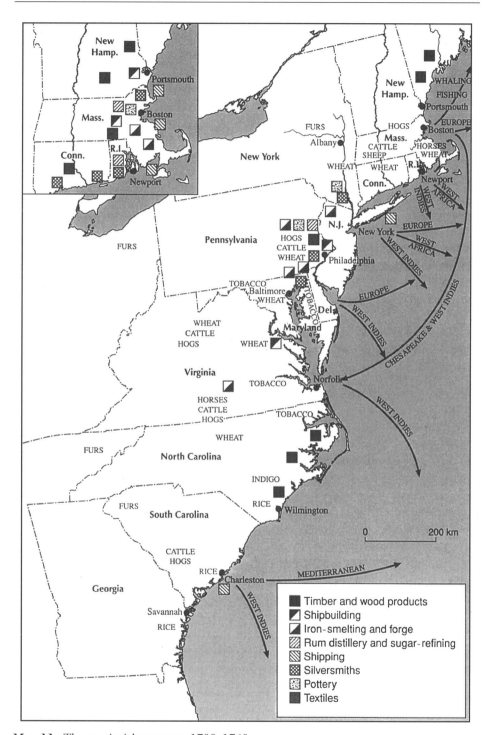

Map 11 The provincial economy, 1700–1760.

ditches, sluice gates, and reservoirs to control the water supply. A dry spring or early summer could mean disaster if the reservoirs ran dry, while too much rain might lead to flooding at the wrong time. For this reason some planters began experimenting with river tidal flows to get a more dependable supply of water, but the technology and capital to do this were not widely available during the colonial period.

Another crop developed in South Carolina after 1740 was indigo. Its production at this time was the result of attempts by the planters to diversify in response to the problems caused by the war in Europe. When boiled in special vats, the leaves of this plant yielded a brilliant violet dye, which was especially prized before the invention of chemical substitutes. The advantage of indigo was that it could be grown on land where rice cultivation was not possible. The disadvantage was that it was not easy to produce, since the periods of fermentation, distillation, and drying were difficult to assess, making quality control a nightmare. Nevertheless, production rose steadily, helped after 1748 by a bounty of sixpence a pound from Parliament. Indigo provided an export value of approximately £100,000.

Cotton, the crop usually associated with the Deep South in nineteenth-century North America, was still almost unknown. The short-staple variety was impracticable to harvest on any scale until Eli Whitney invented his famous gin, though some slaves and poor whites spun a little yarn for their own use. Otherwise, all the colonies at this time imported sea island cotton from the West Indies if they wanted fabric from this material.

The first southern colonizers had envisioned a mixed economy of commerce, manufacturing, and farming, but their hopes had been sadly disappointed. Timber was plentiful, but shipbuilding was restricted by a lack of skilled labor. In the eighteenth century, however, a lumber industry developed using water-powered saw mills. Its principal product was staves for making barrels to export the South's cash crops. Shingles for roofing and clapboard were also produced, and found a ready market in the West Indies, where all wood products were scarce. Sales of these products brought in perhaps £50,000.

Timber also supported the naval stores industry. As the century progressed, the Royal Navy required ever larger quantities of pitch and tar for making vessels watertight, as well as turpentine for varnishing woodwork. Until the eighteenth century these items were obtained mainly from the Baltic, but political uncertainty in that area eventually induced the navy to seek alternative supplies from the North American colonies. To encourage this Parliament passed an act in 1704 providing for bounties on the production of masts, hemp, pitch, and tar. The pitch and tar industry was especially important for the Carolinas, since both had a vast supply of suitable pine trees. The resinous timber was heated slowly to make the tar run out without catching fire. Initially the industry flourished in South Carolina, but as rice cultivation became more widespread there, production shifted to North Carolina. The export value of this product was about £60,000 annually.

The continued expansion of cash crops in the South was made possible by the growth of the labor force, primarily through the purchase of African slaves. As was pointed out in Part II, before 1700 Virginia and Maryland had relied on indentured servants, although South Carolinians had always preferred slaves, including both Native Americans and Africans. The eighteenth century witnessed a rapid increase in the size of the African labor force in both the upper and lower South, as planters sought to extend their holdings and increase their profits. In 1680 Virginia had 3,000 slaves and 15,000 indentured servants. By 1715 the ratio of slaves to indentured laborers was almost exactly the reverse, with 23,000 slaves in the province, and another 1,000 being imported annually. Even these figures were dwarfed by the dramatic increase between 1743 and 1756. The total number during this period rose from 42,000 to 120,000 as a result of both importation and the fertility of the existing population.

Maryland and the Carolinas experienced similar increases. In 1690 there had been 1,500 enslaved Africans in South Carolina; by 1720 the figure had risen to 12,000, reaching 57,000 in 1760. By then Virginia and South Carolina were each importing over 2,500 enslaved Africans annually; and even North Carolina was buying several hundred. During the 1750s imports often exceeded 7,000 slaves a year.

The reasons for the growth of slavery were varied, as we have seen. White laborers from England became less willing in the late seventeenth century to migrate to the Chesapeake as indentured servants. Most indentured servants left their masters at the end of their service and thereafter became too expensive. According to the Reverend Peter Fontaine of Virginia, in 1750 a free white servant would expect to be paid almost £20 a year, while for another £7 or £8 a planter could "have a slave for life." The cost of slaves relative to indentured servants had significantly decreased since the seventeenth century, especially as the numbers of enslaved Africans being shipped by British traders increased the available supply.

Other reasons probably had to do with the behavior of servants and slaves themselves. British servants who ran away could blend into the surrounding population, while Africans could not. Northern Europeans languished (and often died) in the tropical or semi-tropical conditions found in the southern colonies, while Africans understood how to grow their own food and build adequate housing out of available materials. British servants could resort to the courts for redress if they were mistreated, while African slaves, unused to the English legal system, were less likely to do so.

As slavery became more common and numbers of African slaves grew, racial fears and antipathies also became more virulent, making it easier for owners to exploit blacks than whites. Most plantation tasks were of a dull, routine nature. While white indentured servants were apt to resist such work, both male and female slaves could be forced to put up with them.

It was traditionally assumed that slave-ownership was limited to the wealthy few. Scholarship has now shown that it was more widespread, especially in the tidewater, where 40 percent of households in many counties had three or more slaves. Even in the piedmont 20–30 percent of households owned one or two slaves. Of course ownership was distributed unevenly, many households having only one, while others had half a dozen or more. Large plantations with more than 20 slaves were relatively scarce and were found most frequently in South Carolina, where rice and indigo cultivation and the production of naval stores were expensive businesses which could be undertaken only by large producers.[10]

---

[10]   The claim that slave-owning was relatively widespread in the Chesapeake is advanced by Allan Kulikoff, in *Tobacco and Slaves: The Development of Southern Cultures in the Chesapeake, 1680–1800* (Chapel Hill, 1986). His argument that large concentrations of Africans were rare is challenged by Philip D. Morgan and Michael L. Nicholls in "Slaves in Piedmont Virginia, 1720–1790," *William and Mary Quarterly*, 46 (1989), 211–51, who found that in many piedmont counties 30 percent of Africans lived on plantations of 21 slaves or more.

Despite the widespread ownership of slaves, their use did not go unquestioned. Many South Carolinians feared that slaves would become too numerous and eventually overpower them. Accordingly, attempts were made in the early 1730s to restrict slave imports by imposing a tax, linked to a promise of 50 acres of land without quitrents for 10 years for every white person settling new townships in the back-country. The Crown saw the tax on slaves as a restriction on trade and disallowed the measure.

Similar efforts to restrict the slave trade were made in Virginia, though concern there was not as great as in South Carolina, since Africans were not a majority of the population. Nevertheless, some thoughtful Virginians already recognized that white planters there were influenced by a system of economic incentives that would inevitably lead to greater reliance on plantation agriculture and slavery. Hiring wage laborers was expensive, so most planters invested instead in slaves, a cheaper investment in the long run. This meant that there were few opportunities for free laborers. White men sought instead to become planters, and as a result did not spend time learning the skills that in the North would lead to better wages and opportunities for advancement. As a result there were fewer skilled coopers, smiths, joiners, wheelwrights, leather workers, weavers, and bricklayers in the South than in the North. The full consequences of this lack were not felt until the onset of the Industrial Revolution in the nineteenth century, when the South was to find itself increasingly disadvantaged by its lack of skilled labor and commercial acumen.

One possible alternative to slave labor was the use of convicts. In 1718 Parliament passed a law providing for their transportation to America. While occasional convicts had been sent over since the time of the Restoration, the numbers now greatly increased, reaching a total of 30,000 by 1760. Some two-thirds went to the Chesapeake, where they worked in gangs like the slaves, serving sentences between seven and 14 years. The advantage for employers was that convicts were cheaper than any other hired labor. No purchase or transportation charges were incurred, nor were freedom dues payable when their sentences were completed. Not all were hardened criminals; many were first offenders convicted of minor crimes for whom transportation was a chance to make good. However, the practice did not become popular with most colonials, and the convicts were invariably blamed for increases in crime. Benjamin Franklin suggested America should send her rattlesnakes to England in "return for the Human Serpents sent us by the Mother Country." A larger problem was that there were not enough convicts to supply the demand for labor, so slaves were preferred.

Although slavery was now the predominant form of labor, its prevalence did not cause the disappearance of white servitude. Considerable numbers of indentured servants continued to be imported into the Chesapeake, especially from Ireland. Most masters still preferred a mixed labor force to give them some control over their African slaves. Others had to invest in servants because they required a smaller initial outlay. In all, 18,000 came to Maryland between 1718 and 1760.

The employment of slaves, convicts, and indentured servants was confined largely to the production of staples for export. Fifty percent of the white population were subsistence farmers with no labor other than their own. Although this chapter has focused on colonial exports, at least 80 percent of all economic activity was purely domestic, a fact which has led some historians to suggest that the role of exports in shaping the colonial economy has been grossly exaggerated.[11]

Small-scale tenant and freehold farmers were especially numerous in the backcountry of Virginia, Maryland, and North Carolina, where most families grew a little tobacco in exchange for other essentials. In the lower South the common surpluses were wheat, horses, cattle, and hogs. Since there were few towns to buy their produce, their opportunities were necessarily limited. Towards the end of the colonial era, however, corn and wheat began to be exported to the Mediterranean and West Indies. Even the poorest farm families wanted to market some produce so that they could improve their lot. By 1760 farmers in the Shenandoah Valley and south side of Virginia were trading up to one-quarter of their produce in the market.[12]

Almost no manufacturing took place in the South, except for the production of pig and bar iron. Most foundries were concentrated in Maryland close to the Delaware, though there were some furnaces scattered throughout Virginia and North Carolina. Another obvious aspect in which the southern colonies differed from their northern neighbors was lack of towns, which for many southerners explained the failure of their economy to diversify. Of course, South Carolina had a commercial center at Charleston and Maryland the beginnings of a port at Baltimore by 1760. Virginia, however, remained stubbornly rural despite numerous attempts by the House of Burgesses to establish towns.

The lack of diversification in the southern economy has induced much speculation. It is usually attributed to the institution of slavery, which absorbed the region's available capital while burdening it with a labor force with limited skills. In addition southerners preferred to invest in the area which they knew best and in which they had the greatest competitive edge: growing cash crops.

Certainly diversification was not a major worry in the eighteenth century. The South paid its way vis-à-vis Britain, something that the North found more difficult. Nor did it feel itself to be a beleaguered or inferior region. The planter class bought the best goods from Europe and displayed far more obvious wealth than did the northern elites.

---

[11]   Edwin J. Perkins, *The Economy of Colonial America* (New York, 1988).

[12]   For the development of the Virginian piedmont, see Robert D. Mitchell, *Commercialism and Frontier: Perspectives on the Early Shenandoah Valley* (Charlottesville, 1977); and Richard R. Beeman, *The Evolution of the Southern Backcountry: A Case Study of Lunenburg County, Virginia, 1746–1832* (Philadelphia, 1984). The commercialization of backcountry farming is also discussed by Allan Kulikoff in "The Transition to Capitalism in Rural America," *William and Mary Quarterly*, 46 (1989), 120–44; *The Agrarian Origins of American Capitalism* (Charlottesville, 1992); and "Households and Markets: Toward a New Synthesis of American Agrarian History," *William and Mary Quarterly*, 50 (1993), 342–55. In addition, see Winifred Rothenberg, "The Market and Massachusetts Farmers, 1750–1855," Journal of Economic History, 41 (1981), 283–5; and Richard L. Bushman, "Markets and Composite Farms in Early America," *William and Mary Quarterly*, 55 (1998), 351–74. The contrary view that community-oriented values dominated colonial economic activity is advanced by James A. Henretta, "Families and Farms: *Mentalité* in Pre-industrial America," William and Mary Quarterly, 35 (1978), 3–32; and *The Origins of American Capitalism: Collected Essays* (Boston, 1992). See also James A. Henretta and Gregory H. Nobles, *Evolution and Revolution: American Society, 1600–1820* (Lexington, Ky., 1987).

Indeed, the per capita income of the region's white inhabitants was twice that of either New England or the middle colonies.[13]

3   NORTHERN FARMING AND COMMERCE

While the South was dominated by the production of cash crops, the northern British mainland colonies from an early stage had a more varied economy. This diversity increased during the eighteenth century, though somewhat paradoxically the actual percentage of persons engaged in agriculture remained around 85 percent. The region nevertheless had a growing commercial sector and even the beginnings of manufacturing, though mainly of a craft or cottage kind.

Northern farm sizes ranged from between 50 and 100 acres to 300 acres. Not all the land could be cultivated at one time. Like his southern counterpart, the northern farmer exhausted his soil and then moved on to freshly cleared land. In general a man could harvest only between five and ten acres. So even with two or three sons and a couple of servants, a farmer could not cultivate more than 50 acres, though a much larger pasturage could be handled.

The most common products on the northern farm were hogs and corn. Indian corn was an extraordinarily productive crop and easy to grow. It provided bread for the family and fodder for the animals, especially hogs, which were said to fatten best on this crop. The usual method of cultivation was to sow the plants at regular intervals in small hillocks, which were created by scraping the surface of the soil with a hoe, an unavoidable procedure in ground not yet clear of roots and stumps. But even in well-cultivated land, this method was often used, since it avoided the necessity of plowing – no mean consideration for small-scale farmers who had neither plow nor draft animals. Approximately 1,200 to 1,500 could be planted to the acre. On the larger farms, especially in Pennsylvania, wheat became an increasingly popular and valued crop, since it produced a finer flour than Indian corn and hence better bread. Barley and rye were also grown in some areas. These crops all required the ground to be plowed.

The other pillar of British North American agriculture, the hog, was also easy to raise. Hogs foraged for themselves and provided meat for much of the year. By the latter part of the colonial period, however, cattle were also becoming popular, especially in New England, as better pasture became available following the importation of European grasses. Unfortunately, the readiness of farmers to let their cattle forage made breeding improvements difficult and also meant the loss of much valuable manure, something that European visitors were quick to criticize.

---

[13]   For the distribution of income, see Alice Hansen Jones, *Wealth of a Nation To Be: The American Colonies on the Eve of the Revolution* (New York, 1980); and section 5 of this chapter. Historians have traditionally seen the southern economy, with its concentration on a few staples, as an anomaly, compared to the diversification of the North. During the 1980s several scholars suggested that it was New England and the Middle Colonies that were anomalous in the wider context of the Americas, where cash-crop economies were the norm. See Jack P. Greene and J. R. Pole, *British Colonial America: Essays in the New History of the Early Modern Era* (Baltimore, 1984), and McCusker and Menard, *The Economy of British North America*.

All farm families tried to produce what their members needed, at least insofar as purchased substitutes were unavailable. Poultry provided extra protein, while most farms had a good orchard. Beer was brewed with barley malt, and in the spring the maple trees could be tapped for syrup. Many farm families also kept some sheep; their wool, although coarse, made excellent working garments. Unfortunately, the lack of pasture resulted not only in inferior fleeces but also in the loss of much wool in the scrubby terrain. For this reason some farmers cultivated flax for making linen yarn.

Although northern farmers had no southern-style cash crops to sell, they were still keen to market their produce. The opportunities were twofold. One was the growth of towns, especially the seaports along the coast, which by mid-century had a total population of 120,000. The other was the development of export markets to the West Indies and southern Europe.

Prosperous commercial farming was confined largely to the coast or major river valleys like the Hudson, Connecticut, and Delaware, which offered not only the best land but also water transport. The majority of northern farmers were not blessed with such resources, especially in New England, where the rivers were not generally navigable, the soil was often rocky, and the climate harsh. As a result most of the population in these areas engaged mainly in subsistence farming.

Since the time of Jefferson, Americans have glorified the small farmer as a self-sufficient individual who provided for himself and his family without depending on outsiders or entangling himself in the marketplace. This idealization should be qualified on a number of counts. In the first place, the image of the individual farmer is a myth. It was virtually impossible to run a farm without at least two adults, typically a husband and a wife, to divide the necessary labor, usually with substantial assistance from children, servants, or slaves. Second, subsistence did not equal self-sufficiency, something that no farm family could ever attain completely. Farmers always needed tools or other equipment and of necessity bartered surpluses to secure them. Third, a farm family's existence was by no means enviable. Farming was a hard business, dependent on the climate, and precarious too should either adult be injured or fall sick. Hence farmers always aimed to increase production beyond mere subsistence level. If they were fortunate they might secure additional land and purchase servants or slaves, in which case a family might live in greater comfort. Subsistence farming was never seen as anything other than a prelude to entering the market.[14]

The principal provisions exported by the east coast producers were pickled beef and pork from New England; wheat from New York; and wheat, flour, and bread from Pennsylvania and New Jersey. Because it was the easiest farm commodity to sell, most New England farmers kept a few head of cattle on their limited pasture, driving them to Boston and other seaports for slaughter and pickling. This practice became so common that meat exports from New England reached a value of approximately £80,000 by mid-century, the most important area of production being the Connecticut River

---

[14] On the Jeffersonian image of farming, see Joyce Oldham Appleby, "Commercial Farming and the 'Agrarian Myth' in the Early Republic," *Journal of American History*, 68 (1982), 833–49. On the impracticability of being self-sufficient, see Bettye Hobbs Pruitt, "Self-Sufficiency and the Agricultural Economy of Eighteenth-Century Massachusetts," *William and Mary Quarterly*, 41 (1984), 333–64, and Bushman, "Markets and Composite Farms." The continued glorification of farming has been greatly reinforced by the perceived decline in the quality of urban life.

Figure 18 West Indian slaves processing indigo. From Pierre Pomet, *A Compleat History of Drugs* (1725). Slave-based societies in the West Indies provided the northern colonies in British North America with their main market for food and other products, since West Indian planters generally did not grow enough food to feed the slave population.

Valley. The middle colonies also produced some meat, though from the early days they concentrated on the cultivation of grain, especially wheat. Pennsylvania in particular produced some of the finest flour, instituting a rigorous inspection system in 1725 to maintain its high quality. Pennsylvania and New Jersey in addition exported some corn and peas, and the total annual value of their combined exports amounted to about £300,000 by 1760.

As in the South, the principal export markets were southern Europe and the West Indies. By 1750 the value of shipments of flour and pickled meat to southern Europe amounted to some £150,000 a year. Equally important, those trading there brought little back with them, thus ensuring a net gain to the balance of payments. Most cargoes comprised wine from Madeira and the Canary Islands.

The annual value of victuals exported to the West Indies was about £200,000 during the same period. This market existed because planters in Barbados, Jamaica, and other British West Indian islands now devoted virtually all of their resources to the production of sugar, and had to import food to provision both themselves and their slaves. Exports to the West Indies in turn financed further trade transactions. Most captains returned from their provisioning voyages with cargoes of sugar and molasses, the thick syrup that was drained off from the sugar. Molasses was an important commodity because it could be fermented and distilled into rum, a useful stimulant after a long day's work and a valuable anesthetic in the event of injury. Rum was also a key item in the trade with Native Americans. Its manufacture consequently supported over 100 refineries and distilleries in the northern colonies, with the heaviest concentration around Boston and Newport. Other goods imported from the Caribbean included cocoa, coffee, cotton, and mahogany.

A variant on direct trade between British North America and the West Indies was the so-called triangular voyage via Africa to purchase slaves. The volume of slaving voyages on ships owned by North American merchants has been difficult to estimate because of incomplete data; however, the best currently available evidence shows that about 2,000 slaving voyages set out from North American mainland ports between 1714 and 1807, carrying some 200,000 slaves. British carriers transported more than 10 times as many slaves as North Americans did during the same period. Nevertheless, the shipment of slaves was a lucrative business for a small group of North American merchants. The most active slave traders were from Newport, Rhode Island, while a few also operated from New York.[15]

At the start of the eighteenth century the dominant force in the export of victuals was Boston, whose merchants had pioneered the trade in provisions with the West Indies and elsewhere. When supplies from its own hinterland proved scarce, the Boston merchants had scoured the other colonies for alternative sources, effectively replacing the Dutch as general carriers. By the third decade of the eighteenth century, however, both Philadelphia and New York were developing their own commerce at Boston's expense, resulting in a stagnation in its growth after 1720.

New Englanders were involved in two other forms of commerce: fishing and whaling. Fish was a common ingredient in many colonial diets and was similarly important in southern Europe, where the Catholic Church proscribed the eating of meat on Fridays. Like rice, fish could be shipped directly, not being an enumerated product, and consequently numerous vessels were employed for this purpose. What made the industry so important in New England was the region's proximity to the great fishing banks of Maine and Newfoundland. Each catch was usually dried or pickled with salt and put into barrels. The highest-quality fish were dispatched to Europe, while the inferior refuse fish were sent to the West Indies to feed the slaves. Fishing was New England's most valuable industry, its exports amounting annually to some £150,000.

Whaling constituted a similarly valuable commerce both for the domestic market and for export to England. Whale meat was an important addition to the colonial diet, while the fat could be made into candles or used as oil for lamps and for tanning leather. Whale bone was also used for decorative combs and for stays in women's corsets. Lastly, the intestines of the whale produced the odoriferous ambergris, which was used as an ingredient of perfume. The whaling industry has traditionally been associated with Nantucket, but whalers operated from most New England and eastern Long Island ports, mainly patrolling the areas around Newfoundland and Greenland; the searching of the Seven Seas occurred only in the nineteenth century. Annual export values of whale products were in the region of £50,000 by 1760.

---

[15] For a critique of the traditional view of the slave trade, see Gilman M. Ostrander, "The Making of the Triangular Trade Myth," *William and Mary Quarterly*, 30 (1973), 635–44. For its relative importance to Rhode Island, see Jay Coughtry, *The Notorious Triangle: Rhode Island and the African Slave Trade, 1700–1807* (Philadelphia, 1981). By 1740, six percent of its shipping was clearing for Africa. For a summary of the most recent data, see David Eltis, "The Volume and Structure of the Transatlantic Slave Trade: A Reassessment," *William and Mary Quarterly*, 58 (2001), 17–46, esp. table at 43.

Although the fur trade had declined in relative importance since the seventeenth century, it remained significant for the merchants of Albany and other centers near the frontier. Indeed a fierce rivalry continued between New York, Pennsylvania, and of course New France for access to the Great Lakes and Ohio country. The principal pelts were deer and beaver. Deer hides were used for making leather goods like saddles, bags, belts, and shoes. Beaver pelts were prized for making hats. It is difficult to put a total value on the trade, but it probably averaged around £30,000 a year for the northern colonies.

Another important commodity industry in the north was lumber. In the early settlement period each man cut his own crude requirements. However, as areas became well established, settlers increasingly demanded finished products for their timber-frame and clapboard houses. Such quality necessitated water-powered saw mills. By the middle of the eighteenth century all the colonies had such mills near the fall line. New Hampshire was particularly blessed in this respect, having both timber and water power near the coast. For this reason New England exported more timber than any other region, mainly to the West Indies, where many of the sugar islands lacked even firewood. Consequently, on voyages there vessels usually carried items like hoops for making casks, boards, and posts for building houses, and shingles for covering roofs. Though the annual export value of such commodities was about £60,000, this was one industry whose products were intended mainly for the domestic market.

Maine and New Hampshire, like the southern colonies, also benefited from the 1704 Naval Stores Act. Their forests produced the timber for the very large masts required for the battleships of the Royal Navy. Here, too, bounties were paid to encourage production, and the result was an important trade, centered on Portsmouth, worth perhaps £20,000 in an average year.

Commerce provided employment for hundreds of ships and thousands of seamen. In addition the export of provisions required a sizable processing industry for their preparation and packing. Warehouses were needed to store the goods, middlemen to distribute them once they had arrived, and clerks to settle accounts between customers who lived thousands of miles apart. Increasingly complicated logistics led to the emergence of counting houses. Insurance was also increasingly used, as was credit. Although no banks were actually set up during the colonial period, attempts were made to establish one in Boston. Here was the economic sophistication and diversification that eluded the Chesapeake economy.

Another way in which commerce benefited the North was by stimulating manufacturing. So much tonnage required a considerable shipbuilding industry to sustain it. Ships needed replacing on average every 10 to 15 years and had to be repaired in between. The northern colonies were extremely well placed to develop shipbuilding; they had almost inexhaustible supplies of timber and could supply practically all the materials required for the construction of the largest ocean vessels, in addition to having a skilled labor force.

Much of what the colonists built they exported to Britain. Indeed, it was frequently the practice to sell both the ship and the cargo on arrival there. The reputation of colonial builders was such that by 1760 their yards were producing 25,000 tons a year, one-third of all British requirements. This trade was an important element in enabling the northern colonies to pay their way, contributing perhaps £140,000 annually to their balance of payments.

As the century progressed, other types of manufacturing also began to develop, although unlike shipbuilding, they were devoted mainly to supplying the domestic market. Most of these enterprises were concentrated either around the Delaware, where Quaker pragmatism was conducive to manufacturing skills, or in southern New England, where a similar environment and concentration of skills existed.

Among the more important manufacturing processes were the smelting of iron and production of metal wares. John Winthrop, Jr. had made the first attempt to produce iron in Massachusetts in the 1640s. But the industry did not become established until the second decade of the eighteenth century. Most of the furnaces for producing pig iron, slitting mills for fashioning it into bars, and forges for making finished goods were concentrated in the two key regions of the Delaware and southern New England. By 1750 colonial iron output was sufficiently important for Parliament to pass an act controlling the industry, by which time British North America was producing one-eighth of the world's pig iron.

Also concentrated in these two areas was the silver industry, with numerous workshops in Connecticut and the towns of Philadelphia, New York, and Baltimore. Here also were located other key metalworkers, notably gunsmiths and clockmakers. Another significant craft industry was cabinetmaking. As British colonial standards of living improved, so did the demand for furniture designed in the latest European fashion.

Other manufacturing industries which had developed by 1760 were pottery and glass. Both had existed as cottage industries from the early days, but the production of finer pieces had to await technical improvements and a more skilled workforce. By 1760 a number of factories had been established in the two main areas of manufacturing. The paper industry, too, established mills in these two areas.

One other incipient manufacturing activity was woolen and linen goods. During the seventeenth century, colonists imported cloth from England. By the eighteenth century, domestic production began to emerge as well, with specialist weavers producing cloth for sale in shops out of wool spun at home. The native wool was coarse and unable to compete with English cloths, but British producers were sufficiently apprehensive to have an act passed in 1699 prohibiting the export of colonial woolens. They need not have worried, since the colonists never had enough yarn to meet even their own domestic needs.

All this activity meant that the northern economy required additional labor to sustain its multifarious activities, especially skilled personnel like coopers, smiths, tanners, weavers, shipwrights, printers, and clerks. In New England this demand could be met from the resources of the local population. Not all fathers had sufficient land for their sons after 1700, as the population grew, and many younger sons had to be apprenticed to ensure themselves of a livelihood. Others did casual labor when not required on the family farm. One consequence was the emergence of a flexible multiskilled workforce.

The middle colonies, in contrast, continued to use the system of indentured servants as the mainstay of their labor force. Almost 100,000 were imported from the British Isles in the period 1700–75, while another 35,000 came from Germany. About half of all servants went to Pennsylvania, with Philadelphia becoming the great entrepôt for them. One result of indenture was an absence of the English apprenticeship system with its restrictive guilds. Employers either recruited already trained servants from Europe or chose suitable persons from the many eager young men anxious to learn a trade. The opportunities for developing skills were always greater in British North America than in Europe.

One resource which was not usually employed to solve the northern labor shortage to a significant extent was African slavery. Northern cereals and husbandry were less labor-intensive than southern cash crops. And since the growing season was shorter and the winters longer, there was less year-round work. In these circumstances the family, including a few indentured laborers and perhaps one slave, was usually sufficient to work most farms. Additional hands or casual labor could be found from the local white community if required. The same was true of manufacturing. Employers generally preferred to employ indentured servants, living and working as they did in close proximity to one another. An additional disincentive was the cost. African slaves cost considerably more than indentured servants, and most northern farmers (in contrast to the staples producers in the South and the West Indies) did not earn profits high enough to justify the investment.

One other question that has concerned historians is the extent to which the northern (and southern) economies were true capitalist systems operating through a market economy. Many key ingredients were certainly there, particularly in the North. Property could be sold without restrictions like primogeniture and entail (which did exist in some southern colonies), facilitating the accumulation of capital. Markets for labor were developing, with an incipient system of wage labor in the North which allowed the workforce to be deployed in a flexible and efficient manner, unencumbered by the restrictive practices of guilds and other craft associations. Sumptuary laws had been dispensed with, leaving individuals free to spend their money. They could also use their capital for investment without fear of prosecution for usury. Compared to the seventeenth century, the economy was now predominantly a cash-based one rather than one determined by barter and exchange.

On the other hand, many restrictions still operated, including restraints on wages, prices, and working conditions, and there was as yet no modern banking system. Moreover, in a society where most inhabitants still lived on small family farms, prices were never determined solely by impersonal economic forces. Also important were social factors like the good of the community and the personal needs of the household. Most farmers, for instance, assisted their neighbors at certain times of the season, receiving help in return, which made cooperation rather than competition the underlying principle of economic activity.[16]

4 THE MERCANTILIST SYSTEM

We have already seen that the colonial economy had to function within the parameters of the navigation laws, or the mercantilist system, to ensure that the colonies' trade and domestic economy were regulated for the benefit of the mother country. This system had become fully articulated by the eighteenth century.

---

[16] Unsurprisingly, historians have not been able to agree when a true market economy emerged. See Chapter 7, n. 6 for the historiography concerning this topic.

Though we have seen that the system stimulated the expansion of British trade, there has been considerable debate about its impact on colonial economies. Some historians have asserted that it strangled development, others that it was an irrelevance; still others have claimed that it was beneficial.[17] The truth undoubtedly lies somewhere in between.

Industrialization in the mother country brought a number of advantages to the colonists. First, it increased demand for colonial raw materials, which enjoyed a protected market, since high tariffs excluded foreign producers from selling in Britain. Second, it supplied capital to the colonists. As members of the landed classes still sent younger sons or relatives to build up estates, so merchants similarly sought trade outlets and partners, extending credit to their colonial contacts. Equally important was the export of human capital, especially skilled labor.

As the pace of industrialization quickened, Britain was also able to supply the best and cheapest manufactured goods to colonial buyers. These included machinery like saws, cogs, axles, crankshafts, and gears; nails, hooks, files, chisels, hammers, shovels, knives, plows, and anchors; implements of war, notably cannon, firearms, shot, and gunpowder; and navigational instruments like compasses and sextants. The wealthy imported British fabrics made from wool, linen, cotton, lace, silk, and felt. Many other household goods, such as lanterns, taps, mirrors, curtain rings, pewter, cutlery, kettles, sieves, measuring cans, and brass items like candlesticks could also be obtained from the mother country at ever lower prices. So, too, could books and fine-quality paper.

Being part of the British mercantilist system brought the colonists other advantages too, one of which was the benefit of insurance from Lloyds, which helped the flow of trade and furthered colonial economic development. Another was the protection afforded by the British navy. In wartime British trade suffered less disruption than that of any other European state. This continuity was crucial in a period of so much strife, with major wars from 1689 to 1713, 1739 to 1748, and 1755 to 1762. Moreover, after 1700 an increasing number of warships were employed in commerce protection, so that by 1720 the day of pirates like Teach and Kidd was over. In addition, mercantilism offered the collective advantages of British financial policies, which allowed many goods shipped for re-export incentives in the form of

---

[17] One of the earliest critics of the navigation system was George W. Bancroft, *History of the United States*, 10 vols (Boston, 1834–74). Bancroft was a member of the Whig nationalist school and was anxious to justify America's separation from Britain in 1776. Like most nineteenth-century writers, he was overly influenced by Adam Smith and the doctrines of free trade. In the early twentieth century, Progressive historians also criticized mercantilism, believing that its restrictions left the colonies in debt. See especially Charles A. Beard and Mary R. Beard, *The Rise of American Civilization*, 2 vols (New York, 1930); and Lawrence A. Harper, *The English Navigation Acts: A Seventeenth-Century Experiment in Social Engineering* (New York, 1939). This view was challenged by members of the imperial school. They, too, were products of the Progressive era but had more obvious Anglo-Saxon leanings which led them to emphasize the benefits of the British connection. See especially Charles McLean Andrews, *The Colonial Period of American History*, 4 vols (New Haven, 1934–8); and Oliver M. Dickerson, *The Navigation Acts and the American Revolution* (Philadelphia, 1951). Most recent writers have been favorable to the navigation laws as a system of economic management, notably McCusker and Menard, *The Economy of British America*; and Gary M. Walton and James F. Shepherd, *The Economic Rise of Early America* (New York, 1979). The latter emphasize the advantages of competitive shipping rates, capital investment, and access to technology.

customs repayments. After 1704, Britain also gave various bounties to colonial industries which would otherwise not have been viable, notably naval stores.

The expansion of trade combined with the growth in the number of available ships, itself a side effect of the navigation laws, contributed to making transatlantic shipping more frequent and more efficient. By the eighteenth century, the time required to travel across the ocean was considerably shorter than it had been a century earlier. Maps and navigational techniques had improved with time and experience, and monthly packet boats began traveling from London to the West Indies in 1702. The British navy's suppression of piracy by the 1720s made overseas voyages more regular and predictable. Shipping costs declined, benefiting both farmers who produced goods for export and colonial consumers, who could purchase goods for lower prices. An unanticipated benefit of the greater frequency of transatlantic crossings was the improvement of communications between Great Britain and its colonies. Eventually a regular mail service was established between London and a few of the mainland colonies, and families and friends began to send letters back and forth on a regular basis. Books, pamphlets, and sermons reached Boston and Philadelphia within months after they went into print in London. News reached the colonies while it was still reasonably fresh. By the middle of the century newspapers were being printed in virtually all of the mainland cities, carrying British political and diplomatic news, satirical essays from the *Spectator*, and information about British fashions. The increased flow of news and information stimulated consumer demand in the colonies for new and fashionable British products, creating an incentive for greater economic activity. Increased transatlantic communications would even have an impact on colonial culture, increasing colonial sympathy for and identification with Great Britain.[18]

A final aspect of British imperial policy which profoundly impacted colonial society was free immigration. Most other European powers controlled the flow of people to their colonies so as to exclude subversive elements. Both the French and the Spanish, for example, prohibited Protestants from emigrating to their colonies in New France and Spanish Florida.[19] Britain, on the other hand, placed few obstacles in the way of troublesome elements like the Quakers and was even ready to open the door to the refugees of other nations, such as French Huguenots, many of whom were skilled craftsmen or persons with capital. Britain's liberal policy continued into the eighteenth century. Although fewer immigrants came now from England, new arrivals included large numbers of Scots, Irish, and Germans. Some historians estimate that as many as 300,000 or more new immigrants entered the 13 continental colonies in the period 1700–79.[20] This open-door policy helped to facilitate the extraordinary speed with which British North America was settled.

---

[18] See Ian K. Steele, *The English Atlantic, 1675–1740: An Exploration of Communication and Community* (New York, 1986).

[19] However, as noted in Chapter 5, section 1, it is not clear that many French people would have immigrated even in the absence of government restrictions.

[20] For this estimate (as well as a discussion of the range of estimates in the historical literature), see Christopher Tomlins, "Indentured Servitude in Perspective: European Migration into North America and the Composition of the Early American Labor Force, 1600–1775," in Cathy Matson, ed., *The Economy of Early America: Historical Perspectives and New Directions* (University Park, 2006), 146–82, esp. table at 176.

Unfortunately no economic system can satisfy all its constituent elements. The British liked to assert that mercantilism was complementary: Britain sold its manufactures to the colonies, while they sent their produce in return. The disadvantage of being taxed for enumerated exports was theoretically offset by the advantage of a protected market. In practice the system did not work so well. In the Chesapeake a planter might receive £5 on a 1,000-pound hogshead of tobacco. After the shippers had added their charges and the Crown had collected duties of nearly £17, the same hogshead sold for £25. The amounts suggest a less than adequate return, as is also indicated by the fact that the Virginia and Maryland planters were constantly in debt to their British factors.

The question of Virginian indebtedness is a complex one, however. Contemporaries in Britain argued that such debts were the result of extravagance; the planters were simply too much given to importing expensive luxuries. Later historians believe that the planters should have been more efficient and made greater efforts to control the tobacco trade itself. Others have seen the planters' indebtedness as evidence of their creditworthiness and their debts as basically an investment in the system.[21] What is not in doubt is that some planters resented their dependency on British merchants and that this may have been one reason why the Virginian elite later supported the Revolution so ardently.[22]

To some extent the Virginian tobacco industry was the victim of its own success. The planters overproduced, causing the depressions of 1704–13, 1720–34, and 1756–65, with their consequent loss of income. The eighteenth-century Chesapeake also demonstrated the classic weakness of a single-crop economy: reliance on tobacco left the planters especially vulnerable to market forces because they had little else to supplement their income. The same difficulties afflict many developing countries today.

Another, more obvious flaw in the argument that mercantilism was complementary is that New England and the middle colonies actually produced few raw materials for the mother country. This problem was partially solved by their supply of foodstuffs to the West Indies, which restored the principle of complementarity. Unfortunately, the middle colonies expanded so fast that by 1720 Britain was unable to use all that they produced. As a result surplus foodstuffs were sold to the French and Spanish colonies. Although this practice did not contravene the navigation laws in peacetime, the colonists began buying so much cheap French and Spanish sugar for their return voyages that the British islands then found themselves being undercut on their own market. The result was the Molasses Act of 1733, whereby all foreign sugar products imported into the colonies had to pay a duty of sixpence a gallon.

Had this act been enforced, it would have dealt a serious blow to the northern economy. However, customs machinery in the period 1714–60 was still rudimentary. The coast was divided into a number of districts, but they were poorly staffed. Many of

---

[21] For a discussion of Virginian indebtedness, see Warren M. Billings, John E. Selby, and Thad W. Tate, *Colonial Virginia: A History* (New York, 1986).

[22] See especially T. H. Breen, *Tobacco Culture: The Mentality of the Great Tidewater Planters on the Eve of the Revolution* (Princeton, 1985). Similar resentments existed among the rice growers of South Carolina, according to Kenneth Morgan, "The Organization of the Colonial Rice Trade," *William and Mary Quarterly*, 52 (1995), 443–6.

the officers were corrupt and levied only a nominal duty of one penny a gallon, though the low yield suggests that some illicit trade must also have occurred.

This situation has led to the assertion that the mercantilist system was in fact maintained by smuggling. The extent of illegal trading is difficult to assess; as with social security fraud today, the perpetrators did not keep records. People certainly talked as though smuggling was common, though the evidence suggests that outside the West Indies most merchants obeyed the rules, especially when trading with Europe, since North American vessels were very conspicuous and could be easily policed by their British counterparts. Even in the West Indies there was a tendency to abide by the law. A Newport ship-owner instructed the master of one vessel on a voyage to St. Eustatius in 1750 as follows: "You may perhaps meet with some Frenchman . . . who may propose to make a French bottom of your vessel; but desire that you will not take up with any such proposal, as I would not have you go on any illicit trade."

Religion was one reason for such a law-abiding attitude, since conscience clearly dictated that it was improper to deny the king his due. Quakers were especially insistent on the ethical conduct of business and had a vested interest in ensuring that others kept within the law. If there were infractions, these are likely to have occurred as a result of the 1733 Molasses Act, which seemed to have been passed to allow British sugar planters to live in idleness and luxury.

The increasing development of manufacturing in the northern colonies indicates a third discrepancy in the theory of complementarity. Shipbuilding, especially, ought to have been the preserve of the mother country, but the demands of British merchants for cheap ships overrode the cries of protest from British shipbuilders, who did not have the advantage of cheap timber. Protectionism prevailed, however, in other areas where colonial producers were seen as a threat. Wool, for example, was one of the oldest industries in England, accounting in the past for 80 percent of her exports. By the end of the seventeenth century the industry was under attack not only from America but from Ireland too. Accordingly a Woolen Act was passed in 1699 stating that no wool or finished items were to be exported from Ireland or the colonies, even to a neighboring province. All domestic produce must be sold where it was made. The hat industry, too, was regulated in this way. When this long-established British trade found itself in danger of losing its traditional markets to colonial producers, a ban was placed on the export of colonial hats in 1732. Regulations were also laid down concerning the number of apprentices who must be employed in the trade, ostensibly to maintain quality but in reality to restrict production. No slaves could be employed, and all apprentices had to serve for seven years.

The third major activity to be regulated in the interests of Britain was the iron industry, where the conflict was similar to that in the shipbuilding industry. British smelters wanted all colonial activity banned, while the makers of finished goods wanted cheap pig and bar iron from the colonies. The latter group eventually won. In 1750 Parliament enacted legislation banning the colonists from building or operating any "mill or other engine for slitting or rolling of iron, or any plating forge . . . or any furnace for making steel," but in accordance with the principle of complementarity, no duties were to be levied on the import of any pig or bar iron. The North American colonies were to produce the raw materials, Britain the finished products, the latter of course being the more profitable activity.

The same reasoning led Britain to annul various colonial laws encouraging local manufactures. In 1705 the Privy Council disallowed a Pennsylvania law encouraging shoemaking. The following year it was New York's turn to have a sail-making venture condemned. In 1756 a Massachusetts law to facilitate the production of linen suffered a similar fate.

It is difficult to say how effective these prohibitions were, since governors and other officials had neither the information nor an inspectorate to enforce them. In any case, British concern was generally premature. The quality of British North American wool, for instance, was too poor to be exported. The number of slitting mills and forges for iron was relatively small, and the infant industry was not seriously inconvenienced. The ability to ship as much pig and bar iron as could be produced seems to have satisfied the North American iron industry. There was no outcry before 1760.

Nevertheless, these prohibitions on colonial manufacturing suggest that by 1750 there had been a qualitative change in the operation of the mercantilist system caused by British recognition that its economy now depended as much on the export of manufactured goods as on the import of cheap raw materials. In the seventeenth century the colonists had been encouraged to produce as many goods as possible: now they were being restricted in what they could do. It has been argued that this indicates that the system was being increasingly managed for the benefit of special interests, notably the merchants of London, in contrast to the seventeenth century when the aim had been to strengthen the kingdom as a whole. The evidence on this point is not conclusive, since the original navigation laws had been largely prompted by English merchant interests. Nevertheless the continued commitment of Britain to a system designed to benefit the imperial center certainly contained the potential for discord in the future.[23]

5 MONEY AND TAXATION

One problem faced by all the colonies in the period 1689–1760 was a lack of specie. The condition used to be attributed to a chronic imbalance of payments with Britain, but modern scholars have largely discounted this interpretation. Although exports to the mother country often equaled only half the value of imports, the imbalance was generally corrected by colonial surpluses on trade with the West Indies and southern Europe.[24]

Even so the domestic economy was invariably short of specie. Minting fresh coinage was not permissible, since this was a Crown prerogative. The colonies in any case had

---

[23] The shift to the protection of Britain's manufacturing was first noted by George Louis Beer, *British Colonial Policy, 1754–1765* (New York, 1907). For the thesis about special interests, see John J. McCusker, "British Mercantilist Policies," in Stanley L. Engerman and Robert E. Gallman, eds, *The Cambridge Economic History of the United States*, Vol. 1: *The Colonial Era* (Cambridge, 1996), 337–62. For a discussion of special interests before 1700, see Joyce Oldham Appleby, *Economic Thought and Ideology in Seventeenth-Century England* (Princeton, 1978).

[24] For the old view about the imbalance of payments see Curtis P. Nettels, *The Roots of American Civilization* (New York, 1938). For more recent analyses see Walton and Shepherd, *The Economic Rise of Early America*; and McCusker and Menard, *The Economy of British North America*.

little gold or silver to mint. Barter solved the problem on the frontier, but it was a hindrance elsewhere as the colonial economy became more sophisticated.

One alternative was the use of commodity money, the most common forms of which were tobacco and wampum, though the latter was largely a seventeenth-century device. Most colonies passed acts regulating such items in terms of their sterling value. North Carolina, for instance, rated 16 commodities in 1715, including tobacco, corn, wheat, tallow, leather, beaver, butter, cheese, pitch, whale oil, pork, and beef.

The difficulty was fixing the value of a commodity satisfactorily. In times of a glut, the commodity was devalued and the creditor was hurt; in times of scarcity, the debtor was at a disadvantage. In addition, commodities used in payments could often be spoiled or become unmarketable. Complaints were made in New Haven that worthless wampum was being put into the church collection plate, to the distress of the minister and his family. Although the provincial assemblies constantly tried to regulate commodity prices, it was an almost impossible task.

A third option was the use of bills of exchange, whereby those wishing to settle an account or buy some goods would go to a local merchant and buy a bill that was negotiable with a third party with whom the purchaser wanted to do business. This procedure was really only feasible for merchants or persons dealing in large sums, usually overseas or in another colony.

Most colonists had to make do with whatever specie was available: Spanish pesos or pieces of eight, Flemish ducatoons, Portuguese crusadoes, Dutch guilders or florins, German and Danish talers or dollars, and French ecus. Apart from their bewildering variety, such specie often had variations in their silver or gold content. Many coins were also clipped. Nevertheless, some specie was better than none, and many colonial legislatures passed laws placing higher values on certain coins to attract them to their province. The ploy was rarely successful, since it merely stimulated other colonies to do the same. This practice so alarmed British merchants, who were apprehensive of being paid in artificially inflated coin, that in 1704 the Privy Council issued a proclamation regulating the value of foreign coins according to their silver content. In the future such specie was not to exceed the sterling equivalent by more than one-third. Three years later Parliament enacted legislation to this end, though with only limited effect.

By this time the colonies had discovered a new solution to their lack of money, namely the printing of paper. Essentially two types of paper currency were issued during the colonial period: tax anticipation bills, or notes to be redeemed from tax receipts, and asset-backed currency. Tax anticipation notes were first issued by Massachusetts in 1690 to finance the expedition of Sir William Phips against Québec. The bills had to be repaid within a short time at the insistence of the British merchants, who feared that otherwise they would be paid in depreciated paper. The Board of Trade in consequence was under constant pressure either to prevent their issue or to ensure that such notes were not legal tender and obligatory in the settlement of debts. Nevertheless, the device was too useful to ignore, especially in wartime, and other colonies followed Massachusetts' example: South Carolina in 1703, New York and New Jersey in 1709, and North Carolina in 1712.

Most of the notes were in denominations of between 5 shillings and £20 and were more like bills of credit than modern currency. The individual had to purchase them from the provincial treasurer and pay interest for the privilege of doing so. The advantage was that they could be circulated more widely than bills of exchange, which were restricted to the name of the eventual payee.

So useful did these emissions prove that a number of colonies continued their use long after the official redemption date, sometimes to pay their government expenses, sometimes to redeem other bills, and sometimes as a means of stimulating the economy. However, their unpopularity in London led some colonies to experiment with the second type of paper money: asset-backed currency based on land. The most notable scheme was that of Pennsylvania in 1723 whereby individuals could obtain notes ranging from £10. 10s. to £100. 0s. from the local loan office. The borrower had to pay five percent interest and provide as security land twice the value of the total loan, for what was effectively a mortgage. That same year New Jersey adopted a similar scheme, using the interest on the notes to meet the expenses of government.

The benefit of paper currency was not lost on some royal officials. As Governor William Burnet of neighboring New York explained in November 1724, such schemes had widespread advantages: "The officers of the government might otherwise be kept out of their money for a very long time and have difficulty to subsist." Essential expenditures like repairs to the fort and diplomatic contacts with Native Americans would also suffer. Indeed, Burnet asserted, "Under good regulation, these acts are both of service to the trade of the plantations and of Great Britain." Burnet also pointed out that the colonists were merely imitating Parliament, anticipating revenues by means of paper.

In the aftermath of the 1720 South Sea Bubble in Britain, in which thousands of investors were ruined by fraudulent share schemes, Burnet's arguments were not appreciated. Hence in 1725 the Privy Council ordered South Carolina to redeem its £55,000 of outstanding bills. Nevertheless, the need for a circulating medium led to the acceptance of two New Jersey acts in 1730 and 1733 for an emission of £60,000 and one in Maryland. The following year Connecticut managed to secure an issue of £35,000 "to promote trade." Even the South Carolina assembly managed to pass another bill in 1736 for an emission of £210,000, arguing that its trade was in great distress for want of a circulating medium.

The problem of sustaining the value of such currency became acute only in the late 1730s when there was a renewed threat of war. By then the Massachusetts pound was trading at £5. 5s. to £1 sterling; and the South Carolina currency at £7. 19s. to £1. Fearing new issues of depreciated paper, the Privy Council sent a circular letter in August 1740 telling the governors to allow no more emissions. If any such acts did have to be passed, they must contain a suspending clause until they had been approved in Britain. The following year the Board of Trade ordered the Massachusetts assembly to retire all its paper money, except for £30,000 to finance its government.

In response, a group of merchants decided to set up a Land Bank to print notes, using their landholdings as security. The idea had been mooted during the previous decade, but it was the recall of the provincial bills which now led to its execution. A more conservative group then proposed a rival Silver Bank, with notes redeemable in silver. Both groups proposed to operate without a charter from the provincial legislature. At this point the British vetoed both measures by declaring that they fell within the scope of the 1720 Bubble Act, which had been passed to prevent just such enterprises.

The closing of the Land Bank hurt a number of people, including the father of Samuel Adams.

Nonetheless, the Privy Council's attempts to restrict the issue of paper proved difficult in the 1740s, for military expenditures would not wait. A number of issues were accordingly made, much to the dismay of British officials. The New England colonies were particular offenders, though they were provoked by the need to meet the cost of capturing Louisburg in 1745. Worse, their emissions were not well managed, lacking any redemption date or security in the form of tax revenue. By the end of the war the exchange rate had slumped to £12 of Massachusetts currency for £1 sterling. Fortunately Massachusetts was owed a large sum in reimbursement for its war effort, and Thomas Hutchinson persuaded the assembly to use this to redeem its near worthless currency.

Despite this far-sighted initiative, Parliament passed an act in 1750 requiring the redemption of all existing bills in New England. In future, only sufficient paper for the government salaries and other necessary expenditures could be issued, and this amount had to be redeemed in two years, though in an emergency the period could be extended to five years. Such notes were not to be legal tender, thus restricting their use as a circulating medium.

Nevertheless, further emissions continued to be made, especially of asset-backed paper, which suffered little depreciation due to the rising value of the land offered as collateral. Hence New Jersey was allowed another £60,000 worth of bills in 1754 in recognition of its earlier judicious handling of paper. As the Board of Trade commented, the previous issues were "found to be the least burthensome method of levying taxes for the support of government" and had "also been of great service in enabling the inhabitants to extend and improve their trade." The bills were not to be legal tender.

Even that restriction had to be lifted to stimulate the colonial war effort during the final conflict with the French and their Indian allies. The British merchants then renewed their clamors, even though Virginia stipulated in its first issue of 1755 that any discount would be made good in the settlement of sterling debts. The issue of paper was to be one element in the subsequent conflict between Britain and the colonies after 1760.

The supply of money generally seems to have sufficed. Even Britain in the eighteenth century had to manage with a mixture of barter, commodity money, paper, and coin. The colonial economy was no exception.

One aspect of the colonial economy which was favorable throughout the period was tax rates. Though the colonies had to pay the navigation duties, which could be heavy, the burden fell on the consumer rather than on the population at large. In contrast, internal taxation was light, since the government expenses were low except in wartime. The bureaucracy was tiny, and there was no standing army or fleet. Poor relief was the responsibility of the local authorities. Spending on roads or other facilities was minimal.

One reason for the popularity of paper money was that it could finance extraordinary expenditures in wartime, though ultimately such issues had to be redeemed and other obligations met. To this end taxes were most commonly levied on land or personal property. Poll taxes on adult males over 16 were another option; in the Chesapeake an export duty on tobacco was imposed, and excise duties on liquor were also adopted. But with the exception of quitrents, none was so onerous as to cause significant protest before 1760.[25]

6 THE STANDARD OF LIVING: POVERTY AND PROSPERITY

Whatever the restraints of the mercantilist system, the colonies developed at a remarkable pace throughout the later colonial period. Growth was by no means even, there being periods of stagnation. Nevertheless, the evidence suggests that the system cannot have been too restrictive. Colonial trade with Britain grew by 700 percent in the period 1689–1760, while the population of the British North American colonies increased from 250,000 to around 1.5 million. At the same time average per capita income rose by at least 0.5 percent a year in real terms, so that the standard of living for most of the population improved by between 50 and 100 percent. The British North American colonies were among the first societies to escape the Malthusian cycle in which increased resources merely stimulated population growth and ultimate decline in per capita income. British North Americans never experienced the kind of famines which afflicted most European societies until the nineteenth century.

One indication of colonial well-being was the reaction of visitors. In the seventeenth century it was the wild appearance of the continent which drew comment, whereas by the 1750s visitors were impressed by the general prosperity of the inhabitants. Most white men appeared to have land, and European travelers noticed little poverty or unemployment. As a British officer commented, "Everybody has property and everybody knows it." The general progress was well symbolized by the rise of Philadelphia, a town that did not exist in 1682, but which by 1760 was on a par with Dublin, Edinburgh, or Bristol. Benjamin Franklin, too, constantly emphasized the material benefits of living in British North America. After a trip through Scotland he commented, with characteristic irony, "I should never advise a nation of savages to submit to civilization," suggesting that he thought even the Indians in North America were better off than tenant farmers in the British Isles.

The same points were made more prosaically by Thomas Hutchinson in his *History of Massachusetts.* He wrote, "Property is more equally distributed in the colonies ... especially those to the northward of Maryland than in any nation in Europe. In some towns you see scarce a man destitute of a competence to make him easy." The reason, of course, was the availability of land, which led "most men as soon as their sons grow up endeavour to procure tracts in some new township where all except the eldest go out one after another with a wife, a yoke of oxen, a horse, a cow or two and maybe a few goats and husbandry tools ... A small hut is built and the man and his family fare."

Though a few such statements could be misleading, other types of evidence such as wills and contemporary depictions of household furnishings tend to support the view

---

[25] For the accepted view that taxation was light, even during the final French and Indian War, see Lawrence Henry Gipson, *Connecticut Taxation, 1750–1775* (New Haven, 1933). That Parliament by no means reimbursed all the costs of that struggle and that considerable taxation was necessary is argued by Harold E. Selesky in *War and Society in Colonial Connecticut* (New Haven, 1989).

that living standards were improving, at least for the middling ranks of the settler population. Whereas in the seventeenth century most decedents left a few tools, some rough furniture, and livestock, eighteenth-century inventories often reveal a much richer standard of living, including china rather than coarse pottery, silverware, furniture, clocks, warming pans, and other household items designed for decoration or comfort rather than mere survival. Additional evidence can be obtained from the records of colonial imports. After 1700 these increasingly included what earlier would have been considered inessential luxury items: tea, coffee, French wines, Indian silks and calicos, glass, porcelain, and even furniture. Previously colonials had made their own, found substitutes, or done without. The first 60 years of the eighteenth century witnessed a consumer boom which seems to suggest a standard of living 20 percent higher than in Britain, for the middle classes at least.[26]

Of course, this wealth was not evenly spread, even within the colonial elite. The evidence from wills for the year 1774 reveals that the Charleston area of South Carolina, with its large rice plantations, had by far the highest concentration of wealth, with the estates of decedents there averaging £2,337. The next most wealthy area was Ann Arundal in Maryland, with an average inventoried estate of £660. Slaveholding planters in the South were substantially wealthier than elites elsewhere, including northern merchants. Philadelphia, for all its commerce, had an average estate of no higher than £396, while the figure in Suffolk County, Massachusetts, was just £312. New York City was even lower with a mere £278, suggesting the presence of many middling people who enjoyed a comfortable existence, rather than a conspicuously wealthy upper class.[27]

How was this prosperity achieved? One answer was greater efficiency. Although historians have generally condemned the British North American colonial farmer for his wasteful land usage, improvements did occur through greater knowledge of the climate and terrain. Some modest technological improvements occurred in manufacturing and commerce, though less so in farming. Most colonials were still using tools similar to those of their seventeenth-century ancestors, though implements like plows were now used more widely. In addition, the colonial period was generally one of price stability. The price of manufactured goods actually fell as production methods improved and transport became cheaper, giving settlers greater purchasing power. Throughout the period the colonists continued to enjoy that almost unique combination of abundant land, cheap food, and unlimited fuel.

Lastly, the growth in living standards was ironically fueled by consumer behavior itself. Many historians now argue that British American colonists underwent their own

---

[26]   Considerable work is now being done on the eighteenth-century consumer revolution. See Carole Shammas, *The Pre-industrial Consumer in England and America* (New York, 1990); and Ronald Hoffman, Cary Carson, and Peter J. Albert, *Of Consuming Interests: The Style of Life in the Eighteenth-Century* (Charlottesville, 1993). Some historians have attempted to link the growth in consumption to the separation from Britain. T. H. Breen, *The Marketplace of Revolution: How Consumer Politics Shaped American Independence* (New York, 2004), argues that the growth of a consumer economy in the British colonies gave people a common set of experiences which facilitated the development of trust and a shared identity. Breen observes that the consumer economy also allowed colonists to employ consumer boycotts as a tactic for resisting British imperial policies during the American Revolution.
[27]   For further information, see Alice Hanson Jones, *Wealth of a Nation to Be.*

consumer revolution in the eighteenth century. Whereas colonial families had once sought to replicate the familiar and traditional as they made decisions about food production and architectural styles, they now began to hunger for the new. Colonial elites led the way, developing new tastes in architecture, furniture, food, clothing, and manners so that they could present themselves as "refined" or "genteel" in the eyes of the British gentry. Middling people followed suit, adopting new customs like drinking tea out of imported china teacups, signaling new aspirations to refinement or, at least, comfort.

As consumer behavior changed, moral judgments of consumption changed along with them. Until the end of the sixteenth century only gentlefolk were expected to live sumptuously as a sign of their rank and a means whereby the social order could be maintained. Ordinary people, it was assumed, would merely be corrupted by such consumption into idleness and vice. (The purpose of sumptuary laws, which virtually all colonial governments enacted in the seventeenth century, was to prevent ordinary people from engaging in excess consumption.) By the end of the seventeenth century such attitudes had changed in favor of personal improvement. Now it was argued that many of these same luxuries were items of refinement which could be defended on moral grounds as leading to gentility.

Changes in consumer behavior and attitudes had two consequences for colonial economies. One was a surge in demand. The other was an increase in production. Colonial people underwent what has been called an "industrious revolution," spending more of their hours in labor so as to be able to buy new objects to improve their standard of living. The Protestant work ethic was now geared to the god of consumption.

The contemporary statements of Franklin, Hutchinson, and others have encouraged the belief that British North America was the first society to banish poverty. Interestingly, Hutchinson did not say that no towns experienced any deprivation, and modern historians have shown that poverty was a growing problem in cities like Boston, New York, and Philadelphia. In the case of Boston the first serious poverty occurred after the 1690–1713 war. That conflict had precipitated a boom in shipbuilding and privateering; when it ended many seamen and carpenters were left in straitened circumstances. War widows were also badly hit. Indeed, the advent of peace ushered in a period during which the population of Boston actually fell. By 1740, 25 percent of the town's inhabitants were living below the poverty line. Responding to this catastrophe, prominent Bostonians constructed workhouses and a linen factory where the unemployed might work and repay the cost of their upkeep. Unfortunately, this attempt to use private capital to solve unemployment in Boston was not a success: the factory was unable to compete with low-priced imports and had to close after a few years. Other towns were similarly affected by the scourge of poverty, and by 1760 even Providence had a workhouse.

Though Benjamin Franklin is known for his optimistic conviction that any man in British North America could become an economic success, Franklin's Philadelphia belies his claims by demonstrating the reality of urban deprivation in the eighteenth century colonies. Many artisans and laborers there were rarely above the poverty line. This was especially the case in winter, when perhaps a quarter of the workforce required relief. Many tried to avoid this humiliation, since recipients of public assistance had to wear a large letter P (for pauper) on their garments. Even when the economy was

DOCUMENT 15

Benjamin Franklin on the Protestant ethic: the advice of Poor Richard, reprinted in Kenneth Silverman, *Benjamin Franklin: The Autobiography and Other Writings* (New York, 1986), 216–17

The following maxims were published by Franklin in his Poor Richard's Almanac. Questions to consider: *To what extent are the values Franklin espouses here still shared by Americans? To what extent is Franklin making fun of these values?*

The Taxes are indeed very heavy; and if those laid on by the Government were the only ones we had to pay, we might more easily discharge them; but we have many others, and much more grievous to some of us. We are taxed twice as much by our *Idleness*, three times as much by our *Pride*, and four times as much by our *Folly* . . . However let us hearken to good Advice, and something may be done for us; *God helps them that help themselves, as Poor Richard says*, in his Almanack of 1733 . . .

How much more than is necessary do we spend in Sleep! forgetting that *The sleeping Fox catches no Poultry*, and that *there will be sleeping enough in the Grave, as Poor Richard* says. If Time be of all things the most precious, *wasting Time* must be, as Poor Richard says, *the Greatest Prodigality*, since, as he elsewhere tells us, *Lost Time is never found again*; and what we call *Time-enough always proves little enough*: Let us then be up and be doing, and doing to some Purpose; so by Diligence shall we do more with less Perplexity. *Sloth makes all things difficult, but Industry all easy*, as Poor Richard says; and *He that riseth late, must trot all Day, and shall scarce overtake his Business at Night*. While *Laziness travels so slowly, that Poverty soon overtakes him*, as we read in Poor Richard, who adds . . . *Early to Bed, and early to rise, makes a Man healthy, wealthy and wise.*

robust, many seamen, shoemakers, and journeymen tailors earned barely enough to feed, clothe, and house their families. As a result they were never able to amass enough capital to break out of their cycle of poverty, no matter how hard they worked or observed the aphorisms of Franklin's *Poor Richard*.[28]

Nor was poverty limited to the towns. New England farming communities increasingly warned away strangers for fear they would become a charge on the inhabitants. In Virginia the House of Burgesses passed a law in 1723 against vagabonds who were becoming a burden on the parish and county authorities. According to the most recent calculations, 30 percent of the population in that colony were poor even by the standards of the time. A similar picture pertained for Maryland, while in South Carolina the governor calculated that 6,000 of its 26,000 white population lived in dire poverty, with another 10,000 possessing only the bare necessities of life.

---

[28]   The issue of urban poverty is dealt with by Gary P. Nash, *The Urban Crucible: Social Change, Political Consciousness, and the Origins of the American Revolution* (Cambridge, Mass., 1979); and Billy G. Smith, *The "Lower Sort": Philadelphia's Laboring People, 1750–1800* (Ithaca, 1990).

Historians are also now aware how large was the proportion of tenant farmers – perhaps 30 percent of all those engaged in agriculture. Since 20 percent of the population were laborers, this figure actually indicates that close to 50 percent of white males owned no land. Of course, tenancy could be the first step on the ladder to ownership; and many young men with no land were simply waiting to inherit from their parents or relatives. A study of conditions in Connecticut suggests that most males owned no land on reaching adulthood. However, by the time they were married they possessed an average of around 40 acres, which had typically increased to 100 acres by age 40. Only five percent remained permanently poor. On the other hand tenancy rates rose during the eighteenth century, especially in the South.[29]

Finally, although optimistic European observers rarely acknowledged them, the African slaves who comprised some 20 percent of the colonial population lived in forced, permanent poverty. Slaves were permitted, even encouraged, to grow crops and raise poultry or hogs in order to supplement their own diets. Slaveholders in North America had an economic incentive to keep their slaves sufficiently well fed so that they would be able to work. But by the eighteenth century slaves had little or no legal right to any property of their own, and were rarely able to acquire the kinds of consumer goods that were becoming widely available to European farmers. African Americans' standards of living improved little, if at all, over the course of the eighteenth century. Their poverty offered a stark contrast to the growing prosperity of most whites.

Thus it can still be asserted that most white persons in British colonial North America had a better chance of a comfortable existence at some point in their lives than did their counterparts in the mother country, which was why most of them, or their ancestors, had come in the first place. At the same time, poverty was growing in the cities and in parts of the South, and increasingly defined the lot of African slaves. Indeed its marks were probably now especially visible in a world where rising prosperity was coming to seem the norm.

---

[29]   For the view that tenant farming was widespread and led to poverty, see Gregory A. Stiverson, *Poverty in a Land of Plenty: Tenancy in Eighteenth-Century Maryland* (Baltimore, 1977); Gloria L. Main, *Tobacco Colony: Life in Early Maryland, 1650–1720* (Princeton, 1983); and Sharon V. Salinger, *"To Serve Well and Faithfully": Labor and Indentured Servants in Pennsylvania, 1682–1800* (New York, 1987). Salinger points out how difficult it was for servants to make the transition to owning property in Pennsylvania. For a more optimistic account of tenancy, see James T. Lemon, *The Best Poor Man's Country: A Geographical Study of Early Southeastern Pennsylvania* (Baltimore, 1972); Sung Bok Kim, *Landlord and Tenant in Colonial New York: Manorial Society, 1664–1775* (Chapel Hill, 1978); and Lucy Simler, "Tenancy in Colonial Pennsylvania: The Case of Chester County," *William and Mary Quarterly,* 43 (1986), 542–69. The details on Connecticut can be found in Jackson Turner Main, *Society and Economy in Colonial Connecticut* (Princeton, 1985).

11

Settler Families and Society

1648   Massachusetts passes a law condemning rebellious children over 16 to death for striking their parents.

1690   The first birth control devices become available in London.

1693   John Locke publishes his *Thoughts Concerning Education*.

1700   The European American population in British North America reaches 250,000. Gender ratios in the Chesapeake become more balanced.

1751   Benjamin Franklin publishes his *Observations Concerning the Increase of Mankind*.

1770   The European American population in British North America reaches 1.7 million.

Colonial America: A History to 1763, Fourth Edition. Richard Middleton and Anne Lombard.
© 2011 Richard Middleton and Anne Lombard. Published 2011 by Blackwell Publishing Ltd.

1 NEW WORLD FAMILIES

TWENTY-FIRST-CENTURY westerners are quick to conjure up an image of what families were like in the past. We imagine them as more stable and supportive than our own, envisioning them as mainstays of generational continuity that included grandparents, parents, children, and extended family members all living under the same roof. It is an appealing image. However, insofar as it applies to the families of seventeenth-century Englishmen and settlers in the British North American colonies, the image is based more upon myth than reality. Empirical evidence painstakingly gathered by historical demographers since the 1960s has provided a more realistic picture of the contours of actual family life in early modern England and its colonies. If we want to understand why families mattered to the development of British North American societies, it is important for us to begin with that picture.[1]

Historians once thought that settler families in colonial British America were smaller and less stable than families in the Old World. English people in the seventeenth century, the story went, lived from birth through adulthood in stable extended families surrounded by loving relatives from multiple generations. Only in the colonies were those extended families exchanged for nuclear families whose members moved frequently, always looking for greener pastures.

Demographic evidence has shown historians that in fact this traditional view of Old World family life was vastly distorted. Most English families in the seventeenth century were nuclear in structure, headed by an adult male who lived with his wife and young children in a single household which they did not typically share with extended family members. Although households commonly included additional members besides the parents and children, they were generally servants, unrelated to the household head. Moreover, families were anything but cradles of support for children from birth to adulthood. Most English parents could not afford to provide property sufficient to support more than one of their children in adulthood. Therefore younger children were apprenticed or bound out to service, often by their early teens. Although they might return home after one employment ended and before another began, once they reached adulthood most young people in seventeenth-century England left the villages where

---

[1] The new demographic history began appearing in the late 1960s. See especially Peter Laslett, *The World We Have Lost: England Before the Industrial Age* (New York, 1973); and Peter Laslett, ed., *Household and Family in Past Time: Comparative Studies in the Size and Structure of the Domestic Group* (Cambridge, 1972). For summaries of much of the subsequent research, see Keith Wrightson, *English Society, 1580–1680* (New Brunswick, 1982), and Roy Porter, *English Society in the Eighteenth Century* (New York, 1982). These studies in demography came about because social changes in Europe, not least the democratization of political structures, generated interest in the history of the common man. An early survey of the new methodology and its implications for American history can be found in Philip J. Greven, Jr., "Historical Demography and Colonial America," *William and Mary Quarterly*, 24 (1967), 438–54. The first major demographic works on colonial America were Philip J. Greven, Jr., *Four Generations: Population, Land, and Family in Colonial Andover, Massachusetts* (Ithaca, 1970); and John Demos, *A Little Commonwealth: Family Life in Plymouth Colony* (New York, 1970). Later studies include Vivian C. Fox and Martin H. Quitt, eds, *Loving, Parenting, and Dying: The Family Cycle in England and America, Past and Present* (New York, 1980); John Demos, *Past, Present, and Personal: The Family and the Life Course in American History* (New York, 1986); and Barry Levy, *Quakers and the American Family: British Settlement in the Delaware Valley* (New York, 1988).

they had been born and settled elsewhere. Nor did they find life easy or stable once they left. It was not uncommon for young people to fail at earning a living, and a substantial number therefore remained single, drifting from one place to another throughout adulthood. Their world was hardly one of stable havens in which people lived continuously from one generation to the next.[2]

While white settler families in colonial British North America replicated some of these patterns, the distinct challenges and opportunities of economic life in the colonies changed the experience of family life (for most white settlers) in important ways. By the late seventeenth century (and much earlier in New England), nearly all young adults from white families married and began families. Their families were also considerably larger than the average English family. British American and other European American settlers had more children and were more likely to acquire servants and slaves than their counterparts in the home islands. And although they lived in nuclear families (much as in England), they were much more likely than English parents to keep their children at home with them until adulthood. The first question we need to answer is why these distinctive patterns of family life developed in colonial British America.

Family formation was critical to the success of settler societies in North America. As we have seen from the example of the early Chesapeake, new societies did not survive and develop if they could not sustain their populations. Although a society could maintain a stable population for some time through immigration, its long-term prospects depended on people's ability and willingness to bear and rear children, and the lowering of mortality rates to a point where births at least kept pace with deaths. Since authorities in the English colonies discouraged intermarriage between whites and Native Americans (a policy distinctly different from those of the Spanish and French colonies in North America), the capacity of Anglo-American settler societies to reproduce themselves depended on developing a balanced gender ratio and reasonable longevity within the settler population. These two conditions were achieved within a generation in New England and most of the middle colonies. They took longer in the Chesapeake, but even there, by the beginning of the eighteenth century, the white population had developed a reasonably balanced gender ratio through natural repro- duction and the importation of a larger percentage of female servants. And from 1700 onwards, white births in the Chesapeake outnumbered deaths. Thus white settler populations in all regions by the eighteenth century had developed demographic conditions that encouraged family formation.[3]

---

[2]   For the now discredited theory that extended English families gave way in the colonies to nuclear families, see Bernard Bailyn, *Education in the Forming of American Society: Needs and Opportunities for Study* (Chapel Hill, 1960).

[3]   The discussion in this chapter is limited to the family experiences of white settlers. African slaves on the North American mainland would overcome a similar demographic imbalance, begin to form families, and become remarkably successful in reproducing their population by about 1750. However, the nature of family life for enslaved people would be very different than for the free white population. By the end of the seventeenth century, African Americans in many of the colonies were prohibited from marrying whites, and slaves were legally prohibited from marrying at all. Given these constraints, African American family experiences were distinct from those of whites. It will be important for us to focus on some of the differences, so African American family experiences will be discussed separately in Chapter 14.

Once that happened, settlers married at a remarkable rate. In this respect, Anglo-American colonial societies were strikingly different from societies in Europe, particularly in seventeenth-century England. Studies of New England, for example, have shown that the proportion of the adult population which remained single throughout their lives was well under 10 percent, and white populations elsewhere in the colonies had similarly high rates of marriage by the eighteenth century. In contrast, in England during much of the seventeenth century a quarter of the adult population never married at all.

Typically marriages took place shortly after the man had acquired enough property to start a farm, a fact that points us towards the main reason for the differences in marriage patterns between England and North America. In England, population was high and land scarce. In the British North American colonies, conditions were reversed. Especially after the wars of the seventeenth century forced most Native American groups to move away from Anglo-American settlements, land became widely available for purchase and settlement. What remained necessary to make it productive was labor. And marriage was the easiest way to solve the labor problem. Households with at least two members were a virtual necessity, since nobody in this commercially undeveloped economy could run a farm all alone. Unless the farm produced a profitable enough crop to be able to hire or purchase labor, a partnership was a necessity, and marriage provided the most familiar and predictable institutional mechanism for such a partnership.

The ready availability of land not only encouraged many people to marry, it allowed them to marry relatively young. Abundant land was cheap land, and that meant young people could acquire it either through purchase or tenancy without spending many years earning and saving their money to build up capital. So white settlers in colonial British North America not only married more frequently than young people in England; they also married earlier. The average marriage age by the eighteenth century in New England was about 22 for women and about 26 for men, on average two years earlier than the average marriage age in England. Among Quakers in the middle colonies the average marriage age was slightly higher than in New England (but still lower than in England), between 22 and 23 for women, and 26 to 27 for men. In the Chesapeake before 1680, as we have seen, marriage ages were very high for both men and women, since men had a hard time finding women to marry and women who came as servants had to wait until their service was completed (usually at age 24) before being allowed to marry. But by 1700, once settler societies in the Chesapeake matured and indentured servitude became less common, young people there began to marry at strikingly young ages as well. For example, the average marriage age for native-born whites in Somerset County, Maryland between 1670 and 1740 was about 23 for men, and under 19 for women.[4]

Having married young, white settlers typically produced very large families. For example, during the seventeenth century the average number of children born to each couple in the town of Andover, Massachusetts was 8.2. What was remarkable was that seven of these survived to age 21. Across the Atlantic the average survival rate tended to

[4] Statistics are from Henry A. Gemery, "The White Population of the Colonial United States, 1607–1790," in Michael R. Haines and Richard H. Steckel, eds, *A Population History of North America* (Cambridge, 2000), 143–90, especially table 5.2.

DOCUMENT 16

Benjamin Franklin, "Observations Concerning the Increase of Mankind, Peopling of Countries, &c." (1751, published 1755), in *The Papers of Benjamin Franklin*, edited by Leonard W. Labaree et al. (New Haven, 1961), Vol. 4, 225–34

Benjamin Franklin wrote this essay in 1751 but did not publish it until the lead-up to the French and Indian War in 1755. When the essay was republished in several London magazines, some material including the last paragraph was omitted. Questions to consider: *How would a high fertility rate among the white settler population affect the societies they created in North America? How might it affect their expectations? What kinds of assumptions does Franklin make in this essay about ethnicity and race? What is surprising about them?*

Land being thus plenty in America, and so cheap as that a labouring Man, that understands Husbandry, can in a short Time save Money enough to purchase a Piece of new Land sufficient for a Plantation, whereupon he may subsist a Family; such are not afraid to marry; for if they even look far enough forward to consider how their Children when grown up are to be provided for they see that more Land is to be had at Rates equally easy, all Circumstances considered.

Hence Marriages in America are more general, and more generally early, than in Europe. And if it is reckoned there, that there is but one Marriage per annum among 100 Persons, perhaps we may here reckon two; and if in Europe they have but 4 Births to a Marriage (many of their Marriages being late) we may here reckon 8, of which if one half grow up, and our Marriages are made, reckoning one with another at 20 Years of Age, our People must at least be doubled every 20 Years . . .

. . . [T]here are supposed to be now upwards of One Million English Souls in North-America . . . This Million doubling, suppose but once in 25 Years, will in another Century be more than the People of England, and the greatest Number of Englishmen will be on this Side the Water. What an Accesion of Power to the British Empire by Sea as well as Land! What Increase of Trade and Navigation! . . .

And since Detachments of English from Britain sent to America, will . . . increase so largely here; why should the Palatine Boors be suffered to swarm into our Settlements, and by herding together establish their Language and Manners to the Exclusion of ours? Why should Pennsylvania, founded by the English, become a Colony of *Aliens*, who will shortly be so numerous as to Germanize us instead of our Anglifying them . . .

Which leads me to add one Remark: That the Number of purely white People in the World is proportionably very small. All Africa is tawny. Asia chiefly tawny. America (exclusive of the newcomers) wholly so. And in Europe, the Spaniards, Italians, French, Russians, and Swedes are generally of what we call a swarthy Complexion; as are the Germans also, the Saxons only excepted, who with the English, make the principal Body of White People on the Face of the Earth. I

> could wish their Numbers were increased. And while we are, as I may call it, *Scouring* our Planet, by clearing America of Woods, and so making this Side of our Globe reflect a brighter Light to the Eyes of Inhabitants in Mars or Venus, why should we in the Sight of Superior Beings, darken its People? Why increase the Sons of Africa, by Planting them in America, where we have so fair an Opportunity, by excluding all Blacks and Tawneys, of increasing the lovely White and Red? But perhaps I am partial to the Complexion of my Country, for such Kind of Partiality is natural to Mankind.

be only between four and five out of approximately seven births. Average numbers of births per white couple in the colonies decreased somewhat during the eighteenth century (as did survival rates), but family sizes were still well above the British norm. In the South, the average number of children born to families during the second half of the eighteenth century was a stunning 9.6 children per woman.[5]

Though the main reason for the size of colonial settler families was simply that women had more years to bear children, another contributing factor had to do with the North American environment. New England, in particular, was a healthy place. During the seventeenth century it was relatively isolated from the epidemics which regularly swept across Europe, an isolation which (along with the cold weather) made diseases relatively rare and produced lower levels of infant mortality and greater life expectancies than in Europe. Although the commercialization of New England's economy during the eighteenth century ended its isolation and brought more European epidemic diseases, mortality rates were not as devastating as in the Old World. American colonists enjoyed a better diet than Europeans, meaning that no one starved; the famines that were so common in Europe simply did not occur. Most farmers had enough land, and no one was dependent on a single crop.

The large size of settler families would have a profound impact on patterns of development in British North America during the eighteenth century, because they meant a very rapid rate of settler population growth. The white population in the English colonies in 1700 was approximately 250,000. Between 1700 and 1770 the number of new European immigrants who flowed into the colonies was approximately 300,000. Remarkably, by the end of the period (in 1770) the total white population of the colonies had grown to 1.7 million, an extraordinary increase made possible by very high rates of fertility.[6] Meanwhile, as the settlers thrived, Native American populations continued to be ravaged by warfare and disease. The settler population in effect became a juggernaut that pressed its way onto Native American land, forcing the Indians to assimilate or migrate to new territory where there was less competition for resources.[7]

Birth rates in most societies today are nowhere near as high as those found in colonial British North America, for we have experienced what historical demographers call the

---

[5] Gemery, "White Population of the Colonial United States," table 5.2.

[6] Imports of enslaved Africans will be discussed in Chapter 14.

[7] For a comparison of the family patterns of English and Native American New Englanders, see Gloria Main, *Peoples of a Spacious Land: Families and Cultures in Colonial New England* (Cambridge, Mass., 2001).

"fertility transition," the point when couples began to limit their fertility. Why did Anglo-American couples in the seventeenth and eighteenth centuries have so many children? The absence of birth control technology is part of the answer, of course. Although sheaths made of sheep's gut could be purchased in London from the 1690s, they were unavailable to colonists (indeed they were not widely available in the United States until the late nineteenth century). Yet families could have limited their fertility without artificial birth control. Women in Native American societies managed to limit their fertility to one pregnancy every three or four years by prolonging the breastfeeding of small children in order to inhibit ovulation. And in the early nineteenth century, both American and French women began limit the sizes of their families by abstaining from sexual intercourse when they wanted to avoid pregnancies.

To put the question another way, why did women in British North American settler communities not limit their pregnancies in the ways these other women did? Ideology provides a partial explanation. The Christian religion taught that God would provide bountiful blessings through a loving union between husband and wife. Large families may have offered solace and security to immigrants who had left their own families of origin far behind. However, the most basic explanation is that having lots of children made economic sense. Land was abundant, but it was valuable only to the extent there was labor to clear the trees and make the capital improvements needed for it to become productive. Children provided cheap, obedient labor. If they could be put to work milking cows and tending chickens when they were young, they cost very little, and as teenagers they could more than repay the cost of their upkeep in the value they added to a family farm.[8]

Colonial British North Americans' need for children's labor on family farms would shape family life in other ways as well, especially in the North and in the piedmont regions of the South where farmers relied on family labor. Colonial settlers' children typically stayed with their families through adolescence. Unlike the experience of English teenagers, who were sent into service during their mid-teens and returned home only intermittently thereafter, white colonial children remained at home and remained dependent on their parents until adulthood. A poorly developed labor market meant that teenaged sons and daughters were their parents' laborers of choice, and also that teenagers had fewer opportunities to earn a living away from their own homes.

To us, it may seem cold or heartless to think about children in terms of their economic value. To European settlers in the colonies it would not have seemed heartless at all. Members of these families understood full well that each of them was responsible for a share of the family's productive work. Families worked together so that everyone in them could survive and thrive. Even in the mid eighteenth century the relative scarcity of goods for purchase made household production as well as local trading vital to family well-being. Growing up in such a society was a different kind of experience than it is for middle-class children in the United States and Europe today, and childhood had a different set of meanings.

---

[8] For a particularly clear explanation of the economic relationships involved in family farming, see Daniel Vickers, *Farmers and Fishermen: Two Centuries of Work in Essex County, Massachusetts, 1630–1830* (Chapel Hill, 1994).

2 CHILDREN

Historians have sometimes suggested that in western Europe before the eighteenth century, childhood did not exist. Children were treated as little adults, expected to bear adult responsibilities at ages when we think of them as unformed innocents who need special nurturing from adults and time to develop.[9] Obviously, the assertion that childhood was nonexistent cannot be literally correct, since childhood dependence is universal. Every society has to find ways to care for and train young children if they are to survive. But certainly the experience of childhood was different in British colonial societies than in our own. Children were expected to work at a young age, and could be thrust into positions of great responsibility long before we would consider them to be ready for adulthood.

Most evidence suggests that British colonial parents wanted children very much, and welcomed them into their families with joy. Mothers nursed their infants, and paid close attention to certain aspects of infant and toddler care.[10] Still, some colonial childrearing practices would seem (to us) surprising, suggesting that the goals of early childhood care were somewhat different from our own.

One of the most striking patterns in infant and toddler care was an apparent concern with making sure that babies grew straight, stood, and began walking as quickly as possible. Infant clothing, for example, seems to have been designed with these goals in mind. Babies were tightly swaddled for about the first three months, wrapped in linen bands that effectively prevented them from moving. Once they were out of swaddling clothes, babies were often put into corsets worn under the clothes, which held their bodies upright and straight. Babies of seven or eight months were discouraged from crawling. Instead various devices were used to speed the transition to standing and walking, the most popular being standing stools, go-carts, and leading strings. Parents' evident concern with straightness, as well as the seeming haste with which children were urged to stand and walk, are puzzles that need to be explained. Some historians speculate that the concern stemmed from the premise that children were essentially bestial and uncivilized and would fail to develop properly unless they were consciously molded. Others posit the more practical explanation that such practices helped mothers care safely for their children while simultaneously performing their household work. Infants who are swaddled typically stay calm and still, which would have been helpful for mothers who had to work constantly in gardens and kitchens. Toddlers who are kept in standing stools are easily kept out of trouble, and small children who can move about independently can entertain themselves. So efficiency of effort was probably a major goal of early childrearing practices.[11]

In most settler families, once children learned to walk until about age six they were left mainly to their own devices, although under the watchful eye of an older child or servant. During these years boys and girls were dressed in identical long garments, these

---

[9] This argument was most fully articulated by Philippe Aries, *Centuries of Childhood: A Social History of Family Life* (1960), trans. Robert Baldick (New York, 1962).

[10] There is little evidence that colonial women hired wet nurses, as wealthy Englishwomen sometimes did.

[11] See Karin Calvert, *Children in the House: The Material Culture of Early Childhood, 1600–1900* (Boston, 1992).

being the easiest to wash and pass on from one child to the next. Few children could expect new clothes. Toys were rare; most children played imaginatively with whatever was lying around the house. Older children played games with their siblings, either indoors or outdoors as weather permitted. Early education from adults was generally minimal – parents were too busy running the farm or managing the household to spend much time with young children.

This pattern of childrearing meant that women mothered extensively rather than intensively. This contrasts with the present day, when most women rear children for just one period of their lives and devote as much time as possible to their upbringing. It may be that upper-class mothers had more time for their children, since they could employ servants and slaves to do their housework. But working-class women and farmer's wives had no option but to continue with their daily chores.[12]

Some historians, especially in the past, have argued that parents in the colonial era withheld their affection from young children. Childrearing advice published before about 1740 suggests that emotional detachment was to some extent the ideal. Orthodox opinion held that too much affection was undesirable, since it made adults self-indulgent and children selfish. Hence the advice was to ignore the cries of infants, who were assumed to be either exercising their lungs or expressing their frustration at not being gratified in some excessive want. Notwithstanding the advice, there is considerable evidence that parents became emotionally attached to their children, became extremely anxious when children were ill or had accidents, and grieved deeply when they died. But our ideal of parents paying close attention to small children in order to nurture their verbal and emotional development would not have been a familiar one to most seventeenth- and eighteenth-century colonists. Very small children were not the center of their parents' attention.

Around the age of six decisive changes occurred. Boys were given breeches, while girls remained in skirts. The change in clothing marked an important step on the road to adulthood. Both sexes began to be given small tasks, the girls helping their mothers and older sisters in the kitchen or dairy, the boys doing light farm work with their fathers. In New England and the middle colonies most children would also receive some schooling for a few hours each morning.

At this point both girls and boys began to receive sustained attention from the parent of their own gender, since now they could be trained for the work they would do as adults. Girls spent increasing amounts of time with their mothers, learning the skills of household production. Since most boys would become farmers, they now began to spend time with their fathers, learning when and how to sow and harvest the crops. A small proportion of boys from the richer families progressed to a grammar school and even college in preparation for a career as a minister, lawyer, or merchant. Also, as

---

[12] The view that childrearing was extensive rather than intensive and thus involved less individual attention to children is argued by Laurel Thatcher Ulrich, *Good Wives: Image and Reality in the Lives of Women in Northern New England, 1650–1750* (New York, 1982); and Catherine M. Scholten, *Childbearing in American Society: 1650–1850* (New York, 1985). The emotional commitment of mothers to their children is emphasized by Mary Beth Norton in *Liberty's Daughters: The Revolutionary Experience of American Women, 1750–1800* (Boston, 1980).

colonial society developed, some boys around the age of 10 began an apprenticeship, normally lasting about nine years, during which the apprentice lodged with the master. That boys received so much attention was not accidental. In this patriarchal society, it was assumed that they were more capable of being educated than girls. Putting boys into a relationship with a responsible adult male mentor was seen as critical to getting them to abandon childish ways and become responsible adults, capable of heading their own families. The theory behind out-placement was to provide children with an education and skills – and to ensure that they remained under the tutelage and supervision of a responsible adult who could teach them the skills they would need to be productive adults. Again in theory, the relationship between master and servant was supposed to be similar to that between parent and child – stern but affectionate.

The practice of out-placement could be quite different from the theory, especially for the children of the poor. Fatherless children and orphans as young as five were sometimes "put out" to live with families of strangers. The receiving master was supposed to provide a certain level of care and education in return for the child's labor, but in fact that education was rarely one that would enable boys to become independent householders later on, or girls to marry well. Servitude for poor children, historians have found, was more like welfare than education; it provided a way to relieve communities of the cost of their support. This had been true in early seventeenth-century England as well. There, poor children in their early teens were routinely kidnapped and transported to Virginia or Barbados, where they served without contracts until they reached adulthood (if they survived). With no adults capable of advocating for them, such children could be treated with appalling cruelty.[13]

Although adults focused most of their energies on training older children, there were some regional and religious exceptions. Dissenting Protestants paid a great deal of attention to childhood as a stage of moral development, and believed that parents had to devote more than an ordinary amount of attention to their children's spiritual well-being to ensure their salvation. Puritans arrived at this conclusion in one way, Quakers in another, but the end result was similar – both Puritan and Quaker parents were more intensely involved in their children's spiritual educations than their nondissenting counterparts.

Because the Puritans did the most writing about childhood, their views are the best known. They believed (in common with most Englishmen of their time) that children were the product of original sin. But unlike most Englishmen, they also believed that salvation was available only to the elect, who could not sit idly by waiting for God's grace. Parents therefore had to carefully prepare their children for salvation. From as young an age as possible, children had to be carefully and systematically taught to suppress their impulses so they could avoid the temptations of Satan and learn to understand God's will. Historians frequently cite the Puritans' admonition that

---

[13] Edmund S. Morgan, *The Puritan Family: Religion and Domestic Relations in Seventeenth-Century New England* (New York, 1966), 77, argues that New England families adopted this practice to protect themselves from being excessively indulgent. The economic reasons behind such family disruption are emphasized in Helena M. Wall, *Fierce Communion: Family and Community in Early America* (Cambridge, Mass., 1990), 97–125. Poor children are discussed in Ruth Herndon, *Unwelcome Americans: Living on the Margin in Early New England* (Philadelphia, 2001).

children's "natural pride" be "broken and beaten down" in early childhood, and the Puritans (like virtually all Englishmen) advocated the use of moderate corporal punishment. Its purpose, though, was not to destroy their children's self-esteem, but to teach them self-control. Puritan parents were also to warn children of the need to prepare their souls for death: a meaningful message, since children in the colonial world usually had at least one sibling who died before attaining their majority. And finally, parents needed to teach their children how to read, usually starting around age four or five, so that they could understand the Scriptures.

Strikingly, from our point of view, the Puritans believed much of this parental involvement should come from the father, who as the head of a godly household had a special responsibility to attend to his children's spiritual development. Cotton Mather, the famous Massachusetts minister, worked as hard as anyone to live up to the Puritans' paternal ideal, taking it as his calling to "consider how to enrich [children's] minds with valuable knowledge; how to instill into their minds generous, gracious, and heavenly principles; how to restrain and rescue them from the paths of the destroyed, and fortify them against their peculiar temptations." Certainly the task could not be left to the young persons themselves for "'tis folly for them to pretend unto any Wit and Will of their own." In pursuit of his own advice, Mather questioned his six children every night, asking them what they had done during the day, whether they had "sought the Face of God and read His Word." At meal times Mather sought to make the conversation "facetious as well as instructive." For Mather, parenting was an important part of his role as an adult man.[14]

Quaker ideas about childrearing are usually contrasted with those of the Puritans, since the Quakers were considerably more optimistic about children's natural capacity for virtue. They believed that children, like the rest of humanity, were innately good. According to Quakers, each soul was born with an inner light that could lead the individual to salvation. They recoiled from the coercive childrearing techniques of the Puritans and other contemporaries, opposing coercion of any kind as contrary to God's will. But Quakers were similar to Puritans in their belief that parents should be intensely involved in their children's moral education. The purpose of such involvement was not to tame children's corrupt natures but to prevent their children's inner light from being corrupted by the example of the outside world. Parents had to teach their children to achieve the behavioral ideals of kindness, gentleness, and truthfulness by providing them with proper examples, supported occasionally by verbal admonition and constant, patient love. Another difference from the Puritans was the Quakers' expectation that the parent responsible for providing these early examples would usually be the mother.[15]

During the eighteenth century, Enlightenment era British writers began to join the chorus of voices calling for closer parental involvement in young children's moral and intellectual training. The first and most influential such writer was John Locke, who argued in his *Essay Concerning Human Understanding* (1690) and *Some Thoughts Concerning Education* (1693) that children were born as moral blank slates and must be

---

[14] Quoted in Fox and Quitt, eds, *Loving, Parenting, and Dying*, 313.
[15] Levy, *Quakers and the American Family*.

taught through example and environment to control their passions and develop their rational capacities. Though Locke's emphasis on the use of moral suasion and affection differed from the Puritans' belief in coercion, Locke's emphasis on early childhood education was similar to that of the Reformed Protestants in their focus on understanding children as individuals and on beginning to shape their moral development at an early age. Other Enlightenment writers like Francis Hutcheson, too, suggested that children had an innate moral sense, which would flourish if it was nurtured by parents in infancy and early childhood. These ideas became increasingly popular among colonists as books from British presses became available in colonial cities during the eighteenth century, and wealthier colonists appear to have devoted increasing amounts of time to their children during early childhood compared to the past.[16] At the same time, emerging new ideas about children probably heightened perceptions of children's helplessness and dependence.

Even as new questions were being raised about children's moral development early in life, so too were questions being asked about the age at which children stopped needing adult tutelage and became responsible for making their own decisions. Although scholars used to assume that young people in colonial (and British) society always reached the "age of majority" at 21, it now appears that neither British nor colonial societies had a consistent age of majority before the late eighteenth century. Before the 1750s, children could be treated as legally capable adults at surprisingly young ages. Propertied boys could serve in the House of Commons as well as the Virginia House of Burgesses during their teens. Poor children were routinely sent out to service as toddlers, and could be hanged for felonies at age eight. Girls could legally "consent" to sexual intercourse with an adult male (thus providing him with a defense to a charge of rape) as young as eight or nine.

By the mid to late eighteenth century, however, these seemingly anomalous legal rules were clearly changing. Children were by now usually excluded from voting or serving in political offices, and their treatment as morally responsible individuals was being postponed until they reached an age that we would consider more developmentally appropriate. This increase in the age of majority went hand in hand with the gradual reconceptualization of childhood as a malleable, unformed period in which capacities for reasoned decision-making had yet to be developed. As historian Holly Brewer has argued, these changes were connected with the gradual rethinking of the basis for religious and political communities that took place from the Reformation through the Enlightenment. Membership in communities was coming to be based less on inherited status, and more upon the capacity for carefully reasoned moral decision-making and consent. The new attention being paid to the need to nurture moral reasoning skills during childhood and adolescence coincided with the new concern

---

[16] For the influence of Enlightenment ideas about childhood in eighteenth-century colonial America, see Jay Fliegelman, *Prodigals and Pilgrims: The American Revolution against Patriarchal Authority, 1750–1800* (Cambridge, 1982). Another view is that the rising standard of living, coupled with increasing longevity, encouraged people to plan not only for their children but for their grandchildren too and provided an additional incentive to develop a close and loving relationship. This view is argued by Daniel Blake Smith in *Inside the Great House: Planter Family Life in Eighteenth-Century Chesapeake Society* (Ithaca, 1980). See also his review article, "The Study of the Family in Early America: Trends, Problems, and Prospects," *William and Mary Quarterly*, 39 (1982), 3–28.

among religious and political philosophers with the capacity for reason. Instead of thrusting children as quickly as possible into adult responsibilities, the new thinking was that children should wait until they were morally and intellectually mature before they assumed adult roles. Gradually, childhood would come to be thought of as a special stage of life in which people needed careful supervision so as to develop into capable, thinking moral beings.[17]

3 PATRIARCHAL AUTHORITY

Because other institutions such as the aristocracy and the church were so weak, household government played a more important role in the British North American colonies than it did in Britain. Colonial families in British North America were not only institutions for rearing children; they were also institutions of government, welfare services, and social control.[18] Colonial households were patriarchal in form, with the father as the unquestioned head to whom all of the members owed obedience. Fathers had extensive legal powers over their wives, children, and teenaged as well as adult servants and slaves. In turn fathers owed their dependents various obligations: economic support, protection, moral guidance, and a certain amount of religious training (though the degree of obligation to servants and slaves was considerably less than was owed to kin). The theory was that heads of households made up the political community; when men voted on taxes or enforced laws, they did so not only for themselves but also on behalf of their dependents. When men fulfilled their duties to their dependents, they were seen as serving the public good. Even after household government became less patriarchal and more paternalistic during the eighteenth century, the theory of the household as the foundation of political society persisted.[19]

The list of obligations was long. Fathers were supposed to provide adequate support for their children, as well as religious instruction and a good moral example. They were to prepare their sons for adulthood, either by leaving them property or by teaching

---

[17] The declining autonomy of children is dealt with in Holly Brewer, *By Birth or Consent: Children, Law, and the Anglo-American Revolution in Authority* (Chapel Hill, 2005).

[18] Since around 1990, there has been a revived interest in exploring the establishment, evolution, and persistence of patriarchal forms of authority in early America. This interest grew in part from questions about why the American feminist movement had failed to achieve one of its main goals, the ratification of the Equal Rights Amendment. Mary Beth Norton, *Founding Mothers and Fathers: Gendered Power and the Forming of American Society* (New York, 1996), argues that a highly patriarchal political ideology prevailed in New England, while a more modern political ideology (which also insisted on male dominance in the family) developed in the Chesapeake. Carole Shammas, *A History of Household Government in America* (Charlottesville, 2002), argues that white male household heads had exceptional powers over Anglo-American households until the mid nineteenth century. Holly Brewer's findings on the declining autonomy of children (cited above) also support the general thesis that parental authority grew during the eighteenth century, rather than declined.

[19] The patriarchal model of the family received considerable reinforcement from the political theories of Sir Thomas Filmer, who used a model of the patriarchal family to justify absolute monarchy in the seventeenth century. Filmer argued that all government authority flowed from the father's authority over dependents. John Locke, a critic of absolutism, argued that the family was a private realm, separate from the state. For a discussion of the Filmer and Locke models of the family, see Mary Beth Norton, *Founding Mothers and Fathers*.

them a trade. They were legally required to control unruly behavior and prevent disturbances of the peace by children and servants. Parents (particularly fathers) were expected to supervise the marriage choices and courtship behavior of their children and servants, with the expectation that they would ensure marriages that served the children's long-term interests. Fathers were to assist their daughters by providing them with adequate dowries. And when they died fathers were to divide up their property among their family members in a way that would provide, at a minimum, for the people who had contributed the most to their households, usually the widow and the eldest son.

To enable them to carry out these expectations, fathers in the British North American colonies had what most of us would consider to be astonishing legal powers, especially in seventeenth-century New England where the ideal of patriarchal government was most influential. In fact, male household heads in the colonies had significantly more legal authority over dependants than their British counterparts. Men were legally entitled to control their children's labor, an entitlement that gave them various kinds of coercive powers: the power to take a child's wages and earnings; to indenture a child to a master, whether or not he liked it; and to decide how a child should be educated. They could also control the decisions of servants, which might seem perfectly just – except that (in the colonies) servants were not typically entitled to leave a household they disliked, and many of them had no choice as to the households in which they were placed until they were emancipated.

Fathers were also charged with maintaining order within their families. Legal institutions in the colonies were weak, and authorities relied heavily on male household heads to ensure that the young people and women under their authority behaved properly and did not create trouble for the rest of the community.[20] Fathers had the legal power (and the legal obligation) to discipline children and servants if they became unruly or disobedient, although they were supposed to use discipline in moderation and only when truly necessary. Fathers (and mothers) were legally entitled to strike their children and servants, and all of the colonies passed laws imposing penalties on children and servants who threatened or struck either parent. The most notorious was the Massachusetts statute of 1648 imposing the death penalty on children over age 16 who cursed at or refused to obey their parents. Prosecutions under such laws were rare (and no colony ever imposed the death penalty on a rebellious child), but they did clearly define the expectation that young people were supposed to obey their parents. Fathers and mothers also had the legal power, as well as the duty, to oversee their children's marriage choices. All of the colonies had laws on their books by the seventeenth century requiring the consent of a parent (usually the father) or master for a valid marriage, a legal requirement not enacted in England until 1752.[21]

Although male household heads in Great Britain had some of the same formal legal powers as in the colonies, white men in the colonies typically possessed more actual power over dependants than was enjoyed by their counterparts at home. One previously noted factor was that colonial men had more children, most of whom lived at home

[20] Chapter 12 will deal at greater length with the powers of husbands over their wives.
[21] Ruth Bloch, *Gender and Morality in Anglo-American Culture*, 1650–1800 (Berkeley, 2003), ch. 4.

until they reached adulthood. Thus white children in the colonies lived under paternal authority for a greater proportion of their lives than children in Britain. Colonial men were also more likely (overall) to own servants or slaves, especially during the eighteenth century, or to have purchased the indentures of poor people.

Before the Reformation, institutions like monasteries and guilds had provided havens for poor people and their children. But in the sixteenth and seventeenth centuries, local governments in England instead began binding out poor people, especially children, to work in households until they reached adulthood. In the colonies, where other government institutions, like churches, had few resources, local governments relied even more heavily on male household heads to provide economic support as well as supervision and discipline for the poor. If they could not find family members willing to take them in, local colonial governments placed orphans, poor children, widows, unwed mothers, debtors, even indigent elderly people into the households of strangers, essentially requiring them to work as household servants for years in return for their bed and board. The result was a society in which adult male household heads had formal control over the vast majority of the population. One historian has estimated that in the colonies, by 1774, 80 percent of the population (including wives, children, servants, and slaves) lacked the legal freedom to leave the households in which they resided without the permission of the male household head.[22]

A final source of coercive power over children (though not servants) in British North America was colonial fathers' virtually unlimited right to disinherit their children upon their deaths. Since fathers owned most or all of a family's productive property, this could be a very significant power. Colonial fathers often possessed more power to disinherit children than British fathers because they were more likely to hold unrestricted ownership rights to their land, especially in the northern colonies. Legally a man's authority to dispose of his land as he chose was limited (in law) only by the widow's dower right, which gave her the right to use (though not to sell or otherwise dispose of) a third of the property that the couple had built up during their marriage. The main exception to this pattern of paternal power over land was among elite families in the South. Southern families commonly tied up their land in entails, a legal mechanism used frequently in Britain to require that land be passed down through the lineage for generations. Entail weakened the powers of fathers over their children, since it prescribed how land would be disposed of and deprived fathers of the ability to disinherit children.[23]

It would be logical to ask why anyone would put up with a system that was so undemocratic. Part of the answer, certainly, has to do with ideology. Early modern Europeans (particularly the Puritans) commonly viewed young people as less rational

---

[22] For statistics on dependency, see Carole Shammas, "Anglo-American Household Government in Comparative Perspective," *William and Mary Quarterly*, 52 (1995), 122. The large numbers are partly explained by the high number of slaves, and partly by the fact that over half the population in the colonies were minors. The proportion of the colonial population made up of servants and slaves was also considerably higher in the colonies, 26 percent as compared with 7 percent in England during the same period.

[23] Shammas, "Anglo-American Household Government." For the importance of entail in the colonies, see Holly Brewer, "Entailing Aristocracy in Colonial Virginia: 'Ancient Feudal Restraints' and Revolutionary Reform," *William and Mary Quarterly*, 54 (1997), 307–46.

than adult men, and less capable of self-government. As noted above, notions of children as unformed or morally undeveloped strengthened notions that children needed fathers to guide and supervise their behavior. Another factor was a tendency within dissenting Protestantism to idealize fatherhood. It was commonplace in colonial culture to depict these powerful patriarchs as benevolent, wise, generous, and just, and to minimize or deny the extent to which men abused their powers. In other words, various powerful ideological currents led towards the same conclusion: that adult white men were the most rational, morally responsible members of the community. Therefore they should have the power to make decisions for everybody else.[24]

By the eighteenth century the idea that fathers should have absolute power over their children was becoming discredited, having been jettisoned along with the much reviled theory of absolute monarchy. However, other ideological tendencies continued to prop up paternal authority over young people and servants, though an authoritarian style of discipline did become less popular. The Protestant idealization of fathers as benevolent figures persisted at least until the American Revolution. The growing Enlightenment era emphasis on reason highlighted children's lack of rationality, thereby making them seem in greater need of paternal guidance and protection. Meanwhile, the authority of masters over their slaves was being strengthened in the eighteenth century by developing racial ideologies suggesting that nonwhite adults were supposedly less capable of making rational moral decisions than adult white men.

Another part of the answer may be that young people had several strategies for limiting or avoiding parental tyranny before the mid eighteenth century that did not involve outright resistance. Neighbors and friends could exert considerable pressure on household heads who acted in clearly immoral or irresponsible ways to change their behavior. Thus, dependants of a violent or unreasonable master could occasionally get help to change their situation. Also by the eighteenth century the development of a market for young people's labor in a few urban areas offered boys, if not girls, another way to resist parental tyranny: running away. The most famous runaway in colonial America was undoubtedly Benjamin Franklin. Having been bound as an apprentice to his elder brother James, a printer, Franklin became unhappy with his master's heavy-handed management style and ran away to Philadelphia in his late teens, with help from some friends. Another less famous youngster with a similar story was Ashley Bowen, a Massachusetts boy whose father apprenticed him to a sea captain at age 13 after his mother died. Bowen's master was a savage brute who bullied, starved, and beat the boy for four years, until Bowen found a way to escape and signed on with the master of another ship bound for the Caribbean.[25]

A more common safeguard against parental tyranny may simply have been that fathers were often as dependent on their teenaged children, particularly their sons, as their children were on them. The scarcity of labor (combined with the abundance of land) gave some adult sons more bargaining power in negotiating the terms of their

---

[24] Moral justifications for patriarchy (which were strongest in New England) are covered in Norton, *Founding Mothers and Fathers*, and Anne Lombard, *Making Manhood: Growing Up Male in Colonial New England* (Cambridge, Mass., 2003). For the importance of family life to New England men's identities, see Lisa Wilson, *Ye Heart of a Man: The Domestic Life of Men in Colonial New England* (New Haven, 1999).
[25] Ashley Bowen's story is recounted in Daniel Vickers with Vince Walsh, *Young Men and the Sea: Yankee Seafarers in the Age of Sail* (New Haven, 2005).

relationships than the legal rules might have seemed to permit. Nowhere was the interdependence of fathers and sons great than in seventeenth-century New England, where sons typically worked for their fathers until well into adulthood. Meanwhile fathers compensated their offspring by subdividing their own farms and building houses for each of the sons so that they could continue working for their fathers even after marrying and beginning families of their own. Sons thus benefited from the arrangement even though they did not strike out on their own and become financially independent.[26]

During the eighteenth century, fathers continued to need their sons for work on family farms. Yet by this time it seems that adult sons had begun to make different kinds of bargains with their parents in exchange for their labor. Fewer eighteenth-century fathers had enough land to induce their sons to remain near home past their mid-twenties. Farms could not be subdivided forever, and moving further west became a more attractive option for more young men. Now New England fathers left most of their land to a designated son, usually the eldest or the youngest, and repaid the labor of their other sons by providing them with training in trades so that they could earn extra money, or by helping them to purchase land elsewhere. These strategies encouraged young men to develop greater independence, and sons in these later generations became more likely to move away from their home towns when they reached adulthood.

Eighteenth-century Quaker fathers in Pennsylvania and New Jersey continued to exert considerable influence over their children's marriage choices, pressing their children to marry within the church. However, they too tended to encourage married adult children to live on their own rather than working on parental land. Consistent with their emphasis on moral suasion and their opposition to coercion in childrearing, Quakers offered land outright to their children once they married, usually providing a farm within a year of the marriage, rather than withholding it until the parents died. Of course Quaker fathers in Pennsylvania and New Jersey had less reason than Puritan fathers in New England to withhold their sons' portions, since they were not as dependent on their sons for farm labor. They were relatively wealthier than farmers in New England, and often earned enough cash from their wheat harvests to purchase German or Scots-Irish indentured servants who could do their work instead.[27]

The pattern of increasing independence for adult children during the eighteenth century was not universal. As a group, southern fathers in some ways asserted *more* control over their teenaged children during the eighteenth century than they had during the earlier decades. During the seventeenth century fathers in the Chesapeake, with its high mortality rates, had typically named their widows as the executors of their estates, hoping that giving their wives control over their property would more likely enable them to keep the children together under one roof and maintain continuity in the family. However, during the eighteenth century, after mortality had declined,

---

[26]   On mobility in New England, see Greven, *Four Generations*, 122–6; and Linda Auwers Bissell, "From One Generation to Another: Mobility in Seventeenth-Century Windsor, Connecticut," *William and Mary Quarterly*, 31 (1974), 79–110. For the theory that fathers forced sons to stay by threatening to disinherit them, see Greven, *Four Generations*. For the theory that labor scarcity gave sons bargaining power, see Vickers, *Farmers and Fishermen*.

[27]   On Quaker families, see Levy, *Quakers and the American Family*.

fathers became likely to live long enough to see their children grow up. Men stopped entrusting their widows with executorships and came to rely on male relatives to oversee their property instead, which suggests that most southern families were becoming more patriarchal, in contrast to the pattern found elsewhere in the colonies.

Nevertheless one group of southern Anglo-American fathers consistently struggled to assert any control at all over their sons. By 1750 rich, landowning fathers in Virginia and Maryland had strikingly independent, even insolent, teenaged children. Some historians have suggested that these families had become more permissive and child-centered, encouraging sons to become independent and self-confident so that they could effectively function in a competitive society. Typically gentry families did not need their children for labor, since they depended on slaves instead; therefore, relationships between fathers and sons were less intense among the southern gentry than in small farming families. Another explanation for the absence of patriarchal control in some southern gentry families may be that children had less need for their fathers' economic assistance. As mentioned above, gentry families in the Chesapeake began during the seventeenth century to tie up their land in entails, which guaranteed that land would pass to prescribed heirs regardless of what a father wanted. If family lands were tied up through entails, fathers could not disinherit their disobedient sons. Fathers' lack of power may help to explain their children's independence.[28]

By the mid eighteenth century, ideological as well as economic trends were making it easier for grown children to criticize and even openly resist tyrannical fathers. As John Locke's political theories became popular in the wake of the Glorious Revolution in 1689, his ideas about childrearing began also to be widely read by well-educated colonial settlers. In his *Essay Concerning Human Understanding* (1690) and *Some Thoughts Concerning Education* (1693), Locke argued that parents should moderate their discipline with a little indulgence to secure their children's gratitude and affection. The child would then respond more readily to the challenge of adulthood. Locke also suggested that a sense of shame was generally more effective than fear, for the former would naturally induce a desire for self-improvement. Corporal punishment should be administered only as a last resort, since it could make a child resentful and less open to reason and moral persuasion. The new attitude was reflected in depictions of the biblical prodigal son. Earlier versions stressed the folly and ruin that would result for children who defied their parents. By 1740 or so the emphasis had shifted to the need for parental affection and forgiveness to prevent children leaving in the first place.

Locke's influence helped to popularize a softer version of patriarchy. He denied that any authority was absolute or divinely appointed, since it had to be contractual, giving protection to all members of the family (though Locke still believed in the

---

[28] The structure of gentry families is examined in Daniel Blake Smith, *Inside the Great House*. A recent account of the troubled relationships between father and children in one plantation household is Rhys Isaac, *Landon Carter's Uneasy Kingdom: Revolution and Rebellion on a Virginia Plantation* (New York, 2004). It used to be thought that primogeniture and entail were rare even in the South. South Carolina had abandoned entail in its legal code of 1712, while Virginia was believed to have largely given up the practice, a view based on C. Ray Keim, "Primogeniture and Entail in Colonial Virginia," *William and Mary Quarterly*, 25 (1968), 545–86. However, recent work by Holly Brewer suggests otherwise. See "Entailing Aristocracy in Colonial Virginia," in which she shows that up to three-quarters of all estates were entailed at the time of the Revolution when Jefferson brought in his bill abolishing the practice.

natural superiority of men). The manner in which fathers were expected to assert their authority as parents began to change, as authoritarian styles of parenting became less acceptable and paternalistic styles gained popularity. Although fathers could still exert enormous influence over the lives and decisions of their children until they married and started their own households, paternal authority became more amenable to negotiation.[29]

One sign of adult children's increasing assertiveness in relationships with parents was their new insistence by about 1740 on making their own courtship and marriage decisions. Traditional patterns of sexual behavior had permitted couples to become sexually intimate before marriage provided they married promptly if the woman were to become pregnant. Puritans in New England had virtually transformed these patterns during the seventeenth century by encouraging strict paternal control as well community oversight over young people's sexual behavior. However, after 1740 or so traditional patterns of courtship re-emerged as parents, even in New England, relaxed their control over their children's courtships. Social interactions between young men and women became substantially more relaxed than they had been a century earlier, and sexual intimacy before marriage became unexceptional. The best indication of the new attitudes was a considerable increase in the rate of bridal pregnancy. During the seventeenth century, the percentage of brides who became pregnant before they married never rose above 10 percent in New England. By the mid eighteenth century, the rate had increased to around 30 percent. Parents, of course, continued to have the legal right to withhold their consent to children's marriages, but were unlikely to refuse when their daughters were already pregnant. Adult children had thus found an effective way to decide for themselves whom they would marry, and when.[30]

4 SOCIAL STRUCTURE: RANK AND CLASS

People in the United States have long prided themselves on having a classless society. Historians used to agree, offering three reasons in support: (1) that the frontier was a great leveler; (2) that, in crossing the Atlantic, immigrants to British North America left class distinctions behind; and (3) that North America was a land of opportunity. In the

---

[29] The argument that the decline of patriarchy was linked to the American Revolution is made by Melvin Yazawa, in *From Colonies to Commonwealth: Ideology and the Beginnings of the American Republic* (Baltimore, 1985); and by Fliegelman, in *Prodigals and Pilgrims*. Kenneth A. Lockridge, *On the Sources of Patriarchal Rage: The Commonplace Books of William Byrd and Thomas Jefferson and the Gendering of Power in the Eighteenth Century* (New York, 1992) offers a different reason for the decline, arguing that misogyny accounted for the patriarchal impulses of many men and that such attitudes were becoming less acceptable as a result of the Enlightenment. Cornelia Hughes Dayton, *Women Before the Bar: Gender, Law, and Society in Connecticut, 1639–1789* (Chapel Hill, 1995), argues that patriarchal and misogynistic views in New England were actually strengthened as the legal system became anglicized. Allan Kulikoff, *Tobacco and Slaves: The Development of Southern Cultures in the Chesapeake, 1680–1800* (Chapel Hill, 1986), also argues that patriarchy was increasing in the eighteenth century.

[30] Richard Godbeer traces the dramatic changes in sexual mores and behavior during the eighteenth century as the colonists developed a more individualistic set of ideas about desire and sexual identity, in *Sexual Revolution in Early America* (Baltimore, 2002).

words of Benjamin Franklin, the question was not what a person was, but what a person could do. Ability, not birth, determined status and rewards in life.[31]

Along with the perception that British North Americans invented the nuclear family, the perception that class did not exist in colonial British North American societies is one more example of American exceptionalism that contemporary historians have debunked. Of course the colonists did leave behind them the strict hierarchical structures of Europe. No feudal aristocracy or peerage existed in British North America as in Britain. But immigrants did not arrive in British North America as equals. As we have seen, the Virginia Company had dispatched a number of gentlemen to help build the colony; the Puritans were led by gentry families like the Winthrops, Saltonstalls, and Vanes; Lord Baltimore sent over his brother and a number of gentry to Maryland; while the Carolinian proprietors planned a leading role for their aristocracy. Even Penn relied on his connections with the aristocracy and on a monied class to get his settlement established.

Domination by the elites was reinforced by religious sanction. As John Winthrop asserted on board the *Arabella* in 1630, "God Almighty, in his most holy and wise providence, has so disposed of the condition of Mankind" that "some must be rich, some poor, some high and eminent in power and dignity, others mean and in subjection." In fact, British colonial societies were shot through with social inequality from the very beginning. Class distinctions became considerably more visible during the eighteenth century as colonial societies grew wealthier and elites accumulated property and prestige. British North Americans did not, however, experience class in the same ways as the British.

To understand class divisions in colonial British North America it is helpful to begin by looking at concepts of social hierarchy found in seventeenth-century England. Contemporaries sometimes described English society as comprised of two estates: the nobility and the commons. The nobility was a legally defined category; everybody else was simply part of the commons. Other descriptions of English society were rather more nuanced. Although people did not speak of "classes," they described the social order in terms of "rank," "degrees," and "sorts." Most people thought of the "upper sort" as including both the nobility and the gentry, that is, people whose lands gave them independent incomes so that they did not have to work. Comprising the "middling sort" were a wide variety of people who worked for a living, including wealthy merchants, shopkeepers, lawyers, clergymen, ship captains, highly skilled

---

[31] It was a foreign visitor, J. Hector St. John Crèvecoeur, who first propounded the notion that America was exceptional in its social structure. In an oft-quoted passage from his *Letters from an American Farmer* (1782), he asked: "What then is the American, this new man?" The answer was clear: "He is an American, who leaving behind him all his ancient prejudices and manners, receives new ones from the new mode of life he has embraced, the new government he obeys, and the new rank he holds . . . Here individuals of all nations are melted into a new race of men, whose labors and posterity will one day cause great changes in the world." "From involuntary idleness, servile dependence, penury and useless labor" in Europe the newcomer "has passed to toils of a very different nature, rewarded by ample subsistence." The belief in the egalitarian nature of American life was then passed down in American mythology. Among the more notable expositions on this theme in the twentieth century was that by Louis Hartz, *The Liberal Tradition in America* (New York, 1955). For a more recent discussion, see Jack P. Greene, *The Intellectual Construction of America: Exceptionalism and Identity from 1492 to 1800* (Chapel Hill, 1993).

artisans in high-status trades like silversmithing, and so on. Independent yeoman farmers were often a separate category, deserving of considerable respect because of their independence (but comprising only a minority of farmers, since most farmers were tenants or owned too little land to be considered independent). There was also the "lower sort," which included lower-paid artisans, poor farmers, unskilled laborers, ordinary seamen, servants, and the vagrant poor. Categories were not carefully defined (except for the nobility or peerage), but status roughly corresponded with wealth, especially landed wealth. It has been estimated that though the aristocracy and the gentry comprised only 2 or 3 percent of the population in early seventeenth-century England, they owned perhaps 65 percent of the land. Virtually all important offices in county and parish governments were held by members of the gentry, who were also eligible to serve in the House of Commons.

Similar sorts of categories were used to describe people in colonial British North American societies, but they appear to have acquired different meanings. A titled aristocracy never developed in the British North American colonies. Still, by the end of the seventeenth century, local elites had emerged who thought of themselves as members of the gentry in every colony. New York was dominated by the Anglo-Dutch dynasties of Van Rensselaer, Livingston, Stuyvesant, Bayard, and Philipse; Virginia was controlled by the planter families of Beverley, Randolph, Carter, Harrison, Lee, and Byrd; and South Carolina had its Pinckneys, Rutledges, Draytons, and Manigaults. Massachusetts had long been dominated by its Puritan ministers and magistrates, the Mathers and the Winthrops being the pre-eminent examples, who by the end of the seventeenth century shared a place at the top of the social scale with members of merchant families like the Dudleys, Hutchinsons, Pynchons, and Sewalls. In every province this gentry dominated social and political life, especially at the level of the provincial council. In New York during one decade 25 of the 28 councillors were from the landed families of the Hudson Valley. Similarly, in Virginia, nine families made up one-third of the council in the period 1700–60, while in Connecticut 25 names accounted for two-thirds of that body.

What about the rest of the population? Fifty years ago many scholars suggested that British colonial North American society was equal because it offered unrivaled economic opportunity, at least for the immigrants who came here from Europe. Robert E. Brown in particular argued that the presence of the frontier made land both plentiful and cheap, while the high level of wages opened its purchase to all whites. Since property was the only qualification men required in order to vote or to hold office, entry into the political and social life of a colony was unrestricted. Brown called this situation economic democracy, a society in which the majority of the white population was middle-class.[32]

Unfortunately, the Brown thesis contained several flaws, which most historians now recognize. In the first place, though land may have been cheap in many areas, the frontier itself was far from having a leveling effect. Settlers simply did not arrive there in an equal condition, for of course the scions of the rich were able to secure the best tracts from their relatives on the council and gain a head start before coming west with slaves

---

[32] Robert E. Brown, *Middle-Class Democracy and the Revolution in Massachusetts, 1691–1780* (Ithaca, 1955).

or servants. Such "pioneers" included William Byrd of Virginia, who purchased 100,000 acres in what became Lunenburg County; and John Pynchon, who developed the frontier settlement of Springfield, high up the Connecticut River in western Massachusetts.[33]

In the second place, as settlement expanded, the price of land rose, putting it out of the reach of many ordinary settlers in some areas by the eighteenth century. As we have seen, by 1700 in Virginia only half the free adult male population owned land and 50 percent of these did not have the necessary 100 acres to make life comfortable. The extent of tenant farming rose substantially during the eighteenth century. The same was true in Maryland. In Talbot County 150 men owned land and slaves, 220 owned some land, but 420 owned no land at all. In neighboring Prince George County during the 1730s the average tenant was worth just £26; the owner of a small farm was worth £117; but a planter with slaves possessed almost £600. Perhaps most significant is the fact that some 60 percent of households still possessed less than £100.

In the North, the distribution of land was more balanced, though by the middle of the eighteenth century inequality was growing there too. In Dedham, Massachusetts, the top five percent of the population owned a mere 15 percent of the property in the town by 1730. But in cities, where merchants and ship-owners were able to amass considerable wealth, the gap was greater. In Boston the top five percent owned about 46 percent of inheritable wealth on the eve of the Revolution, while the lowest half of the population owned just 5 percent. In Philadelphia the top five percent owned more than 55 percent of inheritable wealth by the same period.[34]

It was these discrepancies that helped to create an upper class in the British mainland colonies. Still, it was an upper class not particularly secure in its claims to gentry status. Most of the upper class in the North, for example, owed its wealth to commerce, not land. Members of the southern upper class did their best to replicate the British gentry, solidifying their pedigrees through intermarriage and carefully settling substantial amounts of wealth on their eldest sons. But they still lacked the long history, and with it the claim to inherited authority, of the British gentry. Perhaps hoping to buttress their stature, the families of the upper classes began distancing themselves from the rest of society around the beginning of the eighteenth century. Their way of life changed. They built conspicuously large houses and furnished them with luxuries imported from Europe. They bought carriages, wore clothing made from imported fabrics in the latest European fashions, and gave greater attention to their personal hygiene and appearance. Their patterns of consumption seemed designed to affirm to the world, as well as to themselves, that they really were gentlemen, entitled to respect and deference. The

---

[33] The Brown thesis incurred considerable criticism at the time of publication, not least for its flawed statistical methodology. See John Cary, "Statistical Method and the Brown Thesis on Colonial Democracy," *William and Mary Quarterly*, 20 (1963), 251–76. For the thesis on frontier democracy see Frederick Jackson Turner, *The Frontier in American History* (New York, 1920).

[34] For wealth distribution in Maryland, see Paul G. E. Clemens, *The Atlantic Economy and Colonial Maryland's Eastern Shore: From Tobacco to Grain* (Ithaca, 1980); for Dedham, see Kenneth A. Lockridge, *A New England Town, the First Hundred Years: Dedham, Massachusetts, 1636–1736* (New York, 1970); for Boston and other cities, see Gary B. Nash, *The Urban Crucible: Social Change, Political Consciousness, and the Origins of the American Revolution* (Cambridge, Mass., 1979) and *Race, Class, and Politics: Essays on American Colonial and Revolutionary Society* (Urbana, 1986).

new elite sought, too, to educate their children in a way that befitted the children of the gentry, sending them to school and later college, where they could develop a network of acquaintances. Such children mixed only with their peer group and soon absorbed the manners and attitudes of a governing class.

We have already seen that at the other end of the social scale, colonial societies by the eighteenth century were also seeing the emergence of real poverty. As land grew more crowded with the growth of settler populations, some young people whose parents could not provide for them took to the roads in search of work, particularly after about 1760. Some among them migrated to the larger towns and seaports, hoping to ply their trades or looking for jobs as dockworkers, laborers, or sailors. Though paid work was often available in urban areas, wage laborers and artisans were extremely vulnerable to disruptions of the market caused by wars and economic downturns. Epidemics, too, could be devastating. New York's yellow fever epidemic in 1702, for example, killed 10 percent of the city's population and left one in five families headed by a widow. Wages for many urban workers (especially women) were so low that when work disappeared as a result of a temporary downturn, they could not support their children without binding them out to masters or sending them to beg in the streets. When people grew truly desperate, they could apply for public alms; some five to seven percent of urban people received public assistance during the eighteenth century, either in almshouses or in the workhouses that were built in cities like Boston and Newport to attempt to make poor relief pay for itself. Others, not yet on the verge of starvation or death from exposure, did not qualify for alms and thus are not counted in that figure. Although most historians have found that poverty in British North American urban areas was not as extensive as in London or other contemporary European cities, the poor were just as vulnerable in the colonies as elsewhere.[35]

Some historians have argued that the growth of commerce in British North America helped produce a distinctive working class, since the market economy, with its differentiation between owners and operatives, reduced labor from having a dignified status to that of a mere commodity. Distinctions of wealth and class were clearly on the increase during the eighteenth century. There is also evidence that some of the poorer sorts of people, especially in colonial cities, may have developed a distinct set of cultural values during the eighteenth century that made it possible to criticize elite claims to authority under some circumstances. On the other hand any self-conscious working class in the British colonies was still small. One reason is the majority of workers were still servants who lived with their masters in considerable intimacy. The segregation of the workplace from the home by the payment of a flat wage had yet to be adopted on a large scale, though as we have seen, many northern cities had a population of wage laborers by 1760. Unlike wage workers who lived in their own neighborhoods, servants had relatively few opportunities to complain to others outside their household or to develop a thorough critique of their situation, since so much of their time was supervised by their masters. Another factor was that many servants later became masters and property-owners, although they rarely became rich. A true working class would not

---

[35] See James Henretta, "Economic Development and Social Structure in Colonial Boston," *William and Mary Quarterly*, 22 (1965), 75–92; Billy G. Smith, "Poverty and Economic Marginality in Eighteenth-Century America," *Proceedings of the American Philosophical Society*, 132 (1988), 85–118.

emerge until industrialization produced both capitalist and propertyless classes which were mutually antagonistic. This sort of division had yet to occur except on southern plantations, where the workers were enslaved.[36]

The evidence of growing disparities of wealth is at odds with Brown's thesis about a universal middle class. On the other hand, to people who had come to the colonies from Great Britain or other European countries as immigrants, colonial societies looked considerably less class-stratified than societies back home. Even with the growing disparities between the rich and poor, the "middling sort" in the British mainland colonies was substantial. Landownership was considerably more widespread than in Great Britain, where most rural people were tenants, poor farmers, and hired laborers. Indeed landownership was widespread enough that the majority of free white men could at least dream of achieving a competence – becoming a yeoman or an independent artisan, capable of supporting himself with the help of his dependants, and enjoying the respect of his wife and children. Even if tenancy was increasing, land was available enough and wages high enough to ensure that most free white men in the British North American colonies could marry at a relatively young age and have children of their own. And in many regions, it would be possible to develop strategies so that the majority of a man's sons could become independent household heads themselves, a prospect virtually unthinkable for most men in contemporary Britain.

For white men from modest origins, this was enough to hope for. A yeoman or an independent artisan could earn enough to be entitled to the respect and deference of a wife and a household full of children, and of his community as well. The colonies were hardly classless societies, and no settler would have said they were. But that they offered so many the opportunity to achieve the status of a patriarchal household head was enough to make most white men feel very confident and optimistic about their futures – as long as enough land remained available to keep that opportunity open for them and for their sons.

---

[36] The emergence of a proletariat is implicit in Nash, *The Urban Crucible*. For a recent interpretation, see Ronald Schultz, *The Republic of Labor: Philadelphia Artisans and the Politics of Class, 1720–1830* (New York, 1993). The concept of class has been used less commonly by historians writing about British America than by historians writing about Europe.

12

White Women and Gender

1656	New Haven permits divorce for adultery, desertion, bigamy, or male impotence.
1664	Maryland provides that white women who marry enslaved African men must become indentured servants to their husbands' masters.
1691	Virginia prohibits interracial marriage.
1700	Witchcraft accusations end.
1718	Pennsylvania grants sole trader status to abandoned wives or those with absent husbands.
1739–42	Elizabeth Timothy manages the *South Carolina Gazette*.
1741	Eliza Pinckney introduces indigo to South Carolina.
1744	South Carolina grants sole trader status to married women engaged in business.
1745	Widow Roberts runs a coffee house in Philadelphia.
1749	Elizabeth Murray Smith (Inman) starts her dry goods and millinery business in Boston.
1766	Mrs Catherine Blaikley, "an eminent midwife" from Williamsburg, dies aged 76, having presided over 3,000 births.

Colonial America: A History to 1763, Fourth Edition. Richard Middleton and Anne Lombard.
© 2011 Richard Middleton and Anne Lombard. Published 2011 by Blackwell Publishing Ltd.

1 GENDER AND THE SETTLER EXPERIENCE IN THE SEVENTEENTH CENTURY

T
HOUGH BRITISH NORTH American societies expanded the opportunities, power, and prestige available to middling white men, these opportunities were by no means equally shared with the women in their families. Women in British settler societies were subject to a restricting set of legal rules and gender norms that created strong incentives for most women to defer to men, limiting their choices and their power. White women had few opportunities for real independence in the economically undeveloped, mostly rural societies of colonial British North America, and African American women had even fewer. At the same time, women were vital economic participants in these societies. Men who aspired to become independent yeomen or artisans depended in great measure not only on their own efforts, but on the daily, sustained productive energies of their wives. To some extent contemporaries recognized these women's economic contributions to their households, and indeed married women enjoyed a somewhat higher status than unmarried women in most cases. However, women's economic contributions to their society would not be recognized as a basis for expanding women's legal rights until long after the end of the colonial period.[1]

All societies, obviously, include both men and women, but societies differ dramatically in the ways in which they allocate power and divide up responsibilities between them. Scholars use the term "gender" to refer to the way in which a society differentiates between the two sexes. A society's "gender system" is the way in which this differentiation creates expectations for behavior and apportions power between men and women. Societies also develop values and beliefs that provide their members with seemingly logical or common sense explanations for their particular system of gender, which in many societies is linked with ideas about status categories such as class and race. The term "gender ideology" refers to these values and beliefs.

---

[1]   Historians once thought that white women's economic importance in colonial British America, along with their relative scarcity during the early colonial period, gave them an unusually high status, so that they enjoyed a kind of "golden age" during the colonial period compared to the nineteenth century. See Elizabeth A. Dexter, *Colonial Women of Affairs: Women in Business and the Professions in America Before 1776* (Boston, 1931); Julia Cherry Spruill, *Women's Life and Work in the Southern Colonies* (Chapel Hill, 1938); and Richard B. Morris, *Studies in the History of American Law, with Special Reference to the Seventeenth and Eighteenth Centuries* (1930; 2nd edn, Philadelphia, 1959). Later works to endorse the thesis include John Demos, *A Little Commonwealth: Family Life in Plymouth Colony* (New York, 1970); and Roger Thompson, *Women in Stuart England and America: A Comparative Study* (Boston, 1974). Today, the "golden age" thesis is no longer seriously defended. A partial list of challenges includes: Mary Beth Norton, *Liberty's Daughters: The Revolutionary Experience of American Women, 1750–1800* (Boston, 1980); Marylynn Salmon, *Women and the Law of Property in Early America* (Chapel Hill, 1986); Cornelia Hughes Dayton, *Women Before the Bar: Gender, Law, and Society in Connecticut, 1639–1789* (Chapel Hill, 1995); Kathleen Brown, *Good Wives, Nasty Wenches, and Anxious Patriarchs: Gender, Race, and Power in Colonial Virginia* (Chapel Hill, 1996); Elaine Forman Crane, *Ebb Tide in New England: Women, Seaports, and Social Change, 1630–1800* (Boston, 1998); Cynthia A. Kierner, *Beyond the Household: Women's Place in the Early South, 1700–1835* (Ithaca, 1998); Terri Snyder, *Brabbling Women: Disorderly Speech and the Law in Early Virginia* (Ithaca, 2003). Indeed, some historians argue that women's legal status was more constricted in the colonies than in Great Britain.

One important part of the gender system in English (later British) North American settler societies during the colonial period was a draconian set of legal rules which helped to prop up a male-dominated system of family and social life and created strong incentives for women to defer to their husbands and fathers, or at least not openly challenge their dictates.[2] These legal rules made most women legally subordinate to fathers, masters, husbands, and even, if they became widows, to their grown sons, for most of their lives. As young women, they were subject to the legal rules governing either master–servant or parent–child relationships, including the requirement that neither servants nor children could marry without the consent of the household head with whom they lived. (They could not, however, be forced to marry against their will.) Though free adult women could marry, they would be regulated by a set of legal rules that gave enormous power to their husbands.

Thanks to the legal doctrine of *coverture*, developed in England during the late Middle Ages and strengthened during the seventeenth century with the growing systematization of the common law, a wife lost the legal right to control or manage any real property (that is, land) she had brought into a marriage. She lost all legal rights to any personal property she had owned before the marriage, along with any wages she earned during her husband's lifetime. In general, she would be unable to appear in court to defend her own interests in actions involving her property or contracts. Although in New England her husband was prohibited from hitting her, most colonies did not explicitly prevent a husband from "correcting" his wife as long as he did not cause her excessive physical injury. Because any property that she and her husband produced or purchased during the marriage would legally belong to him, the only right she had to it when he died was her dower right, that is, a right to use (but not to sell) one-third of her family's property. In most families that meant the widow was relegated to a back room of the house she had once inhabited with her husband, after her son and his family took it over.

Seventeenth-century Anglo-American gender ideology rationalized women's subordination to men on various grounds. Among these the most common was the theory that women were intellectually weak and ruled by their passions and therefore needed the moral and intellectual guidance of men. Typical of such views was a pamphlet *The Lady's New Year's Gift, or, Advice unto a Daughter*, published in London in 1688 and frequently reprinted. The author began by observing to his reader what seemed (to him) a fundamental truth: "There is *Inequality* in the *Sexes*, and that for the better Oeconomy of the World, the Men, who were to be the Law givers, had the better share of *Reason* bestowed upon them; by which means your Sex is the better prepared for the *Compliance* that is necessary for the performance of those *Duties* which seem to be most properly assigned to it." He continued: "We are made of differing *Tempers*, that our Defects may the better be Mutually Supplied: Your sex wanteth our *Reason* for your *Conduct*, and our *Strength* for your *Protection*; Ours wanteth your *Gentleness* to soften and entertain us." While seventeenth-century male writers sometimes described women in positive terms, they usually emphasized virtues that reinforced women's

---

[2] In the early years of colonization, these legal rules applied more or less equally to women of all races. As time went on the legal rules surrounding marriage became applicable mostly to white women, since increasingly they would be the only women allowed to marry, as will be explained in section 2 of this chapter. The additional constraints imposed on enslaved African women are discussed in Chapter 14.

subordination to men in a family setting. The ideal woman was a faithful and loving consort, strictly obedient to her husband's commands, and an industrious help-meet who worked to do her husband's bidding on his farm or in his shop.

Seventeenth-century gender ideology included more overtly misogynistic ideas as well, emphasizing women's supposed sexual unreliability, their inability to manage money, and their vanity or greed. All of these qualities supposedly required women to have men to govern over them. These views were to a certain extent reinforced by the Bible, especially the early chapters on the creation. It was Eve who had eaten the apple and brought about the Fall, thanks to her greater susceptibility to temptation. As punishment she had been told, "Thy desire shall be to thy husband and he shall rule over thee." The repercussions of stories like these were profound: every aspect of a woman's life was affected by the assumption that she was physically, mentally, and morally inferior and must at every stage be kept dependent.

Given the legal disadvantages of marriage, it is worth asking why free women in the North American colonies married at all. The reason is that marriage generally offered greater autonomy and status than remaining single. In the rural areas and small towns where most settlers lived, women had few employment options outside the household context, other than washing or household service. Most spinsters lived with relatives in a demeaning dependency. As wives, women would become partners in an economically self-supporting household. It was virtually impossible for a household to achieve economic independence without the economic contributions of at least two adults, generally a husband and a wife. And thanks to their importance to a household's economic wellbeing, wives' household work could garner the respect of their neighbors in ways it rarely, if ever, does in a modern industrialized society.

Seventeenth- and eighteenth-century convention in British North America divided productive work for the household by gender. Men were supposed to provide their wives with the supplies they needed for housekeeping – flour, firewood, meat, and the like. Women were supposed to turn those supplies into the products that their households needed to stay fed and reasonably comfortable, without going into debt. Doing all of this effectively required intelligence and skill. Wives managed the garden as well as the dairy, kept the fires lit, provided the household with clothing, preserved food, cooked, spun, baked bread, made cheese, and kept their larders well stocked and organized. It was largely women's efforts and skills that determined what standard of comfort a family would enjoy.

Indeed, wives were understood to bear considerable responsibility for the economic well-being of their families. A wife was a deputy husband, expected to promote her family's economic interests in whatever way necessary. That meant she provided back-up labor if her husband needed her in his shop or in his fields. It meant she would manage her husband's property or run his business if he was away, represent his interests in dealing with creditors, even go to court to defend his interests (though not her own individual ones). When her husband died, the widow could be the executor of his estate, conduct negotiations for her children's marriages, and run the family business until her adult sons took it over. Sometimes she would continue to manage that business herself for the rest of her life.

Whether married or single, a free woman could usually also sell or trade anything extra that she produced – her cider or eggs or butter – to obtain other necessities and household products. If she were married, she could generally market her goods without interference from her husband, since it was understood that in marketing her surplus produce she was supplementing the resources available to her household. In addition, there were a few other ways for women to earn extra cash. The most lucrative opportunity available to free women in most regions of the colonies was midwifery, which was dominated by women at least until the 1760s, when some male doctors began to offer gynecological services. Midwives learned their trade through practice and experience, and if they became successful, could command considerable fees.

Although women in the Anglo-American colonies must have noticed the cultural message that they were incompetents who needed men to guide them, for the most part married women defined their identities in terms of their contributions to building economically successful family farms and businesses. Most of the few diaries left behind by eighteenth- and early nineteenth-century white women emphasize economic activities: work done, goods produced, trades completed.

Women also reinforced the importance of their household work by emphasizing domestic skills in the training they gave their daughters, as well as young female servants. Girls in farming families spent years learning the arts of making cider and beer and cheese, slaughtering hogs, drying and curing meat, manufacturing soap, carding wool, knitting, and spinning good, strong thread. As they grew older, girls made significant contributions to household labor alongside their mothers. In exchange for their labor, most young white women in the colonial era expected their parents to

Figure 19 Typical eighteenth-century kitchen hearth from the Abraham Browne, Jr. House, Watertown, Massachusetts. Courtesy of Peabody Essex Museum, Salem, Massachusetts.

reward them for their economic contributions to the household by providing them with a dowry, or marriage portion, before they wed. The dowry usually consisted of household goods, blankets and bedding, tools for the kitchen, and possibly furniture, though if there was more wealth in the family it could include livestock or even land. Young women and their parents often spent years amassing the goods that would make up the dowry, which would make an important contribution to a couple's ability to become economically self-supporting.[3]

Even household architecture and furnishings in the seventeenth century reflected the emphasis on women's domestic production. Early immigrants to the North American colonies initially constructed simple cottages, mainly one-room affairs with a stone hearth for cooking and a loft to sleep in. New Englanders began to improve their houses within a few decades (unlike settlers in the Chesapeake, whose structures remained crude and poorly built for years, reflecting the instability of their society). Yet even when affluent seventeenth-century New Englanders began to improve their houses, the features they added were designed to make household production more efficient, such as cellars for food storage and a separate kitchen at the back. Aesthetic improvement and even comfort remained low priorities. Furniture was plain and utilitarian, consisting of simple wooden tables, benches, stools, beds, and coffers, with rush mats on the floor.

2 REGIONAL VARIATIONS

Though becoming a wife in an economically independent household was a widely shared ideal, women's chances of achieving that ideal – or of achieving autonomy as a single adult – varied from one region to another, reflecting different regional economies and religious cultures. In addition, women faced different kinds of options and constraints depending on their social status as well as their age and point in the life course. Increasingly, by the end of the seventeenth century these options would also be linked to race, with white women enjoying considerably greater opportunities than African women.[4]

Young single women who arrived in the Chesapeake during the seventeenth century were vulnerable and had little support. Most single white women arrived as indentured servants, alone, without family members who could protect them. The status of a female servant here was unenviable. She would confront years of back-breaking field labor in an unfamiliar and inhospitable place before being freed from her indenture, usually at around 24 or 25. She would be legally prohibited from marrying until her service ended (as would a male servant). With a gender ratio among her neighbors of three to six men for each woman, she would probably be isolated from contact with other women, and

---

[3] Paragraphs on white women's economic roles in household production are based on Laurel Thatcher Ulrich, *Good Wives: Image and Reality in the Lives of Women in Northern New England, 1650–1750* (New York, 1982), and Linda Sturtz, *Within Her Power: Propertied Women in Colonial Virginia* (New York, 2002).

[4] A fuller analysis of these regional variations may be found in Carol Berkin, *First Generations: Women in Colonial America* (New York, 1996).

vulnerable to sexual predation from men. She would have virtually no legal protection and would face enormous legal and social restrictions.

The story of Anne Orthwood provides a vivid illustration of a female servant's vulnerability in the early Chesapeake. An impoverished young woman from Bristol, England, with few prospects at home, Anne entered a four-year indenture and arrived in Virginia in 1662 at age 23. There she was sold and went to live in her new master's large, mostly male, household, including his family, a nephew, and nine or ten other servants and slaves besides herself. At some point Anne began a sexual relationship with her master's nephew under somewhat ambiguous circumstances. The man may have offered to buy out her contract and marry her, or he may have coerced her into accepting his advances. A servant woman who had been raped by her master or one of his male relatives had little legal recourse, since charges of rape were almost never successful with all-male juries and judges. In fact, a single woman ran great risks if she accused a man of rape. A woman who admitted to a sexual relationship potentially faced punishment for fornication. A servant woman without the money to pay her fine (or a master willing to pay it for her in exchange for an extra year of her service) would be punished with a public whipping on her bare back. In the face of such odds, unmarried women rarely brought rape charges against men who assaulted them.

Whatever the actual circumstances of her relationship with the master's nephew, Anne became pregnant. Virginia's legal system would place most of the burden of this pregnancy and its aftermath on her alone. Under a law passed by the House of Burgesses in 1660, a female servant who gave birth during her term of service was required to repay her master for what she had cost him, including his loss of her work at full capacity during her pregnancy. Usually that meant an extra two years of service was added to her existing indenture. Then there was the problem of the baby. The local community would pursue the father to pay for child support, although the father could typically cover these costs by indenturing the baby to serve a master until he reached adulthood. In this case, Anne died shortly after giving birth, bearing the ultimate burden of an unwanted pregnancy. The surviving baby, named Jasper, was put out to a wet nurse and then bound out – at approximately six months of age – to a tobacco planter's family to work as a servant until he turned 24.[5]

In the face of such profound restrictions on their freedom, servant women sometimes rebelled against prescriptive moral standards. They formed clandestine relationships, and induced abortions or committed infanticide to conceal unwanted pregnancies. They ran away and married in secret, and argued against magistrates and ministers instead of displaying the deference expected of women towards their social superiors. Such assertiveness could help a woman to escape from a dismal situation, gain a short-term respite from the pressures of her situation, or blow off steam. Yet there were great risks for those who refused to conform. Runaways were penalized by being forced to serve extra time if they were caught. While abortion was legal, at least early in the pregnancy, it was unreliable, and women could die from a badly performed procedure. Women convicted of infanticide were hanged. Women could be fined (or whipped) for

---

5   For the ubiquity of sexual assaults against servants and the difficulty of prosecuting them, see Sharon Block, *Rape and Sexual Power in Early America* (Chapel Hill, 2006). For the story of Orthwood and of her son's subsequent efforts to be emancipated from his indenture, see John Ruston Pagan, *Anne Orthwood's Bastard: Sex and Law in Early Virginia* (New York, 2003).

uttering quarrelsome or "riotous" speech. Thus the pressures to conform to social expectations were great.[6]

A white woman who outlived her indenture had considerable incentives to marry once she was freed. True, as a married women her freedom would still be circumscribed by her status as a *feme covert*. She would have no legal control over her own property, no right to make contracts on her own behalf, no right to the custody of her children in the case of marital separation. She was still likely to die in childbirth, if she did not die of malaria. The average life expectancy of a white woman in the early Chesapeake was around 40, compared to a male life expectancy of about 46, thanks to the added mortality risks associated with pregnancy. If her marriage was an unhappy one, she had no recourse to divorce under the laws of any of the southern colonies (and a woman who ran away from her husband forfeited all rights to her children and any property in the marriage). Still, as a married woman she would have considerably more autonomy than a servant or a single woman. As a wife, she would be in charge of household production, which was vital to a family's well-being. She would also have considerable authority over children, household servants, and the allocation of household resources.

With the high ratio of men to women in the Chesapeake before the late 1600s, a free woman would probably also have a number of options in choosing a husband. In fact her marriage could become an important route to upward mobility since married women here were likely to become widows with property. A woman's marriage was unlikely to be a long one; the average marriage in seventeenth-century Chesapeake lasted only 10 to 15 years before the death of one of the partners. But if she was the survivor, not only would she receive her dower right (giving her control over a third of her husband's land, servants, and slaves for her lifetime), but she would have considerable control over the rest of her husband's property, held in trust for her children. Chesapeake men knew they were likely to die before their children were grown, and wrote wills leaving their widows with more than their dower thirds, often naming them as executors of their estates as well. Men's hope was to maximize their chances of keeping their children together, so in many cases they gave their widows control over considerable amounts of property to manage on behalf of their children. This meant that many widows controlled significant financial assets when they entered the marriage market for a second or third time. Thus widows in the Chesapeake during the seventeenth century assumed more financial responsibilities during their lifetimes (and had more bargaining power in arranging the terms of subsequent marriages) than did most English women.[7]

---

[6] Information on abortion is extremely difficult for historians to find, since procedures were done in secret so as to avoid the scandal associated with premarital pregnancy. The harrowing story of a botched abortion in eighteenth-century Connecticut is recounted in Cornelia Hughes Dayton, "Taking the Trade: Abortion and Gender Relations in an Eighteenth-Century New England Village," *William and Mary Quarterly*, 48 (1991), 19–49. In this case, the male participants were prosecuted because the woman died, but had the abortion been successful it would have been legal.

[7] Property held by a widow on behalf of her children typically did not become the property of her new husband if she remarried, though it could be invested in ways that benefited him. The lives of white women in the Chesapeake are covered in Lorena Walsh and Lois G. Carr, "The Planter's Wife: The Experience of White Women in Seventeenth-Century Maryland," *William and Mary Quarterly*, 34 (1977), 542–71, and Mary Beth Norton, "The Evolution of White Women's Experience in Early America," *American Historical Review*, 89 (1984), 593–619.

Though marriage would continue to be a route to higher status for women throughout the colonial period, after about 1660 that status in the Chesapeake became increasingly restricted on the basis of race. During the earliest years of colonial settlement, prevailing gender norms had permitted marriages between whites and blacks. In fact there was considerable social interaction between white and African servants and small farmers, and interracial marriages were not uncommon. Many English people appear to have viewed skin color as an adaptive response to climate; the idea that race was a sign of profound differences between different groups of people had not yet developed. Then beginning in the 1660s legislators in Virginia and Maryland began to impose a variety of penalties on women who entered into mixed-race unions. To a large extent these new rules seem to have been designed to strengthen the property rights of owners over children born to their female servants and slaves. Lawmakers began to pass laws prohibiting interracial marriage, specifying that children born to enslaved African women would become slaves belonging to the women's owners, and barring enslaved African women and men from marrying at all. They imposed harsh penalties on white women who bore mixed-race children out of wedlock. By 1700 or so such laws were being put into place in all of the major slaveholding colonies, and many of the northern colonies eventually followed suit.

The long-term consequences of these laws on the lives of women and men were profound. Enslaved African women in most colonies could not marry legally at all. Even free African women had few potential marriage partners, since they could marry neither enslaved African men nor white men, and were cut off in many cases from legal marriage as a route to respectability and increased status. Since African women were generally barred from legal marriages, their sexual relationships were usually defined as outside the bounds of the law. Black women became increasingly subject to harsh stereotypes that portrayed them as less virtuous and more sexually lascivious than white women.

Free white women who wanted the heightened status that came with marriage now had to marry white men, for the legal disadvantages of sexual relationships with black men were severe. Since interracial marriage had been prohibited, all mixed-race children would by definition become bastards, legally excluded from inheriting property from their fathers. In addition, the mixed-race children of poor free white or black mothers were often bound out as servants, not until age 21 like poor white children but for 10 years longer, to 31. White women who gave birth to mixed-race children could be fined, publically humiliated, or forced to become indentured servants for extended periods, even if they had been free at the time they gave birth. For white women, then, many of the social benefits of marriage – enhanced status, the companionship of their children, the satisfaction of seeing their children marry and have their own children – would be available to them only if they chose white partners.

The effect of these new legal rules was to begin to define female status in racial terms. In English society married women usually enjoyed a higher status than unmarried women, since wives had considerable control over household resources, children, and servants, and enjoyed a presumption of sexual respectability that unwed women often did not. In British North American societies, especially in the South, that higher status would now be associated not only with marriage but with whiteness, since white women were virtually the only women allowed to marry. Also, since white women could become wives only by marrying white men, any intimacy between white women and black men would be stigmatized. By the eighteenth century, the allegation that a white woman had had sex with a black man became the most vicious and debasing insult that could be leveled against her, reflecting the extent to which white women's reputations for chastity were now becoming bound up with the notion of white purity.[8]

Women's options in seventeenth-century New England also depended on their marital status, although their prospects were typically quite different from those of their counterparts in the South. Young, single white women in New England typically lived in nuclear families with their parents or other adult relatives. In general they were less vulnerable to sexual assault by men from outside their families, since their sexual behavior was supervised by their fathers. On the other hand they had even less sexual freedom than single women in the South. New England colonial governments expected fathers to prevent disorder in their families, and pregnancy outside of wedlock was a serious form of disorder. If fathers failed to supervise their children adequately, town governments had other mechanisms for ensuring sexual chastity. Young people could be fined for being out late at night without parental consent. Legal penalties for fornication and unwanted pregnancy were more likely to be imposed here than in the South. Another difference from the South was that in seventeenth-century New England these penalties fell upon both the man and the woman. Young people who committed fornication could be publicly whipped or heavily fined, even if they married after the behavior had occurred. Early New Englanders took these prohibitions seriously. In seventeenth-century England, rates of premarital pregnancy were as high as 25 percent (that is, one-quarter of all newly married women had a first child before they had been married for eight months), but the corresponding rate in New England during the same period was less than five percent. Daughters (and sons) in New England not only had to obtain paternal consent before they could marry; in some jurisdictions their would-be suitors even had to get a father's consent before beginning a courtship.[9]

Once a white woman in New England married, on the other hand, she could expect to enjoy a long life, a relatively stable marriage, and many children. The average life expectancy for a seventeenth-century white woman in New England once she reached her twenty-first birthday was about 61. Of course as a *feme covert* she would have little or no control over property for as long as her husband lived. In fact her control over separate property was less than it would be for a wife living in England during the same period. Upper-class families in England were able to place legal restrictions on any real estate belonging to their daughters so that it could not be alienated by the husband, usually by placing their property into a trust. In seventeenth-century New England,

---

[8] Racial restrictions on marriage and sexual relations had a profound effect on the lives of African American women and men, whose experiences will be discussed more fully in Chapter 14. Since the 1990s, much scholarship has examined the racial dimensions of colonial gender ideology and sexual regulation, reflecting historians' perception that scholarship on American women's history had been distorted by its insufficient focus on the experiences of women of color. Consideration of racial restrictions on marriage and sexual relations in the British mainland colonies may be found in Brown, *Good Wives, Nasty Wenches*; Kirsten Fischer, *Suspect Relations: Sex, Race, and Resistance in Colonial North Carolina* (Ithaca, 2002); and Richard Godbeer, *Sexual Revolution in Early America* (Baltimore, 2002).

[9] Legal penalties for fornication and other courtship-related transgressions are discussed in Cornelia Hughes Dayton, *Women Before the Bar*. On marriage regulation in the colonies, see Ruth H. Bloch, *Gender and Morality in Anglo-American Culture, 1650–1800* (Berkeley, 2003), ch. 4.

though, trusts were unenforceable. The Puritans looked with suspicion on devices that aristocratic families could use to perpetuate their control over future generations, and instead sought to maximize the control that male household heads had over family property. Wifely independence was not something that Puritan governments wanted to encourage.

The one device which the Puritans did permit for protecting women's separate property was a jointure, or marriage settlement, according to which the bride's family contributed a sum of money or personal property as a dowry. In return, the groom or his family set aside an equivalent amount in real estate in the bride's name. The property was still managed by the husband but could not be alienated to pay off creditors. If the couple did subsequently wish to sell, they could do so only with the agreement of the wife. In reality, this requirement offered little protection to a woman, since all that her husband needed to sell her property was her signature on a document that he had her sign at home.

Although the Puritans discouraged the preservation of separate property for women, they did take seriously the ideals of marital harmony and marital love. It is hard to measure how many husbands abided by their ministers' admonitions to behave kindly and lovingly towards their wives, but many Puritan men, writing in diaries or letters, described their marriages in highly idealistic terms. And in an attempt to ensure that marriages remained harmonious, Puritans also provided certain legal protections for wives in colonial New England that other colonies did not. They were virtually unique in the Western world in allowing absolute divorce, under limited circumstances, since they took the view that marriage could be dissolved if one partner violated its terms so badly that the marriage could not continue. New Haven's legal code in 1656, for example, allowed a full divorce with permission to remarry for wives who had been abandoned, wives whose husbands were impotent, wives (or husbands) of bigamists, and victims of adultery. Puritans also seem to have taken allegations of spousal abuse more seriously than colonists in the South, intervening through the courts to police and fine wife-batterers. On the other hand, once fines had been imposed, Puritan magistrates insisted that women in abusive marriages go back to their husbands and admonished both spouses to behave lovingly towards each other in the future. Cruelty was not a permissible ground for obtaining a divorce in New England until the 1780s. And New Englanders' vigilance in policing male misbehavior appears to have declined during the eighteenth century, after the Puritans lost control over several of the New England governments and legal systems became anglicized.[10]

White women probably had the greatest range of options, on the whole, in the middle colonies of New York, New Jersey, and Pennsylvania. Unique circumstances in these colonies offered greater opportunities for women who chose to remain unmarried and encouraged the development of relatively egalitarian marriages. Under Dutch law in New Netherland before 1664, daughters tended to inherit the same shares of family property as sons when their parents died, and married Dutch women kept their own property when they married. Married Dutch women in New Amsterdam also retained their ability to make contracts (and to sue to enforce them) under Dutch law. Legal

---

[10]   For the life expectancies of women in New England, see Philip J. Greven, Jr., *Four Generations* (Ithaca, 1970), 61; for the law of divorce and the anglicization of the legal system, see Dayton, *Women Before the Bar*, ch. 3.

control over property gave women economic options, and a considerable number of women (wives as well as widows) operated their own shops in New Amsterdam during the seventeenth century. Quaker women in Pennsylvania and New Jersey, too, enjoyed unusual influence within their churches, where they were allowed to preach the inner light and even to serve in missions, often traveling hundreds of miles in the company of one or two colleagues. The Quakers encouraged marriages in which both women and men would be spiritual help-meets to each other, and Quaker women assumed a more important role in parenting than was typical in late seventeenth- and early eighteenth-century white colonial families. Some Quaker writers encouraged women *not* to marry if they could not find partners who would encourage their spiritual development.[11]

Still, the extent of women's autonomy even in the middle colonies should not be exaggerated. After the English took over New York in 1664, Dutch families there began slowly to give up their relatively egalitarian marriage customs and conform instead to English law and custom. Dutch men began leaving all their real estate to their sons. Instead of dividing marital property equally between husband and wife, courts adopted the English practice of restricting the widow to one-third of the husband's estate. Since women in New York had no mechanism under English law to enforce their contracts, many of them stopped trading or running shops on their own. There had been 134 female traders in New Amsterdam in 1653, but by 1774 in the considerably larger city of New York there were no more than 43.[12] Quaker wives were subject to the same legal handicaps in Pennsylvania and New Jersey as wives in the other English colonies, becoming *femes coverts* when they married and having no access to marital trusts to protect separate property. Widows were rarely allowed to administer their husbands' estates without interference, and were almost never involved in trade or in managing money. Everywhere in the English colonies, the gender system was heavily weighted in favor of free, married white men, who had considerably more economic power than their wives and daughters.

Gender ideology applied to men as well as to women, and here too it helped to rationalize and strengthen a patriarchal social system and to encourage marriage. Colonial gender ideology suggested that manly men were rational, self-controlled, and responsible, and therefore the logical candidates to lead their households and govern their wives. At the same time, colonial gender ideology in many ways suggested that free white male household heads were morally superior to many other *men* as well as to women. The ideal man praised in most sermons and advice literature was almost never young, dependent, or black. Youths, servants, and enslaved Africans were consistently depicted as passionate, uncontrolled, violent, and irresponsible, while the supposed paragons of virtuous manhood were usually older than 30, free, and white. This ideological construction of manhood helped provide a logical explanation for a world in which married, adult white men owned most of the property, made most legal and political decisions, and possessed the ability to govern almost everybody else.

---

[11] For a discussion of options for single white women, see Karin Wulf, *Not All Wives: Women of Colonial Philadelphia* (Philadelphia, 2000).

[12] Studies of women in colonial New York include Linda Briggs Biemer, *Women and Property in Colonial New York: The Transition from Dutch to English Law, 1643–1727* (Ann Arbor, 1983); David Narrett, *Inheritance and Family Life in Colonial New York City* (Ithaca, 1992).

Gender norms suggesting that married household heads were more manly than young rakes also provided a considerable incentive for men to marry and begin families. Since manly men were thought to be more potent, that is more capable of siring children, men also had an incentive to father large families to prove their manhood. The abundant supply of relatively cheap land provided the means for families to support themselves economically, as long as everybody worked. In fact, norms combined with economic opportunities to encourage men to channel their energy into productive work. A married man who provided adequately for his family was considered to be more manly than a bachelor or a poor provider. If he provided an ample supply of economic necessities for his wife to use in her half of the family enterprise, he was entitled to deference from his wife, children, and servants. The duty to provide was a condition of the right to rule. Neighbors were likely to shake their heads with disapproval at a household head whose wife complained of being left without provisions, or whose child was poorly dressed or malnourished. Thus a man's standing in the community depended to some extent not only on having a wife who bore many children but also on having a wife whose hard work allowed her family a comfortable standard of living.[13]

When demographic conditions prevented considerable numbers of men from marrying, as in the Chesapeake during the seventeenth century, men sometimes developed alternative ways to assert their manhood. The men who took part in Bacon's Rebellion, for example, evidently believed that standing up to the perceived injustices of their government and defending their communities against Indian trespassers was more important than demonstrating their rationality, responsibility for a family, or self-control. Indeed white men in the British American colonies would display a disturbing tendency to assert their manhood through collective displays of vigilante violence against Native Americans, a tendency that very likely became more pronounced in backcountry regions during the eighteenth century. Assertions of the right to use violence were always a component of male gender norms. On the other hand, the ideal man in the British North American colonies was decidedly *not* the aristocrat who would have been idealized in much of Europe at this time. The ideal colonial man was praised for his productivity, not his adherence to a chivalric code of honor or his valiant conduct in battle. At least until the mid eighteenth century, colonial Anglo-American men proved their manhood as patriarchs rather than as soldiers or warriors.

3   GENDER IN A COMMERCIALIZING CULTURE: THE EIGHTEENTH-CENTURY REFINED LADY

The expansion of transoceanic commerce in the eighteenth century brought the societies of British North America into the empire, transforming the Atlantic coastal

---

[13] Historical studies of masculinity and male gender ideology are relatively recent. British American manhood and masculinity are explored in Kathleen Brown, *Good Wives, Nasty Wenches*; Lisa Wilson, *Ye Heart of a Man: The Domestic Life of Men in Colonial New England* (New Haven, 1999); Anne Lombard, *Making Manhood: Growing Up Male in Colonial New England* (Cambridge, Mass., 2003); and Thomas A. Foster, *Sex and the Eighteenth-Century Man: Massachusetts and the History of Sexuality in America* (Boston, 2006). Brown and Foster explore the growing connection between ideal manhood and whiteness.

settlements from isolated frontier outposts into increasingly prosperous and commercial British provinces. As the transmission of news and information speeded up and consumer goods became more available, colonists' expectations about appropriate standards of living began to change. Gender ideology, which had been closely tied to ideas about economic productivity and household living standards, changed along with the colonists' new economic reality. Nowhere was this transformation more visible than in the ideas of the emerging colonial gentry.

The growth of transatlantic communications made wealthy colonists in British North America both more aware of, and in a sense more connected to, the concerns and values of the British middle and upper classes during the eighteenth century. Ships that crossed the Atlantic carried not only goods but also travelers, newspapers, and mail. Visitors and letters provided a means to exchange news and strengthen relationships with friends or family members in Great Britain. Rich colonial planters and merchants began to send their sons to school in England, where they learned how to behave like British gentlemen. When the sons came home to run their fathers' businesses and plantations, they brought their new, more sophisticated manners and tastes along with them. Even the children of merchants and planters who could not afford a metropolitan education for their offspring soon had models close to home to show them what it meant to act and live like members of the British gentry. Among other things, it meant that achieving economic independence as a farmer or a business owner was no longer sufficient for a man who wished to be treated like a gentleman. In addition to independence, he had to become refined.

Refinement was a multifaceted ideal. It required people to master a particular code of behavior that had been popularized among members of the aristocracy during the previous century and was now becoming widely adopted by members of the gentry and upper middle classes in Britain. Refinement was more than simple respectability. Refined people were expected to behave more courteously than ordinary people, adopting the more sophisticated manners, conversational styles, eloquence, and even posture that were becoming recognized as the hallmarks of upper-class status in Britain. Becoming refined also meant developing particular consumer preferences and tastes, in order to demonstrate that one knew how (and could afford) to live like a gentleman or a lady. Proper housing was the first prerequisite for a refined life, and colonial merchants and planters adopted it enthusiastically.

During the first six decades of the eighteenth century, the housing of the colonial elite improved steadily in quality. The fashion favored a colonial Georgian style, featuring columns, friezes, pediments, and other decorative devices popular in ancient Greece and Rome. At the front of the typical house was a large hall, perhaps with a colonnaded entrance, which could be used for entertaining. Windows were much larger and the ceilings higher than the structures of the seventeenth century, giving the houses an airy feeling. Interiors were more finished than in the past, featuring plastered or paneled walls and wallpaper instead of the crude board surfaces of seventeenth-century walls. Second-floor bedrooms were now added to houses in order to separate public spaces from sleeping areas. Kitchens, too, were located in an adjacent block or in the rear, separate from dining rooms and parlors. Formal gardens surrounded the house to enhance its appearance, emphasizing through symmetry the triumph of civilization over the wilderness.

Figure 20 Thomas Hancock House, Boston. Courtesy of the Massachusetts Historical Society, Boston.

Within these elegant settings, gentlemen and ladies were expected to entertain, in ways that gave them opportunities to demonstrate their good tastes through their displays of luxurious consumer goods. Graceful houses provided the appropriate backdrop for refined, genteel behavior. Serving tea required china tea sets, table linens, and upholstered chairs on which one's guests could sit. Formal dinners involved complete sets of silver and china, while for evening social gatherings a household needed card tables, punch bowls, liquor decanters. The trestle tables and stools of seventeenth-century houses were replaced by Queen Anne drop-leaf tables, sideboards, and chairs, all with matching cabriole legs and pad feet. By the end of the colonial period the elaborately carved designs of Thomas Chippendale, often with a Chinese motif, were becoming popular. All of these objects were props in a seemingly endless round of entertaining which allowed members of the new colonial gentry to exhibit their refined tastes and genteel status.[14]

The new spatial arrangements in elite households were designed not only to display the wealth and sophistication of the owners, but also at least in part to demonstrate that their wives did not work. A man could spend his days haggling with other merchants or supervising his slaves, but having a wife who appeared to be a lady of leisure suggested that he was of the same social status as members of the British gentry. Of course appearance could belie reality. On southern plantations, elite women actually had considerable managerial responsibilities for supervising servants and organizing food

---

[14] The development of architectural and furnishing styles as an aspect of refinement and gentility in the colonial upper classes is discussed in Richard L. Bushman, *The Refinement of America: Persons, Houses, Cities* (New York, 1992).

preparation and consumption. During one year, for example, the wife of Robert Carter of Nomini Hall had to oversee the consumption of 27,000 pounds of pork, 20 head of cattle, 550 bushels of wheat, 4 hogsheads of rum, and 150 gallons of brandy. But when guests were present, the wives of planters and merchants appeared in beautiful and delicate dresses looking like they had never set foot in a kitchen, while servants and slaves performed the visible labor. Their elegant, fashionable clothing made from imported silk and satin fabrics demonstrated not only that these women had the leisure time to dress like ladies but also that their husbands were sophisticated gentlemen with refined tastes in women. Meanwhile new standards of behavior also emphasized that elite white women were removed from the public world, and it became improper for such women to travel alone or otherwise appear in public places without male protection.[15]

Particularly in the South, the emergence of a new female gender ideal in the families of the elite changed priorities for the education of upper-class girls. Instead of teaching daughters to become housewives, genteel mothers trained their girls to develop the social polish they would need to be the wives of gentlemen. Necessary skills included French, music, and dancing, in addition to the manners of the tea table, along with reading, basic arithmetic, and beautiful handwriting. Young women's reading habits came to include a wider variety of reading materials than in the past, particularly as imported novels became available. But by and large, elite young women were not given the same level of education as their brothers, and were expected to spend much of their time socializing or engaged in busy work while they waited to be introduced to appropriate suitors. Clothing, dancing skills, or musical accomplishments could provide means of self-expression, but in general there were not many avenues for meaningful work. Elite young women quickly became stereotyped as frivolous and wasteful.

An occasional woman like Eliza Lucas Pinckney provided an exception. She was the daughter of a British army officer and South Carolina planter, George Lucas, who gave her an unusually thorough education that included more reading in law, science, and literature than an average upper-class girl would have received in addition to training in the social skills expected of a gentleman's wife. Lucas entrusted her with the management of his plantations while absent on military service. Both father and daughter were interested in developing imported plants, especially from the West Indies, including indigo, ginger, cotton, and cassava. The most successful was indigo, though it was not easy to grow since both the soil and the processing of the leaves required careful preparation. The first crop was harvested in the early 1740s, and in 1744 Eliza Pinckney produced only seeds so that her neighbors might also begin to cultivate the plant. Indigo exports were sufficiently promising by 1748 for Parliament to offer a bounty of sixpence a pound to encourage production.

The new standards of refinement not only shaped ideas about class and gender; they also impacted economic behavior. Eighteenth-century gentlemen in North America became eager consumers of imported manufactured goods, including calicoes from India, silks from China, fustians from England. They bought glassware,

[15] Eighteenth-century expectations for upper-class women are discussed in Brown, *Good Wives, Nasty Wenches*, chs 8 and 9.

porcelain, and beaver hats from British manufacturers, and specialty food items such as tea, chocolate, coffee, sugar, and wine from producers elsewhere in the empire. Some luxury items could be manufactured in the colonies, and local craftsmen developed the capacity to meet the growing demand for Queen Anne tables and fine silverware. However, most goods had to be imported. The cost of maintaining such consumption levels was high, but an upper-class family could hardly do without. After all, the consumption of certain kinds of goods was a crucial component of refinement, and without refinement the colonial gentry could not claim to be genteel. Unfortunately, as we have seen, the cost of maintaining a genteel lifestyle was often higher than even the most successful tobacco exporters could pay for, and the great planters of Virginia and Maryland had become chronically indebted to their British factors by the middle of the eighteenth century.

4 GENDER IN A COMMERCIALIZING CULTURE: MIDDLING AND WORKING WHITE WOMEN

Though most white women in North America during the eighteenth century were not members of the genteel elite, the commercialization of eighteenth-century colonial culture impacted middling white women's lives as well. The availability of imported consumer goods encouraged many people outside the colonial elite to aspire to higher standards of living. Economic independence, or competence, remained a powerful ideal for middling men and women. Yet the ideal was increasingly becoming broader. No longer was it enough to provide food, shelter, and the resources necessary for the next generation to become self-supporting. Increasingly something like comfort was expected as well, at least in long-settled areas of the colonies.

One clear marker of changes in the standards of living of middling people during the eighteenth century was the improvement in housing in older villages and towns. Middle-ranking farmers or self-employed craftsmen often now lived in rectangular houses, consisting of two main rooms on the first floor and two bedrooms between the eaves, with a lean-to kitchen at the rear. The typical construction was clapboard over a timber frame, with brick becoming more common in city dwellings. Houses now had glass windows, though with smaller panes and overall dimensions than in the houses of the gentry.

Manufactured consumer goods, too, became more readily available for purchase by ordinary white households after about 1730, especially in urban areas. Shops in Boston, Newport, New York, Philadelphia, and Charlestown carried an array of goods: imported cloth, ribbons, hats, pins and needles, glassware, paint, books, wine, tea, chocolate, sugar, tobacco, iron hardware and tools, locally manufactured candles and soap. Since women were the members of a family who made most decisions about how to feed and clothe a family, it was largely women who made purchases from these shops. During the eighteenth century, middling households became more likely to own products like teapots, china cups, glassware, napkins, and silver or pewter cutlery, not the luxuries of the elite but nevertheless objects that made their daily lives more comfortable. Semblances of refinement, too, crept into middling white women's daily lives as they adopted the rituals of drinking tea with other women, or served their families breakfast on china tableware instead of the wooden trenchers or plain ceramic bowls their mothers and grandmothers would have used. Women's clothing became more fashionable and more colorful, representing a new means of self-expression, especially for young women.[16]

Life in colonial towns and cities in the eighteenth century not only provided more access to consumer goods; it also gave some urban women more autonomy than their counterparts who lived in rural areas. Urban wives were more likely to earn wages or to work in shops alongside their husbands, where they could develop sidelines marketing to female customers. Wives of haberdashers and dry goods merchants, for example, developed profitable businesses as milliners and dress-makers, often acquiring sufficient business skills to continue if their husbands died. One of the more notable milliners was Elizabeth Murray Smith (Inman) of Boston, who in 1749 established a small dry goods shop before her marriage to a Boston merchant. After his death she returned to the millinery business before deciding to remarry. This time she protected her right to trade by insisting on a prenuptial agreement, and when her second husband died, Murray became one of the wealthiest individuals in town. For a white British North American woman, Murray was exceptional in her dedication to a career, and in her constant encouragement of other young women to follow her example by developing entrepreneurial skills. However, other women followed suit in less visible types of businesses. It was not uncommon for urban women, usually widows, to keep grocery shops and drug-stores, or to sell alcohol at inns and taverns.

Other commercial opportunities for white women in urban areas arose as a result of the growing demand for fashionable products and European news and information. The first woman to capitalize on the English fashion for coffee houses was the Widow Roberts in Philadelphia in 1745. Ten years later Mary Ballard more ambitiously advertised her coffee house in Boston, where gentlemen could expect to find all the regular colonial newspapers, together with the best English magazines, which they could peruse while drinking their tea, coffee, and chocolate. A few exceptional widows found niches as printers. Dinah Nuthead inherited her husband's printing press at St. Mary's and was sufficiently successful to be appointed printer to the Maryland assembly. Similarly, Elizabeth Timothy inherited the *South Carolina Gazette*, Charleston's first newspaper, which her husband had taken over. Although she had six small children and was pregnant with a seventh, she successfully continued the paper until her eldest son was ready to take over.

White women in cities were more likely to live without husbands, in part because wage-earning opportunities were more available in urban than in rural areas. The most

---

[16] Consumption patterns have been the subject of considerable historical scholarship. See, for example, Carole Shammas, *The Pre-industrial Consumer in England and America* (Oxford, 1990) and Cary Carson, Ron Hoffman, and Peter Albert, eds, *Of Consuming Interests: The Style of Life in the Eighteenth Century* (Charlottesville, 1994).

Figure 21　Portrait of Mrs James Smith (Elizabeth Murray), 1769, by John Singleton Copley. The artist has paid close attention to the details of Smith's dress, made from imported cloth as befitted a woman from a family in the mercantile elite. Museum of Fine Arts, Boston. Gift of Joseph W. R. Rogers and Mary C. Rogers. Courtesy of the Museum of Fine Arts, Boston.

successful were widows with their own businesses. Also, a small but growing number of northern urban women now decided to remain unmarried, encouraged in some cases by the example of some Quakers who argued that a single state was spiritually preferable to marriage and offered women opportunities for meaningful lives devoted to religious and literary pursuits. Both widows and single women were *femes soles*, a legal status that allowed unmarried women to make contracts, buy and sell goods, sue to protect their rights, and testify in court. In a commercial economy, these legal rights had considerable value.[17]

Although a slightly higher proportion of white women in British North America chose to remain unwed during the eighteenth century, the desirability of the unmarried state should probably not be exaggerated. By the eighteenth century single white women had considerably more freedom from their parents than earlier generations, including the freedom to conduct their own courtships. Middling white women in the eighteenth century were more likely to expect that romance and love would be a part of courtship, and these expectations probably made them more eager to marry, not less. Moreover, bearing children out of wedlock was still deeply taboo for middling white women, even if it was now acceptable for them to be pregnant at the time of the wedding. Thus despite white women's greater sexual freedom in the eighteenth century, they continued to wed.[18]

Also, notwithstanding the examples of a small number of female business owners, economic opportunities for most single women remained seriously limited. Among the most disadvantaged single women were those who were technically married but whose husbands had deserted them, since they could not make contracts or sue to enforce their rights. A few colonies provided partial reforms to alleviate their situation. The Pennsylvania assembly in 1718 gave *feme sole* trader status to any woman whose husband was away for a long period – a mariner, for example – or had abandoned her. Such a status allowed her to make contracts, keep her profits, sue and be sued in court. The main purpose of the law was not to benefit women but to prevent them from being a burden on the community. Once the husband returned the woman lost her sole trader status. South Carolina's assembly in 1744 allowed all businesswomen the status of sole traders, regardless of whether their husbands could be found, a gesture which paradoxically acknowledged some southern men's sense of entitlement to leave their wives and take up with mistresses with impunity.

Poor single mothers and women who were separated from their husbands typically lived on the edge, making whatever money they could by offering domestic services, from wet nursing to mending, washing, starching, and ironing clothes. Increased demand for laundering services may have been a by-product of the consumer revolution, as families aspiring to be part of the gentry demanded cleaner clothes as well as more fashionable ones. Such women's wage work paid extremely poorly. Women workers on average earned between one-quarter and one-half of what men earned for their labor, and poor urban women were never more than a few rungs up from the almshouse. The feminization of poverty was an eighteenth-century phenomenon as much as it is a modern one.

Social commentators were quick to observe – and criticize – the impact of the emerging commercial culture on women in eighteenth-century colonial cities. Moral writers were perhaps most disturbed by the new social fluidity seemingly made possible

---

[17] Karin Wulf discusses the reasons for the small but growing population of single women in Philadelphia in *Not All Wives.*

[18] Rising expectations of romantic love are dealt with in Ruth Bloch, "Changing Conceptions of Sexuality and Romance in Eighteenth-Century America," *William and Mary Quarterly,* 60 (2003), 13–42, and Richard Godbeer, *Sexual Revolution.*

by an enthusiastic embrace of consumer goods among middling and even lower sorts of people. The consumer revolution blurred social boundaries; a servant girl with an eye for fashion and talent as a seamstress could wear clothes that made her look a great deal like her mistress. For many critics increased access to consumer goods seemed to be conducive to pride; in other words, it encouraged people to forget their station in society. Writers also warned that the new addiction to fashion would corrupt men's daughters, making them self-centered and demanding, and destroying their virtuous modesty. And they warned that the wives of ordinary tradesmen were coming to demand so many expensive new luxuries, from silk for their dresses to chocolate and coffee and china for their tables, that they would ruin their husbands and bankrupt their families. Concerns about women's wasteful and ruinous tastes for fancy clothing were not limited to moral writers either. The diaries of wealthy eighteenth-century colonial men are full of entries about their efforts to control their wives' and daughters' spending on clothes and household goods, suggesting that eastern white women were in the forefront of changing expectations for colonial standards of living. The tone of the complaints, in turn, suggests that male household heads felt anxious about their ability to live up to the new standards.

The frequent repetition of several key ideas in this new moral critique of consumerism suggests that male writers believed women's consumer behavior was threatening, not only family order but also men's ability to command deference and respect from women. Young men were warned to beware fashionable young women who would try to entrap them into marriages in which they would insist on being supported in grand style. Fathers were urged to control their daughters' spending habits lest they demand so much that their parents' funds would be depleted. Often, masculinity itself seemed to be threatened. Writers complained that women tempted men to buy things they did not need, like powdered wigs, which turned them from manly men into effeminate fops. A common warning was that the consumer marketplace could unleash uncontrollable desires, which would make men vain and effeminate. None of this evidence shows that gender relationships were really being transformed by the growth of commerce, or that the patriarchal family was really under threat. Rather it suggests that the growth of a consumer economy created tensions within patriarchal families as women's spending was interpreted through the lens of a traditional gender ideology that portrayed women as irrational, vain, and unable to manage money.[19]

Changes in consumer behavior, most visible in colonial towns, were less apparent in rural areas, where the majority of white families in the colonies still lived. Housing styles in newer-settled communities, for example, remained fairly primitive, with log cabin construction actually becoming more popular during the eighteenth century than previously (although the houses of prosperous rural families were more likely than in the past to have plastered interior walls and glass windows). Wives, daughters, and servants in these families continued to be responsible for considerable amounts of

---

[19] These same tensions may help to explain why urban colonial men and women in North America so enthusiastically participated in boycotts of imported British consumer goods during the 1760s. Demonstrating self-control and producing homespun instead of using imported cloth was a way to prove to themselves and others that colonial men were more manly, and colonial women more industrious, than the men and women of the British empire who were trying to impose new imperial controls on them.

household production. They still sewed, processed food, and manufactured most household products. Yet even in rural areas eighteenth-century women changed their routines of household production as local economies became more market-oriented, with the ultimate goal of increasing their families' standards of living.[20]

Historians know from the rising number of spinning wheels found in household inventories that eighteenth-century northern colonial white women spent more time spinning than their mothers and grandmothers had. Relative rarities during the seventeenth century because of their expense, spinning wheels were owned by 50 percent of colonial households by the eighteenth century. More butter churns and cheese-making supplies, too, were being acquired by colonial households, suggesting that women were spending more time manufacturing dairy products. Other rural women took up soap manufacture and candle-making. Women in New England became weavers, taking over a craft that in England had been dominated by men since the fifteenth century. All of these occupations were time-consuming and difficult, requiring many extra hours of work each week that could otherwise have been devoted to socializing or relaxing.

Why did eighteenth-century white women spend so much extra time working to produce yarn, butter, cheese, soap, and cloth, on top of the endless routine of food-processing, cooking, and other household tasks that still had to be done? The most likely explanation is that manufacturing household products enabled rural women to participate in the market. They could take their candles and butter and yarn to the local storekeeper and bargain to buy other household goods, such as imported tea and sugar. Producing more goods at home gave women a way to participate in the consumer revolution without having to depend on cash provided by their husbands and fathers. By selling their own products and buying other commodities, they could raise their household standards of living while demonstrating that they could manage their own money and behave rationally. Alternatively, women could use products that they manufactured at home in order to raise standards of household comfort *without* having to increase household financial outlays for the purchase of consumer goods. In many New England households, homemade tablecloths and coverlets and blankets provided substitutes for imported cloth, allowing families to increase their material wealth even without participating in the cash economy.[21]

Ordinary white women's lives were thus moving in the opposite direction from those of their counterparts in the gentry. Instead of becoming ladies of leisure, the wives and unmarried daughters of rural families worked harder than ever in the eighteenth century, especially in the North. By the nineteenth century, such young women's textile-manufacturing skills, industrious work habits, and need for dowries would make them ideal workers in New England's emerging textile industry. The mill girls of Lowell, Massachusetts and other towns throughout New England would become

---

[20]   Log cabins were easy and cheap to construct, making them attractive to young white men eager to start households before having saved much money. Carole Shammas, "The Housing Stock of the Early United States: Refinement Meets Migration," *William and Mary Quarterly*, 64 (2007), 549–90. No record of how these men's wives felt about living in log cabins has been found.

[21]   Changes in eighteenth-century colonial women's work and women's contributions to a changing material culture are explored by various authors, particularly Laurel Thatcher Ulrich, *The Age of Homespun: Objects and Stories in the Creation of an American Myth* (New York, 2001).

DOCUMENT 17

An Act to Enable Femes Coverts to Convey Their Estates, Georgia, 1760, reprinted in W. Keith Kavenagh, *Foundations of Colonial America: A Documentary History* (New York, 1973), Vol. 3, 2505–6

The fear of dower rights on some properties inhibited land sales and the ability of owners to develop their estates. Like all southern colonies, Georgia made provision to ensure that the wife was a willing party to such transactions. Question to consider: *Would the following legal rule have protected women from husbands who wanted to coerce them to sell their property?*

II. Whereas it is necessary to secure the property of future purchasers of lands and tenements as well to prevent husbands disposing without the consent of the wife what of right did or would belong to them ... where a *feme couvert* has or may have any right in part or the whole of the lands and tenements to be conveyed and the said *feme couvert* does willingly consent to part with her right by becoming a party with her husband and in the sale of such lands and tenements, in such cases as these the said *feme couvert* shall become a party with her husband in the said deed of conveyance and sign and seal the same before the chief justice or assistant judges, or one of his Majesty's justices of the peace for the parish where such contracts shall be made, declaring before the said judge or justice that she has joined with her husband in alienation of the said lands and tenements of her own free will and consent without any compulsion or force used by her husband to oblige her so to do. Which declaration shall be made in the following words: "I, A.B., the wife of C.D. do declare that I have freely and without any compulsion signed, sealed and delivered the above instrument of writing passed between E.F. and C.D.; and I do hereby renounce all title or claim of dower that I might claim or be entitled to after the death of C.D., my said husband."

virtually the first North American factory workers, continuing in the long tradition of rural northern women who defined their lives through their productive work.

The growth of a commercial economy in the eighteenth century expanded white women's spheres of action in diverse ways. Their ability to make decisions not only as consumers but often as producers of goods no doubt gave them a sense of satisfaction, and may in the long run have increased their expectations for autonomy and self-determination. More important to the larger story of colonial North America, their economic decisions helped to transform the British North American economy. Women's aspirations to improve family standards of living helped stimulate demand for imports of consumer goods, which rose on a per capita basis by about 50 per cent between 1720 and 1770. Women's increasing productivity in household manufacturing contributed significantly to local economies, helping to generate the growth that paid for increases in consumption. In the long run, the vitality of these colonial economies and their growing importance as markets for British consumer goods would capture the attention of British government advisors, even changing the strategic priorities of the British empire during the 1750s.

Nevertheless it would be some time still before the expectations created by a commercial culture would begin to change women's legal status so as to give them control over their property and their economic decisions. If anything, white middle-class women's economic activity became increasingly invisible during the nineteenth century, as Anglo-American gender ideology changed to imagine white men as competitive, economically productive citizens and white women as virtuous and delicate ladies who did no visible work. Whatever the rationale, they still lacked most of the rights of men.

13

British North American Religion, Education, and Culture, 1689–1760

1689	Parliament passes the Toleration Act.
1693	The College of William and Mary is chartered. John Locke publishes his *Thoughts Concerning Education*.
1701	The Society for the Propagation of the Gospel (SPG) is founded. Yale is founded to train a more orthodox New England ministry.
1704	*The Boston News-Letter* begins publication.
1706	The Anglican Church is established in South Carolina. Francis Makemie forms the first presbytery in Philadelphia.
1708	The Connecticut churches adopt the Saybrook Platform.
1722	The first Anglican church in Connecticut is established.
1726	William Tennent's Log College is founded at Neshaminy.
1727	The Junto Club (later the American Philosophical Society) is founded by Benjamin Franklin in Philadelphia.
1729	Jonathan Edwards is appointed minister at Northampton.
1731	The Library Company of Philadelphia is created. The first public music concert is given in Boston.
1739	George Whitefield arrives in America.
1746	The Presbyterian College of New Jersey is established at Elizabethtown (and moved to Princeton in 1754).
1751	Franklin's Academy of Philadelphia is established.
1752–4	Lewis Hallam's theater company tours the colonies.
1754	King's College, New York (later Columbia College) is chartered.

Colonial America: A History to 1763, Fourth Edition. Richard Middleton and Anne Lombard.
© 2011 Richard Middleton and Anne Lombard. Published 2011 by Blackwell Publishing Ltd.

1 RELIGION

THE RAPIDLY INCREASING flow of information, news, and consumer goods between the colonies and Great Britain would not only change consumer behavior and gender ideology but also affect religious ideas, educational expectations, manners, literary tastes, and even perceptions of national identity among ordinary colonists. Colonial culture changed so rapidly during the eighteenth century that its disparate strands can be difficult to make sense of. At times it seemed that colonial culture was becoming more rational, influenced by the Enlightenment and the scientific ideal. At other times it appeared that colonial culture was becoming more emotional with the growing popularity of evangelical Protestantism. Much like cultural change in the modern era, these trends can seem contradictory and impossible to reconcile. Yet one common thread runs through the many manifestations of cultural change during the era. Over time, colonial societies were becoming more integrated into the larger British empire. Their inhabitants were growing more aware of British religious movements, intellectual debates, politics, and wars. As time went on they were coming to think of themselves as Britons.

Clearly religion remained the most important aspect of colonial life, even in the South. Although sectarian differences generally became less divisive after 1689, religion was still a crucial element in people's lives, and provided one of the main lenses through which ordinary colonists viewed their world.

Many characteristics of seventeenth-century religions persisted in the eighteenth century. God was still seen as a vengeful deity who punished the wicked by sending them to hell. Only a minority would go to heaven. Nevertheless, important developments had taken place. In New England the need to expand the elect had led some ministers to extend the communion. The first tentative steps in this direction had been taken by Thomas Hooker in seventeenth-century Connecticut. Towards the end of his ministry, Hooker had opened communion at Hartford to all adults of good behavior, believing that only God could judge whether someone was of the elect. At the same time he urged everyone to prepare for salvation. Hooker argued that God had not necessarily made up his mind about every individual. Grace might still be achieved if the covenant were observed.

Hooker's ideas were later adopted at Northampton, further up the Connecticut Valley, where Solomon Stoddard was the minister. Opponents like Cotton Mather understandably argued that Hooker and Stoddard were preaching a covenant of works, meaning that salvation could be achieved by doing good works rather than through faith or God's grace. Nevertheless, Stoddard was not prevented from continuing these practices when the Massachusetts synod of ministers was convened in 1679 to discuss the issue of church declension. Increasingly others followed his lead, notably the Brattle Street Church in Boston. After 1740 most churches began offering communion to all who appeared of a godly disposition, effectively ending the distinction between the elect and the rest of the congregation. All that was now required in most places to take communion was a satisfactory preparatory examination before a minister.[1]

Other philosophical influences were also at work. By the start of the eighteenth century the European intelligentsia were moving towards a more rational, less theological explanation of the world, based on the scientific work of Galileo and Newton and the deductive philosophy of Locke. An intellectual revolution was in progress which even the churches could not escape. Especially important was the view that man was not the product of original sin. A benign deity had given humanity reason so that it could understand the environment and benefit therefrom. Opinion, in other words, was shifting towards those who believed in free will rather than predestination as the answer to salvation. Among those affected by these intellectual currents were the two Mathers. Although they continued to believe in an elect chosen through grace, they now sought to reconcile theological explanations of the world with the new insights of the natural sciences. Hence the elder Mather accepted the scientific explanation for the periodic appearance of comets, but also affirmed that they were God's way of indicating his divine purposes. Cotton Mather argued similarly for the workings of providence when he published his views on the natural world in *The Christian Philosopher* in 1721.

This intellectual approach helped narrow the gap between the Congregational and Presbyterian churches, since both subscribed to many of the new ideas. One sign of this rapprochement was the readiness of the two Mathers to attend the consecration of a Presbyterian church in Boston. Clearly the Massachusetts establishment had come a long way since the time of Robert Child. Exclusivity was now less important than standing together against the growing irreligion of the population at large.

The most dramatic closing of the gap between these two churches occurred at the Connecticut synod of 1708, when the Congregational ministry adopted the Saybrook Platform, which effectively instituted a Presbyterian form of discipline. Another sign of the retreat from Congregationalism was that the ordination of the clergy was now done entirely by the laying on of ministerial hands rather than those of the laity. The ministers felt that their congregations contained too many unregenerate elements for the old practice to continue, though another reason may have been the disproportionate number of women now comprising most congregations. The result was a further distancing of the ministers from their flock.[2] The drift towards clericalism caused considerable disquiet and may have been one cause of the subsequent Great Awakening.

---

[1] On the abandonment of the requirement that all candidates relate their conversion experience, see Baird Tipson, "Samuel Stone's Discourse against Requiring Church Relations," *William and Mary Quarterly*, 46 (1989), 786–803. Stone was Hooker's deputy at Hartford. The importance of Stoddard is argued by Perry Miller in *The New England Mind from Colony to Province* (Cambridge, Mass., 1953). This view is challenged by Paul R. Lucas, *Valley of Discord: Church and Society along the Connecticut River, 1636–1725* (Hanover, NH, 1976). More recently Stoddard's influence has been reasserted by Philip F. Gura in "Going Mr Stoddard's Way: William Williams on Church Privileges, 1693," *William and Mary Quarterly*, 45 (1988), 489–98.

[2] The view that congregationalism as a form of church government was in decline is challenged by James F. Cooper, Jr., *Tenacious of Their Liberties: The Congregationalist in Colonial Massachusetts* (New York, 1999).

Officially or unofficially, most colonies continued to have an established church. In most of New England it remained the Congregational Church. The Massachusetts charter of 1691 stated that "there shall be a liberty of conscience allowed in the worship of God to all Christians, except papists." This provision was interpreted to mean that each town could levy tithes for the support of a Congregational minister. Liberty of conscience did not mean the right to equal treatment. Not until 1727 and 1728 were laws passed exempting Anglicans, Baptists, and Quakers from the payment of tithes for the support of the Congregational ministry. Even then it was a case of applying for an exemption rather than an automatic right.

Connecticut and New Hampshire similarly tried to exclude other religious groups. Connecticut did grant the Baptists the right to worship in 1708, but they still had to pay tithes and obtain permission from the county court to hold their services. In this hostile climate the Anglicans did not manage to form their first church there until 1722. Between 1727 and 1729 the tithe requirement was finally abated for most denominations, including Quakers, though the exemption was still hedged by various restrictions and Connecticut was far from accepting genuine toleration. The presumption remained that minority religious groups undermined the established order and ought to be discouraged.

The only province in New England not to have an established church was Rhode Island. Here the legacy of Roger Williams prevailed: all churches had to be supported by their congregations without the aid of a tithe. The result, as Cotton Mather sarcastically observed, was that Rhode Island had "Antinomians, Familists, Anabaptists, Antisabbatarians, Arminians, Socinians, Quakers, Ranters – everything in the world but Roman Catholics and real Christians."

Elsewhere, except for Pennsylvania and Delaware, the Anglican Church superficially reigned supreme. It had prospered in the aftermath of the Glorious Revolution, securing establishment in the Carolinas, Maryland, and part of New York. One sign of its growing confidence was the founding in 1701 of the Society for the Propagation of the Gospel in Foreign Parts, the SPG, which dispatched numerous missionaries, books, and pamphlets to the colonies. The Anglicans were also helped by the desire of several groups to ingratiate themselves with the British authorities. By 1750 many Dutch in New York City had joined Trinity Church, and Huguenots acted similarly in South Carolina. By the end of the colonial period the Anglicans had built over 400 churches, including 70 in New England. The Dutch Reformed Church in contrast had barely 60 congregations, concentrated in New York and New Jersey.

The newfound confidence of the Anglicans was reflected in the building of Christ Church, otherwise known as the Old North Church in Boston in 1723. Its steeple dominated the Puritan capital, compelling the Congregational community to respond with a similar adornment for the Old South Church in 1729. Other churches were given steeples also in an attempt to dominate the skyline. But perhaps most shocking to Congregationalists was the defection to Anglicanism in 1722 of the rector of Yale, Timothy Cutler, and another leading minister, the Reverend Samuel Johnson.

Despite these successes, the Anglican Church suffered from a number of weaknesses. In the South it tended to remain the religion of the planter class, who seemingly adopted it for reasons of social snobbery rather than conviction. Conversation among the congregation after the service was usually about tobacco prices and social matters rather than the content of the sermon. Among the backcountry farmers it was unable to compete with the Baptists and Presbyterians. Although the South structured its local government around the parish vestry, the arrangement did not usually benefit the Anglican Church, since many vestries contained persons belonging to other denominations.[3]

One fundamental weakness of Anglicanism was its lack of locally trained clergy. The failure to create an American bishopric contrasted sharply with the position of the other major denominations, which had no such problems in the ordination of their ministers. The decision to place the colonies under the episcopal authority of the bishop of London in 1691 did not help, since he was too remote to exert effective leadership. Hence the church, like other institutions of the English establishment, was starved of local input and later withered like the proverbial seed in stony ground on the outbreak of the Revolution in 1776.

In addition to Rhode Island, Pennsylvania and Delaware were by the eighteenth century two other provinces not to have an established church. The Quaker conviction that religion was a matter for the individual meant that uniformity was not sought there. Only Catholics were excluded from full toleration, at the insistence of the authorities in the mother country.

Three churches – Presbyterian, Lutheran, and German Reformed – enjoyed major growth during the eighteenth century. There had been Presbyterians in America since the time of Robert Child, but they remained an insignificant group. Indeed, the church was not properly organized until 1706 when Francis Makemie, an Edinburgh-trained Scots-Irishman, succeeded in bringing the various English, Welsh, Scots, and Irish congregations together under a presbytery in Philadelphia. The subsequent arrival of more Scots following the Act of Union in 1707 and, more important, of the Scots-Irish from northern Ireland after 1717, led to such remarkable growth that by the end of the colonial period Presbyterians made up the largest denomination in the middle colonies and had significant support in Virginia and the Carolinas. By then they comprised nearly 400 congregations.

The Lutheran and German Reformed churches also flourished because of immigration, in this case from Germany. Most of the new immigrants went to Pennsylvania, though some later took the great road down the Shenandoah into the backcountry of North and South Carolina. The Lutherans, like the Church of England, subscribed to salvation through faith and similarly retained much of the former Roman liturgy. The Reformed churches, on the other hand, were strictly Calvinist and believed in purging their worship of all traces of Catholicism. By 1760 the Lutherans had around 200 churches and the German Reformed 150.

Finally, mention should be made of the German Pietist sects, the Mennonites, Amish, Dunkers, and Moravians. The Mennonites and Amish believed in the supremacy of the laity, reliance on the gospel, and the need for personal religious experience. They were in many respects close to the Quakers. The Dunkers, on the other hand, were the German equivalent of the Baptists, believing in the need for adult immersion. All

---

[3] For the Baptist advance in Virginia, see Rhys Isaac, *The Transformation of Virginia, 1740–1790* (Chapel Hill, 1982).

three were inward-looking, concerned about their own salvation, and were limited to a few scattered communities in eastern Pennsylvania.

The Moravians, in contrast, affected to believe in St. Paul's dictum about going out to preach to the world. Another difference was that they claimed to be part of the Lutheran Church, though in reality they were much closer to the Quaker movement. Despite their outward stance, their numbers were small even in Pennsylvania, where they comprised perhaps 2,000 believers. Their main proselytizing success proved to be with the Native American peoples, where the simplicity of their message about the love of Christ and their readiness to interpret Indian dreams made them welcome. Their most important mission was at the Delaware village of Shamokin, near the forks of the Susquehanna River.

Obviously this was a theologically diverse population. Yet the bitter sectarian disputes of the seventeenth century had waned, at least for the time being. The defeat of the Catholic James II and the accession of the Protestant William and Mary, it has been suggested, helped to promote a new sense of pride among Britons that they were part of a Protestant nation.[4] The Toleration Act of 1689 guaranteed dissenting Protestants the right to worship without interference by the state. While the Puritans on both sides of the Atlantic had been forced to compromise and guarantee religious toleration, New Englanders took as much pride as any Britons in being the subjects of a Protestant monarch. Congregationalist ministers like John Wise explained to their flocks that while the Crown might govern secular affairs it was still the "New England Churches" who governed men's souls. Indeed the New England churches believed they were as quintessentially English as any church in existence. "[T]here is in the Constitution of our Church Government more of the English Civil Government in it, and it has a better Complexion to suit the true English Spirit, than is in the English Church."

None of this new sense of common purpose implied a loss of commitment by church leaders to their individual denominations. In fact, many churches worried during the early decades of the eighteenth century that their flocks were sinking into irreligion and godlessness. An inquiry at the end of Queen Anne's War in Connecticut concluded that the spirit of the original covenant had "departed from us" and called for an inquiry into the state of religion.

Historians now believe that no serious declension in religious belief was taking place.[5] Nevertheless, attempts continued to be made to enhance the appeal of the

---

[4] Linda Colley, *Britons: Forging the Nation, 1707–1837* (New Haven, 1992), has argued that Protestantism provided the unifying force that helped to create a sense of shared British identity in England, Wales, and Scotland after 1707. The same argument has been made recently with respect to the British colonists by Brendan McConville, *The King's Three Faces: The Rise and Fall of Royal America, 1688–1776* (Chapel Hill, 2006).

[5] See Patricia U. Bonomi, *Under the Cope of Heaven: Religion, Society, and Politics in Colonial America* (New York, 1986); and Jon Butler, *Awash in a Sea of Faith: Christianizing the American People* (Cambridge, Mass., 1990). Butler argues that, except for New England, the North American colonies were essentially unchurched in the seventeenth century, a situation that began to change only after 1700 with the imposition of more effective discipline and organization. An increase in religious faith was also found by Christine Leigh Heyrman, *Commerce and Culture: The Maritime Communities of Colonial Massachusetts, 1690–1750* (New York, 1985).

churches by relaxing membership requirements and adopting a more rational approach. Paradoxically these attempts at modernization were to cost the major churches dear. As sermons became ever more theoretical and philosophical in content, they provided opportunities for the Baptists to pick up converts from denominations which had lost their fire. The Baptists, as we have seen, had first arrived in the 1650s, preaching the need for adult baptism and attacking the idea of state-supported churches. Their simple style was beginning to win them many converts, especially in the South, where their ministers courageously journeyed to the furthest habitations. By the late colonial period they had perhaps 300 congregations.

The most persuasive challenge to the major churches came from the phenomenon known subsequently as the Great Awakening, which began in a number of different places on both sides of the Atlantic as individual ministers, mainly of a Calvinist variety, sought to revive religious feeling through evangelical methods.[6] Their efforts involved placing greater emphasis on the four Gospels with their message of glad tidings and salvation, stressing the need for individual religious experience rather than formal acknowledgment of established doctrine. The Calvinist churches, with their greater concern about heaven, hell, and the millennium, were perhaps more open to such appeals. Accordingly, one of the first churches in the colonies to adopt this method was Theodore Frelinghuysen of the Dutch Reformed church in the Raritan Valley in 1726. His success in rousing his congregation was emulated by other ministers, notably the venerable Solomon Stoddard, who was still seeking to recreate the First Church of Christ at Northampton, Massachusetts. In New Jersey the evangelical style of preaching was first adopted by the Presbyterian William Tennent and his son Gilbert, a close associate of Frelinghuysen. They in turn inspired Jonathan Edwards, Stoddard's successor at Northampton, to deliver a series of sermons aimed at stopping young people from "night walking, and frequenting the tavern" and other "lewd practices." This was in 1735. Two years later Edwards claimed in his published account, *Faithful Narrative*, that 500 persons had been saved.

The movement's most important boost came with the arrival of George Whitefield, an Englishman who had already achieved fame in Britain as an extraordinarily effective preacher and one of the founders of Methodism. Methodists were generally Anglicans who, like many denominations, found that their church had lost its vitality in the face of abstract theology and the defense of established privileges. They preached a new evangelical message that all men could be saved if they turned to God. In some respects the Great Awakening was a return to the old belief in salvation through faith and God's saving grace, though without the concept of an exclusive elect. This was in stark contrast to most churches which veered implicitly towards a brand of Arminianism that was linked to the concept of free will and the belief that humanity could save itself.

All this the Great Awakening rejected, seeking instead to center religion once more on the heart rather than the head, on faith rather than reason, and on grace rather than good works. Even more important than its theology was the movement's style; its proponents reached out to the mass of the population by preaching in fields in what became the first mass revivals of modern times.

---

[6] The term "Great Awakening" was first used in 1841.

Whitefield himself came to British North America in 1739 on the first of seven tours. Beginning in Savannah, Georgia, he proceeded up the coast to Philadelphia before returning via the backcountry to Charleston. In August 1740 he traveled to New England, after drawing crowds of many thousands all along his route. In Philadelphia he impressed even the cynical Benjamin Franklin with the power of his delivery, the simpleness of his message, and his ability to be heard.

Whitefield's greatest triumphs, however, came in New England, where his itinerant style of preaching was as yet hardly permitted. When pulpits were denied him, he took to the fields, followed by huge crowds. Everywhere he subjected his listeners to the certainty of hellfire and eternal damnation unless their repentance was immediate and complete. Thousands wept for their sins.

Whitefield and his imitators posed a serious challenge to the established churches. The speed of their conversions and their indifference to denominational boundaries inevitably caused dispute. Many ministers, recognizing the revivalists' appeal, opened their doors in the belief that these techniques would help rekindle the religious zeal of their own congregations. Others, notably Charles Chauncey of Boston's First Church, rejected this approach, feeling that such enthusiasm was of little value in awakening real spirituality and that only a proper appreciation of Christ could bring an individual real grace. Among the doubters, the need for caution was soon reinforced by the antics of James Davenport, who urged his followers to give away their worldly goods, including much of their clothing, and follow him dancing and singing through the streets of Boston and other New England towns.

The result was an internal split in many churches, notably among the Presbyterians of the middle colonies and the Congregationalists of New England, where both denominations established rival congregations in many towns. Among the Presbyterians divisions were especially bitter after Gilbert Tennent published his pamphlet *The Danger of an Unconverted Ministry*, which attacked the conservatives. The two groups came to be known as the New and Old Lights, representing the radical and conservative wings respectively. Some of these rifts healed after a few years; others remained. Many New Lights subsequently found that the Baptist Church met their desire for a more informal, less institutionalized religion.

The dilemma posed by the twin challenges of revivalism and orthodoxy is aptly illustrated by the career of Jonathan Edwards himself. As we have seen, Edwards, like many ministers, tried to adapt the new enthusiasm to revitalize the existing Congregational Church. The theme of his most famous sermon, delivered in 1741, was "Sinners in the Hands of an Angry God," during which individual members of the congregation cried out "What shall I do to be saved?" and "Oh, I am going to hell." However, Edwards soon came to distrust the idea of simple conversion, emphasizing instead the old Calvinist view that God could not be bargained with. Repentance had to be deep and sustained. Being of the elect was still the key to salvation. He increasingly felt that the revivals could only create a better environment in which God's purpose might be revealed. Significantly, this attempt to return to the old standards cost Edwards his pulpit in 1750.

Some historians believe that there were social and economic factors behind these divisions, noting that the supporters of the Great Awakening tended to be drawn from the young, the new commercial classes, and the poorer elements of the population, notably artisans, small farmers, and traders. Opponents, on the other hand, were largely drawn from the governing elite and merchant aristocracy. All three of the former desired to challenge the existing religious order, the exclusiveness of the political establishment, or the restrictive nature of the economy. Thus in Connecticut, the New Lights were strong in the growing commercial center of New London and recently settled towns of the interior. The Old Lights in contrast were dominant in the older towns of Hartford and New Haven. However, the evidence is by no means conclusive; for while most New Lights wanted to break the existing religious mold, they were by no means in favor of political reform or the development of a market economy with its trend towards consumerism.[7]

The area least affected by the Great Awakening in its early stages was the South, partly because the Anglican Church dominated the tidewater and partly because the backcountry was so isolated. The Anglicans were afraid of the impact that the new style of religion might have on their slaves. During the 1750s, however, Baptists like Shubal Stearns traveled through the piedmont preaching the message of salvation, so that by the end of the decade revivals were still common there long after they had ceased elsewhere. The uneven impact of the Great Awakening has led some scholars to question whether the revivals should be described as part of a single phenomenon (even though its supporters believed it was a clear manifestation of God's work).[8]

Finally, some historians have suggested a link between the Great Awakening and the American Revolution, arguing that revivalism destroyed the old deference for established institutions and made it easier for the colonists to break free from Britain politically and intellectually. Furthermore, the Calvinist emphasis on an elect and the popularity of millennial thought reinforced the colonial view that they were a special people, like the children of Israel, who would be released from their bondage. Lastly, it has been argued, the Awakening provided an opportunity for an intercolonial exchange of ideas, thus helping further the development of a shared Anglo-American identity.

Certainly, the emphasis on personal salvation strengthened those elements in colonial culture which placed the individual ahead of the group and paved the way for a more

---

[7]   The suggestion that the Awakening tended to attract the young is made by Peter S. Onuf, "New Lights in New London: A Group Portrait of the Separatists, 1740–1745," *William and Mary Quarterly*, 37 (1980), 627–44. The argument that it created divisions between new and old commerce is suggested by Rosalind Remer, "Old Lights and New Money: A Note on Religion, Economics and Social Order in 1740 Boston," *William and Mary Quarterly*, 47 (1990), 566–73. The view that the Awakening stimulated nonelite political consciousness is made by Gary B. Nash, *The Urban Crucible: Social Change, Political Consciousness, and the Origins of the American Revolution* (Cambridge, Mass., 1979); Isaac, *The Transformation of Virginia*; and Mark Valeri, *Law and Providence in Joseph Bellamy's New England: The Origins of the New Divinity in Revolutionary America* (New York, 1994). Valeri points out that class differences affected the ministry itself. Among those writers stressing the movement's wider appeal are Edwin Scott Gaustad, *The Great Awakening in New England* (New York, 1957), and James Walsh, "The Great Awakening in the First Church of Woodbury, Connecticut," *William and Mary Quarterly*, 27 (1971), 543–62.

[8]   For the debate over the origins of the term, see Jon Butler, "Enthusiasm Described and Decried: The Great Awakening as Interpretative Fiction," *Journal of American History*, 69 (1982), 305–25. The view that the Great Awakening was largely a publicity stunt is argued by Frank Lambert, *Inventing the "Great Awakening"* (Princeton, 1999).

democratic culture in the nineteenth century. Equally important was the revivalists' adoption of the open-air mass meeting, where not much was required for religious topics to be supplanted by political and social ones. It was this dangerous implication of revival meetings which made so many Old Lights wary of the new movement.

Nevertheless, most scholars downplay the importance of the links. They stress the time lag between the Great Awakening and the Revolution, especially in New England and the middle colonies. Another point is the fragmented nature of the movement and the fact that it had an international dimension: it was not specifically a North American phenomenon. Evangelical revivals swept across Europe, especially England and Scotland, during the same decades. Moreover, if Calvinist theology and millenarianism were so strong, they are curiously absent from the rhetoric of the leaders of the Revolution (although there is evidence of a strongly millennial current in popular culture which helped to build support for independence.) Finally, the idea that the New Lights provided the core leadership of the Revolution is not borne out by the subsequent careers of many Old Lights, notably Charles Chauncey, who took the lead in the controversy about a North American episcopacy and remained a strong supporter of the patriot cause.[9]

A more recent view suggests that the Awakening strengthened the sense of British national identity which was already emerging in the British North American colonies, rather than making them feel more distinctively American. One of its long-term consequences was to further break down sectarian barriers as people from diverse denominations became swept up in the revivals together. Rather than aiming for doctrinal purity, the evangelicals often spoke to their listeners simply as Christians. The new preaching styles they popularized became influential in many denominations. The Awakening also helped to stimulate the growth of the nonestablished denominations of the Baptists and of Methodism, both of which were more welcoming of the poor and the illiterate than most of the older sects. Thus it seems likely that the Awakening contributed to a sense among many of the British colonists that they were part of a chosen nation of Protestant believers committed to God's purposes. That nation was clearly British.

---

[9] The thesis that the Great Awakening prepared the way ideologically for the Revolution is advanced most explicitly by Alan Heimert in *Religion and the American Mind from the Great Awakening to the Revolution* (Cambridge, Mass., 1966); William G. McLoughlin, "The Role of Religion in the Revolution," in S. G. Kurtz and J. H. Hutson, eds, *Essays on the American Revolution* (Chapel Hill, 1973); and J. C. D. Clark, *The Language of Liberty, 1660–1832: Political Discourse and Social Dynamics in the Anglo-American World* (Cambridge, 1993). The argument that the Awakening stimulated new forms of communication is advanced by Harry S. Stout, "Religion, Communications, and the Ideological Origins of the American Revolution," *William and Mary Quarterly*, 34 (1977), 519–41. Millennialism during the Revolutionary era is explored in Ruth Bloch, *Visionary Republic: Millennial Themes in American Thought, 1756–1800* (New York, 1985). Among those questioning the links are Butler, *Awash in a Sea of Faith*, who stresses the Revolution's secular nature; and Bonomi, *Under the Cope of Heaven*, who affirms both the time lag between the two events and the fact that the Great Awakening occurred during a period of political stability. The international connections with Europe are stressed by Perry Miller, *Errand into the Wilderness* (Cambridge, Mass., 1956), and the intercolonial impact by Richard Hofstadter, *America at 1750: A Social Portrait* (New York, 1973).

DOCUMENT 18

Benjamin Franklin on George Whitefield, reprinted in Kenneth Silverman, ed., *Benjamin Franklin: The Autobiography and Other Writings* (London, 1986), 116–19

This description of Whitefield's preaching techniques comes from Benjamin Franklin, who admired Whitefield's ministry without being fully persuaded by his message. Questions to consider: *What impact would attendance at one of Whitefield's sermons be likely to have had on a rural person who had spent his whole life living in the same small village? Why do you think Whitefield was so effective?*

In 1739 arrived among us from England the Reverend Mr Whitefield who had made himself remarkable there as an itinerant preacher. He was at first permitted to preach in some of our churches; but the clergy taking a dislike to him, soon refused him their pulpits, and he was obliged to preach in the fields. The multitudes of all sects and denominations that attended his sermons were enormous, and it was a matter of speculation to me, who was one of the number, to observe the extraordinary influence of his oratory on his hearers and how much they admired and respected him, notwithstanding his common abuse of them, by assuring they were naturally "half beasts and half devils." It was wonderful to see the change soon made in the manners of our inhabitants, from being thoughtless or indifferent about religion, it seemed as if all the world were growing religious, so that one could not walk through the streets in an evening without hearing psalms sung in different families of every street . . .

I happened soon after to attend one of his sermons, in the course of which I perceived he intended to finish with a collection and silently resolved he should get nothing from me. I had in my pocket a handful of copper money, three or four silver dollars, and five pistoles in gold. As he proceeded, I began to soften and concluded to give the coppers. Another stroke of his oratory made me ashamed of that and determined me to give the silver; and he finished so admirably that I emptied my pocket wholly into the collector's dish, gold and all . . .

Some of Mr Whitefield's enemies affected to suppose that he would apply these collections to his own private emolument, but I who was intimately acquainted with him (being employed in printing his sermons and journals, etc.) never had the least suspicion of his integrity, but am to this day decidedly of opinion that he was in all his conduct a perfectly honest man.

2 EDUCATION

The United States has a long tradition of providing free schooling for its citizens and was the first nation to do so. The origins of this achievement can be traced back to the colonial period.

We have seen that the first educational establishments, notably those in New England, were motivated by religious considerations. Persons wishing to be saved must be conversant with the word of God and therefore required the ability to read the Bible. Another consideration was the need for a trained ministry.

To these ends schools and colleges were established from an early stage in New England. A Massachusetts law of 1647, the first to regulate education, stated that if parents neglected to instruct their children, the selectmen could apprentice them so that they could "read and understand the principles of religion and the capital laws of the country." Connecticut passed a similar law in 1650.

In smaller communities most instruction was provided in "dame" schools, where the teacher was a female member of the church. Only the larger towns could afford a qualified master to run a grammar school, and these were restricted to boys. Nevertheless, by 1700 in New England some 70 percent of men and 45 percent of women could read and write. The figures continued to climb throughout the colonial period as communities became more settled, but literacy remained essentially a religious rather than a secular quest. This is reflected in the principal book used by children after 1686, the *New England Primer*, which, apart from the alphabet and a list of syllables, contained mostly hymns, prayers, biblical stories, and accounts of Protestant martyrs. Not until the 1760s were materials like *Tom Thumb's Song Book* and Daniel Defoe's *Robinson Crusoe* used. The value of education in advancing a person's skills and livelihood was not generally accepted until after the Revolution.[10]

Outside New England, schooling was more haphazard, on account of different attitudes among the other churches. Most left the attainment of salvation to guidance by the minister rather than personal study by the individual. Such elitist views were especially prevalent in the Anglican Church. The rector's sermons, services, and parish visits were thought to be sufficient guidance for the congregation, though education was seen as a legitimate part of the missionary process. Those least concerned with education were the Baptists and Quakers, who relied on inspiration and spontaneity, for which neither formal training nor literacy was necessary, though this attitude started to change once these sects became more institutionalized.

In the middle and southern colonies schooling was accordingly left to individual parishes and communities. Large towns like New York and Philadelphia had schools by the end of the seventeenth century, though their emphasis remained religious. The first school in New York was established by the Dutch Reformed Church, followed in 1710 by Trinity School, an SPG foundation. In Philadelphia the first educational institution was the Friends' School, founded by the Quakers in 1689, in part to maintain their tribal purity which made separate educational facilities seemingly necessary. Elsewhere, especially in the South, the only instruction available was by private tutor, though many parents did their best to pass on their skills. In reality, appreciation of the need for education had not advanced much beyond the time of Sir William Berkeley, who

---

[10] The traditional view was that America's commitment to mass education laid the foundations for its phenomenal progress in the past 200 years. See Bernard Bailyn, *Education in the Forming of American Society: Needs and Opportunities for Study* (Chapel Hill, 1960). For the argument that religion remained the basis of education, see Kenneth Lockridge, *Literacy in Colonial New England: An Enquiry into the Social Context of Literacy in the Early Modern West* (New York, 1974).

proudly boasted that Virginia had neither printing presses nor free schools, which he believed was a blessing, since they merely encouraged sedition and rebellion.

As the eighteenth century progressed, the need for better schools outside New England was recognized not just by the churches. This increased awareness in part reflected a growing need for clerks and other literate persons in commerce, law, and administration. The growth of education was also a response to the Enlightenment, as the more affluent began to sense that they could improve themselves materially as well as morally if they were educated.

These factors resulted in greater efforts to provide schooling. In Maryland attempts were made in 1723 to set up county schools for the poor, albeit unsuccessfully, while in the Charleston area a number of "free" schools were established where only the better off had to pay. This increase in schools in turn led more people to contemplate a career in teaching, which had now become accepted as a separate vocation from the ministry, though many people continued to practice both. Another aid to educational expansion was an increase in the number of legacies left to schools. The consequence was a respectable increase in literacy even in Virginia, where perhaps two-thirds of males could read documents and sign their names by 1760, though an ability to read did not necessarily mean an ability to write. Pennsylvania had roughly the same literacy level.

The figure for women's literacy is less definite. Since women were expected to marry and wives could not normally participate in business transactions, girls were offered less education. In particular, girls were not taught to sign their names, so tended to sign documents with a mark even if they knew how to read. For this reason, it has been difficult for historians to measure women's literacy. However, women often *did* know how to read the Bible. For the daughters of the elite, music, penmanship, and foreign languages were sometimes added, in order to give girls some social polish. Female

Figure 22 "A Westerly View of the Colledges ... " (Harvard College), attributed to Paul
Revere. Courtesy of the Peabody Essex Museum, Salem, Massachusetts.

literacy was undoubtedly aided by the new form of literature, the novel. Especially influential was Samuel Richardson's *Clarissa*, which took the form of an exchange of letters between two young women.

We have already seen that New England was also at the forefront of higher education with the founding of Harvard in 1636 in Cambridge, Massachusetts, to provide a trained ministry. The college was never intended solely as a seminary, for in addition to theological topics, instruction was offered in "good literature, arts and sciences." Nevertheless, until the end of the colonial period any male wishing to graduate in anything other than classics, divinity, and philosophy had to journey across the Atlantic for his education. The most popular subjects were medicine in Edinburgh and law in London.

Life at Harvard was very formal. Freshmen were not allowed to wear gowns or carry canes, and all undergraduates had to doff their caps on passing the president's house. They were similarly required to salute at 50 yards when meeting the president in the street and had to acknowledge professors and tutors at 40 and 25 yards respectively.

Harvard remained the only institution of higher learning in British North America for 50 years until the College of William and Mary was established at Williamsburg in 1693 as a belated response by the Anglican community there to the need for a trained ministry. The lack of a higher institution to prepare Anglican clergy had hampered the Episcopalian cause, although with no bishop in the American colonies, candidates still had to cross the Atlantic to be ordained. The first president and founding father was a Scottish Episcopalian, James Blair, who always intended William and Mary to be a college as well as a seminary to cater to the needs of the Virginian planters.

Blair's friendship with John Locke was reflected in the college's curriculum, which provided for the study of medicine and law in addition to the more traditional classics and theology. In 1717 the first chair in natural philosophy and mathematics was created. But though generously endowed, the college languished because of internal squabbles. A serious fire also destroyed most of the main building in 1705. As a result some planters continued to send their sons to England for their education, especially in law.

By the turn of the eighteenth century, Harvard had begun to adopt more liberal attitudes in religious matters, reflecting the growth of Arminian views. Not everyone welcomed this trend, and as a result Yale was founded in New Haven in 1701 to produce ministers of a more orthodox stance. The curriculum at the new college was similar to that of Harvard in the previous century, having a heavy emphasis on classics, divinity, and philosophy. In due course Yale, too, found that it could not divorce itself from the intellectual currents which were sweeping Europe. By 1760 it was little different from its rival.

The middle colonies had to wait longer for an institution of higher learning. New York lacked a single dominant religious group, while Quaker Pennsylvania felt no need of one, having no trained ministry. The Quakers in any case laid more emphasis on the "university of life," as Benjamin Franklin termed it. However, as the Presbyterians grew in strength, they became increasingly eager to have some institution to train their ministers. A few candidates attended Harvard, and in 1726 William Tennent established a "log college" at Neshaminy in Bucks County, Pennsylvania, which trained some 20 ministers before closing its doors through lack of funding. Accordingly, in 1746 a group of New Light Presbyterians, led by Jonathan Dickinson, a Yale-trained New Englander, with the enthusiastic support of the Neshaminy-trained ministers, founded the College of New Jersey. Initially this operated from Dickinson's house in

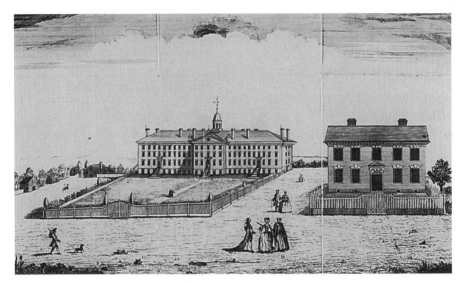

Figure 23   College of New Jersey (later Princeton University). Engraving by Henry Dawkins, 1764. A northwest prospect of Nassau Hall with a front view of the president's house. Department of Rare Books and Special Collections, Princeton University Library.

Elizabethtown, before moving on his death to Newark. Finally, in 1754 new premises were established at Princeton, though the college was not known by that name until the 1760s. From the beginning it was interdenominational; indeed, its third president was Jonathan Edwards. And like Harvard, Yale, and William and Mary, Princeton had many students who were not candidates for the ministry.

Meanwhile, under Benjamin Franklin's guidance, in 1751 the Academy of Philadelphia had been founded, with the distinction of being the first secular institution to impose no religious test for admission. Initially it was designed to be only a school, but in 1755 a three-year undergraduate program was added, after which its name was changed to the Academy and College of Philadelphia. From the beginning its aim was to promote knowledge as an end in itself. As Franklin argued in his initial appeal, this was the surest way to advance "the happiness both of private families and of commonwealths." Franklin was heavily influenced by his Quaker surroundings and by the educational philosophy of Locke. The academy therefore placed a heavy emphasis on what was useful. Among the proposed subjects were arithmetic, accounts, geometry, and astronomy. Also included were English and history, to show "the beauty and usefulness of virtue"; natural history and botany, to contribute to the "improvement of agriculture"; and mechanics, "by which weak men perform such wonders, labour is saved, [and] manufactures expedited." The academy also taught Greek and Latin, which were useful in the study of divinity, law, medicine, and modern languages. Franklin's academy has often been seen as the forerunner of the future public school system of the United States. It was certainly no coincidence that the University of Pennsylvania was later to be the first institution of higher learning to have a medical school, in 1765.

Lastly, in 1754 New York obtained its first institution of higher learning with the establishment of King's College. The Anglicans had tried to charter a college in 1746

DOCUMENT 19

On training to be a lawyer: the early career of John Adams, 1758, reprinted in L. H. Butterfield, ed., *The Diary and Autobiography of John Adams* (Cambridge, Mass., 1961), Vol. 1, 54–5

The law was just beginning to become more professional when John Adams set out to be a lawyer after graduating from Harvard. This segment of his diary describes the subjects he was advised to master in order to practice law. Questions to consider: *Was the legal profession open to any person in the colonies who wanted to enter it? What kinds of skills, knowledge, and qualities was Adams urged to cultivate in order to become a lawyer?*

Went in the morning to Mr Gridleys, and asked the favour of his Advice what Steps to take for an Introduction to the Practice of Law in this Country. He answered "get sworn" [i.e. at the bar] . . .

ADAMS: But in order to that, sir, as I have no Patron, in this County.
GRIDLEY: I will recommend you to the Court. Mark the Day the Court adjourns to in order to make up Judgments. Come to Town that Day, and in the mean Time I will speak to the Bar for the Bar must be consulted, because the Court always inquires, if it be with the Consent of the Bar.

Then Mr Gridley inquired what Method of Study I had pursued, what Latin Books I read, what Greek, what French. What I had read upon Rhetorick. Then he took his Common Place Book and gave me Lord Hale's Advice to a Student of the Common Law, and when I had read that, he gave me Lord C[hief] J[ustice] Reeves' Advice [to] his Nephew, in the Study of the common Law. Then He gave me a Letter from Dr. Dickins, Regius Professor of Law at the University of Cambridge, to him, pointing out a Method of Studying the civil Law. Then he turned to a Letter He wrote himself to Judge Lightfoot, Judge of the Admiralty in Rhode Island, directing a Method of Studying the Admiralty Law. Then Mr. Gridley run a Comparison between the Business and studies of a Lawyer or Gentleman of the Bar, in England, and that of one here. A Lawyer in this Country must study common Law and civil Law, and natural Law, and Admiralty Law, and must do the duty of a Counsellor, a Lawyer, an Attorney, a solicitor, and even of a scrivener, so that the Difficulties of the Profession are much greater here than in England . . .

I have a few Pieces of Advice to give you Mr. Adams. One is to pursue the Study of the Law rather than the Gain of it. Pursue the Gain of it enough to keep out of the Briars, but give your main Attention to the study of it.

The next is not to marry early. For an early Marriage will obstruct your Improvement, and in the next Place, twill involve you in Expence.

Another Thing is not to keep much Company. For this application of a Man who aims to be a lawyer must be incessant. His Attention to his Books must be constant, which is inconsistent with keeping much Company.

but had been prevented by the Presbyterians in the assembly, where neither group was sufficiently dominant to dictate its wishes. When King's College finally opened, therefore, it was effectively a nondenominational institution. Its curriculum was centered on "the learned languages" and "liberal arts and sciences." Entrants had to be able to read and write, have basic arithmetic, and possess a good knowledge of Greek and Latin. It, too, added a medical school in 1767.

By 1760, then, six colonies had institutions of higher learning. Five of them were in the North, reflecting the concentration of dissenting churches there. All were exclusively male. An increasing number of students no longer intended to be ministers, having more secular ends in view. For a growing segment of the elite and the upper middle classes, saving the world was no longer a primary aim. But although all the colleges were broadening their curriculum, they still only partially met the needs of professions like law and medicine. Nor did the situation change dramatically in the 1760s. Of the three new institutions of higher education founded before the Revolution, two – Rutgers (Dutch Reformed) and Brown (Baptist) – were overtly religious; and Dartmouth, though affecting to be interdenominational, provided a traditional curriculum based on Christianity and the classics. Until the Revolution, those who could not afford to study law and medicine in Europe had to graduate from a colonial college and then practice with someone already qualified in the profession (see Document 19).

3 THE ANGLICIZATION OF TASTE

Traditionally, historians viewed the eighteenth century as a time when the British North American colonies were becoming distinctively American. Many historians today have concluded that in reality the colonies were becoming anglicized as the century progressed.[11]

Originally, when the colonists first came over during the seventeenth century, they were clearly English in their cultural attitudes. Then over time the unfamiliar environment compelled them to adapt their styles of life, modifying dress, food, housing, and farming methods. In many cases they borrowed agricultural techniques, crops, and

---

[11] The thesis of anglicization is associated with the work of John M. Murrin, "Anglicizing an American Colony: The Transformation of Provincial Massachusetts" (unpublished PhD thesis, Yale University, 1966). Other works in this genre are David Grayson Allen, *In English Ways: The Movement of Societies and the Transferral of English Local Law and Custom to Massachusetts Bay in the Seventeenth Century* (Chapel Hill, 1981); and T. H. Breen, "An Empire of Goods: The Anglicization of Colonial America, 1690–1776," *Journal of British Studies*, 25 (1986), 467–99. See also Richard L. Bushman, "American High-Style and Vernacular Cultures," in Jack P. Greene and J. R. Pole, eds, *Colonial British America: Essays in the New History of the Early Modern Era* (Baltimore, 1984), 345–83. The contrary position is argued by Jon Butler, *Becoming America: The Revolution Before 1776* (Cambridge, Mass., 2000), which argues that British North American societies became more modern after 1680, but not more British. Butler stresses the distinctiveness of the North American societies, which were more ethnically diverse and religiously pluralistic and produced higher per capita standards of living and a more participatory form of politics than developed in Britain.

even cuisine from Native Americans and adapted it to their own cultures. A landscape full of unfamiliar animals and potentially hostile native inhabitants caused the colonists to change their language and adopt new words from Native American languages. They developed a simplified standard of living more appropriate to an environment in which consumer goods were hard to come by.

Yet with the advent of the eighteenth century, colonists in the more settled areas became eager to acquire British goods and manners and to develop British tastes. They bought British books and copied London furniture styles. They aspired to become more sophisticated and "polite." In some respects, they were no different from their counterparts at home, for Great Britain itself was in the throes of a consumer revolution, in which the emerging middle classes were adopting the fashions, dress, and lifestyles of the aristocracy.[12] In addition the British colonists had some of their own distinct reasons for emulating the British gentry. As discussed in the previous chapter, during the late seventeenth century an established colonial elite had emerged whose members aspired to be recognized as part of the gentry class. Fulfilling these aspirations required them to conform to the standards of refinement, in terms not only of living standards and consumer preferences but also of education, manners, and even artistic tastes. Second, the new efficiency of transatlantic communication in the eighteenth century had increased the amount of information available to people in the British North American colonies about what was going on in Britain. Their greater awareness of their connection with Great Britain gave colonial people a strong sense of pride and shared commitment to the mother country. A third factor was the increasing availability of consumer goods, which spurred even ordinary people to aspire to become more fashionable. Since London and other major British cities were recognized as the centers of fashion, becoming more fashionable by definition meant emulating the British.

Several historians argued that the anglicization of British North American culture also heightened the colonists' awareness of class differences. Indeed more affluent colonists were eager to distinguish themselves from ordinary people by observing the new code of genteel refinement which had begun in the royal households of Europe before spreading to the gentry and commercial classes. Among its requirements was politeness of speech, especially the use of "please" and "thank you." Refinement also required individuals to be clean and their surroundings to be neat. Particular attention was given to improving eating habits through the use of cutlery, plates, chairs, and linen rather than hands, bowls, and stools, which latter methods inevitably led to stained and smelly clothing. The aim everywhere was to elevate and refine in order to create a pleasing impression. Those who thought of themselves as polite invariably looked

---

[12] The rise of "politeness" or "refinement" in England has been traced to the rise in wealth and political power of the commercial class. In England the middle class, defined as people who made their livings in business, had traditionally been looked down upon by the aristocracy. During the eighteenth century members of this group began to think of themselves as gentlemen, entitled to respect not because of their titles but because of their manners, tastes, and educational achievements. See for example Paul Langford, *A Polite and Commercial People: England, 1727–1783* (Oxford, 1989).

down on ordinary people with their unrefined manners and undeveloped sensibilities and tastes.[13]

At the same time, manners offered a relatively fluid way of demarcating class boundaries. Unlike the traditional British idea that membership in the elite depended on birth and inherited status, the concept of refinement which was developing in the northern colonies tended to stress that it was a person's ability to display polite behavior, dress fashionably, and attain a particular level of education that made him a gentleman. Thus a man from an urban artisan's family like Benjamin Franklin, or a man from a moderately prosperous but essentially undistinguished farming family like John Adams, could aspire to rise to the upper middle class by becoming well educated and learning to act the part of a gentleman. In the South, access to upper and upper middle-class status appears to have depended upon more traditional markers, such as distinguished family connections and ownership of considerable quantities of land (and slaves), although refinement was important here too.[14] However, in the more commercially oriented North, where merchants dominated the society, refinement could turn a man with money into a gentleman within a single generation.

The desire among merchants, professionals, upwardly mobile artisans, and planters to be thought of as refined, sophisticated, and "polite" helps to explain a great deal about the culture that developed in the long-settled areas of the eastern seaboard by 1700. Of course members of this group represented a minority of the colonial population, even if their group was growing. The differences (and to some extent the similarities) between their cultural sensibilities and those of the vast majority of the population can be seen in a survey of the kinds of reading material consumed by the literate population.

4   LIBRARIES, LITERATURE, AND THE PRESS

The earliest libraries in British North America belonged to private individuals and were relatively small and few in number. The first collection of a public nature was set up in Boston's town house and comprised mainly the books of Robert Keayne, a merchant who died in 1656 and bequeathed his collection to the town. Most of its stock was of a religious nature.

---

[13]   The doyen of refinement was Lord Chesterfield, though his *Letters of Philip Dormer Stanhope, Earl of Chesterfield to His Son*, were not published until 1774. Richard Bushman makes the argument about gentility and its contribution to the emergence of an eighteenth-century colonial elite in *The Refinement of America: Persons, Houses, Cities* (New York, 1992).

[14]   Dallett Hemphill, *Bowing to Necessities: A History of Manners in America, 1620–1860* (New York, 1999), finds that comportment and physical self-control, both attributes which aspiring members of the middle classes could attain, were increasingly emphasized in the conduct books that circulated in the northern colonies after 1740. Hemphill argues that northern ideals of gentility and refinement were noticeably different from southern ideals, which stressed family connection more than behavior. See her "Manners and Class in the Revolutionary Era: A Transatlantic Comparison," *William and Mary Quarterly*, 63 (2006), 345–72. Another aspect of gentility and refinement after 1750 was the display of sensibility, or sympathy for the feelings of others. See Sarah Knott, *Sensibility and the American Revolution* (Chapel Hill, 2009).

Book-collecting, like education, had been motivated largely by religion in its early stages. At the turn of the eighteenth century Dr Thomas Bray, one of the founders of the SPG, established several libraries, primarily for the benefit of the Anglican clergy. Among the most notable were those at Annapolis, Maryland and at Charleston, South Carolina.

As the century progressed men from the merchant and planter classes began to demand more secular collections, leading to the founding of private subscription libraries. The first of these was the Library Company of Philadelphia in 1731, in which development the indefatigable Franklin played a prominent role. It was funded by a subscription of 40 shillings and prominent among its early purchases were various works on science. The scheme proved sufficiently successful for Charleston to establish a similar library in 1748, followed by New York City in 1754. The joining fee for the latter was £5, with an annual subscription thereafter of 10 shillings. The New York Society Library, as it was called, inherited a collection of books originally donated by Bray, but it quickly set about expanding its selection to meet the changing tastes. A new form of literature, the novel, proved popular, especially works by Richardson and Smollett. By 1760 some 20 such libraries had been established. All were private libraries created for the use of the subscribers; none were public libraries in the modern sense of being open to ordinary people.

Outside the main towns, people had to buy their own books. As they were relatively expensive, purchasers were generally members of the clergy, lawyers, and the small but increasing number of well-educated people who affected to believe in the enlightened mind, not least the Virginia plantocracy. Among the more notable collections were those of Robert Carter, who had 1,200 volumes at his death in 1732, and Cotton Mather, whose collection amounted to some 3,000 volumes when he died in 1727.

The content of library collections by mid-century provides good evidence that men who aspired to be part of the colonial elite were expected to have read, or at least to be aware of, the major European poets, philosophers, and scientific thinkers, along with some of the classics. A good subscription library would contain the poetry of Pope, Dryden, Milton, and Spenser; the plays of Shakespeare, Molière, Congreve, and Addison; the novels of Smollett, Richardson, Fielding, and Sterne; and the political and philosophical works of Montesquieu, Voltaire, Locke, Sidney, Swift, Bolingbroke, and Hume. Also indispensable were a good selection of the classics: Cicero, Tacitus, Livy, Seneca, Aristotle, Terence, Virgil, and Homer; the historical works of Robertson, Hume, and Clarendon; and the scientific works of Buffon and Newton. Finally, no library was considered complete without some sermons and the legal works of Coke, Bracton, and Fortescue.

Few of these books were published in the colonies, though an increasing number of printing presses were being established. The first press opened in Boston in 1638, but it was mainly for official business. Most of its other publications were of a religious nature, for example, the Bay Psalm Book in 1640. The literary output of this as well as of later local presses gives a good idea of the types of books that ordinary colonists were likely to read. Religious tracts and essays were always popular. A perennial bestseller was Foxe's *Book of Martyrs*, an account of the sufferings of Protestants who had been executed during Queen Mary's reign. Another literary genre to attain popularity in New England was the narratives of those captured by Indians during the various wars with the Indians and the French, the most notable being that of Mary Rowlandson, which first appeared in 1682.

Outside of New England the development of printing was considerably slower. Nevertheless, by the eighteenth century nearly all the colonies had at least one press for producing official documents, while the larger provinces had several. In 1738 the first non-English press appeared in Pennsylvania to cater to the colony's German community.

Relatively few books were written by colonial British North Americans before 1760, and even fewer of these were actually published there, though the number was growing. In 1702 Cotton Mather produced his *Magnalia Christi Americana* in Boston. This work consisted of a history of New England, supposedly from the ecclesiastical point of view of explaining divine providence, although it included most of the key events concerning the colony's settlement and expansion. Three years later Robert Beverley, Jr. produced his *History and Present State of Virginia*, a more secular account. This work was the first to be written in the mainland British colonies from a consciously American point of view. The newfound pride of the Virginian elite led the Reverend Hugh Jones to produce a similar volume in 1726, entitled the *Present State of Virginia*. Elsewhere the desire to understand the North American environment stimulated John Lawson to write his *New Voyage to Carolina* in 1707 and Cadwallader Colden to produce his *History of the Five Indian Nations* in 1727, while in 1757 William Smith published his *History of the Province of New York*. By then most provinces had seen some work published about their history or physical environment.

Apart from works of a religious, historical, or topographical nature, the most regularly printed work was the almanac. This useful compendium of information about the political and physical world was an indispensable tool for upwardly mobile urban artisans and merchants. Since almanacs were cheaper and more widely distributed than books, there is reason to think they were read by a broader cross-section of the population as well, along with the Bible and locally published religious tracts. The most famous almanac was Franklin's *Poor Richard's Almanac*, which first appeared in 1732, though there were a number of competing publications.

The first weekly newspaper in the colonies was the *Boston News-Letter*, founded in 1704. The second was the *Boston Gazette*, established in 1719. That same year marked the appearance of Philadelphia's first newspaper, the *American Mercury*, on which the youthful Franklin was employed. New York followed in 1725 with the *New York Gazette*, while Charlestonians saw the appearance of the *South Carolina Gazette* in 1732. By 1760 Boston had four newspapers and five other printing establishments, Philadelphia two newspapers and three other presses, New York three newspapers, and Charleston two. Other newspapers were published in Williamsburg, Annapolis, Germantown, New Haven, New London, Newport, and Portsmouth. The distribution, if not the sale, of newspapers was assisted by the establishment of a post office in 1710, which had a network of some 65 offices by 1770, serving all 13 continental colonies.

Newspapers were aimed squarely towards an audience of merchants and their relatively well-to-do customers. Most contained advertisements for the sale of goods and the arrival and departure times of ships. The news they reported was almost entirely news of European events, reflecting the increasing interest of merchants and the rural gentry in metropolitan culture. When Franklin and his partner David Hall took over Pennsylvania's second newspaper, the *Pennsylvania Gazette*, in 1729, they announced that they would provide more coverage of public events, history, diplomatic affairs, and matters of cultural and scientific interest. Their model was the London *Spectator*, which was popular on both sides of the Atlantic. It does not seem to have bothered readers that the news and information found in the newspapers rarely touched upon local events. Their identities were becoming increasingly bound up with their self-concept as educated and sophisticated Britons. Moreover their livelihoods were increasingly dependent on transatlantic trading, so it made sense for them to stay informed about international diplomacy and war. Awareness of European affairs helped them to assess their investment risks.

5 SCIENCE AND THE ARTS

The eighteenth century was an age of science, and upper-class British North Americans were keen students. They were loath to think of themselves as unsophisticated provincials; they wanted to stay up to date with most important new ideas. Moreover, living in a new world, many of them were genuinely eager to understand their environment, and found many of the traditional religious explanations no longer convincing. In this context the Enlightenment in Europe, with its stress on understanding the universe through analysis and observation, proved an important influence.

Philadelphia was perhaps the most important center of science and technology, its position reflecting the Quaker belief in reason and the notion that God had given man his intellect to understand his environment. Equally, it was no coincidence that from 1743 Philadelphia was the home of the American Philosophical Society, the first colonial institution dedicated to scientific enquiry. Five of its first nine trustees were Quakers or had been members of the Society of Friends.

The most famous of the trustees was Benjamin Franklin, though of course he was not a Quaker. He was a New Englander by birth but had left Boston when still a youth. It was Franklin who was instrumental in getting the society started. He conducted numerous experiments himself, notably those in which he identified electricity's positive and negative qualities. Out of his observations came the lightning conductor, a useful invention which reduced the risk of fire. This was one of the attractions of science: the production of useful gadgets which would improve the quality of life. Later, Franklin helped devise a stove which required less air, burned more slowly, and gave out greater heat, thus making homes less draughty and easier to keep warm.[15]

Another Philadelphia Quaker interested in science was James Logan, who helped classify the flora and fauna of North America. Also resident in the city was John Bartram, who in 1728 established the first botanical garden and later traveled throughout the known portions of the continent collecting plants. It was in Philadelphia, too, that David Rittenhouse, a clockmaker, subsequently built the first orrery, or model for explaining the planetary system.

Of course scientific inquiry was not restricted to Philadelphia. Paradoxically, Boston, the home of Puritanism, was not without its cognoscenti. We have seen that many

---

[15] However, the links between science and technology remained relatively weak. See Brooke Hindle, *The Pursuit of Science in Revolutionary America, 1735–1789* (Chapel Hill, 1956).

Figure 24 Portrait of Benjamin Franklin at the age of 54. Engraving by James McArdell after Benjamin Wilson. Benjamin Franklin Collection, Sterling Memorial Library, Yale University Library.

ministers accepted the new scientific revolution to keep their theology relevant, and some even engaged in scientific inquiry themselves. Increase Mather, in cooperation with Dr Zabdiel Boylston, experimented with inoculation after learning of its use in Africa from his slave Onesimus, persuading some inhabitants of Boston to adopt the practice during a smallpox epidemic in 1721.[16] In general New Englanders excelled in the more theoretical sciences. Thomas Robie identified the nature of a meteor. John Winthrop IV, the Harvard professor of mathematics and natural philosophy, worked on sunspots, the transit of Venus, the lunar eclipse, and Halley's comet.

---

[16] The experiment caused considerable controversy at the time, since most people believed that it would spread the disease. These fears subsided only when Boylston subsequently demonstrated that about 15 percent of the naturally infected died, compared with 2.4 percent of those inoculated.

All these individuals recognized the desirability of a forum in which to exchange their ideas. One such was of course the Royal Society in London, to which no fewer than 18 British Americans belonged during the colonial period. Colonials contributed substantially to the society's published transactions, and the establishment of a British North American post office in 1710 facilitated the dissemination of its ideas. Traveling across the Atlantic, however, was not feasible on a regular basis.

Accordingly, in 1727 Franklin and several others established the Junto Club in Philadelphia. This group, which helped John Bartram to continue his observations about the botanical nature of the North American continent, later expanded to become the American Philosophical Society. Elsewhere, several New Yorkers attempted to establish a similar project in 1748 with their Society for the Promotion of Useful Knowledge. Despite its title it was designed to complement the activities of the Royal Society, though its name exhibited that later American tendency to view all knowledge as potentially useful. In any event it failed to survive. So too did the American Philosophical Society. Before 1760 colonial science was not yet ready to stand on its own feet. Its practitioners remained essentially field workers for scientists in Europe, on whom they depended for the manufacture of accurate instruments and the publication of learned materials. The American Philosophical Society was re-established on a permanent basis only in 1768.

The fine arts meanwhile were in their infancy, with only a tiny leisured class to patronize aspiring artists. Although portraiture became increasingly popular during the eighteenth century as middle- and upper middle-class people commissioned portraits of themselves and their families, most of the work was done by amateur artists. Generally they were engravers or house painters who practiced portraiture to enhance their incomes. No painters developed the artistry and skill necessary for critical recognition among Europeans until after 1760. However, several artists emerged in the 1760s who were to win recognition at the highest level, notably John Singleton Copley, Benjamin West, and Charles Willson Peale. All had to travel to Europe to complete their training.

Classical music was also embryonic. During the seventeenth century the Puritans had been opposed to elaborate music and the use of musical instruments in church, which they considered to be relics of Catholicism within the church. Therefore people sang psalms entirely without musical accompaniment (and usually with no melody or harmony either). However, by the eighteenth century there was a movement to improve church music by teaching people how to sing by note. Organs began to appear in some Anglican churches early in the century, although no Congregationalist church allowed one before 1770. Upwardly mobile urban people began to patronize music and dancing schools, and planters hired music and dancing teachers for themselves and their children. Concerts began to be arranged in the principal towns, where there were sufficient violinists, cellists, flautists, and other instrumentalists to perform the works of composers such as Handel, Bach, and Vivaldi. The first formal concert of classical music took place in Boston, in 1731. By the 1750s New York had a regular series of subscription concerts. The performers were almost all amateurs, there being as yet no professional class of musicians.

The theater was a greater challenge. Until the 1700s going to a play was considered the equivalent of visiting a brothel and most colonies banned both forms of entertainment. Even in the eighteenth century many (especially in New England) considered theater immoral, but the colonial upper classes' growing aspirations for sophistication and refinement induced some desire to see the works of great dramatists performed. The first permanent theater was established in Williamsburg in 1716 when two dancers, Charles and Mary Stagg, obtained permission to erect a stage. Here they produced a number of plays for several years. Slowly other groups emerged, mostly of a private or amateur nature. The most popular productions were George Farquhar's *The Recruiting Officer* and Joseph Addison's *Cato*. By the 1730s all the major cities had hosted some kind of theater. Several theatrical groups toured the colonies in the late 1740s and early 1750s, by which time Shakespeare had become the most popular playwright. No play, however, had yet been written or performed by a colonial author.

6 POPULAR CULTURE

Buying books, attending college, joining learned societies, and going to classical concerts were activities reserved for those who aspired to be part of the colonial elite. Most colonists had neither the money nor the inclination for these activities. It was not that they lacked time for entertainment – there were only rare periods in a year when work could not be interrupted, and farmers had a great deal of time on their hands during the winter. However, their main types of entertainment were different – less "refined," but just as important to their sense of who they were.

Colonial British North Americans, like early modern people throughout the Western world, were sociable people, and their amusements mostly involved spending time with family and neighbors. There was little privacy. Family members spent much of their time together in a central room within their houses; neighbors often stopped by to share work and gossip. Socializing was routine. In the South, visitors stopped in and stayed to be entertained. Communal work activities like barn-raisings, corn-huskings, and quilting bees were opportunities for parties with food, drink, and other entertainment. Singing was popular and often accompanied by instruments such as the fiddle or the cittern, a stringed instrument resembling a mandolin or a banjo. When space allowed dancing was popular.

Despite the fact that most colonial people worked in or around their own houses, they had fairly frequent occasions for leaving home and socializing outside their neighborhoods as well. The most frequent opportunity for socializing was the weekly Sabbath. During the seventeenth century, dissenting Protestants had warned against treating Sundays as occasions for recreation – they were supposed to be devoted to family religious instruction, edifying sermons, and prayers. But even for the strictest seventeenth-century Puritans, Sundays offered a chance to socialize. And in the South, the visiting and chatting that took place before and after religious services sometimes seemed to be more important to the participants than the service itself.

In summer other occasions for social activity arose at markets, fairs, and meetings of the county court. In the South these three events were often combined. The courts gave planters a chance to discuss business and traders to exhibit their goods, while those wishing to see an attorney could do so at the same time. Inevitably such occasions also attracted traveling showmen. Bear-baiting and cock-fighting were common, drinking at the local tavern more so. Local groups of musicians invariably gathered, and those who wished to could dance. Some of the gentry might also arrange a horse race on which bystanders could bet.

Northern court meetings tended to be more decorous, though entertainments were customary at ceremonies like the installation of a governor or celebration of the king's birthday. Here again fringe activities would be organized so that those attending could combine business with pleasure.

Men had more opportunities to socialize than women. One major event for young men was the militia training day, which in some colonies took place every couple of months. By the eighteenth century the threat of Indian attack was no longer imminent in long-settled areas of the east coast, and militia training days involved only a few hours of drills, a few times a year. During the rest of the day young men partied and took part in athletic contests, devoting so little attention to their military drills that one observer in 1704 sarcastically referred to militia training in New England towns as the "Olympiack games." Election days were similarly occasions for men to gather and socialize, although since the men attending these events tended to be older and more established, they were not as rowdy.[17]

Socializing was of course an activity that took place across society, regardless of class. By the eighteenth century, though, even the most ordinary kinds of social activities were becoming demarcated by class lines. Taverns are a good example. By the eighteenth century virtually every community along the eastern seaboard had a tavern or an inn, usually run out of somebody's house. In towns and cities, taverns were more numerous. Of course all provided alcoholic beverages, a pleasure that was available on a daily basis, and most catered primarily to men. Provided consumption was not excessive, most men saw no contradiction between going to church in the morning and visiting the tavern at night. Taverns provided them with an opportunity to socialize, talk business, and increasingly discuss political issues after 1760. It was the *kind* of tavern that one frequented, and the kinds of entertainments offered there, that were now beginning to differentiate these men by class. Taverns aimed at artisans and laborers provided pugilistic contests and covert gaming. Those aimed at the upper classes provided newspapers, billiard tables, playing cards, and rooms for private meetings. Some upper-class men formed clubs that met regularly at such establishments, including the first Masonic lodges in Philadelphia in 1730 and Boston, Charleston, and Savannah shortly afterwards.[18]

There was at least one type of social occasion that served to reinforce people's common identity as members of a larger group: the celebration of holidays. When the Puritans abolished the celebration of Christmas and other saints' days and replaced them with occasional days of thanksgiving, they had engaged in a conscious attempt to

---

[17]   The description was offered by Sarah Kemble Knight, *The Journal of Madam Knight,* ed. Malcolm Frieberg (Boston, 1972), 20, quoted in Bruce Daniels, *Puritans at Play: Leisure and Recreation in Colonial New England* (New York, 1995), 98.

[18]   For the impact of taverns on colonial society, see especially David W. Conroy, *In Public Houses: Drink and the Revolution of Authority in Colonial Massachusetts* (Chapel Hill, 1995); Peter Thompson, *Rum Punch and Revolution: Taverngoing and Public Life in Eighteenth-Century Philadelphia* (Philadelphia, 1999); and Sharon Salinger, *Taverns and Drinking in Early America* (Baltimore, 2002). Salinger challenges an earlier view that taverns contributed to social leveling, showing that taverns in fact became increasingly differentiated by class during the eighteenth century. Upper-class men drank with other gentlemen, not with ordinary folks.

create a shared sense of membership in a biblically ordained, godly commonwealth. Thanks to their efforts, the celebration of saints' days never took hold in the New England colonies. However, after the Glorious Revolution a number of official royal holidays began to be celebrated throughout the British North American colonies. One of these was the king's birthday, which people everywhere commemorated by lighting bonfires, holding parades, shooting off fireworks and drinking toasts. Royal holidays were declared every time a new governor arrived to govern one of the provinces. By the 1730s, new holidays had been declared to celebrate the birthdays of the queen and the Prince of Wales.

Probably the most important of the new British holidays, especially in New England, was the annual celebration of Pope's Day on November 5. Pope's Day commemorated the failure of an event in 1605 known as the Gunpowder Plot, when Catholics led by Guy Fawkes had attempted to blow up Parliament. The anniversary of this event was marked by ceremonies and parades all over Britain, where it was called Guy Fawkes' Day. After the Glorious Revolution it came to be celebrated in many British North American towns and cities as well. Nowhere was Pope's Day embraced more enthusiastically than in the towns and cities of New England, where it became an occasion for demonstrating vociferously against Catholicism. Boston's celebrations were the most colorful. At the beginning of the day church leaders provided sermons denouncing Catholicism. Then artisans and laborers from all over the city organized parades in which they dressed up in costumes, built floats to carry effigies of the pope, the devil, and the deposed king James II (the "Catholic Stuart Pretender"), and paraded to the town common where they burned the effigies in a great bonfire. The celebration was lubricated with plenty of alcohol and by the 1750s came to involve contests between rival gangs from either end of town to see which could more effectively destroy the other's pope.[19]

Despite the disorder it produced, Pope's Day was widely approved by colonial officials. Like sending children to be educated in England or imitating the manners and clothing of the aristocracy, encouraging Pope's Day celebrations helped to reinforce loyalty to the British empire. Like the people who participated in the revivals of the Great Awakening, urban people who built floats and bonfires on Pope's Day learned that what they all shared was their commitment to the higher cause of defending Protestantism against the Catholic threat. All of these practices changed colonial aspirations and linked people emotionally to a larger entity, what they imagined as a Protestant British empire. It encouraged people to think of themselves as Britons, loyal subjects of a great empire, entitled to the respect and the rights that were due to them as Englishmen. Their future was bright, full of optimism that as Britons, they would continue to grow prosperous and powerful.

---

[19] For the argument that the adoption of these royal holidays helped to generate feelings of loyalty to the monarchy that were even stronger in the colonies than in Britain, see Brendan McConville, *The King's Three Faces*, ch. 2.

14

Slavery and the African American Experience, 1689–1760

1619	The first Africans arrive in Virginia.
1638	Slavery is first mentioned in the laws of Maryland.
1662	A Virginia law declares that children take the status of their mother.
1691	South Carolina passes an act for the better ordering of slaves.
1693	Spain offers to free any slave escaping to Florida who becomes a Catholic.
1699	Free African Americans are required to leave Virginia.
1705	Virginia institutes a slave code.
1712	Nine whites are killed by slaves in New York; 18 slaves are executed for allegedly conspiring to assist them.
1720	Slaves become the majority in South Carolina.
1723	Virginia passes an act to deal with slave conspiracies.
1730	A majority of Chesapeake African Americans are now American-born.
1732	South Carolina attempts to ban the import of slaves.
1735	Slavery is banned in Georgia.
1738	Florida acknowledges the freedom of all slaves who escape to Florida.
1739	The Stono Rebellion in South Carolina is put down.
1740	South Carolina revises its slave code.
1741	A slave conspiracy is suspected in New York; 30 slaves and four whites are executed.
1750	Slavery is permitted in Georgia.

Colonial America: A History to 1763, Fourth Edition. Richard Middleton and Anne Lombard.
© 2011 Richard Middleton and Anne Lombard. Published 2011 by Blackwell Publishing Ltd.

1 SLAVERY: AN EVOLVING INSTITUTION

T HE STORY OF African American slavery is one of the most important stories in the history of the United States. It has also been one of the most difficult to tell. North American slavery involved unspeakable violence and cruelty, along with endurance and heroic resistance. The slave trade from Africa to the Americas produced one of the greatest diasporas of all time, bringing about the forced relocation of between 9 and 12 million West and west-central Africans to the Americas. Because of slavery, an enormous population of Africans became part of colonial British American societies and collectively asserted a major influence on the development of colonial cultures and social institutions. In the North American colonies, one of every five settlers was of African origin.

In past generations, historians most often told the story of slavery from the point of view of Anglo-Americans. They emphasized the ways that Europeans perceived African people, focused on the things that white enslavers did to African people, or told the story of how a small group of Europeans fought to end slavery. The experiences of Africans themselves were virtually absent from the narrative except as slavery's victims. More recently historians have shifted their focus to include the points of view of enslaved Africans and African Americans themselves. While making clear that the experience of slavery was a terrible ordeal, historians pay more attention now to the ways in which Africans asserted themselves and became embedded within the fabric of British North American societies. This broader gaze has resulted in a new understanding of the ways that African Americans influenced colonial North American culture as a whole and resisted slavery whenever they could. Historians have now also recognized that the institution of slavery was not static, but evolving.

North American slavery changed considerably during the first century of its existence. During the earliest decades of colonial development, we have seen that enslaved people like Anthony Johnson could sometimes become free men, marry, own land, and even own servants or slaves of their own. Slavery as a social and legal institution permitted enough flexibility that some enslaved people could maneuver their way through the system and gain significant control over their own lives.

This institutional flexibility resulted in part from English settlers' lack of experience with slavery before the seventeenth century. The institution of slavery had not been recognized under English law since before the Norman Conquest, having been replaced by serfdom. Temporary servitude offered the closest legal analogy – and masters were expected to treat servants with the solicitude owed to a family member. Laws in the Chesapeake and New England during the early years thus allowed slaves to earn extra money, assert their rights in the courts, and even purchase their own freedom and acquire property. Some slaves were able to form patronage relationships with masters who gave them protection and helped them to improve their situations.[1]

Institutional flexibility also developed from the experiences and actions of the slaves themselves, experiences shaped by the demography of slavery during the earliest

---

[1] Dutch laws in New Netherland, too, allowed slaves to work for wages and eventually earn their freedom under some circumstances.

generations. Before 1680 most slaves brought to North America had already spent time living in the West Indies, in Brazil, or along the West African coast. These Africans were "Creoles," meaning they were already somewhat assimilated to European culture. As Creoles they had often learned the rules and understood how to maneuver within European societies.[2] In North America they lived side by side with white servants and freed persons of both races, and were able to form relationships with other servants, creating integrated communities. They often even married across racial lines. These were, as historian Ira Berlin has explained, "societies with slaves," meaning they included slaves but were not organized around slavery.

During the last two decades of the seventeenth century, the institution of slavery on the mainland began to change. By 1680, planters in the Chesapeake had a well-established staple crop economy based the production of tobacco for export to Europe. Over the next few decades planters in South Carolina would follow suit, developing a staple crop economy based on the production of rice (and later indigo), also for export. To produce these commodities, planters needed labor above and beyond what a family could provide. By now young English people were becoming reluctant to emigrate to the southern colonies, since their prospects would be better if they stayed in England or became servants in Pennsylvania or the Jerseys. Native Americans east of the Mississippi had proved unsuitable for work in a plantation setting. That left Anglo-American planters in South Carolina, Maryland, and Virginia looking elsewhere for labor.

Meanwhile, thanks to the large numbers of slaves now being shipped from West Africa to Barbados, Jamaica, and the Leeward Islands, supplies of enslaved Africans were becoming more plentiful. The Atlantic slave trade had already reached substantial numbers between 1600 and 1700, with approximately 1.3 million Africans being shipped to the Spanish, Portuguese, English, Dutch, and French colonies. After 1700, when British carriers came to dominate the trade, the slave trade ballooned in size. Between 1700 and 1800, British merchants alone transported over three million slaves from Africa to the Americas, while carriers of other nationalities (primarily French, Dutch, Portuguese, and Spanish) transported an additional three million or more. The growing volume of transatlantic shipments made African slave traders the obvious suppliers of labor for plantations in the mainland colonies. Slavers transported approximately 350,000 slaves to British North America during the eighteenth century, while carrying about four times that number to the British West Indies.

As Africans through their sheer numbers became a more obvious presence in settler societies, the relationship between African and European populations was altered. Between 1690 and 1750 the total black population in the mainland British North American colonies grew dramatically from about 10,000 to about 240,000. In 1680 Virginia had about 3,000 slaves and 50,000 whites; by 1760 the number of slaves had risen to 120,000, making up 40 percent of the population. South Carolina experienced an even more dramatic change in its demographic structure. In 1690 there were only 1,500 African slaves in the colony; by 1730 the colony had 10,000 whites but 20,000 African Americans and appeared to one observer "more like a Negro country than a

---

[2] For information about Creoles, see Ira Berlin, "From Creole to African: Atlantic Creoles and the Origins of African American Society in Mainland North America," *William and Mary Quarterly*, 53 (1996), 251–88, and *Many Thousands Gone: The First Two Centuries of Slavery in North America* (Cambridge, Mass., 1998).

country settled by white people." The composition of the population was coming to resemble that of the British West Indies, where the total black population by 1760 had reached about 260,000, comprising about 86 percent of the population.[3]

As the total number of Africans in the southern population increased, their demographic origins changed as well. After 1700, responding to the increased demand, slave-traders began to transport captives directly from West Africa to North American ports instead of going first to the West Indies.[4] The Africans who arrived during the eighteenth century thus had no previous experience with Europeans. To the European settlers, these new arrivals seemed more foreign and less culturally familiar than their predecessors. The newcomers practiced traditional African religions, wore traditional hairstyles, filed their teeth, and wore strange clothing. Their bodies and faces bore tattoos or scars from initiation rituals that European settlers did not understand. They spoke no English. To the settlers, these practices marked the newcomers as heathens, profoundly different from themselves and from their white servants.[5]

Much as British West Indian planters had done in the middle of the seventeenth century, British North American planters now began to treat these new arrivals as outsiders rather than like their other servants. They gave the newcomers less responsibility and kept them at arm's length. Instead of housing them with the family, where they could form personal relationships with their masters, they placed slaves in separate, poorly constructed shacks. Slaves became more isolated from poor whites. Legal restrictions on slaves were tightened, and their opportunities to maneuver through the system narrowed. British North American planter societies had at last become "slave societies," societies organized around the control of slaves.

Historians have for many years debated the question of whether racism preceded slavery, or was created by it. Some stress that Europeans had long associated blackness with sin, evil, and pollution, even before the Atlantic slave trade began. The idea that Africans had been enslaved as a result of Noah's curse upon his son Ham was widely repeated. Such racist beliefs, these historians argue, predisposed the English to embrace African slavery when English servants became less available.[6] Other historians, however, point to evidence suggesting that racial ideas were only one component of sixteenth- and seventeenth-century Europeans' thinking about Africans. Englishmen before the late 1600s were more conscious of differences based upon rank, lineage, and religion than they were of physical differences such as skin color or facial structure. Only in the eighteenth century did European scientists begin to develop theories suggesting that people should be classified according to skin color and other physical traits, and that

---

[3] Figures are from Richard R. Johnson, "Growth and Mastery: British North America, 1690–1748," 287, and Richard B. Sheridan, "The Formation of Caribbean Plantation Society, 1689–1748," 400, both in *The Oxford History of the British Empire*, Vol. 2: *The Eighteenth Century*, ed. P. J. Marshall (New York, 1998).

[4] Susan Westbury, "Slaves of Colonial Virginia: Where They Came From," *William and Mary Quarterly*, 42 (1985), 228–37.

[5] The arguments made in this section are primarily drawn from Ira Berlin, *Many Thousands Gone*.

[6] For the emphasis on early English racism towards Africans, see Winthrop Jordan, *White Over Black: American Attitudes toward the Negro, 1550–1812* (Chapel Hill, 1968), and Alden T. Vaughan and Virginia Mason Vaughan, "Before *Othello*: Elizabethan Representations of Sub-Saharan Africans," *William and Mary Quarterly*, 54 (1997), 19–44.

groups of people classified in this way possessed inherently different qualities of moral character and intelligence.[7]

The development of new racial ideologies in the late seventeenth and eighteenth centuries went hand in hand with legal changes that increasingly separated the experiences of African slaves from those of white servants or farmers. Maryland's first slave legislation, passed in 1664, laid down that all "Negroes or other slaves hereafter imported into the province shall serve" for life, as should their children. A particular focus of these new laws, as we saw in Chapter 12, was to prevent interracial unions. Thus, Maryland's 1664 legislation provided that any white woman so forgetful of her status as to marry a slave would have to serve the master of her husband until his death, and her offspring would also be slaves. When Virginia recognized slavery in 1662, its legislature passed an act stating that the child of any Englishman born to a slave mother would take slave status, effectively discouraging white men from marrying enslaved African women. A 1691 act went further, explicitly banning interracial marriages. Other laws barred slaves from marrying at all, and otherwise closed old avenues to freedom and upward mobility. In an act passed in 1668, the Virginia legislature declared that baptism did not change the status of slaves. In 1670 the legislature prohibited free African Americans from purchasing "Christian servants," meaning whites, on the assumption that Africans could never be Christian and certainly could not rule over whites. Finally, in 1705 the Virginia House of Burgesses passed a comprehensive slave code that effectively reduced all African Americans, unless already free, to perpetual slavery. Step by step, it had created a system of laws designed to create social distance between blacks and whites.

Legal codes in South Carolina developed along the same lines. Once rice became the basis for a plantation economy and slave imports began to increase, the legislature took action to separate blacks and whites. Since South Carolina had never had as many white indentured servants or poor whites as the Chesapeake, there was less concern about interracial alliances between poor whites and enslaved blacks. But here too the legislature prohibited servants and slaves from trading with one another, barred white women from having sexual relations with black men, and prohibited slave marriages. As the slave population grew larger, more comprehensive slave codes were put into place.

A major motivation for the slave codes was fear, since there was now a real possibility that this larger, more culturally foreign population of enslaved Africans would retaliate against their white masters. In 1723 the Virginian authorities introduced a bill for the "More effectual punishing Conspiracies and Insurrections." In the future any slave guilty of conspiracy was to suffer death. Those committing perjury were to be nailed by the ear, whipped, and then have that ear cut off. Meetings of slaves were also banned, except when working or attending divine service with their masters, and no African American was to be freed "except for some meritorious services ... allowed by the Governor and Council." This clause was inserted solely to reward informers who betrayed serious conspiracies. A similar tightening of the laws occurred elsewhere.

---

[7] For the emphasis on the evolution of racial ideologies in the eighteenth century, see David Brion Davis, *The Problem of Slavery in Western Culture* (Ithaca, 1975); Anthony L. Barker, *The African Link: British Attitudes to the Negro in the Era of the Atlantic Slave Trade, 1550–1807* (London, 1978), and Emily C. Bartels, "*Othello* and Africa: Postcolonialism Reconsidered," *William and Mary Quarterly*, 54 (1997), 45–64.

Pennsylvania, hardly a hotbed of slave uprisings, provided that if more than four African Americans met together without permission they were to be whipped. In New York, after 1712 when a group of slaves killed nine whites who were trying to extinguish a fire, the assembly prohibited more than three slaves from congregating together without the consent of their owner.

These developing legal rules succeeded in creating a system that defined Africans as outside the bounds of civil society. A 1692 Virginia law explicitly barred slaves accused of committing capital crimes from asserting a right to trial by jury, or a right to appeal a conviction. South Carolina created special courts that used summary processes to try slaves accused of crimes. Even Pennsylvania, despite its reputation for humaneness, provided for African slaves to be tried not by a full jury but by two justices and six "of the most substantial freeholders." Civil rights that white men were coming to take for granted were explicitly denied to blacks, as laws were passed to prohibit even free blacks from possessing arms, from assembling together in large gatherings, and from voting. Slaves were prohibited from moving freely on public roads without authorization from their masters, and from conducting ceremonies or rituals in secret. Legal punishments that an eighteenth-century Anglo-American public would no longer have tolerated if imposed on whites were now imposed only on blacks, in ways that accentuated their degraded legal status. A 1691 South Carolina law provided that any African or Native American slaves showing violence to a white person for a second time were to have their noses slit and their faces burned. In Virginia after 1705, a slave who struck a white man would receive 39 lashes. In South Carolina after 1714, the same behavior was a capital crime. South Carolina law explicitly provided that slaves could be castrated or burned alive for certain crimes.

Perhaps most oppressive for enslaved people were the ways in which the legal system removed them from its protection and left them under the virtually unchecked control of their owners. In place of a system of discipline organized by the patriarchal family, which was coercive but limited by the moral oversight of neighbors and friends, the slave codes made masters legally immune from prosecution for most acts of violence towards their slaves short of premeditated murder. A 1669 Virginia law, for example, provided that a slave-owner or overseer who killed a slave in the course of a beating was to suffer no penalty, since it could never be presumed that a man would destroy his own property except for good reason. Masters became free to use extraordinary brutality towards slaves without interference from neighbors or courts. Slaves who resisted their masters' authority could be flogged, tortured, humiliated, permanently removed from their families – all with public sanction. Robert "King" Carter, the most powerful planter in Virginia, was in 1708 granted official permission to cut off the toes of two of his female slaves in order to punish them for persistent disobedience. South Carolina planters not uncommonly cut slaves' hamstrings or amputated one of their feet as punishment for running away. Obviously slaves who had been maimed in these ways were less valuable to their owners, but the slaveholders' violence did have a purpose (perverse as it was). Public demonstrations of sadistic violence towards disobedient slaves were essentially terror tactics that enabled owners to control their other workers through intimidation. The legal system tacitly endorsed this kind of privately imposed terror by refusing to stop it.

The new codes not only sanctioned unprecedented violence by masters; they highlighted the centrality of race as the characteristic that determined status. They defined slavery not only as a lifetime status, but also as an inherited one, invariably passed on to one's children. They closed off the possibility for slaves to achieve freedom for themselves or their children by being baptized or marrying a free person. They made it more difficult for a slave to purchase his or her freedom. The effect of these rules in combination was to destroy the old system whereby it was relatively common for slaves to earn their freedom, and replaced it with a system in which virtually all blacks could be assumed to be slaves. Meanwhile, local colonial governments enlisted the help of poor whites in enforcing the new system of discipline over slaves by creating all-white militias to catch runaways and punish disobedient slaves. The effect of the militias was to define white men as the enforcers of law and blacks as lawbreakers. They created a system of slavery more clearly based on race than any previous one, and created a racial divide in British North American societies that permanently relegated Africans and their descendents to a degraded status.[8]

2 SLAVES' EXPERIENCES

Slavery imposed extraordinary constraints on the lives of Africans in British North America. Yet slave codes and the relations of power that they supported were not the only things that defined the scope of experience for enslaved Africans. Collectively, they not only survived but transcended the obstacles they faced, eventually forging African American communities and cultures that coexisted alongside and intersected with the cultures of European American settlers. That process of cultural creation and adaptation has continued to make vital contributions to American collective life since it began in the eighteenth century. To understand it, we must look not only at the institution of slavery, but at the experiences of slaves.[9]

The ordeal of a newly enslaved person began, of course, in Africa. Most slaves transported to the British North American colonies in the eighteenth century came from the Slave Coast, a region of West Africa that now comprises the states of Benin, Nigeria, Cameroun, Gabon, the Republic of the Congo, and Angola. Smaller numbers

---

[8] Berlin, *Many Thousands Gone*.

[9] There was once considerable debate among historians over the humaneness of slavery. Ulrich B. Philips, *American Negro Slavery* (New York, 1929), argued that slavery was essentially benign, as did Margaret Mitchell in her novel Gone *with the Wind* (New York, 1936). Both were southerners, part of a movement of southern writers who sought to rehabilitate the reputation of the antebellum South. Their views of slavery's humaneness have now been thoroughly repudiated. In *The Peculiar Institution: Slavery in the Ante-Bellum South* (New York, 1956) Kenneth M. Stampp, writing after the first Supreme Court judgments against segregation, argued that the slaves and their masters were in a mutually antagonistic relationship, a view supported since 1956 by numerous other writers. One problem with this approach has been that the slaves themselves were portrayed merely as slavery's victims rather than as participants in shaping American history. More recently the trend has been to suggest that the African Americans adapted as best they could to the realities of slavery, developing their own culture and lifestyle and influencing the societies they shared with whites. See for example Allan Kulikoff, *Tobacco and Slaves: The Development of Southern Cultures in the Chesapeake, 1680–1800* (Chapel Hill, 1986), as well as works by Ira Berlin, Philip Morgan, and numerous other historians cited in this chapter. For a cautionary note on this approach, see Jean Butenhoff Lee, "The Problem of Slave Community in the Eighteenth-Century Chesapeake," *William and Mary Quarterly,* 43 (1986), 333–61.

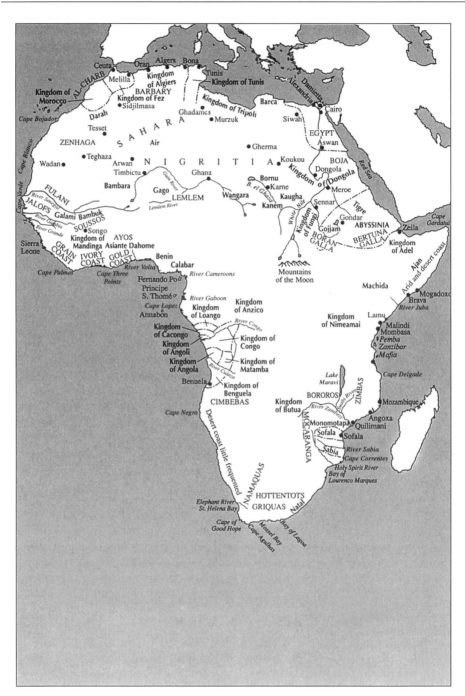

Map 12   Africa as known to Europeans in the mid eighteenth century. Based on D'Anville's map of 1749, one of the best and most accurate maps of Africa made before the era of modern European exploration.

originated in Senegal, Guinea, Sierra Leone, Liberia, the Ivory Coast, and Ghana. People from these regions identified with a wide variety of ethnic and political groups, including the Dahomey, Mali, Songhay, Asante, Yoruba, Benin, Igbo, Luango, Kongo, and Luba, among others. Most captives belonged to inland nations that were at war with the coastal African nations that actually ran the slave trade. A small number of slaves came from East Africa and Madagascar, where Arab traders were active.

The nightmare of slavery began with capture, followed by a forced march to the coast, invariably as part of a group of captives tied together with ropes around hands and necks. The journey often lasted weeks or even months. On arrival, captives were sold to European traders, who, after branding their purchases, put them on board a vessel for the Americas. Revolts on board slave ships were very common, so traders adopted procedures designed to intimidate the captives and deter collective uprisings. Families were routinely sold apart, except for nursing infants who were left with their mothers. The captives were stripped and shaved to prevent disease, a degrading and deperso- nalizing procedure, and separated into all-male or all-female groups for the duration of the voyage. The journey across the Atlantic was extraordinarily traumatic. Most captives had never seen the sea, and its strangeness increased their desperation. Some believed that their European captors were cannibals who had eaten their own people before turning to Africans. Many committed suicide even before the ships sailed. During the voyage, slaves were kept chained below deck on platforms, each having a space 18 inches across and six feet deep to lie on. The most a slave could do was sit, for the height of the deck above was usually about four and a half feet. Toilet facilities were at best an open tub.[10]

In good weather the slaves might be taken on deck for exercise to the beat of a drum or cat-o'-nine-tails. In bad weather, or if the crew were fearful of being overpowered, the slaves were kept chained permanently below deck in conditions whose horror can only be imagined. One doctor commented about his ship, "The floor of their rooms was so covered with the blood and mucus, which had proceeded from them in consequence of the flux, that it resembled a slaughterhouse." The "flux" was usually dysentery, which was quick to take hold. In such circumstances it was surprising that so many slaves survived the voyage. Certainly slave-traders expected a substantial proportion of their cargo to perish before arrival. Modern estimates suggest that on average between 12 and 18 percent died, though individual voyages would vary, depending on the weather, length of voyage, and care of the crew. Diseased slaves were often thrown overboard. But whatever the casualty rate, a deep melancholy afflicted every slave ship, each voyage being punctuated by incessant weeping, hysteria, refusal to eat, and attempted suicide.

Male slaves generally outnumbered females on these slaving voyages. Part of the reason for this gender imbalance was slaveholders' preferences for strong young males. On the other hand European slave-traders also bought considerable numbers of

---

[10]   The human experience of the Atlantic slave trade is explored in Stephanie Smallwood, *Saltwater Slavery: A Middle Passage from Africa to the American Diaspora* (Cambridge, Mass., 2007) and Marcus Rediker, *The Slave Ship: A Human History* (New York, 2007).

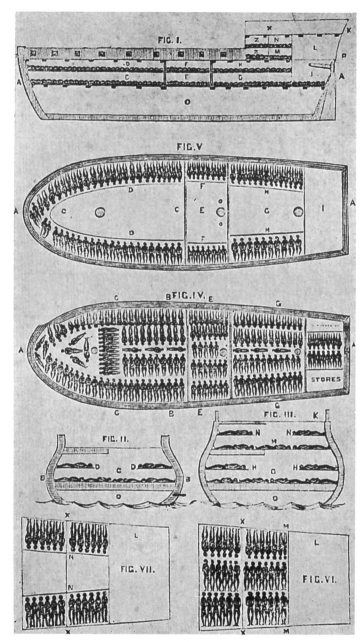

Figure 25   Plan of slave ship *The Brookes*. From Elizabeth Donnan, ed., *Documents Illustrative of the History of the Slave Trade to America* (Washington, DC, 1930–1935), Vol. 2. The sketch was originally drawn by opponents of the slave trade and may exaggerate the overcrowding on the ship.

women and children, in part because they had to take the individuals that African slave-traders supplied. The result was a gender imbalance in the slave population of approximately two males to every female – considerably closer to balance than the European servant population in the early years.[11]

On arrival at their final destination, the slaves were put up for sale, either individually or as a group. Though mothers and nursing infants were customarily kept together, no regard was otherwise paid to the relationship of one slave to another. The purchasers were concerned mainly with the health of the new arrivals, though there is some evidence that planters from South Carolina preferred individuals from Senegal, Gambia, and Sierra Leone because they were familiar with rice cultivation. Virginia and Maryland planters, on the other hand, had few preferences regarding the origin of their slaves. In any case, the planters often had to take what they were offered, which generally meant purchasing slaves from Angola and the Congo.

Historians once assumed that since African cultures and language groups are so diverse, the slaves on slave ships had nothing in common. Newer findings suggest that slaves tended to be shipped together from the same region, so in some cases slaves traveling together on the same ship spoke similar languages or even knew one another. If so, this could be a helpful source of support. Whether they were shipped with people from their own communities or with total strangers, newly captured slaves were forced very quickly to figure out whom they could trust. Instead of thinking of themselves as members of particular villages or kingdoms, captives might begin to see their fellow passengers as comrades to whom they were bound by their shared misfortune, rather than as foes. It was the first step in defining a new identity that would enable them to survive in the New World.[12]

Accurate numbers are difficult to establish, but it is thought that around 55,000 Africans were shipped to the Chesapeake area in the period 1700–40, 50,000 of them directly from Africa. South Carolina imported approximately 40,000 slaves during the same period. Thereafter imports into the Chesapeake began to decline, with fewer than 1,000 arriving annually. In contrast, South Carolina continued to buy at least 2,000 Africans a year until the conflict with Britain made the trade more difficult. Even then the trade continued, if at a reduced level.[13]

Having arrived in North America, a slave was sold once again to a colonial buyer, usually the owner of a plantation. From this point forwards his or her life would be dominated by one activity: labor. Since the prime economic activity of the South was the production of cash crops, most adult male and female slaves were employed in

---

[11] See David Eltis, *The Rise of African Slavery in the Americas* (New York, 2000); G. Ugo Nwokeji, "African Conceptions of Gender and the Slave Traffic," *William and Mary Quarterly*, 58 (2001), 47–67.

[12] Historians who emphasize the shared ethnic identities of slaves in the Americas include John Thornton, *Africa and Africans in the Making of the Atlantic World, 1400–1800*, 2nd edn (Cambridge, 1998), Michael Gomez, *Exchanging our Country Marks: The Transformation of African Identities in the Colonial and Antebellum South* (Chapel Hill, 1998), and Gwendolyn Midlo Hall, *Slavery and African Ethnicities in the Americas: Restoring the Links* (Chapel Hill, 2007). For an emphasis on change and fluidity in the identities of Africans once they were enslaved, see Robin Law, "Ethnicity and the Slave Trade: 'Lucumi' and 'Nago' as Ethnonyms in West Africa," *History in Africa*, 24 (1997), 205–19.

[13] According to Philip D. Morgan, *Slave Counterpoint*, 59, during the eighteenth century, Virginia imported a total of 77,650 African slaves and South Carolina 110,900.

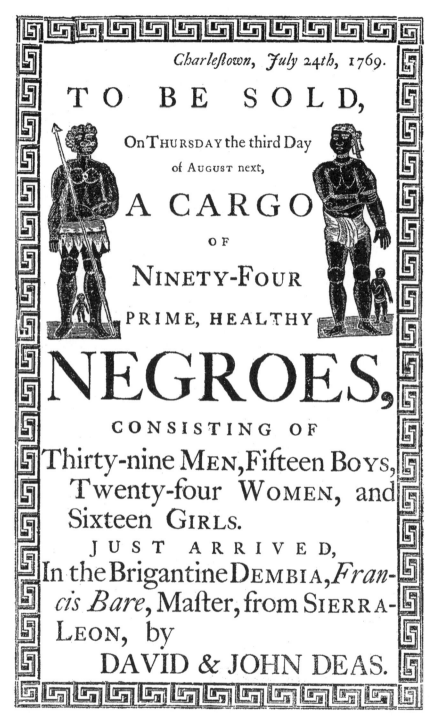

Figure 26   Advertisement for a sale of slaves, Charlestown, July 24, 1769. From *William and Mary Quarterly*, 53 (1996), 141. Courtesy American Antiquarian Society.

DOCUMENT 20

A slave market, circa 1755, reprinted in Karen Ordahl Kupperman, ed., *Major Problems in American Colonial History: Documents and Essays* (Lexington, Mass., 1993), 454

Questions to consider: *How might the experiences described here affect a recently enslaved person's sense of himself or herself? How might they affect his or her perceptions of the Europeans who participated in the slave markets?*

We were not many days in the merchant's custody, before we were sold after their usual manner, which is this: On a signal given (as the beat of a drum), the buyers rush at once into the yard where the slaves are confined, and make their choice of that parcel they like best. The noise and clamor with which this is attended, and the eagerness visible in the countenances of the buyers, serve not a little to increase the apprehension of terrified Africans, who may well be supposed to consider them as the ministers of that destruction to which they think themselves devoted. In this manner, without scruple, are relations and friends separated, most of them never to see each other again. I remember, in the vessel in which I was brought over, in the men's apartment, there were several brothers, who, in the sale, were sold in different lots; and it was very moving on this occasion, to see and hear their cries at parting. O, ye nominal Christians! might not an African ask you – learned you this from your God, who says unto you, Do unto all men as you would men should do unto you? Is it not enough that we are torn from our country and friends, to toil for your luxury and lust of gain? Must every tender feeling be likewise sacrificed to your avarice?

fieldwork, organized either in gangs or by individual tasks. The employment of one system as opposed to the other could make a great deal of difference to an enslaved person's daily routine, and to the amount of autonomy that he or she could assert.

Masters in the Chesapeake generally worked their slaves in gangs where they could be watched, either by the masters themselves or by white overseers. Such supervision was necessary with tobacco, it was said, since each plant had to be carefully tended throughout the season. This system had its disadvantages. The pace tended to be that of the slowest member, and the slaves had less incentive to work diligently. Whenever the overseer's eye was turned, furtive secession from labor invariably occurred. As one owner commented, the slaves "work hard and seem diligent, while they think anybody is taking notice of them, but when their masters' and mistresses' backs are turned, they are idle and neglect their business."

A lack of commitment was hardly surprising, since the cultivation of cash crops was both tedious and onerous. Tobacco, for instance, required much stooping, especially when the seedlings were being transplanted in the spring, since each plant had to be placed in a small mound of earth at the rate of 350 a day. Not surprisingly, it was at this

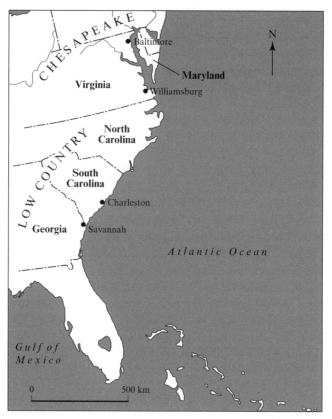

Map 13   Major British North American slaveholding regions: the Chesapeake (Virginia and Maryland) and the low country (South Carolina and Georgia).

time that slaves in the Chesapeake were most likely to run away. Next came a period of constant hoeing to control weeds, interspersed with inspections of each plant to destroy hornworms and caterpillars. In addition, the heads and suckers of each plant had to be removed to encourage growth in a few selected leaves only. These labors continued until the fall when it was time to harvest the crop, after which the leaves had to be dried and have their stalks removed before being packed into large barrels, called hogsheads, for export. The whole process, from germinating the seeds in February to the packing of the barrels in November, took about nine months of unremitting labor.

Slaves in South Carolina generally were able to avoid gang labor since planters here preferred the task system. The South Carolina low country was unhealthy, so planters lived in their mansions in Charleston if they could and left their plantations under the management of white overseers or stewards, assisted by trusted black foremen or drivers. Groups of slaves were assigned particular tasks, such as clearing ditches or weeding rice fields, so that their completion of those tasks could be readily monitored without the need for constant supervision. The task system in turn provided an incentive for each slave to complete the assignment; once the day's tasks were completed, the remaining hours in the day belonged to the slave.

Rice was even more onerous and physically demanding to grow than tobacco. At new plantations the swampy land first had to be cleared after which ditches and banks were constructed to control the flow of water into and out of the fields. Reservoirs also had to be built to supply water at certain times of the season. Only around April could the sowing of the seed begin, which was done in the African manner by making a small hole with the heel before covering the seed with a flick of the toes. For the next three months the fields had to be constantly hoed, to control the weeds which grew prolifically in such a wet and warm environment. It was at this time that many masters offered their slaves additional food and even rum to keep them at their work. The intensity of labor eased a little in August when the fields were flooded a second time, which helped control the weeds, though some owners used the intermission to divert their workers to the production of indigo. Finally, from mid-September the harvesting and processing of the crop began. The plants first had to be cut and dried after which threshing and winnowing were necessary to separate the grains. Then came the worst part, the removing of the inner film, which, until the 1760s, had to be done by hand with a mortar and pestle. This process began in late November and could take weeks or even months to complete, producing arms that constantly ached and hands that were covered with calluses.

Indigo, the other major cash crop grown in South Carolina and later in Georgia, was another entity that required constant attention by the workforce. Apart from hoeing, it too was subject to the hazard of caterpillars and grasshoppers, which had to be plucked by hand to prevent the crop from being destroyed. The plants were usually cut twice, first in July and again in late August. Production of the dye began immediately after cutting to avoid a loss of quality. First the cuttings were steeped in a fermentation vat for 12–15 hours. Next the contents were removed to a second container where the liquid was constantly stirred to oxidize it before being transferred to a third vessel in which lime was added to precipitate the blue sediment which was the object of the exercise. This was then strained through muslin bags, dried, and cut into cakes for dispatch (see Figure 18). For the slaves none of this work was particularly pleasant since the process created a foul stench which attracted flies. Mercifully the production season was considerably shorter than that for tobacco and rice.

Slaves' work routines become more varied and somewhat less onerous with time, thanks to the introduction of technological improvements towards the end of the colonial era. In Virginia and Maryland, the shift to wheat production created more opportunities for workers to develop skills as mowers, threshers, and cradlers. Plows and horse-drawn carts began to be used more widely, which made the preparation of the ground and harvesting marginally easier. In South Carolina and Georgia some rice planters invested in threshing machines and pounding mills driven by draft animals, which spared workers the most debilitating part of the production process. Also beneficial to slaves in the lower South was the adoption after 1760 of tidal power to water the crops, which allowed the fields to be flooded more frequently, dramatically reducing the growth of weeds and the need for constant hoeing. There is evidence that some enslaved people developed real skills and indeed took considerable pride in certain types of agricultural work. Indigo production in particular was considered an art.

For most plantation slaves, though, work requirements were incessant and exhausting. The working day began at dawn and continued until noon when slaves had a break for lunch, which usually consisted of hominy or hoe cakes, though many owners added some bacon or ham a couple of times a week. Work was then resumed until either the assignment was completed or sunset approached. Some colonies attempted to regulate the working day. In South Carolina the slave code of 1740 stated that slaves were not to work more than 15 hours in the spring and summer, and no more than 14 hours during the rest of the year. However, no machinery existed for enforcing these regulations.[14]

When their tasks were done, the slaves had control over the rest of their time. Such control did not, however, translate into being at leisure. Most mainland British American plantation owners expected their slaves to feed themselves, at least partly, by growing corn and vegetables and by raising hogs and chickens. Most mainland slaves therefore had gardens, which seem to have been tilled on a family basis.[15] These plots were an activity which could bring pride to the workforce as each family vied to produce the largest squash and corn. Archaeological evidence reveals that slaves supplemented their diet with meat from wild animals, notably opossum, raccoon, turtle, deer, squirrel, duck, and rabbit. Additional protein was also obtained from fish in nearby streams and rivers.

Raising their own food gave some slaves in the South a degree of economic autonomy. The most popular entrepreneurial activity among slaves was the raising of livestock, and most families kept a few chickens or hogs. Especially in South Carolina, where the task system gave slaves more time for such pursuits, enterprising slaves took their surplus to the local market or bartered with the neighboring community. Indeed, many plantation owners found they could not compete with their own labor force for the supply of fowl and bought from them instead. Other slaves used their spare time to set traps and go hunting, subsequently selling their catches to the white population. Profits could be used to acquire tools, cooking utensils, furniture, and occasionally horses, though slaves had no legal rights to the property they might possess.

In addition to raising their own food, slaves were also responsible on many plantations for the upkeep of their housing. When not gardening, therefore, they worked on their homes. As the eighteenth century progressed, slave quarters appeared like small villages on the larger plantations, comprising a series of one- or two-roomed huts. Skilled carpenters from within the slave population usually built these structures. In South Carolina, as in the West Indies, housing was often similar to that found in West Africa, comprising an earthfast timber frame with wattle-and-daub sides under a gable roof covered with thatch. Chimneys were usually made of sticks covered in clay (see Figure 27). In the Chesapeake, on the other hand, slave cabins resembled the frontier cabins of European settlers. One distinctive feature of slave housing in the Chesapeake was the provision of a root cellar for storing garden produce and other possessions. In the lower South, lofts, not cellars, seem to have been more common, because of the swampy ground. However, owners invested little in the construction of slave quarters, so dirt had to suffice for floors instead of sawed boards, and shutters were used for windows in lieu of glass.

Like white females, African American women were responsible for domestic chores, notably gardening, cooking, and making clothes. The difference was that enslaved

---

[14] In *Slave Counterpoint*, Philip Morgan extensively explores the ways in which work routines in rice, tobacco, indigo, and wheat production shaped the lives of slaves in the different regions of the South.

[15] Gardens were not usually a feature of slave life in the West Indies, since slaves on sugar plantations were expected to devote all of their labor to sugar production.

Figure 27 "View of Mulberry, House and Street, 1805," by Thomas Coram. This drawing
depicts the slave quarters on the Mulberry plantation in South Carolina. Gibbes
Museum of Art/Carolina Art Association Collection Charleston.

women were expected to spend the vast majority of their time doing fieldwork rather
than domestic work. This expectation was so widespread that in Virginia it was
institutionalized in the tax code; white women were exempt from taxes because they
spent their time working in the household, but black women were taxed (like men)
because they spent their days producing tobacco. The result was that enslaved African
American women had less time or resources for the kinds of productive domestic work
that raised the living standards of white settler families.[16] Slaves' living standards
remained impoverished as a result. Straw often had to suffice for bedding, and garments
were usually made from cloth supplied by the owners. The most common material was
Osnaburg, a coarse drab linen, though this could be brightened using vegetable dyes.
As to footwear, most slaves went barefoot or wore sandals fashioned out of wood
or leather.

Although most slaves lived and worked on plantations, a small number lived in urban
areas in the South. Here they usually worked as domestic servants in the households of
rich planters. Some of these slaves had the chance to acquire skills, since urban masters

---

[16] The experiences of enslaved women in British North America were initially obscured both from American
women's history and from the history of American slavery, though more recently historians have sought to
bring their experiences to light. Scholarship on enslaved women in the colonial period includes Jacqueline
Jones, "Race, Sex, and Self-Evident Truths: The Status of Slave Women during the Era of the American
Revolution," in Ronald Hoffman and Peter J. Albert, eds, *Women in the Age of the American Revolution*
(Charlottesville, 1989), 293–337; Kathleen Brown, *Good Wives, Nasty Wenches, and Anxious Patriarchs:
Gender, Race, and Power in Colonial Virginia* (Chapel Hill: 1996); David Barry Gaspar and Darlene Clark
Hine, eds, *More than Chattel: Black Women and Slavery in the Americas* (Bloomington, 1996); and Jennifer
Morgan, *Laboring Women: Reproduction and Gender in New World Slavery* (Philadelphia, 2004).

were often flexible in how their slaves were employed. In Charleston and Savannah owners on occasion allowed their slaves to hire themselves out, provided they returned at the specified time with an agreed sum of money. Such privileged slaves could move about with considerable freedom, keeping their own wages and even living on their own. Sometimes they could even form families, acquire consumer goods, and establish businesses that catered to other people of African descent. With the opportunities available to them in an urban consumer economy, they developed a different cultural style than plantation slaves. For example, many urban slaves, both male and female, wore fashionable European clothing as a way of expressing their individuality, despite attempts by the South Carolina and Georgia legislatures to prohibit them from wearing fancy dress.

Slaves in the North experienced a third variation of life in slavery, one with its own freedoms but also considerable constraints. Slaves in the northern colonies were far less numerous than in the South. Still, slavery was expanding here too as indentured servitude began its gradual eighteenth-century decline. By 1770, slaves in New York City made up about 14 percent of the population, and they were present in other northern cities as well. Slaves were most commonly employed as household servants and general laborers, especially in the maritime industries. Some were used on the larger cereal farms of Pennsylvania, New Jersey, and the Hudson and Connecticut river valleys, while others became skilled craftsmen. Some northern societies (especially in New England) continued to be "societies with slaves," rather than "slave societies," with slaves typically being incorporated into work routines that were shared by white workers. The main difference between the working roles of enslaved blacks and indentured whites was that female slaves were required to do fieldwork and white female servants almost never were. As in the South, the difference in work roles quickly became a marker of black women's degraded status relative to whites.

Although enslaved northern men often enjoyed considerable autonomy because of their work, in some ways their conditions were becoming as onerous as those in the South, with additional problems. Newly imported Africans became ill and died at a disproportionate rate in cold northern climates. Northern blacks were no less ostracized by whites than in the South but were more likely to be isolated from other blacks. Northern owners also discouraged their slaves from forming family relationships. In this respect, their lives were far lonelier and more alienating that those of slaves in the South.

3 THE AFRICAN AMERICAN FAMILY

African American family life in the southern colonies took years to develop, for the same reasons as inhibited the growth of white southern family life in the seventeenth century. Like Europeans, African Americans had to undergo a seasoning process as they adjusted to their new environment. Almost without exception the slaves were debilitated by the rigors of their passage, which included not just the sea crossing but also the journey along the coast. They then had to face the perils of smallpox and respiratory diseases like pleurisy, so that about 25 percent of those who survived the passage perished in the first year. This high mortality would have cut short many potential relationships. Disease, poor diet, and the physical and psychological trauma of the passage also affected the fertility of many African women.

Another inhibition to family life was the imbalance in gender ratios. Two out of every three arriving slaves were males. Also, most slaves imported before 1720 were scattered on isolated plantations and found themselves living either on their own or in predominantly male groups. This situation could change only if more women and girls were imported or if the existing population began to reproduce itself. In New England and the middle colonies the situation was even worse than in the South, because the number of African slaves was small and they were widely dispersed. For these reasons, the African American population failed to reproduce itself in the early decades. Just as in the British West Indies, deaths of Africans outnumbered births, and the population grew only because of the constant inflow of new slave imports.

As the eighteenth century progressed, however, this pattern reversed itself in both the upper and lower South, to the extent that the second generation was surprisingly fertile. Several reasons account for this turnaround. The work regimen in the North American mainland colonies was not as harsh as in the West Indies, and enough slaves survived to bear children, creating a small Creole population. Children born in North America appear to have had a better chance of survival than new immigrants, since they received some environmental immunity from their mothers. Nature also ensured an equal number of male and female births, so that the sex ratio began to correct itself. As the number of enslaved people increased, so the opportunities for social intercourse improved. Also, the second generation had not experienced the trauma of the passage; they typically reached adulthood as members of intact communities, and were more ready to build lives for themselves with other people whom they loved.

As a result, most North American-born African women formed relationships from early puberty, ensuring their high fertility through early first births. This fertility in turn had a dramatic effect on the sex ratio and the balance between imported and native-born slaves. In 1725, 60 percent of the slave population in the Chesapeake was still African-born. By 1750 this proportion had dropped to 30 percent, in spite of recent levels of importation. At the same time 40 percent of the slave population in many tidewater areas was now female. A similar process was also happening in the lower South. The population began to grow dramatically; much like the white settler population, women bore multiple children who had a good chance of surviving to adulthood and having children of their own. In the words of one historian, therefore, second-generation African Americans had proved a "prolifick people."[17]

Enslaved African Americans who tried to create stable family lives faced great obstacles. Among the most pernicious of these was the lack of legal recognition, since white slave codes did not recognize the slaves' marriages. Most African American children legally belonged to the master, rather than to their father as white children did. Families could be torn apart in a variety of circumstances. Owners might choose to sell some of their slaves to pay off a debt; they might die and their estates be broken up; they

---

[17] Statistics on fertility and population growth are discussed in Allan Kulikoff, "'A Prolifick People': Black Population Growth in the Chesapeake Colonies, 1700–1790," *Southern Studies*, 16 (1977), 391–428. See also Allan Kulikoff, *Tobacco and Slaves.* Jennifer Morgan, *Laboring Women*, observes that enslaved women were the major agents in creating Creole African American communities, in deciding to bear children.

might purchase new lands in the interior and send part of their labor force to work there; or they might give their children plantations of their own, with slaves to work on them. In all these instances African American families could be split up in an instant with no redress. For some the pain was so great that suicide or insanity resulted. When Henry Laurens of South Carolina considered breaking up some of his slave families in the 1760s, he predicted *"great distraction among the whole."*

African American women were also extremely vulnerable to predatory white men, and sexual harassment and rape were a constant threat. Enslaved women had no legal protection from sexual assault, and enslaved men could do little to protect their wives, daughters, and sisters from being victimized by their masters or other white men on their plantations. Even if masters refrained from sexual coercion, they were not above exploiting their position for sexual favors. Black women were most vulnerable in South Carolina and Georgia, where there was a culture of tolerance towards interracial sex, stemming from planters' links with the West Indies, the absence of many owners' families in Charleston, and the fact that such liaisons were easier to conceal because the rice plantations were relatively self-contained and remote from the white population. By contrast, in the Chesapeake and northern colonies such liaisons were more difficult to hide and were usually condemned on both moral and social grounds. Occasionally an enslaved woman might accept a white man's advances as a way to improve her status and gain a little more control over her life. The mixed-race children of white men's slave mistresses were often allowed a privileged status and better working conditions than other slaves (though they were rarely freed). The number of mixed-race children is difficult to quantify, since they were rarely acknowledged by their fathers. Just under 10 percent of the slave population in the Chesapeake was identified as of mixed race by 1750, although the extent of racial mixing was probably higher.

Unlike the parents of young people in European American families, enslaved African American parents had little control over the marriage decisions of their children. Most unions were decided by the couple themselves on the basis of mutual attraction. Both owners usually had to approve when the man and the woman lived on separate plantations. However, approval was not usually a problem since owners recognized that slave unions facilitated a more contented labor force, and would produce offspring that would enrich them directly. Slave marriages were usually simple affairs, held after the working day was over. The man began the proceedings by giving his bride a brass ring or other token of his attachment, after which friends and relatives gathered for a celebration. If the owners approved the match, they might contribute a hog and barrel of rum for the gathering. Unlike with European American marriages, there would be no dowry or gift of property to help the new couple get started. Since slaves had no legal right to own property, their families would not provide a mechanism for passing on property to children and helping them to achieve economic independence as white families did. Slavery would impose enforced poverty on African Americans for well over two centuries.

Because enslaved African Americans had so little power to protect their children, families had to adapt. West African societies were mainly patrilineal, the children taking the name and status of their father. Enslaved couples were more likely than not during the eighteenth century to live together in nuclear family units. But in many cases, African American families became matrilineal because they had to. With marriage legally prohibited, enslaved fathers had no legal right to participate in the upbringing of their children. Small children were usually kept with the mother if a family was split up. Since female slaves might of necessity have several partners during their lives, the mother was the one who provided the child's identity and place.[18]

Another adaptation in African American families was their greater reliance on extended kin networks rather than the nuclear family to care for and nurture children. Infants were normally looked after by elderly relatives or other slaves who were too old to labor, since their mothers were sent back to work shortly after giving birth. Older children were usually left to play among themselves until the age of 8 or 9. They would then be rated as a quarter-hand and given small tasks until the age of 16 or so, when they would be sent into the fields or assigned such other work as they were considered best fitted for. It was these young adults who were most likely to be sent to another plantation or sold. Fortunately, the spreading patterns of kinship meant that they would usually be accompanied by an uncle, brother, half-brother, sister, half-sister, cousin, nephew, or niece. Thus while European American families in British North America were typically nuclear, African American families were often extended. It was this extended kinship network that protected African Americans from childhood through adulthood, to the extent it was possible to do so.

4 AFRICAN AMERICAN CULTURE

By the middle of the eighteenth century, a sense of community became possible on the larger plantations in South Carolina and in the more populated areas of the Chesapeake. The formation of a distinct communal identity among African Americans was most pronounced in the low country regions of South Carolina and Georgia, where slaves usually lived on large all-black or mostly-black plantations. Here, they had time to congregate without white interference, and were truly able to create a separate universe, apart from European American society and culture. In the Chesapeake, slaves tended to live on small or middling farms, surrounded by a majority white population with whom they had significant day-to-day interactions. Here, communal identity was forged out of a different kind of experience, which was more integrated with that of European Americans.

While African American communities were forged through all kinds of shared experiences, they found their fullest expression when enslaved people had time to socialize. Sundays were generally allowed to be a day of rest. With the benefit of their master's absence either at church or visiting relatives, slaves would often invite the workforce from neighboring plantations. Although slaves were generally forbidden to travel, they came nonetheless, using back roads or paths to evade white police patrols. Indeed, such routes were well established by the middle of the eighteenth century. Most masters ignored these gatherings in the interests of harmony, unless they became too unruly or disrupted work the next day.

---

[18] The ordeal of enslaved women on one plantation in colonial Jamaica is vividly described in Trevor Burnard, *Mastery, Tyranny, and Desire: Thomas Thistlewood and His Slaves in the Anglo-Jamaican World* (Chapel Hill, 2004).

Enslaved people mostly came together to eat, drink, talk, smoke tobacco, dance, and relax. The participants provided food from their own gardens and livestock and usually prepared drink from corn or wild fruit, perhaps assisted with sugar from the main house. They played music on drums, flutes, and banjos, sang, danced, told stories, and took part in athletic contests. Card-playing, gambling, and cock-fighting provided other popular forms of entertainment.

Historians have spent considerable energy uncovering the extent to which African American forms of cultural expression retained elements of African cultures. Some African influences in eighteenth-century African American culture are readily apparent. West African styles of rhythm and movement had a powerful influence on the music and dancing styles of African Americans throughout the mainland colonies. African influences were also present in the ways that African Americans made banjos, drums, mats, baskets, and wood carvings. The African origins of a game like mancala, in which the participants captured each other's counters from shallow containers, are even clearer. The importation of plants like okra, black-eyed peas, yams, sorghum, and watermelons also allowed the continuation of African cooking, as did the importation of guinea fowl. Recently, archaeologists have added to the list of African cultural influences. In particular they have shown that African skills were widely implemented in the making of Colono earthenware, which African women apparently preferred to the iron pots supplied by their masters.[19] African influences also persisted in hairstyles and items of personal decoration. Many female slaves continued to braid their hair and to wear African-style jewelry in the form of colored glass necklaces, beaded armbands, bracelets, and brass earrings. Cowry shells also remained popular as decorative charms to ward off disease and other misfortune. Materials used for decorative purposes did not always come from Africa, of course, but enslaved African people often injected their own meaning into many artifacts of North American or European origin.[20]

In other areas, such as language, the influence of African culture was more complex. Even though most slaves came from West Africa, they still spoke a variety of languages that were not mutually comprehensible. It is calculated that there were several hundred languages at the beginning of the African diaspora. Hence newly enslaved captives were often unable to communicate with one another, unless they were fortunate enough to be lodged with members of their own people. The most famous African American of the colonial period, Olaudah Equiano, an Igbo prince, commented on his arrival at age 12 in Virginia in 1757, "I was now exceedingly miserable, for . . . I had no person I could speak to that I could understand." Slaves adapted by creating a variety of different Creole languages in different parts of the British colonies, incorporating English vocabulary along with West African words and elements of West African syntax. In North America the most distinctive of these was the Gullah dialect spoken in the islands off the coast of South Carolina. Although built around a base of English, Gullah contained some 250 words from Angola, Senegambia, and Sierra Leone, and retained

---

[19] See especially Leland Ferguson, *Uncommon Ground: Archaeology and Early African America, 1650–1800* (Washington, DC, 1992); and Anne Elizabeth Yentsch, *A Chesapeake Family and Their Slaves* (Cambridge, 1994).

[20] See Patricia Samford, "The Archaeology of African American Slavery and Material Culture," *William and Mary Quarterly*, 53 (1996), 87–114.

African speech patterns, grammar, and syntax. It was incomprehensible to whites, and therefore enabled its African American speakers to communicate without interference from their masters.[21] Slaves in the Chesapeake, on the other hand, spoke English, reflecting their greater exposure to Anglo-American settlers.

Another area where African culture was partially preserved was in naming patterns, though here too assimilation into British colonial culture took place as children were increasingly given the name of one of their master's family. Some owners like Robert Carter of Virginia deliberately imposed English names on new slaves to undermine their African background and make them easier to control. However, English homonyms often allowed the semblance of an African name to be preserved, as in Joe for Cudjo; and many children continued to be called, albeit in English, after the day, month, season, or festival on which they were born, as was the custom in many parts of Africa. In any case slaves typically used their own names when not in the presence of their master or overseer.

A last critical aspect of African culture which survived for a time was religion, especially on southern plantations. Before 1750 slave-owners in British North America made only cursory attempts at converting their slaves to Christianity, fearing, among other things that conversion might lead to a demand for emancipation, even though most colonies had passed laws precluding this possibility. Thus when the South Carolina brothers Hugh and Jonathan Bryan attempted to convert their slaves after a visit by George Whitefield, they were quickly told to desist by neighboring planters. In addition, there was a clear reluctance among planters to share their religion, since their racial prejudice made them unwilling to accept that they might go to the same heaven as their slaves.

For most of the colonial period, therefore, the slaves were allowed considerable autonomy in spiritual matters, especially on the large rice plantations of the lower South where contact with the white population was minimal. Some Africans from Senegambia and the Gold Coast were clearly practicing Muslims, judging by the advertisements for runaway slaves with Islamic names. Even more continued to observe traditional African religious practices. Most West Africans believed in a supreme Creator under whom there were various lesser gods, usually associated with natural phenomena like thunder, lightning, rain, earth, fertility, spring, summer, and fall. All had the power to do good or ill, and it was considered important to propitiate them by invoking various forms of Obeah or magic through the use of charms and talismans called *minkisi* supplied by a person knowledgeable about magic. Since African religion and medicine were closely

---

[21]   See Margaret Washington Creel, *"A Peculiar People": Slave Religion and Community-Culture among the Gullahs* (New York, 1988). The idea that African Americans retained part of their African roots was first stated by the activist W. E. B. Du Bois, who received considerable support from the anthropologist Melville J. Herskovits's *Myth of the Negro Past* (New York, 1941). Most of Herskovits's material related to Brazil and the Caribbean, and its relevance to America was fiercely denied by E. Franklin Frazier in *The Negro Family in the United States* (Chicago, 1939). Scholarly opinion in the past 30 years has moved back towards the position taken by Du Bois and Herskovits, following the work of Sydney Mintz and Richard Price, *An Anthropological Approach to the Afro-American Past: A Caribbean Perspective* (Philadelphia, 1976); and the novel by Alex Haley, *Roots* (New York, 1976). See especially John Thornton, *Africa and Africans in the Making of the Atlantic World, 1400–1680* (New York, 1992); Ferguson, *Uncommon Ground*; Gomez, *Exchanging our Country Marks*; and Hall, *Slavery and African Ethnicities*.

intertwined, *minkisi* often took the form of amulets or medicine bags into which various herbs and charms were placed, depending on the effect to be achieved, for *minkisi* could be used for good or harmful purposes. Most objects were worn as decoration for personal protection. However, if someone was to be punished, the charm would be placed near that person's house.

Equally important to African religious practice was ancestor worship. All Africans believed that their ancestors' spirits could protect the living, and for this reason they commonly tossed a small amount of food and drink on one side before starting a meal in memory of departed relatives. Even more important, proper offerings had to be made at funerals to propitiate the departed member of the family, for example, placing broken crockery on the grave to free the deceased person's spirit. It was also customary for Africans to be especially demonstrative when accompanying the body to the grave, celebrating the return of the dead person's soul to their ancestral spirits in Africa. This behavior contrasted vividly with the silence maintained by mourners at white funerals.

Even in the area of religion, however, acculturation began to take place as the native-born increased in number. Creoles spoke English and were therefore easier to convert, as well as more willing to accept Christianity. Certain similarities with African religions may have made Christianity appealing, notably the idea of one supreme being, the presence of lesser spirits, the concept of reincarnation, the belief in miracles, the importance of water baptism, and the need for blood sacrifice. In addition, Christianity dealt with suffering, exile, the promise of freedom, and the punishment of evil at the day of judgment. Of course, some enslaved people probably also hoped that baptism might lead to emancipation as a reward for being good and faithful servants. Christianity also gave Creole slaves the opportunity to differentiate themselves from those recently arrived from Africa; and in the last resort a Christian slave was less likely to be sold than a heathen one.

Where masters failed to offer religious instruction, as was generally the case in the South, slaves increasingly filled the gap themselves. From 1750 they received considerable help from the Baptists, who had no slave-owners among their membership and were far more egalitarian in their doctrines than the Anglicans. The interest was quickly reciprocated. African Americans were often drawn to the informality and evangelical style of the Baptists, as well as their emphasis on universal salvation. African religions customarily placed great importance on divine revelation; thus the Baptist appeal to salvation through the mediation of the Holy Spirit had an obvious attraction, as did the possibility of conversion without the need to master a complex theology. A further attraction may have been the practice of adult immersion, which bore similarities to African water cults. Also appealing was the fact that the Baptists demanded no specially trained ministry; a simple license from an existing minister and an ability to preach were all that was required though no African American became a minister until the 1770s. Lastly, the Baptist use of singing and emphasis on trauma during conversion seem to have complemented earlier African religious practices, notably the "ring shout" when participants formed a circle, drumming their feet and clapping their hands, while they sang and danced.

The Baptists began making inroads among the African American community in the aftermath of the Great Awakening, when Shubal Stearns and other ministers passed through the southern backcountry. The first predominantly African American Baptist congregation was established at Lunenburg in 1758 near the estate of William Byrd III. Estimates suggest that up to 40 percent of the African American population in the Chesapeake had converted to some form of Christianity by 1760, though the figure for the lower South was much less owing to the slaves' isolation and the higher level of imports. One owner there confessed even in 1779 that his slaves remained as "great strangers to Christianity, and as much under the influence of Pagan darkness, idolatry and superstition, as they were at their first arrival from Africa."

Thus, although specific cultures disappeared, new African American cultures were built out of African elements. Most notable were the lack of distinction between the natural and supernatural world, particular styles of rhythm and dance, and the sense of time as cyclical rather than linear. All these elements gave African Americans a style of expression and belief that was quite different from those of either Europeans or Africans. What was emerging among the second generation was a shared African American ethnic identity which replaced the narrower tribal or national identities of native Africans. This is not to say that all Creole blacks had a common identity, given the lack of contact between the different regions of British North America. Nevertheless, many had created vibrant new American cultural identities distinct from those of Europeans in the colonies by the mid-1700s.

Finally, some scholars now believe that African American cultures exerted a deep influence on the culture of southern whites. Styles of religious worship, music, healing, and cooking in the South all appear to have been shaped by African American influences. The most noticeable influence was surely in the area of language, as African words and speech patterns came to be commonly used in southern white people's spoken language. As one traveler commented towards the end of the eighteenth century, "common country folk talk very much like Negroes."[22]

5 FREE AFRICAN AMERICANS

Not all Africans in British North America were slaves. Even after 1700, a small number of slaves continued to secure their freedom, or obtained their manumission as a reward for loyalty over a long period of time. Others were freed because they were infirm, though most provinces had laws against this practice.

Estimating the number of free African Americans is no easy task. In Virginia there may have been as many as 2,000 by 1760, despite a law of 1699 that required all newly freed slaves to leave the colony. Free African Americans may thus have represented between two and three percent of the total African American population in the colony, sufficient for a clause to be included in a 1723 statute banning the manumission of African American slaves without the permission of the legislature.

In South Carolina the ratio of free to slave was smaller, perhaps one percent, or between 200 and 300 individuals by 1760. The contrast to Virginia may have been the result of the more rigorous enforcement of a law of 1722 ordering all freed slaves to

---

[22] See especially Mechal Sobel, *The World They Made Together: Black and White Values in Eighteenth-Century Virginia* (Princeton, 1987).

leave the province. White South Carolinians, as always, were terrified of slave rebellions, and feared the presence of free blacks who could help to organize them.

In the North the proportion of free African Americans was higher, but because they made up such a small percentage of the general population, the actual number of free African Americans was small. In Connecticut perhaps 20 percent of the province's 2,000 African Americans enjoyed such status by 1760. In New York, on the other hand, the percentage had shrunk, from 20 percent of the African American population in the seventeenth century to only seven percent in the eighteenth. The total throughout the North amounted to only a few thousand, or one out of ten blacks living north of Maryland.

The position of free African Americans everywhere was far from enviable. In Virginia they could not marry whites or enslaved blacks, could not vote or hold any office, were excluded from the militia, were forbidden to use firearms, and could testify only in court cases involving other African Americans. Miraculously, some still managed to get a small piece of land, usually as tenants. Others used such skills as they had to hire themselves out, mostly as laborers. Some found employment in Williamsburg and other towns where they could use their craft skills. A few owned farms and enjoyed some degree of prosperity, but many apparently slipped back into servitude. Apart from the economic pressures they experienced, they remained continually vulnerable to bullying neighbors, blackmail, or kidnap plots. Use of the courts in these circumstances was not easy.

Conditions were not much better in the North even where these remained "societies with slaves" rather than "slave societies." In eighteenth-century New York free African Americans were not allowed to own real estate. Those masters who liberated slaves had to provide sureties of £200, since "it is found by experience that the free Negroes of this colony are an idle slothful people and prove very often a charge." They were always the first suspects in any crime and were also severely fined if they helped slaves to abscond. Free blacks faced similar discrimination in Massachusetts, where they were normally excluded from the militia and forced to work on the highways instead. They could not vote or sit on juries, and after 1705 they were forbidden to marry whites. Not the least of their difficulties was dealing with economic discrimination. While slaves found it relatively easy to get work, since their masters arranged it for them, free African Americans found work opportunities extremely limited and were pushed into the poorest housing. Although they could use the courts, they were always at a disadvantage before a white jury, and their attempts to purchase property often met with outright refusal. Freedom in such circumstances was bittersweet indeed.

There was still one place where free blacks could live with dignity during the eighteenth century. This was the settlement of Gracia Real de Santa Teresa de Mose in Florida. Mose owed its existence to a 1693 Spanish offer of freedom to any African American slave in the English colonies who converted to Catholicism. The Spanish had always been more liberal in their attitude to slavery and manumission, though their policy was not entirely disinterested. By encouraging slaves to abscond, they hoped to weaken the economy of South Carolina while strengthening that of Florida.

News of this offer soon spread among South Carolina's African American population, and during the early decades of the eighteenth century a trickle of refugees made

DOCUMENT 21

"Afro-Floridians to the Spanish King, 1738," translated by John DuVal and reprinted in Kathleen DuVal and John DuVal, eds, *Interpreting a Continent: Voices from Colonial America* (Lanham, 2009), 179–80

This letter was written by former slaves to the king of Spain, thanking him for a decision by Florida's governor to reconfirm the earlier decree granting freedom to runaways, which some local Spaniards had recently tried to ignore. Questions to consider: *How would the presence of this settlement have affected relationships between Africans and whites in South Carolina, just a few hundred miles to the north? Why do you think that the writers of this letter promised to fight against the English and to serve the king of Spain?*

My lord:
All the Black people who escaped from the English plantations, obedient and loyal slaves to Your Majesty, declare that Your Majesty has done us true charity in ordering us to be given freedom for having come to this country and for being Christian and following the true religion that saves us ... [O]beying laws which Your Majesty decreed, the present governor, Don Manuel de Montiano, has set us free, for which we greatly appreciate Your Majesty and thank him for this most royal kindness.

Likewise, the Governor has offered and assured us that he will establish a place for us, which is called Gracia Real, where we may serve God and Your Majesty, cultivating the land so that there may be fruit in this country.

We promise your Majesty that, whenever the opportunity arises, we will be the cruelest enemies to the English and will risk our lives in the service of Your Majesty, even to spilling the last drop of blood, in defense of the great crown of Spain and our holy faith.

Thus Your Majesty may order any amount of service from us because we are his faithful slaves all of our life and we will always pray Our Lord to guard Your Majesty's life and the life of all the Royal Family throughout the slow years that we poor people need.

Saint Augustine, Florida, 10 June 1738.

the difficult and dangerous journey to St. Augustine. The largest influx occurred during the Yamasee War, when a number of slaves joined the Indians in their southward flight. By 1738 there were enough refugees for the establishment of a separate community of about 100 people two miles north of St. Augustine.

Mose was ostensibly under the command of a Spanish officer, assisted by a priest, since the new settlement was designed as a military outpost for the Spanish capital. But because only the priest lived in the village, the day-to-day life of the settlement was under the control of one of its own freedmen, Francisco Menéndez. He had arrived in

Florida in 1724 and first organized the male inhabitants into a militia. Otherwise Mose was similar to a Spanish Indian mission. The inhabitants lived in small thatched huts and tilled the land around the fort, fishing in the nearby waters to make ends meet. Some worked for wages in St. Augustine.

The British regarded the settlement at Mose as a threat to their sovereignty, and James Oglethorpe attempted to destroy it during his 1740 expedition against St. Augustine. The inhabitants were evacuated to the Spanish capital for protection. Menéndez and his militia played an important role in Mose's recapture a few weeks later. Thereafter, the settlement struggled, with only about 60 inhabitants. Nonetheless, Mose continued to serve as beacon for slaves in the lower South hoping to live in freedom.

6 RESISTANCE TO SLAVERY

African Americans resisted slavery's oppression in a wide range of ways. The most common was to sabotage the system by passive resistance. Working slowly, doing poor-quality work, or pretending sickness were common behaviors but hard for owners to detect. Acts of sabotage such as breaking tools, minor theft, and even arson were widespread. Masters learned to avoid unnecessary confrontations over minor infractions of this type, which are common in any society that fails to provide adequate incentives for workers to be efficient or careful.

Another form of resistance was running away. During the colonial period, especially in the far South, slaves sometimes sought the help of groups hostile to the British colonists in their attempts to escape. Runaways in South Carolina or Georgia often tried to reach St. Augustine, where they would be freed and sheltered by the Spanish. Other runaways obtained the help of the Indians, who sometimes adopted the fugitives into their own nations or kept them as slaves for the sachems' own use. In the Chesapeake, runaway slaves sometimes tried to go to a town like Williamsburg, where they could pass as free among the free African American community.

Quite often, slaves ran away temporarily. Sometimes the reason was to escape harsh treatment by an unsympathetic master, or to negotiate better working conditions. Most commonly, though, slaves ran away to see their families, whose members were frequently split up. Family members could hide them temporarily, then the runaways usually returned of their own accord after a few days. The price of a permanent escape was the abandonment of loved ones, and that was a price many enslaved people were unwilling to pay.

Organized rebellions occurred as well, most successfully in places where blacks outnumbered whites and where there were large numbers of recently arrived Africans in the population. Plans to try to overthrow the slaveholding regime in the mainland colonies were discovered in New York in 1708, 1712, and 1741, as well as in the Chesapeake in 1709, 1710, 1722, and on several occasions during the late 1720s. Most of the time rebellions were stopped before bloodshed occurred, with the exception of the New York uprising in 1712 when a group of slaves set fire to a building and then killed nine white men who were attempting to put it out. Even then, however, rapid retaliation by New York authorities prevented the uprising from spreading.

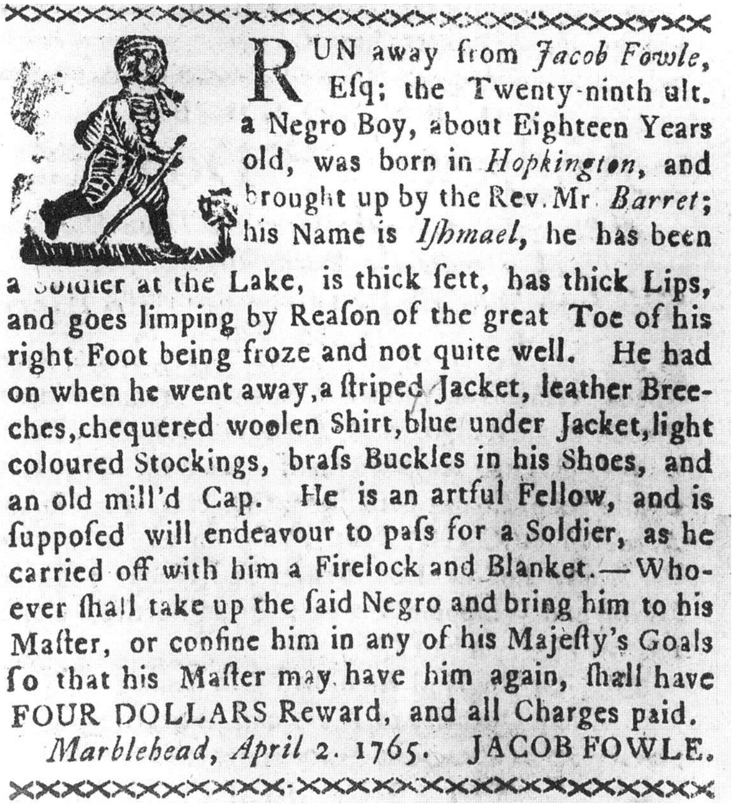

> RUN away from *Jacob Fowle*,
> Efq; the Twenty-ninth ult.
> a Negro Boy, about Eighteen Years
> old, was born in *Hopkington*, and
> brought up by the Rev. Mr. *Barret*;
> his Name is *Ifhmael*, he has been
> a Soldier at the Lake, is thick fett, has thick Lips,
> and goes limping by Reafon of the great Toe of his
> right Foot being froze and not quite well. He had
> on when he went away, a ftriped Jacket, leather Bree-
> ches, chequered woolen Shirt, blue under Jacket, light
> coloured Stockings, brafs Buckles in his Shoes, and
> an old mill'd Cap. He is an artful Fellow, and is
> fuppofed will endeavour to pafs for a Soldier, as he
> carried off with him a Firelock and Blanket.—Who-
> ever fhall take up the faid Negro and bring him to his
> Mafter, or confine him in any of his Majefty's Goals
> fo that his Mafter may have him again, fhall have
> FOUR DOLLARS Reward, and all Charges paid.
> *Marblehead, April* 2. 1765. JACOB FOWLE.

Figure 28 Advertisement for the return of a runaway slave, *Boston Gazette*, April 8, 1765. From *William and Mary Quarterly*, 53 (1996), 145. Courtesy American Antiquarian Society.

The largest slave revolt on the mainland was the Stono Rebellion in South Carolina in 1739. War was in the offing with Spain, and the authorities in St. Augustine had offered refuge to all slaves who fled the British settlements. In addition, the large number of Christian Angolans from the Kingdom of Kongo who had recently been imported into South Carolina may have given the uprising exceptional cohesion. The Kongo had converted to Roman Catholicism at the end of the fifteenth century, following contact with the Portuguese. The offer of sanctuary in Catholic Florida, therefore, was doubly appealing.[23] On the morning of Sunday, September 9, a group of 15 slaves attacked a store, seized some guns, and killed some of the local whites. When they advertised their success by drum beat to encourage others to join, several dozen answered the call; but the action also alerted the local white militia. In a short exchange 14 slaves were killed while the rest fled south towards Florida, recruiting more slaves as they traveled. Eventually, after a battle between the well-armed white militia and a rebel band numbering about 100, the slaves were defeated and the rebellion came to a close.

---

[23] For the Kongo connection, see John Thornton, "The African Dimension of the Stono Rebellion," *American Historical Review*, 96 (1991), 1101–13.

DOCUMENT 22

A suspected African rising prevented, 1680, reprinted in Warren M. Billings, *The Old Dominion in the Seventeenth Century: A Documentary History of Virginia, 1606–1689* (Chapel Hill, 1975), 160

This document illustrates the response of Virginia officials to a suspected slave uprising. Question to consider: *Why did the council decide to prohibit Africans from assembling to bury their dead?*

His excellency was pleased this day in Council to acquaint the Council that he had even then received from Mr Secretary Spencer intelligence of the discovery of a Negro plot, formed in the Northern Neck for the destroying and killing his Majesty's Subjects the inhabitants thereof, with a design to carrying it through the whole Colony of Virginia, which being by God's Providence timely discovered before any part of the designs were put in execution, and thereby their whole evil purposes for the present defeated. And Mr Secretary Spencer having by his care secured some of the Principal Actors and contrivers, and the Evil and fatal Consequences that might have happened, being by this Board seriously considered, have found fit to order that the Negro Conspirators now in custody be either safely secured until the next General Court, to the Intent they may then be proceeded against according to Law, or if it be found more necessary for the present safety of the country that they be brought to a Speedy trial, that then his Excellency will be pleased to direct a Commission to Mr Secretary Spencer, Col Richard Lee and Col Isaac Allerton, three of His Majesty's Council Inhabitants in the Northern Neck to sit, hear and try according to law the Negro Conspirators, and to proceed to sentence or condemnation and execution, or to such other punishments as according to law they shall be found Guilty of, by such examples of justice to deter other Negroes from plotting or contriving either the death, wrongs or injuries of any of his Majesty's subjects.

And this Board having considered that the great freedom and liberty that has been by many masters given to their Negro Slaves for walking abroad on Saturdays and Sundays and permitting them to meet in great numbers in making and holding of funerals for Dead Negroes gives them the opportunities under pretension of such public meetings to consult and advise for the carrying on of their evil and wicked purposes and contrivances, for prevention whereof for the future, it is by this Board thought fit that a proclamation do forthwith issue, requiring a strict observance of the several laws of this colony relating to Negroes and to require and command all Masters of families having Negro Slaves not to permit them to hold or make any solemnity or funerals for any deceased Negroes.

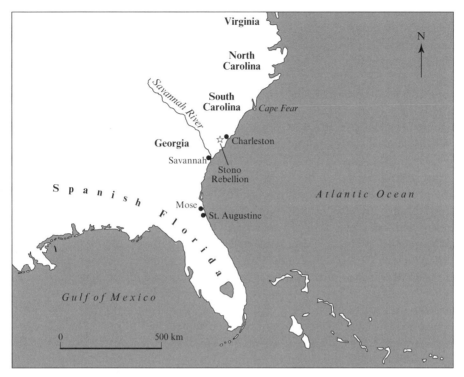

Map 14 Stono Rebellion, South Carolina (indicating Charleston, Savannah, St. Augustine, and Mose, Florida). Reproduced with permission of Yale University Press.

Colonial responses to slave rebellions and conspiracies were undeniably brutal. In the aftermath of the New York uprising in 1712, authorities rounded up dozens of slaves, tried 43 of them, and executed 18 using methods that included burning at the stake and breaking on the wheel. Following the Stono Rebellion, South Carolina whites inflicted a series of brutal reprisals, in which offenders were burned, dismembered, and made to suffer a slow death by being suspended in chains until the birds and other animals had plucked out their eyes and eaten their flesh.[24] Retaliation in the aftermath of the alleged New York slave conspiracy of 1741 was the most vicious, especially considering that the alleged conspiracy had resulted only in a series of fires with no injuries to people. Seventeen slaves and four whites were hanged, 13 slaves were burned at the stake, and 72 slaves were transported and sold to new owners in the Caribbean for allegedly plotting to destroy the city.[25]

---

[24] Punishments for white offenders who committed treason, which colonial authorities would have considered approximately analogous to slave rebellion, were hardly less gruesome. Those guilty of treason were first hanged by their necks, then cut down while still conscious so that their bowels could be cut out and burned in front of them, after which they were beheaded and their bodies cut into four parts.

[25] Historians have disagreed about the actual extent of the 1741 New York conspiracy. For the conclusion that it was not the major plot imagined by New York authorities, see Peter Hoffer, *The Great New York Conspiracy of 1741: Slavery, Crime, and Colonial Law* (Lawrence, 2003), and Jill Lepore, *New York Burning: Liberty, Slavery, and Conspiracy in Eighteenth-Century Manhattan* (New York, 2005).

The savagery of official repression in the aftermath of both real and imagined slave conspiracies undoubtedly helped to deter further uprisings, functioning like the sadistic punishments inflicted by masters upon slaves to instill terror. It became clear that even knowing a person who talked about rebellion could get a person killed. Slaves in the mainland colonies realized that violent rebellion was suicidal, since these colonial societies had substantial numbers of white men who had been trained and armed through their local militias to suppress slave rebellions. And once African Americans began to form families, the risks of rebellion outweighed the possible rewards. Even so, thousands of slaves grasped at the chance of liberation during the American Revolution, when the British military offered to free slaves who agreed to serve in the king's army.

Slave resistance in the Caribbean colonies provides an instructive contrast. There, slaves outnumbered whites by about ten to one, meaning that rebellions were far more likely to succeed. During the eighteenth century, major slave rebellions occurred in the British colonies of Jamaica and Grenada, and in Dutch, Spanish, Danish, and French colonies elsewhere in the Caribbean. The most successful of these was the Haitian Revolution in 1791, which resulted in the overthrow of the French government on the island of St. Domingue.

Resistance by slaves produced little awareness in the minds of eighteenth-century white colonists of the injustices created by slavery. A few denominations showed an interest in the spiritual well-being of the Africans after 1700, and the Society for the Propagation of the Gospel attempted to teach some slaves to read. The concern for African American souls increased with the onset of the Great Awakening when both Wesley and Whitefield condemned the spiritual neglect of the slaves. Among those who responded was Samuel Davies, a New Light Presbyterian, who from 1747 began preaching to slaves in Hanover County, Virginia.

Nevertheless, before 1760 the morality of slavery itself was rarely questioned. A few isolated whites protested the institution: Francis Pastorius at Germantown in 1688, and Samuel Sewall, a Boston merchant and Massachusetts superior court judge, in 1700. But not until John Woolman published *An Epistle of Advice and Caution* in 1754 did the Quakers begin to take a firm stand against slavery. The following year their Philadelphia meeting disowned any member still in the slave trade and advised all others to manumit their slaves as soon as possible. Yet the rest of the white population found slavery too essential to contemplate its abolition.

In the absence of widespread questions about its morality, slavery continued to expand and to become more entrenched in British North American societies. Its legacy would be vast. The African American population would continue to grow, amounting to about a fifth of the colonial population in British North America by the time of the American Revolution. After the Revolution African American slaves and their descendents would continue to play a vital part in the creation of an American culture. Their work would underpin the wealth of the richest single class of Americans, the southern planter class, until the institution was destroyed by the American Civil War. Yet the poverty enforced by their enslavement would keep most African Americans from passing on family farms and other forms of property to their children until well into the twentieth century, whereas most European Americans in the English colonies had come to take such wealth for granted by 1700. Americans would remain in the grip of the system of race relations created by slavery until well after the Civil Rights movement of the 1960s. Slavery was the dark underside of American liberty and opportunity, and its legacy would continue to haunt Americans for centuries to come.

15

Expanding Spanish and French Empires in North America

1565	St. Augustine founded by Pedro Menéndez de Avilés.
1595	The Franciscans arrive to convert the Florida Indians.
1598	Juan de Oñate conquers the Pueblo towns on the Rio Grande.
1610	The founding of Santa Fe.
1630	The conversion of the Apalachees in western Florida begins.
1670	The founding of Charlestown (later Charleston).
1672	Catholic Mohawks begin to settle at Kahnawake.
1673	The French discover the Mississippi.
1680	The revolt of the Pueblo peoples.
1681	French begin to assist Illinois and Miami peoples in wars with the Iroquois. The revolt of the Apalachicolas or the Lower Creeks.
1684–7	The failure of La Salle to establish a colony in the Gulf of Mexico.
1693	Spanish return to New Mexico led by Diego de Vargas.
1699	The French establish themselves at Biloxi.
1702–8	The final destruction of the Spanish missions in Florida, except at St. Augustine.
1716	Spanish missions established in East Texas.
1718	New Orleans founded by the French as the capital of Louisiana.
1729	The defeat of the Natchez Indians by the French.
1733	The founding of Georgia.

Colonial America: A History to 1763, Fourth Edition. Richard Middleton and Anne Lombard.
© 2011 Richard Middleton and Anne Lombard. Published 2011 by Blackwell Publishing Ltd.

L ONG INTO THE eighteenth century both Britain and France continued to be tantalized by the possibility that some great source of riches might still be found in the North American West. It was true that no explorer had managed to find a fabulously wealthy civilization north of the Rio Grande, and pragmatic English and French investors had found ways during the seventeenth century to make money through other means than plunder. Yet dreamers continued to imagine that it might be possible to find great mineral deposits in the West, or better yet a water route leading through the continent to the Pacific which could facilitate trade with China or Japan or with the immensely rich Spanish colony of Peru. Indeed the French and British governments both remained open to the possibility that the control of North America might give them a decisive strategic advantage over their rivals. Spain, meanwhile, maintained a number of colonies in North America for the purpose of guarding the rich silver mines in New Spain and Peru upon which its imperial ambitions continued to ride.[1]

For nearly two centuries, the Spanish, French, and British conducted a three-way chess game to control the continent. Their contest would be vitally important for all the peoples of North America, for it impelled continued exploration and interaction between Europeans and Indians ever further west and north. Spanish colonizers in Florida, New Mexico, and Texas and French colonizers in Canada, the Great Lakes region, Illinois, and Louisiana would create alliances and change diplomatic relationships. They would introduce European microbes, plants and animals, trade goods and religions into the societies of vast numbers of indigenous North American peoples. Meanwhile for British North Americans, the various colonies created by the Spanish and the French would be profoundly significant, shaping the development of their colonial societies by destabilizing their borders and limiting their ability to expand across space.[2]

---

[1] Since there is in fact no water route across North America to the Pacific, historians have until recently discounted the historical significance of French and British attempts to find one. However, Paul W. Mapp, *The Elusive West and the Contest for Empire, 1713–1763* (Chapel Hill, 2011), shows that expectations for a western water route were a key factor shaping French, British, and Spanish territorial objectives until the end of the Seven Years War in 1763.

[2] The borderlands, in other words the regions once claimed by Spain and France that later became part of the United States and Canada, have long been of interest to historians, though historians' approaches to the subject have changed. Early scholarship on both the Spanish and French borderlands sought to find points of comparison between the British and other European colonies and focused much attention on differences in imperial policy and administration. Francis Parkman, for example, contrasted French colonial policy and administration with that of the British colonies in *France and England in America*, rev. edn (1883), portraying the French as absolutist despots in contrast to the supposedly liberty-loving English. For the Spanish borderlands, the seminal work was Herbert Eugene Bolton, *The Spanish Borderlands: A Chronicle of Old Florida and the Southwest* (New Haven, 1921). Today, much of the inquiry has shifted towards interactions between Indians and Europeans in both French and Spanish colonies. David J. Weber provides a synthesis of scholarship on the Spanish colonies north of the Rio Grande in *The Spanish Frontier in North America* (New Haven, 1992). For a summary of more recent trends in the history of the Spanish borderlands, see David J. Weber, "The Spanish Borderlands: Historiography Redux," *History Teacher*, 39 (2005), 43–56. An example of the new focus on interactions between Indians and Europeans is James Brooks, *Captives and Cousins: Slavery, Kinship, and Community in the Southwest Borderlands* (Chapel Hill, 2002), which argues that Spanish colonists became tied together in relationships of exchange with many groups of Indians in a complex economy based on trade, slavery, and kinship. Examples of historical works that show how interactions between the French and the Indians took shape and influenced the lives of both include Denys Delage, "L'alliance franco-amerindienne, 1660–1701" [The French–Indian Alliance, 1660–1701], *Recherches amerindiennes au Québec*,

1 FLORIDA

As we have seen, Spain began its first colony north of Mexico for defensive purposes, when it established a permanent settlement in St. Augustine, Florida, in 1565 in order to sustain its claim to the area and protect its Treasure Fleets as they made their way through the Straits of Florida. The colony was effectively a joint venture in which the Spanish Crown supplied naval and military assistance while the colony's leader, Pedro Menéndez de Avilés, financed the costs of settlement. In exchange he received the right to exploit all lands to the north of New Spain, as Mexico was then called. Menéndez initially established five separate forts along the coast.[3] However, they proved difficult to defend, and after an attack by Sir Francis Drake on St. Augustine in 1586, it was decided to concentrate resources at St. Augustine. Almost the entire Hispanic population of 500 was now concentrated in just one settlement, and half of this comprised the garrison. It was an expensive colony to maintain. Yet the Spanish government helped bear the cost because of its strategic importance, which was reinforced after 1607 with the establishment of the English colony at Jamestown in the Chesapeake.

The Spaniards were never able to attract significant numbers of European settlers to their colony in Florida. Although several hundred thousand Spaniards emigrated to the New World,[4] they found little to appeal to them in comparison with the opportunities offered in Mexico to the south. Therefore the Spanish government sought to control the region not by sending Spanish settlers but by converting the native peoples to Christianity. Conversion meant Hispanicization and a loyal Indian population, which it was hoped would consolidate Spanish control, solve the endemic labor problem, and allow sustained development. Also, conversion of the native peoples had been one of the conditions of the papal bull of 1493 authorizing Spain to take possession of the New World, and the Spanish government felt some obligation to carry out its mandate.

Early conversion efforts had little success. Although 10 Jesuit missions were established between 1566 and 1572, all were abandoned in the face of violent resistance

---

19 (1989), 3–15, and Richard White, *The Middle Ground: Indians, Empires, and Republics in the Great Lakes Region, 1650–1815* (New York, 1991). Some historians argue that the concept of Atlantic history (discussed in Chapter 2) perpetuates historians' excessive focus on the coastal British North American colonies and their relationship with Great Britain, calling instead for a "continental approach" to American history that focuses on the contest between Spanish, French, British, and Indian peoples to control the trans-Mississippi West. The critique is summarized in James A. Hijaya, "Why the West is Lost," *William and Mary Quarterly*, 51 (1994), 276–92. Some recent examples of a continental approach to early American history are Alan Taylor, *American Colonies* (New York, 2001); Colin G. Calloway, *One Vast Winter Count: The Native American West Before Lewis and Clark* (Lincoln, Nebr., 2003); Kathleen DuVal, *The Native Ground: Indians and Colonists in the Heart of the Continent* (Philadelphia, 2006); Ned Blackhawk, *Violence over the Land: Indians and Empires in the Early American West* (Cambridge, Mass., 2006); and Paul W. Mapp, *The Elusive West*.

[3] The Point of Santa Elena had been the original choice of Philip II in 1557 for a military and naval base. Two attempts were made to establish the site in the years 1559–60; both failed.

[4] It is calculated that, by 1650, approximately 450,000 Spaniards had emigrated to the New World.

Figure 29 Portrait of Pedro Menéndez de Avilés/Josef Camaron lo dibo. Engraving by Francisco de Paula Martí, 1791. Library of Congress, Washington, DC.

by the local population (as noted in Chapter 3). Nevertheless the Hispanization policy had not been abandoned. Beginning in 1595, members of the Franciscan order replaced the Jesuits, and over the next six decades managed to convert 26,000 Indians (at least by their own calculations), served by some 70 Franciscan priests.

The Franciscans in Florida generally sought to convert the native peoples without resort to force, having concluded by the end of the sixteenth century that conversion at the point of a sword was both bad theology and self-defeating, since it merely stimulated hostility and resistance. Instead the priests sought to make Christianity attractive by making themselves appear to have access to important magic. They walked barefoot in hair shirts over long distances, which appeared to the Indians to demonstrate their extraordinary bravery and endurance. They wore ornate vestments, used sacred images, chanted music, and recited the liturgy. By 1595 many of the Indians seem to have become open to the possibility that these practices could protect them against natural disasters, especially the diseases that had recently begun to sicken them, but did not apparently affect the newcomers. The friars in addition offered the possibility of access to European goods, which the Indians found both beautiful and useful.

Once a foothold had been established, the Franciscans' techniques became more heavy-handed. They would usually build a church and invite potential adherents to live nearby, for it was a maxim of the friars that converts must live within the sound of the mission bell. Church attendance could then be encouraged, simple catechisms taught, and attention paid to the formal observance of Christian sexual mores. Then pagan idols could be smashed and native rituals discountenanced. The last stage was baptism, after which converts were expected to attend services regularly and go to confession.

Equally important to successful conversion was the process of secular acculturation, since it was assumed that pagans could not become true Christians until they lived like Christians. Hence the Franciscans required their converts to dress, cook, talk, and comport themselves like Spaniards. Particular attention was devoted to the education of the young, since they were more malleable and less resistant to new ideas and could become powerful allies in the battle to win the hearts and minds of a community. Converts who resisted this process of acculturation, by seeking to leave the church or by questioning its doctrines, were brutally punished.

The missions, of course, were never simply spiritual entities, for no friar could succeed unless he enjoyed material support from the host community. Indeed a principal reason for converting the native peoples was to turn them into productive subjects of the Crown. Hence the importance of work in the service of God was constantly emphasized. Meanwhile the world of work was also important for the process of acculturation. By introducing the natives to new crops, livestock, and systems of agriculture, the friars hoped to change their entire way of life. Horses, cattle, sheep, goats, pigs, and chickens were all introduced, as were European crops like wheat and barley and fruits like oranges, peaches, watermelons, and pomegranates. Similarly, useful skills like carpentry, joinery, and metal-working were encouraged to keep the native men and women within constant reach of the friars and control of the Spanish. By 1620 this pattern had allowed the Franciscans to establish missions among the Guales along the coast as far north as Santa Catalina, in present-day Georgia, and among the Timucuas around St. Augustine.

Hoping to expand their influence further, the Spanish next encouraged the creation of missions across northern Florida to the western Timucua and Apalachee peoples. Apart from excluding the English, they also hoped to open a road to New Spain around the Gulf of Mexico. The Franciscans established their first formal missions among the Apalachees in the 1630s, when loss of population had made them vulnerable enough to look favorably on an alliance with the Spanish. There was soon a string of new posts across northern Florida to the Gulf of Mexico near Tallahassee and beyond. In return for Spanish protection and religious instruction, the Apalachees were expected to provide food and labor not only for the missions but also for the maintenance of a road to St. Augustine, along which they sent considerable quantities of corn.

Although the Spanish had obviously managed to establish missions in Florida, the strategy of Hispanicization failed in the long run to attain the regional control for which they had hoped. During the high-water mark of the mission system, the period 1635–75, the Franciscans operated between 40 and 70 missions, organized in four provinces: Timucua in central Florida; Guale along the Georgia coast; Apalachee on the northeastern edge of the gulf; and Apalachicola to the west. Yet the existence of these missions belied a persistent dissatisfaction among the Indians with the Spaniards'

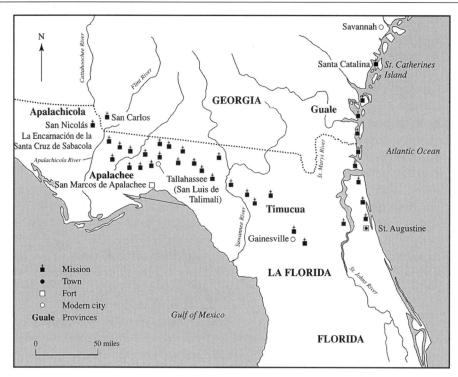

Map 15 Missions in Spanish Florida, circa 1674–1675. From David Weber, *The Spanish Frontier in North America* (New Haven, 1992), 101 (map drawn specifically for Professor Weber's book by Don Bufkin).

heavy-handed methods.[5] To the Indians, the most offensive aspect of the Spanish system was the *repartimiento*, whereby the Spanish levied tribute in money, goods, or services. In theory the *repartimiento* was limited to periodic labor on public works, for which the Indians were to be paid, the most important requirements being the maintenance of the Camino Real (or royal road), the carrying of supplies to St. Augustine, and the building of fortifications. But in practice the system was open to abuse, both by the friars and by the Spanish ruling class, who forced Christian Indians to work on the settlers' farms instead of tending their own crops. The Indians

---

[5] Herbert Bolton, one of the earliest historians of the Spanish borderlands, proposed in *The Spanish Borderlands* that in its early years the Spanish mission system in Florida experienced a "golden age." Bolton was endeavoring to counteract the "black legend" about the Spanish era as one of economic repression and religious intolerance, rather than one of reciprocity and self-sufficiency. Bolton's "golden age" thesis was subsequently challenged by Robert Allen Matter, *Pre-Seminole Florida: Spanish Soldiers, Friars and Indian Missions, 1513–1763* (New York, 1990), who argued that the missions were far from successful, either spiritually or economically, since they merely hastened the extirpation of the Indian population. A similar view is taken by Amy Turner Bushnell, *Situado and Sabana: Spain's Support System for the Presidio and Mission Provinces of Florida* (Athens, Ga., 1994).

demonstrated their unhappiness in a series of revolts, notably by the Guales in 1645 and the early 1680s; the Apalachees in 1647; the Timucuas in 1655; and the Apalachicolas in 1675 and 1681. Only the last of these, by the Apalachicolas, or Lower Creeks, succeeded. Most of these revolts were suppressed and their leaders hanged, but in the aftermath of the crackdowns many Indians, including converts, ran away from the missions and removed themselves from the Spanish sphere of influence. An even more serious problem that worked to undermine Spanish control was the unintended effect of Spanish diseases on the local population, whose numbers became substantially diminished during the first century of Spanish occupation. The Apalachee population, for instance, was around 30,000 in 1617, but by 1676 was little more than 8,000.[6]

The result of the Indians' defection was that the Spanish were not as strong as they might have been to face the challenge posed by the arrival of the English. News arrived in 1670 that the English had established a colony in South Carolina. Spain and England were now technically at peace and on the point of signing a treaty respecting each other's possessions across the Atlantic. However, both sides recognized that the activities of the other were incompatible with their own pretensions regarding the area. The Spanish still wanted to possess as much of North America as possible by converting and holding the allegiance of the native people. The newcomers were equally determined to restrict, if not entirely destroy, the Spanish hold on Florida so that they could develop a market for deerskins and slaves.

As a result hostilities commenced, despite the treaty of 1670. The Spanish attempted a pre-emptive strike on Charleston in 1675, though without success. One major problem was the defection of local Indians to the Carolinians. The Yamasee and the Creek Indians helped the English to attack the Guale missions, attracted by offers of guns, horses, and cheap trade goods. The English had considerably more trade goods to offer than the Spanish, so they were more desirable allies. Moreover, having seen how the Spaniards treated their Christian converts, the Yamasees and the Creeks had little interest in helping them to remain in the area. Within six years the Guale missions had been destroyed.

The English threat to Florida was not limited to eastern Florida, for in 1686 news arrived that Dr Henry Woodward, an English trader and envoy of the Carolina proprietors, had appeared among the Apalachicola or Lower Creek people with a large train of packhorses loaded with weaponry. This would clearly be a prelude to an attack on the Apalachee missions with their valuable grain supplies. The Spanish accordingly launched pre-emptive strikes against both the Apalachicola and against Charleston itself. Neither scheme was a success. The Charleston expedition got no further than Edisto Island, while the invasion of Apalachicola merely encouraged the Creeks to hit back, having been newly convinced that the Spanish presence in the area should not be tolerated.

---

[6] For a discussion of the population of the southeastern nations during this period, see Marvin T. Smith, "Aboriginal Depopulation in the Post Contact Southeast," in Charles Hudson and Carmen Chaves Tesser, eds, *The Forgotten Centuries: Indians and Europeans in the American South, 1521–1704* (Athens, Ga., 1994), 257–75.

Unfortunately for the Spanish, the English and their newfound allies were not the only threat to Spanish hegemony in the region, for in 1684 they learned that the French, under René Robert Cavelier, Sieur de La Salle, were attempting to establish a colony in the Gulf of Mexico. The Spanish determined to first destroy the French settlement and then establish a permanent base of their own. It proved a case of easier said than done. The Gulf above the Rio Grande, with its swamps, bayous, and shallow waters, was almost unknown to the Spanish and it took nearly three years to find the French settlement, by which time it had been abandoned. Establishing a Spanish fort in the area took even longer because of financial constraints and the difficulty of finding a suitable site. Not until 1698 was the decision made to build the new post at Pensacola and within months it was shown to serve no useful purpose. In the first place it was irrelevant to the defense of the Apalachee missions. Secondly, with the signing of a peace treaty in Europe in 1697, the Spanish found it diplomatically impossible to uproot the French when they did finally establish themselves at Biloxi Bay in 1699, just a few miles from Pensacola itself.

However, the problems of Spain and their Indian allies in Florida really began only in 1702 with Queen Anne's War, or the War of Spanish Succession. As we have seen, the English in Charleston tried to drive the Spanish out of Florida entirely in 1702, raiding St. Augustine and destroying all the remaining missions along the east coast and on the St. Johns River. South Carolina's governor tried again in 1703, invading the province of Apalachee with the help of Creeks and Yamasees, destroying some 14 missions, and executing several Spanish officials when they were unable to ransom themselves. The bitter animosity of the British towards Spanish Catholics was demonstrated by South Carolina's treatment of one friar, Father Parga, who had his legs hacked off before being burned at the stake. The result was the enforced evacuation of Apalachee by both the Spanish and the native peoples, who were dispersed in every direction. Finally, late in 1708, the English launched a third raid, this time against western Timucuas, completing the ruin of the Spanish mission system in Florida. During this period some 10,000 Christian Indians were either killed, enslaved, or forced to run away. A pitiful remnant of about 300 took refuge under the guns of the Spanish fort at San Marcos, it being unsafe even to venture into the town.

By 1708 the Spanish missions had largely failed and many had been abandoned. In effect the colony was reduced to one principal settlement, the town of St. Augustine. After 1708 the only other posts were a few satellite missions between St. Augustine and the St. Johns River, though a mission and fort were subsequently rebuilt in 1718 at St. Marks on the northeast shore of the Gulf for the remnants of the Apalachee people. The colony also received an influx of several hundred Yamasees, following their war with South Carolina. However, the prosperity of the colony could not recover while border warfare continued. Spanish acceptance of the Yamasee refugees, along with the runaway slaves harbored at Mose,[7] angered the Carolinians since they interpreted this as an indication of Spain's underlying hostility.

To prevent further reprisals by the Yamasees, the South Carolinians in 1721 established a fort at the mouth of the Altamaha River. In 1727, retaliating for continued

---

[7]   For further information on Mose, see Chapter 14, section 5.

Yamasee raids, a South Carolina force fought its way almost to the gates of St. Augustine itself. Although Spanish diplomatic pressure was successful in getting the fort on the Altamaha removed, the tranquility did not last. In 1733 George II granted the area between the Savannah and Altamaha rivers for the new colony of Georgia, creating a new strategic buffer for South Carolina against potential attacks by both Spain and France to the south.

Border warfare continued to batter the colony in the 1740s. The Spanish colony survived the subsequent conflict known as King George's War, managing to beat back a siege by British forces commanded by Georgia governor James Oglethorpe in late 1739 and 1740. Spanish troops once again successfully defended themselves against a second British attack in 1741, and retaliated with their own attack against Georgia in 1742, though they were forced to withdraw. However, the population in St. Augustine and the immediate region was only about 3,000 by mid-century. Of these, some 500 were soldiers, 1,500 ethnic Spanish, and the remainder Hispanicized Indians, African slaves, and free blacks living in Mose. The other two settlements, St. Marks and Pensacola, each had perhaps 150 soldiers and 500 other inhabitants. Everywhere the missions had shrunk. By 1759 there were only 79 Indians in the two villages near St. Augustine and just 25 at St. Marks.

Despite the failure to sustain a large local population in Florida, Spain continued to hold its fortified settlements for defensive purposes. The emergence of British and French colonies in the southern latitudes of North America had, if anything, increased the need to protect the borders of New Spain. Military garrisons were expensive for the Spanish Crown, but they were necessary to keep the British and the French from expanding any further.

2 NEW MEXICO

The colonization of New Mexico began, like that of Florida, because it served the strategic goals of the Spanish Crown. After the exploration of the area by Francisco Vázquez de Coronado in 1540–2, no further effort was made to settle the region for the next 50 years, since the area had little in the way of mineral wealth to offer Spanish adventurers. However, by the 1590s other considerations had come to the fore. The government of New Spain needed to protect the silver mines of Zacatecas in northern New Spain from Indian raids, which were a constant problem. Spanish authorities also believed that somewhere to the north lay the long-sought passage to China, which it was imperative to discover before it fell under foreign control. The presence of the relatively advanced Pueblo civilizations made New Mexico an appealing site for a colony, since some adventurer might be willing to finance the venture in exchange for the right to exploit the Indians' labor in an *encomienda*-style plantation system. *Encomenderos* had originally been appointed to fight the Moors in Spain. In return for defending the frontier the Crown gave them the right to exact tribute from any subject peoples.

King Philip II granted a commission to colonize the area and convert the native people in the area to Don Juan de Oñate in 1598. A Mexican-born Spanish aristocrat with extensive interests in the Zacatecas mines, Oñate was expected to bear all the expenses of the conquest. In return he would have extensive rights over the land, with the power to award the status of *hidalgo*, a lesser nobleman, to his principal followers. No royal forces would accompany him, since Oñate was unlikely to meet European opponents.

Oñate crossed the Rio Grande in April 1598. Accompanying him were some 500 persons, including 130 soldiers, 10 Franciscans, and sundry colonists with their wives, children, servants, and slaves. The Pueblo communities offered little resistance; they had experienced visits from the Spaniards over many years, and most had ended in considerable loss of Indian life. It made sense, therefore, to treat the newcomers with deference. Indeed, it seems that some Pueblos actually welcomed the Spaniards as protectors against the nomadic Apaches, whose raids had recently increased. Oñate accordingly continued northwards along the Rio Grande, taking over a pueblo on the west side of the river for his headquarters, which he renamed San Gabriel. However, the site soon became overcrowded and proved unsuitable for defense. Within 10 years Oñate had moved his capital 20 miles southwards to a place that he named Santa Fe.

The Pueblo Indians quickly realized that Oñate was not the ally and protector they had hoped for. He expected the Pueblos to provide tribute in the form of labor and food, and his men tortured and killed the native people in order to obtain it. When the Pueblo of Acoma resisted the Spanish extortion by killing 11 of Oñate's men, the *adelantado* responded by offering the inhabitants a choice of slavery or death. The Acoma declined the offer; their town sat atop a seemingly impregnable *mesa*, and they thought they were safe. Tragically, they were mistaken in their belief. During the subsequent fighting, at least 500 men and 300 women and children were killed, out of a total population of 1,380. The Spaniard then put the survivors on trial. All except children under 12 were condemned to 25 years' servitude. Males over 25 then had one foot cut off, as a reminder to other Pueblos of the consequences of rebellion.

The viceroy of New Spain removed Oñate from power in New Mexico because of his brutality towards the Indians and placed the colony under royal control. The viceroy curbed the worst excesses of the Spanish settlers and encouraged Franciscan missionaries to convert the Indians, hoping to pursue the same strategy of Hispanicizing the local population that was being pursued in Florida and elsewhere in New Spain. Initially the friars enjoyed remarkable success. By the late 1620s they had established almost 50 churches and residencies along a 200-mile stretch of the Rio Grande. The arrival in 1629 of eight more friars allowed additional missions to be established further afield among the Acoma, Zuni, and Hopi peoples.[8]

The Indians in New Mexico very likely had a variety of reasons for deciding to convert to Christianity, many of them similar to those of the Indians in Florida. To some extent they undoubtedly complied with the friars out of fear; having seen at Acoma what Spanish soldiers were capable of, they judged cooperation to be a better course than resistance. Another factor was the desirability of Spanish protection against the Apaches, semi-nomadic peoples who often raided the Pueblos. A third was the apparent immunity of the Spanish from the diseases that afflicted the native peoples so severely.

---

[8] The question of whether the villages of the Zunis and Hopis actually accepted Christianity, or simply tolerated the friars to avoid military reprisals, is noted by Weber, *The Spanish Frontier in North America*, 97–8.

And just as in Florida, the Indians may have been open to the idea that the Franciscans had supernatural powers. Their first arrival in 1598 coincided with the ending of a drought, a coincidence that proved so potent that the friars thereafter always attempted, when on a new mission, to arrive just before the rainy season. In addition, the friars wore opulent vestments and engaged in strange, elaborate ceremonies. They performed medical feats that helped to give them an appearance of magic and invincibility.

It has been argued that a final factor explaining the Indians' conversions was that both the friars' behavior and the Christian liturgy could be understood in ways that were compatible with traditional Pueblo beliefs. In this view, flagellation seemed to demonstrate that the friars had extraordinary powers, since it could be equated with the native practice of flogging their leaders to see if they could endure pain. The friars' abstinence from sexual activity could be seen as confirmation that these were men of extraordinary power. Pueblo men abstained from sex before hunting and war, believing this gave them greater power, both spiritual and physical. To abstain permanently seemed miraculous. The Indian Corn Mother became the Virgin Mary, while the cult of the rain spirits, or *katsinas*, was incorporated into the veneration of the saints. The traditional prayer sticks used to summon the rain spirits were replaced by the cross.[9]

But though the Indians may have imagined Christianity as a new source of magic that could be added to traditional practices and beliefs, the Franciscans expected them to relinquish all traces of their old culture once they had been baptized. As in Florida, conversion went hand in hand with a restructuring of Indian civil society. The adoption of European-style farming, especially the keeping of domestic animals, considerably strengthened Spanish authority since it meant a downgrading of hunting, the prerogative of the former civil chiefs. Men's role as warriors was undermined, since warfare was now primarily the responsibility of the Spanish. The priestly class had been discredited by their failure to conjure sufficient magic to defeat the Spanish. Indian icons were destroyed and replaced with those of the cross and the Virgin Mary. The priests even took control over the institution of marriage and sought to change Indian sexual mores, which had permitted both polygamy and serial monogamy. They insisted that Indian women cover their bodies and imposed harsh punishments for what they perceived as a lack of chastity, with no appreciation of Indian attitudes to fertility and sex.

Despite the missionaries' success in converting the Indians to Christianity, New Mexico failed to flourish economically. The arid climate made New Mexico unattractive to Spanish settlers, compared to a place that could support the production of tropical commodities like sugar. Thus the Hispanic population never exceeded 1,500 during the seventeenth century, though the number of Indians acknowledging Spanish authority may have been as high as 17,000. The settlers supported themselves mainly by ranching and raising crops. But besides livestock, the only other export commodity – an illegal one under the royal ordinance of 1573 – was the sale of slaves. Prisoners captured

---

[9] The argument is made by Ramón Gutiérrez, *When Jesus Came, the Corn Mothers Went Away: Marriage, Sexuality, and Power in New Mexico, 1500–1846* (Stanford, 1991). For a critique, see Alison Freese, ed., "Pueblo Responses to Ramon Gutiérrez's *When Jesus Came, the Corn Mothers Went Away*," in *American Indian Culture and Research Journal*, 17 (1993), 141–77. Freese and her coauthors, all of whom are Native Americans, suggest that contemporary Pueblo traditions contradict Gutiérrez's interpretation. In particular they deny that their ancestors would have seen the Spanish as possessing supernatural powers of any kind, or that precontact Pueblo cultures were as sexually uninhibited as Gutiérrez suggests.

from the Apache could always be sold in New Spain as labor for the mines. The practice, however, invited retaliation by the Apache on the outlying Pueblo communities, causing considerable economic destruction. Another constraint on trade was the colony's isolation. San Gabriel and Santa Fe were almost 800 miles from the nearest Spanish settlements in northern Mexico. Even El Paso, founded in 1659, was nearly as remote. New Mexico in consequence could expect a supply convoy only once every three years, and frequently the period was longer. This meant that there were few trade goods to offer to the local Indians, making it difficult for the Spanish to maintain good relations with the local Indians or to forge new ties.

Another constraint on growth was the Spanish reliance on the *encomienda* system. Unlike Florida, New Mexico's soldiers were not supported by the Crown, and instead levied tribute from the Indians in both goods and services, which, when added to the friars' demands for labor to build, repair, and feed the missions, amounted to a harsh exploitative regime. What made the situation even more repressive was that the demands on each individual increased as the Indian population declined, and many Indians effectively fell into permanent servitude.

Ultimately the Pueblos realized that the Franciscans were not the powerful shamans they had initially seemed to be. Not only the Spanish soldiers but some friars as well sexually abused Indian women and appropriated Indian land for their own use. Moreover by the last quarter of the seventeenth century the religion of the conquistadors had seemingly lost much of its magic. The ravages of disease continued, as did other natural calamities like droughts, which were severe in the 1660s and 1670s. Moreover the Spanish had failed to shield the Pueblos from Apache raids, which simultaneously undermined respect for their temporal power.

Finally, in 1680 the Pueblo peoples decided to combine against their oppressors. The difficult climatic conditions of the 1660s and 1670s, combined with the ever increasing demands of the Spanish for tribute and a renewed attempt to suppress Pueblo dancing and *kivas*, drove a majority of the native inhabitants secretly to agree on a concerted bid for freedom. Led by a dynamic shaman named Popé, thousands of Indians rose up against the Spanish in August 1680. The rebels attacked farms, churches, and Santa Fe itself, as the rebellion spread to dozens of communities ranging over an area of more than 100 miles. After six weeks, the governor decided to abandon the capital and retreat down the Rio Grande to El Paso, whither another 1,500 had already fled. By the end, about 400 Spanish had been killed, including 21 missionaries.

The Pueblo people of New Mexico had reached the same conclusion as the followers of King Phillip in New England, only they had implemented it more successfully: by working together they had driven out the European invaders. In the weeks that followed the rebellion, Popé encouraged his followers to destroy all traces of the Spanish occupation, both secular and religious, in an effort to cleanse and restore the native way of life. The Indians destroyed altars and crosses, restored the *kivas*, and resumed the practice of polygamy. They were so successful that for more than a decade after the Pueblo Revolt, the Spanish abandoned New Mexico entirely.

Eventually, however, the Spanish decided to try to reconquer the colony because of the need for a military outpost to guard against French attacks on the northern frontier of New Spain. By the 1680s, the Spanish had become aware that the French were searching for a waterborne route to the Pacific. Then they learned that the

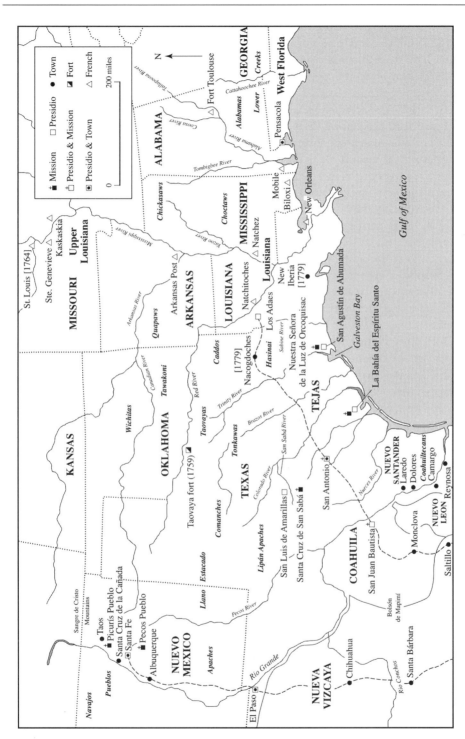

Map 16 Spanish, French, and Indian settlements in the Gulf of Mexico in the mid eighteenth century. From David Weber, *The Spanish Frontier in North America* (New Haven, 1992), 185 (map drawn specifically for Professor Weber's book by Don Bufkin). Reproduced with permission of Yale University Press.

French were trying to create a colony on the Texas coast, threatening Spanish control over the Gulf of Mexico. To protect its claims in North America, the Spanish Crown would have to maintain a continued military presence in New Mexico. Therefore in 1691, Spanish authorities appointed Diego de Vargas as governor of the province with the charge of restoring Spanish authority. Vargas reorganized the refugees at El Paso, who were in large part able to regain the initiative because the Pueblo communities were once more divided among themselves. Popé had alienated many of his supporters by acting in the manner of a Spanish governor and by now many Pueblos were ready to play the Spanish off against their rivals. These divisions allowed Vargas to return with military reinforcements in 1693, fighting his way into Santa Fe in an effort to restore Spanish authority in the Pueblos.

However, the Franciscans found that without a continuous military presence they could no longer remain in their missions, as before. When another rebellion broke out, Spanish authorities undertook a number of reforms, abandoning the *encomienda* system and replacing it with the less extortionate *repartimiento* labor requirement. The Spanish government sent in paid, professional military men to defend the colony instead of relying on the *encomenderos*. They also made religious concessions as the Franciscans recognized the need to be more accommodating of native customs and beliefs.

During the eighteenth century, the colony struggled more than ever. During the long absence of the Spanish, some of the Plains peoples including the Comanches had acquired abandoned Spanish horses and become adept at using them in hunting and warfare. Moreover, with French settlements in the Mississippi Valley, some of these peoples were now able to obtain European guns. The defense of Spain's northern frontier now became much more difficult as mounted raiders launched surprise attacks, using their new firearms, to carry off captives from the Pueblos to be sold as slaves. Meanwhile the Spanish were still unable to provide the trade goods that would have genuinely strengthened their alliances with local Indians.[10] Although the Spanish population grew gradually, the native population had declined to about 10,000 by 1750, as people from the Pueblos drifted away. Even with the Spanish government's commitment to sustain the colony, New Spain's northern frontier had become dangerously unstable.

3 THE GROWTH OF NEW FRANCE

In contrast to the Spanish colonies, the French colony of New France had grown and prospered economically during the latter decades of the seventeenth century and the

---

[10] The reasons for Spanish deficiencies in trade were twofold. Spanish manufacturing was weak, and the mercantilist system restricted the flow of goods to its colonies. Historians have advanced many reasons for the economic decline of Spain: the expulsion of the Moors and Jews, the most dynamic elements in the population; the excessive dependence on bullion, which fueled inflation and undermined Spanish manufactures; a mercantilist system, which was totally designed for the benefit of metropolitan Spain; the Catholic Church, which laid insufficient stress on the work ethic; and a culture that glorified war and adventure at the expense of more mundane economic activity. See J. H. Elliot, *Spain and Its World, 1500–1700: Selected Essays* (New Haven, 1989).

settled area within the colony had spread. There were now a number of royal trading posts inhabited by fishermen and traders near Tadoussac, at the entrance to the St. Lawrence River, along with whaling and fishing camps along the Atlantic coast to the north in Labrador and Newfoundland. About 1,100 French farmers and fishermen lived in Acadia to the south, mostly in Port Royal, on what is now Nova Scotia. The towns of Québec, Trois-Rivières, and Montréal (also called Ville-Marie) had grown, and settlers lined the banks of the St. Lawrence River in between them. The fertility of the French Canadians was high, just as in New England to the south, and in the cold, healthy climate of New France life expectancies were longer than for contemporaries in Europe. As a result the settler population continued to expand rapidly through natural increase. The total population of New France would grow to about 25,000 by 1720, and by 1760 it would nearly triple again, reaching almost 75,000.

During the latter half of the seventeenth century, French settlers around the St. Lawrence region had begun shifting away from their almost exclusive reliance on the fur trade to develop a subsistence-based, family farming economy. Since farmers all wanted access to the St. Lawrence River, the main transportation route within the colony, farms were laid out along its banks in narrow vertical strips which often extended out away from the river for more than a mile. The result was a settlement pattern which brought farmers not only close to the water but close to one another. By the eighteenth century a visitor traveling down the river from Québec to Montréal would have seen a farmhouse every 200 yards or so, interrupted every so often by a manor house, a mill, or a church. The rural families who lived in these farmhouses lived much like their counterparts in New England. They grew corn and wheat and raised cattle, sheep, and pigs to feed their own families, and by the 1720s were able to sell a small surplus of grain to buyers in Montréal and Québec and other French colonies in North America and the West Indies. In many respects the St. Lawrence Valley resembled British colonies further south. However, their societies were developing some distinct differences.

Though its farms produced commodities similar to those found in New England, French Canadian society remained a more aristocratic society; most of the land was owned by large landlords, called *seigneurs*, but farmed by renters known as *habitants*, who paid their landlords annual dues or rent. Since the land produced few if any profitable products during the seventeenth century, the *seigneurs* did not grow rich from their rents. However, they still enjoyed more prestige than the ordinary settlers. For example, members of seigneurial families were preferred for civil offices within the colonial government and members of the officer corps in the regular army were almost always *seigneurs*. Members of seigneurial families also tended to share the values of the French aristocracy, stressed the importance for young men of earning honor and glory for their families through military service. As a result the Canadian *troupe de marines* included an unusually large number of noble officers from local families, many of them eager to prove themselves in battle.

Settler families in New France, like those in the British colonies, were patriarchal in the sense that they assumed the superior authority of a male household head. Yet French household heads possessed somewhat less power over their dependents than their counterparts further south. French law made it difficult for a father to disinherit his children, meaning he could not exercise as much control over them in practice as a

British colonial father could. Moreover French women in New France fared considerably better than white women in the British colonies in several respects. For one thing, married French women retained substantially more control over marital property than did British wives, owning half of all marital property rather than losing control over all of it. French widows received their half of the marital property outright after their husbands died instead of being limited to the use of only a third. For another, elite French women had more occupational choices than British colonial women. While most French Canadian women married and defined their lives largely in terms of their productive household work, those who could afford the payment of a "dowry" could remain single, enter a Catholic convent, and engage in teaching and charitable work. Women in female religious communities possessed considerably more autonomy than wives and daughters.

Just as in other colonies in North America, African slavery had gained a small foothold in New France by the eighteenth century. Since the agricultural economy produced minimal profits, farmers had no incentive to import slaves on a large scale. Nevertheless wealthy settlers in Canada brought in small numbers of African slaves purchased in the Caribbean or the British colonies (as well as Pawnee slaves from the far west) to work as household servants. As in other "societies with slaves," Africans were not invariably excluded from the society of poor whites or prevented from developing relationships with white patrons. Their situation was not enviable, however, for they faced the same kinds of problems as Africans in New England. The cold climate of New France was inhospitable and alienating for people of African origin. Even more important, because the number of Africans in New France remained tiny, opportunities for marriage and family life were limited. Life in New France often entailed isolation and loneliness for Africans who had been brought there involuntarily.

Government authority over the settlers in New France was considerably more centralized than authority in the British colonies. The governor-general, *intendant*, and bishop cooperated to govern the colony, assisted by a sovereign council of *seigneurs* along with governors and deputy *intendants* to help carry out their policies at the local level. The governor-general, answerable to the Crown, was in charge of military affairs and commanded the French regulars who were permanently garrisoned in the colony. The *intendant* enforced the laws and carried out economic policy. There was no elective assembly. Although the royal government conducted annual public assemblies in which the governor and the *intendant* listened to the people's views on matters of policy, these assemblies had no power to veto government decisions.

In sharp contrast to the town meetings that had developed in some of the British colonies, local government entities in New France were not independent decision-making bodies but administrative agencies responsible for carrying out government policy and mobilizing the militia when instructed to do so. A *capitaine de milice* was responsible for organizing militia companies, in which all white men in the colony between the ages of 16 and 60 were expected to serve, and providing the settlers with appropriate military training. The governor-general appointed militia captains to command the militia companies, and also to help enforce the law when necessary. Despite the absence of local autonomy, these institutions aroused little resistance from the settler population. Militia captains were *habitants* rather than *seigneurs*, which helped them to win the trust of their subordinates and to help mediate between local populations and the *intendant*. Another feature of government that helped to mitigate potential resentment was that most *habitants* paid no taxes. Certainly in comparison to peasants in France during the eighteenth century, the *habitants* in New France were lightly governed. Thus despite its top-down structure, the government did not seem oppressive to most of the colonists.

This relationship between the colonial government and the French settler population provided an important advantage to the French. For even though the population of New France remained small relative to the British population further south, it could be mobilized rapidly and efficiently to defend the colony when needed. Of course the settlers did not provide the colony's sole military force. The professional soldiers in the *troupe de marines* along with the colony's Indian allies would provide its first line of defense in case of an attack, and were usually on the front lines in any offensive action.

Another major difference between society in New France and the societies that were developing in the British colonies further south was the presence of Native Americans in or near white settlements, and the frequency of interactions between the Indians and the French. French settlers frequently encountered Indians in their day-to-day lives, particularly during the summer when Indian hunters and trappers visited Montréal in large numbers to sell their furs. During the late seventeenth century the royal government in New France followed a policy of trying to assimilate the Indians into French society by encouraging marriages between French men and Indian women as well as the adoption of Indian children by white families. Although the policy had been abandoned by the eighteenth century, the government continued to encourage Christian Indians to settle in Catholic *reserves* right next to the French settlements. A group of Huron refugees had settled at Lorette, north of Québec, sometime after being driven from their villages in Huronia during the 1640s. South of Québec was the Abenaki village of St. Francois. Considerable numbers of Christian Mohawks had settled southwest of Montréal in Kahnawake by 1700 on land owned by the Jesuits, and more Christian Iroquois migrated to Kahnawake as well as a second Jesuit *reserve*, Kanesatake, during the eighteenth century.

Because the French government depended so heavily on the Indians in these communities to help defend the colony against the British, French leaders avoided antagonizing the Indians by interfering with tribal sovereignty. Thus the *reserve* Indians spoke French but retained substantial control over their own political affairs and preserved a great deal of cultural autonomy, in stark contrast to the Christianized Indians in Florida and New Mexico. The Kahnawake and Kanesatake Mohawks declined to submit to French law, adopted Jesuit teachings selectively, and largely managed to maintain their traditional gender roles. Women continued to farm the land in the same manner as their mothers and grandmothers had, planting corn, squash, and beans all together in hillocks, while men proved their manhood by joining war parties for the French government, bringing back extra income and plunder for their clans. Tribal governing structures continued to operate. As long as French ports remained open and trade goods continued to arrive from Europe, alliances between the French and their Indian neighbors remained strong. Meanwhile the French were building additional military alliances with new groups of Native Americans in the West.

4 THE FRENCH UPPER COUNTRY, OR *PAYS D'EN HAUT*

With the supply of furs dwindling in the St. Lawrence Valley, French traders had begun as early as the 1660s to venture further west to search for new Indian trading partners who could supply them with furs. Louis XIV and his minister Jean-Baptiste Colbert initially tried to discourage the westward expansion of the fur trade, fearing it would be expensive to defend. The colony needed to concentrate on building up the settler population in Canada and strengthening government authority before expanding into an area it could not possibly control. Westward expansion might be worthwhile to prevent competition from other European competitors in the fur trade, but there was little immediate danger of such competition during the 1660s. Still, Colbert eventually concluded that the exploration of the West should be allowed. He and other advisors continued to hope the explorers would discover a water route to the Pacific, or at least to some warm-water port that could communicate with Canada year-round. Indeed after 1670, when an English company established a fur-trading colony in Hudson Bay, the need to explore the West became more urgent. Whichever power became the first to find a water route to the Pacific could control the continent.

French parties were therefore sent off to explore the Great Lakes to the west of Lake Huron as well as the rivers to the north, west, and south. By 1670 the Great Lakes had been traversed and claimed for France. Exploration of the rivers proceeded rapidly as well. In 1669, René Robert Cavelier, Sieur de La Salle, traveled south on the Ohio River, though he returned without finding anything of great interest. Then in 1673, Father Jacques Marquette, a Jesuit missionary now working at the northwestern tip of Lake Huron, and Louis Joliet, a trader and explorer from Québec, traveled from the Bay of Green Bay up the Fox River and proceeded south on the Wisconsin River until they reached the Mississippi. Marquette and Joliet continued downstream on the Mississippi far enough to realize that it led directly to the Gulf of Mexico before they finally turned around near the mouth of the Arkansas River in July, fearing they might encounter the Spanish.

Once these expeditions had shown the way, Canada's governor-general, the Comte de Frontenac, took the lead himself in organizing the westward expansion of the trade. Fort Frontenac was built on the eastern tip of Lake Ontario in 1673. La Salle received the right to establish trading posts on the Mississippi, provided that he would explore the river to its mouth within the next five years. Within a few years there was string of trading posts at geographically strategic points throughout the Great Lakes region, which the French called the *pays d'en haut*, or the upper country. Other posts along with Fort St. Louis and Fort Crevecoeur had been constructed along the Illinois River south of Lake Michigan, a region known as Kaskaskia. In addition the French built Fort Prudhomme on the Mississippi in what is today Tennessee.

Actual French occupation of these newly claimed lands was thin. French traders traveled through them, but their purpose here was to obtain furs and ship them back to Montréal to sell, not to establish villages or settlements. By 1680 there were some 800 traders in the *pays d'en haut*. Most operated without permits and spent much of the year living among the Indians, typically taking Indian wives and becoming assimilated into

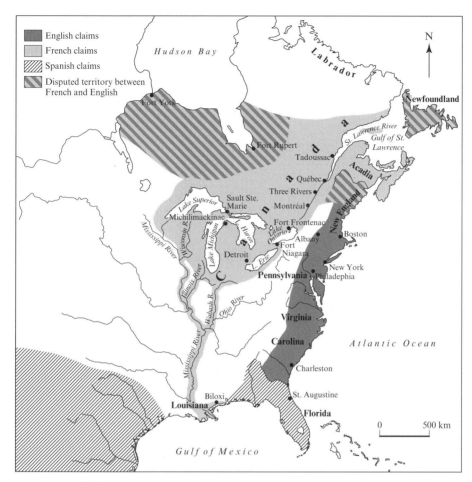

Map 17   French claims in North America, circa 1700, showing major forts in the Great Lakes region, the Mississippi and Illinois rivers, and major settlements in New France.

their villages. A small number of soldiers were sent to protect the trading posts during the 1680s. But for the most part traders spent their time far from the protection of the garrisons. Meanwhile, the Iroquois, asserting that they had the right to control the passage of trade through much of the area, became increasingly aggressive. France's ability to maintain a continued presence in this region would depend on its success in sustaining alliances with trading partners who were willing to help counter the Iroquois.

The Indians who lived in the *pays d'en haut* by 1680 were a motley group made up mostly of recently arrived refugees from tribal lands further to the east. From the 1640s to the 1660s, the Iroquois, armed with Dutch guns, had made war on the various peoples who lived in the Ohio and Illinois valleys, forcing them to flee their homelands and move further west. The refugees of these wars now lived west and south of the Great Lakes. They included members of the Fox, Huron-Petun, Illinois, Miami, Kickapoo, Noquet, Ojibwa, Ottawa, Potawatomi, Sauk, and Wyandot peoples, along with other, smaller bands. Most were Algonquian speakers; a few spoke Iroquoian languages but were not members of the Five Nations. The region's original inhabitants, the Menominees and Winnebagos, had been so weakened by disease and war that they were willing to accept newcomers, so the refugees had settled here in villages, clustered close together and without any clear sense of territorial boundaries. Surrounded by strangers, they were wary of one another. Old rivalries bubbled up. In a few cases mixed groups had formed new kinship ties, intermarrying or exchanging gifts in order to produce the bonds of mutual obligation that could help them to survive. But for the most part they remained divided.

These disparate groups might never have become allied with one another but for the fact that the Iroquois fell on them again after 1680. A short-lived truce between the Five Nations and the French had ended when the English and the Iroquois created the Covenant Chain alliance in New York. Now the Iroquois had resumed their attacks, not only against the allies of New France around Québec and Montréal but also against the Illinois and the Miamis. French leaders in Québec and Montréal realized that the Iroquois posed a major threat to French interests, since if they could destroy each of these tribes one at a time, Canada would be cut off and the French fur trade would disappear. What was needed was a French effort to unify their different western allies and trading partners. The French therefore agreed to an alliance with the Illinois and the Miamis in 1681, and began to organize a loose coalition between the various peoples who lived in the region.[11]

The coalition was fragile at first, but in the long run became surprisingly effective. French traders in the West took steps to help defend their various trading partners and to provide them with supplies. La Salle brought Miamis, Illinois, and Shawnees together into his garrison. The French leader at Michilimackinac, Governor La Barre, provisioned the fort for a siege. Unfortuantely La Barre lost his nerve and betrayed the Illinois to the Iroquois; however, the French government promptly sent a replacement governor to Michilimackinac, repudiated La Barre's agreement with the Iroquois, and renewed French support for the Illinois and the Algonquians. The alliance between the French and the Algonquians was never completely secure, since both the Indians and the French always feared the other would abandon the coalition and make a separate peace with their enemies. But French Canadians increasingly realized that this large-scale French–Algonquian alliance was necessary to their own survival, since it could provide them with a buffer against attacks by the Iroquois and the English, and help them to keep the English from expanding their colonies even further. In time, the alliance turned the tables on the Iroquois. By the 1690s, with combined French and Algonquian forces launching attacks on Iroquois villages, killing warriors and burning cornfields, the Five Nations had been put on the defensive. The Iroquois' own participation in the disastrous English expeditions against Montréal and Québec, as we have seen, magnified the scope of their losses, finally convincing the Iroquois to agree to the general peace established by the Grand Settlement of 1701.

---

[11]   For a thorough exploration of this alliance and its evolution, see Richard White, *The Middle Ground*. The narrative presented here tracks White's argument. Susan Sleeper-Smith, *Indian Women and French Men: Rethinking Cultural Encounter in the Western Great Lakes* (Amherst, 2001), argues that the Catholic kinship communities forged by marriages between Native women and French men helped Native American communities around the Great Lakes persist, even with attempts to remove them during the nineteenth century.

Since neither the French nor any of the disparate Algonquian allies in the West had the power to enforce their will on the others, working together in a coalition meant having to establish mutual trust. One institutional mechanism which enabled the creation of cross-cultural confidence was marriage. The loss of warriors in the recent wars had created a shortage of men in many Algonquian kin groups. Families therefore encouraged young Algonquian women to marry French traders. These marriages were advantageous to both parties since they brought traders into kinship networks within Indian communities, and gave the women and their families special access to European trade goods. Women who married French traders gained considerable power and prestige, since they played such vital roles both in their marriages and in their families of origin. The mixed-race children of these marriages often served important functions within the French–Algonquian coalition as well. Because they typically spoke both Algonquian and European languages and understood the expectations of both groups, they could mediate between them in arranging trade deals and resolving disputes.

Misunderstandings between members of such culturally distinct groups were common, so it was vital for all parties to develop effective mechanisms for dispute resolution. Indeed, the failure to find a middle ground could sometimes be lethal, especially in cases involving violent crimes. The French legal system dealt with crime by insisting upon the punishment of the guilty offender, which usually meant executing the offender if the crime was murder. The problem was that if the French (or any of their allies) executed an Indian to punish him for his crimes, his kin would be bound to take revenge on the kin of the executioner. Algonquian legal systems dealt with violent crime by requiring compensation to be offered to the victim's family in the forms of gifts of goods or slaves, in order to prevent the killing from setting off a cycle of revenge killings between kin groups. To prevent the kind of destabilizing consequences that these blood feuds were likely to cause, the French developed new protocols to satisfy all sides: criminals were imprisoned and tried for their crimes but they paid for their crimes by compensating their victims' families rather than being executed. Such compromises allowed all parties to feel that justice had been served, thereby avoiding further dissension and violence.

Another kind of misunderstanding had to do with the meaning of trade. French traders, at least initially, had expected their trades with the Indians to be governed by the same laws that governed the marketplace, the laws of supply and demand. The Algonquians, though, persisted in seeing their transactions with the French as exchanges of gifts. They expected these gift exchanges to be made in accordance with traditional protocols. For example if the Indians offered gifts that they considered valuable, like moose hides or wampum, and the French turned them down because they preferred furs that they could market in Europe, the Indians accused them of being greedy and refused to trade with them in the future. The French had to accept the Algonquians' terms because they needed the Algonquians as allies against the Iroquois, and because they knew the Algonquians could always go to the English for trade goods if they became offended with the French. Thus, just as in Canada, French vulnerability gave the Indians considerable bargaining power.

By 1700 the French–Algonquian alliance had become so central to French imperial policy in North America that the French government was willing to operate the western fur trade at a loss in order to preserve it. During the 1690s an oversupply of furs caused prices to drop, and the French government considered shutting down virtually all of its western trading posts, which by now had expanded west of the Great Lakes into the territory of the Sioux. However, in the end, the French continued to supply trade goods to the Indians despite their declining profits. By 1700 Louis XIV had decided that the western alliance was critical to France's future policy in North America. Instead of concentrating only on the fur trade, France's objective now would be to control the North American West. Officials in New France were ordered to build military posts from the Great Lakes to the Gulf of Mexico, which could be used to stop the English, as well as positioning France to take over some or all of the Spanish colonies, if necessary. Meanwhile French traders and priests were to maintain the loyalty of the western tribes, thereby controlling the bulk of North American territory.

The task of sustaining the French–Algonquian alliance became more complicated after 1710, since the Iroquois had declared their neutrality and stopped attacking the western Algonquians. In addition, in the years after 1713, British traders began to venture west in order to engage in commerce with the western nations. Now that they could trade with the British without interference from the Iroquois, some of the Algonquians sought to assert their independence from the French. In particular, the Fox, in the area of the Wisconsin River, became so confident in their ability to act as independent agents that they tried to bar the French from crossing their lands in order to trade with the Sioux further to the west. The Fox even attempted to negotiate a separate alliance with the Iroquois and the British. The French government retaliated by launching a concerted assault against the Fox, using 400 French soldiers along with about 1,200 of their Algonquian allies to attack Fox villages. The major goal of this heavy-handed action by the French against the Fox was to demonstrate to the rest of their western allies the dire consequences of turning against the French.

As time went on, however, the French lost the ability to control the terms of the alliance. Other Algonquian allies decided that surviving members of the Fox should be allowed to rejoin the coalition, despite French opposition, and mediated their return. Having lost the power to dictate terms to their Algonquian allies, the French became even more adept at the rituals of gift-giving so that they could prevent particular chiefs and villages from defecting to the British. Though the changing balance of power made their alliances more expensive, French leaders continued to cultivate them, at times even operating the fur trade at a loss.

Why were these alliances so important to the French? Clearly alliances were helpful in consolidating fur-trading relationships in the West. But when the expense of gifts undercut the profitability of the fur trade, why did French leaders continue to invest so heavily in their alliances? One reason is that their friendships with the Indians were vital to their strategic interests, because the Indians not only kept the British from venturing into the *pays d'en haut* and Kaskaskia; they also shielded Canada from British attack. The French population in Canada was continuing to grow, reaching 40,000 by 1737, and 55,000 by 1755, and its economy had at last begun to prosper, as merchants developed a small shipbuilding industry and farmers began to export some of their grain and livestock to the French West Indies for sale to French plantation-owners. A second and possibly more important reason, it has recently been shown, is that French officials continued to hope that control over the West would eventually yield profits greater than those available through the fur trade. Perhaps they could still find a river leading to the

Pacific, or discover mineral deposits west of the Mississippi that would yield riches like those of New Spain. The potential future value of the West justified spending considerable amounts of money to keep it.[12]

From a British point of view, of course, the French commitment to its loose alliances with the Algonquians had the effect of encircling the British colonies, hemming them into the area east of the Allegheny Mountains and preventing their expansion westwards. Meanwhile another barrier to the expansion of their colonies was being developed further south, where a French colony had been established in 1699 at the mouth of the Mississippi River. It was called Louisiana.

5 LOUISIANA

Since 1682 the French had been trying to establish themselves in the Gulf of Mexico and the Mississippi Valley. Their reasons were varied. The French wanted to expand their empire. They had been distracted from overseas ventures by domestic political and religious strife for much of the previous century. Now, under Louis XIV, France had become the most powerful country in Europe, a seventeenth-century equivalent of a twenty-first-century superpower. It seemed fitting that France should now take her place in the imperial order. The French sugar islands of Martinique and Guadeloupe in the West Indies had been highly successful, but were not sufficient to make France an imperial power like Spain or even England, whose colonial possessions were rapidly expanding. In the late seventeenth century hopes remained high of finding mineral wealth in the West as well as a passage to the Pacific, in order to gain access to trade with China, Japan, and Peru. Controlling the Mississippi would be critical to achieving these ambitions. A base on the Gulf of Mexico might even allow France to invade Mexico by sea, or to capture other Spanish possessions in the West Indies. Finally, there was the fur trade. Now that the trade was being expanded into the Great Lakes region and the Illinois country, the French wanted to develop it further to the south as well.

By 1678, La Salle had a formal commission from Louis XIV to explore the full length of the Mississippi. He had his first view of the river in December 1680, but required another year to assemble sufficient men and supplies for his main expedition. He finally entered the Mississippi on February 6, 1682. As he proceeded downstream he noted much promising countryside, both for hunting and for agriculture. The mouth of the river was reached on April 6, 1682 where three days later formal possession was proclaimed on behalf of Louis XIV. The party then retraced its passage up the Mississippi.

La Salle recognized that establishing French claims to the territory would require physical occupation. Accordingly, in February 1684 he proposed the establishment of a colony 200 miles up the Mississippi to render it safe from Spanish attack. His request

---

[12]   Paul Mapp, in *The Elusive West*, argues that historians have failed to understand the importance of the West to French intentions because the traditional perspective of colonial North American history was too narrow. Historians' focus on the British colonies on the east coast obscured the fact that French policy-makers wanted to control the Mississippi River corridor and Louisiana because this would give them control over the unexplored trans-Mississippi West.

was granted and he set off in July 1684 with four ships, including a royal frigate, heading directly for the Gulf of Mexico with approximately 200 soldiers and 300 colonists. Hopes were high, but unbeknown to them, disaster awaited them, just as it had for earlier Spanish explorers of the region. La Salle's main problem was finding the mouth of the river. Unwittingly he thought his first sighting of the mainland was the coast of Apalachee, when in reality he was 300 miles west of his objective. A temporary refuge, Fort St. Louis, was built in Matagorda Bay, near the mouth of the San Antonio River, while further attempts were made to find the Mississippi amid the islands, bayous, and channels that dotted the area. Further setbacks were not long in coming. One of La Salle's ships went aground, while the naval officer in charge of the frigate, having failed to find the mouth of the Mississippi further east, returned to France. This left La Salle with no shipping, since his other two vessels had remained at Santo Domingo. He then made three attempts, from 1685 to 1687, to set off on foot to find the Mississippi and get help from New France. On the third such attempt, in January 1687, he was murdered by his own mutinous soldiers, most of whom, together with the settlers, died of starvation, disease, or death at the hands of the Indians. By the spring of 1689, when the Spanish finally succeeded in finding Fort St. Louis, it was an abandoned ruin.

The same concerns that had fueled support for La Salle resurfaced at the end of the century, though France was now less worried about Spanish attack, since the two nations were at peace. The 1697 Treaty of Ryswick had ceded to France the western portion of Hispaniola or the island of Santo Domingo (now Haiti), providing her with a convenient base from which to launch a new attempt at colonization. In addition, the French remained concerned that the English might try to establish themselves in the region. Accordingly, when a new proposal for a colony in the lower Mississippi Valley was submitted to Louis XIV by Pierre Le Moyne, Sieur d'Iberville, and his younger brother, Jean-Baptiste Le Moyne, Sieur de Bienville, it was readily accepted and a force similar to that of La Salle's commissioned. This time, though, the brothers were more careful in their choice of subordinates. Iberville left France in October 1698 and, like La Salle, reached the Gulf coast via Santo Domingo towards the end of January 1699. He rediscovered the mouth of the Mississippi, and founded two settlements: one at Biloxi Bay in 1699, and the other at Mobile, not far from the recently established Spanish post at Pensacola, in 1702.

Trade with the Indians was one of the goals of this new French colony from the beginning. The area around Mobile and Biloxi was inhabited by people the French called the "*petite*" nations, a diverse set of small tribal groups who had been devastated by disease and who welcomed the French as traders and potential allies. The coastal peoples provided the French with food and deerskins in exchange for guns and other trade goods. As the French advanced into the interior, they came into contact with larger, more powerful nations. Among the more important were the Creeks who lived to the east of Mobile; the Natchez people on the Mississippi River above the future New Orleans; the Choctaws on the upper reaches of the Pearl River; the Chickasaws further north between the Yazoo and Tennessee rivers; the Cherokees, to the north in the Appalachian Mountains. In addition, the Caddo Indians lived west of the Mississippi, and the Quapaw and Osage Indians to the west of the Mississippi in the Arkansas Valley, north of modern-day Texas. Although the French government was eager to establish alliances with the Indians, they were rather less successful here than in the north.

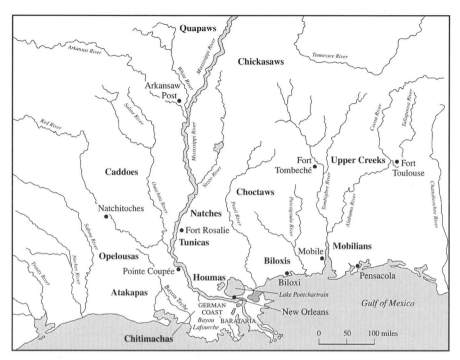

Map 18 The lower Mississippi Valley in the 1730s. From Daniel H. Usner, Jr., *Indians, Settlers and Slaves in a Frontier Exchange Economy: The Lower Mississippi Valley Before 1783* (Chapel Hill, 1992), 51. Copyright © 1992 by the University of North Carolina Press. Used by permission of the publisher.

One reason for the difficulty was that in this region many of the Indians had pre-existing trade ties, and in some cases rivalries, with the British in South Carolina. Contact was first made with the Creeks after the founding of Mobile in 1702, when an attempt was made to wean them from their trading alliance with the English. The same reasoning led to the building in 1717 of Fort Toulouse at the junction of the Coosa and Tallapoosa rivers. Unfortunately the French, like the Spanish, did not always have sufficient goods of the right quality and price. The French attempted to overcome this want by sending various chiefs to France to impress them with the wealth and power of their nation. Greater attempts were also made to understand Indian culture. Many, like Bienville, learned Indian languages, while young French boys were sent to live with the natives so that they could become interpreters. Still, though the French made some headway with the Upper Creeks, their success was limited, since British traders could offer a better and more varied supply of goods.

The French had a different set of difficulties in establishing trading relationships with the Quapaw and Osage Indians north and west of Louisiana in the Arkansas Valley. The Indians here were willing to trade, having begun by this time to realize the utility of European trade goods. Yet because their lives had not been greatly disrupted by warfare caused by European intrusions in the east, they had less need for French friendship than the French had for an alliance with them. Therefore the Indians dictated the terms of the relationship and the French had to follow their diplomatic protocols, provide lavish gifts, and adapt to local customs in order to remain in the region.[13] Further north, in the upper Mississippi Valley, the French exerted more influence, establishing new mission posts in the upper Mississippi Valley at Kaskaskia, Cahokia, and Peoria. As a result, by the early 1700s the French fur trade had expanded its reach to the entire length of the Mississippi as well as far into the West.

The French were also able to establish successful relationships with the Natchez and Choctaw peoples, who provided deerskins rather than furs, a lucrative source of exports worth £50,000 each year, with the figure exceeding £100,000 on occasion. Around Louisiana, just as 100 years earlier in New France, the French and the Indians became deeply interdependent. The French population was small, and the Indians provided not only deerskins but often food as well.

Attempts to find an agricultural commodity in Louisiana initially met with little success. The lower Mississippi Valley was not suitable for European agriculture and, starved of resources, had nothing to stimulate its development. The only agriculturally productive parts of the new colony were those where more traditional styles of farming were possible. Many of the province's 400 settlers went northwards to the Illinois settlements, which now began to produce wheat to provision the rest of the colony. Even this modest success was seemingly put in jeopardy in 1712 when the French king granted a monopoly on Louisiana's trade to a leading French merchant Antoine Crozat, by way of repayment for helping finance the recent war in Europe. Crozat quickly organized a survey which defined more precisely the limits of Louisiana, and set about establishing trading posts on all the important rivers, notably on the Red River at Natchitoches, as the Spanish shortly discovered.

Crozat, too, found it hard to make a profit, and in 1717 handed over his patent to a subsidiary of the Company of the Indies. This was just before the 1721 South Sea Bubble, when speculative fever was rife in both Britain and France and there was plenty of money for investment schemes, especially in exotic faraway places. In many respects Louisiana now experienced a phase similar to that of Virginia under the lead of Sir Edwin Sandys after 1619. Like Sandys, the new directors believed that population growth was the key to success. During the next four years they sent some 7,000 white immigrants and 2,000 West African slaves, mainly from Senegal, to the colony. Just as at Jamestown, lands were granted to certain privileged individuals or concessionaires for the development of plantations. A well-sited levee along the Mississippi was chosen in 1718 for the capital, which was to be called New Orleans.

Louisiana experienced rapid growth in the years 1717–26, although, as at Jamestown, many of the new arrivals died or went back home. The census of 1726 indicated a total population of just under 4,000. Of the whites, 1,663 were *habitants* who were free to work for themselves and acquire land, another 245 were *engagés* or indentured servants who still had contractual obligations to complete, and 332 were military personnel. Slaves accounted for the rest, comprising 1,385 blacks

---

[13]   Kathleen DuVal in *The Native Ground* argues that the Indians in the Arkansas Valley retained the upper hand in their relationship with Europeans until the nineteenth century, controlling their "native ground" to a far greater extent than did the inhabitants of the Great Lakes region.

and 159 Indians.[14] But the most dramatic change, compared to the pre-1718 colony, was the emergence of tobacco plantations, which spurred the importation of most of the African slaves.

The shift to a plantation economy and the attendant growth of the settler population placed considerable new pressure on the relationship between the colony and local Indians. Unlike the harmonious relationship between Frenchmen and Indians in New France, Louisiana developed a relationship with the Natchez that resembled the relationship between Virginia and its neighbors 100 years earlier, when the Indies Company began to encourage tobacco planting near the Indians' principal settlements. French farming damaged the Natchez people's hunting grounds, while French livestock destroyed their crops. This pressure was added to an already difficult diplomatic situation; the French had managed to offend the Natchez, who were descendents of the Mississippi mound-building cultures, by treating them without proper respect. The Natchez were also now aware of the dangers of living too close to the white settlers and their diseases. From 1722 onwards they retaliated against the encroachments of the settlers by attacking their livestock and crops. The French in return took hostages and demanded compensation. The final straw came in 1729 when the French commander at Fort Rosalie ordered the Natchez to vacate one of their principal settlements so that he could establish a plantation for himself. The Natchez became determined to attempt what Opechancanough had tried to do at Jamestown: liquidate the entire white presence so as to preserve their culture and livelihood.

Despite rumors of the Indians' impending design, the French at Fort Rosalie were totally surprised when the plan was executed on November 28, 1729. Within hours some 235 French men, women, and children had been killed and nearly 300 African slaves taken. Indeed, some of the Africans were apparently involved in the uprising, along with the Natchez. However, African slaves at New Orleans did not rebel, though there was widespread fear that they might do so. Also many of the neighboring peoples, most importantly the Choctaws who were traditional rivals of the Natchez, now rallied to the French cause. The French were accordingly able to mobilize sufficient forces to hunt down the rebels, who were either killed or sold into slavery in Santo Domingo, though some managed to take refuge with the Chickasaws and Creeks.

Although the colony survived the Natchez war, the Indies Company's control did not. The members decided that Louisiana was too unprofitable a prospect to be worth keeping, and surrendered their charter to the king in January 1731. The day-to-day management of the colony was now delegated to a royal governor, the veteran Bienville. Yet the colony became no more profitable under royal control. The market for Louisiana tobacco failed to develop. Indigo, another cash crop, was equally disappointing, while sugar was not thought to be feasible because of the length of the growing season. Many planters accordingly had to turn to the more mundane occupation of providing France's Caribbean islands with timber, naval stores, cereals, and cattle. The one profitable enterprise remained the deerskin trade.

---

[14]   This information is from Daniel H. Usner, Jr., *Indians, Settlers and Slaves in a Frontier Exchange Economy: The Lower Mississippi Valley Before 1783* (Chapel Hill, 1992). Usner stresses the continuing interdependence between the French and their Indian allies, well into the eighteenth century.

Continued French reliance on the deerskin trade ensured that interdependence between the French and the local people around Louisiana would remain strong. With the defeat of the Natchez, the Choctaws now became the principal allies of the French. The Choctaws, a Muskogean-speaking people, had at least 20,000 inhabitants, but had long been disadvantaged by the difficulty of securing arms to fight their traditional enemies, the Creeks and Chickasaws. In many ways they now formed a partnership similar to the one between the Iroquois and New York. Though their relations were not always harmonious, the advantages of the French alliance were ultimately too great for most Choctaws to ignore. The disastrous conflict between the French and the Natchez was not repeated with any other important nation, and the French alliance with the Choctaws remained secure.

By the 1740s Louisiana had proved only a partial success for France. Strategically, the French had achieved their main objective. They had built an alliance with a powerful local people that enabled them to control the mouth of the Mississippi and maintain a presence at a key location on the Gulf of Mexico. They had attracted planters and were building a plantation economy. However, the colony was nowhere near as profitable as the French colonies in the West Indies. And no progress had been made towards finding a route to the Pacific, or mineable ore. Some were beginning to ask whether this colony, expensive as it was to administer, was worth keeping.

6   TEXAS

Though Spain had eventually been forced to accept a French presence at Biloxi Bay in 1699, that did not mean that the Spanish had resigned themselves to losing the area. Rather it stimulated them to take preventive action to limit the damage. The principal fear was competition from French traders, which would loosen New Mexico's dependence on New Spain (and New Mexico's influence over the local Indians). A secondary concern was that the French might use their coastal bases in Louisiana to attack key Spanish possessions like Panama, or even to launch an invasion of Mexico. The result was renewed Spanish interest in the region, especially the area that came to be Texas, which until the end of the seventeenth century had been entirely neglected.

Spanish interest in Texas began in 1689 after Spain learned of La Salle's expedition down the Mississippi. Determined to stop France from claiming territory on the Gulf of Mexico, Spanish authorities decided to gain control of the region through their usual strategy of using Franciscan missions to win over the native inhabitants. Their main target this time was the Caddo peoples living between the Trinity, Sabine, and Red rivers. The Caddos were attractive because, like the Pueblo Indians in New Mexico, they were relatively sedentary and had a well-developed agriculture. The hope was that the Caddos, like the Pueblo peoples, would be open to Christian conversion.

The first plan, drawn up in 1690, was for a mission near the Trinity River, 500 miles north of the Rio Grande. The danger as always was that the post would be too remote to defend or to have any real effect. The likelihood of this was greatly increased when Father Mazanet, the mission leader, dismissed most of his escort, fearing that the soldiers would set the Caddos a bad example. In the event an outbreak of disease rather than the behavior of the military defeated the venture. The Caddos rightly blamed the Spanish for the arrival of smallpox and ordered the friars to leave, which they did. No immediate attempt was made to return. The problems in New Mexico and the failure of La Salle meant that for the moment Spain had neither the resources nor the need for such a venture.

However, by the turn of the eighteenth century a French presence on the Mississippi had become a reality and the Spanish recognized that, unless they reoccupied East Texas, French influence among the native tribes would grow, threatening Spanish claims to the Gulf. Accordingly, in 1716 an expedition was dispatched under Captain Domingo Ramón to make contact once more with the Caddo peoples. Ramón's force was small, just 75 persons, among whom were 20 soldiers and 10 friars. By the time Ramón reached the Natchitoches tribe on the Red River he found a French post already there. Since France and Spain were now at peace, Ramón had to accept this fait accompli and establish instead two mission posts nearby, called San Miguel de los Adaes and Dolores de los Ais, from which he hoped to contain any further French incursion. But to prevent East Texas from being totally isolated, the viceroy of New Spain simultaneously ordered the building of a mission on the San Antonio River to act as a way station between the two. The new town, begun in 1718, was to be called San Antonio.

Despite this peaceful progress the Spanish soon faced further challenges to their position in East Texas. In 1719 Spain went to war with England, France, and Austria over her territorial claims in Italy. This provided the French with an opportunity to attack the Spanish in the Gulf. First Pensacola and then the East Texas missions were overrun, leaving San Antonio as Spain's most advanced post. Not that the Spanish were prepared to accept such an outcome permanently. An army of 500 men was assembled on the Rio Grande by the Marquis de San Miguel de Aguayo, but by the time he was ready to attack, peace had already been signed in Europe. Aguayo, therefore, merely had to escort the French trespassers back to their former post at Natchitoches.

Before returning to New Spain, Aguayo arranged to leave a more formidable garrison of 250 men, 100 of whom were quartered at Los Adaes. This now became the provincial capital, despite its closeness to the French at Natchitoches. Militarily Spain was not to be threatened again in East Texas during the colonial period, though this was largely the result of Franco-Spanish friendship in Europe rather than of Aguayo's military arrangements.

Unfortunately, there was one major weakness in the Spanish position: the missions lacked economic viability. With the rigid trade restrictions in effect in New Spain, the Spanish could not get supplies of trade goods from Mexico. In turn this prevented them from establishing a viable relationship with the local Indians. The Caddo peoples expected high-prestige gifts such as guns, hatchets, and manufactured cloth if the Spanish were to retain their respect. Without generous distribution of presents the missions had little to offer the Indians. Meanwhile the French at nearby Natchitoches had trade goods in abundance. Without gifts or powerful magic to offer, the Spanish missions had little potency, and conversions were infrequent. Since the Franciscans could not get the Indians to settle at their missions and work on their farms, at times they could not even feed themselves, having to buy what they needed from their French neighbors. Three of the East Texas missions were accordingly abandoned in 1731 and their personnel withdrawn to Los Adaes or San Antonio. But even at the latter they were not safe. As the French expanded their own trading relationships further west, new groups of Indians acquired French guns and Spanish horses. Armed bands of Apaches now raided San Antonio so often in search of cattle and horses that the beleaguered settlers begged Spanish officials to sue for peace.[15]

Insecurity stunted the colony's growth. By 1730 the province still had only 500 Hispanic people, with perhaps another 1,000 Hispanicized natives. Economic prospects improved a little in 1749 when peace was agreed with the Apaches, which allowed more extensive ranching. The market, though, was only a local one, being restricted to the supply of food and other services to the military. This was not a recipe for growth. Even by 1760 the three principal settlements of San Antonio, Los Adaes, and La Bahia (near the mouth of the San Antonio River) had barely 1,200 Hispanic inhabitants. Like Florida and New Mexico, Texas was retained entirely as a defensive outpost. It was costly for the Spanish government to maintain and produced nothing in revenue.

7 SIGNIFICANCE FOR THE BRITISH COLONIES

Despite their costs, the Spanish colonies, like the French, appeared to be in North America to stay. None was hugely profitable, although New France and Louisiana were self-sustaining. The Spanish and French governments were willing to provide support even for those colonies that continued to struggle, however, because of their strategic importance to imperial interests in North America. Spain needed a buffer to guard its valuable possessions in New Spain to the south. France had achieved effective control over the Mississippi River corridor, and hoped that in the future this control would guarantee its hegemony over the trans-Mississippi west, although with the yet undiscovered resources it must contain. In 1750, both powers were determined to retain control over their North American colonies long into the future.

To the British colonists along the Atlantic coast, it did not really matter whether the Spanish and French colonies were cost-effective for their sponsors. What mattered was simply that the colonies were there. Both native-born and immigrant farmers in the British colonies wanted cheap land for their families, and eighteenth-century speculators hoped to profit by acquiring western land that could be sold to them. However, by 1750 the competition between Spain and France to control the Gulf of Mexico and the trans-Mississippi west had created a balance of power that effectively blocked the British colonies from expanding beyond the Allegheny Mountains. French alliances with thousands of Native Americans in the *pays d'en haut* and along the Mississippi River corridor had given them control over the center of the continent. Furthermore the French were determined to maintain their hegemony there, despite its considerable cost, because they believed it gave them a decisive geopolitical advantage in their imperial contests with Great Britain and Spain. By 1750, there was every reason for the British to expect that France would be a permanent rival to their west, limiting the geographical expansion of their own Atlantic seaboard colonies in North America for the imaginable future.

---

[15] Juliana Barr, *Peace Came in the Form of a Woman: Indians and Spaniards in the Texas Borderlands* (Chapel Hill, 2007), shows that the peoples of Texas, much like the peoples in the Arkansas Valley, dictated the terms of their relationship with Europeans rather than vice versa. They refused to adapt to Spanish cultural norms, insisting that the Spanish adapt to their customs instead.

16

Native American Societies and Cultures, 1689–1760

1675–78	Massachusetts and the Abenaki peoples are at war.
1677	New York agrees the Covenant Chain with the Iroquois.
1680s	Delaware people sell some of their land to Pennsylvania. Shawnees begin to leave Ohio Valley, migrating to Pennsylvania and Carolina.
1701	The Iroquois sign a treaty of neutrality with the French.
1712	The Tuscarora people in North Carolina are defeated. Most migrate to Pennsylvania.
1713	By the Treaty of Utrecht the British claim the eastern part of the Micmac homeland.
1715	The Catawbas emerge in the South Carolina piedmont region.
1717	The Yamasees are defeated in South Carolina and migrate to Florida.
1720s	Delaware and Shawnee peoples begin migrating to the Ohio Valley.
1722	The Tuscaroras join the Iroquois League (and are granted full membership in 1750).
1724	The Abenaki village at Norridgewock is destroyed. Many Abenakis migrate to St. Francis.
1729	The Natchez people are defeated and join the Chickasaws.
1737	Pennsylvania claims more land from the Delawares following the Walking Treaty Purchase.
1744	The Iroquois force the Delawares to move to the upper Susquehanna.
1751	A peace treaty is agreed at Albany between the Catawbas and the Iroquois.

Colonial America: A History to 1763, Fourth Edition. Richard Middleton and Anne Lombard.
© 2011 Richard Middleton and Anne Lombard. Published 2011 by Blackwell Publishing Ltd.

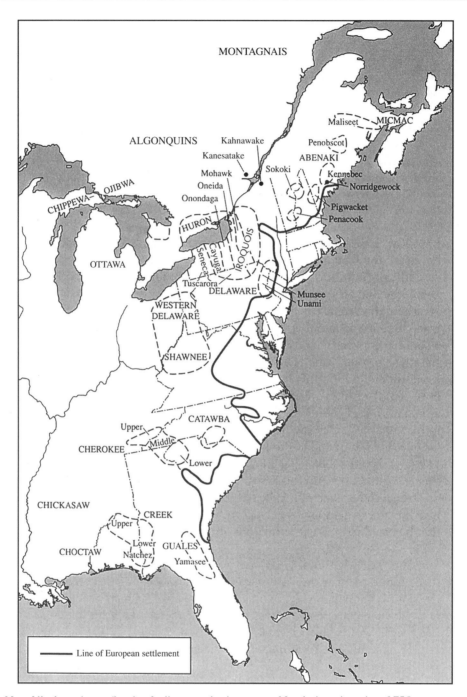

MONTAGNAIS

Maliseet   MICMAC

ALGONQUINS   Kahnawake   Penobscot

Kanesatake   ABENAKI

Mohawk   Sokoki

OJIBWA   Oneida   Kennebec

CHIPPEWA   Onondaga   Norridgewock

HURON   Pigwacket

Penacook

OTTAWA   Cayuga

Seneca   IROQUOIS

Tuscarora

DELAWARE   Munsee

WESTERN   Unami

DELAWARE

SHAWNEE

CATAWBA

Upper

CHEROKEE   Middle

Lower

CHICKASAW   CREEK

Upper

CHOCTAW   Lower   GUALES

Natchez   Yamasee

——— Line of European settlement

Map 19   Locations of major Indian peoples in eastern North America, circa 1750.

1 NATIVE AMERICAN SOCIETIES IN THE EIGHTEENTH CENTURY

B
Y THE EIGHTEENTH century the lives of Native American peoples in eastern North America had changed a great deal since their ancestors' first encounters with Europeans two centuries earlier. The challenges of trade with Europeans, environmental change, and competition over resources had transformed their world. Old World diseases had wrought untold devastation and populations had declined dramatically. Beginning in 1675 with King Philip's War and Bacon's Rebellion and ending with the Yamasee War from 1715 to 1717, a series of wars had produced catastrophic disruptions in virtually every Indian community east of the Appalachian Mountains. The Native American death rate in these wars was horrendous, typically far greater than casualties for whites since it was usually the Indians who were on the front lines of the fighting. To be captured and sold into slavery was another disaster, causing terrible damage not only to the individuals who had been enslaved and sent to the West Indies but to the families and clans who had been left behind.

And yet Native Americans were still to play a central part in the unfolding story of the European colonization of North America. The total Indian population on the continent north of the Rio Grande very likely still outnumbered the colonial European population in the middle of the eighteenth century. Even more important, relationships between Native Americans and Europeans were no longer new. Two hundred years of shared history had taught the Indians what to expect from Europeans and given them new strategies for negotiating and maneuvering to protect their own interests. Although those Indians who had remained within the boundaries of British settlement by now had very little bargaining power in their relationships with the British, those who lived in or had moved to borderlands between two different European powers often had a great deal. In addition, by 1750 many Indian peoples had grown in political sophistication and acquired considerable savvy about how to protect their interests against the threats posed by colonizers.

Even peoples whose societies had been devastated by warfare had considerable resilience, adopting a variety of strategies that enabled them to persist and to exert significant influences on events. Some stayed in villages under the jurisdiction of European American colonial governments. Others drifted north, west, and south from their traditional homelands and joined new communities. Some joined groups whose members spoke similar languages and included distant kin. Others placed themselves under the protection of more powerful forces, whether the Iroquois, the Creeks, the French, or the Spanish. Some were adopted into new tribes as captives and embraced new cultural practices, assimilating in order to survive. Still others found their way to settlements of refugees, like the peoples of the *pays d'en haut*. All of them struggled to regroup, learn the lessons of their experiences, and find new strategies for living in a world that had seemingly become dominated by conflict and catastrophe.

Even as Native Americans reorganized themselves, patterns of culture were changing within the societies of which they were a part. Trade with Europeans had drawn a vast number of Indians into the Atlantic economy, as producers of furs and skins and as consumers of various manufactured goods, from guns to cloth to cooking pots. In some areas, the land they inhabited had been transformed by European cattle, pigs, and plows. In others, the forests were still thick with game, but competition for access to it had grown. Diplomatic alliances with Europeans had altered languages, religious practices, kinship patterns, and gender roles. Even the names by which people called themselves were often new.

In the past, historians often viewed these changes as evidence of the destruction of Native American cultures. The use of consumer goods led to acculturation, and thus (it was argued) to the loss of traditional ways of life. Hunting for game led to overhunting in order to meet European demand, which led in turn to the degradation of the natural resources on which Indians' traditional ways of life depended. European missionaries destroyed traditional religions, just as European wars and diseases destroyed lives. The story these historians told was one of unmitigated tragedy.[1]

More recently historians have argued that the cultures of the Eastern Woodlands peoples in the eighteenth century were evolving and changing, but not dying out. These historians would suggest that culture is not static or timeless; religions change as they are adapted to new circumstances, but that they are no longer "traditional" does not typically mean they have ceased to shape the worldviews of their adherents. In fact, various characteristics of many Native American cultures may have made them unusually open to innovation and persistence when challenged. Openness to trade allowed Native Americans to incorporate new goods into existing ways of life. The practice of adopting captured women and children into new tribes enabled Native Americans to revitalize their kin groups after members had been lost. The ability to relocate provided tribes with a mechanism for survival in case of war or environmental damage. Historians who emphasize evolution and change in Indian culture tell a story of heroic endurance.[2]

Both stories have elements of truth, especially when we consider the diversity of experience among Native Americans in eastern North America during the eighteenth century. Some peoples were forced to make enormous compromises and virtually disappeared. Others preserved considerable autonomy from Europeans and retained vibrant and powerful societies. Their experiences spanned a wide spectrum.

At one end of the spectrum were peoples who lived within the boundaries of the British colonies, most of whom were eventually forced to submit to British legal and political authority and to give up much of their independence. The Indians of southern New England were one such group. Before King Philip's War, the Indians had made up nearly a quarter of the local population in southern New England, with approximately

---

[1] This approach was prevalent in the 1970s and early 1980s. For examples, see Calvin Martin, "The European Impact on the Culture of a Northeastern Algonquian Tribe: An Ecological Interpretation," *William and Mary Quarterly*, 31 (1974), 3–26; Kenneth M. Morrison, "'That Art of Coyning Christians': John Eliot and the Praying Indians of Massachusetts," *Ethnohistory*, 21 (1974), 77–92; Richard White, *The Roots of Dependency: Subsistence, Environment, and Social Change among the Choctaws, Pawnees, and Navajos* (Lincoln, Nebr., 1983).

[2] The emphasis on adaptation and persistence has become more common since 1990, and can be seen in works such as Richard White, *The Middle Ground: Indians, Empires, and Republics in the Great Lakes Region, 1650–1815* (New York, 1991); Daniel K. Richter, *The Ordeal of the Longhouse: The Peoples of the Iroquois League in the Era of European Colonization* (Chapel Hill, 1992); Gregory Evans Dowd, *A Spirited Resistance: The North American Struggle for Unity, 1745–1815* (Baltimore, 1992); Colin G. Calloway, *New Worlds for All: Indians, Europeans, and the Remaking of Early America* (Baltimore, 1997), and Daniel K. Richter, *Facing East from Indian Country: A Native History of Early America* (Cambridge, Mass., 2001).

18,000 Indians living alongside about 60,000 English settlers. By the end of the war, half of the Indians had died, been captured and sold into slavery, or fled to new homes in the north. Despite the fact that the survivors had mostly remained loyal to the English during the war, New England government authorities were now profoundly suspicious of them all and imposed tight restrictions on their movements. In Massachusetts, all Indians were ordered either to live in Christian families (as servants) or to resettle in one of four Christian Indian villages, Natick, Wamesit, Hassanamesit, and Punkapaug.[3]

The Indians were now expected to earn their livelihoods in the same manner as the English settlers, a task that proved extremely difficult. Although Indians in southern New England had always done some farming, they were unwilling to adopt English agricultural methods and forms of ownership that would erode their community-based society. Surrounded by land that had been cleared of forests, the men could not hunt. Instead they hired themselves out when they could as whalers or trackers, or signed on as soldiers during the many wars with France. Although they undoubtedly would have preferred to hunt, all of these jobs allowed them to utilize skills as hunters or warriors that were traditionally sources of respect for Native American men. Women made baskets, brooms, and pottery, which they sold to their Anglo-American neighbors. Often they were unable to maintain their independence. Burdened by debt and having few possessions of value besides their land, many Indians sold their land to white settlers simply to survive. Some became indentured servants, while others became itinerants and vagrants. Itineracy created unbalanced sex ratios, undermining family structures and fertility. By 1760 the ratio of female to male was approximately two to one not least because so many men had been killed in the wars with France.

Despite these obstacles, Indians and their descendents in southern New England continued to think of themselves as peoples separate and distinct from the English, adapting creatively to their new circumstances in order to survive. Forced to live in villages with strangers, they created new, ethnically mixed communities with their former rivals. Niantics, Narragansetts, Wampanoags, Nipmucks, and Pequots now defined themselves as the same people. Others adapted and survived by intermarrying with other people of color. African Americans, like Indians, had an unbalanced sex ratio, with men outnumbering women owing to the vagaries of the slave trade. Although New England colonial authorities discouraged both Indians and African Americans from marrying whites, they did not interfere with marriages between Indian women and African American men. The offspring of these blended multicultural families grew up understanding that they were of Indian or part-Indian descent, even though government officials now often classified them as "Negro" or "black."[4]

Similar processes took place elsewhere in the British colonies. In Virginia, members of peoples who had once been part of the powerful Powhatan Confederacy, such the

---

[3] For population statistics, see James David Drake, *King Philip's War: Civil War in New England* (Amherst, 1999), 169, 182.

[4] For the persistence of Indian identity in Massachusetts, see Daniel R. Mandell, *Behind the Frontier: Indians in Eighteenth-Century Eastern Massachusetts* (Lincoln, Nebr., 1996); and Jean M. O'Brien, *Dispossession by Degrees: Indian Land and Identity in Natick, Massachusetts, 1650–1790* (Cambridge, 1997). For the feminization of Indian poverty, see Ruth Wallis Herndon and Ella Wilcox Sekatau, "The Right to a Name: Narragansett People and Rhode Island Officials in the Revolutionary Era," in Colin G. Calloway, ed., *After King Philip's War: Presence and Persistence in Indian New England* (Hanover, NH, 1997), 113–40.

Chickahominy, Mattaponi, and Pamunkey, remained inside the boundaries of the colony, where they were expected to assimilate and live in the manner of the English settlers. A treaty signed in the aftermath of Bacon's Rebellion supposedly guaranteed them certain lands and rights similar to those enjoyed by the colonists. But, as in Massachusetts, their lands were slowly encroached upon by whites, confining them to a few small enclaves. The Virginia legislature created new barriers to their ability to become full members of Virginia society, prohibiting intermarriage with whites in 1691 and banning Indians from testifying in court in 1705. Young men were compelled to labor for their white neighbors instead of relying upon hunting for their livelihoods, with the result that tribes became dispersed and their languages were lost.

Just as in southern New England, Indians within Virginia adapted to these setbacks by adopting and intermarrying with outsiders. They took in people from other tribes as well as free African Americans and poor whites, creating new bonds of kinship to incorporate new members much as Native American clans had always done when their populations declined. Families formed through this process of racial intermingling continued to identify themselves as Indians or part-Indians until the twentieth century, preserving plant lore and indigenous techniques for hunting and fishing even while they lived in much the same manner as their poor white neighbors. A similar process was evident in Maryland.[5]

Although some Eastern Woodlands peoples had obviously been forced to make extraordinary compromises with the British by the 1700s, other peoples managed to retain a substantial degree of autonomy despite the pressures created by European colonization. Several factors contributed to their success. The first of these was their ability to pick up their belongings and migrate to a new location when their survival became threatened. Migration minimized unnecessary conflict with settler populations, helped to prevent further attacks by Native American enemies, and enabled people to find better hunting grounds when their own forests became depleted. A second factor was many Native American peoples' willingness to incorporate newcomers and reconstitute their communities. As people moved, they created new alliances, formed new villages and confederations, and redefined their tribal identities. And a final factor, perhaps the most important, was that peoples who occupied territory between competing imperial governments learned that they were better off playing one nation against the other than sticking firmly with a single European ally. A closer look at some of the other major groups who lived along the borders of the British colonial settlements by the early 1700s illustrates this range of possibilities.

2 THE NATIONS OF THE NORTHERN FRONTIER

The most powerful of all the Eastern Woodlands peoples in the North were still the members of the Iroquois League: the Seneca, Cayuga, Onondaga, Oneida, and

---

[5] See, for example, Theodore Stern, "Chickahominy: The Changing Culture of a Virginia Indian Community," *Proceedings of the American Philosophical Society*, 96 (1952), 157–225.

Mohawk peoples. For much of the seventeenth century the Iroquois had managed to control a substantial share of the fur trade by making war on other groups, and sustained their population by using the mourning war tradition to replace their losses. For five decades they carried out attacks on their enemies, culminating in 1684 with their humiliating defeat of the French. As we have seen, however, there were limits to the Iroquois strategy of making war in order to survive, and after 1684 the French not only reinforced their colony but united the surrounding peoples in alliance against the Iroquois. By the end of the century the members of the Five Nations were exhausted. Their wars had become wider and more destructive than traditional warfare, and were damaging their society. Their population at the end of the century was in serious decline. Finally, the dwindling supply of game around the eastern Great Lakes region meant that the Iroquois would soon have little of value to trade for European goods. Their fear was that they would be of use to their English allies only as a buffer against the French.

Even in the face of these dire circumstances, however, the Iroquois were able to manipulate both the French and the British in ways that allowed them to increase their power and revitalize their society. As discussed in Chapter 9, in 1701 one group of Iroquois leaders entered into a pledge of neutrality with New France while another group simultaneously agreed to renew the so-called Covenant Chain with the British. By adopting a policy of effective neutrality they were able to play one European power against the other.[6] One advantage of the arrangement was to give the Iroquois access to new economic resources. Their own supply of furs had been depleted, but neutrality enabled them to serve as middlemen in negotiating new trading relationships with French-allied Indians in the west who had abundant supplies. Sometimes this broker-age role was explicit, as in 1710 when they invited both British traders and Ottawa hunters to Onondaga to negotiate a trading alliance. At other times the Iroquois simply insisted on trade or gifts in exchange for allowing people from the west to cross Iroquois land on their way to trade at Albany. Meanwhile the Iroquois could now trade with both the British and the French themselves.

Neutrality was useful too in enabling the Iroquois to stay out of highly destructive wars with the French. Iroquois culture continued to prize military prowess in the eighteenth century, but after 1701 most Iroquois military campaigns were directed against distant tribes living in the Carolinas and Virginia instead of against close allies of the French. The Catawbas in particular were a favored target in part because they did not have a powerful empire to provide them with unlimited military support. Making war on the Catawbas allowed young Iroquois warriors to prove themselves in battle and to gain prestige and confidence, enabling the Iroquois to renew cultural cohesion without being suicidal.

---

[6] This meant in practice that the Seneca, Cayuga, and Onondaga nations maintained their links with the French, while the Oneida and Mohawk peoples continued their traditional friendship with the British. The fullest study of the Iroquois' evolving strategies for dealing with Europeans is Richter, *The Ordeal of the Longhouse.*

DOCUMENT 23

> The Iroquois reject English missionaries, circa 1710, reprinted in Karen Ordahl Kupperman, ed., *Major Problems in American Colonial History: Documents and Essays* (Lexington, Mass., 1993), 489
>
> *This exchange between Iroquois leaders and the Governor of New York, the Indians complain about their relationship with the British.* Questions to consider: *Why did they reject the offer of missionaries? Why were they interested in having blacksmiths to instruct them in metal working? Does this exchange suggest that their interactions with the British were causing the Iroquois to abandon their culture, or does it suggest something else?*
>
> It appears by the answer of one of the Indian chiefs or Sachems to Governor Hunter, at a conference in this town [Albany], that the English do not pay so much attention to a work of so much consequence as the French do, and that they do not send such able men to instruct the Indians, as they ought to do. For after Governor Hunter had presented these Indians, by order of Queen Anne, with many clothes and other presents, of which they were fond, he intended to convince them still more of her Majesty's good-will and care for them, by adding *that their good mother, the Queen, had not only generously provided them with fine clothes for their bodies, but likewise intended to adorn their souls by the preaching of the gospel; and that to this purpose some ministers should be sent to them to instruct them.* The governor had scarce ended, when one of the oldest sachems got up and answered *that in the name of all the Indians, he thanked their gracious good queen and mother for the fine clothes she had sent them; but that in regard to the ministers, they had already had some among them . . . who instead of preaching the holy gospel to them had taught them to drink to excess, to cheat, and to quarrel among themselves because in order to get furs they had brought brandy along with which they filled the Indians and deceived them.* He then intreated the governor to take from them these preachers, and a number of other Europeans who resided amongst them, for, before they came among them the Indians had been an honest, sober, and innocent people, but now most of them had become rogues. He pointed out that they formerly had the fear of God, but that they hardly believed his existence at present; that if he (the governor) would do them any favor, he should send two or three blacksmiths amongst them, to teach them to forge iron, in which they were inexperienced.

Another mechanism which enabled the Iroquois to revitalize their culture was their practice of inviting various refugee groups to settle in Iroquois-controlled territory and then claiming jurisdiction over the refugees by virtue of their authority under the Covenant Chain. For example, the Iroquois had driven the Susquehannocks out of the Susquehanna Valley in Pennsylvania during the 1670s, whereupon the Susquehannocks resettled in Maryland. After their defeat at the hands of Bacon's militia in 1675,

Governor Andros invited the Susquehannocks to resettle in New York and placed them under the protection of members of the Iroquois League. The Iroquois now extended that practice. In 1701, in treaty negotiations with Pennsylvania, the League claimed to have acquired jurisdiction by right of conquest over various peoples who had settled in the Susquehanna Valley during the 1690s, including some Susquehannocks (known as Conestogas) and Shawnees. By 1720, more groups had arrived, including Delawares, Nanticokes, and Conoys, over whom leaders of the Iroquois League made similar claims. These people, called "Props of the Longhouse," were expected to provide military assistance to the Iroquois if needed, and to provide a buffer against hostile tribes coming north to invade Iroquois territory. In reality League influence over these peoples was not as great as it appeared, yet the Iroquois carefully cultivated the illusion that they were the leaders of an empire with many allies.

In 1727 Pennsylvanian authorities, frustrated by the need to negotiate with multiple tribes on the western borders of their settlements, proposed to renew the Covenant Chain by designating the Iroquois League as the representative of all the tribes in the region. By granting the League this kind of diplomatic recognition, Pennsylvania further strengthened its members' power and prestige. At the same time Pennsylvania became a valuable new ally and trading partner, allowing Iroquois peoples to broker new trading relationships with new groups of Indians with access to furs.

In one case, the Iroquois invited one of these tributary groups into the League. The Tuscaroras who lived in Carolina were an Iroquoian-speaking people with whom the Iroquois shared many cultural affinities. Several Tuscarora headmen approached the Five Nations in 1710 to seek peace with them, though before any treaty could be concluded, the Tuscaroras became involved in the Tuscarora War. After the war ended in 1713, as many as 2,000 Tuscaroras moved northwards to ask for shelter among the Five Nations. In 1722 the Iroquois invited the Tuscaroras to join the League, and around 1750 conferred on them the status of Sixth Nation, with representation on the grand council at Onondaga.

The Iroquois were able to maneuver effectively in a colonial world in part because they occupied strategically important territory: on the border between two competing empires, they guarded the principal pathways to the west by way of the Mohawk River. In addition their numerical strength, amounting perhaps to 15,000 people, and their prowess in warfare gave them a reputation for being more powerful than they actually were.[7] The reality was that by 1701 the Iroquois had been seriously weakened by war and disease, and they were far from unified. Yet for the next 50 years their ability to sustain the illusion of their power convinced both the British and the French colonial governments to supply them with arms and trade goods and to offer them diplomatic ties so as to ensure they did not give their full support to the other. In essence the Iroquois were able to use the mystique of their own power to regain the power they had lost, and to continue to play a decisive role in the development of North American politics and diplomacy.

---

[7] For the historiography of the Iroquois, see Daniel K. Richter and James H. Merrell, eds, *Beyond the Covenant Chain: The Iroquois and Their Neighbors in Indian North America, 1600–1800* (Syracuse, 1987); and Dean R. Snow, *The Iroquois* (Cambridge, Mass., 1994).

Map 20 Major Native American powers of the northern frontier, circa 1725.

Figure 30 Portrait of Sagayenkwaraton (baptized Brant), named Sa Ga Yeath Qua Pieth
Tow, King of the Maquas (Mohawk). Painting, 1710. The cloak was a gift in
London, while the white cloth shirt was a standard item among the trade goods made
available by British traders. Note that the wearer has taken these items of European
clothing and incorporated them into a distinctly indigenous style of dress and self-
presentation. The National Archives of Canada.

A much smaller group of Iroquois peoples, mostly Mohawks, retained their
independence by converting to Catholicism and joining the other Catholic, French-
allied Indians in the *reserves* at Kahnawake and Kanesatake in New France. These
Indians appeared on the surface to have become thoroughly French. They spoke
French, wore French clothing, and worshiped in French Catholic churches guided by
Jesuit priests. Yet they retained considerable political and cultural autonomy, since the
government of New France relied on them for military support and was therefore
careful not to make too many demands. Unlike the Indians who had stayed in New
England after King Philip's War, for example, the *reserve* Iroquois had never had to

agree to submit to the jurisdiction of French courts. Nor did they tolerate the kind of heavy-handed discipline that the Franciscans had imposed at their missions in Florida and New Mexico. The Catholic Iroquois maintained ties of kinship with the British-allied League Iroquois, and along with those kinship ties came a strong sense of shared cultural identity.

Still, life in the *reserves* was no utopia. The problem was that the French expected their Indian allies to go to war on their behalf. In general the *reserve* Iroquois refused to fight against other Iroquois, but they could not altogether ignore the demands of the French allies. Therefore in general they attacked British settlers in New England instead, inviting sometimes devastating reprisals from the British colonial governments. Maintaining their independence was a delicate balancing act.

Another highly successful Native American population group could be found in a string of villages stretching from present-day Vermont and New Hampshire north to New Brunswick. Made up of the Micmacs of Acadia (Nova Scotia) and New Brunswick and various Abenaki peoples in what is now Maine, Vermont, and New Hampshire, these Algonquian-speaking peoples were all part of a loose-knit confederacy known as the Abenaki Confederacy.

The Micmacs who lived in the north relied mostly on hunting and fishing for their subsistence, which meant their villages were less permanent than those of the nations in southern New England. The Micmacs were staunch allies of the French, whose fishermen they had first encountered in the 1530s. Trading with the French for furs gave them access to hatchets, guns, textiles, and other useful items. Meanwhile their northern location, along with the relatively small size of the French population, insulated them from interference from French settlers. Their relationship enabled the Micmacs to enjoy the prosperity that came from trade with the French without losing the resources that had traditionally sustained their culture.

For the Micmacs the most serious threat to their culture arrived in 1713 when the Treaty of Utrecht consigned Micmac lands in Nova Scotia to Britain and British settlers began to move into the region. The French government was reluctant to become openly involved in time of peace. Nevertheless the Micmacs determined to fight for their homes with the encouragement of a Jesuit priest, the Abbé Le Loutre, who had a mission at Bay Verte on the isthmus connecting Nova Scotia to the mainland. A series of raids was launched to confine the British to their principal settlement at Annapolis Royal, and until 1750 the Micmacs were indeed generally successful in their endeavors to defend their homes.

Their Abenaki neighbors to the south faced greater challenges, but they too managed to hold their own against colonization for many years. The Abenakis included a number of nations, known collectively as the eastern and western Abenakis. Among the eastern Abenaki peoples were the Maliseets, Kennebecs, Pigwackets, and Penobscots. The western Abenakis included the Sokoki and Penacook peoples. Like the Micmacs, the Abenakis were primarily hunters, fishermen, and gatherers, but members of the western Abenakis also found it advantageous to engage in agriculture, and as a result their settlements were more sedentary than those of the Micmacs. Nevertheless their ability to move, either in family groups or in larger bands, ultimately helped them to avoid the devastation suffered by the Indians of southern New England.

DOCUMENT 24

The Micmacs ridicule the French, 1677, reprinted in Colin G. Calloway, *The World Turned Upside Down: Indian Voices from Early America* (Boston, 1994), 50–2

Though allies of the French, the Micmacs remained skeptical of European culture. Questions to consider: *What can the following episode tell us about the relationship between the Micmacs and the French? What can it tell us about the differences between Micmac society and French society?*

Thou sayest of us also that we are the most miserable and most unhappy of all men, living without religion, without manners, without honour, without social order, and, in a word, without any rules, like the beasts in our woods and in our forests, lacking bread, wine, and a thousand other comforts which thou has in superfluity in Europe ... I beg thee now to believe that, all miserable as we seem in thine eyes, we consider ourselves nevertheless much happier than thou in this, that we are very content with the little that we have; and believe also once for all, I pray, that thou deceivest thyself greatly if thou thinkest to persuade us that thy country is better than ours. For if France, as thou sayest, is a little terrestrial paradise, art thou sensible to leave it? And why abandon wives, children, relatives, and friends? Why risk thy life and thy property every year, and why venture thyself with such risk, in any season whatsoever, to storms and tempests of the sea in order to come to a strange and barbarous country which thou considerest the poorest and least fortunate of the world? Besides, since we are wholly convinced of the contrary, we scarcely take the trouble to go to France, because we fear, with good reason, lest we find little satisfaction there, seeing, in our own experience, that those who are natives thereof leave it every year in order to enrich themselves on our shores. We believe, further, that you are also incomparably poorer than we, and that you are only simple journeymen, valets, servants, and slaves, all masters and grand captains though you may appear, seeing that you glory in our old rags and in our miserable suits of beaver which can no longer be of use to us, and that you find among us, in the fishery for cod which you make in these parts, the wherewithal to comfort your misery and the poverty which oppresses you. As to us, we find all our riches and all our conveniences among ourselves, without trouble and without exposing our lives to the dangers in which you find yourselves constantly through your long voyages. And, whilst feeling compassion for you in the sweetness of our repose, we wonder at the anxieties and cares which you give yourselves night and day in order to load your ship. We see also that all your people live, as a rule, only upon cod ... until things come to such a pass that if you wish some good morsels, it is at our expense; and you are obliged to have recourse to the Indians, who you despise so much, and to beg them to go a-hunting that you may be regaled. Now tell me this one little thing, if thou hast any sense: which of these two is the wisest and happiest – he who labours without ceasing and only obtains, and that with great trouble, enough to live on, or he who rests in comfort and finds all that he needs in the pleasure of hunting and fishing? ... Learn now, my brother, once and for all, because I must open to thee my heart: there is no Indian who does not consider himself more happy and more powerful than the French.

The Abenakis' relationship with the English in the New England settlements was originally cordial, and they traded with both the English and the French for decades after the arrival of the first settlers. Like most groups that had contact with Europeans the Abenakis were exposed to unfamiliar diseases, which caused population losses. However, during much of the seventeenth century they were relatively successful in replenishing their lost population by absorbing refugees from further south. The largest influx of refugees came after King Philip's War, when between 1,000 and 2,000 Algonquian-speaking peoples from southern New England migrated north and were taken into Abenaki villages or allowed to live under Abenaki protection.

By the time of King Philip's War the Abenakis' relationship with the English had become considerably less amicable, since English settlers had begun moving into their territory in the middle of the seventeenth century. The settlers endangered Abenaki villages and drove away their game, cheated them in trade and demanded that they give up their guns. Some Abenakis therefore joined the rebellion against the English in 1675, opening up a second front of King Philip's War in Maine. Even though the English ultimately prevailed over Indian resistance in southern New England, the Abenakis actually won the war in Maine. By the end of 1676 they had driven most of the English settlers out of their villages in Maine to seek shelter in Massachusetts. When Massachusetts authorities finally signed a peace treaty ending the war in April of 1678, they had to agree to pay a token tribute to the Indians, rather than vice versa.[8]

During the 1680s, English people began returning to their former settlements in New Hampshire and southern Maine. The Abenakis once again were faced with the problem of having to compete with the settlers for the use of their own land. Some Abenakis sought French support in raids against the English. Yet the French government proved a reluctant ally, fearing that it would antagonize the English by attacking them on English territory. The French Catholic Church provided a welcome alternative. Many Abenaki families migrated north to St. Francis, a Jesuit mission village in Québec, beginning in the 1680s. Here they found shelter from English hostilities, which could be devastating. Like other Indians who lived in the *reserves* along the St. Lawrence and Ottawa rivers, they typically converted to Catholicism but did not dramatically change their cultural practices. Chiefs and tribal councils retained their authority, and Indian languages continued to be spoken. Men continued to hunt to supplement what women produced on their farms. Children were raised to think of themselves as members of Abenaki peoples, not as French.

Other Abenakis remained in northern New England, where they continued to resist the encroachment of the settlers on their lands. With the beginning of King William's War Abenakis began a series of raids on English villages, destroying houses and taking prisoners in the hope that they could convince the settlers to abandon their towns and go back to their homelands. Attacks resumed during Queen Anne's War, terrifying the

---

[8] The northern front in King Philip's War is covered in Jenny Hale Pulsipher, *Subjects unto the Same King: Indians, English, and the Contest of Authority in Colonial New England* (Philadelphia, 2005).

settlers as entire villages were destroyed and the survivors taken prisoner and marched north to Montréal and Québec.

After the wars more Abenakis moved north to avoid further conflict, while those who remained behind continued to be caught up in hostilities with the British. The people most immediately affected by the tide of British settlement were the Norridgewock Indians of the Kennebec River, home to another French mission run by Father Sébastien Rale. The Norridgewocks repeatedly tried diplomacy to reach an amicable settlement with their new neighbors, since they had no wish to become the clients of France and were keen to trade with the British. All attempts to negotiate, however, were frustrated by the unacceptable demands of the Massachusetts authorities, who insisted on hostages to secure conformity with their wishes. Rale himself tried constantly to mediate between the parties, seeking to do what was best for his mission in a difficult situation. The British, however, believed Rale was an evil priest who connived with French authorities in the sending of war parties against peaceful British settlements, a view later perpetuated by the nineteenth-century American historian Francis Parkman.[9]

In fact the Norridgewock Indians were forced to struggle alone in their conflict with Massachusetts, since the French were not willing to provide effective assistance against a British colony during peacetime. Neither did other Abenakis provide much military assistance. They lacked a political structure for coordinating broad military action, and by now most Abenaki peoples had decided to seek neutrality in order to avoid conflict. Their main interest, as in the past, was to obtain essential European goods through trade. And by now they had learned that their best chance to continue trading was to maintain good relations with both European nations.

The attempt of the Norridgewock people to protect their way of life finally ended in 1724 when Governor Shute of Massachusetts sent an expedition to destroy Rale's mission. Rale, an old man in his late sixties, was scalped and brutally killed by the Massachusetts soldiers. The remnants of the Norridgewock Abenakis fled to the French settlement of St. Francis, and a neutralist faction gained control in most Abenaki communities as people decided that diplomacy was a more prudent course than violent resistance. In 1727 the Abenakis concluded a treaty with Massachusetts. It was hardly a panacea, since further disagreements arose soon afterwards. Yet the Abenakis' decision to remain neutral, as well as the decision of many Abenaki families to migrate north into New France, enabled them to escape further conflict for several decades. Like the Iroquois they had learned that avoiding conflict with either the British or the French offered their best chance to maintain trade ties with Europeans and retain their independence.

One group of northern Indians who waged a more difficult struggle to retain their autonomy after 1700 were the Algonquian-speaking Lenni Lenapes, now known as the

---

[9] Francis Parkman, *France and England in North America*, 7 vols (Boston, 1865–92). The contrary viewpoint is argued by Kenneth M. Morrison, *The Embattled Northeast: The Elusive Ideal of Alliance in Abenaki–Euramerican Relations* (Berkeley, 1984). For an analysis of Parkman's writings, see Francis Jennings, "Francis Parkman: A Brahmin among Untouchables," *William and Mary Quarterly*, 42 (1985), 305–28.

DOCUMENT 25

An attempt to cheat Indians of their lands, New Jersey, 1716, reprinted in W. Keith Kavenagh, *Foundations of Colonial America: A Documentary History* (New York, 1973), Vol. 2, 1595–6

Unscrupulous whites commonly used fraudulent deeds to rob Indians of their land, which led many Indians to distrust all paper documents. Some British colonial officials, especially in New Jersey and Pennsylvania where the Quakers were sympathetic, attempted to protect them from such practices. This description of a hearing before a Quaker Justice of the Peace illustrates one such attempt. Questions to consider: *What can this interchange tell us about the relationship between Quaker officials, non-Quaker white settlers, and Delaware peoples? Do you think the Quakers' efforts to protect the Indians were likely to have been successful?*

John Kay came before me, Jacob Doughty, one of the King's Justices of Peace for the County of Burlington.

Myself [John Kay] with several others sent for John Weitherill and heard the Indian's complaint against him, which was that said John Weitherill had come to said Indian King and treated him with cyder and made him drunk, and that he came again to him the next morning and would have given him more cider and told him he sold him some land the night before, being land which said Indian King and other Indians lived on, and had set his hand to a deed or writing for the sale of said land. The said Indian King declared he remembered nothing of selling any land to said John Weitherill or setting his hand to any paper and further said he had always refused to sell that land and had reserved it for himself and the Indians to live upon and that the Indians had a right in it and would never suffer him to sell it. He had also promised them that he would not sell it and that he loved to live near John Wills and other Englishmen whom he called his bretheren and ... if John Weitherill had got him to sign any paper it was by defraud and cheating him and that he could neither eat, drink, nor rest with quiet until that writing or paper was destroyed.

We used what endeavours we could with John Weitherill to persuade him to deliver the writing to the Indian King and make him and the rest of the Indians easy, telling him how unjust such an action it was and the dangerous consequences that might thereby happen, but could not prevail with him to give any satisfaction.

Eventually the governor of New Jersey interceded, and the deed was destroyed.

Delawares, in Pennsylvania. Originally the Delawares had inhabited much of southern New York and New Jersey, but by the late seventeenth century they had been pushed back by white settlement to the region around the Delaware River. By 1700 they numbered perhaps 4,000 people. Never a single nation, the Delawares were divided into two linguistic groups: the Munsees, or northern Delawares, and the Unamis, or lower Delawares. The Delawares were largely agrarian in their means of subsistence, growing corn and legumes, though like all Eastern Woodlands Indians they relied on hunting for meat. They lived mainly in small, semi-permanent villages, some of which were stockaded, though others were merely a series of dwellings scattered along a convenient stretch of river.

Delaware relations with the English were for many years fairly harmonious, not least because William Penn had made particular efforts in the 1680s to negotiate proper land purchases. The Delawares were content to sell some territory, seeing the advantage of trade and assistance against other, more aggressive neighbors. The Quakers, almost alone out of all the English settlers, showed respect for the indigenous inhabitants and their customs. Yet despite the Quakers' well-intentioned solicitousness for their Delaware neighbors, the relationship compromised the Indians' independence almost from its inception.

As early as 1700 the Delawares were being pushed away from their homelands along the lower Delaware River by European settlers. Some moved further upriver to the fork between the Delaware and the Lehigh rivers. Others, as we have seen, moved to the Susquehanna Valley which by now was becoming a relatively heterogeneous place thanks to the resettlement here of the Delaware, Shawnee, Nanticoke, Conoy, and Conestoga Indians. Here Delawares became "Props of the Longhouse," since this was a region where the Iroquois claimed to have jurisdiction by right of conquest. The Delawares did not see themselves as Iroquois subjects, but made nominal acknowledgments of Iroquois authority so as to avoid conflict.

After Penn returned to England, Indian policy in Pennsylvania fell largely into the hands of his former secretary, James Logan. Pennsylvania had no militia to protect it from hostile Indians, should they attack the colony. So during the 1720s Logan began to further strengthen the colony's relationship with the Iroquois, in hopes that the Iroquois could serve as a proxy defense force to guard the colony's inhabitants against attackers. Under the terms of the treaty agreed by Pennsylvania and the Iroquois in 1727, the Iroquois purported to sell Pennsylvania most of the land in the Susquehanna Valley in return for Pennsylvania's recognition of their right to sovereignty over the Indians in the region. Of course it was not the Iroquois at all, but rather Delawares, Shawnees, and other recently resettled peoples who actually inhabited that land. As result of the treaty, the claims both of the Iroquois and of Pennsylvania to the Susquehanna grew stronger, while those of the actual inhabitants were weakened.

In the 1730s Penn's sons, Thomas and John, took over the proprietorship of Pennsylvania, with the assistance of James Logan. All three were more interested in developing their lands than in protecting the Indians, having abandoned the Quaker moral commitment to treat the native inhabitants with Christian compassion. The situation was the more volatile because numerous Germans and Scots-Irish were now entering Pennsylvania in search of land. The arrival of the new immigrants offered the Penns the prospect of huge profits from land sales if they could remove the native inhabitants.

The result was a new mechanism to dispossess the Delawares from their homeland on the upper Delaware River, called the "Walking Purchase" of 1737. Thomas Penn claimed to have discovered an ancient deed granting his father an area extending from the junction of the Delaware and Lehigh rivers as far as a man could walk in one and a half days. The Delawares grudgingly agreed to respect the deed, believing it would require them to give up only a relatively small area. Unbeknownst to them, Thomas Penn had arranged for a relay of runners to mark out the boundary along a trail they had secretly blazed in advance. The runners ran a distance of 70 miles to the west, enabling the Penns to claim over one million acres of new territory. The Delawares could do nothing to stop them. They had trustingly based their security for 50 years on their original treaties with William Penn. Although they totaled about 4,000 people, their warriors were too few and their settlements too exposed for outright resistance.

Not that the Penn brothers had a completely free hand, since they still had to deal with the Quakers in the assembly. It was partly to circumvent this obstacle that Thomas and John Penn again enlisted the aid of the Iroquois. The two sides had several interests in common. Apart from land, the Penns wanted to open trade with the western tribes, which they could do only with the agreement of the Iroquois. The latter believed that the subjection of the Delawares would increase their power and influence. Accordingly, in 1744 a treaty was concluded at Lancaster. The Iroquois claimed suzerainty over the Delawares on the upper Delaware River, whom they claimed to have conquered and reduced to the status of women, and told them to move to the other Delaware settlements on the Susquehanna River. The Delawares were forced to leave. The Pennsylvania proprietors received the lands thus vacated, along with the blessing of the Iroquois for a western trade route.

The combined pressure of the proprietors and the Iroquois League was too strong for the Delawares to fight against. A few, like Chief Teedyuscung, adopted Christianity in an abortive attempt to keep their lands. Others sought refuge with the Moravian missionaries at Gnadenhutten near Bethlehem or moved to the Susquehanna Valley. But many refused to accept such clearly fraudulent proceedings and migrated westward to the Ohio River Valley. Here they encountered a friendly group of people whose members were also migrating west in order to avoid conflict with the Pennsylvania proprietors and the Iroquois: the Shawnees.

Known as the "greatest travelers in America," Shawnees had already ranged across vast distances by the eighteenth century. After being driven by the Iroquois from their homeland in the Ohio Valley by the 1680s, various groups of Shawnees moved to South Carolina, Pennsylvania, Virginia, and what would later become Alabama and Kentucky in order to escape from English and Iroquois domination. In Pennsylvania at the end of the seventeenth century the Shawnees had lived peacefully near the Delawares. Then during the first half of the eighteenth century, many Shawnees began returning to the Ohio Valley, sometimes migrating around the same time as their former Delaware neighbors. The Delawares and the Shawnees soon represented a formidable combination, not least because of their mutual resentments against both the British and the Iroquois.[10]

---

[10] Colin Calloway discusses the early history of the Shawnee in *The Shawnees and the War for America* (New York, 2007).

In the Ohio Country Delawares and Shawnees settled at sites along the Allegheny River which had once served as hunting camps for their warriors. Here they were joined by a group of Senecas (called Mingoes by local peoples) who had moved away from their ancestral Iroquois homelands. Living in new villages that dotted the countryside along the Allegheny and Ohio rivers, Delawares, Shawnees, and Mingoes mingled with French-allied Indians from the *pays d'en haut* who had settled along the western portions of the Ohio. Before many years their communities became thoroughly multiethnic much like the refugee communities of the western Great Lakes during the late seventeenth century.

Life in the Ohio Country offered the western Delawares considerably more indepen-dence than their eastern kinfolk who had stayed in Pennsylvania. Great Britain and France both claimed the right to sovereignty over the region, which meant that both British and French traders and missionaries all came through the region periodically. Colonial governments saw traders and missionaries as emissaries who could win Indian allies and strengthen their territorial claims, but for the Delawares and the Shawnees they presented new opportunities for freedom. Both the Delawares and the Shawnees distrusted the British (and the British-allied Iroquois). At the same time, they felt no historical attachment to the French. This left them free to trade with any nation they wished. Both British and French traders competed fiercely for their loyalty. British traders consistently offered better-quality goods for lower prices, especially during the 1740s when a war cut off French merchants' ability to ship goods to New France. Meanwhile the French worked harder to maintain the reciprocal ties so important to alliances with the Indians.

In the Ohio Country it seemed that the once embattled Delawares had at last discovered the key to freedom. Their favorable location gave them access to trade goods, and yet they did not have to do the bidding of any single European power in order to obtain them. Having resettled in a borderland where they were dominated by neither the French nor the British, they were able to play the one off against the other. This renewed independence may have helped to inspire some western Delawares to begin thinking about spurning their European alliances altogether. It was around this time that some visionary leaders among the western Delaware people began to develop a new philosophy which taught that only by abandoning the ways of the white man could they ever again enjoy their former happy state.

The other major population group inhabiting the region from the Mississippi River to the Ohio, as we saw in Chapter 15, were the peoples of the *pays d'en haut*, comprised of various Algonquian-speaking refugee groups including Ottawas, Potowatomis, Ojibwas, Mississaugas, Wyandots, and others from the western Great Lakes region. At the beginning of the century they had been united by their enmity towards the Iroquois and their common alliance with the French. By the 1720s they had reconciled with the Iroquois and learned the same lesson as the Delawares had learned about dealing with Europeans. Instead of relying on an alliance with one imperial power, it was to their advantage to maintain a relationship with two. During much of the eighteenth century the people of the *pays d'en haut* traded with the British in Albany and Oswego as well as with the French in Montréal. Their ability to spurn the assistance of the French allowed them to make their own decisions. At the same time they had begun to think differently about their relationships with one another, becoming more closely tied across tribal lines in a loose, multiethnic coalition. Membership in this broad group would one day serve them well.

3 THE NATIONS OF THE SOUTHERN FRONTIER

In the South, native peoples living outside the settled regions of the British colonies negotiated their relationships with European colonizers in many of the same ways as did the peoples of the North. The presence of Spain in Florida and (after 1699) of France in Louisiana could be an advantage, giving many Native Americans in the South options to play different European traders off one another. On the other hand trade could mean becoming ensnared in debilitating relationships of dependence. For some, alliances brought new resources and autonomy. For others, especially those who inadvertently became caught up in the perverse cycle of the Carolina slave trade or in the bloody Indian wars that tore through the South from 1703 to 1717, the costs of those alliances could be devastating. Some peoples scattered and regrouped, becoming part of new nations. Some migrated to new locations, sought the protection of stronger allies, and cultivated ties to more than one set of European traders in order to avoid becoming overly dependent. Between 1720 and 1750, most of the native peoples who remained in the region achieved relatively stable relationships with their European neighbors thanks to their new strategies for maneuvering through the world they now shared with British, French, and Spanish colonizers.

A traveler in Florida around 1660 would have encountered a variety of peoples living in and around Spanish missions (see Chapter 15). Though their numbers had been much reduced by disease during their many years of contact with the Spanish, the Apalachees, Timucuas, and Guales still possessed coherent cultures and traditions. Had that traveler gone north and west from Florida, through what would later become Georgia, he would have encountered the Lower and Upper Creeks. Some 15,000 strong and living in about 60 villages, the Creeks subsisted on a mixture of farming and hunting. Further west, but still east of the Mississippi, were the powerful and densely populated nations of the Choctaws, the Chickasaws, and the Natchez. North of the Creeks and along the Carolina coast lived a diverse group of peoples, including the Cherokees in the west, and Yamasees, Savannahs, Catawbas, and Tuscaroras along the coast. Many of these peoples had traditional rivalries with one another, but a relatively stable balance of power before 1670 had kept friction under control and allowed these societies to coexist.

From 1670 onwards the Native American slave trade in Carolina had disrupted relationships between many of these peoples and created tremendous instability. Thereafter, English demand for captives, their Indian allies' own desire for trade goods, and English conflicts with Spain combined to make things worse. By the end of the Indian wars in 1717, a total of between 30,000 and 50,000 Indian people had been enslaved, and the total Native American population in the region had declined by perhaps 60 percent.[11] The question for us is to what extent those who were left were able to adapt and to assert their autonomy as independent peoples.

---

[11] Allan Gallay, *The Indian Slave Trade: The Rise of the English Empire in the American South, 1670–1717* (New Haven, 2002), 298–9.

The Tuscaroras' numbers had been reduced from 5,000 to perhaps 2,500. As we have seen, as many as 2,000 surviving Tuscaroras migrated north where they were offered sanctuary by the Five Nations on the upper reaches of the Susquehanna River. The remainder opted to stay in North Carolina instead. Here they were grouped by the provincial authorities in a reservation on the north side of the Roanoke River under a single sachem, Tom Blount. Elevation of one individual in this way was alien to Native American culture and helped to weaken their clans. Moreover, the Tuscaroras, who had previously been important participants in the fur trade, no longer had access to furs and trade with the western nations. Soon white settlements began to encroach on the reservation, and the North Carolina authorities proved even less ready than New Englanders to protect the native peoples from unscrupulous land speculators. In deepening poverty, the remnants frequently had to sell their land. Their numbers dwindled further, and by 1760 many had moved north to join their relatives in Iroquoia.

Leaving the area was generally a better strategy than staying among the British. The Savannahs (the British name for the Shawnees in South Carolina) had been a major trading partner of the Carolinians, but began to leave the region by the early 1700s. Most migrated to join their Shawnee relatives in the Susquehanna Valley in Pennsylvania, and many eventually went on from there to the Ohio Valley. The Yamasees likewise left the region to seek refuge with another confederacy after their own defeat by South Carolina and its Creek allies in 1717. Since they spoke a Muskogean language, they traveled south to join the Muskogean-speaking Guales in northern Florida and became allied with the Spanish. Spain now maintained alliances with a mixed coalition that included Yamasees, Apalachees, Guales, and Lower Creeks. In time new communities formed out of these mixed populations, along with a number of escaped African slaves. Members of the resulting nation called themselves Seminoles.

Forming a new nation out of the remnants of older ones could be an effective strategy for long-term survival, a process perhaps best illustrated by the experiences of the Catawba peoples. Until 1715 the term "Catawba" was unknown, being a phrase of convenience first coined by the Europeans to describe the Esaw, Sugaree, and Shuteree tribes living on the Catawba River in the vicinity of Sugar Creek, in the Carolina piedmont region. All of these peoples had originally come from the Siouan area of the plains sometime in the sixteenth century. By the early eighteenth century they lived on the border between North and South Carolina, sandwiched between the Tuscaroras to the east and the Cherokees to the west. Then around 1715 they came together to form a single nation since they needed the support of a larger coalition in order to survive. Their new community was not large, numbering perhaps 2,500 members total with some 570 warriors in 1715. Following the Yamasee War they were joined by the remnants of other Siouan peoples, among whom were the coastal Waccamaws and Santees and the more inland Congarees, Saponis, Ocaneechees, and Cheraws. A Scotsman who traded with them during the 1740s reported hearing 20 different languages spoken in the Catawba settlements that he visited. In large part because of their flexibility and willingness to work together, the Catawbas managed to hold their own against larger competing nations at least until the 1750s. Each tribe lived in its own village with a council of headmen held periodically to help bridge their differences.

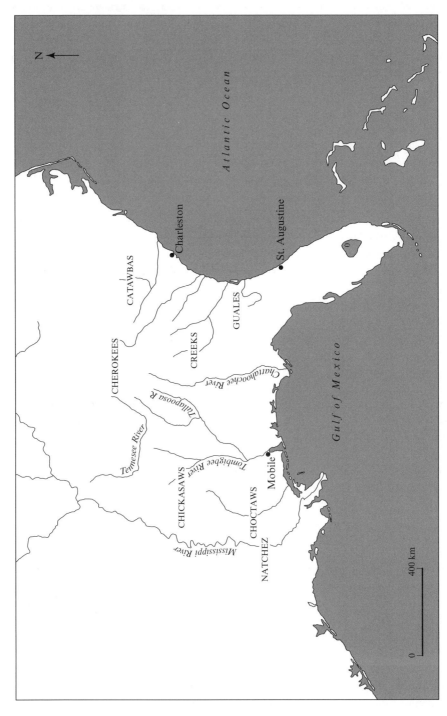

Map 21 Major Native American powers of the southern frontier, circa 1725.

Ties were also reinforced by communal hunting, war parties, and trade. Although their consolidation was not complete, it was strong enough for these Siouan peoples to sustain their sense of common identity for many years.

Making war against other powerful confederacies in the region probably helped unify the Catawbas, and certainly helped them to retain their cultural integrity. Like the Iroquois, the Catawbas practiced the mourning war ritual, and were drawn into frequent battles against Iroquois war parties coming down from the North. After 1722 Iroquois raiders were joined by Tuscaroras, who resented the Catawbas' role in driving them out of North Carolina. The Catawbas more than held their own, and won a reputation for themselves as some of the most fearsome warriors east of the Mississippi. The fighting became so intense that the provincial authorities in Virginia, South Carolina, and New York attempted in the 1740s to end the warfare in order to unite the native peoples against the French. A treaty was accordingly signed at Albany in 1751, but it proved of limited duration. The mourning war ritual had its own imperatives, and the Catawbas continued to fight individual Iroquois clans despite the agreement at Albany.

The Catawbas' reputation may have helped them to win a place as South Carolina's most vital Native American ally until at least the 1740s. Up to this point in its history the colony's government lacked the power to police its own borders or to defend its settlers against a host of potential enemies. Like the government in Pennsylvania, South Carolina needed groups of friendly Indians who could be employed as guardians of their frontier, absorbing the brunt of attacks from the north that might otherwise have fallen on British settler communities. The South Carolinians also needed an ally who could be used in tracking down runaway slaves. The Catawbas filled both of these roles. Meanwhile the experience of the Yamasee War had made the colonists nervous about the possibility of future Indian uprisings, so they worked hard to maintain amicable relations with the Catawbas. Thus the Catawbas occupied an enviable position with access to British trade goods and British diplomatic protection, enabling them to prosper for at least three decades.

Nevertheless, by the 1750s the Catawbas were increasingly under threat. The main problem was the advancing line of white settlement. Since 1729 the authorities in Charleston had encouraged development of the backcountry to protect the coastal plantations from another Indian war. Now a new tide of settlement was approaching from the North, along the great wagon road from Pennsylvania through Virginia and North Carolina. The settlers cut down the trees, drove away the game, cleared the land, erected fences, built roads, diverted streams, stocked the countryside with domestic livestock, and destroyed the Catawba economy in the process. Earlier the Catawbas had been able to conduct a thriving trade in skins to meet their needs. Now they were increasingly dependent on the colonial government – even for food when a drought occurred in 1755. Only their reputation as warriors sustained them in the eyes of the colonists.

The Catawbas recognized their precarious situation, and as early as 1748 they debated the wisdom of joining the Chickasaw or Creek nations. Essentially they had three options: removal, resistance, or reservation status. Removal to unknown lands was both risky and unappealing. Resistance was no longer realistic, since they had become vastly outnumbered. The majority wished to stay and decided the best way was through accommodation. At a meeting in 1754 the Catawbas promised to respect the colonists' laws, explaining that recent thefts of livestock and other items had merely been the result of exuberance on the part of the younger warriors. They hoped that gratitude for past services and current usefulness would ensure them a future.

As long as the Spanish, French, Cherokees, Creeks, and Chickasaws posed a threat, the South Carolina government in Charleston continued to welcome the Catawbas. Indeed the Catawbas were even able to play the South Carolinians off against the Virginians and North Carolinians, who were anxious for their support. But should the military balance shift decisively in favor of the British, such bargaining power would be lost. As it was, the Catawbas were now on the verge of being a dependent people, with a homeland little more than a reservation.[12]

By the late 1740s it had become clear that another people had replaced the Catawbas as South Carolina's most vital Native American ally: the Iroquoian-speaking Cherokees. One of the most numerous Indian peoples, they had a population of around 12,000 at the turn of the eighteenth century. The Cherokees resided in the mountains of southern Appalachia, where the borders of Georgia, the Carolinas, and Tennessee now meet, concentrated in three groups – the lower, middle, and upper towns – comprising some 60 settlements. Like the Iroquois, their towns were based on clans and were politically independent. Also like the Iroquois, Cherokee clans never fought each other. Diversity in their foreign relationships was not incompatible with harmony at home.

The Cherokees had been the key to South Carolina's success in the Yamasee War, as they turned against the Creek–Yamasee coalition to side with the British in exchange for promises of trade goods. Once the Yamasees had been defeated, many of the Cherokees continued to trade with the British and to promise military support. Still, not all Cherokees welcomed British traders. The lower and middle towns favored the British, or at least tried to remain neutral. The upper towns looked to the French at New Orleans, reflecting their different economic interests and location on the tributaries of the Tennessee River. This disunity proved helpful to the lower Cherokees, who were able to convince the British to make periodic concessions to them in order to secure their allegiance.

The Cherokees faced a major challenge to their autonomy when a devastating smallpox epidemic in 1738 and 1739 killed half their population. Some Cherokee bands retreated north. However, the Cherokees remained able to convince the British that they were indispensable allies. British fear of attacks from French-allied Indians to their west made them eager for Cherokee support and they repeatedly reconfirmed their ties through a series of treaties during the 1740s and 1750s.

---

[12]   For the Catawbas' story up to the 1840s, see James H. Merrell, *The Indians' New World: Catawbas and Their Neighbors from European Contact through the Era of Removal* (Chapel Hill, 1989). Although the Catawbas had enjoyed remarkable success before 1755, their descent into reservation status occurred more quickly than anyone anticipated. In 1759 smallpox killed over half the tribe, reducing their number to 500. At the same time the defeat of the French and Cherokees meant that Catawba warrior skills were no longer marketable. The Catawbas responded by requesting that their lands be surveyed to distinguish and protect them from white claims, effectively establishing a reservation.

West of the Cherokees was another powerful nation whose friendship the British also tried to cultivate. A Muskogean-speaking people, the Chickasaws had a population of about 5,000. Because the Chickasaws lived near the Mississippi River it was relatively easy for them to attack the French colony in Louisiana. The Chickasaws' longstanding animosity towards the Choctaws, who became allied with the French, made them desirable allies and trading partners to the British. South Carolina's government kept them supplied with guns and trade goods for many decades, and they rewarded British efforts by periodically attacking French settlements. For both the Cherokees and the Chickasaws, geographical position was the advantage that guaranteed their favorable treatment by the British.

The largest nation in the Southeast, and probably the most successful of all in retaining their autonomy after 1715, were the Creeks. "Creek," like "Catawba," was a term of convenience to describe a number of tribes, some of which did not even speak a Muskogean language. After the Yamasee War they would incorporate remnants of the Guales of northern Florida and the Yamasees of South Carolina, and after the late 1720s they would incorporate Natchez refugees who had been driven from their homes by the French. However, the heart of the confederacy comprised two groups of Muskogean-speaking settlements on the Alabama and Chattahoochee rivers, usually referred to as the Upper and Lower Creeks, though the latter were known as the Apalachicolas by the Spanish. The principal settlements of the Upper Creeks were Abeika, Okfuskee, and Okchai; those of the Lower Creeks, Coweta, Cussita, and Oconee. Estimates of the Creek population varied from 15,000 to 20,000 people, distributed between some 60 settlements. What is not in doubt is that their readiness to accommodate other groups had made them one of the most powerful confederacies in eastern North America.

The Creeks managed more successfully than any other southern nation to keep their options open by playing the British against the Spanish and the French. Although the Creeks had traded with the British since shortly after the founding of Carolina, they learned to be wary of British traders for their sharp dealing and unreliability. In 1715 the Creeks supported the Yamasees in their war with South Carolina. Nevertheless the British wanted their continued assistance against the Spanish and the French, and patched up relations with the Creeks in 1716. After the founding of Georgia in 1733, contacts were further increased and British traders from Charleston, Augusta, and Savannah kept the Creeks well supplied with trade goods like cloth and metal tools which they brought into Creek towns on packhorse trains. The problem for the British was that this method of transport was an expensive one for heavier goods such as firearms. The Upper Creeks therefore went to the French post at Fort Toulouse at the convergence of the Coosa and Tallapoosa rivers to buy guns, since the French could transport them here by water at a significantly lower cost.[13]

The Creeks experienced very little European acculturation other than the import of tools, weapons, and cloth. After the Spanish had been expelled from Apalachicola in 1681, no missionaries had been allowed to establish their value systems or challenge traditional Creek religious practices. Even in economic matters the Creeks felt able to deal with the Europeans on an equal footing. Signs of change became evident only

---

[13] For Creek relations with the French, see Chapter 15, section 4.

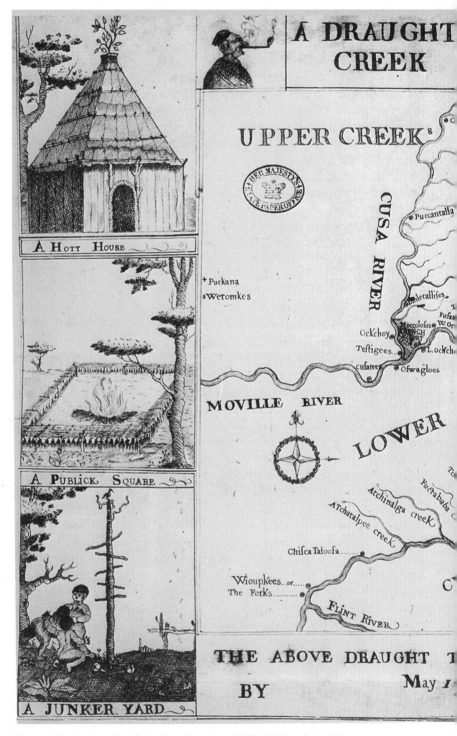

Figure 31 A draught of the Creek nation, 1757. National Archives.

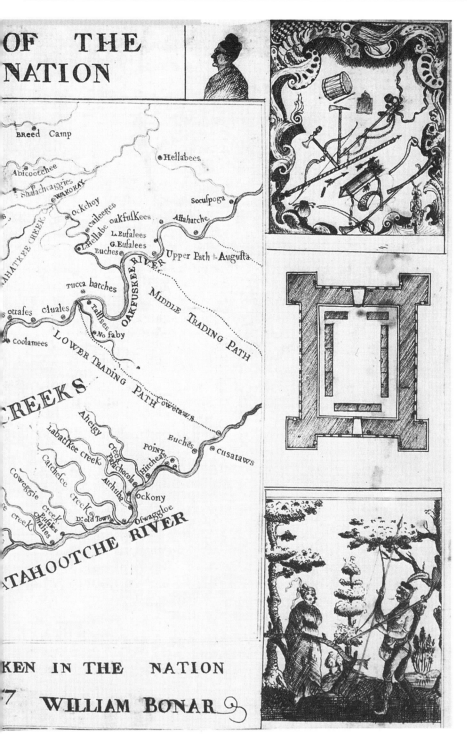

OF THE
NATION

BReed Camp

Abicootchee

Shalacheagries
WAKOKAY

Hellabees

ockchoy
caileeges
Hellabe oakfulkees
L.Eufalees
G.Eufalees
Euches

Soculpoga

Altaharche

Upper Path Augulta

OAKFUSKEE RIVER

rucca hatches

ottafes cluales
Tallsee
Nofaby

coolamees

MIDDLE TRADING PATH

LOWER TRADING PATH

Cowetaws.

CREEKS

Ahelgy Creek
Labatkee creek
Catchelee creek
Coweggie creek
creek Euffee
Challee
D: old Town
Palachoola
Archiba
ockony
Ofwaggloe

Euches
cusataws
POINT
Hitchees

TAHOOTCHE RIVER

KEN IN THE NATION

7 WILLIAM BONAR

Figure 31   (*Continued*)

around 1760 when white-tailed deer became scarce through overhunting and some Creek chiefs began to keep cattle.

4 ADAPTATION OR DECLINE?

It is clear that Native Americans in every region made vigorous efforts to retain their autonomy and their distinctive identities as peoples, though some were obviously more successful than others. Two factors helped those groups who succeeded: a favorable location that allowed them to avoid losing their lands to European colonizers, and an ability to manipulate relationships between two competing colonial powers to their own advantage. Meanwhile even those who were the most successful in retaining their independence experienced cultural changes as a result of their relationships with Europeans.

Thanks to their eagerness to trade with Europeans, virtually all Native Americans from the Atlantic coast to the Great Plains became caught up in the consumer revolution that was sweeping through the Atlantic world during the eighteenth century. Indians adopted European-made objects including firearms and ammunition, iron hatchets and brass kettles, cloaks made out of English woolens, ready-made shirts, scissors, fishhooks, and spoons. It would be a mistake to imagine them as pawns of British traders, for Indians were selective consumers and refused to purchase things they could not use. In fact they asserted their desires so effectively that manufacturers sometimes changed their product lines in order to meet indigenous North American demand. Nor did traditional expectations of reciprocity in trade disappear simply because Indians' trading partners now included Europeans. Eighteenth-century Native Americans still expected the mutual exchange of gifts to lead to friendship and peaceful relations. They found it offensive that Europeans expected to bargain and to sell goods at higher than customary prices when they became scarce in the marketplace.

Even though the Indians retained considerable autonomy as consumers and showed no interest in becoming part of a capitalist European culture, purchasing items in the marketplace inevitably brought about changes in their economic behavior. In order to obtain the European goods they coveted, Native Americans needed to produce something that Europeans valued, whether furs, deerskins, or slaves. Before contact with the Europeans, the local inhabitants generally killed only enough game to provide meat and clothing for themselves. Once Europeans arrived, however, local peoples had new incentives to hunt more intensively. Now men spent more of their time hunting for furs or going on slaving raids instead of hunting for meat. Women spent more of their time preparing skins for sale. Time that had once been spent in food and clothing production was often reallocated to producing products for sale in the marketplace. One result of the realignment of labor was that Indians began to neglect traditional skills like pottery-making and weaving. Having lost the ability to produce cooking pots and cloth for themselves, they had to produce more furs so that they could buy what they needed. Meanwhile another unintended side effect of this increased reliance on trade with Europeans was to lower the status of women, since the furs produced by men commanded a higher value in the marketplace than the food and other products made by women. While the horticultural revolution had produced greater equality in gender relations within Native American societies, the consumer revolution had the opposite effect.[14]

Commercial hunting also put pressure on the Indians' ecosystems. Traditional hunting practices limited the amount of game that was killed. Now Indians often hunted the game to extinction. This in turn disrupted relationships between tribes. Once a tribe had killed all of the beaver in its hunting grounds, its members had an incentive to conquer other tribes so that they could hunt in their lands instead. The Iroquois' many wars during the seventeenth century were partly driven by this desire to gain more land for hunting beaver once their own supplies were depleted. It was deeply ironic that Native Americans were placing more pressure on their woodland ecosystems at the very same time that British American farmers were shrinking the amount of available forest. By the eighteenth century over-hunting combined with the clearing of land had already resulted in an environmental calamity for all the east coast peoples.

The Indians' trade relationships with Europeans also drew them into new military conflicts that changed the practice of warfare. Before 1607 Native American conflicts had been limited, since their prime purpose had mostly been to avenge earlier losses and not to conquer entire tribes. Now the Europeans introduced them to a more destructive style of warfare. European guns were far more lethal than bows and arrows when used for fighting. European wars were also fought on a larger scale, since their purpose was to conquer territory by destroying its inhabitants' claims to the land. The Europeans therefore urged their Indian allies to destroy entire towns and enslave entire confederations. The escalation of warfare in turn heightened competition over resources, exacerbating antagonisms already provoked before the arrival of Europeans by climate-induced scarcity. Nations now felt compelled to secure a monopoly of the game in their area so that they could be assured access to European guns and ammunition, which they needed so as to protect themselves from attacks by their rivals. Perhaps one-quarter of the native population perished because of the violence unleashed by these mutually destructive struggles.[15]

Despite all of these damaging consequences of increased involvement with Europeans, some consequences of that involvement had the potential to strengthen Native Americans' ability to resist. The new place of sustained warfare in the lives of many Native American groups had produced significant changes in customary practices of political organization. Indian political structures had traditionally been organized around highly autonomous villages or clans. However, as communities were disrupted by disease and warfare and their members regrouped, they often developed more effective techniques for coordinating the actions of multiple villages and clans. As we

---

[14] Scholarly views on the effects of trade with Europeans on Native American economies have evolved over the past four decades. Historians writing in the 1970s tended to emphasize that it caused dependence and destroyed indigenous societies and cultures. See, for example, Calvin Martin, *Keepers of the Game: Indian–Animal Relationships and the Fur Trade* (Berkeley, 1978). Recent historical treatments emphasize that trade caused evolutionary change, but not rapid decline or dependency. See, for example, Kathryn E. Holland Braund, *Deerskins and Duffels: The Creek Indian Trade with Anglo-America, 1685–1815* (Lincoln, Nebr., 1993); Matthew Dennis, *Cultivating a Landscape of Peace: Iroquois–European Encounters in Seventeenth-Century America* (Ithaca, 1993); Colin G. Calloway, *New Worlds for All*, ch. 4.

[15] Changes in Native American warfare are dealt with in Calloway, *New Worlds for All*, ch. 5.

have seen, tribal leaders in the *pays d'en haut* after 1700 became more skilled at negotiating so as to hold together their broad coalition. Similarly the Catawbas created tribal councils in order to bring together their disparate members into a more unified group. Another adaptation was to enlarge existing coalitions or confederacies, as the Iroquois did with their incorporation of the Tuscaroras. By 1750 Native Americans had become considerably more likely to perceive themselves as having interests in common with other Native Americans than before European contact began, although old rivalries (along with European alliances) continued to play a central role in shaping relationships between Indian nations.[16]

Thus the situation of many Native American societies east of the Mississippi was fairly secure by the 1750s. They were relatively strong, despite the ravages of disease, because of the presence of three competing imperial powers: Britain, France, and Spain. France's economic and military strategy in North America required the maintenance of trade ties and alliances with the Indians so as to contain the British. Meanwhile the British and Spanish colonies' fears of their European rivals ensured that they would maintain trade ties and alliances with other Indians so as to protect themselves. Many Indians had come to see themselves as sharing common interests with peoples from other tribal groups. If the Indians were to come together into a unified coalition, if they could learn to exploit the divisions between the various Europeans on the continent, they might still turn themselves into a major military force with which Europeans would have to reckon.

---

[16] For a summary of findings on economic, military, and political changes in Indian societies during the eighteenth century, see Gary B. Nash, *Red, White, and Black: The Peoples of Early North America*, 5th edn (Upper Saddle River, 2006), 229–39.

17

Immigration and Expansion in British North America, 1714–1750

1685	The revocation of the Edict of Nantes by Louis XIV increases the Huguenot exodus from France.
1704	The first sewer is built in Boston.
1707	The Act of Union between England and Scotland opens the door to Scottish emigration to America.
1709	Swiss Mennonites arrive at Pequea Creek, Pennsylvania.
1710	Palatine Germans settle on the Schoharie River, New York.
1717	The first Scots-Irish arrive in the Delaware and at Boston.
1720	Massachusetts passes an act to discourage Irish immigration. Lutheran and German Reformed immigration into Pennsylvania begins.
1730	The first settlements in the Shenandoah Valley are established.
1732	A charter is issued for the establishment of Georgia.
1735	The first Moravians arrive in Pennsylvania.
1740	Settlers arrive in the North Carolina piedmont.
1749	A lighting scheme is introduced on Philadelphia's streets.
1750	Settlement begins in the South Carolina backcountry.
1760	Philadelphia becomes the third largest city in the British empire. Fire destroys 400 houses in Boston.

Colonial America: A History to 1763, Fourth Edition. Richard Middleton and Anne Lombard.
© 2011 Richard Middleton and Anne Lombard. Published 2011 by Blackwell Publishing Ltd.

1 THE GERMANS AND SCOTS-IRISH

T HE SEVENTEENTH CENTURY is usually portrayed as a period of settlement, the eighteenth century as one of consolidation. Before 1700, English men and women streamed forth to found a series of colonies driven by economic and religious necessity. Thereafter immigration dried up. But while this portrait may have held true for New England, it is not correct for the rest of the colonies. The South greatly increased its importation of African slaves, while all the colonies outside New England attracted new sources of white settlement.

What is true is that there was a relative decline in emigration from England after 1700. One reason was a lessening of religious persecution, another was an improvement in living standards there. A third was industrialization, which provided new opportunities at home. Even so, British North America continued to lure people from England, as the hope of a better existence still had considerable appeal, especially for those who had friends and relatives there. Others, perhaps 30,000, came as a result of the 1718 Transportation Act. It is likely that 75,000 persons of English extraction went to North America in the period 1700–60.

A steady stream of Scots also crossed the Atlantic. The inhabitants of the northern kingdom had been excluded from England's overseas possessions during the seventeenth century. Some Lowland Scots did settle in East New Jersey around Perth Amboy, after its purchase by Scottish Quakers. But after the 1707 Act of Union the door was open. Some Scots left as a result of the Jacobite uprisings of 1715 and 1745; many more departed for economic reasons. In time these Scottish immigrants were to be especially important in commerce, not least the tobacco trade. Perhaps 20,000 Scots came to North America in this period.

A further group to appear before the turn of the eighteenth century were the Huguenots, or French Protestants. Most came following Louis XIV's revocation of the Edict of Nantes in 1685, which until then had assured them of religious toleration. The Huguenots were generally welcomed, as their numbers were not large enough to constitute a threat and they brought many valuable skills as coopers, gunsmiths, clockmakers, and textile workers. These skills, added to their thrift and diligence, soon enabled them to prosper. They improved their position still further by learning English and integrating with the rest of the community, even to the extent of joining the existing Anglican Church. Perhaps 5,000 Huguenots had arrived by 1750. They were especially numerous in New York, where they founded the town of New Rochelle, and in South Carolina.

A few hundred Jews also came to North America from Britain during the latter part of the colonial period. While they faced clear discrimination, their commercial talents enabled them to prosper in the major seaports of Newport, New York, Philadelphia, and Charleston, where the first North American synagogues were established. By the time of the French and Indian War, merchants like David and Moses Franks of Philadelphia were sufficiently established to secure contracts for supplying the British army with provisions.

The two most important sources of white immigration in the eighteenth century, however, were from Germany and Ireland. In both countries the population was

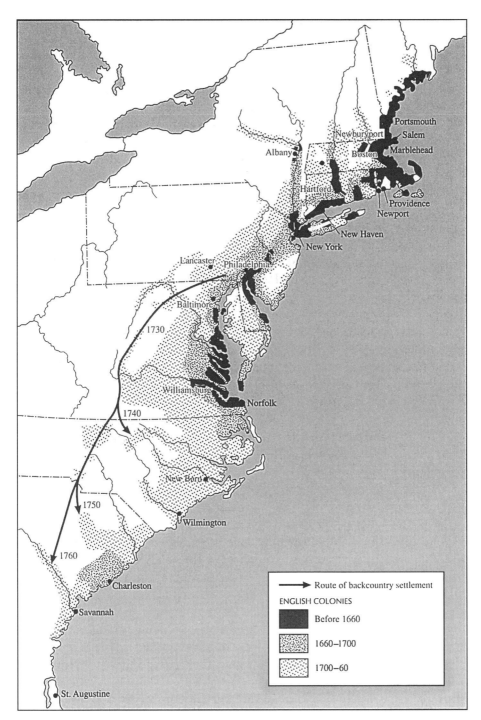

Map 22 Immigration and expansion, 1700–1760.

initially driven from Europe rather than attracted to North America, their uprooting being the familiar product of the search for economic opportunity and a desire for greater religious freedom.

The first Germans to come to British North America arrived with Francis Pastorius in 1683 at the invitation of William Penn. Their numbers were small. German emigration became substantial only after 1690, the year in which the Palatine prince decided to become a Catholic. Severe persecution ensued as he attempted to convert his subjects. In addition the devastation of the principalities of Baden, Württemberg, and the Palatine during the wars of 1689–1713 led many to consider emigration as the only possible escape. Most Germans looked for refuge elsewhere in central and eastern Europe: America was never the promised land for more than a small minority during the colonial period. German emigration proceeded in two main waves. First came the Pietist sects, erroneously called Palatines, like the Mennonites and Dunkers. Later came a second, larger wave from among members of the established Lutheran and Reformed churches after European hostilities had ended in 1713.

Initially, departures were necessarily restricted by the fighting in Europe, though some emigrants did escape. In 1709 a group of Swiss Mennonites made their way to Pequea Creek in Lancaster County, Pennsylvania. The following year 2,500 Rhinelanders arrived in New York, assisted by financial aid from the British government. The Whig ministry believed that Dutch commercial success in the seventeenth century had resulted partly from that nation's tolerant religious policy. Hence the exodus of German and French Protestants might be put to good use, especially, it was hoped, in producing hemp for the navy.

In the event a change of ministry meant that no further aid was forthcoming, and it was some time before the refugees finally found shelter on the Schoharie Creek to the west of Albany. The lack of suitable land and the indifference of the New York authorities led most Germans to look instead to Pennsylvania, where the early Mennonites had received a welcome because their Pietist beliefs were close to those of the Quakers. Soon other groups were arriving in the Delaware, notably the Amish people, an offshoot of the Mennonites, who settled in Lancaster County. Other newcomers were the Dunkers, or Baptists, who found homes there and in Berks County.

The end of the war in Europe brought a new exodus around 1720. These emigrants increasingly belonged to the main Lutheran and German Reformed churches, and their reasons for emigrating were more economic than religious. The Upper Rhineland in particular was experiencing a population explosion that meant ever smaller farms and less opportunity. In the mid-1730s, however, the Moravians, an evangelical branch of the Lutheran Church, began to arrive, following their expulsion from Austria by the archbishop of Salzburg.

The total number of German-speaking immigrants during this period is difficult to assess, but it certainly approached 100,000 and led to one-third of Pennsylvania's population being of German origin by 1760. The numbers were so high that fears were expressed for the survival of the English inhabitants. In 1727 a bill was passed requiring all immigrants to take an oath of loyalty, and in the early 1740s there was talk of barring from office anyone who did not speak English, the first demonstration of that later phenomenon known as nativism. As Benjamin Franklin commented, "Why should the

Palatine boors be suffered to swarm into our settlements, and by herding together, establish their language and manners, to the exclusion of ours."[1] He was referring not only to the continued use of the German language but also to the fact that Germans lived in their own enclaves, socialized in their own taverns, drank coffee rather than tea, worshiped in their own churches, and seemingly failed to become politically involved. Recent scholarship suggests that the Germans were not keen to assimilate; they defined for themselves a distinctive identity as Palatines and resisted pressures to become more like their English neighbors, at least initially.[2]

The Germans were to prove able colonists. Most of them were peasants who needed only settled conditions to prosper, being hardworking, God-fearing, and thrifty. Not all farmed immediately. Many came as redemptioners, hoping to pay off the costs of passage either by borrowing from relatives already there or by becoming servants for a time. This practice was bitterly criticized by the Reverend Gottlieb Mittelberger, who came to America in 1750 to investigate. He asserted: "It often happens that whole families, husband, wife and children, are separated by being sold to different purchasers, especially when they have not paid any part of their passage-money." Mittelberger was anxious to dissuade others from coming and accordingly painted a picture of hardship on the voyage and disappointment on arrival. In fact, since most redemptioners traveled in groups and possessed property, usually only one or two had to be sold into servitude, and they were generally redeemed by the rest of their family within a short time. Some German emigrants in any case saw servitude as an apprenticeship that was useful to complete before buying a farm. Some took 10 to 15 years to purchase a property of their own.

Unlike most English-speaking colonists, the Germans, or at least the Mennonites, cherished their farms and sought to improve the land rather than merely to exploit it. This attitude often encouraged them to take over farms which the original owners had decided were no longer viable. And like the Puritans in New England, they rarely moved until the pressure of population forced the third generation to look elsewhere for land. The result was that they generally prospered, and their husbandry was one reason that Pennsylvania prospered in turn. Though one of the last provinces to be founded, Pennsylvania contained over 300,000 people by 1760, making it the third most populous colony in America and the one with the highest per capita income.

The second major ethnic group to arrive in the period 1715–60 were the Scots-Irish from northern Ireland, where religious persecution also played a part. Although the Presbyterian Scots-Irish had been brought to Ireland by the Protestant James I, they suffered considerable persecution, not least the requirement to pay tithes to the established Episcopalian Church. Then in 1665 the Anglican-dominated Parliament in Dublin passed an Act of Uniformity requiring all ministers to conduct services according to the Book of Common Prayer. The effect was to bar Presbyterian ministers

[1] Quoted in Stephanie Grauman Wolf, *Urban Village: Population, Community, and Family Structure in Germantown, Pennsylvania, 1683–1800* (Princeton, 1976), 138–9.
[2] The speed of assimilation is questioned by A. G. Roeber, *Palatines, Liberty, and Property: German Lutherans in Colonial British America* (Baltimore, 1993); Aaron S. Fogleman, *Hopeful Journeys: German Immigration, Settlement, and Political Culture in Colonial America, 1717–1775* (Philadelphia, 1996); and Philip Otterness, *Becoming German: The 1709 Palatine Migration to New York* (Ithaca, 2004).

not only from holding church services, including marriage ceremonies and funerals, but also from operating schools. However, for the first 35 years the act was enforced only intermittently. Then at the turn of the eighteenth century a more militant Anglican Church, as elsewhere, attempted to make its supremacy effective in practice as well as in theory. This culminated in the 1704 Test clause of the Popery Act which barred all dissenters from holding any public office in central or local government.

The Scots-Irish had economic grievances too. Although Ireland was a dominion of the British Crown, it had been excluded from the mercantilist system, like Scotland before 1707. The worst blow had been the 1699 Woolen Act prohibiting Irish wool exports to Britain. This ban particularly hurt the northern province of Ulster, where a textile industry was developing. Finally, most Scots-Irish were tenant farmers. Many of their leases were due to lapse in 1717, and the only prospect they faced was higher rents. The coming of peace in Europe induced many merchants to offer passage on their outward voyages, and for some Scots-Irish the chance proved irresistible.

Accordingly, in 1717 several shiploads of emigrants set off from Ireland to seek a better life. In a few cases whole congregations emigrated, though when the restrictions against the Presbyterian ministry were eased shortly thereafter, this phenomenon ended.[3] Once a precedent had been set, however, others were ready to follow, especially since the economic problems remained. Initially, many headed for New England, believing that they would be welcomed there. When the inhabitants discovered that the newcomers were Presbyterians, however, relations quickly deteriorated, culminating in the burning of the newcomers' church at Worcester. Hostility was so great that in 1720 the Massachusetts assembly passed a bill to discourage any further immigration from Ireland. A few groups did manage to establish themselves in New Hampshire and Maine, where the settling of the frontier was considered more important than the maintenance of religious orthodoxy. Among the new settlements were the towns of Londonderry and Belfast.

Initially the southern colonies were also unattractive to the emigrants from Ireland. The domination of Maryland, Virginia, and the Carolinas by the plantation system with its slave workforce restricted both the demand for white labor and the availability of land, though attempts were made to lure them to the South Carolina backcountry in the 1730s with bounties to increase the white population. Another apparent obstacle was the presence of the Anglican Church, which made further persecution a possibility.

New York had little appeal because its manorial system left little freehold land available for settlement. After being tenants in Ireland the emigrants were determined not to have any more landlords. Nor was there any need to do so, for as the former governor of New York Lord Bellomont observed, "What man will be such a fool as to become a base tenant . . . when for crossing the Hudson River that man can for a song

---

[3] In 1719 the Dublin Parliament, under pressure from the more liberal Whig ministry in England, passed a limited Toleration Act allowing Presbyterians to hold religious services. At the same time it passed a Partial Indemnity Act which suspended the Test clause, allowing Presbyterians to hold public office on a grace-and-favor basis. Some of the restrictions on Irish trade with the American colonies were also relaxed in 1731 by an act of Parliament, 4 George II, c. 15. Marriages between Presbyterians were eventually legalized in 1737, though not for mixed marriages, which still had to be performed by an Anglican minister. The formal ban on office-holding was removed only in 1780, while tithes remained payable until 1870.

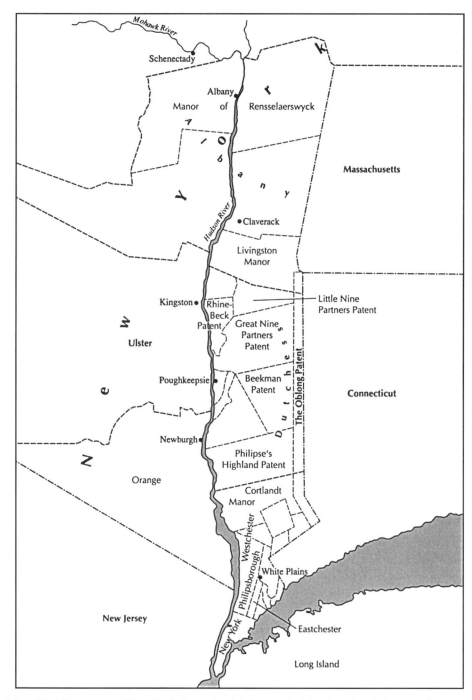

Map 23 The manors of New York. From Patricia Bonomi, *A Factious People* (New York, 1971). Reproduced by permission of Patricia U. Bonomi.

DOCUMENT 26

Gottlieb Mittelberger on the perils of crossing the Atlantic, 1750, reprinted in Merrill Jensen, ed., *English Historical Documents*, Vol. 9: *American Colonial Documents to 1776* (New York, 1955), 464–9

This passage by a German immigrant describes the conditions on Atlantic crossings in the eighteenth century. Questions to consider: *What kinds of expectations do you think these immigrants had of America? How might the experience of the passage have affected the identities of the new immigrants who came over?*

When the ships have for the last time weighed their anchors near the city of Kaupp [Cowes] in Old England, the real misery begins with the long voyage. For from there the ships, unless they have good wind, must often sail 8, 9, 10 to 12 weeks before they reach Philadelphia. But even with the best wind the voyage lasts 7 weeks.

During the voyage there is on board these ships terrible misery, stench, fumes, horror, vomiting, many kinds of seasickness, fever, dysentery, headache, heat, constipation, boils, scurvy, cancer, mouth-rot, and the like, all of which come from old and sharply salted food and meat, also from very bad and foul water, so that many die miserably.

Add to this want of provisions, hunger, thirst, frost, heat, dampness, anxiety, want, afflictions and lamentations, together with other trouble, as the lice abound so frightfully, especially on sick people, that they can be scraped off the body. The misery reaches the climax when a gale rages for 2 or 3 nights and days, so that every one believes that the ship will go to the bottom with all human beings on board. In such a visitation the people cry and pray most piteously ...

That most of the people get sick is not surprising, because, in addition to all other trials and hardships, warm food is served only three times a week, the rations being very poor and very little ... The water which is served out on the ships is often very black, thick and full of worms, so that one cannot drink it without loathing, even with the greatest thirst ...

At length, when, after a long and tedious journey, the ships come in sight of land, so that the promontories can be seen, which the people were so eager and anxious to reach, all creep from below on deck to see the land from afar, and they weep for joy and pray and sing, thanking and praising God ... But alas!

When the ships have landed at Philadelphia after their long voyage, no one is permitted to leave them except those who pay for their passage or can give good security; the others, who cannot pay, must remain on board the ships till they are purchased ... The sick always fare the worst, for the healthy are naturally preferred first, and so the sick and wretched must often remain on board in front of the city for 2 or 3 weeks, and frequently die ...

purchase a good freehold."[4] Accordingly it was to New Jersey and Pennsylvania that the newcomers looked. Only there did the Quakers ensure the absence of religious persecution; and only Pennsylvania offered freehold land on easy terms, not least because the proprietary family was anxious to increase the value of its holdings.

Pennsylvania thus offered a preferable alternative, since there was still so much unsettled land in the colony. A steady stream of Scots-Irish arrived in Pennsylvania at the rate of over 2,000 a year in the peak periods of 1717–19, 1727–9, 1740–3, and the early 1750s, when economic conditions were at their worst in Ireland. Perhaps a third of those emigrating went as families with sufficient resources to pay their passage and buy land on arrival. The rest, mainly single young men and women, took the traditional option of traveling as indentured servants. The men might hope in due course to buy land or become craftsmen. The women could look forward to a good marriage at the end of their service as the best means of securing a better life.

Initially, the newcomers, at least those who had the means, went to Lancaster County and the frontier areas of Cumberland and York, including the Susquehanna Valley and its tributary, the Juniata River. They were assisted by the readiness of the proprietary family to buy out the Native Americans, though by the 1730s most of the best land in eastern Pennsylvania had been distributed. To the west lay only the uninviting Allegheny Mountains, but land was known to exist in the Shenandoah, or Great Valley of Virginia. The newcomers, accordingly, began trekking down through Maryland to the junction of the Shenandoah and Potomac rivers at Harper's Ferry. They were encouraged to make the journey because the northwestern part of Virginia was not suitable for plantation agriculture, while the Anglican Church there was too weak to pose a threat. The Virginian authorities in any case welcomed the newcomers as a means of protecting their frontiers from attack by the French and their Indian allies. The settlers might also prevent runaway slaves from setting up maroon communities (settlements of fugitives and Native Americans who lived independently from white societies). Lastly, the Virginian elite wanted to sell them lands which they had patented for this purpose. Accordingly, in 1738 Frederick and Augusta counties were organized where new arrivals could apply for a survey and obtain a patent. Prices ranged from £3 to £11 a hundred acres, depending on location and availability.

The Scots-Irish settlers making this trek were joined by many Germans, Scots, and people of English descent. The coastal areas were experiencing a demographic explosion of their own thanks to the extraordinary rate of reproduction among descendents of the early English settlers. In the period 1720–60 Connecticut's population rose from 60,000 to 140,000; Maryland's from 60,000 to 160,000; and Virginia's similarly from 130,000 to 310,000. The children of English settlers needed farms of their own, and land was becoming almost unobtainable in the tidewater, except for the wealthy. Members of all groups therefore moved west. In Frederick County in the Shenandoah 38 percent of the population were English, 30 percent German, and only 28 percent Scots-Irish, though for the valley as a whole the figures were 25 percent English,

---

[4] Quoted in Michael Kammen, *Colonial New York: A History* (New York, 1975), 179. This view has been challenged by Sung Bok Kim, *Landlord and Tenant in Colonial New York: Manorial Society, 1664–1775* (Chapel Hill, 1978).

31 percent German, and 38 percent Scots-Irish. Since the mountains remained forbiddingly impenetrable, the settlers turned southeast from the Shenandoah, arriving in the backcountry of North Carolina from 1740 onwards. Here they found what had until now been a sparsely populated area. By 1750 an advanced guard of settlers had reached South Carolina, where they were welcomed as a protective screen against the still powerful Cherokee, Catawba, and Creek nations. South Carolina also saw them as a useful balance to the province's large number of slaves. In these regions the new settlers were more exposed to the Indians, of course, than colonists in the long-settled regions nearer to the coast.

It is hard to calculate precisely the total number of Scots-Irish immigrants to America; the most scholarly assessment suggests that about 100,000 people left Ireland in the period 1717–60. Higher estimates have been given but seem suspect in light of the limited Scots-Irish population in Ireland. The immigrants were not a unified group; they were theologically divided and left Ireland for a variety of reasons.[5] Of course emigration from Ireland could have included other groups, like the descendents of those who settled following Cromwell's conquest since passenger lists for the period 1717–20 reveal many departures from ports outside Ulster, notably Dublin, Cork, and Waterford. Many Catholics may also have taken ship, changing their religion and anglicizing their names so that they could make a fresh start on the other side of the Atlantic. As early as 1692 Edward Randolph had noted that Somerset County in Maryland was "pestered with Scotch and Irish." The presence of Catholic immigrants could explain why the authorities in Massachusetts acted with such hostility.[6] Even in Pennsylvania they were not warmly welcomed. Pennsylvania's elites denigrated them as wild and uncivilized.

In any event, Scots-Irish settlers were sufficiently numerous to make up 10 percent of the population by the end of the colonial period. Their presence was especially noticeable in Pennsylvania, where they constituted over 30 percent of the population. In time this influence was to have a profound effect on the politics of that province. Until 1760, however, the newcomers were too isolated and underrepresented to have much impact in Philadelphia, let alone in the southern colonies, though the evidence from Opequon Creek in Frederick County, Virginia, suggests that they played their part in local government as justices of the peace and members of the militia, along with their German neighbors.[7]

Compared with the Germans, the Scots-Irish were not good farmers. They were more like earlier English settlers, concerned only with exploiting the land quickly. They preferred to cut the trees down, build a crude log cabin, and grow whatever was possible

---

[5] Patrick Griffin emphasizes the lack of a unified identity among the Ulster Scots in *The People with No Name: Ireland's Ulster Scots, America's Scots Irish, and the Creation of a British Atlantic World, 1689–1764* (Princeton, 2001).

[6] For a discussion of Catholic emigration to America before 1776, see David N. Doyle, *Ireland, Irishmen and Revolutionary America, 1760–1820* (Cork, 1981), 59–61; and Kerby A. Miller, *Emigrants and Exiles: Ireland and the Irish Exodus to North America* (New York, 1985), 137–49.

[7] Warren R. Hofstra argues that ethnic divisions in the backcountry were less severe than along the coast, in "Land, Ethnicity, and Community in the Opequon Settlement, Virginia, 1730–1800," in H. Tyler Blethen and Curtis W. Wood, Jr., eds, *Ulster and North America: Transatlantic Perspectives on the Scotch-Irish* (Tuscaloosa, 1997).

regardless of the long-term consequences for the land. This attitude explains why so many of them moved after a few years. The French visitor J. Hector St. John Crèvecoeur later commented that, on average, out of every 12 families emigrating to America, nine Germans succeeded, seven Scots, but only four Scots-Irish. However, when making his comparison, Crèvecoeur selected the Mennonites, who were exceptional even among the Germans, and more recent work suggests that, where the Scots-Irish secured good land, their farming practices differed little from those of other European settlers.[8]

The Scots-Irish have enjoyed a reputation as frontierspeople. Certainly a number of them did excel as traders and frontierspeople, though not all Irish frontierspeople were of Scots-Irish descent. George Croghan, for example, came from Dublin of Anglican parents. But the vast majority of the Scots-Irish stayed on the eastern side of the Allegheny Mountains, since conditions in Tyrone and Fermanagh bore little resemblence to the terrain and climate of North America. As one settler from Belfast commented on arriving in South Carolina: "We were oppressed with fears, on divers account, especially of being massacred by the Indians, or bitten by snakes, or torn by wild beasts, or being lost and perishing in the woods." Settling one frontier in Ireland did not necessarily qualify them to do so again.[9]

In reality the Scots-Irish, like most groups, became frontier settlers only by necessity. The frontier was where the land was cheapest or could be squatted on without payment of rent. Once settled, the Scots-Irish, like all Europeans, did their best to destroy the frontier by cutting down the trees, plowing the land, and building roads, houses, and churches. They, too, wanted to send their surplus produce to market so that they could enjoy a better standard of living. Roaming the woods had little attraction in itself, except for the tiny minority who traded with the native peoples. For the Presbyterian Scots-Irish, as for the Puritans of New England, the wilderness was a dark, forbidding place, occupied only by savages and wild beasts. They began leaving their communities in the Shenandoah Valley, for example, only when the growth of population by 1783 required members of the third generation to find new lands in Kentucky and Tennessee.

Not surprisingly, one effect of the Scots-Irish settlement was the deterioration in relations with the Native Americans. The Quakers, as already mentioned, did their best to deal fairly with the indigenous inhabitants. No such compunction swayed the Presbyterian Scots-Irish. For them a Native American was a heathen outside the moral law. Like most European settlers, they believed the native peoples to be guilty of ignoring the parable of the talents. As one squatter told the proprietary land agent, "It was against the laws of God and nature that so much land should be idle while so many Christians wanted it to work on." James Logan noticed early on how the Scots-Irish were "very rough" with the Delawares. The result was a bitter harvest of trouble in the 1750s, when the battle to control the Ohio Valley began.

---

[8] See Blethen and Curtis, eds, *Ulster and North America*.

[9] The view that the Scots-Irish were especially heroic frontier settlers owes much to Theodore Roosevelt, *The Winning of the West* (New York, 1910). Roosevelt was writing at a time when exploitation of the American West was equated with progress. His attitude also reflected his own concept of manhood, typified by his formation of the Rough Riders during the war with Spain in 1898, rather than a historian's view. A more realistic account is to be found in James G. Leyburn, *The Scots-Irish: A Social History* (Chapel Hill, 1962). See also Blethen and Wood, eds, *Ulster and North America*; and David Colin Crass et al., eds, *The Southern Colonial Backcountry: Interdisciplinary Perspectives on Frontier Communities* (Knoxville, 1998).

2 THE FOUNDING OF GEORGIA

The settling of the backcountry was not the only expansion taking place at this time. In the 1730s a more formal colony was begun on the southern flank of South Carolina and named Georgia in honor of the king. The prime mover behind this scheme was Colonel (later General) James Oglethorpe.

A number of considerations prompted his design. After a career in the army Oglethorpe devoted himself to helping the poor of London, notably those imprisoned for debt. He suggested settling them in North America, just as the Elizabethans had sought to do with their beggars. But there were other considerations too. South Carolina, which had become an important colony, was isolated from the other provinces and had many potential enemies. A new settlement on its southern border would offer valuable protection. Several plans had been proposed since the Yamasee War but had failed for want of money. The need for action remained, however. The land south of the Savannah River had until the 1680s been controlled by Spain through its missions with the Guale or Yamasee peoples, and the British government feared that the Spanish might revive their influence. Settlement of a new colony would help to consolidate British claims to the region as well as providing a buffer for South Carolina.

Since money was required, Oglethorpe took his scheme to Parliament. Funding was duly agreed to, though a charter still had to be obtained from the Crown. The charter was issued on June 9, 1732, to a group of 20 trustees, headed by John Viscount Percival. The trustees were granted the status of a corporation with power to elect their own council, grant lands, enact laws, and raise taxes. To avoid a conflict of interest with their charitable aims, however, no trustees could hold any paid office or receive land. In addition, their responsibilities were to terminate after 21 years in favor of the Crown. In the meantime they had to make regular reports to the Secretary of State and Board of Trade and to cooperate with the Crown's revenue officers.

The device of appointing trustees indicated a shift in public attitudes; crude profiteering in the manner of the seventeenth century was no longer acceptable as a model for colonization, though the commercial motives behind the scheme had some similarities with past endeavors. In this case the climate of Georgia was thought to be suitable for growing the mulberry trees on which silkworms spin their cocoons, and every farm was to have 50 bushes. Similar hopes were entertained for potash and viticulture. Moral arguments also resurfaced; the settlement would provide Native Americans with a Christian example and give the colonists an opportunity to redeem themselves by hard work. However, the new venture would not have an established church. Liberty of conscience would be granted to all except papists.

Since the scheme was to benefit the poor, Oglethorpe and Percival placed a limit on the size of landholdings. They were determined that this settlement should not follow the example of the other southern colonies, with their large plantations and discrepancies of wealth. No grant of land was to exceed 500 acres. In addition, the settlers in receipt of charity who had not purchased their lands could neither sell nor alienate their holdings, nor divide them into portions of less than 50 acres. This restriction was

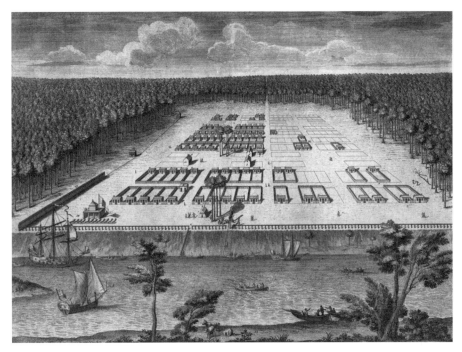

Figure 32 View of Savannah, March 29, 1734. Engraving by P. Fourdrinier, circa 1735. Library of Congress, Washington, DC.

designed to avoid the creation of a class of either very rich or very poor people. Georgia was to remain a land of yeoman farmers.

The paternalistic nature of the settlement was reflected in one other respect. There was to be no assembly, even though such bodies were now established in all the other mainland colonies. The power of making laws was to remain with the trustees, though their enactments had to "be reasonable and not contrary or repugnant to the laws" of England. Finally, the scheme placed considerable emphasis on defense. The new colony was to be laid out in compact townships to which everyone would be confined, thus facilitating defense in general and the formation of a militia in particular.

Prospective settlers were to receive free passage and be given cattle, land, and subsistence until they established themselves. The period of support was not expected to be more than 12 months, for the situation was quite different from that which prevailed in the seventeenth century. As Oglethorpe argued, "Carolina abounds with provisions, the climate is known, and there are men to instruct in the seasons and nature of cultivating the soil." He concluded: "By such a colony many families who would otherwise starve will be provided for ... the people of Great Britain to whom these necessitous families were a burden will be relieved; numbers of manufacturers will be here employed for supplying them with clothes, working tools and other necessaries; and the power of Britain ... will be increased by the addition of so many religious and industrious inhabitants."

The first batch of 114 settlers left England with Oglethorpe towards the end of 1732, arriving at the Savannah River early in 1733. Few of the new arrivals were released debtors, the trustees having vetted the settlers so carefully as to eliminate such people. The passage had been well organized and only two emigrants had died on the voyage, a great improvement over the experience of pioneers a century earlier. Also propitious was Oglethorpe's choice of an easily defensible bluff as the site for the first town, which he then proceeded to survey in a military fashion. The new settlement, Savannah, was laid out as a series of squares, which were in turn divided into house lots, with gardens and farms to the rear.

The settlement received an unexpected boon when the leader of a local Indian village offered to broker an alliance between the British colonists and the Creek Indians. Following the Yamasee War, most of the Guales and Yamasees had withdrawn towards St. Augustine, but a clan of Creeks known as the Yamacraws remained, under their sachem, Tomochichi. Relations between the Yamacraws, the Yamasees, and the Creeks were strained. Hence Tomochichi sought an alliance with the British as a way to bolster his own prestige and enable him to negotiate a reconciliation between his own followers and their Creek kin. Along with Mary Musgrove, the half-Creek wife of a South Carolina trader, Tomochichi helped negotiate a treaty with the main Creek nation recognizing the right of the emigrants to settle. The Creeks in turn welcomed the British as a counterbalance to the Spanish in Florida and the French along the Gulf at Biloxi and Mobile.[10]

Meanwhile the settlers, organized in gangs, began clearing the ground and building houses, spurred by the knowledge that within a year they would be laboring on their own behalf. Soon other groups arrived. Among them were some Moravians from Austria and a boatload of Sephardic Jews from London. Oglethorpe was not pleased about the appearance of the latter, since like most of his countrymen he was deeply anti-Semitic. Nevertheless, he accepted them, since they included several doctors and other individuals with valuable skills.

However promising the initial 12 months, North America was soon to prove once more the graveyard of European experiments in social engineering. The trustees expected gratitude from the recipients of their charity. Instead the settlers grumbled, not least at the restrictions on where they could settle and what they could do with their land. They were particularly alienated by the decision in January 1735 to prohibit slavery. The trustees believed that this ban would encourage the settlement of "English and Christian inhabitants" who alone could be relied on in war. If the dream of a white yeoman society was to be realized, then slavery must be excluded, a point seemingly reinforced by the Stono Rebellion in 1739.[11]

The settlers took a very different view. Most of those arriving in Georgia after the first few years were South Carolinians who viewed being yeoman farmers as a recipe for

---

[10] Julie Ann Sweet, *Negotiating for Georgia: British–Creek Relations in the Trustee Era, 1733–1752* (Athens, Ga., 2005).

[11] The plan to ban slavery was strongly supported by William Byrd II, who commented from his experience of living in Virginia: "I am sensible of many bad consequences of multiplying these Ethiopians amongst us. They blow up the pride, and ruin the Industry of our White People, who seeing a Rank of poor Creatures below them, detest work for fear it should make them look like Slaves." Quoted in Karen Ordahl Kupperman, ed., *Major Problems in American Colonial History: Documents and Essays* (Lexington, Mass., 1993).

poverty. They wanted to become large-scale planters and, based on the experience of other colonies, believed that the use of slaves was the only means of rapid expansion.

The trustees' paternalism was also evident in their attempt to prevent the importation of rum and other spirits. The trustees claimed that the Creeks desired such a ban because of the "great disorders among them occasioned by the use of the said liquors." In reality the trustees feared the effect alcohol might have on their own settlers, some of whom had only recently been plucked from the streets of London, where gin cost a penny a gallon and disorder was equally prevalent.

For a time criticism was diverted by the war against Spain. But after the fighting died down in the early 1740s, the trustees slowly had to give way on various aspects of their model society. The attempt to settle people in compact towns had never been a success. Now the restrictions on both the size of farms and the right to sell had to be removed. From 1742 holdings of up to 2,000 acres were allowed. That same July the ban on liquor was removed, if only to help Georgian merchants trading with the West Indies.

Finally, in August 1750 the trustees conceded the right to own slaves as "an encouragement to the inhabitants." For a time their antislavery views had been supported by Scottish settlers in the community of Darien and German Moravians in the community of Ebenezer. But the South Carolinians in Savannah, the colony's main settlement, kept up their demands. One last straw may have been the encouragement they received from George Whitefield, who argued on one of his revivalist tours that the colony would never prosper unless slavery was adopted. Not that the trustees gave in completely, for under their new decree anyone keeping four slaves had to employ at least one able-bodied white male servant; also, no African Americans were to be trained as apprentices, so as to encourage the creation of a skilled white workforce. In addition, the trustees tried to revive their plans for a silk industry by requiring slave-owners to keep one female trained "in the art of winding or reeling of silk." Lastly an import duty was to be levied on all slaves entering the colony to support the government and pay for a Christian ministry.

These concessions in fact represented almost the last act of the trustees. Two years later they handed over their authority to the Crown and Georgia became a royal colony, with a governor, council, and provincial assembly.

The trustees' stewardship was not without result. By 1752, 4,500 whites and 1,500 Africans had been settled in Georgia. Parliament, however, had expended £137,000 in the process. The trustees' idealistic hopes had faded. Some silk was produced at Ebenezer for a few years, but little remained of the plan to resettle London's poor, develop compact towns, or create a new class of yeoman farmer. Georgia quickly adopted the pattern of South Carolina. Rice plantations, owned by a wealthy elite and worked by African slaves, dominated the tidewater, while small struggling farms were the norm elsewhere.

3 THE URBAN FRONTIER

While the backcountry and frontier areas were being developed, a rather different expansion was taking place in the east. The growth of the British North American town was underway. Until the eighteenth century British colonial towns were little more than

Figure 33   *A Northeast View of Boston*, attributed to William Burgis, circa 1723. Courtesy of Peabody Essex Museum, Salem, Massachusetts 1163.

villages, except for Boston, which by 1689 had a population of 7,000 inhabitants. No other settlement had more than 3,000 people, the figure usually set by demographers today as the minimum necessary for an urban environment.

After 1715 other towns began to grow, shedding off their village origins. By 1720 Boston had 12,000 people but Philadelphia, with some 10,000 inhabitants, was catching up fast. New York had a population of 7,000, while Newport and Charleston each contained close to 4,000 people.

The reason for this pattern of growth was the role these settlements played in the economies of their respective areas. Their first-class harbors provided an entrepôt for their respective hinterlands, both for the marketing of their produce and the distribution of imported goods. This commerce in turn supported a growing number of laborers, artisans, and other craftsmen, together with a professional class of, for example, lawyers and doctors. Hence by 1760 Philadelphia had 23,000 inhabitants, New York 18,000, Boston 16,000, Charleston 8,000, and Newport 7,500. Only Boston had failed to sustain a rapid rate of growth, having already reached a population of 16,000 by 1740. Its restricted hinterland and competition for its traditional trades had resulted in a prolonged period of stagnation.

Figure 33 (*Continued*)

Growth was not limited to these five towns; by 1760 two more Massachusetts seaports, Salem and Marblehead, exceeded 3,000 inhabitants, while a number of other towns were approaching this figure. In New England these included Portsmouth, New Hampshire; Newburyport, Massachusetts; Providence, Rhode Island; and New Haven and Hartford, Connecticut. In the middle colonies, Albany in New York and Lancaster in southeast Pennsylvania were similar in size. In the South, Baltimore, Norfolk, and Savannah were also approaching 3,000 inhabitants. Historians have also detected signs of urban activity in the piedmont of Virginia and North Carolina, where the growing wheat trade was creating centers of commerce.[12]

All these places were ports on the coast or on large rivers leading to the sea. Only Lancaster was a genuine inland center, the result of the rapid influx of German and Scots-Irish settlers. Nevertheless, impressive as the growth of towns was, the number of people living in them as a proportion of the total population had actually declined, from

[12] See especially Joseph A. Ernst and H. Roy Merrens, "'Camden's Turrets Pierce the Skies': The Urban Process in the Southern Colonies during the Eighteenth Century," *William and Mary Quarterly*, 30 (1973), 549–74. However, this thesis about southern backcountry towns has been challenged by Hermann Wellenreuther, "Urbanization in the Colonial South: A Critique," *William and Mary Quarterly*, 31 (1974), 653–68.

Figure 34 *Southeast Prospect of the City of Philadelphia*, by Peter Cooper, circa 1720. The Library Company of Philadelphia.

nine percent to six percent. As fast as the towns had expanded, the countryside had grown even faster. Apparently the prospect of farm life remained more compelling to most immigrants and settlers' children than the alternative of learning a craft and becoming a self-employed urban artisan.

The five major towns posed special problems for their inhabitants, the most serious of which was fire. Boston suffered several bad fires in the seventeenth century, notably in 1676 and 1679, leading to the town's purchase of the first fire engine in British North America equipped with buckets and hand pumps. In 1691 the general court passed an ordinance that all buildings in the town were to be of brick. Still the fires raged, and in 1717 the town organized its first volunteer fire company to replace the militia units which had formerly been used. A bonus of £5 was paid to the first one arriving at the scene of a conflagration. Since the act of 1691 was frequently ignored, their services continued to be in demand. The year 1760 witnessed the worst fire of all, in which 400 houses were destroyed.

Similar legislation was adopted by the other major towns, though Philadelphia and Charleston, with their spacious streets and house lots, were less at risk. But a serious fire in Charleston in 1740 emphasized the need for building regulations to be enforced.

Fire was not the only hazard in the cities. Disease and epidemics were a considerable danger too, not least because of the constant influx of newcomers, the close proximity in which people lived, and the lack of sanitation. The link between these elements was not always understood, though the desirability of keeping the streets clean was recognized. Once again Boston took the lead. Following the example of Christopher Wren in London, it began the construction of sewers beneath the main thoroughfares into which householders could pour their offal and other waste material. The first sewer, completed in 1704, was the work of a private individual, Francis Thresher, but the selectmen were quick to encourage others to follow his example by the promise of compensation. New York began to build its first sewer shortly afterwards. These

Figure 34   (*Continued*)

improvements were one reason the inhabitants of the emerging cities of British North America remained relatively healthy in comparison with their European counterparts.

Drinking water was secured mainly from underground wells, though many citizens wisely avoided using them in summer, preferring fermented beverages instead. Some epidemics were inevitable. Boston suffered several smallpox outbreaks, and yellow fever appeared regularly in Charleston every summer, reaching as far north as New York in 1702 when 500 people perished. By 1750 the adoption of inoculation for smallpox and of quarantine procedures for other diseases substantially reduced the incidence of these particular threats.

Linked to the need for sewers was the need to attend to the condition of the streets. As the population grew, the number of carts and coaches made these intolerable, especially in winter, when rain and snow turned them into a quagmire. Beginning in 1690 Boston once more set the tone by having its streets paved with cobblestones. This improvement was often carried out in conjunction with drainage improvements. By 1760 all the large towns had made considerable progress in this direction.

The reason for Boston's lead in municipal improvements, apart from its being the first town to experience such problems, was its system of government. The annual election of selectmen made it more responsive. Most other towns had nonelective corporations. Charleston was most disadvantaged in this respect, having to rely on commissioners appointed by the provincial legislature, who were frequently unsympathetic to its problems.

Private initiatives were therefore still essential to bring about urban improvements. One of the most notable of these was in public lighting. Before 1750 the only street lighting came from oil lamps provided by individuals on a random and voluntary basis. Then in 1749, a group of Philadelphia's citizens, led by the Quaker John Smith, agreed to provide lamps and pay someone to light them each evening. Their action prompted the assembly to pass an act the next year in support of this initiative. The measure was so well received that within 10 years all the major towns had adopted similar schemes, using whale oil as lighting fuel. However, such improvements rarely extended beyond the wealthier parts of a town, leaving the poorer inhabitants to do without until the following century.

One reason for the popularity of street lighting was another urban problem, crime. Its emergence may have been the result of increased poverty in the 1730s when the first workhouses in British North America were established in Boston, New York, and Philadelphia. Another contribution may have been declining religious zeal among a now cosmopolitan population. In addition, the concentration of so many people undoubtedly provided temptations and opportunities which were not available in the country. With robberies and burglaries on the increase, all the townsfolk wanted better protection, especially at night. Hence, in addition to their lighting, every town made provision for increased night patrols.

By 1760 life for the inhabitants of the five largest towns was quite different from that of the rest of the population. Most townspeople worked for a cash wage and had specialist occupations. As a result they purchased their food, clothing, and other requirements from retail shops or large markets. Everywhere the concept of the just price had been superseded by the mechanism of the marketplace. And although churchgoing remained popular, the ideal of the godly man had been replaced by that of the good citizen, someone who was concerned for the well-being of the community and its environment.

By 1760 the major cities were sufficiently advanced to impress visitors from Europe. The Swede Peter Kalm commented on the "grandeur and perfection of Philadelphia," while one British naval officer said of New York in 1756 that "the nobleness of the town surprised me more than the fertile appearance of the country . . . I had no idea of finding a place in America, consisting of near two thousand houses, elegantly built of brick . . . . Such is this city that very few in England can rival it." Indeed, in their municipal developments, British North American towns were ahead of their British provincial counterparts. Civic pride and the desire for refinement were everywhere evident.

The cities represented the cutting edge of colonial society, where fashion and ideas were most advanced. Some have argued that this was also true of politics. Although only 6 percent of the population lived in them, the towns provided the political leadership and organization that was lacking elsewhere.[13]

---

[13] This theme is argued by Gary B. Nash, *The Urban Crucible: Social Change, Political Consciousness, and the Origins of the American Revolution* (Cambridge, Mass., 1979).

18

British North American Institutions of Government

1691	The Virginian treasury comes under the control of the House of Burgesses. John Locke publishes *Two Treatises of Government*.
1708	Lord Cornbury is recalled as governor of New York for maladministration.
1718	Governor Spotswood is defeated in his appeal to the Virginia electorate.
1719	The Massachusetts House of Representatives claims sole right to name its speaker.
1720	An attempt is made to prevent the South Carolina assembly from adjourning without the Crown's permission. Gordon and Trenchard begin publication of *Cato's Letters* in London.
1725	The Maryland assembly claims sole legislative competence against the provincial council. A Massachusetts explanatory charter gives the governor a veto over the choice of a speaker.
1728	The Crown attempts to obtain a permanent salary for the governor of Massachusetts.
1732	William Cosby is appointed governor of New York.
1734	Gabriel Johnston is appointed governor of North Carolina; the Albemarle region secedes from the assembly.
1735	The Zenger trial takes place in New York. Zenger is acquitted.
1738	The South Carolina assembly attempts to prevent the council from amending money bills.
1740	The Privy Council requires all bills to contain a suspending clause.
1742	The proprietary party is defeated in an election in Pennsylvania.

Colonial America: A History to 1763, Fourth Edition. Richard Middleton and Anne Lombard.
© 2011 Richard Middleton and Anne Lombard. Published 2011 by Blackwell Publishing Ltd.

1747	Governor Wentworth refuses to extend representation for the New Hampshire assembly.
1750	Jonathan Mayhew gives a sermon against "unlimited submission."
1752	The Privy Council instructs that all judicial appointments are to be at the king's pleasure. Georgia becomes a royal colony and is granted an assembly.
1758	Virginia passes the Twopenny Act.

1 THE ROYAL FRAMEWORK

BY THE END of the 1720s colonial government in British North America had acquired the pattern it would retain until the Revolution. The Crown would not attempt to further centralize political control over the colonies until after the French and Indian War, instead allowing them considerable autonomy in running their own political affairs. Every province had a governor, council, and assembly elected by the freemen. However, there were significant differences between one province and another in the manner of selecting the governor and council. In the royal colonies of New Hampshire, Massachusetts, New York, New Jersey, Virginia, and the Carolinas, the king appointed the governor, who in turn chose the council. The only exception was Massachusetts, where the assembly selected the councillors in agreement with the governor.

Under the proprietary system in Maryland and Pennsylvania, the proprietor chose the governor and council subject to the consent of the monarch. In the corporate colonies of Rhode Island and Connecticut, on the other hand, the freemen elected not only the assembly and council but the governor, too, though the king could theoretically exercise a veto.

Before the Glorious Revolution the colonists' political relationship with England had been confined largely to the Crown; and this situation did not change after 1689. Until 1760 Parliament was little concerned with the administration of the colonies beyond ensuring that the mercantilist framework was in place. Their internal management was still the responsibility of the king and was jealously protected as part of the royal prerogative. Most of the routine administration was performed by the Board of Trade, which answered to the Privy Council, where most major decisions about the colonies were made.

The king's principal representative in each colony was the governor. In many respects he performed the same function as the monarch in England. He was head of the executive, approved all appointments on behalf of the king, and was responsible for the execution of the laws. He also summoned the local assemblies by the issue of writs, similarly proroguing or dismissing them in the manner of Parliament. He was in addition commander-in-chief of the local forces with responsibility for the defense of the province. On paper his powers were formidable.

To help administer the colony, the governor had a number of officials, including a secretary, attorney general, deputy auditor, and naval officer. He also had a council, which was a cross between the Privy Council and the House of Lords, with executive, judicial, and legislative functions. This body assisted the governor in all administrative matters and was also the highest provincial court of appeal. In addition, it had legislative responsibilities, constituting an upper house for the passage of bills. The only provincial exception to this rule was Pennsylvania, which had a unicameral legislature under the charter of 1701.

The third branch of English government was the judiciary, which was responsible for dealing with those who broke the law or were in some kind of civil dispute. In medieval times judges had been officers of the king and dismissible at his pleasure. However, since the 1701 Act of Settlement they could no longer be removed except by impeachment in the House of Commons. This granting of tenure during "good behaviour" had been instigated to ensure their independence and to check abuses by the executive branch of government.

The colonial judiciary had not yet attained this eminence. Indeed, in many respects it was still a branch of the executive. Colonial judges did not enjoy security of tenure but could be removed "at the pleasure" of the king. The reasons for this were various. Before 1689 justice had been the responsibility of part-time members of the council, who by definition had only limited knowledge of the law. Thereafter all the colonies created separate bodies to act as a superior court of judicature, probate, and admiralty. Nevertheless, the Crown still felt that colonial judges were not sufficiently trained to be given tenure for life. Perhaps most important was the belief that the colonial judiciary, like colonial assemblies, could not enjoy the same exalted status as its counterpart in England. Mercantilist theory dictated that all colonial institutions be subordinate to the mother country, and making judges independent was incompatible with that aim.

2 LOCAL GOVERNMENT: TOWN MEETING AND COUNTY COURT

Most colonists dealt only with the lowest strata of government. They were remote even from the provincial capital, and very few ever made the journey to the mother country.

The structure of local government varied considerably from province to province. In New England the town was its principal element. Originally, only church members could participate, but since the end of the seventeenth century a property qualification had been instituted instead. The voters elected a wide range of officials: constables, tax assessors, highway surveyors, and tithingmen. Most important were the selectmen, who had general responsibility for the town, determining taxes and dispensing justice for minor offenses. However, one responsibility not granted them was the distribution of town lands, which after 1692 lay with the proprietors or founding families, acting separately. Elections were annual.

The New England provinces also had a system of county courts, consisting of a panel of justices appointed by the governor. Their main business was to act as an intermediate judicial stage between the petty misdemeanors handled by the selectmen and the major crimes involving "life, limb, banishment, or divorce" dealt with by the provincial superior court.

The middle colonies had a more varied system of local government. New York City was governed by a mayor, aldermen, and councillors. Under Governor Dongan's charter of 1686, the aldermen and councillors were elected by the free male inhabitants. Since the posts of mayor, sheriff, recorder, and town clerk were still chosen by the governor, however, the citizens' real power was limited. Like the New England selectmen, the mayor and aldermen acted as justices of the peace.

Most of the rest of the province was divided into counties, with a sheriff and panel of justices appointed by the governor. Some counties, like Suffolk on Long Island, also had towns structured on the New England model, in which all freeholders had the vote. In addition, the Van Rensselaer patroonship remained, though with greatly restricted legal and administrative authority. The other manors merely gave their possessors ownership of the land. Local government was exercised either by the county courts or by town officers elected by the inhabitants.

Pennsylvania had a similarly complex structure of local government but was also in some respects the least representative of the northern colonies. Philadelphia was governed by a closed corporation on the English model with a mayor, aldermen, and councillors, who coopted someone as a vacancy arose. The rest of the province was divided into counties, with a sheriff and bench of justices appointed by the proprietor or his representatives. However, in 1711 the assembly reduced the powers of the justices when it created county tax commissioners, positions which became elective in 1722. The post of sheriff was also partially democratized. The freemen elected two nominees, leaving the governor to make the final choice. There was a similar arrangement concerning the townships into which each county was divided. The inhabitants elected two nominees for constable and local tax assessor, giving the governor the final say. There were no town meetings.

The third middle colony, New Jersey, had a system similar to that of New England; towns elected their own officials and county justices were appointed by the governor. However, the representative element was strengthened by the requirement that the justices, when dealing with administrative rather than judicial matters, were assisted by a panel of supervisors, elected by the freemen of each township in the county.

The southern colonies, in contrast, had almost no representative element in their local government. They followed English practice, especially in the Chesapeake. At the lowest level was the parish, whose governing body was the vestry. This body was invariably self-coopting and chosen from the gentry. Its responsibilities included appointing Anglican ministers, the upkeep of the established church, the provision of welfare for the indigent sick and elderly, and the setting of a parish rate.

The next level of local government in the South was the county court, which consisted of a panel of justices, technically appointed by the governor, but in effect also self-coopting, since they filled vacancies by recommending names to the governor. The justices also selected the sheriff and other court officials. They dealt with most legal matters such as hearing civil actions and petty misdemeanors, the verifying of wills, and the sale of lands. The county courts also shared responsibility with the parishes for roads, bridges, and ferries. The only southern province to diverge from this county court pattern was South Carolina, where most judicial and administrative tasks continued to be handled by the vestries.

Local government was clearly not representative, especially in the South. Only the New England town was fully elective, and historians once paid much attention to its system in the belief that it provided the bedrock of the subsequent democracy in the United States.

It is often supposed that representative institutions are by definition democratic, but as the study of New England itself shows, such an assumption is not valid. During the seventeenth century only church members or proprietors could participate in the affairs of most New England towns, and even then only the wealthier members were elected to positions of authority. Widely shared assumptions held that the best-educated men from the oldest families and the most wealth had the wisdom required of rulers. Popular acquiescence in the authority of the elite was almost complete.

Only in the last two decades of the century was elite domination challenged in a growing number of disputes about taxes, the level of the minister's salary, election returns, and the distribution of town lands. The consensus broke down for various reasons. In Massachusetts, one factor was the granting of a new charter in 1691, under which any male who possessed taxable property worth £20 could participate in town affairs. This qualification was a considerable reduction from the previous requirement of £80 under the 1670 franchise law, but it was still a far cry from the concept of one man, one vote. Nevertheless, more electors meant greater diversity of opinion. The need for voters to be in good standing in the church also seems to have been abandoned at this time. Although the colony still outwardly conformed to the values of its forebears, it no longer had the same commitment to them, perhaps being influenced by the spread of materialism as the towns became more susceptible to market forces.

A further cause of discord among New England townspeople was the monopoly of the proprietary families over the distribution of unsettled lands. This was increasingly resented by the other inhabitants who had subsequently bought land, held office, and paid their taxes – only to remain excluded from entitlement to any dividend. Frequent attempts were made to widen access, but all were defeated by the general court because of its reluctance to interfere with the rights of private property. However, the proprietors of many communities eventually found it prudent to admit to their ranks the more prominent residents who were still excluded from their number.

Analysis of the specific disputes, however, shows that there was another factor responsible for the loss of the consensus on local government: the growth of many towns. Community and agreement were possible when a town comprised just a few families pioneering in the wilderness. Eighty years later the population of many towns had increased several times. In the case of Dedham, founded in 1636, the initial grant from the general court had been very extensive. By the 1700s the spread of the population had effectively created new centers of population at Bellingham, Walpole, and Needham. These communities found it inconvenient to have their affairs managed from Dedham and increasingly wanted their own minister, school, town meeting, and selectmen. The result was a bitter series of disputes which in 1728 compelled the general court to intervene; in the end Dedham had to be divided into three precincts.

Many other New England towns suffered similar disruption. Gloucester had originally been a small farming community. From the second decade of the eighteenth century a thriving port began to develop in the area known as Gloucester Harbor. When a new church was required in the mid-1730s the wealthy merchants there determined to have it rebuilt in their own part of town close to the harbor. The farmers and fishermen of the older Annisquam region of Gloucester resisted bitterly, since their control of the community was already being undermined in other respects. The controversy rumbled on until 1742, when the general court allowed the creation of two separate parishes.[1]

---

[1] See Kenneth A. Lockridge, *A New England Town: The First Hundred Years, Dedham, Massachusetts, 1636–1736* (New York, 1970); and Edward M. Cook, Jr., *The Fathers of the Towns: Leadership and Community Structure in Eighteenth-Century New England* (Baltimore, 1976). For Gloucester, see Christine Leigh Heyrman, *Commerce and Culture: The Maritime Communities of Colonial Massachusetts, 1690–1750* (New York, 1984). The argument that consensus was breaking down is disputed by Michael Zuckerman, *Peaceable Kingdoms: New England Towns in the Eighteenth Century* (New York, 1970).

The primary force behind these disputes was not a demand for democracy but rather a geographically motivated desire for reallocation of local government responsibilities. The towns continued to be run by small enclaves of relatively privileged people, in a manner far removed from the spirit of a modern democracy. One indication of their restrictive nature was their unwillingness to admit strangers, especially if they appeared to have no visible means of support. The first six decades of the eighteenth century witnessed a huge increase in the number of people being "warned out" of towns.

Another reason for dissension after 1740 was religion. During the Great Awakening congregations in many towns became divided between the New and Old Lights over the selection of ministers, destroying the unanimity of the old order. Along the way the inhabitants became accustomed to electioneering, speech-making, and all other aspects of politics. This process in turn prepared the ground for the later growth of a more truly democratic spirit, though only after the colonial period had ended.

Elsewhere local government remained relatively static in the hands of the traditional authorities. In the middle colonies towns did not have large landholdings and no problems arose concerning the location of their churches or government. Any excess population simply emigrated to the next county and sought incorporation as required.

A similar picture pertained in the South, where the planter elites dominated government at both local and provincial levels. Many of those appointed to the county courts were also members of the council or house of representatives and were thus able to use their visits to St. Mary's, Williamsburg, New Bern, or Charleston to confirm themselves or their relatives as sheriffs and county justices.

Not until the last decades of the colonial period did the arrival of a new population in the backcountry pose a challenge to this cozy arrangement. Interestingly, the response varied from one province to another. Virginia acted quickly to establish vestries and county courts. The tidewater elite welcomed the new settlers both as a barrier against the Shawnees and other western Indian peoples and also as a means of increasing the value of their own lands. Accordingly, in 1738 Orange County was established on the eastern side of the Blue Ridge Mountains, followed in 1745 by Augusta County in the valley itself. Although these counties were not elective, they did reflect the newcomers' desire for some framework of government. In addition, the vestries were left almost entirely free of Episcopalian influence, to avoid offending the religious sensibilities of the newcomers.

In the Carolinas, by way of contrast, the authorities paid little attention to the new settlements in the piedmont. North Carolina created counties but staffed them with the tidewater elite, who used their position to further their own interests. In South Carolina the new settlements were simply administered as extensions of the existing coastal parishes. This lack of attention to the political needs of the backcountry population would cause serious trouble after 1760 with the rise of the Regulator movement.

3 THE PROVINCIAL ASSEMBLY: CROWN VERSUS PEOPLE

After 1689 all 12 British mainland North American colonies had an assembly, as did the main British West Indian colonies. As already noted, these had been won only after protracted struggles during the seventeenth century and were looked on as grants of favor rather than of right. Officially that view had not altered, but the Glorious Revolution in England, with its emphasis on property rights, had strengthened the assemblies' position considerably.

Although the origins of the different assemblies had been diverse, by 1700 they had two main functions. The first was to make local laws for the convenience of colonial inhabitants – London was too far away to meet every legislative requirement. Second, the provincials believed that the assemblies, like Parliament, should act as watchdogs. The experience of the seventeenth century had demonstrated that the rights of the individual subject were constantly under threat from the executive branch of government.

The assemblies normally met in the spring or fall, when the roads were passable and the weather temperate. The sessions usually lasted about four weeks. Most representatives were not professional politicians and were anxious to return home to their occupations as farmers and merchants.

The main business was to vote taxes essential to cover the expenses of government, such as the salaries of the governor and the few other permanent officials. Members also addressed any other subjects which required government attention: poor crops, natural disasters, or lapses in law and order. Most sessions were not controversial, though an issue like paper currency might cause dispute.

The right to vote for members of the assembly varied from colony to colony but always required a property qualification. In most places it was equivalent to the English 40-shilling freehold, that is, ownership of a property with a rental value of 40 shillings. In Virginia, for example, the law of 1736 required that a voter possess either 25 acres of improved land with a house of 400 square feet or 100 acres of unimproved land.

Historians have long been divided as to just how democratic the provincial franchise was. At one time it was popular to argue that because wages were high and property was cheap, almost any male could qualify for the vote. In the past 50 years writers have tended to emphasize the hidden costs of landownership, the high incidence of tenant farming, and the presence of considerable poverty in both town and country, all of which suggest a lower proportion of enfranchised settlers, perhaps 50 percent of white males. This was a considerably higher proportion of men than possessed the right to vote in eighteenth-century England, but by modern standards it was very low.[2]

Indeed the fact that virtually all women, African Americans, and Indians were excluded from the political process reminds us that by no means were the British

2 For a discussion of the provincial franchise, see Robert J. Dinkin, *Voting in Provincial America: A Study of Elections in the Thirteen Colonies, 1689–1776* (Westport, 1977). The view that land was cheap, wages high, and voting qualifications easily obtainable is argued by Robert E. Brown, *Middle-Class Democracy and the Revolution in Massachusetts, 1691–1780* (Ithaca, 1955). For a more recent analysis of electoral practices in Virginia, see John Gilman Kolp, *Gentlemen and Freeholders: Electoral Politics in Colonial Virginia* (Baltimore, 1998). He shows that there were wide variations in voter participation depending on the issues and local circumstances. In some counties only 25 percent of males voted; in others the figure was as high as 75 percent. See also Chapter 11, section 4.

American colonies democratic.[3] Nor did they pretend to be, for although the representatives referred to themselves as the popular part of the system, they did so only in contrast to its monarchical and aristocratic components. Before 1760 no one believed that a crude head count could be the basis of political legitimacy. The popular view was that government should be a mixture of monarchy, aristocracy, and democracy, the three legitimate forms of government outlined by Aristotle. Democracy alone was thought likely to degenerate into mobocracy, the worst of all conditions, since property itself would be at risk. Here lies one of the crucial differences between eighteenth-century British North America and the present-day United States. In colonial times the belief that owning property should be a requirement for participation in the political process was virtually unquestioned on both sides of the Atlantic.

Why did ordinary people who did not own property fail to protest their exclusion from the right to vote, or demand the right to be considered for responsible political offices? This question, too, has divided historians. Many argue that colonial political culture was deferential. In other words, ordinary people yielded to the judgment of the better-educated, upper-class elite because they lacked confidence in their own judgments, or were afraid to challenge their "betters." This view has been disputed by other historians who point out that when ordinary colonists decided to protest the decisions of the elite, they could be remarkably forceful in asserting their interests. Poor people in colonial societies generally did not depend for their livelihoods on the patronage of the rich, as they did in the aristocratic societies of western Europe. Nonetheless the concept of deference is helpful for understanding ordinary people's unwillingness to challenge their noninclusive political system. Most people spent their formative years in patriarchal families where they were expected to defer to a property-owning male household head, so the habit of deferring to the decisions of another person would have been well ingrained for many, even as adults. Relatively low levels of literacy (compared to rates of literacy in modern Western societies) may have convinced many that they lacked the wisdom and the understanding needed for political leadership, or even voting. Finally the structures that would later emerge to mobilize the political energies of ordinary people, such as political parties, did not exist in colonial societies.[4]

---

[3] Inevitably there were a few exceptions. In some places in Massachusetts, widows with property were occasionally allowed to vote, as were Indians, in, for example, Stockbridge in western Massachusetts. For more information on the latter, see Brown, *Middle-Class Democracy*, 40–4, 89. Some free African Americans may also have voted in the South until the second decade of the eighteenth century, when both North and South Carolina passed laws to make the franchise exclusively white, as did Virginia in 1723. For more information, see Dinkin, *Voting in Provincial America*, 33. Five colonies also specifically excluded Catholics from the franchise: Virginia, New York, Maryland, Rhode Island, and South Carolina. Another four excluded Jews. See Chilton Williamson, *American Suffrage: From Property to Democracy, 1760–1860* (Princeton, 1960), 15–16.

[4] The concept of deference in the colonial context has been widely employed by various historians including J. R. Pole, "Historians and the Problem of Early American Democracy," *American Historical Review*, 67 (1962), 626–46; Jack P. Greene, "Society, Ideology, and Politics: An Analysis of the Political Culture of Mid-Eighteenth-Century Virginia," in Richard Jellison, ed., *Society, Freedom, and Conscience: The American Revolution in Virginia, Massachusetts, and New York* (New York, 1976); J. G. A. Pocock, "The Classical Theory of Deference," *American Historical Review*, 81 (1976), 516–23; Richard L. Bushman, *King and People in Provincial Massachusetts* (Chapel Hill, 1985). The concept of deference has been challenged by historians from the Progressive school, who argue that ordinary colonial people acted in ways that promoted their self-interests. For a recent critique, see Michael Zuckerman, "Toqueville, Turner, and Turds: Four Stories of Manners in Early America," *Journal of American History*, 85 (1998), 13–42.

The absence of significant or widespread popular challenge to the political structure, however, did not mean that politics in the colonies was peaceful and harmonious. In fact, colonial political leaders engaged in frequent and contentious disputes. Two basic issues were generally at stake. One concerned the rights of the provincial assemblies, the other issues of legislative policy.

The main points of contention in regard to the rights of the assemblies centered on their ability to control their membership, choose a speaker, audit expenditure, and adjourn when they wanted. Since these were all rights enjoyed by the House of Commons, the lower houses generally believed that they should enjoy them too. After all, the men who served in colonial assemblies considered themselves to be gentlemen; why should they not be entitled to the same rights as gentlemen in England, who were represented in the House of Commons? British officials, however, regarded such claims as unacceptable, believing that if granted, they would weaken royal government and undermine the whole purpose of the imperial relationship. In their view the colonies were constitutionally akin to borough corporations, which also held royal charters allowing them to make bylaws and raise local taxes. Such institutions could never be equated with the majesty of Parliament; what the colonists assumed to be rights were in British eyes merely privileges.

Hence when Francis Nicholson was appointed governor of South Carolina in 1720 he was warned how "the members of several assemblies in the plantations have of late assumed to themselves privileges no ways belonging to them." One such assumption was that "of being protected from suits at law during the term of the assemblies." Freedom from arrest was something that only members of Parliament ought to enjoy. Equally unacceptable was the practice of many assemblies to adjourn "themselves at pleasure without taking leave from his Majesty's governor first obtained." This habit suggested that it was the assemblies which were determining business, not the Crown.

The same reasoning induced the Crown to ensure that the speaker of the house was at least approved by the governor, so that some control could be exerted over that body's proceedings. This policy produced a fierce battle in Massachusetts during the 1720s. The clash began in 1719 when the house nominated Elisha Cooke, Jr. to be speaker. The recently arrived Governor Shute vetoed the nomination because Cooke had been critical of his predecessor. The assembly disputed Shute's right to do this and decided to adjourn, whereupon Shute dissolved the house and called new elections. The house remained adamant over its choice of speaker and in the end Shute appealed to the Privy Council, which issued an explanatory charter in 1725 affirming the right of the governor to veto the nominee of the lower house. Significantly, the assembly accepted this ruling, fearing that further obstruction might mean the loss of the 1691 charter.

The extension of representation was another area of dispute. The Crown took the view that representation was a privilege which only it could grant. The lower houses asserted that it was part of their inherent right to determine their own membership. The matter was potentially explosive, since the need for additional representation often arose in light of the continuing westward spread of the population. In practice the lower houses were not always quick to act, since the creation of new constituencies would weaken the influence of the existing tidewater areas. In most colonies the Crown did permit limited increases in representation. Nevertheless, from 1747 to 1752 the issue provoked a bitter dispute in New Hampshire between the assembly and Governor Wentworth, who asserted that membership had been fixed at the time of the original charter and could not be unilaterally increased by the house.

The most heated battles between the Crown and the provincial representatives were fought over the control of finance. Though the assemblies had gained the right of initiating taxation, the Crown continued to fight a rearguard action for a permanent source of revenue, especially to pay the governors' salaries. The British were terrified that their officials would be blackmailed into making concessions if their salaries had to be renewed annually. In reality only one episode lived up to the authorities' apprehensions, after Governor Shute refused to accept the Massachusetts assembly's nomination for the speakership. The house first responded by reducing his stipend and then in 1720 refused to pay him at all. Matters finally came to a head in 1728, when Shute's successor, Governor Burnet, was instructed to demand a permanent revenue, hinting at possible parliamentary action in the event of a negative response. The house refused but did offer the governor an increased stipend on the old conditions. Burnet continued to resist, even proroguing the assembly to Salem, and the issue dragged on until his death in September 1729. In the end the next governor, Jonathan Belcher, accepted the increase and the subject was quietly dropped. The royal representatives were ultimately reluctant to involve Parliament, for fear of reducing the royal prerogative. Equally, the assembly was not unaware that a further confrontation might lead to the loss or amendment of the charter.

Another financial matter which caused dispute was the issue and audit of money. The Crown took the view that taxes were "aids to the king" which gave it the right to dispose of the money as it wished. To this end the governors were strictly enjoined to ensure that all monies were issued through their own hands. But several assemblies argued that what the people had granted should be spent only as they designated.

Unfortunately for the Crown, it had already lost this battle in a number of colonies during the confusion of the late seventeenth century. In Virginia the issue of money since 1691 had been exercised by the treasurer, who was appointed by the house. A similar practice prevailed in South Carolina, where a weakened proprietary government had given way. In the aftermath of Governor Cornbury's corrupt stewardship, New York had adopted the same practice, arguing successfully that the assembly must protect the public from such notorious peculation. Once a precedent had been set it was almost impossible to reverse.

The control of expenditure was most controversial in wartime, when emergency levies were imposed. On these occasions the lower houses frequently specified that commissioners were to accompany the army to supervise military expenditures. Similar tactics were adopted in the financing of presents to the British colonies' Indian allies. The Crown feared that the assemblies would thereby gain control of these important areas of policy and thus undermine the royal prerogative. The Massachusetts assembly caused offense in this respect in 1720 when it tried to supervise the running of several military posts in Maine by the direct vetting of expenditures.

One other matter of constitutional dispute concerned the tenure of judges. In both North Carolina and New Jersey attempts were made to give colonial judges commissions on the English basis of good behavior rather than at the king's pleasure, in order to protect their appointments from executive interference. As already noted, the Crown did not believe that colonial judges were sufficiently competent or mindful of imperial requirements to be given tenure for life. Moreover, as most judges were paid, like governors, only on a yearly basis, they would be substituting dependence on the executive for one on the legislature, an even less desirable relationship. In 1752 the Privy Council issued a general directive that all judicial appointments were to be at the king's pleasure. The issue did not become really contentious until after 1760.

Finally, in several royal colonies attempts were made to restrict the powers of the council on the grounds that it was an arm of the executive, not the legislative, branch of government. The most sensitive area in this respect was the right of councils to amend money bills. In South Carolina the assembly refused the council this right from the late 1730s, claiming the same exclusive power over taxation as the House of Commons did in England. In some provinces the response of the councils was to differentiate between their executive and legislative functions by excluding the governor from the latter deliberations. In New Jersey Governor Lewis Morris voluntarily withdrew when bills from the lower house were under discussion. However, in South Carolina the appointment of expatriates from England led the assembly to demand the council's exclusion from all legislative matters, arguing that it was improper for placemen to be involved in the making of laws.

Intermingled with these constitutional issues were other policy matters which provoked conflict between the Crown and provincial assemblies. Here again, Massachusetts was in the forefront though for a time it seemed that the appointment of a native Bostonian, Jonathan Belcher, as governor in 1730 would help calm the situation after the acrimonious disputes about the speakership and payment of the governor's salary.[5] Belcher decided that the key to a successful administration was to build his own party in the assembly. During his first year he dismissed 51 justices of the peace and other local officials, replacing them with persons linked to potential sympathizers in the assembly. The evidence suggests that he offended more than he cajoled, which proved unfortunate when the Land Bank became a burning issue at the end of the 1730s. By then Belcher had too many enemies to control the situation.

The disallowance of the Land Bank, however, was to prove a turning point in the politics of Massachusetts. In 1741 Belcher was replaced by William Shirley, partly because of intrigues by his opponents and in part because of his poor handling of the bank issue. Though an Englishman, Shirley had first come to the colony in 1731 and had served Belcher as advocate general of the admiralty court. A man of considerable charm and ability, he did not try to change the leadership of the assembly, unlike Belcher, preferring to work with those already there. Shirley's adept handling of the final stages of the Land Bank issue, his subsequent willingness to accept paper money, and his organization of the expedition against Louisburg in 1745 brought the old antagonistic relationship between the executive and the legislature almost to a close.

---

[5]   See Chapter 10, section 5, for details about the Land Bank.

He was also helped by the growth of a Court party and a more pragmatic Country party leadership (see section 4 below). Massachusetts was exceptional among the colonies in the intensity and duration of its quarrels with the Crown, which were exacerbated partly by its long tradition of self-government during the seventeenth century. It took time for these commonwealth traditions to die.

New York had problems of a different kind. Riddled with faction for much of the seventeenth century, in 1702 it had the misfortune to receive Lord Cornbury as governor. Cornbury came with only one end in view, to make himself rich. He siphoned off money from the provincial treasury and made lavish land grants, playing one faction off against another to his own advantage. He also offended many of New York's inhabitants by dressing as a transvestite.[6] He was equally cavalier in his treatment of New Jersey, of which he was simultaneously governor. His final affront was to ignore the Toleration Act of 1689 by imprisoning the Presbyterian minister Francis Makemie in 1707 for preaching. Although Cornbury was related to Queen Anne, the Whig administration in London insisted on recalling him, thus illustrating the new commitment to honesty which permeated government after 1689.

The appointment of Robert Hunter as governor in 1708 initiated a period of relative harmony. Hunter was a cultivated man, whose good manners and fine sense of judgment enabled him to steer between the opposing Leislerian and Anglo-Dutch factions. No less important was his ability to sort out the province's finances, including the grant of a five-year revenue to the Crown, though he achieved this only by acknowledging the right of the assembly to appoint the provincial treasurer, a significant concession in the struggle to control finance. The good relations between the executive and legislature continued under his successor, Governor Burnet, until the latter's removal to Massachusetts in 1727.

Unfortunately New York was to suffer from another high-handed governor in the early 1730s. William Cosby, like Cornbury, was related to the English aristocracy, and he too had accepted a colonial appointment so as to revive his fortune. When he failed to secure some perquisites he created a special court of chancery to handle the case. This episode not only offended the chief justice, Lewis Morris, but also led John Peter Zenger to publish his *New York Weekly Journal*. Ultimately, Cosby upset too many people and in 1736 he too was recalled.

After the departure of Cornbury, New Jersey in contrast witnessed little conflict between the Crown and assembly – at least until the governorship of Lewis Morris, when paper currency became an issue following the Privy Council's ban on further emissions. This led Morris to veto a bill for the issue of £40,000 in 1742, even though the assembly offered him an increased stipend and inserted a suspending clause as requested by the Privy Council. The assembly responded by withholding his salary. Morris then called new elections, but to no avail, even though he dissolved the assembly three more times and purged his council. The issue was resolved only by his death and the appointment of Jonathan Belcher, who was prepared to be

---

[6] This aspect of Cornbury's character has been challenged by Patricia U. Bonomi, "Lord Cornbury Redressed: The Governor and Problem Portrait," *William and Mary Quarterly*, 51 (1994), 106–18. See also Patricia U. Bonomi, *The Lord Cornbury Scandal* (Chapel Hill, 1998), in which she argues that the charges against Cornbury were largely inventions by his political opponents.

Figure 35 Portrait of Major General Robert Hunter (1666–1734), attributed to Sir Godfrey
Kneller, circa 1720. Hunter served as the colonial governor of New York until 1718.
Collection of the New York Historical Society, New York City.

DOCUMENT 27

Lord Cornbury instructed to obtain a permanent salary, 1703, reprinted in W. Keith Kavenagh, *Foundations of Colonial America: A Documentary History* (New York, 1973), Vol. 2, 1118–19

The following passage contains instructions from Crown officials to the royal governor of New Jersey, Lord Cornbury. Questions to consider: *Why was the Crown eager to have the colonial assembly give the governor a permanent salary, rather than voting yearly on whether to renew his salary for the year? Why did Crown officials direct Lord Cornbury not to accept gifts from the assembly? What does the Crown's inability to obtain a permanent salary for the royal governors tell us about the extent of the Crown's power in the colonies?*

Whereas we have appointed you our Governor-in-Chief of our province of New Jersey in America, and there being no provision made, as we yet understand, for the support of yourself or of the governor or lieutenant governor of the said province for the time being, we do hereby signify to you our royal will and pleasure that, at the first meeting of the Assembly after the receipt thereof, you do acquaint them with our expectation that, in regard of our receiving our good subjects of that province under our immediate protection and government, they do forthwith settle a constant and fixed allowance on you our governor ...

In consideration whereof we are hereby pleased to direct that neither you our governor, nor any governor, lieutenant governor, commander-in-chief or president of the council of our said province for the time being, do give your or their consent to the passing of any law or act for any gift or present to be made to you or them by the assembly, and that neither you nor they do receive any gift or present from the Assembly or others, on any account or in any manner whatsoever, upon pain of our highest displeasure and of being recalled from that our government.

more flexible, following his experience as governor in Massachusetts. His salary was paid, even though the Privy Council subsequently vetoed the currency bill. The assembly finally got its way in 1754 when financial necessity overruled the council's objections.

Unlike New York and New Jersey, Virginia experienced a prolonged period of political harmony from 1720 to the early 1750s. In some respects this was surprising, given the earlier conflict between the imperial authorities and the members of the planter elite. Indeed, the 1700s had witnessed an attempt by Governor Spotswood to break the planters' power, culminating in his appeal to the Virginia electorate in 1718 "to choose men of Estates and Family's of moderation ... dutiful to their superiors." The attempt failed, and Spotswood, unable to beat his opponents, joined them, buying large tracts of land and becoming a planter himself. He also humored the grandees by allowing them similar concessions and thus avoiding political controversy. Governor Gooch continued this policy, and the harmony was disrupted only following the appointment of Robert Dinwiddie in 1751. Dinwiddie provoked disputes on two occasions: once after an attempt to impose a minor fee on land grants, and the other when he vetoed an act regulating tobacco prices by the House of Burgesses. The problem in the latter case was the act's failure to include a clause suspending its operation until the consent of the Crown had been obtained.

The suspending clause was not otherwise a serious issue before 1760. Perhaps only five percent of bills were disallowed for want of such a clause, or indeed for any other reason. Connecticut had fewer than six measures challenged in over a hundred years: in South Carolina a mere 20 out of 400 were challenged between 1719 and 1760. Many temporary bills were permitted in recognition that emergency action had been necessary. When measures were disallowed it was usually because they contravened the laws of trade. For instance, the 1723 Virginia tax on imported slaves was annulled at the prompting of British merchants who saw it as a threat to their commercial interests. At no time before 1760, however, did such disallowance threaten a serious constitutional disturbance. The colonies generally accepted the right of the Privy Council to exercise judicial review to ensure compatibility with the laws of Britain.

The proprietary colonies were likewise not free from political controversy between their legislative and executive branches of government. Pennsylvania probably had more disputes than any other colony, continuing the tradition set during the first 20 years when David Lloyd led his country supporters against Penn and his wealthy backers in Philadelphia. In 1716 a bitter dispute over the right of Quakers to affirm rather than take an oath on the Bible in legal and administrative proceedings was stirred up by Governor Charles Gookin, despite the English Toleration Act of 1689 which allowed Quakers to be excused from the oath on conscientious grounds.

There were periods of calm following the death of Penn in 1718. During the 1720s the main areas of contention occurred within the assembly itself when a former governor, William Keith, tried to wrest control from Lloyd in a battle for the speakership. The harmony between the executive and legislature continued even when Thomas Penn arrived in 1732 to restore the fortunes of his family.

The outbreak of war in 1739, however, was another matter, as it immediately raised the issue of defense along the colony's western frontier. This issue had nearly cost William Penn his province 50 years before, and Thomas was determined not to repeat this experience. To meet the crucial need to form a militia, he set about building a party from the minority groups which could challenge the Quaker country party in the assembly. Thomas went so far as to organize gangs of seamen to intimidate the voters, but was signally rebuffed in the 1742 election, not least because the Quakers organized their own guard of shipwrights known as the White Oaks. This defeat led to talk of disfranchising the Quakers, while they in turn considered an appeal to the Crown for a royal charter. The antagonism became even more bitter with the steady distancing of the proprietary family from the Quaker religion. One sign of this was Penn's choice of Richard Peters, an Anglican clergyman, to be provincial secretary.

The dispute over defense dragged on until 1747, when Benjamin Franklin appeared as peacemaker. Though associated with the Quaker party, Franklin was more flexible than the acrimonious Lloyd. Hence a bill was finally passed in 1748 for the support of a volunteer militia. This allowed the non-Quaker population to defend itself without contravening the conscientious objections of the Friends. Fortunately, hostilities with Spain and France did not greatly affect Pennsylvania, involving no more than some privateering between the Capes of Delaware. The issue was to resurface, however, during the French and Indian War, with rather more serious consequences.

Maryland, the other proprietary colony, also had its share of disputes. Although the Calvert family had lost its governing rights in 1689, these had been restored in 1715 following Benedict Calvert's conversion to Anglicanism. Initially it was feared that the family had acted merely for political convenience, since several Catholics immediately claimed positions of authority in the provincial government. In any event the proprietor refused to support them, and Protestant fears were calmed by a further act in 1718, requiring all officeholders to take oaths of loyalty to the Hanoverian monarchs and disavow the temporal authority of the pope. After this anti-Catholic fears subsided.

Thereafter attention in Maryland politics shifted to the relationship between the council and the assembly. In reality this was a continuation of the old battle against the proprietary authority, since the Calverts controlled the council's membership. In 1725 the assembly claimed to be "the people's representatives for whom all laws are made" and proceeded to whittle down the powers of the upper house, denying them in 1740 the right to amend money bills. Disputes also developed concerning the right of the proprietor to a permanent revenue.

The system in existence in most colonies thus produced periodic conflicts between appointed governors and elected legislatures, probably a predictable outcome given that each represented such different interests. Governors and their councils represented proprietors or the Crown. Assemblies represented local landowners. Only the corporate colonies of Connecticut and Rhode Island completely avoided overt tension between their legislative and executive branches of government since both were elected by the local inhabitants, and therefore enjoyed a close harmony of interests.

There was one mechanism for resolving conflicts between the Crown and colonies: the system of agents who represented the provincial assemblies in London. Essentially the agents were lobbyists; their task was to ensure favorable consideration of colonial interests by the authorities at the center of the empire. Among their targets were the Board of Trade and Privy Council, but ordinary members of parliament were also lobbied since they could influence legislation affecting the colonies. The principal merchants who traded with North America were another important target, since they could give valuable support both inside and outside Westminster. The system provided a safety valve whereby the views of the colonists and imperial authorities could be reconciled to the benefit of both.

Some historians have tended to see the disputes between the central and local authorities as evidence that the colonial political system could not have survived in the long run. They argue that the imperial system was too inflexible, saddling the colonies with incompetent officials, offering insufficient reward to native-born white North Americans, and containing fundamental constitutional inconsistencies.[7]

---

[7] See especially Leonard W. Labaree, *Royal Government in America: A Study of the British Colonial System Before 1783* (New Haven, 1930); and Jack P. Greene, *The Quest for Power: The Lower Houses of Assembly in the Southern Royal Colonies, 1689–1776* (Chapel Hill, 1963). The thesis is restated in Jack P. Greene, *Peripheries and Center: Constitutional Development in the Extended Politics of the British Empire and the United States, 1607–1788* (Athens, Ga., 1986).

Certainly the Crown sent too many ineffective place-seekers, most of whom were total strangers to North America. But colonial opposition to them did not constitute disloyalty to the Crown, only a protest against its representatives. Many of these disputes in any case were motivated by local men's desire for office. Once that objective had been attained, those who had vociferously condemned a particular measure or official often adopted what they had so recently denounced. The quality of governors also improved as the century progressed, one reason being the stricter guidelines drawn up by the Board of Trade. Though some infractions of these rules did take place, the worst excesses of Cornbury and his predecessors were not to be repeated. When governors fell foul of the population it was because of their lack of judgment, not because of peculation or extortion. In addition the Crown sent out many good governors, notably the veteran Nicholson and his successor, Spotswood, in Virginia, and the able Robert Hunter of New York. Even appointees in the era of the duke of Newcastle from 1725 to 1760 were not as incompetent as has usually been suggested. Where able men were appointed, comparative harmony was the result, as Shirley demonstrated in Massachusetts.[8]

Another popular explanation of the conflict between the Crown and the assemblies is that the Board of Trade and Privy Council saddled the governors with rigid instructions which prevented them from dealing with each situation as it arose. But most of the hundred-odd articles in these instructions were designed to introduce the incumbent to the routine of provincial administration, while other provisions merely asserted the need for a godly atmosphere. The most controversial directives were those already outlined: to prevent the assemblies from accumulating too many privileges and to ensure that mercantilist policies were observed. In any case, under emergency conditions many governors ignored the strict letter of their instructions and took contrary actions which the Board of Trade and Privy Council retrospectively had to accept. No governor who had shown himself adept was removed for being flexible.

Ironically, it was often locally born governors like Lewis Morris who were most inflexible, not having the confidence of appointees from Britain as to how far they could ignore their instructions. For example, William Burnet accepted a paper money bill from the New Jersey assembly in 1723, even without a suspending clause, in return for a better salary. Morris felt he had no such latitude and suffered prolonged confrontation as his reward.

A further criticism of the colonial system of government has been that it offered too little in the way of rewards for the local elites. No provincials were raised to the peerage,

[8] For a fuller analysis of Shirley, see John A. Shutz, *William Shirley: King's Governor of Massachusetts* (Chapel Hill, 1961). The view that the period was one of drift is argued by James A. Henretta, *"Salutary Neglect": Colonial Administration under the Duke of Newcastle* (Princeton, 1972); and Stanley N. Katz, *Newcastle's New York: Anglo-American Politics, 1732–1753* (Cambridge, Mass., 1968). Both Henretta and Katz were influenced by the British historian Sir Lewis Namier, who argued that patronage was the sole consideration in mid-eighteenth-century British politics. More favorable to Newcastle is Philip S. Haffenden, "Colonial Appointments and Patronage under the Duke of Newcastle, 1724–1739," *English Historical Review*, 78 (1963), 417–35; and Richard Middleton, "The Duke of Newcastle and the Conduct of Patronage during the Seven Years' War, 1757–1762," *British Journal for Eighteenth-Century Studies*, 12 (1989), 175–86. Behind the distribution of offices Newcastle had a serious political objective: the maintenance of the 1689 Revolution settlement.

and only two were rewarded with baronetcies: William Phips for his capture of Port Royal; and William Pepperell for the capture of Louisburg in 1745. Even the imperious Joseph Dudley failed to secure such an honor, while William Byrd II was snubbed on two counts. Not only did he not receive the governorship of Virginia; he also failed to secure a bride from the ranks of the British aristocracy which would have advanced his political influence and self-esteem. Such rebuffs may have fueled resentment against the imperial connection, since many visiting provincials often suffered an identity crisis in Britain, not least when disparaging comments were made about their country being a haven for convicts and the poor.[9]

Many provincials, though, were appointed to the most senior administrative positions of governor or lieutenant governor. In Massachusetts, local men held the governorship for 35 out of the 50 years following the Glorious Revolution, and almost all the men appointed in Rhode Island and Connecticut were colonials, though New England was perhaps the exception. Appointees in Virginia, New York, and South Carolina invariably came from the mother country.

Nevertheless, colonial elites everywhere could look to places on the council and positions in the judiciary. The superior courts were staffed by local men, even though most had no formal legal training. The same was true of the councils, where in addition to executive, legislative, and judicial responsibilities, membership allowed participation in the special perquisite of granting lands. A large number of positions were also available in the county courts, town meetings, and provincial militias, creating in the local inhabitants a strong sense of running their own affairs. The only areas of government not staffed exclusively by colonials were the customs, vice-admiralty judgeships, and a few positions (like colony secretary) for which British-born governors liked to bring over their own men. Until the 1760s thwarted ambition does not appear to have been a serious political problem.

A final reason for asserting that the imperial system was doomed has been that the Crown and the assemblies had incompatible views about their constitutional relationship. The constitutional settlement which followed the Glorious Revolution in Britain placed most actual authority with the King-in-Parliament. Essentially this meant the House of Lords and House of Commons possessed all lawmaking power, though the Crown could still influence Parliament through its patronage towards individual members of Parliament. Colonial political leaders in British North America, however, understood their own legislatures to possess lawmaking power over local colonial affairs. They also believed it was their local legislatures, not Parliament, that protected their liberties against monarchical overreaching. Parliament (they believed) had no place in their political relationship, other than to regulate trade within the empire as it had done with the Navigation Acts. Nothing in this understanding of their constitution prepared them for Parliament's attempts to assert direct legislative authority over the colonies after 1763.

---

[9] For a discussion of Byrd's wounded pride and the alienation of other members of the Virginia gentry, see Kenneth A. Lockridge, "Colonial Self-Fashioning: Paradoxes and Pathologies in the Construction of Genteel Identity in Eighteenth-Century America," in Ronald Hoffman, Mechal Sobel, and Fredrika Teute, eds, *Through a Glass Darkly: Reflections on Personal Identity in Early America* (Chapel Hill, 1997), 274–339.

Ironically the colonists' different understanding of their constitutional relationship with the king may have made the colonists more enthusiastic about the British monarchy than their counterparts in the British Isles. One historian has recently argued that the colonists shared a royalist political culture, bound together by their passionate devotion to a purportedly benevolent Protestant king, at a time when British subjects at home had become more devoted to an abstract concept of the nation. The strength of patriarchal family structures in the colonies may have helped to reinforce expectations among ordinary white colonists that a benevolent political patriarch would protect their interests and promote their welfare.[10]

Thus conflicts between colonial assemblies and appointed governors may have reflected the divergent opinions and interests of their members, rather than a systemic failure of the colonial political system. The colonial intention was not to dismantle or deny the legitimacy of royal government. The assemblies believed that they were merely performing their proper role in watching over the executive. In any case, greater activity by the assemblies did not necessarily mean a decline in the powers of the Crown. And although governors occasionally voiced the need for parliamentary intervention, no one talked of radical restructuring or ultimate separation from Britain, even in Massachusetts. Such talk occurred only after 1760.

4 PARTIES AND FACTIONS IN THE AGE OF WALPOLE

One reason for not seeing the period 1715–60 solely in terms of a developing conflict between the Crown and the assemblies is that both intercolonial and intracolonial disputes were equally prevalent.

Most intercolonial conflict occurred over boundaries. Imprecise wording and lack of proper surveys prior to the drafting of the seventeenth-century charters meant that every colony had some dispute with its neighbors. Connecticut and Rhode Island remained in disagreement over their boundary until 1728. Massachusetts and New Hampshire were in contention during the 1730s. New Hampshire and New York had to negotiate in the 1740s, while from 1748 onwards there were disturbances on the Massachusetts border with New York when squatters invaded the Livingston manor. Pennsylvania and Maryland had a long-running dispute over their border, while Connecticut claimed the northeast corner of Pennsylvania by virtue of its 1664 charter.

Political strife in this period, however, was actually most prevalent between rival groups inside each colony. Disputes were carried on under various guises, for at that time political parties were not considered legitimate. In a just polity where magistrates did their duty, subjects were expected to be loyal. Factiousness was equated with self-interest. Accordingly, all those who were politically active argued that they were acting for the common good. This was the key to legitimacy in government or opposition.

The nature of the struggles varied from colony to colony. In some they revolved around commerce and agriculture. In others they were the result of religious and ethnic

---

[10] Brendan McConville, *The King's Three Faces: The Rise and Fall of Royal America, 1688–1776* (Chapel Hill, 2006).

disagreements. Elsewhere the conflicts can be explained in terms of tidewater versus piedmont. Often it was a mixture of all three.

In Massachusetts the conflict was perhaps one of the clearest cases of commerce versus country. In Boston a nucleus of the wealthier classes, especially those involved in trade with Britain, like the Dudley and Hutchinson families, generally supported the executive. At times they and their allies in the other seaports and market-oriented constituencies were sufficiently powerful to dominate the assembly, where Thomas Hutchinson was speaker for two years. Most of the country towns, jealous of such commercial wealth, opposed them.

The conduct of politics in Massachusetts was influenced by another ingredient. As one historian has shown, a number of politicians in the country party began their careers by shaking the political tree as the prelude to climbing it. Among them were men like James Otis, Sr., Robert Hale, and John Choate. All were effectively professional politicians who used their skills to manage the untutored backcountry members in the Massachusetts assembly. Their behavior did not result in constant battle with the Crown or commercial interests, since an accommodation was their ultimate objective. Even Elisha Cooke, Jr., the most vitriolic member of the country party, indicated a willingness to support Governor Belcher in the 1730s.[11]

In Connecticut political tensions tended to be sectional, with the older towns of the Connecticut River Valley and New Haven arrayed against the more recent eastern settlements, like the burgeoning commercial centers of Norwich and New London. The older towns had been formed by religious covenants which still permeated their political culture. The newer towns, in contrast, had been founded as commercial ventures and reflected their more materialistic origins. They demanded cheap credit through the issue of paper currency, which appalled leaders from the older towns.

In New York the political lines were not always clear. Locals called the divisions "court" and "country," while later commentators preferred the terms "Whig" and "Tory," but "town" and "country" would often be more appropriate, since New York City, with its strong commercial interests, often found itself ranged against the farming communities of the Hudson River and Long Island. Divisions sometimes also took on a religious complexion, especially between the Anglicans and Presbyterians, while ethnicity was a third factor with such a mixture of English, Dutch, Scottish, Huguenot, and German inhabitants.

New York City was generally dominated by the large Anglo-Dutch families, whose interests were increasingly commercial rather than landed and who also tended to be Anglican. Their leaders were Adolphe Philipse and later James DeLancey. The country party was led by Lewis Morris and Philip Livingston. The latter was a Presbyterian. Although large landowners themselves, Morris and Livingston cultivated the support of the "middling sort" of small farming communities of the Hudson, including the Dutch, together with the growing artisan class in New York City. The main arguments after 1710 centered on the question of taxation: should the provincial government be financed by quitrents or customs? Quitrents would bear more heavily on the small

---

[11] See Robert Zemsky, *Merchants, Farmers, and River Gods: An Essay on Eighteenth-Century American Politics* (Boston, 1971). A similar interpretation is followed by Stephen E. Patterson, *Political Parties in Revolutionary Massachusetts* (Madison, 1973); and Bushman, *King and People in Provincial Massachusetts.*

farms: customs burdens would fall chiefly on the commerce of New York. Defense was another intermittent issue. The tidewater area around the city believed that the frontier counties should look after themselves.

During Hunter's governorship, the Morris group dominated, since Hunter wanted to reduce the power of the elite. Governor Burnet initially continued this alliance when he arrived in 1720, but as support for the Philipse faction increased in the assembly, Burnet began to look to them. This was the situation which greeted Governor William Cosby on his arrival in 1731. Cosby's injudicious prosecution of the newspaper publisher John Peter Zenger for seditious libel quickly discredited his political allies. Accordingly, in the mid-1730s the Morris faction once more achieved ascendancy, only to find the situation reversed again in the 1750s when the DeLanceys came back into power. Although both sides claimed to be representing the people, and cultivated their votes at election time, none of this maneuvering involved much principle, for as Philip Livingston confessed during the Cosby episode, "We change Sides as Serves our Interest best not the Country's."

New Jersey was similarly riven by sectionalism, religious antagonism, and differing economic interests. Early in its history it also had a problem with absentee landowners, since many proprietors preferred to be domiciled in the relative comfort of New York or Philadelphia rather than in the wilds of East or West New Jersey.

However, with the governorship of Robert Hunter, most took up residence in the province to provide an effective governing elite, helping to alleviate the divisions between the east and the west. But most important was the development of tolerance between the Anglicans and Quakers, who dominated the upper and lower houses of the general assembly even though they made up only one-quarter of the population. They were helped in their electoral dominance by the inability of the Presbyterians, Dutch Reformed, and Baptists to work together or to vote in sufficient numbers.[12]

Several other factors helped the development of a more cooperative spirit. One was the need for unity to combat the dominance of New York and Philadelphia. Another was that New Jersey fortunately had no exposed frontier to defend. Finally, all the contending parties agreed to keep government to a minimum, thus avoiding contentious issues that bedeviled other provincial governments.

New Jersey's political harmony broke down in the 1740s when doubts arose over the validity of various land titles. Since obtaining their original grant in 1664, the Elizabeth and Newark associates[13] had continued issuing patents well beyond the original area, following additional acquisitions from the Indians, thus causing conflict with the proprietary titles purchased from Berkeley and Carteret. In 1745 the East Jersey proprietors decided to challenge the activities of the Elizabeth and Newark associates in the courts, provoking numerous evictions and riots, during which the inmates of several jails were released. The struggle was then transferred to the council and the assembly. The council, representing the large landowners, demanded a draconian

---

[12] For a revisionist view, see Thomas Purvis, *Proprietors, Patronage, and Paper Money: Legislative Politics in New Jersey, 1703–1776* (New Brunswick, 1986). See also Benjamin H. Newcomb, *Political Partisanship in the American Middle Colonies, 1700–1776* (Baton Rouge, 1995); and Brendan McConville, *Those Daring Disturbers of the Public Peace: The Struggle for Property and Power in Early New Jersey* (Ithaca, 1999). Newcomb plays down the importance of the subsequent land title disputes.

[13] See Chapter 7, section 3 for a discussion of the original grants in New Jersey.

public order act to intimidate the rioters into accepting new proprietary patents requiring the payment of quitrents. The assembly, representing the smaller farmers and property-owners, preferred conciliation, seeing the disturbances as essentially a conflict between two sets of landowners. Eventually the assembly got its way. An amnesty was granted; and tempers cooled when many of the small farmers, who had been unaware of the legal pitfalls of purchasing land in New Jersey, finally had their titles confirmed.

We have already seen that Pennsylvania's politics were dominated by the conflict between the proprietary family and the Quakers. Here too there was an element of town versus country. The wealthy commercial elements in Philadelphia were frequently in conflict with the small Quaker farming communities in Bucks and Chester counties. From the 1720s onwards the demographic balance of Pennsylvania began to change following the influx of large numbers of Germans and Scots-Irish. Until the 1750s these newcomers were too remote or inexperienced to participate regularly in the political process. To the extent that they had political representation at all, they generally supported the Quakers because of the latter's opposition to the attempts of the Penn family to raise the price of land. After 1755 these settlers broke from the Quakers over the issue of frontier defense, and after 1760, they were to undermine both the proprietary and Quaker factions.

In the South the factional fighting was generally less pronounced. A principal reason was that the presence of large numbers of slaves made members of the planter elite readier both to cooperate with one another and to listen to the white small farmers. Their alliance helped to prevent any rebellion by the slaves. The result was a tacit political consensus, which in Virginia led to a mere one-third of constituencies being contested after 1728. This *rapprochement* was briefly threatened in 1735 over the Tobacco Inspection Act, which many small farmers believed would exclude their produce from the market. Otherwise this harmony was marred only by the occasional dispute between the council and the assembly. The council was dominated by older members of the elite, who sought to protect their interests from attack by the younger generation in the house. Another cause of occasional discord was competing economic interests, such as those between the Ohio and Loyal Land companies in Virginia.[14]

The one exception to consensus politics was North Carolina, where the number of enslaved African Americans was significantly smaller. The main conflict here was between the northern and southern parts of the province. The northern counties around Albemarle Sound were settled mainly by people from Virginia who, as in their former colony, produced tobacco. The southern area around Cape Fear had been populated largely by people from South Carolina, who cultivated rice and made pitch and tar for the navy. Until the 1730s the northern counties dominated the legislature. But as the Cape Fear region expanded, it began to demand more representation and the removal of the provincial capital from Edenton to New Bern. These demands were effectively realized in 1734 when Governor Gabriel Johnston, a planter from the Cape Fear region, took office. The northern counties responded by refusing to pay

---

[14] Marc Egnal, *A Mighty Empire: The Origins of the American Revolution* (Ithaca, 1988), suggests that the lines of political action were divided between optimists, who wanted to expand as quickly as possible, and pessimists, who were inclined to conserve what had already been won.

their taxes and seceding from the assembly. Eventually, in 1754 a new governor, Arthur Dobbs, secured a compromise involving a more equitable distribution of seats, though a permanent site for the capital still had to be decided. One factor bringing the two regions closer was the arrival of the Scots-Irish, Germans, and other groups in the piedmont area, who posed a challenge to both north and south.

Any system of government is bound to produce political discord; such conflict is part of the human condition. Perhaps more noteworthy than the occasional lack of harmony was the essential stability of colonial institutions between 1714 and 1760. Compared with the seventeenth century the period after 1715 saw few, if any, serious disturbances. No governors had to flee for their lives, nor were royal troops called upon to put down any insurrection. One reason for this relative calm was the greater stability of Britain itself. Another was the new maturity of the colonies. They were no longer isolated frontier settlements, ready to seize arms at the first alarm, and the change was reflected in their politics, which were now conducted within a clear constitutional framework. It was this very maturity that was to be so important after 1760.

5   TOWARD A REPUBLICAN IDEOLOGY

To what extent did the British North American colonists' political factiousness foreshadow the development of a republican, as opposed to a monarchical, theory of government?

Many historians have argued that an embryonic republican ideology began to develop after 1689, making possible the rapid appearance of an alternative political creed after 1763 when Britain and the colonies came into open conflict.

The sources of this ideology have been variously identified. One was the tradition of Protestant dissent. New Englanders in particular held strong critical views of the Anglican Church and, by implication, the English state. Their views were shared by other dissenting groups like the Presbyterians. None was overtly antimonarchical; their quarrel was with the unreformed church. There was much in their theology, however, which was incompatible with the kind of hierarchical authority that kings had sought to claim during the seventeenth century. James I had asserted in 1603 that no bishops would mean no king. Subsequent events proved him right when Charles I was executed and a commonwealth form of government imposed.

The tradition of religious dissent was subsequently subsumed into the Whig party after the restoration of Charles II. Many Whigs, like the earl of Shaftesbury, Algernon Sydney, and John Locke had served during the Cromwellian era. It was their distrust of monarchical power, allied to a hatred of Catholicism, which led to the Exclusion crisis of 1681 when an attempt was made to deprive James II of his right to the throne. The Whigs also played a key role in 1689 during the Glorious Revolution.

After 1689 most English Whigs became supporters of the Crown, since the monarchy was now constrained by Parliament, where the Whigs had a majority following the revolutionary settlement. But a small band continued to remember their more radical traditions. Among them were the publicists Thomas Gordon and John Trenchard. After 1714 they and other "real" Whigs became increasingly alarmed at the apparent corruption of successive ministries under Sir Robert Walpole, fearing that his use of patronage to control the House of Commons would lead to the reimposition of tyranny. They expressed their opposition in various English publications, notably the *Independent Whig* and *Cato's Letters.* These eighteenth-century "commonwealth"-style papers were sometimes read in British North America, where they reminded their transatlantic readers of the need for vigilance if virtuous government and a free people were to survive. The New York lawyer Andrew Hamilton, exhorting a jury to acquit John Peter Zenger in his 1735 trial for seditious libel, exemplified the "commonwealth" tradition with his argument that citizens had a duty to protect liberty: "like wise men who value freedom [we must] use our utmost care to support liberty, the only bulwark against lawless power, which in all ages has sacrificed to its wild lust and boundless ambition the blood of the best men that ever lived." The Boston minister, Jonathan Mayhew, explained that the protection of liberty could even justify revolution. In a 1750 sermon entitled *Discourse Concerning Unlimited Submission,* he told his congregation on the anniversary of the execution of Charles I: "For a nation thus abused to arise unanimously and to resist their prince even to the dethroning him, is not criminal, but a reasonable way of vindicating their liberties and just rights." Or as Andrew Eliot wrote more succinctly in 1765, "when tyranny is abroad, submission is a crime."

Writings on natural law by Enlightenment philosophers like Pufendorf, Vattel, Grotius, Montesquieu, and Voltaire formed a third strand in the embryonic republican ideology. These philosophers provided a rationale for government based on reason, justice, and the laws of nature. The most influential member of this school was John Locke. Locke's intention on publishing his *Two Treatises of Government* in 1691 was to justify the Glorious Revolution. In practice, his arguments found little support even among English Whigs, for Locke stated that all authority must emanate from the people, to whom both monarch and Parliament were accountable. Government was a trust, and if rulers abused their authority the people could remove them, since their consent alone could confer legitimacy. This radical view offered a basis for government quite different from the existing European notions of divine right, prescriptive inheritance, or even parliamentary omnipotence. Significantly, it was this rationale which colonial British North Americans adopted when denying British authority in 1776.

A fourth strand in this incipient republicanism was provided by the classical historians of Greece and Rome, often interpreted and elucidated by Renaissance authors. These demonstrated how a society could conduct itself in an enlightened, constitutional, and virtuous fashion. Classical republicanism appealed to all those looking for a system of government not based on religion in which the good of the commonwealth came before the interests of the individual. But there were dangers too in such precedents, as history showed. The writings of Plutarch, Livy, Cicero, and Tacitus were full of dire warnings about the fate of the Roman republic, where a decline in virtue had allowed vicious tyrants like Nero and Caligula to take control. How happy in contrast were the Germans, Tacitus asserted, because they had retained their simple ways. These perils were seemingly confirmed by the experience of some eighteenth-century colonials. When John Dickinson studied law in London he was appalled at the apparent corruption of British politics. As he told his father, "It is grown a vice here to be virtuous." He could only reflect that "unbounded licentiousness … is the unfailing cause of the destruction of all empires." The colonists should take note.

Lastly, educated British North Americans were familiar with the writings of Aristotle, the great political scientist of the ancient world. His analysis of the three legitimate forms of government – monarchy, aristocracy, and democracy – taught colonials that, theoretically at least, constitutional monarchy was not the only legitimate system.

Of course such knowledge was limited to the few before 1760. Conventional wisdom suggested that the British constitution was the best, since it uniquely combined all three types of government defined by Aristotle. Natural rights were merely an interesting concept, not something the colonials needed to seek, since they already had their rights as Englishmen. When colonial legislators came into conflict with imperial authority they resorted to English legal precedents like Magna Carta, the Petition of Right, Habeas Corpus, and the Bill of Rights.

It was true that ordinary colonists often expressed their loyalty towards the king, professing their belief that the British king was the most benevolent monarch in the world and their gratitude that they were the subjects of a Protestant monarch. Still, the strength of that loyalty had not really been tested since the accession of William and Mary. What would happen if Parliament attempted to impose policies on colonial governments that they genuinely opposed, and if the king failed to protect their rights as the colonists expected him to? In the absence of institutional structures to prop up monarchical authority, without an aristocracy, a court, or a single established church, would that affection and reverence for the monarchy survive? Time would tell.[15]

---

[15]   Richard L. Bushman, in *King and People in Provincial Massachusetts*, argues that despite its monarchical character, colonial society had already begun drifting subconsciously in a republican direction during the eighteenth century. Brendan McConville (*The King's Three Faces*, ch. 10) argues that a monarchical political culture lasted until the middle of the revolutionary crisis, and that the colonists finally lost their confidence in the monarchy around 1773. Most scholars have argued that the roots of a republican political culture were present before the American Revolution. For other important writings on the topic see Bernard Bailyn, *The Ideological Origins of the American Revolution* (Cambridge, Mass., 1967); Gordon S. Wood, *The Creation of the American Republic, 1776–1787* (Chapel Hill, 1969); Caroline Robbins, *The Eighteenth-Century Commonwealthman: Studies in the Transmission, Development, and Circumstance of English Liberal Thought from the Restoration of Charles II until the War with the Thirteen Colonies* (Cambridge, Mass., 1959); J. G. A. Pocock, *The Machiavellian Moment: Florentine Political Thought and the Atlantic Republican Tradition* (Princeton, 1975); and Edmund S. Morgan, *Inventing the People: The Rise of Popular Sovereignty in England and America* (New York, 1988).

19

Britain, France, and Spain

The Imperial Contest, 1739–1763

1713	The Treaty of Utrecht ends the War of the Spanish Succession.
1720	The French establish a fort at Niagara.
1727	The British build a fort at Oswego.
1739	The War of Jenkins' Ear with Spain breaks out.
1741	The British navy is defeated in the Battle of Cartagena.
1745	The New Englanders capture Louisburg.
1747	The Ohio Company is founded.
1748	The Treaty of Aix-la-Chapelle ends the War of the Austrian Succession. The Treaty of Logstown opens the trail to Pickawillany in the West.
1753	Mohawk leaders declare the Covenant Chain to be broken.
1754	The French establish Fort Duquesne (Pittsburgh) at the forks of the Ohio. A plan of union is unveiled at the Albany Congress.
1755	The French defeat General Braddock with the help of western Indians. The British deport French settlers from Acadia.
1756	The French take Oswego; western Indians join the French war effort in large numbers.
1757	The French take Fort William Henry.
1758	The British take Louisburg, Fort Frontenac, and Fort Duquesne; Delawares agree to peace with British at the Treaty of Easton.
1759	General Wolfe takes Québec.
1760	General Amherst takes Montréal and receives the surrender of New France.
1762	Spain enters the war.
1763	Pontiac's Rebellion begins in the West. The Peace of Paris ends the French and Indian War. Canada and the Ohio Country are ceded to the British. Louisiana becomes a colony of Spain. Spanish citizens leave Florida. The British issue the Proclamation of 1763 limiting western settlement.

Colonial America: A History to 1763, Fourth Edition. Richard Middleton and Anne Lombard.
© 2011 Richard Middleton and Anne Lombard. Published 2011 by Blackwell Publishing Ltd.

1 THE WAR OF JENKINS' EAR

T HE TREATY OF Utrecht in 1713 was followed by 26 years of peace, prosperity, and stability for Britain, France, Spain, and their colonies in North America. However, this era of peace was destined to be disrupted. By the late 1730s the British public had forgotten about the high costs of war and begun to clamor once again for an aggressive foreign policy that would expand British control of overseas commerce and territory. That policy, once enacted, would inevitably involve renewed conflict between the British, the French, and the Spanish in North America, and with their Native American allies.

Several points of contention had emerged between the British and the French in North America since 1713. One was the boundary between New France and the British colonies. Although the British had obtained control over Hudson Bay, Newfoundland, and Acadia (now called Nova Scotia), the 5,000 French settlers living in Acadia fiercely resented their new status and refused to swear loyalty to the British at Annapolis Royal. Meanwhile the French still controlled Ile Royale, the large island to the northeast of Nova Scotia (known today as Cape Breton). As the last remaining territory in New France that directly bordered on the Atlantic seaboard, Ile Royale was strategically vital to French control over the St. Lawrence Valley and the Atlantic fishery. To maximize its advantages there the French had begun to construct a massive new fort on Ile Royale at the town of Louisburg in 1719.

To the west, Britain and France had each established rival trading posts at Niagara and Oswego, each hoping to gain access to the western nations and to restrict the commerce of the other. British presence in the West undercut France's previously undisputed control over the western fur trade and created a potential new source of contention between the two European competitors. Hopes of further eroding French control over the West prompted the Board of Trade in London in 1721 to propose a tripartite policy of building forts, regulating the Indian trade, and settling the backcountry beyond the mountains. However, such a policy would have been expensive and difficult, given the strength of French alliances. As a result the British government did little to claim additional western territory.

Other conflicts involved Britain's relationship with Spain, which by the 1730s had once again become a close French ally. One irritant was the creation of the British colony of Georgia in 1733 on land previously claimed by Spain. A second source of contention was trade. Under the terms of the Treaty of Utrecht, Spain had created a trading agreement (*asiento*) allowing the British South Sea Company to supply Spain's American empire with slaves and one annual shipload of goods. Other than this agreement, Spain insisted upon sole control over trade with its American colonies. British traders, on the other hand, were ambitious to gain more of that trade for themselves. The South Sea Company shamefully abused the *asiento*, constantly restocking its vessel with fresh goods. Smuggling was also rife elsewhere, much of it carried out by colonial ships and abetted by the Spanish Creoles, who needed colonial imports to survive. Spanish officials, however, enforced Spain's mercantilist system through the *guarda costa*, or coast guard, and in the process a number of detainees were ill-treated. Among them was a Captain Jenkins, whose ear was allegedly cut off by a coast guard officer who had boarded his ship. The opposition in Parliament used the episode to embarrass the government of Sir Robert Walpole. Although Walpole himself was inclined towards peace, the furor over the treatment of Britain's commerce compelled him to declare war against Spain.

British expeditions during the war suggest that the Crown still hoped to gain a base from which to attack Spanish American silver fleets. In the early months of 1739 a British expedition under Admiral Vernon managed to capture and briefly occupy the Spanish base of Porto Bello, on the Isthmus of Panama. In 1740 a squadron was sent to the Pacific under the command of Commodore George Anson to attack Spanish ships traveling from Mexico to the Philippines, finally capturing the Manila galleon in 1743. Additional attempts were made to take over Cartagena, the departure point for Spain's treasure fleets in New Granada, as well as Guantánamo, Cuba, and several ports along the Venezuelan coast. The North American colonists were enthusiastic enough about these efforts to raise four battalions from 11 colonies for the Cartagena expedition in 1741. However, the expedition itself was poorly executed and failed, having become a disaster for the colonial volunteers, many of whom died of disease or malnutrition. The colonists also found regular discipline distasteful, since most had enlisted for adventure and profit. They got neither, and their dissatisfaction greatly increased when many were detained for service with the Royal Navy. This insult was not forgotten; when the fleet called at Boston in 1747 for provisions and the recovery of deserters, the result was a serious riot.

Equally unrewarding for the North American colonists was General Oglethorpe's scheme to attack St. Augustine, Florida. Like Vernon, Oglethorpe sought local recruits and succeeded in raising over 1,000 volunteers, many from neighboring South Carolina, similarly lured by the prospect of booty. Alas, here too the colonial hopes were blighted, for after besieging St. Augustine for a month, Oglethorpe decided that his forces were too weak to continue and retreated with little to show for his effort. He was more successful in his defense of Georgia. When the Spanish counterattacked there in 1742, they were decisively repulsed near the settlement of Frederica in the Battle of the Bloody Swamp.

By 1744 the war had become part of the War of the Austrian Succession, and France at last declared war against Britain, thereby shifting the focus of most of the fighting back to Europe and away from the colonies. The British government supplied little assistance in the colonial theater aside from some naval attacks on French ships engaged in trade in the West Indies. Yet even without substantial help from London, British colonists along the northern colonial frontier remained enthusiastic about attacking the French. The call to arms was especially popular in New England, since it continued the old struggle against Catholic New France and revived the settlers' hopes of driving away the Indians. The dangers posed by Louisburg were emphasized in 1744 when its garrison destroyed the British fishing village of Canso at the northern end of Nova Scotia and then besieged Annapolis Royal, which Massachusetts was helping to garrison.

Accordingly in 1745 Governor Shirley persuaded the general court to launch an attack on Louisburg itself. Massachusetts had a proud tradition of organizing its own campaigns, notably the attack on Québec in 1690. Some 3,000 men were quickly voted for the enterprise; contingents also came from Connecticut and New Hampshire. The

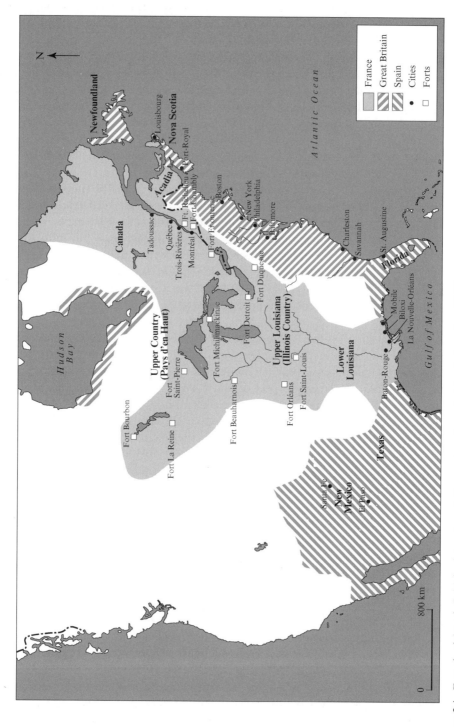

Map 24 French-claimed, British-claimed, and disputed territory in North America, 1755.

operation was greatly assisted by a squadron of Royal Navy frigates under Sir Peter Warren, which ensured that the expedition not only reached its objective but was able to isolate the garrison inside. Morale in Louisburg was low, and the French surrendered on June 16.

The capture of Louisburg inspired wild public enthusiasm (especially in the New England colonies) and stimulated the government in London to look for further success in North America. Orders were sent to New England to have supplies ready for an attack up the St. Lawrence in 1746 and another force in New York prepared to invade Canada via Crown Point. Yet just as in 1709, the colonists' expectations were dashed when the British fleet and army failed to arrive, having been diverted to attack the French coast at the last moment.

New Englanders were even more disappointed when the peace was finally signed at Aix-la-Chapelle in 1748. Having begun the war with high hopes of conquering Spanish and French territory to add to the British empire, Britain was left at the end of the war with no gains in America at all. Especially galling to the colonists was the fact that British negotiators returned Louisburg to the French in exchange for territorial concessions in India and Flanders. Yet the British public continued to demand a more aggressive foreign policy; perhaps it was inevitable that another war with France would soon follow. This time, the provocation for that conflict would be in the West.

2 THE STRUGGLE FOR THE OHIO

By the mid eighteenth century, the vast Ohio River Valley was home to a diverse array of Indian peoples, all of whom by now had a long history of relationships with Europeans. In the western half of the Ohio Valley, an area the French called the Illinois Country, lived remnant bands of Miami, Fox, Wyandot, Ottawa, and Kickapoo peoples, along with diverse other Native American groups. Ever since the 1660s they had been bound together in a loose coalition with the French that served to counter Iroquois power in the West. In the northeastern portion of the Ohio Valley, the Shawnees had been driven out by the Iroquois during the seventeenth century, but by this time they were back, along with Delawares from the Susquehanna Valley in Pennsylvania. Mingoes (western Senecas) were ostensibly here to maintain Iroquois sovereignty over the Shawnees and the Delawares in the Ohio, though in fact the Iroquois now had little real authority this far west and south of their tribal homelands. A few Mahicans and Nanticokes had settled here too, while Ojibwa and Miami bands came here to hunt. Most of the newcomers had longstanding relationships with the British, though many hoped that the Ohio Valley was a place where they might once again become independent of binding entanglements.

French traders had been present in the eastern Ohio Valley for many decades, although not in large numbers since they could obtain better furs from their allies further west and north. By 1749, though, they had some competition. French shipments of trade goods to North America were disrupted by King George's War from 1744 to 1748, thereby weakening the position of the French as the pre-eminent traders west of the Appalachian Mountains. Deprived of their muskets and ammunition, some of the Indians in the region rebelled against the French and even attacked

Fort Miami. Thereafter a number of them turned for their supply of trade goods to British traders from Pennsylvania, particularly a Delaware- and Shawnee-speaking Irishman named George Croghan with exceptional negotiating skills and a knack for finding ways to make a profit. Pennsylvania had already secured Iroquois permission for a route through the Ohio Country under the 1744 Treaty of Lancaster. In 1748 Croghan helped complete negotiations at Logstown for the opening of such a trail. By 1749 Croghan's mule trains had successfully crossed the mountains and opened a series of trading posts, the most notable being the village of Pickawillany on the Miami River. With access to the best commercial trading system in the world, Croghan and other British traders could offer the Indians trade goods at very desirable prices. The Indians' loyalty to French traders visibly waned.

French control over the valley was threatened not only by British traders, but also by British land speculators. The British colonial settler population had continued to grow with extraordinary speed since 1700, thanks to the settlers' high birth rate and the continued flow of new immigrants. Land in the long-settled areas near the Atlantic coast was by now unavailable, but the settlers' adult children and the new immigrants still hoped to acquire farms of their own. A number of forward-thinking investors in the British colonies had formed joint-stock companies in order to claim land in the Ohio country and sell it to settlers, dispossessing the Indians who lived there. The first was the Ohio Company of Virginia, organized in 1747 by Thomas Lee, a large tobacco planter and a member of the Virginia council. Its aims were the promotion of both trade and settlement. Lee initially sought a charter from the Virginia assembly but later decided to apply to the Privy Council instead, perhaps to attract London investors. The grant was for 500,000 acres, on the condition that the company build a fort and settle 100 families within two years on the forks of the Ohio. Although the company planned to sell the land to farmers as soon as it could, for the time being it would make money by competing with the Pennsylvania traders. In 1750 the company dispatched the surveyor Christopher Gist to explore the area and set up a trading post.

The activities of the Ohio Company prompted the establishment of a rival group, the Loyal Land Company, by another set of well-connected Virginia landowners which included John Robinson, the speaker of the Virginia House of Burgesses. These men resented the Ohio Company's direct approach to the Privy Council, preferring that such matters be determined by the local authorities. The Loyal Land Company received a grant of 800,000 acres from the House of Burgesses on what was later to be the borders of Virginia, Kentucky, and Tennessee. It also employed a surveyor, Dr Thomas Walker, who set out on his exploratory mission in the same year as Gist.

To France, these various incursions by British traders and surveyors were alarming. One reason was the threat they posed to French alliances with the Indians, alliances that enabled them to control the corridor that linked New France, the Great Lakes region, and Louisiana via the Mississippi River. Another reason, as Paul Mapp has recently argued, was that British actions seemed to the French to be part of a larger scheme to assert British dominance over the entire continent. The evidence of British designs seemed clear. Between 1739 and 1741 the British had attacked a number of major Spanish American ports, evidently hoping to take over a portion of the Spanish North American empire. Then during the 1740s, British explorers had launched several exploratory expeditions beyond the western shores of Hudson Bay in search of a route to the Pacific. Now the British were moving settlers into the Ohio Valley. To the French government it seemed obvious that the British planned to take over the trans-Mississippi West and use it to gain control over Mexico and access to the Pacific.[1]

The government of New France, believing its own strategic interests in the West were being challenged, initiated a series of moves to regain control over the Ohio Valley. The first was the dispatch of a military force led by Captain Pierre-Joseph Céloron de Blainville in 1749 to assert French title to the region by burying a series of lead plates at points along the upper Ohio. As Céloron traveled through the valley he met with various groups of Shawnees, Delawares, Miamis, and Mingoes, who accepted his gifts but listened skeptically to his lectures about the need to spurn the British and trade only with the French. Then in 1752 the French destroyed the village of Pickawillany, thereby eliminating the presence of the British traders. Next they extended their chain of forts between the Great Lakes and the Mississippi. They strengthened Niagara and built a new post on the shores of Lake Erie at Presque Isle, followed by two more at Venango and Fort Le Boeuf. By 1753 only the Ohio River required fortification to complete the chain.

The French attempt to exclude the British from westward expansion alarmed the government in London, which saw it as a threat to vital British interests. This perception arose in part because of a fundamental shift in Britain's trade. Since the middle of the seventeenth century the sugar islands of the West Indies had been Britain's most prized colonial possessions. By 1750, however, trade with the mainland colonies had begun to surpass that with the West Indies, not least because the export of manufactured goods to colonial consumers in North America was now as important as the importation of enumerated commodities. The British government was beginning to envision a future when the market for its exports might include settlements extending west to the Mississippi. Yet such settlements would never be created if the French continued to control the West. In the words of the duke of Newcastle, King George II's leading minister, "The French claim almost all North America except a line to the sea, to which they would confine all our colonies, and from whence they may drive us whenever they please." And he vehemently affirmed. "That is what we must not, We will not suffer."

Even as the French were working to strengthen their Indian alliances in order to halt British expansion into the West, the British government had reason to be anxious that its own Indian alliances were dissolving. The Iroquois had for years maintained the fiction of the Covenant Chain, namely that they would offer their assistance to the British in case of war. But in fact tribal leaders had long been dissatisfied with their British allies. At a meeting in June 1753, the Mohawk chief Hendrick (or Theyanoguin) had declared the Covenant Chain with the British to be broken. Unhappy with their Albany trading partners and angry about an attempt by land speculators to rob them of their land, many Mohawk warriors had become disgusted with the British. For British officials, the potential loss of their ties to the Iroquois was of grave concern.

The British government accordingly instituted a number of measures. The Board of Trade, under the energetic Lord Halifax, sent a circular letter to the northern colonies

---

[1] Paul W. Mapp, *The Elusive West and the Contest for Empire, 1713–1763* (Chapel Hill, 2011).

urging them to negotiate with the native peoples and, most important, to persuade the Iroquois to resume their traditional alliance. The Board began to expend large sums for the establishment of a new town and harbor in Nova Scotia, to be called Halifax, which had been started in 1749 to secure vulnerable northeastern approaches from the Atlantic. At the same time further pressure was put on the French settlers in Acadia to take an oath of allegiance. And finally the Board ordered the Ohio Company to abide by its charter and establish a fort on the banks of the Ohio River. Everywhere the colonial governments were instructed to meet force with force if they found the French trespassing on the king's territory. To achieve these and other objectives the colonies were to consider establishing a common war chest.

The result was the Albany Congress of June 1754, attended by delegates from New Hampshire, Massachusetts, Connecticut, Rhode Island, New York, Pennsylvania, and Maryland, along with a delegation from the Six Nations of the Iroquois League. The Congress was a landmark in colonial cooperation. Never before had there been such wide participation between colonial governments. True, the New England provinces had long cooperated with one another, while the southern colonies had occasionally given cross-border assistance, as in the Tuscarora and Yamasee wars. Otherwise, previous efforts at cooperation had been confined to meetings of royal officials, like Bellomont's conference of governors in 1700.

Yet, in terms of actual achievements, the Congress accomplished little. The British delegates were unable to regain the trust of the representatives of the Six Nations. A number of gifts were given, but the sachems affirmed that they were tired of fighting Britain's wars without adequate support. One can hardly wonder that they distrusted the British delegates. While the Congress was taking place, negotiators from Connecticut and Pennsylvania each managed to convince separate Iroquois spokesmen to sell them an enormous tract of land in western Pennsylvania, conveniently ignoring the fact that the deeds conflicted with one another.

The conference then turned to the question of a common war fund. This issue provoked a wide-ranging discussion of a plan of colonial union drawn up by Benjamin Franklin. His scheme was that there should be a president general appointed by the Crown and a grand council elected by the colonial assemblies. Representation would depend on each colony's respective population. The grand council, or congress, was to have legislative power, though the president would be able to veto any measure. The new body was to be responsible for defense, relations with native peoples, and lands "not now within the bounds of particular colonies." It would be financed by quitrents on all new grants.

The scheme proved too ambitious to be acceptable either to the Crown or to the provincial assemblies, both of which apprehended a loss of authority; in addition it reminded many New Englanders of the hated Dominion of New England. Nevertheless, it was a remarkable initiative, which was to surface again in 1775.

While the conference was in session, the first hostilities broke out. In 1753 the governor of Virginia, Robert Dinwiddie, had sent a young militia officer, George Washington, to warn the French to stop encroaching on the Ohio. Washington delivered his message and met with various local Delaware, Shawnee, and Mingo representatives, seeking to renew their historical alliances with the British. A few Mingoes professed their willingness to help but most of the Indians ignored his

DOCUMENT 28

The Albany plan of union, 1754, reprinted in W. Keith Kavenagh, *Foundations of Colonial America: A Documentary History* (New York, 1973), Vol. 2, 1374–5

This ambitious scheme proposed to link the colonies together in a defensive union. Question to consider: *How would this plan have changed the way in which the colonies were governed, if it had been enacted?*

The Plan of Union (as finally adopted). It is proposed that humble application be made for an act of Parliament of Great Britain by virtue of which one general government may be formed in America, including all the said colonies, within and under which government each colony may retain its present constitution, except in the particulars wherein a change may be directed by the said act as hereafter follows.

President-General and Grand Council. That the said general government be administered by a President-General, to be appointed and supported by the Crown, and a Grand Council, to be chosen by the representatives of the people of the several colonies met in their respective assemblies.

Election of Members. The [several] House of Representatives ... shall choose members for the Grand Council in the following proportion, that is to say, Massachusetts Bay, 7; New Hampshire, 2; Connecticut 5; Rhode Island 2; New York 4; New Jersey 3; Pennsylvania 6; Maryland 4; Virginia 7; North Carolina 4; South Carolina 4. Total 48.

Place of First Meeting. The City of Philadelphia

New Election. There shall be a new election of the members of the Grand Council every three years ...

Meetings of the Grand Council. The Grand Council shall meet once in every year, and oftener if occasion require, at such time and place as they adjourn to at the last preceding meeting or as they shall be called to meet at by the President-General on any emergency ...

Assent of the President-General and his Duty. The assent of the President-General be requisite to all acts of the Grand Council and that it be his office and duty to cause them to be carried into execution.

Power of the President-General and Grand Council: Treaties of Peace and War. That the President-General, with the advice of the Grand Council, hold or direct all Indian treaties in which the general interest of the colonies may be concerned; and make peace or declare war with Indian nations.

Indian Trade. That they make such laws as they judge necessary for regulating all Indian trade.

Indian Purchases. That they make all purchases, from Indians for the Crown, of lands not now within the bounds of particular colonies or that shall not be within their bounds when some of them are reduced to more convenient dimensions.

New Settlements. That they make new settlements on such purchases by granting lands in the King's name, reserving a quitrent to the Crown.

Laws to Govern them. That they make laws for regulating and governing such new settlements till the Crown shall think fit to form them into particular governments.

Raise Soldiers and equip vessels. That they raise and pay soldiers and build forts for the defense of any of the colonies, and equip vessels of force to guard the coasts . . .

Power to make laws, lay duties. That for these purposes they have power to make laws and lay and levy such general duties, imposts, or taxes as to them shall appear most equal and just.

Quorum. That a quorum of the Grand Council, empowered to act with the President-General, do consist of twenty-five members; among whom there shall be one or more from a majority of the colonies.

Laws to be Transmitted. That the laws made by them for the purposes aforesaid, shall not be repugnant, but as near as may be, agreeable to the laws of England, and shall be transmitted to the King in council for approbation.

Officers, how appointed. That all military commission officers, whether for land or sea service, to act under this general constitution, shall be nominated by the President-General, but the approbation of the Grand Council is to be obtained before they receive their commissions. And all civil officers are to be nominated by the Grand Council and to receive the President-General's approbation before they officiate.

Each Colony may defend itself on an Emergency. That the particular as well as civil establishments in each colony remain in their present state, the general constitution notwithstanding; and that on sudden emergencies any colony may defend itself and lay the accounts of expense thence arising before the President-General and General Council . . .

entreaties, understanding that British expansion into the valley would hardly benefit their people. Early in 1754, Dinwiddie sent a group to construct a fort on the forks of the Ohio. These men were subsequently surprised by a much larger French and Indian force which proceeded to occupy the site themselves. Dinwiddie then sent Washington, now a militia colonel, back with a contingent to expel them. But although Washington routed a small vanguard of the French, he was subsequently surrounded at a makeshift encampment called Fort Necessity, where he was compelled to surrender and admit his guilt for starting hostilities.

Although this episode was intrinsically no more important than many previous skirmishes, on this occasion both crowns felt their prestige was at stake. When news of

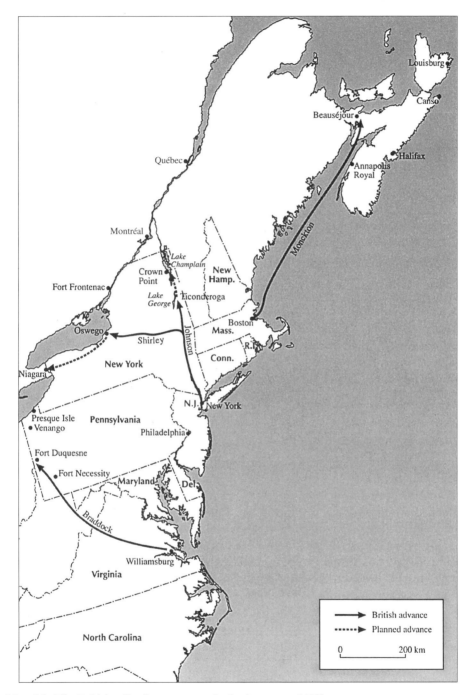

Map 25 The British offensive to secure the backcountry, 1755.

Washington's setback reached London, Newcastle's ministry determined to launch a four-pronged offensive to secure the frontier. First, a force of two regular regiments from Britain under the command of General Braddock was to do what Washington had failed to do on the Ohio. At the same time the middle and New England colonies were to be harnessed in a double offensive. One by Governor Shirley and the New England troops was to go against Niagara. The other under William Johnson, newly appointed commissioner for Indian affairs in Albany, was to advance north with his Mohawk allies and New York volunteers against Ticonderoga and Crown Point, two French forts on New York's northern border. Finally, a mixed force of regulars and provincials was to attack the French post of Beauséjour. Located at the neck of the peninsula joining Nova Scotia to the mainland, this post was seen as the key to French influence in the area.

Braddock arrived in Virginia in February 1755 and conferred with the neighboring governors, but his appearance elicited few offers of assistance. One problem was that the British plans for four simultaneous military expeditions were too ambitious for the highly independent, locally oriented colonial governments to support. Pennsylvania's assembly was especially slow to appropriate funds; its members included pacifists who opposed war in general and were especially reluctant to contribute to an expedition which was being launched from Virginia and likely to benefit that colony. Eventually it voted £20,000 of paper currency but did not include a suspending clause as required in the proprietary instructions. Maryland had no western territory and therefore no interest in the conflict. The Carolinas claimed that they were too poor and had too many other enemies to worry about the struggle for the Ohio. The net result was that Braddock had difficulty acquiring both supplies and transport and was saved only when Franklin, in his capacity as postmaster general, managed to hire some wagons and horses.

Another problem was British ignorance about the terrain on which they would be fighting, especially in the West. Planners of Braddock's expedition had failed to realize that the route from Virginia to Fort Duquesne was a narrow track through dense forest that could not carry wagons full of supplies and cannons without being widened. Nor did they comprehend that a substantial number of Indian allies would be critical to the success of their plans, both for purposes of scouting the territory and to provide military assistance. Although William Johnson and George Croghan had managed through skillful diplomacy to organize a contingent of Iroquois and Delaware warriors to accompany the British soldiers to their destination, the Indians were so offended by Braddock's haughty manners that most of them went home. In the end only eight warriors from the western Iroquois remained with Braddock's forces.

The expedition was a disaster. After crossing the mountains, Braddock's 2,200-man force proceeded at an agonizingly slow pace westwards through the woods. Indian scouts provided the French at Fort Duquesne with ample warning that the British were coming and thus gave the French time to march out and stop their foes. A few miles from the fort, the British came face to face with a mixed force of French regulars, Canadian militias, and over 600 Kickapoo, Miami, Mascouten, Ottawa, Ojibwa, Potawatomi, and Wyandot warriors who had marched out to find them. The Indians fired at them as they were accustomed to do, from behind trees and any other cover they were able to find. The British troops responded in turn as they had been trained to, bravely forming themselves into companies to fire massed volleys towards their enemies. The problem was they could not see their targets since the Indians and their French allies had taken cover. According to Adam Stephens, one of the attendant Virginians, the "Indians crept up hunting us as they would do a herd of Buffaloes ... The British troops were thunderstruck to feel the effects of a heavy fire and see no enemy." Stephens concluded that "you might as well send a cow in pursuit of a hare as an English soldier loaded in his way." Eventually after three hours of heavy fighting General Braddock was killed and the regulars fled from the field. The British suffered enormous casualties, with two-thirds of their men either killed or wounded, and the incident began a fierce debate over whether British troops should be used in America at all.[2]

Further north the colonial forces under Shirley and Johnson were having even more trouble. Although Shirley managed to raise a substantial force of New Englanders, fierce rivalry existed between him and Johnson, reflecting the conflicting interests of New England and New York. Therefore, although Johnson was supposed to recruit some warriors from the Six Nations for Shirley's attack on Niagara, he made little attempt to do so. Both men experienced difficulty supplying their forces. And in the end their expeditions at Lake George and Oswego failed to advance at all. They found the logistics of moving whole armies through a wilderness beyond their means. Johnson's failure was fortuitously disguised by his repulse of a French force under Baron Dieskau, who ill-advisedly attacked his fortifications on Lake George after a long march and without cannon. For this Johnson received a baronetcy.

The only other success was achieved by Colonel Robert Monckton, who commanded an expedition which captured Fort Beauséjour and thus secured Nova Scotia against further attack by land. The Acadians were then offered one last chance to take the oath of loyalty. When they refused thousands of Acadians were rounded up and deported to the mainland, losing most of their property in the process, for their settlements were destroyed to prevent them being reoccupied. Few arrangements were made for their reception, and many died on the journey. The episode received much publicity in New France, and may well have served to inspire the rest of the French Canadian population to dedicate themselves even more fervently to the war, so as to avoid being conquered and suffering a similar fate.[3]

---

[2] The debate over the suitability of deploying British regulars has generated a substantial literature. Most nineteenth-century writers like Francis Parkman argued that the regulars were unsuitable for warfare in America, unlike the colonists who had been brought up to wilderness fighting from birth; this view was also adopted by many more recent writers, notably Howard H. Peckham, *The Colonial Wars, 1689–1762* (Chicago, 1964; and Douglas Edward Leach, *Arms for Empire: A Military History of the British Colonies in North America, 1607–1763* (New York, 1973). The contrary view is argued by Stanley M. Pargellis, *Lord Loudoun in North America* (New Haven, 1933); Lawrence Henry Gipson, *The British Empire Before the American Revolution*, Vol. 6: *The Years of Defeat, 1754–1757*; Vol. 7: *The Victorious Years, 1758–1760* (New York, 1946, 1949); Peter E. Russell, "Redcoats in the Wilderness: British Officers and Irregular Warfare in Europe and America, 1740–1760," *William and Mary Quarterly*, 35 (1978), 629–52; Harold E. Selesky, *War and Society in Colonial Connecticut* (New Haven, 1989); and most recently by Guy Chet, *Conquering the American Wilderness: The Triumph of European Warfare in the Colonial Northeast* (Amherst, 2003). For sympathetic accounts of Braddock, see Stanley M. Pargellis, "Braddock's Defeat," *American Historical Review*, 41 (1936), 253–69; Lee S. McCardell, *Ill-Starred General: Braddock of the Coldstream Guards* (Pittsburgh, 1986); and Fred Anderson, *Crucible of War: The Seven Years' War and the Fate of Empire in British North America, 1754–1766* (New York, 2000), 105–7, who points out that Washington never criticized Braddock for the disaster.

[3] See for this point W. J. Eccles, *The Canadian Frontier, 1534–1760*, rev. edn (Albuquerque, 1983), 173. Eventually many Acadian refugees resettled in southern Louisiana, where they became known as Cajuns.

One immediate result of Braddock's defeat was to produce a series of French and Indian raids on backcountry communities in Pennsylvania, Virginia, and Maryland. From the point of view of the Shawnees and the Delawares, of course, European settlers in the Pennsylvania backcountry were trespassers and invaders who had stolen their land, violating longstanding promises to protect them and to be their friends. The French victory at Fort Duquesne had finally convinced many of the Shawnees and the Delawares that they had nothing more to fear or to gain from the British. At French urging, they attacked backcountry British settlements at will, killing and capturing some 700 Pennsylvanian settlers and pushing back the line of settlement in some places by 50 miles. Backcountry settlers in Virginia and Maryland, too, fled in the wake of Indian assaults. New York did not escape either, for the Iroquois were not willing to control the area as the British had always assumed they would. Only in the Carolinas, where the Cherokees were still allied with the British, did the backcountry remain quiet.

Indian allies were vital to the French war effort, for although the military of New France was extremely effective, it was also very small. Every male in the settler population was part of a militia company and received military training, and military service was held in high esteem, especially for members of seigneurial families. Nevertheless the French were chronically short of men since the settler population in New France was tiny. Therefore French military campaigns typically employed substantial numbers of Indian braves who fought alongside French troops. In August 1756, Delawares and Shawnees from the Ohio Valley joined other traditional allies of the French to help a force of French regulars and Canadian militiamen to a successful siege against the poorly defended Fort Oswego.

Although the Indians had been vital to French success in the battle, their presence became a source of tension between the Canadians and their French commanding officer, the marquis de Montcalm. After the siege at Oswego, the Indians insisted on their customary right to take captives, scalps, and plunder. General Montcalm, who had no experience with North American warfare, was appalled; he believed that the Indians' behavior showed them to be savage and ungovernable. What Montcalm had failed to understand was that the taking of captives and war trophies were vital to Indian warfare, since they provided the proofs of individual courage for which the warriors fought. The Indians, for their part, were pleased with the outcome of the battle, and their enthusiasm for the French cause grew.

Unlike the French, who had effectively mobilized both the Indians and the settler populations to fight for French interests, British colonial governments struggled to raise men who could fight effectively for their empire. Although many colonies still required men to muster a few times a year for militia training days, these exercises had by the eighteenth century become social gatherings that featured more drinking than military drills. Militias were poorly funded in addition to being badly trained. An observer of the Virginia militia in 1739 had noted the "Diversity of Weapons and Dresses, the Unsizeableness of the Men, and the Want of the least Grain of Discipline in their Officers or them." The situation had not improved in 1755. For its part, Pennsylvania had not had a regular militia at all, due to the pacifist commitments of the Quakers in its colonial government. Now, in the wake of raids in the backcountry, the anti-Quaker proprietary faction mobilized public support for military action against

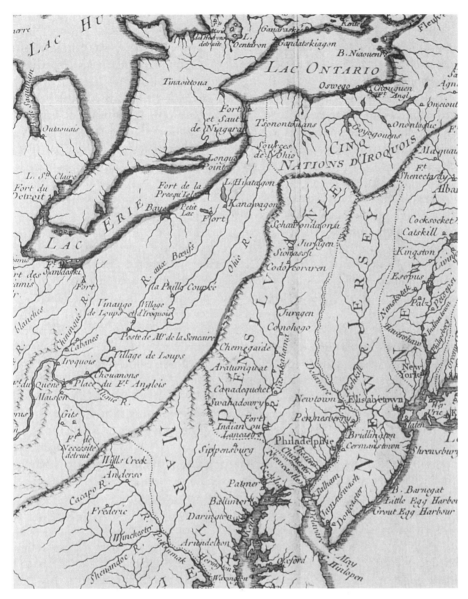

Figure 36 French map of North America, 1756, showing Fort Necessity "détruit" (destroyed), near lower left corner. Photograph by Stephen Davison. Note the detailed information about the locations of Indian as well as European settlements.

the Indians. When beleaguered refugees from the backcountry threatened to take over Philadelphia, the governor declared war in April 1756 and began offering bounties for Indian scalps. The Quakers in the assembly were so horrified by such belligerence that a number of them simply abandoned public service and left the assembly. Yet even under its newly militaristic provincial government the Pennsylvania militia did a poor job defending the backcountry settlements, lacking training, discipline, and equipment. Making things worse, the governor's scalp bounties encouraged vigilante groups to attack neutral Indians instead of hostile ones, creating even greater instability in the backcountry.[4]

The alternative to using the militia was to call for volunteers. However, the system of raising volunteer units in the British colonies had many defects. One problem was young men's reluctance to volunteer. During the early years of colonial settlement, most colonies had imposed an obligation of military service on all free adult white men. However, by the mid eighteenth century military service had ceased to be part of many young men's experience. By now colonial governments had come to rely to a large extent on impressment to fill their limited demands for soldiers rather than calling up all available men. The effect of this policy was generally to limit military service to poor men, since those who could afford it paid for substitutes to serve in their stead. Unlike the young male settler population in New France, young men in most of the British colonies did not think of regular, sustained military service as either a glorious opportunity or a noble duty. Nor was it desirable economically. Military service paid poorly, and most young men from farming families could earn higher wages in civilian occupations, enabling them to save money for the farms they one day hoped to own. For the southern colonies, slave rebellions were an additional concern. Southern governments were reluctant to send too many white men to fight enemies far away, since they needed their white militia members to intimidate the enslaved population at home. A third problem was a lack of military experience, since volunteer units were raised for only one campaign at a time. As the lieutenant governor of New York, Cadwallader Colden, subsequently commented, "Being only levied in the spring and disbanded in the fall they must often disappoint their general's expectations." Poor performance was to be expected "from men educated for the plough or trades in time of peace who never before saw an Enemy."[5]

A century earlier English colonial governments had been able to organize reasonably effective military operations, defending themselves against occasional raids by Spanish or French forces and even prevailing in the end against sizable Indian rebellions such as King Philip's War. Now the British colonies seemed helpless to meet the new military challenge of a full-fledged war with New France. Their populations had ceased to be wary of Indian attacks, since most of the Indians had moved further west. Moreover they were now facing a new kind of threat. Instead of a regional Indian rebellion or localized raids, the British colonies now faced a broad coalition of Indian peoples along with the French who were coordinating their actions. This new foe was better armed, supplied, and organized than past enemies had been. And finally the scale of warfare had changed significantly. Places like Ticonderoga and Niagara were no longer simple

---

[4] Peter Silver, *Our Savage Neighbors: How Indian War Transformed Early America* (New York, 2008), shows that fear created by the Indian attacks in western Pennsylvania not only produced a political crisis in the colonial government but also helped to generate a general hostility towards all Indians along with a new sense of white racial solidarity among the ethnically diverse Pennsylvania settlers.

[5] Cadwallader Colden to Peter Collinson, August 23, 1758, Colden Papers, *New York Historical Society Collections*, Vol. 5 (New York, 1921), 253.

wooden structures; they were built of stone. It required skilled engineers and a siege train to batter them into submission. By early 1756 it was clear to British officials that further British aid would have to be sent to the colonies if the French were to be stopped.[6]

3 THE CONQUEST OF CANADA

The British government resolved to persevere with its objectives in North America, even though France was threatening to invade Britain itself early in 1756. For once it was America which was engulfing Europe in war. First, a new commander, Lord Loudoun, was sent to replace Braddock, who had died in the engagement on the Ohio. Accompanying him were two more regiments of regulars. Plans were also made to raise four battalions from among the German inhabitants of Pennsylvania, to be officered by Swiss and other German-speaking professionals. However, the threat to invade Britain delayed Loudoun's departure, and he arrived too late to prevent the marquis de Montcalm from seizing Oswego in August 1756.

After arriving in North America Loudoun struggled to organize the colonial volunteers who had agreed to join the British war effort. A New England force had been gathered at Lake George under the command of John Winslow, who experienced all the supply difficulties that had dogged Shirley and Johnson the previous year. When Loudoun tried to amalgamate the New England force with his own, he met resistance. Previously the duke of Cumberland, the captain general of the British army, had decreed that no colonial should rank ahead of any regular officer. A British lieutenant could thus give orders to a provincial colonel, creating much resentment in the process, although the colonial lack of military experience partly justified this rule.

The colonial rank and file were equally disenchanted with Loudoun's plans to create a joint force. They had witnessed the severity of regular discipline and had no wish to experience it themselves. For most of them, soldiering was merely an interlude to earn some money and experience a bit of adventure. They were determined not to have their service prolonged past a single campaign, which they feared would be the result if they served alongside the regulars. To New Englanders especially, military service was a contract which both parties must observe. If the government broke its part of the bargain, then desertion was no crime. Their officers recognized this, realizing that they must appeal to their men's better nature rather than command through brute discipline. Such views were quite alien to the British officer corps; they were used to commanding a force made up of poor and working-class British men who became

---

[6] American popular culture has purveyed a myth that the North American settlers excelled in warfare because they had abandoned conventional European tactics and adopted Indian fighting methods. Guy Chet, *Conquering the American Wilderness*, finds that in fact settlers performed poorly in warfare because of their lack of experience and organization. Colonial military efforts (and later the British government) succeeded only when they managed to organize logistical support for large-scale, long-lasting conventional warfare.

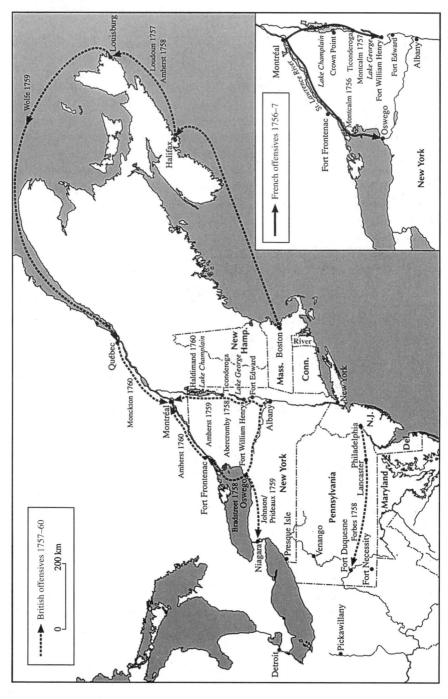

Map 26 The struggle for Canada, 1756–1760.

professional soldiers because they lacked other economic options. British soldiers learned to obey orders without question.[7]

Loudoun also struggled to get the supplies he needed from the provincial assemblies, whose members seemed to him to worry more about preserving their political prerogatives than about defeating the French. In Pennsylvania, even with the Quakers gone, the new assembly remained just as mired in conflict with the proprietors as the previous one. Unwilling to tax the population unless the proprietors paid their fair share, the assembly inserted a clause taxing the proprietary estates into the bill appropriating money for the war, which the Penn family vetoed as a result. In Maryland the lower house remained at loggerheads with the proprietary government, so that even when the house granted supplies, it did so in a manner which the proprietors felt bound to reject. In Virginia, Washington complained bitterly about the attitudes of representatives in the House, whom he called men "tenacious of liberty," who "condemn all proceedings technically illegal, without considering their necessity." The result was that Loudoun was chronically short of funds.

Although Loudoun complained bitterly that the colonial assemblies were lacking in patriotism, members of the assemblies in fact represented constituents who were lacking in cash. Even though settlers in the rural areas of the colonies were relatively prosperous in the sense that they had better food and shelter than their contemporaries in rural England or Scotland, colonial economies also suffered from chronic shortages of currency. Farmers had adapted to the scarcity of specie by going heavily into debt, meaning that the impoundment of livestock or of a crop of corn or wheat would seriously threaten their financial solvency. Under these circumstances, colonial assemblymen were understandably reluctant to burden their rural constituents with additional taxes. Loudoun, however, failed to comprehend why the colonials were unwilling to defer to his commands.

Despite his frustration, Loudoun was determined to adopt a more radical approach to defeating the French, namely an assault on the center of French power in the St. Lawrence. To this end he requested an army of 10,000 regulars and a sizable fleet. His plans coincided with the creation of a new ministry in London headed by William Pitt and the duke of Devonshire. They had come into office on a wave of public anger following the loss of the island of Minorca, which was imputed to the incompetence of the Newcastle ministry. The new government promised a more vigorous conduct of the war, authorizing eight additional regiments, or 8,000 men, plus a fleet of 12 ships of the line with orders to attack Louisburg and Québec.[8]

---

[7]   For an analysis of the colonial soldier, see Fred W. Anderson, *A People's Army: Massachusetts Soldiers and Society in the Seven Years' War* (Chapel Hill, 1984). See also Fred W. Anderson, "Why Did Colonial New Englanders Make Bad Soldiers? Contractual Principles and Military Conduct during the Seven Years' War," *William and Mary Quarterly*, 38 (1981), 395–417. In *War and Society*, Selesky challenges the view that colonial soldiers came from middle-ranking colonial families, arguing that most of the volunteers were from the lowest stratum of society.

[8]   The admission of Pitt to the ministry has traditionally been seen as the beginning of a more dynamic conduct of the war. See Peckham, *The Colonial Wars*, and Leach, *Arms for Empire*. In a more critical analysis, Pargellis, *Lord Loudoun in North America*, suggests that Pitt interfered unnecessarily. For a contrary evaluation of Pitt's war leadership, see Richard Middleton, *The Bells of Victory: The Pitt–Newcastle Ministry and the Conduct of the Seven Years' War, 1757–1762* (Cambridge, 1985). He argues that many of the policies ascribed to Pitt were already in operation before his admission to office and that his powers as a war minister were circumscribed by constitutional constraints.

Loudoun's plan was to transport most of the regulars by sea, leaving a holding force to prevent another incursion such as had happened at Oswego the previous year. Loudoun by now thoroughly distrusted the military capabilities of the provincials but, realizing that he could not do without them, he visited the several provincial capitals between Boston and Philadelphia during the spring of 1757. Yet his brusque manner merely exacerbated the existing conflicts between the civilian and military authorities.

A major point of tension concerned quartering. In Britain, the Mutiny Act allowed the army to quarter its men on local inns and taverns. The colonists argued that this legislation did not apply in North America. Most American taverns in any case were gin shops, with no stables for horses or accommodation for guests. Loudoun accordingly began billeting his men in private houses. The colonists quickly protested, appealing to the English Bill of Rights, which forbade this practice. Loudoun then pointed out that it was inconsistent to accept one act of Parliament but not another. He believed that the colonies were in the same constitutional position as Scotland, where quartering on the local population was allowed. When the magistrates refused to act, Loudoun ordered his officers to take the matter into their own hands, lodging the largest number of men on the offending magistrates themselves. Similar difficulties occurred over the army's demand for wagons and horses, which Loudoun also believed he could demand as of right.

Though tensions undoubtedly plagued Loudoun's relationship with the colonial population, the degree of hostility should not be exaggerated. Most colonials recognized that the army needed quarters, transport, and supplies. In 1755 New York passed an act allowing the impressment of ship's carpenters and boatmen for the Niagara and Lake George campaigns; and in 1756 it provided for the billeting of troops and passed another measure allowing the impressment of carriages. Even Pennsylvania passed an act in March 1756 approving the military use of farmers' wagons. Substantial contributions from New England and the middle colonies enabled Loudoun to sail for Halifax in June 1757 with a considerable armada to await the forces from Britain.

Unfortunately for Loudoun, events in Halifax did not work out as planned. Although he arrived in good time, the forces from Britain did not appear before July, by which time the French had gathered a powerful fleet at Louisburg. Without command of the sea, Loudoun dared not proceed in case his army became trapped on the barren wastes of Cape Breton Island. Even if the French fleet remained in port, Louisburg was almost impossible to attack, since French naval guns could bombard the besieging force.

While the British tried to get organized, the French under General Montcalm were preparing for an assault on Britain's Fort William Henry at the foot of Lake George. Ever since the French success at Oswego, Indians from the Catholic mission settlements (*reserves*) in New France and the *pays d'en haut* had been flocking to Montréal and the forts at Lake Champlain to volunteer for service with the French. By late July of 1757, approximately 2,000 Indian warriors had assembled at Fort Carillon where Montcalm was readying some 6,000 French and Canadian forces for a planned assault on the fort. The garrison there had fewer than 1,500 British and North American soldiers by this time, having recently suffered a number of losses from Indian and Canadian attacks. Additional British regular and colonial forces were available at Fort Edward on the Hudson. Nevertheless, General Webb at Fort Edward decided he was not strong enough to send significant numbers of reinforcements until his own fort had been reinforced by the provincial militias of New England.

Montcalm arrived in early August, laid siege to Fort William Henry, and within a week convinced the British commander to surrender. Montcalm assured him that the British and provincial forces inside the fort would be granted the honors of war, meaning the French would allow them to keep their arms (though not ammunition) and guarantee them the right to travel safely to Fort Edward. What Montcalm had not anticipated was the reaction of his Native American allies. The Indians had expected to be allowed as was customary to take captives and trophies as proof of their bravery in battle, but Montcalm's agreement with the British had deprived them of what they believed was their due. Angry, many of the warriors decided they would take captives and scalps anyway. The night after the surrender, the Indians killed most of the British sick and wounded and took their scalps. The following morning they surrounded the retreating British soldiers and their civilian camp followers, taking prisoners. When Montcalm tried to stop them, the Indians killed a number of the prisoners rather than allow their captives to go free. In all, between 100 and 200 Britons were killed and more than 300 carried off captive.[9]

This defeat concluded what had been a most unhappy year for the British. From April to July the country had no ministry because Pitt and Newcastle were unable to work together. In New England there was even talk of reviving the seventeenth-century Confederation of the United Colonies so that the war could be prosecuted independently of the British. The scheme came to nothing because early in 1758 news arrived that the government, with Pitt firmly back in power, had made important concessions. First, the issue of rank was settled. In the future colonial officers would rank with the regulars, albeit as the most junior in each category. Next, the abrasive Loudoun was to be replaced by a new commander-in-chief, General Abercromby. Third, the British treasury would feed and arm the colonial troops; the provincials would merely have to provide their pay, and even this expense would be reimbursed.

In the colonies, outrage at the news of the defeat at Fort William Henry rapidly solved the problem of recruitment. Especially in New England, anger over "the massacre" at the fort fused with longstanding anti-Catholic resentment towards the French and their alliances with Indians. Male inhabitants of the New England colonies became convinced that this was a war with providential significance and enthusiastically joined the fight. Their newfound enthusiasm was no doubt strengthened by Pitt's new promises of financial support. In Boston, where Loudoun had been seeking 2,000 men, the news of Pitt's letter induced the assembly immediately to vote 7,000 men. A similar response came from Connecticut, while New York also agreed to meet its quota of 2,400. Of the northern colonies, only Pennsylvania proved difficult, though supplies

---

[9] The incident was traditionally used to portray French and native savagery, the implication being that Anglo-Saxon methods were more civilized. This attitude long typified British and American accounts of their various wars. See especially Francis Parkman, *Montcalm and Wolfe* (Boston, 1884), comparing his account of the massacre at Fort William Henry with the attack by Rogers's rangers on the St. Francis Indians in 1759. For a critical analysis of Parkman, see Francis Jennings, "Francis Parkman: A Brahmin among Untouchables," *William and Mary Quarterly*, 42 (1985), 305–28. Recent accounts of the episode are more sympathetic to the Indians, explaining their point of view and motivations for the attack. See Ian K. Steele, *Betrayals: Fort William Henry and the "Massacre"* (New York, 1990), as well as Anderson, *Crucible of War*, ch. 19.

and men were finally secured after the proprietary government had agreed to be more flexible. Even the Virginia House of Burgesses voted to raise two regiments of 1,000 men, now that the major expense would be borne by the British, since this allowed the payment of a large bounty and eliminated the need for a compulsory draft from the militia.

While Pitt's determination to raise thousands of new men boded well for the British, other developments taking place by 1758 were weakening the ability of New France to resist. The western Indians who had participated in the Battle of Fort William Henry had been deeply offended by Montcalm's attempts to stop them from taking captives after the battle. Moreover their people were becoming exhausted by the continuous demands of war. New France had experienced two failed harvests in the previous two years, which meant that both the Indians and the settlers were suffering from food shortages. To make matters worse, the British navy during the previous fall had established blockades that prevented supplies from reaching New France. Not only was it impossible to import food to relieve the starving population, but it was also becoming difficult for traders to supply the guns and gunpowder upon which their Indian allies depended to hunt. Morale and military readiness – as well as the enthusiasm of the Indians for the French cause – were beginning to wane.

For 1758 the British ministry decided upon a three-pronged offensive. General Amherst, supported by the fleet, was to command an army of 14,000 regulars in another attempt against Louisburg and Québec. Abercromby was to advance north from New York towards Montréal with 8,000 British and 20,000 provincial troops. Finally, Brigadier John Forbes, commanding a mixed force of 2,000 regulars and 5,000 provincials, would advance westwards in a new effort to capture Fort Duquesne at the forks of the Ohio.

The British attack on Louisburg was successful, since the French fleet that was intended for its relief was prevented from sailing. The fortress finally capitulated early in July 1758. After Amherst had secured it, however, it was too late to move on to Québec.

Meanwhile, Abercromby had suffered a setback on the northern front, where the largest number of men were deployed. He reached his first objective, the fortress of Ticonderoga, early in July, and then heard that Montcalm was expecting reinforcements of 3,000 Canadians and Indian warriors. Although Ticonderoga was a stone fortification, Abercromby reasoned that if he stormed the outer entrenchments which held most of Montcalm's 6,000 men, he would be able to take the fort at his leisure. It proved a fatal miscalculation. Montcalm had protected his army with a breastwork of trees lined with sharpened stakes. When the assault began, the British were unable to break through the enemy's lines, and over 1,500 regulars and 300 colonials were killed or wounded as a result. The carnage was so severe that Abercromby decided to retreat back down Lake George to reorganize his shattered command.

In August, Abercromby's ambitious quartermaster, Colonel John Bradstreet, achieved an unexpected victory further to the west. Bradstreet had long advocated an attack on the French post of Frontenac on Lake Ontario. He argued that this post must now be denuded of troops, given the operations elsewhere, and that its destruction would strike a blow against the French chain linking Canada with Louisiana and help Forbes in his attempt on Fort Duquesne. Abercromby sensibly agreed, giving

Bradstreet a force of 2,500 men mainly from New York. Bradstreet began his advance in August and found the French defenses negligible. Frontenac was burned, along with several boats and numerous stores. Bradstreet made no attempt to hold the post or to reoccupy Oswego, judging the French ability to retaliate too formidable. Nevertheless, a major blow to French power had been delivered. The destruction of the supplies at Fort Frontenac and the boats that were used to transport them deprived the French of their ability to provision the western forts and deliver trade goods to their Indian allies in the West.

Forbes, too, was successful at Fort Duquesne, though as a result of numerous troubles he reached his objective only in November. The Maryland assembly refused aid even for the 300 troops it had previously supplied at Fort Frederick. Next, Forbes found his Native American allies difficult to control. The Cherokees alone observed Pitt's timetable for an offensive starting in May. When it seemed that the British would never advance, the Indians began to drift away, carrying their supplies with them.

Before the attack, Forbes received assistance from an unexpected quarter. The eastern Delawares, supported by the antiproprietary faction in Pennsylvania, convinced the western Delawares to attend a peace conference with representatives of Pennsylvania, New Jersey, and the Iroquois nations. The eastern Delawares hoped that in exchange for an agreement by their western kin to withdraw from the war, Pennsylvania would repudiate the Walking Purchase and compensate them for the land they had lost. The western Delawares had become exhausted by the war and were interested in finding a way to get out of it if they could do so without sacrificing their independence. Pennsylvania officials promised a better-regulated trade and assured the Delawares that land west of the Alleghenies would be returned to them. In exchange, the western Delawares agreed in October 1758 to stop fighting, under the Treaty of Easton. By this time representatives of other western nations were indicating a similar desire for peace. As a result the French were abandoned at a critical time and there was no repetition of Braddock's defeat. The French commander eventually burned Fort Duquesne rather than surrender it.[10]

Despite the overall success of the 1758 campaign, the British ministry felt that there could be no relaxation of military activity until the whole of Canada had been conquered. Thus for 1759 a similar three-pronged campaign was devised. This time the amphibious forces under General Wolfe were to sail directly for Québec. Amherst himself would succeed Abercromby in an operation to take Ticonderoga and Crown Point before proceeding to Montréal. Finally, General Prideaux and Sir William Johnson would advance on Niagara (Forbes having died at the end of the last campaign). As in 1758, the colonists would be mainly involved in the overland operations.

Wolfe sailed from Halifax on June 4, 1759, arriving off Québec at the beginning of July. For the next 10 weeks he searched in vain for a way through the French defenses until he was able to scale the cliffs, known as the Heights of Abraham, above the city. In the ensuing battle he was killed, as was Montcalm, but he left Québec in British hands.

---

[10]   The central importance of the Treaty of Easton is discussed in Eric Hinderaker, *Elusive Empires: Constructing Colonialism in the Ohio Valley, 1673–1800* (Cambridge, 1997), ch. 4; and Anderson, *Crucible of War*, 267–85.

Figure 37   A view of Québec. From *Popple's American Atlas.* Art Archive.

Amherst's campaign was, by comparison, a pedestrian affair. Once more the provincials found it difficult to keep to Pitt's timetable. With Montcalm at Québec, however, the British capture of Ticonderoga and Crown Point was assured. Amherst then found it necessary to gain naval command of Lake Champlain, by which time it was

Figure 38   *The Death of General Wolfe*, by Benjamin West. Engraving by Wm. Woollett, 1776. Library of Congress, Washington, DC.

too late to advance on Montréal. Nevertheless, his advance meant that the backcountry of New York and western Massachusetts was now secure.

In the West, Prideaux and Johnson were also victorious at Niagara. Again the Indians played a key role in the battle's outcome. Many of the Iroquois were concerned about their waning influence with the Delawares and had decided by late 1758 that a renewed alliance with the British would enable them to regain their prestige among the various Indian nations. Therefore the Iroquois abandoned their policy of neutrality and joined the British war effort. A large number of Iroquois warriors joined Prideaux and Johnson's men as they surrounded Fort Niagara in 1759. However when 30 French-allied Senecas decided to stay inside the fort with the French, the British-allied Iroquois changed their minds and decided not to participate in the battle. When a French relief party arrived, including both Canadian militiamen and warriors from the Great Lakes tribes, the Iroquois changed their minds a second time and decided to fight. The British and their Iroquois allies quickly overwhelmed the French and their allies. Although Prideaux was killed, Johnson carried the operation to a successful conclusion on July 25, 1759.[11]

Although the British had now achieved their original war aims, they would not relax their campaign until the whole of Canada had been conquered. Hence orders were again issued by Pitt for a final campaign in 1760 to win Montréal. The removal of an immediate threat of attack as well as the haughty treatment of provincial forces by British officers made many colonial men reluctant to volunteer for this campaign, even though the same generous financial terms were offered. Governor Thomas Pownall secured only 4,000 men from Massachusetts. Yet with Iroquois support the British had gained the advantage, especially since western and southern Indians were now abandoning the French and making new treaties with the British, desperate for a supply of the arms upon which they had come to depend.

The campaign plan for 1760 was similar to that of the previous year. Three armies were to converge on Montréal. General Murray was to advance from Québec, General Haldimand was to resume the northward movement by way of Lake Champlain, while Amherst himself would advance with the main force via the River Mohawk and Lake Ontario to approach from the west. Significantly, this time the army was accompanied by a large body of Iroquois, though a contemptuous Amherst determined that such fickle allies should not benefit from the plunder they clearly anticipated. The campaign itself was nearly ruined when Murray was defeated by the French under the Chevalier Levis early in the spring before the ice in the river had melted. For a few weeks it was not certain whether Québec itself might fall to the French again. Fortunately for the British, reinforcements arrived by river and the French were forced to retire. Thereafter, all three British armies advanced steadily, finally linking up near Montréal at the beginning of September. The position of the French was now hopeless, and they surrendered on September 7, 1760.

Though the surrender of Montréal effectively ended hostilities between the European powers on mainland America, fighting continued between Britain and

---

[11]   For the importance of the Iroquois decision to fight with the British at Niagara, see Anderson, *Crucible of War*, 330–9. For the sequence of events in this battle, see Richard Middleton, *Pontiac's War: Its Causes, Course, and Consequences* (New York, 2007), 10.

France in both Europe and the Caribbean and had the effect of drawing Spain into the conflict. Spain had remained on the sidelines throughout the war, fearing that a French victory in North America might give France too much power. Then early in 1761 the British navy seized the French island of Martinique. This was a major prize, especially since the British had also conquered another enormously productive French sugar island, Guadeloupe, almost two years earlier. At this point Spain became concerned that the French, growing desperate in the face of its mounting losses, would agree to a territorial settlement that threatened Spanish strategic interests. Therefore Spain formed an alliance with France in August 1761 and entered the war the following May. This gave the British navy a justification for seizing the long-sought prize of Havana, Cuba, from the Spanish in August 1762. Having entered the war too late to make a difference to the outcome in North America, Spain had now lost one of its most important bases in the West Indies. This loss was compounded in October when a British fleet captured Manila in the Philippines.[12]

As a result of these conquests, Britain was able to negotiate a handsome peace by the end of 1762. France would give up its least profitable North American colonies in Canada and the Illinois Country so as to regain possession of its sugar islands of Guadeloupe and Martinique and end the war. Spain would give up Florida in exchange for the return of Cuba. Finally France would give Louisiana, in which its own strategic interest was now vastly diminished, to Spain, who wanted the colony as a strategic buffer to prevent western expansion by the British. Britain would now possess the whole of eastern North America from Hudson Bay to the Mississippi, and Spain would possess Louisiana as well as everything west of the Mississippi. The only link France retained with the continent was two small islands near the Newfoundland fishery.

The question of why the British won the war in North America has provoked considerable thinking among historians recently. The traditional argument was that the British won because they brought more regulars to North America to fight the war, possessed a more effective navy, and had the superior ability to mobilize credit to pay for the cost of war. Certainly these factors were crucial. British naval blockades prevented French ships from supplying New France and its forts, which led to food shortages and starvation for the French and Indian populations. The British government's ability and willingness to borrow and spend vast sums of money to wage war, thanks to the development by the mid eighteenth century of some of the most modern financial institutions in the world, enabled it to pay for the cost of transporting and maintaining a large and well-trained army in North America. Local militias simply lacked the training and the experience to be able to fight effectively in most settings, and Britain's ability to bring in more regular troops gave it a decisive advantage in key battles after 1757.[13]

Yet the traditional emphasis on British military superiority ignored another set of factors which has more recently been given its due by historians: the influence of decisions made by Native Americans as well as the French on the war's outcome. France

---

[12] For the importance of the West in Spanish calculations, see Mapp, *The Elusive West and the Contest for Empire*.

[13] The traditional view was laid out in Lawrence Henry Gipson, *The British Empire Before the American Revolution*, Vol. 6: *The Years of Defeat, 1755–1757*; Vol. 7: *The Victorious Years, 1758–1760* (New York, 1946, 1949). The same argument is implicit in Leach, *Arms for Empire*.

had been able to build and hold an empire in North America despite the fact that its colonial population was smaller than that of the British. It did so because of the trading relationships and alliances it had built with Native Americans from the *pays d'en haut* to the Canadian Catholic mission settlements. It was Native Americans who provided the French with better intelligence and a stronger fighting capacity than the British during the first two years of the war and stymied the British in their original objective of securing the Ohio Valley. Native American raids on backcountry settler communities were highly effective in creating panic among the British settler population and made it difficult for the colonies to organize an effective defense. Indeed, in the end it was Native American decisions to abandon the French that weakened French ability to hold out against British assaults. By 1758 many French-allied Indians were exhausted by the stresses of the war and offended by General Montcalm's diplomatic bungling. The French had become unable to supply them with sufficient trade goods, threatening the Indians' economic well-being as well as their ability to continue fighting.

Believing it was in their people's interest to stop fighting, most of the Indians in the Ohio Valley agreed to peace with the British in 1758. Unfortunately, their decision to make peace with the British contributed to their own destruction. For as long as they could remember, they had done best by playing off Britain, France, and Spain against one another when they could, avoiding conflict with Europeans when they could not. They did not foresee that the French government might lose the war and be driven out of North America entirely, making it impossible for the Indians to pursue their time-honored survival strategies in the future.[14]

4 THE WAR'S CONSEQUENCES

The British victory over the French transformed the balance of power in North America and thereby changed the fates of all the peoples and nations who had fought to control the continent for the century and a half leading up to 1763. Some became more powerful, others less. Just as the story of the colonization of North America had different beginnings for each of its diverse groups of participants, it would have different outcomes as well.[15]

---

[14]   This newer historiography considers not only the Anglo-American but also the French experience in the war. Important contributions include Eccles, *The Canadian Frontier*; Ian K. Steele, *Warpaths: Invasions of North America* (New York, 1994); and Anderson, *Crucible of War*. Recent work typically treats the Indians as central players in the war. See, for example, Matthew Ward, *Breaking the Backcountry: The Seven Years' War in Virginia and Pennsylvania, 1754–1765* (Pittsburgh, 2003). The traditional view was based on an assumption that because the Indians were clan-based rather than state-based societies, they were unable to wage war effectively. Recent experiences around the world with highly destructive wars waged by nonstate actors (such as al-Qaeda) have provoked a rethinking about this assumption. See, for example, Emerson W. Baker and John G. Reid, "Amerindian Power in the Early Modern Northeast: A Reappraisal," *William and Mary Quarterly*, 61 (2004), 77–106, which argues that the Abenaki Indians effectively waged war against New England for nearly 50 years after the end of King Philip's War.
[15]   An indispensable overview of the ways in which the Peace of Paris changed the prospects of each of various groups is provided by Colin G. Calloway, *The Scratch of a Pen: 1763 and the Transformation of North America* (Oxford, 2006).

For the British people in general, the signing of the Peace of Paris in 1763 seemed to herald a glittering era for Britain as a world power with possessions in every corner of the globe. A new king, George III, had recently ascended the throne to begin what promised to be an Augustan age. The British people felt a surge of pride in having defeated France and Spain, a victory that represented not only a great military feat but also the triumph of Protestant liberty in the contest against the absolutist regimes and the hated Roman Catholic Church.

Equally promising were the prospects of most British North American colonists, particularly those of white men. They could anticipate that the removal of the French would open vast new quantities of land for settlement, enabling the sons of family farmers to obtain farms of their own for generations to come. The doubling of the population every 25 years opened up the possibility that within a century North America might become the center of the British empire. And with their long tradition of local political autonomy, these colonists expected that they would continue to be governed by local leaders sympathetic to their interests.

For many new and prospective immigrant men from Europe, the future looked just as bright. New economic opportunities beckoned, especially for those with skills and education. In the future they would also be more likely to become assimilated with the Anglo-American population. Whereas before the war recent immigrants had thought of themselves as members of distinct ethnic and religious groups, their shared wartime experience enduring Indian assaults on their frontier communities had bound many of them together and changed their collective identities. They had begun for the first time to define themselves in terms of race and to refer to themselves as the "white people."[16]

Of course for most white women, children, and servants in the British North American colonies, the opening of territory would be less momentous. While their labor would be just as vital to building self-sustaining farms and households in a frontier economy, they would still be legally dependent on adult male household heads or masters. For enslaved African Americans, too, the future probably looked about the same as before the war. In fact, though they could not have known it, the opening of land would in the long run require the labor of even more slaves and enable the system of slavery to expand and become more entrenched in North American society. As for poor people in colonial cities, opportunities would actually erode once the British army withdrew and stopped contracting with local businesses to outfit its troops and build its ships.

The future seemed gloomier to most French settlers in Canada and the West. French Canadians, numbering about 79,000 in 1762, were shocked that their government had abandoned them and ceded their territory to Britain. Yet despite their disappointment, most would stay in North America. The British government was eager to prevent them from rebelling and therefore guaranteed their religion, property, and legal customs. To a large degree the French Canadians would retain their land, their culture, and their distinctive relations with the Indians. The French in Illinois, on the other hand, had little stomach for the prospect of living under British government. Most of them crossed the Mississippi to found St. Louis, in territory that France had ceded to Spain.

---

[16] Silver, *Our Savage Neighbors.*

They continued to make their living as fur traders, an occupation in which their understanding of Native American cultures gave them continuing advantages over their British competitors.

The French inhabitants of Louisiana, including 4,000 whites and 5,000 enslaved blacks, found themselves now under the government of Spain. They faced an increase in economic regulation, leading to a rebellion by Louisiana merchants and planters against Spanish rule in 1768. Yet despite their fears, their economic prospects would actually improve, thanks to the growth of their economy. Spanish officials encouraged immigration, first by Acadians who began to resettle in the colony from around 1765, and then by Spanish citizens from the Canary Islands. With additional imports of enslaved Africans from the West Indies, the combined settler–slave population in the region would triple by 1783. Meanwhile exports of tobacco, indigo, deerskins and lumber grew at a steady pace.

Spanish people in Florida faced a future as exiles. Although the Peace of Paris guaranteed them the right to continue practicing their religion if they stayed, Catholics in Florida understandably feared a purge by the vastly more numerous British colonists and their governments. When Spain encouraged them to leave by offering them property in Cuba, all 3,000 of the Spanish citizens in the region chose to evacuate. Members of the free black community at Mose and a few Christian Indians left too, along with the Spanish. In Havana refugees faced initial hardships but eventually most survived and became assimilated into Cuban society.

For the European governments who had just engaged in their vast land swap at the Peace of Paris, the future held different challenges – and opportunities. For the French government, the aftermath of the war offered the chance to rebuild its navy and revive its trade. It could also plan for the next war against Great Britain. That war, it turned out, was not so far in the future, and would be one in which a revitalized navy would give France a decisive advantage.

The Spanish government had acquired Louisiana, which threatened to make the costs of administering their northern frontier even heavier than before the war. Spain now faced the additional problem of governing the Indians west of the Mississippi, now that the French were gone. The Spanish would increasingly follow the French example by building alliances through trade. Although such a strategy had proven more effective in retaining the loyalty of the Indians than reliance on missions, it was nonetheless an expensive strategy. Spanish officials still had difficulty supplying trade goods, thanks to trade restrictions imposed by the empire. Moreover Spanish colonizers faced incessant hostility from the Comanche and Apache peoples, who now had horses and guns and were determined to expand their own sphere of influence. The question would be how long Spain could maintain its control.

British government officials were of course enthusiastic about Britain's new acquisitions. Yet the king's ministers understood far better than most British citizens that managing this vast new empire would be difficult. One major problem would be the expense. The British national debt had nearly doubled over the course of the war. By 1763 annual government expenses including interest payments on the debt amounted to about £14 million per year, well in excess of its annual revenues of less than £10 million. Added to its revenue problem was a dramatically new set of challenges in governing North America.

For the past century, since the earliest development of its navigation laws, the British empire had been most successful when it acted as a regulator of trading relationships between the colonies and the mother country. Attempts to exercise simultaneous jurisdiction over English settlers and Native American peoples during the seventeenth century had all failed. The attempt to centralize control over the colonies during the era of James II had resulted in full-scale rebellions in three separate colonies. The British empire would now have to govern a vast new area of territory acquired by conquest, in effect confronting challenges it had failed to meet in the past, only on a larger scale. It would be responsible for maintaining order among the thousands of French Canadians who had suddenly, and unwillingly, been placed under its control, and would need to consolidate its authority over recently evacuated territory in Nova Scotia and Florida. Now that the French government was gone there would be border disputes between different colonies that claimed land to the west and north of the settled areas. The British government would have to mediate these. And it would face an even more difficult challenge in managing its transformed relationship with all of the North American Indians living west of the Allegheny Mountains,[17] especially given the expectations of the settlers in the British colonies that land in the Ohio Valley was about to be opened up to settlement.

The Indians west of the British colonies faced the most difficult dilemma. With the French government gone, they had lost the ability to play the French off against the British so as to maintain their autonomy. Spain would be too preoccupied with defending its possessions in New Mexico, Louisiana, and Texas to pay much attention if British American settlers moved onto Native American land. In any case the Spanish were notoriously poor suppliers of the trade goods on which the Indians' way of life had come to depend. The Indians would have to rely almost entirely on the British for guns and ammunition. And yet, as officials who were charged with maintaining order in Indian country would soon discover, they were far from ready to submit to British domination.

The first sign of problems in the relationship between the Indians and the soon-to-be ascendant British imperial government came in Cherokee country, well before the signing of the Peace of Paris. The Cherokees by 1758 had a population of 10,000 to 12,000 living west of South Carolina. Their alliance with the British had been strong ever since the Yamasee War and they had provided significant assistance in Forbes's campaign against Fort Duquesne during the summer of that year. On their way home from that operation the Cherokees were savagely attacked by some of the backcountry settlers, who had begun to encroach on Cherokee lands. Some of the Cherokees retaliated, and a series of frontier skirmishes followed. South Carolina's government responded by seizing and executing a group of moderate chiefs who were trying to negotiate a truce. By January of 1760 the Cherokees were in a full-scale rebellion. A Scottish Highland regiment, first under Colonel Montgomery in 1760 and then under Colonel Grant in 1761, marched into the Cherokee heartland together with some provincial forces and suppressed the rebellion. In the brutal fashion of eighteenth-century Anglo-Saxon warfare, they destroyed first the lower and then the middle

---

[17]   The Alleghenies are part of the Appalachian Mountains and run for about 400 miles from central Pennsylvania to southwestern Virginia.

Cherokee towns. In the absence of a rival power able to supply them with arms and ammunition, the Cherokees had little leverage. They agreed to peace in 1761.

By 1762 new problems were emerging in the North and West. Having reached new agreements with the British in the waning years of the war, many of the Great Lakes and Ohio peoples expected the British to recognize their land claims and to trade with them on the terms they had once enjoyed in trading with the French. However, the victorious British government soon began to make it clear that it felt no need to stay on good terms with the Indians. The British insisted on keeping soldiers garrisoned at the French forts and trading posts they had taken over during the war, which convinced the Indians that the British were about to repudiate the Easton Treaty and take their land. To make matters worse, General Jeffrey Amherst, the British commander in charge of the western forts, had decided that trading relationships with the Indians were too expensive for the British government to maintain. He issued a new set of regulations that limited the amount of trade goods, particularly ammunition, which the Indians could receive from British traders. This limit was deeply galling, not only violating established trading norms but also starving the Indians of the ammunition they needed in order to hunt.[18]

Other major issues emerged as well. British commanders had promised during the war that the land claims of British-allied Indians would be respected. However, speculators quickly began to move surveyors and settlers into Indian land in northern New York, central Pennsylvania, and the Ohio Valley as soon as the fighting ceased. The British were also demanding that the Ohio and Great Lakes tribes return captives taken during the war. However, the Indians had adopted these captives and regarded them as family members.

Unhappy about the terms being imposed on them by the British, the Indians now faced the question of how best to resist. One strategy that seemed to hold some promise was a pan-Indian alliance. The Iroquois had long understood the value of intertribal coalitions, and thus it is not surprising that the first to propose a pan-Indian alliance against the British were two Seneca chiefs, Tahaiadoris and Kiashuta. They met with tribal leaders in the Ohio Valley in June 1761 to propose an ambitious plan that would unite the Ohio and Great Lakes peoples with the Cherokees and the Iroquois to attack British forts west of the Alleghenies. Although British officials discovered the plan before it could be carried out, other tribal leaders were also beginning to think along the same lines.

In the West, many Native American peoples had started to think of themselves as Indians who shared common interests with other Indians, rather than as members of discrete tribes with separate interests. This new identity, which had been developing for many years, coalesced during the war as peoples from different tribes fought side by side to defeat the British. During the 1750s and 1760s the idea that Native Americans shared a pan-Indian identity came to be expressed by religious leaders, particularly by a

---

[18] Historians have sometimes assumed that the British government adopted more humane policies towards the Indians than those of succeeding American governments, but this view is challenged in Gregory Evans Dowd, *War under Heaven: Pontiac, the Indian Nations, and the British Empire* (Baltimore, 2002). The diplomatic prelude to the war between the British, Western, and Ohioan nations can be found in Middleton, *Pontiac's War*, chs 1–3.

series of Native American prophets who had emerged in the Ohio Valley calling for a nativist revival. A young Delaware named Neolin explained that the "Master of Life" had made the land for the Indians, who had sinned by allowing white people to come into their land and corrupt them with their guns, iron trade goods, and alcohol. Now the Indians had two choices. Either they could continue down the path of alliances with the whites, a path which would lead to suffering and starvation, or they could cleanse themselves of white men's ways and drive the British out of their country. Among those listening to Neolin's message was an Ottawa chief named Pontiac. Soon Pontiac and other leaders were exchanging warbelts throughout the Great Lakes and Ohio region, each agreeing to take action against British forts provided the others would do so too as news of the hostilities arrived. Through a series of surprise attacks beginning in May 1763 the Indians captured all the smaller posts at Michilimackinac, St. Joseph, Miami, Ouiatenon, LeBoeuf, Sandusky, Presque Isle, and Venango, putting many of the garrisons' troops to death. At the same time they laid siege to the main forts at Pittsburgh and Detroit while threatening the communications with Niagara. The only northern Indians who did not join Pontiac's coalition were the Catholic mission Indians from Canada, who remained on the sidelines.[19]

By the end of 1763 the rebellion had succeeded in utterly destabilizing the West. The western Indians took numerous forts, and cut off communications and supply lines to those they could not conquer. They raided British settlements along the western roads, terrifying settlers who fled back east of the Alleghenies. In Pennsylvania the Indians attacked the farms of British settlers who had begun moving into lands in the Susquehanna Valley in violation of the Easton Treaty of 1758. Eventually the British organized an opposition with help from the Iroquois and convinced the Indians in the Ohio Valley to lay down their arms. Further west, peace took years to achieve. Pontiac agreed to stop fighting after meeting with George Croghan in July 1765, and a more formal peace agreement was reached with the Great Lakes nations in August. However, the British did not obtain real control in the Great Lakes region at any time before the American Revolution.

One result of the new instability in the West was to poison the relationship between Indians and colonists in western Pennsylvania, each of whom was increasingly coming to define their identity in terms of their antagonism towards the other. Late in 1763 a number of westerners, mainly Scots-Irishmen from the township of Paxton, sought revenge on the Indians after protesting vociferously that the Pennsylvania legislature had failed to protect them. Christian Indians, living close to white settler communities, were especially vulnerable even though they had maintained peaceful relations with the British throughout the war. In December 1763 a party of some 60 "Paxton Boys" attacked the Indian settlement at Conestoga, murdering six of the inhabitants; the rest took refuge in the Lancaster jail. Despite a proclamation by the governor denouncing the atrocity, the group returned a few days later, broke into the jail, and butchered the remaining 14 Conestogas, who went to their deaths praying to a Christian God for their

---

[19]   The view that the French *habitants* had been responsible for provoking the rebellion, put forth in Francis Parkman, *The Conspiracy of Pontiac and the Indian War after the Conquest of Canada*, 4th edn, 2 vols (1851; Boston, 1905), Vol. 1, 84–6, has been challenged by Dowd, *War under Heaven*. For evidence that the French governor in Louisiana helped to encourage Pontiac's plan, however, see Middleton, *Pontiac's War*, 57–8.

salvation. The Paxton Boys accused them of having secretly conspired to help the western Indians attack settler communities on the frontier. In January 1764 the Paxton Boys marched to Philadelphia with their supporters, threatening to take over the government. It was a sad end to William Penn's "peaceable kingdom."[20]

With these crises unfolding, the British government realized they would need a new policy for managing their new territories and restoring peaceful relations with the Indians peoples in the West. The Proclamation of 1763 prohibited all settlement beyond a line running along the watershed of the Alleghenies, that area being reserved solely for the Indians. The proclamation was designed to centralize control over western lands and to channel new settlement into borderland regions where more British citizens were needed as a buffer against large populations of French and Spanish. An additional object was to reassure the Indians that the British intended to honor their treaties.[21] Two superintendents were appointed to supervise relations with the southern and northern Indians. To meet the costs of these troops being stationed in the West, the Treasury sought a way to raise additional revenue. Since taxpayers at home in Britain were already heavily taxed, the Treasury began to consider ways to make the colonists pay their fair share. It seemed sensible; after all, the military protection being provided in the West would benefit the colonists by making their borders more secure. Unfortunately for the British government all of its new policies began to be announced at a moment when the British North American colonists were looking forward to greater freedom and economic growth.

The British government in 1763 faced an unprecedented challenge. Having tried unsuccessfully to create an empire of conquest in the sixteenth and seventeenth centuries, it had succeeded by 1700 in creating an empire of trade. In 1763 that empire of trade was suddenly augmented by vast new territories in North America, acquired by conquest. Meanwhile the inhabitants of these new territories, including both French settlers and Native Americans, had interests fatally at odds with the interests of the settlers in the 13 original British colonies. Maintaining peace across this enormous area would be a difficult and costly affair.

By now the Indians east of the Mississippi had gained considerable experience in organizing resistance strategies to protect their ways of life. Unfortunately, in the aftermath of Pontiac's Rebellion, they had lost a considerable portion of their populations to the casualties of war, starvation, and disease. Their range of options for resisting European encroachments upon their homelands was growing narrower as a result. Ironically the British government's policies in the West, if they had succeeded, might have allowed the Indians to retain some of their autonomy and to coexist with the settlers for many generations. Sadly, however, those policies offered a weak foundation for their hopes.

---

[20] A recent account of these events may be found in Kevin Kenny, *Peaceable Kingdom Lost: The Paxton Boys and the Destruction of William Penn's Holy Experiment* (New York, 2009).

[21] Though historians have often argued that the proclamation line was intended to protect Native Americans, some evidence suggests the primary British goal was to create an orderly land tenure system so as to protect the property values of speculators and the British government. See Daniel Richter, "Native Americans, the Plan of 1764, and a British Empire that Never Was," in Robert Olwell and Alan Tully, eds, *Cultures and Identities in Colonial British America* (Baltimore, 2006), 269–92.

British North American colonial leaders had already begun predicting the creation of an American empire extending all the way to the Pacific. And all too soon, these same leaders would begin arguing that Parliament was depriving them of their constitutional rights and privileges, commencing the long debate that would lead the 13 British mainland colonies to declare their independence from the empire. Once they managed to break free of Great Britain, the settlers' governments would have little incentive to respect the Indians' territorial claims.

Eventually, European American settlers and their descendents would build ranches and farms and cities on the hunting grounds and the cornfields that had sustained the lives of the earliest Americans for thousands for years. Native American peoples would be forced to adapt, retreating west or onto reserves where their claims to the land and its resources could be conveniently forgotten. And yet they would persist and their stories will continue to be told.

Selected Bibliography ────────────

BIBLIOGRAPHIES

David L. Ammerman and Philip D. Morgan, *Books about Early America: 2001 Titles* (Williamsburg, 1989).

Frank Freidel, ed., *Harvard Guide to American History* (Cambridge, Mass., 1974).

GENERAL TEXTS

Charles M. Andrews, *The Colonial Period of American History*, 4 vols (New Haven, 1934–8; reprinted 1964).

Bernard Bailyn, *The Peopling of British North America: An Introduction* (New York, 1986).

T. H. Breen and Timothy Hall, *Colonial America in an Atlantic World: A Story of Creative Interaction* (New York, 2004).

Jon Butler, *Becoming America: The Revolution before 1776* (Cambridge, Mass., 2000).

Nicholas Canny, ed., *The Oxford History of the British Empire*, Vol. 1: *The Origins of Empire: British Overseas Enterprise to the Close of the Seventeenth Century* (Oxford and New York, 1998).

Edward Countryman, *Americans: A Collision of Histories* (New York, 1996).

J. H. Elliott, *Empires of the Atlantic World: Britain and Spain in America, 1492–1830* (New Haven, 2006).

Jack P. Greene, and J. R. Pole, eds, *Colonial British America: Essays in the New History of the Early Modern Era* (Baltimore, 1984).

David D. Hall, John M. Murrin, and Thad W. Tate, eds, *Saints and Revolutionaries: Essays on Early American History* (New York, 1984).

David Freeman Hawke, *Everyday Life in Early America* (New York, 1988).

Peter Hoffer, *The Brave New World: A History of Early America* (Baltimore, 2006).

Jacob Judd, *Colonial America: A Basic History* (Malabar, Fla., 1998).

Michael Kammen, *People of Paradox: An Inquiry concerning the Origins of American Civilization* (New York, 1972).

Colonial America: A History to 1763, Fourth Edition. Richard Middleton and Anne Lombard.
© 2011 Richard Middleton and Anne Lombard. Published 2011 by Blackwell Publishing Ltd.

Stanley N. Katz, John M. Murrin, and Douglas Greenberg, eds, *Colonial America: Essays in Politics and Social Development*, 4th edn (New York, 1993).

Paul Robert Lucas, *American Odyssey, 1607–1789* (Englewood Cliffs, 1984).

Anthony McFarlane, *The British in the Americas, 1480–1815* (London, 1994).

Peter J. Marshall, ed., *The Oxford History of the British Empire*, Vol. 2: *The Eighteenth Century* (Oxford, 1998).

Donald William Meinig, *The Shaping of America: A Geographical Perspective on 500 Years of History*, Vol. 1: *Atlantic America, 1492–1800* (New Haven, 1986).

Gary B. Nash, *Red, White, and Black: The Peoples of Early America* (Upper Saddle River, 2009).

R. C. Simmons, *The American Colonies from Settlement to Independence* (New York, 1976).

Ian K. Steele and Nancy L. Rhoden, *The Human Tradition in Colonial America* (Wilmington, 2000).

Alan Taylor, *American Colonies: The Settling of North America* (New York, 2002).

Esmond Wright, *The Search for Liberty: From Origins to Independence* (Oxford, 1994).

PRINTED DOCUMENTARY COLLECTIONS

James Axtell, *The Indian Peoples of Eastern America: A Documentary History of the Sexes* (New York, 1995).

Bernard Bailyn and Jane N. Garrett, eds, *Pamphlets of the American Revolution, 1750–1765* (Cambridge, Mass., 1965).

Warren M. Billings, ed., *The Old Dominion in the Seventeenth Century: A Documentary History of Virginia, 1606–1689* (Chapel Hill, 1975).

Paul Boyer and Stephen Nissenbaum, eds, *The Salem Witchcraft Papers: Verbatim Transcripts of the Legal Documents of the Salem Witchcraft Outbreak of 1692*, 3 vols (New York, 1977).

Richard D. Brown, *Major Problems in the Era of the American Revolution, 1760–1791: Documents and Essays* (Lexington, Mass., 1992).

Richard L. Bushman, ed., *The Great Awakening: Documents on the Revival of Religion, 1740–1745* (Chapel Hill, 1989).

Colin G. Calloway, ed., *The World Turned Upside Down: Indian Voices from Early America* (Boston 1994).

Elizabeth Donnan, ed., *Documents Illustrative of the History of the Slave Trade to America*, 4 vols (Washington, DC, 1930–5).

Kathleen DuVal and John DuVal, *Interpreting a Continent: Voices from Colonial America* (Lanham, 2009).

M. Farrand, ed., *Laws and Liberties of Massachusetts* (Cambridge, Mass., 1929).

Jack P. Greene, ed., *Settlements to Society, 1584–1763* (New York, 1966).

Alan Heimert and Andrew Delbanco, eds, *The Puritans in America: A Narrative Anthology* (Cambridge, Mass., 1985).

Merrill Jensen, ed., *English Historical Documents*, Vol. 9: *American Colonial Documents to 1776* (New York, 1955).

W. Keith Kavenagh, *Foundations of Colonial America: A Documentary History*, 3 vols (New York, 1973; paperback edn, 6 vols, 1983).

Karen Ordahl Kupperman, ed., *Major Problems in American Colonial History: Documents and Essays*, 2nd edn (Lexington, Mass., 1999).

Donald S. Lutz, ed., *Colonial Origins of the American Constitution: A Documentary History* (Indianapolis, 1998).

Perry Miller and T. H. Johnson, *The Puritans: A Source-Book of Their Writings*, 2 vols (New York, 1938).

David B. Quinn, ed., *New American World: A Documentary History of North America to 1612*, 5 vols (New York, 1979).

Willie Lee Rose, ed., *A Documentary History of Slavery in North America* (New York, 1976).

Brett Rushforth and Paul Mapp, eds, *Colonial North America and the Atlantic World: A History in Documents* (New York, 2008).

DIARIES, JOURNALS, AND CONTEMPORARY HISTORIES

Adolph B. Benson, ed., *Peter Kalm's Travels into North America: The English Version of 1770* (New York, 1937).

Robert Beverley, *The History and Present State of Virginia* [1705], ed. Louis B. Wright (Chapel Hill, 1947).

Carl Bridenbaugh, ed., *Gentleman's Progress: The Itinerarium of Dr Alexander Hamilton, 1744* (Chapel Hill, 1948).

Colonel Benjamin Church, *Diary of King Philip's War, 1675–1676*, ed. Alan and Mary Simpson (Chester, 1975).

Everett Emerson, ed., *Letters from New England: The Massachusetts Bay Colony, 1629–1638* (Amherst, 1976).

Oscar Handlin and John Clive, eds, *Journey to Pennsylvania* [1756], by Gottlieb Mittelberger (Cambridge, Mass., 1960).

John Lawson, *A New Voyage to Carolina* [1709], ed. Hugh Talmage Lefler (Chapel Hill, 1967).

Michael McGiffert, ed., *God's Plot: The Paradoxes of Puritan Piety, Being the Autobiography and Journal of Thomas Shepard* [1640] (Amherst, 1972).

Alden T. Vaughan and Edward W. Clark, eds, *Puritans among the Indians: Accounts of Captivity and Redemption, 1676–1724* (Cambridge, Mass., 1981).

REFERENCE WORKS

Jacob Ernest Cooke, *Encyclopedia of the North American Colonies*, 3 vols (New York, 1993).

Emory Elliott, ed., *Dictionary of Literary Biography*, Vol. 24: *American Colonial Writers, 1606–1734*; Vol. 31: *American Colonial Writers, 1735–1781* (Detroit, 1984–5).

John Mark Faragher, *The Encyclopedia of Colonial and Revolutionary America* (New York, 1990).

Alan Gallay, ed., *Colonial Wars of North America, 1512–1763: An Encyclopedia*. Military History of the United States, Vol. 5 (New York, 1996).

Daniel G. Reid et al., eds, *Dictionary of Christianity in America* (Downers Grove, 1990).

William C. Sturtevant, ed., *Handbook of North American Indians*, 12 vols (Washington, DC, 1978–2008).

Alden T. Vaughan, ed., *Early American Indian Documents, Treaties and Laws, 1607–1789*, Vols 1–20 (Washington, DC, 1983).

HISTORIOGRAPHICAL WORKS

David Armitage and Michael Braddick, eds, *The British Atlantic World, 1500–1800* (New York, 2002).

James Axtell, "Columbian Encounters: 1992–1995," *William and Mary Quarterly*, 52 (1995), 650–96.

James Axtell, "The Ethnohistory of Early America: A Review Essay," *William and Mary Quarterly*, 35 (1978), 110–44.

James Axtell, "Europeans, Indians and the Age of Discovery in American History Textbooks," *American Historical Review*, 92 (1987), 621–32.

Bernard Bailyn, *Atlantic History: Concepts and Contours* (Cambridge, Mass., 2005).

Bernard Bailyn, "The Challenge of Modern Historiography," *American Historical Review*, 87 (1982), 1–24.

Richard R. Beeman, "The New Social History and the Search for Community in Colonial America," *American Quarterly*, 29 (1977), 422–43.

Wayne Bodle, "Themes and Directions in Middle Colonies Historiography, 1980–1994," *William and Mary Quarterly*, 51 (1994), 355–88.

Jon Butler, "The Future of American Religious History: Prospectus, Agenda, Transatlantic *Problématique*," *William and Mary Quarterly*, 42 (1985), 167–83.

Nicholas Canny, "Writing Atlantic History; or, Reconfiguring the History of Colonial British America," *Journal of American History*, 86 (2000), 1093–14.

E. Wayne Carp, "Early American Military History: A Review of Recent Work," *Virginia Magazine of History and Biography*, 94 (1986), 259–84.

Joyce Chaplin, "Expansion and Exceptionalism in Early American History," *Journal of American History*, 89 (2003), 1431–55.

Peter A. Coclanis, "Atlantic World or Atlantic/World?" *William and Mary Quarterly*, 63 (2006), 725–72.

Charles L. Cohen, "The Post-Puritan Paradigm of Early American History," *William and Mary Quarterly*, 54 (1997), 695–722.

Richard S. Dunn, "The Social History of Early New England," *American Quarterly*, 24 (1972), 661–79.

Alison Games, "Atlantic History: Definitions, Challenges, and Opportunities," *American Historical Review*, 111, no. 3 (2006), 741–57.

Jack P. Greene and Philip D. Morgan, eds, *Atlantic History: A Critical Appraisal* (New York, 2009).

Douglas Greenberg, "The Middle Colonies in Recent American Historiography," *William and Mary Quarterly*, 36 (1979), 396–427.

Philip F. Gura, "The Study of Colonial American Literature, 1966–1987: A Vade Mecum," *William and Mary Quarterly*, 45 (1988), 305–41.

David D. Hall, "On Common Ground: The Coherence of American Puritan Studies," *William and Mary Quarterly*, 44 (1987), 193–229.

David D. Hall, "Witchcraft and the Limits of Interpretation," *New England Quarterly*, 58 (1985), 253–81.

Don Higginbotham, "The Early American Way of War: Reconnaissance and Appraisal," *William and Mary Quarterly*, 44 (1987), 230–73.

Richard R. Johnson, "Charles McClean Andrews and the Invention of American Colonial History," *William and Mary Quarterly*, 43 (1986), 519–41.

Elizabeth Mancke and Carole Shammas, eds, *The Creation of the British Atlantic World* (Baltimore, 2005).

James H. Merrell, "Some Thoughts on Colonial Historians and American Indians," *William and Mary Quarterly*, 46 (1989), 94–119.

Richard Middleton, "British Historians and the American Revolution," *Journal of American Studies*, 5 (1971), 43–58.

Simon Middleton and Billy G. Smith, "Class and Early America: An Introduction," *William and Mary Quarterly*, 43 (2006), 211–20.

H. C. Porter, "Reflections on the Ethnohistory of Early Colonial North America," *Journal of American Studies*, 16 (1982), 243–54.

Anita H. Rutman, "Still Planting the Seeds of Hope: The Recent Literature of the Early Chesapeake Region," *Virginia Magazine of History and Biography*, 95 (1987), 3–24.

Ian Steele, "Exploding Colonial American History," *Reviews in American History*, 26 (1998), 70–95.

Thad W. Tate, "The Seventeenth-Century Chesapeake and Its Modern Historians," in Thad W. Tate and David L. Ammerman, eds, *The Chesapeake in the Seventeenth Century: Essays on Anglo-American Society* (Chapel Hill, 1979).

Daniel Vickers, ed., *A Companion to Colonial America* (Oxford, 2003).

Peter H. Wood, "I Did the Best I Could for My Day: The Study of Early Black History during the Second Reconstruction, 1960 to 1976," *William and Mary Quarterly*, 35 (1978), 185–225.

CHAPTER 1   THE PEOPLES OF EASTERN NORTH AMERICA: SOCIETIES IN TRANSITION

General

William W. Fitzhugh, ed., *Cultures in Contact: The Impact of European Contacts on Native American Institutions, A.D. 1000–1800* (Washington, DC, 1985).

Robert S. Grumet, *Historic Contact: Indian Peoples and Colonists in Today's Northeastern United States in the Sixteenth through Eighteenth Centuries* (Norman, 1995).

Bruce G. Trigger, ed., *Handbook of North American Indians*, Vol. 15: *Northeast* (Washington, DC, 1978).

Bruce G. Trigger and Wilcomb E. Washburn, eds, *The Cambridge History of the Native Peoples of the Americas*, Vol. 1: *North America* (New York, 1996).

Wilcomb E. Washburn, *The Indian in America* (New York, 1975).

The Precontact Background

James Axtell, "The Ethnohistory of Early America: A Review Essay," *William and Mary Quarterly*, 35 (1978), 110–44.

C. Wesley Cowan, "Evolutionary Changes Associated with the Domestication of *Cucurbita pepo*: Evidence from Eastern Kentucky," in Kristen Gremillion, ed., *People, Plants, and Landscapes: Studies in Paleoethnobotany* (Tuscaloosa, 1997), 63–85.

William M. Denevan, ed., *The Native Population of the Americas in 1492* (Madison, Wis., 1976; rev. edn, 1992).

Brian M. Fagan, *Ancient North America: The Archaeology of a Continent* (London, 1990).

Jesse D. Jennings, ed., *Ancient North Americans* (San Francisco, 1978).

Alvin M. Josephy, ed., *America in 1492: The Worlds of the Indian Peoples Before the Arrival of Columbus* (New York, 1992).

Timothy R. Pauketat and Thomas E. Emerson, eds, *Cahokia: Domination and Ideology in the Mississippian World* (Lincoln, Nebr., 1997).

James D. Rice, *Nature and History in the Potomac Country: From Hunter-Gatherers to the Age of Jefferson* (Baltimore, 2009).

Daniel K. Richter, *Facing East from Indian Country: A Native History of Early America* (Cambridge, Mass., 2001).

Neal Salisbury, "The Indians' Old World: Native Americans and the Coming of Europeans," *William and Mary Quarterly*, 53 (1996), 435–58.

Lynda Norene Shaffer, *Native Americans Before 1492: The Moundbuilding Centers of the Eastern Woodlands* (Armonk, NY, 1992).

Bruce D. Smith, *Rivers of Change: Essays on Early Agriculture in Eastern North America* (Washington, DC, 1992).

Bruce D. Smith, ed., *Mississippian Emergence: The Evolution of Agricultural Societies in the Eastern Woodlands* (Washington, DC, 1990).

Bruce C. Trigger, *Natives and Newcomers: Canada's "Heroic Age" Reconsidered* (Montréal, 1985).

The Columbian Impact

Alfred W. Crosby, *The Columbian Exchange: The Biological and Cultural Consequences of 1492* (Westport, 1972).

Alfred W. Crosby, "Virgin Soil Epidemics as a Factor in the Aboriginal Depopulation in America," *William and Mary Quarterly*, 33 (1976), 289–99.

John D. Daniels, "The Indian Population of North America in 1492," *William and Mary Quarterly*, 49 (1992), 298–320.

William M. Denevan, ed., *The Native Population of the Americas in 1492* (Madison, Wis., 1976).

Henry F. Dobyns, *Their Number Become Thinned: Native American Population Dynamics in Eastern North America* (Knoxville, 1983).

Wilbur R. Jacobs, "The Tip of an Iceberg: Pre-Columbian Indian Demography and Some Implications for Revisionism," *William and Mary Quarterly*, 31 (1974), 123–32.

David Jones, "Virgin Soils Revisited," *William and Mary Quarterly*, 60 (2003), 703–42.

Clark Spencer Larsen and George R. Milner, *In the Wake of Contact: Biological Responses to Conquest* (New York, 1994).

Neil Salisbury, "The Indians' Old World: Native Americans and the Coming of Europeans," *William and Mary Quarterly*, 53 (1996), 435–58.

Marvin T. Smith, "Aboriginal Depopulation in the Post Contact Southeast," in Charles Hudson and Carmen Chaves Tesser, eds, *The Forgotten Centuries: Indians and Europeans in the American South, 1521–1704* (Athens, Ga., 1994,), 257–75.

David E. Stannard, *American Holocaust: Columbus and the Conquest of the New World* (New York, 1992).

Russell Thornton, *American Indian Holocaust and Survival: A Population History Since 1492* (Norman, 1987).

John Verano and Douglas Ubelaker, *Disease and Demography in the Americas* (Washington, DC, 1992).

Early Encounters

James Axtell, *After Columbus: Essays in the Ethnohistory of Colonial North America* (New York, 1988).

James Axtell, *Beyond 1492: Encounters in Colonial North America* (New York, 1992).

James Axtell, *The European and the Indian: Essays in the Ethnohistory of Colonial North America* (New York, 1981).

James Axtell, *The Invasion Within: The Contest of Cultures in Colonial North America* (New York, 1985).

Kathleen J. Bragdon, *Native Peoples of Southern New England, 1500–1650* (Norman, 1996).

Colin G. Calloway, *New Worlds for All: Indians, Europeans, and the Remaking of Early America* (Baltimore, 1997).

Robbie Ethridge, *From Chicaza to Chickasaw: The European Invasion and the Transformation of the Mississippian World, 1540–1715* (Chapel Hill, 2010).

Charlotte Gradie, "Spanish Jesuits in Virginia: The Mission that Failed," *Virginia Magazine of History and Biography*, 96 (1988), 131–56.

Charles Hudson and Carmen Chaves Tesser, eds, *The Forgotten Centuries: Indians and Europeans in the American South, 1521–1704* (Athens, Ga., 1994).

Paul Hulton, *America 1585: The Complete Drawings of John White* (Chapel Hill, 1984).

Shepard Krech III, ed., *Indians, Animals and the Fur Trade: A Critique of "Keepers of the Game"* (Athens, Ga., 1981).

Karen Ordahl Kupperman, *Indians and English: Facing Off in Early America* (Ithaca, 2000).

Karen Ordahl Kupperman, *Settling with the Indians: The Meetings of English and Indian Cultures in America, 1580–1640* (Totowa, 1980).

Calvin Martin, *Keepers of the Game: Indian–Animal Relationships and the Fur Trade* (Berkeley, 1978).

Jerald T. Milanich, *The Timucua* (Cambridge, Mass., 1996).

Michael Leroy Oberg, *Dominion and Civility: English Imperialism and Native America, 1585–1685* (Ithaca, 1999).

H. C. Porter, *The Inconstant Savage: England and the North American Indian, 1500–1660* (London, 1976).

Stephen R. Potter, *Commoners, Tribute and Chiefs: The Development of Algonquian Culture in the Potomac Valley* (Charlottesville, 1993).

Helen C. Rountree, *The Powhatan Indians of Virginia: Their Traditional Culture* (Norman, 1989).

Helen C. Rountree, ed., *Powhatan Foreign Relations, 1500–1722* (Charlottesville, 1993).

Helen C. Rountree and Thomas E. Davidson, *Eastern Shore Indians of Virginia and Maryland* (Charlottesville, 1997).

Howard S. Russell, *Indian New England Before the Mayflower* (Hanover, NH, 1980).

Neil Salisbury, *Manitou and Providence: Indians, Europeans and the Making of New England, 1500–1643* (New York, 1982).

Timothy Silver, *A New Face on the Countryside: Indians, Colonists and Slaves in South Atlantic Forests, 1500–1800* (New York, 1990).

Kim Sloan, *A New World: England's First View of America* (Chapel Hill, 2007).

Cynthia Van Zandt, *Brothers among Nations: The Pursuit of Intercultural Alliances in Early America, 1580–1660* (New York, 2008).

Peter H. Wood, Gregory A. Waselkov, and M. Thomas Hatley, *Powhatan's Mantle: Indians in the Colonial Southeast* (Lincoln, Nebr., 1989).

CHAPTER 2   THE AGE OF EUROPEAN EXPLORATION

General

Jared Diamond, *Guns, Germs and Steel: A Short History of Everybody for the Last 13,000 Years* (London, 1997).

The Vikings, Spain, and Portugal

Emerson W. Baker et al., *American Beginnings: Exploration, Culture and Cartography in the Land of Norumbega* (Lincoln, Nebr., 1994).

C. R. Boxer, *The Portuguese Seaborne Empire, 1415–1825* (London, 1968).

J. H. Elliott, *Empires of the Atlantic World: Britain and Spain in America, 1492–1800* (New Haven, 2007).

Paul E. Hoffman, *A New Andalucia and a Way to the Orient: The American Southeast during the Sixteenth Century* (Baton Rouge, 1990).

Gwyn Jones, *The Norse Atlantic Saga, Being the Norse Voyages of Discovery and Settlement to Iceland, Greenland, and America* (New York, 1986).

Karen Ordahl Kupperman, ed., *America in European Consciousness, 1493–1750* (Chapel Hill, 1994).

L. N. McAlister, *Spain and Portugal in the New World, 1492–1700* (Oxford, 1984).

Samuel Eliot Morison, *The European Discovery of America*, 2 vols (New York, 1971).

Anthony Padgen, *Lords of All the World: Ideologies of Empire in Spain, Britain, and France, 1500–c.1800* (New Haven, 1995).

J. H. Parry, *The Discovery of South America* (New York, 1979).

J. H. Parry, *The Spanish Seaborne Empire* (Berkeley, 1990).

William D. Phillips, Jr. and Carla Rahn Phillips, *The Worlds of Christopher Columbus* (Cambridge, 1993).

David Beers Quinn, *North America from Earliest Discovery to First Settlements: The Norse Voyages to 1612* (New York, 1975).

A. J. R. Russell-Wood, *A World on the Move: The Portuguese in Africa, Asia, and America, 1415–1808* (New York, 1993).

Erik Wahlgren, *The Vikings and America* (New York, 1986).

David J. Weber, *The Spanish Frontier in North America* (New Haven, 1992).

Robert S. Weddle, *The Gulf of Mexico in North American Discovery, 1500–1685* (College Station, 1985).

England

K. R. Andrews, N. P. Canny, and P. E. H. Hair, eds, *The Westward Enterprise: English Adventurers in Ireland, the Atlantic, and America 1480–1650* (Detroit, 1979).

David Armitage, "The New World and British Historical Thought: From Richard Hakluyt to William Robertson," in Karen Ordahl Kupperman, ed., *America in European Consciousness, 1493–1750* (Chapel Hill, 1995), 52–75.

Angus Calder, *Revolutionary Empire: The Rise of the English-Speaking Empires from the Fifteenth Century to the 1780s* (New York, 1981).

Nicholas P. Canny, *The Elizabethan Conquest of Ireland: A Pattern Established, 1565–1576* (New York, 1976).

Nicholas P. Canny, "The Ideology of English Colonization: From Ireland to America," *William and Mary Quarterly*, 30 (1973), 575–98.

Nicholas P. Canny, ed., *Europeans on the Move: Studies on European Migration, 1500–1800* (Oxford, 1994).

Nicholas P. Canny and Anthony Pagden, eds, *Colonial Identity in the Atlantic World, 1500–1800* (Princeton, 1987).

J. H. Elliott, *The Old World and the New, 1492–1650* (Cambridge, 1970).

Alison Games, *The Web of Empire: English Cosmopolitans in an Age of Expansion, 1560–1650* (New York, 2008).

R. Hakluyt, *The Principal Navigations, Voyages, Traffiques and Discoveries of the English Nation* (London, 1600; reprinted 1927).

James Horn, *A Kingdom Strange: The Brief and Tragic History of the Lost Colony of Roanoke* (New York, 2010).

Karen Ordahl Kupperman, *Roanoke: The Abandoned Colony* (Totowa, 1984; 2nd edn, Lanham, 2007).

Ken MacMillan, *Sovereignty and Possession in the English New World: The Legal Foundations of Empire, 1576–1640* (Cambridge, 2006).

Peter Mancall, *Hakluyt's Promise: An Elizabethan's Obsession for an English America* (New Haven, 2007).

G. J. Marcus, *The Conquest of the North Atlantic* (New York, 1981).

David B. Quinn, *England and the Discovery of America, 1481–1620* (New York, 1974).

David B. Quinn, *The New American World: A Documentary History*, 5 vols (New York, 1979).

David B. Quinn, *Set Fair for Roanoke: Voyages and Colonies, 1584–1606* (Chapel Hill, 1985).

David B. Quinn and A. N. Ryan, *England's Sea Empire, 1550–1642* (London, 1983).

Africa

Paul Lovejoy, *Transformations in Slavery: A History of Slavery in Africa*, 2nd edn (Cambridge, 2000).

Walter Rodney, *How Europe Underdeveloped Africa*, rev. edn (Washington, DC, 1981).

John Thornton, *Africa and Africans in the Making of the Atlantic World, 1400–1800* (Cambridge, 1993; 2nd edn, 1998).

CHAPTER 3   THE ENGLISH CONQUER VIRGINIA, 1607–1660

The Virginia Company

Charles M. Andrews, *The Colonial Period of American History: The Settlements*, 4 vols (New Haven, 1964).

Robert Applebaum and John Wood Sweet, *Envisioning an English Empire: Jamestown and the Making of an Atlantic World* (Philadelphia, 2005).

Philip L. Barbour, *Pocahontas and Her World* (Boston, 1970).

Philip L. Barbour, *The Three Worlds of Captain John Smith* (Boston, 1964).

Warren M. Billings, ed., *The Old Dominion in the Seventeenth Century: A Documentary History of Virginia, 1606–1689* (Chapel Hill, 1975).

Carville V. Earle, "Environment, Disease, and Mortality in Early Virginia," in Thad W. Tate and David L. Ammerman, eds, *The Chesapeake in the Seventeenth Century: Essays on Anglo-American Society* (Chapel Hill, 1979).

Frederic W. Gleach, *Powhatan's World and Colonial Virginia: A Conflict of Cultures* (Lincoln, Nebr., 1997).

James Horn, *A Land as God Made It: Jamestown and the Birth of America* (New York, 2005).

Ivor Noel Hume, *The Virginia Adventure: Roanoke to James Towne: An Archaeological and Historical Odyssey* (New York, 1994).

William Kelso, *Jamestown: The Buried Truth* (Charlottesville, 2006).

Karen Ordahl Kupperman, "Apathy and Death in Early Jamestown," *Journal of American History*, 66 (1979), 24–40.

Karen Ordahl Kupperman, "Fear of Hot Climates in the Anglo-American Experience," *William and Mary Quarterly*, 41 (1984), 213–40.

Karen Ordahl Kupperman, *The Jamestown Project* (Cambridge, Mass., 2007).

Karen Ordahl Kupperman, ed., *Captain John Smith: A Select Edition of His Writings* (Chapel Hill, 1988).

J. Leo Lemay, *Did Pocahontas Save Captain John Smith?* (Athens, Ga., 1992).

Edmund S. Morgan, "The First American Boom: Virginia 1618–1630," *William and Mary Quarterly*, 28 (1971), 169–98.

Edmund S. Morgan, "The Labor Problem at Jamestown, 1607–1618," *American Historical Review*, 76 (1971), 595–611.

Michael Leroy Oberg, *Dominion and Civility: English Imperialism and Native America, 1585–1685* (Ithaca, 1999).

Helen Rountree, *Pocahontas, Powhatan, Opecancanough: Three Indian Lives Changed by Jamestown* (Charlottesville, 2005).

Darrett B. Rutman and Anita H. Rutman, "Of Agues and Fevers: Malaria in the Early Chesapeake," *William and Mary Quarterly*, 33 (1976), 31–60.

Thad W. Tate and David L. Ammerman, eds *The Chesapeake in the Seventeenth Century: Essays on Anglo-American Society* (Chapel Hill, 1979).

Camilla Townsend, *Pocahontas and Powhatan's Dilemma* (New York, 2004).

Alden T. Vaughan, *American Genesis: Captain John Smith and the Founding of Virginia* (Boston, 1975).

Growth and Consolidation

Warren Billings, *A Little Parliament: The Virginia General Assembly in the Seventeenth Century* (Richmond, 2004).

Warren M. Billings, ed., *The Old Dominion in the Seventeenth Century: A Documentary History of Virginia, 1606–1689* (Chapel Hill, 1975).

Warren M. Billings, John E. Selby, and Thad W. Tate, *Colonial Virginia: A History* (New York, 1986).

T. H. Breen, ed., *Shaping Southern Society: The Colonial Experience* (New York, 1976).

T. H. Breen and Stephen Innes, *"Myne Owne Ground": Race and Freedom on Virginia's Eastern Shore, 1640–1676*, 2nd edn. (New York, 2005).

Kathleen Brown, *Good Wives, Nasty Wenches, and Anxious Patriarchs: Gender, Race, and Power in Colonial Virginia* (Chapel Hill, 1996).

Wesley Frank Craven, *White, Red, and Black: The Seventeenth-Century Virginian* (Charlottesville, 1971).

J. Douglas Deal, *Race and Class in Colonial Virginia: Indians, Englishmen, and Africans on the Eastern Shore during the Seventeenth Century* (New York, 1993).

J. H. Elliott, *Empires of the Atlantic World: Britain and Spain in America, 1492–1830* (New Haven, 2006).

Frederick Fausz, "Fighting 'Fire' with Firearms: The Anglo-Powhatan Arms Race in Early Virginia," *American Indian Culture and Research Journal*, 3 (1979), 33–50.

Frederick J. Fausz, "Merging and Emerging Worlds: Anglo-Indian Interest Groups and the Development of the Seventeenth-Century Chesapeake," in Lois Green Carr, Philip D. Morgan, and Jean B. Russo, eds, *Colonial Chesapeake Society* (Chapel Hill, 1989).

April Lee Hatfield, *Atlantic Virginia: Intercolonial Relations in the Seventeenth Century* (Philadelphia, 2004).

Irene W. D. Hecht, "The Virginia Muster of 1624/5 as a Source of Demographic History," *William and Mary Quarterly*, 30 (1973), 65–79.

Ivor Noel Hume, *Martin's One Hundred* (New York, 1981).

Jon Kukla, "Order and Chaos in Early America: Political and Social Stability in Pre-Restoration Virginia," *American Historical Review*, 90 (1985), 275–98.

Jon Kukla, *Political Institutions in Virginia, 1619–1660* (New York, 1989).

Karen Ordahl Kupperman, *Providence Island, 1630–1641: The Other Puritan Colony* (New York, 1993).

Karen Kupperman, *Settling with the Indians: The Meeting of English and Indian Cultures in America, 1580–1640* (Totowa, 1980).

Edmund S. Morgan, *American Slavery, American Freedom: The Ordeal of Colonial Virginia* (New York, 1975).

John Ruston Pagan, *Anne Orthwood's Bastard: Sex and Law in Early Virginia* (New York, 2003).

James R. Perry, *The Formation of a Society on Virginia's Eastern Shore, 1615–1655* (Chapel Hill, 1990).

Martin H. Quitt, "Immigrant Origins of the Virginia Gentry: A Study of Cultural Transmission and Innovation," *William and Mary Quarterly*, 45 (1988), 629–55.

Bernard Sheehan, *Savagism and Civility: Indians and Englishmen in Colonial Virginia* (Cambridge, 1980).

Engel Sluiter, "New Light on the '20 Odd Negroes' Arriving in Virginia, August 1619," *William and Mary Quarterly*, 54 (1997), 421–34.

Alden T. Vaughan, "Blacks in Virginia: A Note on the First Decade," *William and Mary Quarterly*, 29 (1972), 469–78.

Alden T. Vaughan, "'Expulsion of the Savages': English Policy and the Virginia Massacre of 1622," *William and Mary Quarterly*, 35 (1978), 57–84.

Alden T. Vaughan, *The Roots of American Racism: Essays on the Colonial Experience* (New York, 1995).

Betty Wood, *The Origins of American Slavery: Freedom and Bondage in the English Colonies* (New York, 1997).

CHAPTER 4   THE CONQUEST CONTINUES: NEW ENGLAND, 1620–1660

Plymouth

William Bradford, *Of Plymouth Plantation, 1620–1647*, ed. Samuel Eliot Morison (New York, 1952).

William Cronon, *Changes in the Land: Indians, Colonists, and the Ecology of New England* (New York, 1983).

James Deetz and Patricia Scott Deetz, *The Times of Their Lives: Life, Love, and Death in Plymouth Colony* (New York, 2000).

George D. Langdon, Jr., *Pilgrim Colony: A History of New Plymouth, 1620–1691* (New Haven, 1966).

Neil Salisbury, *Manitou and Providence: Indians, Europeans, and the Making of New England, 1500–1643* (New York, 1982).

Neil Salisbury, "Squanto: Last of the Patuxets," in David G. Sweet and Gary B. Nash, eds, *Struggle and Survival in Colonial America* (Berkeley, 1981), 228–44.

Massachusetts

David Grayson Allen, *In English Ways: The Movement of Societies and the Transferral of English Local Law and Custom to Massachusetts Bay in the Seventeenth Century* (Chapel Hill, 1981).

Virginia DeJohn Anderson, "New England in the Seventeenth Century," in Nicholas Canny, ed., *The Origins of Empire: British Overseas Enterprise to the Close of the Seventeenth Century* (Oxford, 1998), 193–217.

Virginia DeJohn Anderson, *New England's Generation: The Great Migration and the Formation of Society and Culture in the Seventeenth Century* (Cambridge, 1991).

Richard Archer, *Fissures in the Rock: New England in the Seventeenth Century* (Hanover, NH, 2001).

Ben Barker-Benfield, "Anne Hutchinson and the Puritan Attitude toward Women," *Feminist Studies*, 1 (1972), 65–96.

Emery Battis, *Saints and Sectaries: Anne Hutchinson and the Antinomian Controversy* (Chapel Hill, 1962).

Theodore Dwight Bozeman, *To Live Ancient Lives: The Primitivist Dimension in Puritanism* (Chapel Hill, 1988).

T. H. Breen, *The Character of a Good Ruler: Puritan Political Ideas, 1630–1730* (New Haven, 1970).

T. H. Breen, "Persistent Localism: English Social Change and the Shaping of New England Institutions," *William and Mary Quarterly*, 32 (1975), 3–28.

T. H. Breen, *Puritans and Adventurers: Change and Persistence in Early America* (New York, 1980).

T. H. Breen and Stephen Foster, "The Puritans' Greatest Achievement: A Study of Social Cohesion in Seventeenth-Century Massachusetts," *Journal of American History*, 60 (1973/4), 5–22.

Francis J. Bremer, *Congregational Communion: Clerical Friendship in the Anglo-American Puritan Community, 1610–1692* (Boston, 1994).

Francis J. Bremer, *John Winthrop: America's Forgotten Founding Father* (New York, 2003).

Francis J. Bremer, *Puritan Crisis: New England and the English Civil Wars, 1630–1670* (New York, 1989).

Francis J. Bremer, *The Puritan Experiment: New England Society from Bradford to Edwards* (New York, 1976).

Kristina Bross, *Dry Bones and Indian Sermons: Praying Indians and Colonial American Identity* (Ithaca, 2004).

Alfred A. Cave, *The Pequot War* (Amherst, 1996).

Alfred A. Cave, "Who Killed John Stone? A Note on the Origins of the Pequot War," *William and Mary Quarterly*, 49 (1992), 509–21.

Cedric B. Cowing, *The Saving Remnant: Religion and the Settling of New England* (Urbana, 1995).

David Cressy, *Coming Over: Migration between England and New England in the Seventeenth Century* (New York, 1987).

A. L. Cummings, *The Framed Houses of Massachusetts Bay, 1625–1725* (Cambridge, Mass., 1979).

Bruce C. Daniels, *Puritans at Play, Leisure and Recreation in Colonial New England* (Basingstoke, 1995).

Andrew Delbanco, *The Puritan Ordeal* (Cambridge, Mass., 1989).

Richard S. Dunn, *Puritans and Yankees: The Winthrop Dynasty of New England, 1630–1717* (Princeton, 1962).

Stephen Foster, *The Long Argument: English Puritanism and the Shaping of New England Culture, 1570–1700* (Chapel Hill, 1991).

Stephen Foster, *Their Solitary Way: The Puritan Social Ethic in the First Century of Settlement in New England* (New Haven, 1971).

Alison Games, *Migration and the Origins of the English Atlantic World* (Cambridge, Mass., 1999).

Richard Godbeer, "'The Cry of Sodom': Discourse, Intercourse, and Desire in Colonial New England," *William and Mary Quarterly*, 52 (1995), 259–86.

Philip F. Gura, *A Glimpse of Sion's Glory: Puritan Radicalism in New England, 1620–1660* (Middletown, 1984).

David D. Hall, *The Faithful Shepherd: A History of the New England Ministry in the Seventeenth Century* (Chapel Hill, 1972).

David D. Hall, "On Common Ground: The Coherence of American Puritan Studies," *William and Mary Quarterly*, 44 (1987), 193–229.

David D. Hall, *Worlds of Wonder, Days of Judgement: Popular Religious Belief in Early New England* (New York, 1989).

David D. Hall, ed., *The Antinomian Controversy, 1636–1638: A Documentary History* (Durham, NC, 1990).

David D. Hall and David Grayson Allen, eds, *Seventeenth-Century New England* (Boston, 1984).

E. Brooks Holifield, *Era of Persuasion: American Thought and Culture, 1521–1680* (Boston, 1989).

James Holstun, *A Rational Millennium: Puritan Utopias of Seventeenth-Century England and America* (New York, 1987).

Stephen Innes, *Creating the Commonwealth: The Economic Culture of Puritan New England* (New York, 1995).

Francis Jennings, *The Invasion of America: Indians, Colonization and the Cant of Conquest* (Chapel Hill, 1975).

Ronald Dale Karr, "'Why Should You Be So Furious?': The Violence of the Pequot War," *Journal of American History*, 85 (1998), 876–909.

Lyle Koehler, "The Case of the American Jezebels: Anne Hutchinson and Female Agitation during the Years of Antinomian Turmoil, 1636–1640," *William and Mary Quarterly*, 31 (1974), 55–78.

David Thomas Konig, *Law and Society in Puritan Massachusetts: Essex County, 1629–1692* (Chapel Hill, 1979).

Benjamin W. Labaree, *Colonial Massachusetts: A History* (New York, 1979).

Douglas Edward Leach, *The Northern Colonial Frontier, 1607–1763* (New York, 1966).

Perry Miller, *Orthodoxy in Massachusetts, 1630–1650: A Genetic Study* (Cambridge, Mass., 1933).

Edmund S. Morgan, *The Puritan Dilemma: The Story of John Winthrop* (Boston, 1958).

Edmund S. Morgan, *Visible Saints: The History of a Puritan Idea* (New York, 1963).

Dane Morrison, *A Praying People: Massachusetts Acculturation and the Failure of the Puritan Mission, 1660–1690* (New York, 1995).

Margaret Newell, "The Birth of New England in the Atlantic Economy," in Peter Temin, ed., *Engines of Enterprise: The Economic History of New England* (Cambridge, Mass., 2001).

Carla Gardina Pestana, "The City upon a Hill under Siege: The Puritan Perception of the Quaker Threat to Massachusetts Bay, 1656–1661," *New England Quarterly*, 56 (1983), 323–53.

Carla Gardina Pestana, "The Quaker Executions as Myth and History," *Journal of American History*, 80 (1993), 441–69.

Philip Ranlet, *Enemies of the Bay Colony* (New York, 1995).

James P. Rhonda, "'We Are Well as We Are': An Indian Critique of Seventeenth-Century Christian Missions," *William and Mary Quarterly*, 34 (1977), 66–82.

Rosamond Rosenmeier, *Anne Bradstreet Revisited* (Boston, 1991).

Darrett B. Rutman, *American Puritanism: Faith and Practice* (Philadelphia, 1970).

Darrett B. Rutman, *Winthrop's Boston: Portrait of a Puritan Town, 1630–1649* (Chapel Hill, 1965).

Neal Salisbury, "Red Puritans: 'The Praying Indians' of Massachusetts Bay and John Eliot," *William and Mary Quarterly*, 31 (1974), 27–54.

Ivy Schweitzer, *The Work of Self-Representation: Lyric Poetry in Colonial New England* (Chapel Hill, 1991).

George Selement, *Keepers of the Vineyard: The Puritan Ministry and Collective Culture in Colonial New England* (Lanham, 1984).

Darren Staloff, *The Making of an American Thinking Class: Intellectuals and Intelligence in Puritan Massachusetts* (New York, 1998).

David E. Stannard, *The Puritan Way of Death: A Study in Religion, Culture, and Social Change* (New York, 1977).

William K. B. Stoever, *"A Faire and Easie Way to Heaven": Covenant Theology and Antinomianism in Early Massachusetts* (Middletown, 1978).

Frank Thistlethwaite, *Dorset Pilgrims: The Story of Westcountry Pilgrims who Went to New England in the Seventeenth Century* (London, 1989).

Roger Thompson, *Mobility and Migration: East Anglian Founders of New England, 1629–1640* (Amherst, 1994).

Alden T. Vaughan, *The New England Frontier: Puritans and Indians, 1620–1675* (Boston, 1965).

Daniel Vickers, *Farmers and Fishermen: Two Centuries of Work in Essex County, Massachusetts, 1630–1800* (Chapel Hill, 1994).

David Weir, *Early New England: A Covenanted Society* (Grand Rapids, 2005).

Peter White, ed., *Puritan Poets and Poetics: Seventeenth-Century American Poetry in Theory and Practice* (University Park, 1985).

Selma R. Williams, *Divine Rebel: The Life of Anne Marbury Hutchinson* (New York, 1981).

Michael Winship, *The Times and Trials of Anne Hutchinson* (Lawrence, 2005).

Walter Woodward, *Prospero's America: John Winthrop, Jr., Alchemy and the Creation of New England Culture, 1606–1676* (Chapel Hill, 2010).

Larzer Ziff, *Puritanism in America: New Culture in a New World* (New York, 1973).

Rhode Island, Connecticut, and New Hampshire

Sargent Bush, Jr., *The Writings of Thomas Hooker: Spiritual Adventure in Two Worlds* (Madison, Wis., 1980).

James Byrd, *The Challenges of Roger Williams: Religious Liberty, Violent Persecution, and the Bible* (Macon, Ga., 2002).

Jere R. Daniell, *Colonial New Hampshire: A History* (New York, 1981).

Bruce C. Daniels, *Dissent and Conformity on Narragansett Bay: The Colonial Rhode Island Town* (Middletown, 1983).

Timothy L. Hall, *Separating Church and State: Roger Williams and Religious Liberty* (Urbana, 1998).

Sydney V. James, *Colonial Rhode Island: A History* (New York, 1975).

Sydney V. James, *John Clarke and His Legacies: Religion and Law in Colonial Rhode Island, 1638–1750* (University Park, 1999).

Bruce H. Mann, *Neighbors and Strangers: Law and Community in Early Connecticut* (Chapel Hill, 1987).

Perry Miller, *Roger Williams: His Contribution to the American Tradition* (Indianapolis, 1953).

Edmund S. Morgan, *Roger Williams: The Church and the State* (New York, 1967).

Michael Leroy Oberg, *Uncas: First of the Mohegans* (Ithaca, 2003).

Robert J. Taylor, *Colonial Connecticut: A History* (New York, 1979).

David E. Van Deventer, *The Emergence of Provincial New Hampshire, 1623–1741* (Baltimore, 1976).

CHAPTER 5　DIVERSE COLONIES: NEW FRANCE, NEW NETHERLAND, MARYLAND, AND THE WEST INDIES

New France

Denys Delage, *Bitter Feast: Amerindians and Europeans in Northeast North America, 1600–1664* (Vancouver, 1993).

W. J. Eccles, *The Canadian Frontier, 1534–1760*, rev. edn (Albuquerque, 1983).

W. J. Eccles, *France in America*, rev. edn (East Lansing, 1990).

Allan Greer, *The People of New France* (Toronto, 1997).

Peter Moogk, *La Nouvelle France: The Making of French Canada: A Cultural History* (East Lansing, 2000).

Peter Moogk, "Reluctant Exiles: Emigrants from France in Canada before 1760," *William and Mary Quarterly*, 46 (1989), 463–505.

Bruce Trigger, *Natives and Newcomers: Canada's "Heroic Age" Reconsidered* (Montréal, 1985).

Maryland

Lois Green Carr and Russell R. Menard, "Immigration and Opportunity: The Freedman in Early Colonial Maryland," in Thad W. Tate and David L. Ammerman, eds, *The Chesapeake in the Seventeenth Century: Essays on Anglo-American Society* (Chapel Hill, 1979), 206–42.

Lois Green Carr and Lorena S. Walsh, "The Planter's Wife: The Experience of White Women in Seventeenth-Century Maryland," *William and Mary Quarterly*, 34 (1977), 542–71.

Lois Green Carr, Russell R. Menard, and Lorena S. Walsh, *Robert Cole's World: Agriculture and Society in Early Maryland* (Chapel Hill, 1991).

Wesley Frank Craven, *The Southern Colonies in the Seventeenth Century* (Baton Rouge, 1949).

Carville V. Earle, *The Evolution of a Tidewater Settlement: All Hallows Parish, Maryland, 1650–1783* (Chicago, 1975).

David W. Jordan, *Foundations of Representative Government in Maryland, 1632–1715* (Cambridge, 1987).

John D. Krugler, *English and Catholic: The Lords Baltimore in the Seventeenth Century* (Baltimore, 2004).

Aubrey C. Land, *Colonial Maryland: A History* (New York, 1981).

Aubrey C. Land, *Law, Society, and Politics in Early Maryland* (Baltimore, 1977).

Gloria L. Main, *Tobacco Colony: Life in Early Maryland, 1650–1720* (Princeton, 1982).

David B. Quinn, ed., *Early Maryland in a Wider World* (Detroit, 1982).

Russell R. Menard, *Economy and Society in Early Maryland* (New York, 1985).

Russell R. Menard, "From Servant to Freeholder: Status Mobility and Property Accumulation in Seventeenth-Century Maryland," *William and Mary Quarterly*, 30 (1973), 37–64.

Russell R. Menard, Lois Green Carr, and Lorena S. Walsh, "A Small Planter's Profits: The Cole Estate and the Growth of the Early Chesapeake Economy," *William and Mary Quarterly*, 40 (1983), 171–96.

Edward F. Terrar, *Social, Economic, and Religious Beliefs among Maryland Catholic Laboring People during the Period of the English Civil War, 1639–1660* (San Francisco, 1996).

Lorena S. Walsh, "Servitude and Opportunity in Charles County, Maryland, 1658–1705," in Aubrey C. Land et al., eds, *Law, Society, and Politics in Early Maryland* (Baltimore, 1977).

Lorena S. Walsh, "'Till Death Us Do Part': Marriage and Family in Seventeenth-Century Maryland," in Thad W. Tate and David L. Ammerman, eds, *The Chesapeake in the Seventeenth Century: Essays on Anglo-American Society* (Chapel Hill, 1979).

Lorena S. Walsh and Russell R. Menard, "Death in the Chesapeake: Two Life Tables for Men in Early Colonial Maryland," *Maryland Historical Magazine*, 49 (1974), 211–27.

The English Civil War

Carla Gardina Pestana, *The English Atlantic in an Age of Revolution, 1640–1661* (Cambridge, Mass., 2007).

New York

C. R. Boxer, *The Dutch Seaborne Empire, 1600–1800* (New York, 1965).

Thomas J. Condon, *New York Beginnings: The Commercial Origins of New Netherland* (New York, 1968).

Ada van Gastel, "Van der Donck's Description of the Indians: Additions and Corrections," *William and Mary Quarterly*, 47 (1990), 411–21.

Graham Russell Hodges, *Root and Branch: African Americans in New York and East Jersey, 1613–1863* (Chapel Hill, 1999).

Jaap Jacobs, *The Colony of New Netherland: A Dutch Settlement in Seventeenth-Century America* (Ithaca, 2009).

Francis Jennings, *The Ambiguous Iroquois Empire: The Covenant Chain Confederation of Indian Tribes with English Colonies* (London, 1984).

Michael Kammen, *Colonial New York: A History* (New York, 1975).

Donna Merwick, *Possessing Albany, 1630–1710: The Dutch and English Experience* (Cambridge, 1990).

Donna Merwick, *The Shame and the Sorrow: Dutch–Amerindian Encounters in New Netherland* (Philadelphia, 2006).

Simon Middleton, "Order and Authority in New Netherland: The 1653 Remonstrance and Early Settlement Politics," *William and Mary Quarterly*, 67 (2010), 31–68.

Daniel K. Richter and James Merrell, eds, *Beyond the Covenant Chain: The Iroquois and Their Neighbors in Indian North America, 1600–1800* (Syracuse, 1987).

Oliver A. Rink, *Holland on the Hudson: An Economic and Social History of Dutch New York* (Ithaca, 1986).

George L. Smith, *Religion and Trade in New Netherland: Dutch Origins and American Development* (Ithaca, 1973).

William Smith, *The History of the Province of New York* (London, 1757; reprinted New York, 1972).

Petrus Stuyvesant, *Correspondence, 1647–1653*, trans. Charles T. Gehring (Syracuse, 1998).

Allen W. Trelease, *Indian Affairs in Colonial New York: The Seventeenth Century* (Ithaca, 1960).

Bruce G. Trigger, "The Mohawk–Mahican War, 1624–1628: The Establishment of a Pattern," *Canadian Historical Review*, 52 (1971), 276–86.

Delaware

John A. Monroe, *Colonial Delaware: A History* (New York, 1978).

The West Indies: Seventeenth Century

Hilary McD. Beckles, "The Hub of Empire: The Caribbean and Britain in the Seventeenth Century," in Nicholas Canny, ed., *The Origins of Empire: British Overseas Enterprise to the Close of the Seventeenth Century* (Oxford, 1998), 218–40.

Richard S. Dunn, *Sugar and Slaves: The Rise of the Planter Class in the English West Indies, 1624–1713* (London, 1972).

Larry Gragg, *Englishmen Transplanted: The English Colonization of Barbados, 1627–1660* (Oxford, 2003).

Russell Menard, *Sweet Negotiations: Sugar, Slavery, and Plantation Agriculture in Early Barbados* (Charlottesville, 2006).

Richard B. Sheridan, *Sugar and Slavery: An Economic History of the British West Indies, 1623–1775* (Baltimore, 1973).

CHAPTER 6   THE RESTORATION ERA

The Return of Charles II

Robert M. Bliss, *Revolution and Empire: English Politics and the American Colonies in the Seventeenth Century* (New York, 1990).

Wesley Frank Craven, *The Colonies in Transition, 1660–1713* (New York, 1968).

J. R. Jones, *Charles II: Royal Politician* (London, 1987).

J. P. Kenyon, *Stuart England* (London, 1978).

J. M. Sosin, *English America and the Restoration Monarchy of Charles II: Transatlantic Politics, Commerce and Kinship* (Lincoln, Nebr., 1981).

The Mercantilist System

Charles M. Andrews, *The Colonial Period of American History, Vol. 4: England's Commercial and Colonial Policy* (New Haven, 1938).

Joyce Oldham Appleby, *Economic Thought and Ideology in Seventeenth-Century England* (Princeton, 1978).

Michael Braddick, *Nerves of State: Taxation and the Financing of the English State, 1558–1714* (Manchester, 1996).

Robert Brenner, *Merchants and Revolution: Commercial Change, Political Conflict, and London's Overseas Merchants, 1550–1653* (Cambridge, 1993).

K. G. Davies, *The North Atlantic World in the Seventeenth Century* (Minneapolis, 1974).

Ralph Davis, *The Rise of the Atlantic Economies* (Ithaca, 1973).

New York

Thomas J. Archdeacon, *New York City, 1661–1710: Conquest and Change* (Ithaca, 1976).

Randall H. Balmer, *A Perfect Babel of Confusion: Dutch Religion and English Culture in the Middle Colonies* (New York, 1989).

Thomas E. Burke, *Mohawk Frontier: The Dutch Community of Schenectady, New York, 1664–1710* (Ithaca, 1991).

David G. Hackett, *The Rude Hand of Innovation: Religion and Social Order in Albany, New York, 1652–1836* (New York, 1990).

Michael Kammen, *Colonial New York: A History* (New York, 1975).

Cathy Matson, "'Damned Scoundrels' and 'Libertisme of Trade': Freedom and Regulation in Colonial New York's Fur and Grain Trades," *William and Mary Quarterly*, 51 (1994), 389–418.

Robert C. Ritchie, *The Duke's Province: A Study of New York Politics and Society, 1664–1691* (Chapel Hill, 1977).

Donald G. Shomette and Robert D. Haslach, *Raid on America: The Dutch Naval Campaigns of 1672–1674* (Columbia, 1988).

George L. Smith, *Religion and Trade in New Netherland: Dutch Origins and American Development* (Ithaca, 1973).

Dennis Sullivan, *The Punishment of Crime in Colonial New York: The Dutch Experience in Albany during the Seventeenth Century* (New York, 1997).

Allen W. Trelease, *Indian Affairs in Colonial New York: The Seventeenth Century* (Ithaca, 1960).

The Carolinas

James Axtell, *The Indians' New South: Cultural Change in the Colonial Southeast* (Baton Rouge, 1997).

Judith A. Carney, *Black Rice: The African Origins of Rice Cultivation in the Americas* (Cambridge, Mass., 2001).

S. Max Edelson, *Plantation Enterprise in Colonial South Carolina* (Cambridge, Mass., 2006).

S. Max Edelson, Gwendolyn Midlo Hall, Walter Hawthorne, David Eltis, Philip Morgan, and David Richardson, "AHR Exchange: The Question of Black Rice," *American Historical Review*, 115 (2010), 123–71.

Walter Edgar, *South Carolina: A History* (Columbia, 1998).

David Eltis, Philip Morgan, and David Richardson, "Agency and Diaspora in Atlantic History: Reassessing the African Contribution to Rice Cultivation in the Americas," *American Historical Review* 112 (2007), 1329–58.

Alan Gallay, *The Indian Slave Trade: The Rise of the English Empire in the American South, 1670–1717* (New Haven, 2002).

Hugh T. Lefler and William S. Powell, *Colonial North Carolina: A History* (New York, 1973).

Daniel C. Littlefield, *Rice and Slaves: Ethnicity and the Slave Trade in Colonial South Carolina* (Baton Rouge, 1981).

Noleen McIlvenna, *A Very Mutinous People: The Struggle for North Carolina, 1660–1713* (Chapel Hill, 2009).

Donna Spindel, *Crime and Society in North Carolina, 1663–1776* (Baton Rouge, 1989).

Rebecca Starr, *A School for Politics: Commercial Lobbying and Political Culture in Early South Carolina* (Baltimore, 1998).

Clarence L. Ver Steeg, *Origins of a Southern Mosaic: Studies of Early Carolina and Georgia* (Athens, Ga., 1975).

Richard Waterhouse, "England, the Caribbean, and the Settlement of Carolina," *Journal of American Studies*, 9 (1975), 259–81.

Richard Waterhouse, *A New World Gentry: The Making of a Merchant and Planter Class in South Carolina, 1670–1770* (New York, 1989).

Robert M. Weir, *Colonial South Carolina: A History* (New York, 1983).

CHAPTER 7 THE LATER YEARS OF CHARLES II

Virginia: Bacon's Rebellion

Virginia DeJohn Anderson, *Creatures of Empire: How Domestic Animals Transformed Early America* (New York, 2004).

Warren M. Billings, ed., *The Old Dominion in the Seventeenth Century: A Documentary History of Virginia, 1606–1689* (Chapel Hill, 1975).

Warren M. Billings, John E. Selby, and Thad W. Tate, *Colonial Virginia: A History* (New York, 1986).

T. H. Breen, "A Changing Labor Force and Race Relations in Virginia," in *Puritans and Adventurers: Change and Persistence in Early America* (New York, 1980).

Kathleen Brown, *Good Wives, Nasty Wenches, and Anxious Patriarchs: Gender, Race, and Power in Colonial Virginia* (Chapel Hill, 1996).

Wesley Frank Craven, *White, Red, and Black: The Seventeenth-Century Virginian* (Charlottesville, 1971).

J. Douglas Deal, *Race and Class in Colonial Virginia: Indians, Englishmen and Africans on the Eastern Shore during the Seventeenth Century* (New York, 1993).

David W. Galenson, "The Social Origins of Some Early Americans: Rejoinder," with a reply by Mildred Campbell, *William and Mary Quarterly*, 36 (1979), 264–86.

James Horn, *Adapting to a New World: English Society in the Seventeenth-Century Chesapeake* (Chapel Hill, 1994).

James Horn, "Servant Emigration to the Chesapeake in the Seventeenth Century," in Thad W. Tate and David L. Ammerman, eds, *The Chesapeake in the Seventeenth Century: Essays on Anglo-American Society* (Chapel Hill, 1979).

Russell R. Menard, "From Servants to Slaves: The Transformation of the Chesapeake Labor System," *Southern Studies*, 16 (1977), 355–90.

Edmund S. Morgan, *American Slavery, American Freedom: The Ordeal of Colonial Virginia* (New York, 1975).

Michael Leroy Oberg, *Dominion and Civility: English Imperialism and Native America, 1585–1685* (Ithaca, 1999).

Anthony S. Parent, *Foul Means: The Formation of a Slave Society in Virginia, 1660–1740* (Chapel Hill, 2003).

Martin H. Quitt, *Virginia House of Burgesses, 1660–1706: The Social, Educational, and Economic Bases of Political Power* (New York, 1989).

John C. Rainbolt, *From Prescription to Persuasion: Manipulation of Eighteenth Century Virginia Economy* (Port Washington, 1974).

Darrett B. Rutman and Anita H. Rutman, "'Now Wives and Sons-in-Law': Parental Death in a Seventeenth-Century Virginia County," in Thad W. Tate and David L. Ammerman, eds, *The Chesapeake in the Seventeenth Century: Essays on Anglo-American Society* (Chapel Hill, 1979).

Darrett B. Rutman and Anita H. Rutman, *A Place in Time: Middlesex County, Virginia, 1650–1750* (New York, 1984).

Carole Shammas, "English-Born and Creole Elites in Turn-of-the-Century Virginia," in Thad W. Tate and David L. Ammerman, eds, *The Chesapeake in the Seventeenth Century: Essays on Anglo-American Society* (Chapel Hill, 1979).

William L. Shea, *The Virginia Militia in the Seventeenth Century* (Baton Rouge, 1983).

Stephen Saunders Webb, *1676: The End of American Independence* (New York, 1984).

Susan Westbury, "Women in Bacon's Rebellion," in Virginia Bernhard, Betty Brandon, Elizabeth Fox-Genovese, and Theda Perdue, eds, *Southern Women: Histories and Identities* (Columbia, 1992).

Massachusetts and New England

Virginia DeJohn Anderson, *Creatures of Empire: How Domestic Animals Transformed Early America* (New York, 2004).

Virginia DeJohn Anderson, "King Philip's Herds: Indians, Colonists, and the Problem of Livestock in Early New England," *William and Mary Quarterly*, 51 (1994), 601–24.

Sacvan Bercovitch, *The American Jeremiad* (Madison, Wis., 1978).

Colin G. Calloway, ed., *After King Philip's War: Presence and Persistence in Indian New England* (Hanover, NH, 1997).

James F. Cooper, Jr., *Tenacious of Their Liberties: The Congregationalist in Colonial Massachusetts* (New York, 1999).

James D. Drake, *King Philip's War: Civil War in New England, 1675–1676* (Amherst, 1999).

Richard S. Dunn, *Puritans and Yankees: The Winthrop Dynasty of New England, 1630–1717* (Princeton, 1962).

Richard P. Gildrie, *The Profane, the Civil, and the Godly: The Reformation of Manners in Orthodox New England, 1679–1749* (University Park, 1994).

Stephen Innes, *Creating the Commonwealth: The Economic Culture of Puritan New England* (New York, 1995).

Stephen Innes, "Land Tenancy and Social Order in Springfield, Massachusetts, 1652–1702," *William and Mary Quarterly*, 35 (1978), 33–56.

Francis Jennings, *The Invasion of America: Indians, Colonization and the Cant of Conquest* (Chapel Hill, 1975).

Yasuhide Kawashima, *Igniting King Philip's War: The John Sassomon Murder Trial* (Lawrence, 2001).

Benjamin W. Labaree, *Colonial Massachusetts: A History* (New York, 1979).

Jill LePore, *The Name of War: King Philip's War and the Origins of American Identity* (New York, 1999).

Patrick M. Malone, "Changing Military Technology among the Indians of Southern New England, 1600–1676," *American Quarterly*, 25 (1973), 48–63.

John Frederick Martin, *Profits in the Wilderness: Entrepreneurship and the Founding of New England Towns in the Seventeenth Century* (Chapel Hill, 1991).

Perry Miller, *The New England Mind: The Seventeenth Century* (New York, 1939).

Gerald F. Moran and Maris Vinovskis, "The Puritan Family and Religion: A Critical Reappraisal," *William and Mary Quarterly*, 39 (1982), 29–63.

Dane Morrison, *A Praying People: Massachusetts Acculturation and the Failure of the Puritan Mission, 1600–1690* (New York, 1995).

Mark A. Peterson, *The Price of Redemption: The Spiritual Economy of Puritan New England* (Stanford, 1997).

Robert G. Pope, *The Half-Way Covenant: Church Membership in Puritan New England* (Princeton, 1969).

Jenny Hale Pulsipher, "Massacre at Hurtleberry Hill: Christian Indians and English Authority in Metacom's War," *William and Mary Quarterly*, 53 (1996), 458–86.

Jenny Hale Pulsipher, *Subjects unto the Same King: Indians, English, and the Contest for Authority in Colonial New England* (Philadelphia, 2005).

David M. Scobey, "Revising the Errand: New England's Ways and the Puritan Sense of the Past," *William and Mary Quarterly*, 41 (1984), 3–31.

Richard C. Simmons, *Studies in the Massachusetts Franchise, 1631–1691* (New York, 1989).

Armstrong Starkey, *European and Native American Warfare, 1675–1815* (London, 1998).

Robert J. Taylor, *Colonial Connecticut: A History* (New York, 1979).

Mark Valeri, "Religious Discipline and the Market: Puritans and the Issue of Usury," *William and Mary Quarterly*, 54 (1997), 747–68.

Kyle Zelner, *A Rabble in Arms: Massachusetts Towns and Militiamen during King Philip's War* (New York, 2009).

New Jersey and Pennsylvania

Edwin B. Bronner, *William Penn's "Holy Experiment": The Founding of Pennsylvania, 1681–1701* (New York, 1962).

Jon Butler, "'Gospel Order Improved: The Keithian Schism and the Exercise of Quaker Ministerial Authority in Pennsylvania," *William and Mary Quarterly*, 31 (1974), 431–52.

Wesley Frank Craven, *New Jersey and the English Colonization of North America* (Princeton, 1964).

Mary Maples Dunn, *William Penn, Politics and Commerce* (Princeton, 1967).

Richard S. Dunn and Mary Maples Dunn, eds, *The World of William Penn* (Philadelphia, 1986).

M. B. Endy, Jr., *William Penn and Early Quakerism* (Princeton, 1973).

Joseph E. Illick, *Colonial Pennsylvania: A History* (New York, 1976).

Barry Levy, *Quakers and the American Family: British Settlement in the Delaware Valley* (New York, 1988).

John A. Munroe, *Colonial Delaware: A History* (New York, 1978).

Gary B. Nash, *Quakers and Politics: Pennsylvania, 1681–1726* (Princeton, 1969).

William M. Offutt, Jr., *Of "Good Laws" and "Good Men": Law and Society in the Delaware Valley, 1680–1710* (Urbana, 1995).

John E. Pomfret, *Colonial New Jersey: A History* (New York, 1973).

Jean R. Soderland et al., eds, *William Penn and the Founding of Pennsylvania, 1680–1684: A Documentary History* (Philadelphia, 1983).

Thomas Sugrue, "The Peopling and Depeopling of Early Pennyslvania: Indians and Colonists, 1680–1720," *Pennsylvania Magazine of History and Biography*, 116 (1992), 3–31.

CHAPTER 8   JAMES II AND THE GLORIOUS REVOLUTION

England and General Accounts

M. Ashley, *James II* (London, 1977).

J. Childs, *The Army, James II and the Glorious Revolution* (Manchester, 1980).

Richard R. Johnson, "The Imperial Webb: The Thesis of Garrison Government in Early America Considered," *William and Mary Quarterly*, 43 (1986), 408–30.

J. R. Jones, *The Revolution of 1688 in England* (London, 1972).

David S. Lovejoy, *The Glorious Revolution in America* (New York, 1972).

Brendan McConville, *The King's Three Faces: The Rise and Fall of Royal America, 1688–1776* (Chapel Hill, 2006).

Carla Gardina Pestana, *Protestant Empire: Religion and the Making of the Atlantic World* (Philadelphia, 2009).

J. M. Sosin, *English America and the Revolution of 1688* (Lincoln, Nebr., 1982).

Owen Stanwood, "The Protestant Moment: Antipopery, the Revolution of 1688–1689, and the Making of an Anglo-American Empire," *Journal of British Studies*, 46 (2007), 481–508.

Ian Steele, "Governors or Generals? A Note on Martial Law and the Revolution of 1689 in English America," *William and Mary Quarterly*, 46 (1989), 304–14.

Stephen Saunders Webb, "Army and Empire: English Garrison Government in Britain and America, 1569–1763," *William and Mary Quarterly*, 34 (1977), 1–31.

Stephen Saunders Webb, "The Data and Theory of Restoration Empire," *William and Mary Quarterly*, 43 (1986), 431–59.

Stephen Saunders Webb, *The Governors-General: The English Army and the Definition of Empire, 1569–1681* (Chapel Hill, 1979).

Stephen Saunders Webb, *Lord Churchill's Coup: The Anglo-American Empire and the Glorious Revolution Reconsidered* (New York, 1995).

J. R. Western, *Monarchy and Revolution: The English State in the 1680s* (London, 1972).

Massachusetts

Bernard Bailyn, *The New England Merchants in the Seventeenth Century* (Cambridge, Mass., 1955).

Michael G. Hall, *The Last American Puritan: The Life of Increase Mather* (Middletown, 1987).

Richard R. Johnson, *Adjustment to Empire: The New England Colonies, 1675–1715* (New Brunswick, 1981).

Benjamin W. Labaree, *Colonial Massachusetts: A History* (New York, 1979).

David Levin, *Cotton Mather: The Young Life of the Lord's Remembrancer, 1663–1703* (Cambridge, Mass., 1978).

Robert Middlekauf, *The Mathers: Three Generations of Puritan Intellectuals, 1596–1728* (New York, 1971).

Michael J. Puglisi, *Puritans Besieged: The Legacies of King Philip's War in the Massachusetts Bay Colony* (Lanham, 1991).

New York

Joyce D. Goodfriend, *Before the Melting Pot: Society and Culture in Colonial New York City, 1664–1730* (Princeton, 1991).

Adrian Howe, "The Bayard Treason Trial: Dramatizing Anglo-Dutch Politics in Early Eighteenth-Century New York City," *William and Mary Quarterly*, 47 (1990), 57–89.

Michael Kammen, *Colonial New York: A History* (New York, 1975).

Charles H. McCormick, *Leisler's Rebellion* (New York, 1989).

Donna Merwick, "Becoming English: Anglo-Dutch Conflict in the 1670s in Albany, New York," *New York History*, 42 (1981), 389–414.

Donna Merwick, *Possessing Albany, 1630–1710: The Dutch and English Experience* (Cambridge, 1990).

John M. Murrin, "English Rights as Ethnic Aggression: The English Conquest, the Charter of Liberties of 1683, and Leisler's Rebellion in New York," in William Pencak and Conrad Edick Wright, eds, *Authority and Resistance in Early New York* (New York, 1988), 56–94.

Robert C. Ritchie, *The Duke's Province: A Study of New York Politics and Society, 1664–1691* (Chapel Hill, 1977).

David William Voorhees, "The 'Fervent Zeale' of Jacob Leisler," *William and Mary Quarterly*, 51 (1994), 447–72.

Maryland

Lois Green Carr and David William Jordan, *Maryland's Revolution of Government, 1689–1692* (Ithaca, 1974).

David W. Jordan, *Foundations of Representative Government in Maryland, 1632–1715* (New York, 1988).

Aubrey C. Land, *Colonial Maryland: A History* (New York, 1981).

Aubrey C. Land, Lois Green Carr, and Edward C. Papenfuse, eds, *Law, Society, and Politics in Early Maryland* (Baltimore, 1977).

Russell R. Menard, *Economy and Society in Early Colonial Maryland* (New York, 1985).

Lorena S. Walsh, "Staying Put or Getting Out: Findings for Charles County, Maryland, 1650–1720," *William and Mary Quarterly*, 44 (1987), 89–103.

CHAPTER 9   THE ERAS OF WILLIAM AND MARY, AND QUEEN ANNE

British Imperial Policy

J. M. Sosin, *English America and Imperial Inconstancy: The Rise of Provincial Autonomy, 1696–1715* (Lincoln, Nebr., 1985).

J. M. Sosin, *English America and the Revolution of 1688: Royal Administration and the Structure of Provincial Government* (Lincoln, Nebr., 1982).

I. K. Steele, *Politics of Colonial Policy: The Board of Trade in Colonial Administration, 1696–1720* (New York, 1968).

The Wars of William and Anne

Emerson W. Baker and John G. Reid, *The New England Knight: Sir William Phips, 1651–1695* (Toronto, 1998).

John Demos, *The Unredeemed Captive: A Family Story from Early America* (New York, 1994).

Peter A. Dorsey, "Going to School with Savages: Authorship and Authority among the Jesuits of New France," *William and Mary Quarterly*, 55 (1998), 399–420.

Evan Haefeli and Kevin Sweeney, *Captors and Captives: The 1704 French and Indian Raid on Deerfield* (Amherst, 2003).

Philip S. Haffenden, *New England in the English Nation, 1689–1713* (Oxford, 1973).

Gilles Havard, *The Great Peace of Montreal of 1701: French–Native Diplomacy in the Seventeenth Century* (Montréal, 2001).

Eric Hinderaker, "The 'Four Indian Kings' and the Imaginative Construction of the First British Empire," *William and Mary Quarterly*, 53 (1996), 487–526.

Richard R. Johnson, *Adjustment to Empire: The New England Colonies, 1675–1715* (New Brunswick, 1981).

Douglas Edward Leach, *Arms for Empire: A Military History of the British Colonies in North America, 1607–1763* (New York, 1973).

Douglas Edward Leach, *The Northern Colonial Frontier, 1607–1763* (New York, 1966).

Richard I. Melvoin, *New England Outpost: War and Society in Colonial Deerfield* (New York, 1989).

Marcus Rediker, *Between the Devil and the Deep Blue Sea: Merchant Seamen, Pirates and the Anglo-American Maritime World, 1700–1750* (Cambridge, 1987).

Daniel K. Richter, "Cultural Brokers and Intercultural Politics: New York–Iroquois Relations, 1664–1701," *Journal of American History*, 75 (1988–9), 40–67.

Robert C. Ritchie, *Captain Kidd and the War against the Pirates* (Cambridge, Mass., 1986).

John D. Runcie, "The Problem of Anglo-American Politics in Bellomont's New York," *William and Mary Quarterly*, 26 (1969), 191–217.

The Salem Witchcraft Trials

Paul Boyer and Stephen Nissenbaum, *Salem Possessed: The Social Origins of Witchcraft* (Cambridge, Mass., 1974).

Paul Boyer and Stephen Nissenbaum, eds, *The Salem Witchcraft Papers: Verbatim Transcripts of the Legal Documents of the Salem Witchcraft Outbreak of 1692*, 3 vols (New York, 1977).

Elaine G. Breslaw, *Tituba, Reluctant Witch of Salem: Devilish Indians and Puritan Fantasies* (New York, 1996).

Laurie Winn Carlson, *A Fever in Salem* (Chicago, 2000).

John P. Demos, *Entertaining Satan: Witchcraft and the Culture of Early New England* (New York, 1982).

John P. Demos, "John Godfrey and His Neighbors: Witchcraft and the Social Web in Colonial Massachusetts," *William and Mary Quarterly*, 33 (1976), 242–65.

John P. Demos, "Underlying Themes in the Witchcraft of Seventeenth-Century New England," *American Historical Review*, 75 (1970), 1311–26.

Richard P. Gildrie, *Salem, Massachusetts, 1626–1683: A Covenant Community* (Charlottesville, 1975).

Richard Godbeer, *The Devil's Dominion: Magic and Religion in Early New England* (New York, 1992).

Richard Godbeer, *Escaping Salem: The Other Witch Hunt of 1692* (New York, 2004).

Larry Gragg, *The Salem Witch Crisis* (Westport, 1992).

David D. Hall, "Witchcraft and the Limits of Interpretation," *New England Quarterly*, 58 (1985), 253–81.

David D. Hall, *Witch Hunting in Seventeenth-Century New England: A Documentary History, 1638–1692* (Boston, 1990).

Peter Charles Hoffer, *The Devil's Disciples: Makers of the Salem Witchcraft Trials* (Baltimore, 1996).

Peter Charles Hoffer, *The Salem Witchcraft Trials: A Legal History* (Lawrence, 1997).

Carol F. Karlsen, *The Devil in the Shape of a Woman: Witchcraft in Colonial New England* (New York, 1987).

Richard Latner, "Salem Witchcraft, Factionalism, and Social Change Reconsidered: Were Salem's Witch-Hunters Modernization's Failures?" *William and Mary Quarterly*, 65 (2008), 423–48.

Bryan F. Le Beau, *The Story of the Salem Witch Trials: "We Walked in Clouds and Could Not See Our Way"* (Upper Saddle River, 1998).

Mary Beth Norton, *In the Devil's Snare: The Salem Witchcraft Crisis of 1692* (New York, 2002).

Benjamin Ray, "The Geography of Witchcraft Accusations in 1692 Salem Village," *William and Mary Quarterly*, 65 (2008), 449–78.

Elizabeth Reis, *Damned Women: Sinners and Witches in Puritan New England* (Ithaca, 1997).

Bernard Rosenthal, *Salem Story: Reading the Witch Trials of 1692* (Cambridge, 1993).

Keith Thomas, *Religion and the Decline of Magic* (New York, 1971).

Richard Weisman, *Witchcraft, Magic and Religion in Seventeenth-Century Massachusetts* (Amherst, 1984).

The Carolinas

Converse D. Clowse, *Economic Beginnings in Colonial South Carolina, 1670–1730* (Columbia, 1971).

Alan Gallay, *The Indian Slave Trade: The Rise of the English Empire in the American South, 1670–1717* (New Haven, 2002).

Richard Haan, "'The Trade Does Not Flourish as Formerly': The Ecological Origins of the Yamasee War of 1715," *Ethnohistory*, 28 (1981), 341–58.

Hugh T. Lefler and William S. Powell, *Colonial North Carolina: A History* (New York, 1973).

Harry Roy Merrens, *Colonial North Carolina: A Study in Historical Geography* (Chapel Hill, 1964).

H. Roy Merrens, ed., *The Colonial South Carolina Scene: Contemporary Views, 1697–1774* (Columbia, 1977).

Steven J. Oates, *A Colonial Complex: South Carolina's Frontiers in the Era of the Yamasee War, 1680–1730* (Lincoln, Nebr., 2004).

William Ramsey, *The Yamasee War: A Study of Culture, Economy, and Conflict in the Colonial South* (Lincoln, Nebr., 2008).

M. Eugene Sirmans, *Colonial South Carolina: A Political History, 1663–1763* (Chapel Hill, 1966).

Clarence L. Ver Steeg, *Origins of a Southern Mosaic: Studies of Early Carolina and Georgia* (Athens, Ga., 1975).

Peter H. Wood, *Black Majority: Negroes in Colonial South Carolina from 1670 through the Stono Rebellion* (New York, 1974).

Pennsylvania

Richard S. Dunn and Mary Maples Dunn, eds, *The World of William Penn* (Philadelphia, 1986).

J. William Frost, *A Perfect Freedom: Religious Liberty in Pennsylvania* (New York, 1990).

Ned C. Landsman, "The Middle Colonies: New Opportunities for Settlement, 1660–1700," in Nicholas Canny, ed., *The Origins of Empire: British Overseas Enterprise to the Close of the Seventeenth Century* (New York, 1998), 351–74.

Gary B. Nash, *Quakers and Politics: Pennsylvania, 1681–1726* (Princeton, 1968).

Frederick B. Tolles, *Meeting House and Counting House: The Quaker Merchants of Colonial Philadelphia, 1682–1763* (Chapel Hill, 1948).

Frederick B. Tolles, *Quakers and the Atlantic Culture* (New York, 1960).

CHAPTER 10   THE ECONOMY AND LABOR SYSTEM IN BRITISH NORTH AMERICA

General

Peter Coclanis, ed., *The Atlantic Economy during the Seventeenth and Eighteenth Centuries: Organization, Operation, Practice, and Personnel* (Columbia, 2005).

Marc Egnal, *Divergent Paths: How Culture and Institutions Have Shaped North American Growth* (New York, 1996).

Marc Egnal, "The Economic Development of the Thirteen Continental Colonies, 1720–1775," *William and Mary Quarterly*, 32 (1975), 191–218.

Marc Egnal, *New World Economies: The Growth of the Thirteen Colonies and Early Canada* (New York, 1998).

Stanley L. Engerman and Robert E. Gallman, eds, The Cambridge Economic History of the United States, Vol. 1: *The Colonial Era* (Cambridge, 1996).

David W. Galenson, *White Servitude in Colonial America: An Economic Analysis* (New York, 1981).

Nancy F. Koehn, *The Power of Commerce: Economy and Governance in the First British Empire* (Ithaca, 1994).

John J. McCusker, *Essays in the Economic History of the Atlantic World* (New York, 1997).

John J. McCusker and Russell R. Menard, *The Economy of British North America, 1607–1789* (Chapel Hill, 1985).

John J. McCusker and Kenneth Morgan, *The Early Modern Atlantic Economy* (Cambridge, 2001).

Judith A. McGaw, ed., *Early American Technology: Making and Doing Things from the Colonial Era to 1850* (Chapel Hill, 1994).

Cathy Matson, ed., *The Economy of Early America: Historical Perspectives and New Directions* (University Park, 2006).

Michael Merrill, "Putting 'Capitalism' in Its Place: A Review of Recent Literature," *William and Mary Quarterly*, 52 (1995), 315–26.

Edwin J. Perkins, *The Economy of Colonial America* (New York, 1988).

Ian K. Steele, *The English Atlantic, 1675–1740: An Exploration of Communication and Community* (New York, 1986).

Gary M. Walton and James F. Shepherd, *The Economic Rise of Early America* (New York, 1979).

James Walvin, *Fruits of Empire: Exotic Produce and British Trade, 1660–1800* (Basingstoke, 1997).

The Southern Plantation System

Richard R. Beeman, *The Evolution of the Southern Backcountry: A Case Study of Lunenburg County, Virginia, 1746–1832* (Philadelphia, 1984).

T. H. Breen, *Tobacco Culture: The Mentality of the Great Tidewater Planters on the Eve of the Revolution* (Princeton, 1985).

Trevor Burnard, *Creole Gentlemen: The Maryland Elite, 1691–1776* (New York, 2002).

Joyce Chaplin, *An Anxious Pursuit: Agricultural Innovation and Modernity in the Lower South, 1730–1815* (Chapel Hill, 1993).

Paul G. E. Clemens, *The Atlantic Economy and Colonial Maryland's Eastern Shore: From Tobacco to Grain* (Ithaca, 1980).

D. L. Coon, "Eliza Lucas Pinckney and the Reintroduction of Indigo Culture in South Carolina," *Journal of Southern History*, 42 (1976), 61–76.

Christine Daniels, "'WANTED: A Blacksmith who Understands Plantation Work': Artisans in Maryland, 1700–1810," *William and Mary Quarterly*, 50 (1993), 743–67.

Max Edelson, *Plantation Enterprise in Colonial South Carolina* (Cambridge, Mass., 2006).

A. Roger Ekirch, "Bound for America: A Profile of British Convicts Transported to the Colonies, 1718–1775," *William and Mary Quarterly*, 42 (1985), 184–200.

A. Roger Ekirch, *Bound for America: The Transportation of British Convicts to the Colonies, 1718–1775* (Oxford, 1987).

Charles Farmer, *In the Absence of Towns: Settlement and Country Trade in Southside Virginia, 1730–1800* (Lanham, 1993).

David W. Galenson, *Traders, Planters, and Slaves: Market Behavior in Early English America* (Cambridge, 1986).

Laura Croghan Kamoie, *Irons in the Fire: The Business History of the Tayloe Family and Virginia's Gentry, 1700–1860* (Charlottesville, 2007).

David Klingaman, "The Significance of Grain in the Development of the Tobacco Colonies," *Journal of Economic History*, 29 (1969), 269–78.

Allan Kulikoff, "Households and Markets: Toward a New Synthesis of American Agrarian History," *William and Mary Quarterly*, 50 (1993), 342–55.

Allan Kulikoff, *Tobacco and Slaves: The Development of Southern Cultures in the Chesapeake, 1680–1800* (Chapel Hill, 1986).

Johanna Miller Lewis, *Artisans in the North Carolina Backcountry* (Lexington, Ky., 1995).

Daniel C. Littlefield, *Rice and Slaves: Ethnicity and the Slave Trade in Colonial South Carolina* (Baton Rouge, 1981).

Russell R. Menard, "From Servants to Slaves: The Transformation of the Chesapeake Labor System," *Southern Studies*, 16 (1977), 355–90.

Kenneth Morgan, "The Organization of the Colonial American Rice Trade," *William and Mary Quarterly*, 52 (1995), 433–52.

Jacob M. Price, *Capital and Credit in British Overseas Trade: The View from the Chesapeake, 1700–1776* (Cambridge, Mass., 1980).

Mary M. Schweitzer, "Economic Regulation and the Colonial Economy: The Maryland Tobacco Inspection Act of 1747," *Journal of Economic History*, 40 (1980), 551–69.

Lorena Walsh, *Motives of Honor, Pleasure, and Profit: Plantation Management in the Colonial Chesapeake, 1607–1763* (Chapel Hill, 2010).

Betty Wood, *Women's Work, Men's Work: The Informal Slave Economies of Lowcountry Georgia* (Athens, Ga., 1995).

Northern Farming and Commerce

Bernard Bailyn and Lotte Bailyn, *Massachusetts Shipping, 1697–1714* (Cambridge, Mass., 1959).

Richard Lyman Bushman, "Markets and Composite Farms in Early America," *William and Mary Quarterly*, 55 (1998), 351–74.

Charles F. Carroll, *The Timber Economy of Puritan New England* (Providence, 1973).

Jay Coughtry, *The Notorious Triangle: Rhode Island and the American Slave Trade, 1700–1807* (Philadelphia, 1981).

Bruce C. Daniels, "Economic Development in Colonial and Revolutionary Connecticut: An Overview," *William and Mary Quarterly*, 37 (1980), 429–50.

Henry A. Gemery and Jan S. Hogendorn, eds, *The Uncommon Market: Essays in the Economic History of the Atlantic Slave Trade* (New York, 1979).

Joseph A. Goldenberg, *Shipbuilding in Colonial America* (Charlottesville, 1976).

Ellen Hartigan-O'Connor, *The Ties that Buy: Women and Commerce in Revolutionary America* (Philadelphia, 2009).

James A. Henretta, "Families and Farms: *Mentalité* in Pre-industrial America," *William and Mary Quarterly*, 35 (1978), 3–32.

Adrienne D. Hood, "The Material World of Cloth: Production and Use in Eighteenth-Century Rural Pennsylvania," *William and Mary Quarterly*, 53 (1996), 43–66.

Stephen Innes, ed., *Work and Labor in Early America* (Chapel Hill, 1988).

Sung Bok Kim, *Landlord and Tenant in Colonial New York: Manorial Society, 1664–1775* (Chapel Hill, 1978).

Allan Kulikoff, "The Transition to Capitalism in Rural America," *William and Mary Quarterly*, 46 (1989), 120–44.

James T. Lemon, *The Best Poor Man's Country: A Geographical Study of Early Southeastern Pennsylvania* (Baltimore, 1972).

Barry Levy, *Town Born: The Political Economy of New England Towns from Their Settlement to the Revolution* (Philadelphia, 2009).

John J. McCusker, *Rum and the American Revolution: The Rum Trade and the Balance of Payments of the Thirteen Continental Colonies* (New York, 1989).

Cathy Matson, *Merchants and Empire: Trading in Colonial New York* (Baltimore, 1998).

Michael Merrill, "Cash is Good to Eat: Self-Sufficiency and Exchange in the Rural Economy of the United States," *Radical History Review*, 4 (1977), 42–69.

John M. Murrin and Rowland Bertoff, "Feudalism, Communalism, and the Yeoman Freeholder: The American Revolution Considered as a Social Accident," in Stephen G. Kurtz and James H. Hutson, eds, *Essays on the American Revolution* (Chapel Hill, 1973).

Margaret Ellen Newell, *From Dependency to Independence: Economic Revolution in Colonial New England* (Ithaca, 1998).

Gilman M. Ostrander, "The Making of the Triangular Trade Myth," *William and Mary Quarterly*, 30 (1973), 635–44.

Richard Pares, *Yankees and Creoles: The Trade between North America and the West Indies before the American Revolution* (Cambridge, 1956).

Bettye Hobbs Pruitt, "Self-sufficiency and the Agricultural Economy of Eighteenth-Century Massachusetts," *William and Mary Quarterly*, 41 (1984), 333–64.

Marcus Rediker, *Between the Devil and the Deep Blue Sea: Merchant Seamen, Pirates, and the Anglo-American Maritime World, 1700–1750* (New York, 1987).

Winifred B. Rothenberg, "The Emergence of a Capital Market in Rural Massachusetts, 1730–1838," *Journal of Economic History*, 45 (1985), 796–99.

Winifred B. Rothenberg, *From Market-Places to a Market Economy: The Transformation of Rural Massachusetts, 1750–1850* (Chicago, 1992).

Sharon V. Salinger, *"To Serve Well and Faithfully": Labor and Indentured Servants in Pennsylvania, 1682–1800* (New York, 1987).

Ronald Schultz, *The Republic of Labor: Philadelphia Artisans and the Politics of Class* (Oxford, 1993).

Max George Schumacher, *The Northern Farmer and His Markets during the Colonial Period* (New York, 1975).

Mary M. Schweitzer, *Custom and Contract: Household, Government and the Economy in Colonial Pennsylvania* (New York, 1987).

Daniel Vickers, *Farmers and Fishermen: Two Centuries of Work in Essex County, Massachusetts, 1630–1850* (Chapel Hill, 1994).

Peter O. Wacker and Paul G. E. Clements, *Land Use in Early New Jersey: A Historical Geography* (Newark, NJ, 1993).

The Mercantilist System

Thomas C. Barrow, *Trade and Empire: The British Customs Service in Colonial America, 1660–1776* (Cambridge, Mass., 1967).

Curtis P. Nettels, "British Mercantilism and the Economic Development of the Thirteen Colonies," *Journal of Economic History*, 12 (1952), 105–14.

Alison G. Olson, "The Board of Trade and London–American Interest Groups in the Eighteenth Century," *Journal of Imperial and Commonwealth History*, 8 (1980), 33–50.

David R. Owen and Michael C. Tolley, *Courts of Admiralty in Colonial America: The Maryland Experience, 1634–1776* (Durham, NC, 1995).

James F. Shepherd and Gary M. Walton, *Shipping, Maritime Trade, and the Economic Development of Colonial North America* (Cambridge, 1972).

Ian K. Steele, *The English Atlantic, 1675–1740: An Exploration of Communication and Community* (New York, 1986).

Thomas M. Truxes, *Irish–American Trade, 1660–1783* (New York, 1989).

Money and Currency

Leslie V. Brock, *The Currency of the American Colonies, 1700–1764: A Study in Colonial Finance and Imperial Relations* (New York, 1975).

John J. McCusker, *Money and Exchange in Europe and America, 1600–1775: A Handbook* (Chapel Hill, 1978).

Robert Craig West, "Money in the Colonial American Economy," *Economic Inquiry*, 16 (1978), 1–15.

Poverty and Prosperity

T. H. Breen, "Baubles of Britain: The American and Consumer Revolutions of the Eighteenth Century," *Past and Present*, 119 (1988), 73–104.

T. H. Breen, *The Marketplace of Revolution: How Consumer Politics Shaped American Independence* (New York, 2004).

Cary Carson, Ronald Hoffman, and Peter J. Albert, eds, *Of Consuming Interests: The Style of Life in the Eighteenth Century* (Charlottesville, 1994).

Robert E. Cray, Jr., *Paupers and Poor Relief in New York City and Its Rural Environs, 1700–1830* (Philadelphia, 1988).

Alice Hanson Jones, *Wealth of a Nation To Be: The American Colonies on the Eve of the Revolution* (New York, 1980).

David Harvey and Gregory Brown, *Common People and Their Material World: Free Men and Women in the Chesapeake, 1700–1830* (Williamsburg, 1995).

Douglas Lamar Jones, "The Strolling Poor: Transiency in Eighteenth-Century Massachusetts," *Journal of Social History*, 8 (1975), 28–49.

James T. Lemon and Gary B. Nash, "The Distribution of Wealth in Eighteenth-Century America: A Century of Change in Chester County, Pennsylvania, 1693–1802," *Journal of Social History*, 2 (1968), 1–24.

Gloria L. Main, "Inequality in Early America: The Evidence from Probate Records of Massachusetts and Maryland," *Journal of Interdisciplinary History*, 7 (1977), 559–82.

Gary B. Nash, "Poverty and Poor Relief in Pre-Revolutionary Philadelphia," *William and Mary Quarterly*, 33 (1976), 3–30.

Gary B. Nash, *The Urban Crucible: Social Change, Political Consciousness, and the Origins of the American Revolution* (Cambridge, Mass., 1979).

Simon Newman, *Embodied History: The Lives of the Poor in Early Philadelphia* (Philadelphia, 2003).

Carla Gardina Pestana and Sharon V. Salinger, eds, *Inequality in Early America* (Hanover, NH, 1999).

Carole Shammas, *The Pre-industrial Consumer in England and America* (New York, 1990).

Lucy Simler, "Tenancy in Colonial Pennsylvania: The Case of Chester County," *William and Mary Quarterly*, 43 (1986), 543–69.

Billy G. Smith, *The "Lower Sort": Philadelphia's Laboring People, 1750–1800* (Ithaca, 1990).

Billy G. Smith, ed., *Down and Out in Early America* (University Park, 2004).

Gregory A. Stiverson, *Poverty in a Land of Plenty: Tenancy in Eighteenth-Century Maryland* (Baltimore, 1977).

Daniel Vickers, "Competency and Competition: Economic Culture in Early America," *William and Mary Quarterly*, 47 (1990), 3–29.

Lorena S. Walsh et al., "Toward a History of the Standard of Living in British North America," *William and Mary Quarterly*, 45 (1988), 116–70.

CHAPTER 11   SETTLER FAMILIES AND SOCIETY

General

James A. Henretta et al., eds, *The Transformation of Early American History: Society, Authority, and Ideology* (New York, 1991).

Ronald Hoffman, Mechal Sobel, and Fredrika Teute, eds, *Through a Glass Darkly: Reflections on Personal Identity in Early America* (Chapel Hill, 1997).

Families and Gender Relations within Families

Linda Auwers Bissell, "From One Generation to Another: Mobility in Seventeenth-Century Windsor, Connecticut," *William and Mary Quarterly*, 31 (1974), 79–110.

Kathleen Brown, *Good Wives, Nasty Wenches, and Anxious Patriarchs: Gender, Race and Power in Colonial Virginia* (Chapel Hill, 1996).

John Demos, *A Little Commonwealth: Family Life in Plymouth Colony* (New York, 1970).

John Demos, *Past, Present, and Personal: The Family and the Life Course in American History* (New York, 1986).

Firth Haring Fabend, *A Dutch Family in the Middle Colonies, 1660–1800* (New Brunswick, 1989).

David Hackett Fischer, *Growing Old in America* (New York, 1977).

David H. Flaherty, *Privacy in Colonial New England* (Charlottesville, 1972).

Jay Fliegelman, *Prodigals and Pilgrims: The American Revolution against Patriarchal Authority, 1750–1800* (New York, 1982).

Vivian C. Fox and Martin H. Quitt, *Loving, Parenting, and Dying: The Family Cycle in England and America, Past and Present* (New York, 1980).

J. William Frost, *The Quaker Family in Colonial America: A Portrait of the Society of Friends* (New York, 1973).

Philip J. Greven, Jr., *Four Generations: Population, Land, and Family in Colonial Andover, Massachusetts* (Ithaca, 1970).

Philip J. Greven, Jr., "Historical Demography and Colonial America," *William and Mary Quarterly*, 24 (1967), 438–54.

Michael Haines and Richard H. Steckel, eds, *A Population History of North America* (Cambridge, 2000).

Ronald Hoffman, Salley Mason, and Eleanor Darcy, eds, *Dear Papa, Dear Charley: The Peregrinations of a Revolutionary Aristocrat, as Told by Charles Carroll of Carrollton and His Father, Charles Carroll of Annapolis . . .* (Chapel Hill, 2001).

Rhys Isaac, *Landon Carter's Uneasy Kingdom: Revolution and Rebellion on a Virginia Plantation* (New York, 2004).

Winthrop D. Jordan and Sheila L. Skemp, eds, *Race and Family in the Colonial South* (Jackson, 1987).

Susan Klepp, *Revolutionary Conceptions: Women, Fertility, and Family Limitation in America, 1760–1820* (Chapel Hill, 2009).

Peter Laslett, ed., *Household and Family in Past Time: Comparative Studies in the Size and Structure of the Domestic Group* (Cambridge, 1972).

Gerda Lerner, *The Creation of Patriarchy* (Oxford, 1986).

Barry Levy, "The Birth of the 'Modern Family' in Early America: Quaker and Anglican Familes in the Delaware Valley, Pennsylvania, 1681–1750," in Michael Zuckerman, ed., *Friends and Neighbors: Group Life in America's First Plural Society* (Philadelphia, 1982), 26–56.

Barry Levy, *Quakers and the American Family: British Settlement in the Delaware Valley* (New York, 1988).

Jan Lewis, "Domestic Tranquility and the Management of Emotion among the Gentry of Pre-Revolutionary Virginia," *William and Mary Quarterly*, 39 (1982), 135–49.

Jan Lewis, *The Pursuit of Happiness: Family and Values in Jefferson's Virginia* (New York, 1983).

Kenneth A. Lockridge, *On the Sources of Patriarchal Rage: The Commonplace Books of William Byrd and Thomas Jefferson and the Gendering of Power in the Eighteenth Century* (New York, 1992).

Anne Lombard, *Making Manhood: Growing Up Male in Colonial New England* (Cambridge, Mass., 2003).

Gloria Main, *Peoples of a Spacious Land: Families and Cultures in Colonial New England* (Cambridge, Mass., 2001).

Gerald R. Moran and Maris A. Vinovskis, *Religion, Family, and the Life Course: Explorations in the Social History of Early America* (Ann Arbor, 1992).

Edmund S. Morgan, *The Puritan Family: Religion and Domestic Relations in Seventeenth-Century New England* (New York, 1966).

David E. Narrett, *Inheritance and Family Life in Colonial New York City* (Ithaca, 1992).

David J. Russo, *Families and Communities: A New View of American History* (Nashville, 1974).

Carole Shammas, "Anglo-American Household Government in Comparative Perspective," *William and Mary Quarterly*, 52 (1995), 104–44.

Carole Shammas, *A History of Household Government in America* (Charlottesville, 2002).

Daniel Blake Smith, *Inside the Great House: Planter Family Life in Eighteenth-Century Chesapeake Society* (Ithaca, 1980).

Daniel Blake Smith, "The Study of the Family in Early America: Trends, Problems, and Prospects," *William and Mary Quarterly*, 39 (1982), 3–28.

Daniel Scott Smith, "The Demographic History of Colonial New England," *Journal of Economic History*, 32 (1972), 165–83.

Daniel Scott Smith, "Parental Power and Marriage Patterns: An Analysis of Historical Trends in Hingham, Massachusetts," *Journal of Marriage and the Family*, 35 (1973), 406–18.

Daniel Scott Smith, "A Perspective on Demographic Methods and Effects in Social History," *William and Mary Quarterly*, 39 (1982), 442–68.

Lawrence Stone, *The Family, Sex, and Marriage in England, 1500–1800* (New York, 1977).

Helena M. Wall, *Fierce Communion: Family and Community in Early America* (Cambridge, Mass., 1990).

John J. Waters, Jr., "Family, Inheritance, and Migration in Colonial New England: The Evidence from Guilford, Connecticut," *William and Mary Quarterly*, 39 (1982), 64–86.

John J. Waters, Jr., "Patrimony, Succession, and Social Stability: Guilford, Connecticut in the Eighteenth Century," *Perspectives in American History*, 10 (1976), 131–60.

Robert V. Wells, "Demographic Change and the Life Cycle of American Families," *Journal of Interdisciplinary History*, 11 (1971), 273–82.

Lisa Wilson, *Ye Heart of a Man: Domestic Life of Men in Colonial New England* (New Haven, 1999).

E. A. Wrigley and R. S. Schofield, *The Population History of England, 1541–1871: A Reconstruction* (London, 1981).

Children and Childhood

Gillian Avery, *Behold the Child: American Children and their Books, 1621–1922* (Baltimore, 1992).

Ross W. Beales, Jr., "In Search of the Historical Child: Miniature Adulthood and Youth in Colonial New England," *American Quarterly*, 27 (1975), 378–98.

Holly Brewer, *By Birth or Consent: Children, Law, and the Anglo-American Revolution in Authority* (Chapel Hill, 2005).

Karin Calvert, *Children in the House: The Material Culture of Early Childhood, 1600–1900* (Boston, 1992).

John Demos, *Spare the Child: The Religious Roots of Punishment and the Psychological Impact of Physical Abuse* (New York, 1991).

Philip J. Greven, *The Protestant Temperament: Patterns of Child Rearing, Religious Experience, and the Self in Early America* (New York, 1977).

Barry J. Levy, "'Tender Plants': Quaker Farmers and Children in the Delaware Valley, 1681–1735," *Journal of Family History*, 3 (1978), 116–35.

Peter Gregg Slater, *Children in the New England Mind in Death and in Life* (Hamden, 1977).

Nancy Hathaway Steenburg, *Children and the Criminal Law in Connecticut, 1635–1855: Changing Perceptions of Childhood* (New York, 2005).

Glenn Wallach, *Obedient Sons: The Discourse of Youth and Generations in American Culture, 1630–1860* (Amherst, 1997).

Sexuality

Ruth Bloch, "Changing Conceptions of Sexuality and Romance in Eighteenth-Century America," *William and Mary Quarterly*, 60 (2003), 13–42.

Thomas Foster, *Sex and the Eighteenth-Century Man: Massachusetts and the History of Sexuality in America* (Boston, 2006).

Richard Godbeer, *Sexual Revolution in Early America* (Baltimore, 2002).

Susan E. Klepp, "Lost, Hidden, Obstructed, and Repressed: Contraceptive and Abortive Technology in the Early Delaware Valley," in Judith A. McGaw, ed., *Early American Technology: Making and Doing Things from the Colonial Era to 1850* (Chapel Hill, 1994).

Clare Lyons, *Sex among the Rabble: An Intimate History of Gender and Power in the Age of Revolution, Philadelphia, 1730–1830* (Chapel Hill, 2006).

Daniel Scott Smith and M. S. Hindus, "Premarital Pregnancy in America, 1640–1971: An Overview and Interpretation," *Journal of Interdisciplinary History*, 5 (1975), 537–70.

Merril D. Smith, *Sex and Sexuality in Early America* (New York, 1998).

Roger Thompson, *Sex in Middlesex: Popular Mores in a Massachusetts County, 1649–1699* (Amherst, 1986).

Social Structure and Status

Holly Brewer, "Entailing Aristocracy in Colonial Virginia: 'Ancient Feudal Restraints' and Revolutionary Reform," *William and Mary Quarterly*, 54 (1997), 307–46.

Robert E. Brown, *Middle-Class Democracy and the Revolution in Massachusetts, 1691–1780* (Ithaca, 1955).

Lois Green Carr, Philip D. Morgan, and Jean B. Russo, eds, *Colonial Chesapeake Society* (Chapel Hill, 1989).

John Cary, "Statistical Method and the Brown Thesis on Colonial Democracy," *William and Mary Quarterly*, 20 (1963), 251–76.

Edward Countryman, "Stability and Class, Theory and History: The South in the Eighteenth Century," *Journal of American Studies*, 17 (1983), 243–50.

Bruce C. Daniels, ed., *Power and Status: Office Holding in Colonial America* (Middletown, 1986).

Jack P. Greene, *The Intellectual Construction of America: Exceptionalism and Identity from 1492 to 1800* (Chapel Hill, 1993).

James A. Henretta, *The Evolution of American Society, 1700–1815: An Interdisciplinary Analysis* (Lexington, Mass., 1973).

James A. Henretta and Gregory H. Nobles, *Evolution and Revolution: American Society, 1600–1820* (Lexington, Mass., 1987).

Stephen Innes, *Labor in a New Land: Economy and Society in Seventeenth-Century Springfield* (Princeton, 1983).

Sung Bok Kim, "A New Look at the Great Landlords of Eighteenth-Century New York," *William and Mary Quarterly*, 27 (1970), 581–614.

Kenneth A. Lockridge, *The Diary, and Life, of William Byrd II of Virginia, 1674–1744* (Chapel Hill, 1987).

Carla Gardina Pestana and Sharon V. Salinger, eds, *Inequality in Early America* (Hanover, NH, 1999).

Darrett B. Rutman and Anita H. Rutman, *A Place in Time: Middlesex County, Virginia, 1650–1750* (New York, 1984).

Daniel Vickers with Vince Walsh, *Young Men and the Sea: Yankee Seafarers in the Age of Sail* (New Haven, 2005).

Robert Zemsky, *Merchants, Farmers and River Gods: An Essay on Eighteenth-Century American Politics* (Boston, 1971).

Michael Zuckerman, "Tocqueville, Turner, and Turds: Four Stories of Manners in Early America," *Journal of American History*, 85 (1998), 13–42.

CHAPTER 12   WHITE WOMEN AND GENDER

Overviews of Gender Ideology, Culture, and the Experiences of White Women

Carol Berkin, *First Generations: Women in Colonial America* (New York, 1996).

Ruth Bloch, *Gender and Morality in Anglo-American Culture, 1650–1800* (Berkeley, 2003).

Kathleen Brown, *Good Wives, Nasty Wenches, and Anxious Patriarchs: Gender, Race, and Power in Colonial Virginia* (Chapel Hill, 1996).

Lois Green Carr and Lorena S. Walsh, "The Planter's Wife: The Experience of White Women in Seventeenth-Century Maryland," *William and Mary Quarterly*, 34 (1977), 542–71.

Patricia Cleary, *Elizabeth Murray: A Woman's Pursuit of Independence in Eighteenth-Century America* (Amherst, 2000).

Elaine Forman Crane, *Ebb Tide in New England: Women, Seaports, and Social Change, 1630–1800* (Boston, 1998).

Mary Maples Dunn, "Saints and Sisters: Congregational and Quaker Women in the Early Colonial Period," *American Quarterly*, 30 (1978), 582–601.

Larry D. Eldridge, ed., *Women and Freedom in Early America* (New York, 1997).

Sharon M. Harris, ed., *American Women Writers to 1800* (New York, 1996).

Ellen Hartigan-O'Connor, *The Ties that Buy: Women and Commerce in Revolutionary America* (Philadelphia, 2009).

Kevin J. Hayes, *A Colonial Woman's Bookshelf* (Knoxville, 1996).

Esther Katz and Anita Rapone, *Women's Experience in America: An Historical Anthology* (New Brunswick, 1980).

Linda K. Kerber, *Women of the Republic: Intellect and Ideology in Revolutionary America* (Chapel Hill, 1980).

Catherine Kerrison, *Claiming the Pen: Women and Intellectual Life in the Early American South* (Ithaca, 2006).

Cynthia A. Kierner, *Beyond the Household: Women's Place in the Early South, 1700–1835* (Ithaca, 1998).

Lyle Koehler, *A Search for Power: The Weaker Sex in Seventeenth-Century New England* (Urbana, 1980).

Gerda Lerner, *The Majority Finds Its Past: Placing Women in History* (New York, 1979).

Debra Myers, *Common Whores, Vertuous Women, and Loveing Wives: Free Will Christian Women in Colonial Maryland* (Bloomington, 2003).

Mary Beth Norton, "The Evolution of White Women's Experience in Early America," *American Historical Review*, 89 (1984), 593–619.

Mary Beth Norton, *Founding Mothers and Fathers: Gendered Power and the Forming of American Society* (New York, 1996).

Mary Beth Norton, *Liberty's Daughters: The Revolutionary Experience of American Women, 1750–1800* (Boston, 1980).

Jean Soderland, "Women's Authority in Pennsylvania and New Jersey Quaker Meetings, 1680–1760," William and Mary Quarterly, 44 (1987), 722–49.

Linda E. Speth and Alison Duncan Hirsch, *Women, Family, and Community in Colonial America: Two Perspectives* (New York, 1983).

Linda Sturz, *Within Her Power: Propertied Women in Colonial Virginia* (New York, 2002).

Paula A. Treckel, *To Comfort the Heart: Women in Seventeenth-Century America* (New York, 1996).

Laurel Thatcher Ulrich, *Good Wives: Image and Reality in the Lives of Women in Northern New England, 1650–1750* (New York, 1982).

Alan D. Watson, "Women in Colonial North Carolina: Overlooked and Underestimated," *North Carolina Historical Review*, 58 (1981), 1–22.

Karin Wulf, *Not All Wives: Women of Colonial Philadelphia* (Ithaca, 2000).

Women and the Law: Legal Status, Property, and Speech

Linda Briggs Biemer, *Women and Property in Colonial New York: The Transition from Dutch to English Law, 1643–1727* (Ann Arbor, 1983).

Cornelia Hughes Dayton, *Women Before the Bar: Gender, Law, and Society in Connecticut, 1639–1789* (Chapel Hill, 1995).

Joan R. Gundersen and Gwen Victor Gampel, "Married Women's Legal Status in Eighteenth-Century New York and Virginia," *William and Mary Quarterly*, 39 (1982), 114–43.

David Narrett, *Inheritance and Family Life in Colonial New York City* (Ithaca, 1992).

Mary Beth Norton, "Gender and Defamation in Seventeenth-Century Maryland," *William and Mary Quarterly*, 44 (1987), 3–39.

Deborah A. Rosen, *Courts and Commerce: Gender, Law, and the Market Economy in Colonial New York* (Columbus, 1997).

Deborah A. Rosen, "Women and Property across Colonial America: A Comparison of Legal Systems in New Mexico and New York," *William and Mary Quarterly*, 60 (2003), 355–82.

Marylynn Salmon, "Equality or Submersion? Feme Covert Status in Early Pennsylvania," in Carol Ruth Berkin and Mary Beth Norton, eds, *Women of America: A History* (Boston, 1979).

Marylynn Salmon, *Women and the Law of Property in Early America* (Chapel Hill, 1986).

Marylynn Salmon, "Women and Property in South Carolina: The Evidence from Marriage Settlements, 1730–1830," *William and Mary Quarterly*, 39 (1982), 655–85.

Carole Shammas, Marylynn Salmon, and M. Dahlin, *Inheritance in America: From Colonial Times to the Present* (New Brunswick, 1987).

Terri Snyder, *Brabbling Women: Disorderly Speech and the Law in Early Virginia* (Ithaca, 2003).

Sexuality and Its Legal Regulation

Ruth Bloch, "Women and the Law of Courtship in Eighteenth-Century America," in *Gender and Morality in Anglo-American Culture, 1650–1800* (Berkeley, 2003), 78–101.

Sharon Block, *Rape and Sexual Power in Early America* (Chapel Hill, 2006).

Kathleen Brown, *Good Wives, Nasty Wenches, and Anxious Patriarchs: Gender, Race, and Power in Colonial Virginia* (Chapel Hill, 1996).

Cornelia Hughes Dayton, "Taking the Trade: Abortion and Gender Relations in an Eighteenth-Century New England Village," *William and Mary Quarterly*, 48 (1991), 19–49.

Cornelia Hughes Dayton, *Women Before the Bar: Gender, Law, and Society in Connecticut, 1639–1789* (Chapel Hill, 1995).

Kirsten Fischer, *Suspect Relations: Sex, Race, and Resistance in Colonial North Carolina* (Ithaca, 2002).

Thomas A. Foster, *Sex and the Eighteenth-Century Man: Massachusetts and the History of Sexuality in America* (Boston, 2006).

Richard Godbeer, *Sexual Revolution in Early America* (Baltimore, 2002).

Clare Lyons, *Sex among the Rabble: An Intimate History of Gender and Power in the Age of Revolution, Philadelphia, 1730–1830* (Chapel Hill, 2006).

John Ruston Pagan, *Anne Orthwood's Bastard: Sex and Law in Early Virginia* (New York, 2003).

Courtship and Marriage

Ruth Bloch, "Changing Conceptions of Sexuality and Romance in Eighteenth-Century America," *William and Mary Quarterly*, 60 (2003), 13–42.

J. A. Leo Lemay, ed., *Robert Bolling Woos Anne Miller: Love and Courtship in Colonial Virginia, 1760* (Charlottesville, 1990).

Daniel Scott Smith, "Parental Power and Marriage Patterns: An Analysis of Historical Trends in Hingham, Massachusetts," *Journal of Marriage and the Family*, 35 (1973), 406–18.

Lawrence Stone, *The Family, Sex, and Marriage in England, 1500–1800* (New York, 1977).

Robert V. Wells, "Quaker Marriage Patterns in a Colonial Perspective," *William and Mary Quarterly*, 29 (1972), 415–42.

Childbearing and Fertility

Susan Klepp, *Revolutionary Conceptions: Women, Fertility, and Family Limitation in America, 1760–1820* (Chapel Hill, 2009).

Judith Walzer Leavitt, *Brought to Bed: Childbearing in America, 1750–1950* (New York, 1986).

Catherine M. Scholten, *Childbearing in American Society: 1650–1850* (New York, 1985).

Women's Work

Joan M. Jensen, *Loosening the Bonds: Mid-Atlantic Farm Women, 1750–1850* (New Haven, 1986).

Jean P. Jordan, "Women Merchants in Colonial New York," *New York History*, 58 (1977), 416–36.

Cynthia A. Kierner, *Beyond the Household: Women's Place in the Early South, 1700–1835* (Ithaca, 1998).

Gloria L. Main, "Gender, Work, and Wages in Colonial New England," *William and Mary Quarterly*, 51 (1994), 39–66.

Rebecca Tannenbaum, *The Healer's Calling: Women and Medicine in Early New England* (Ithaca, 2002).

Laurel Thatcher Ulrich, "Wheels, Looms, and the Gender Division of Labor in the Eighteenth Century," *William and Mary Quarterly*, 55 (1998), 3–38.

Divorce

Thomas Buckley, *The Great Catastrophe of My Life: Divorce in the Old Dominion* (Chapel Hill, 2002).

Nancy F. Cott, "Divorce and the Changing Status of Women in Eighteenth-Century Massachusetts," *William and Mary Quarterly*, 33 (1976), 586–614.

Merril D. Smith, *Breaking the Bonds: Marital Discord in Pennsylvania, 1730–1830* (New York, 1991).

Widowhood

Vivian Conger, *The Widow's Might: Widowhood and Gender in Early British America* (New York, 2009).

Deborah Gough, "A Further Look at Widows in Early Southeastern Pennsylvania," *William and Mary Quarterly*, 44 (1987), 829–39.

Alexander Kayssar, "Widowhood in Eighteenth-Century Massachusetts: A Problem in the History of the Family," *Perspectives in American History*, 7 (1974), 83–118.

Lisa Wilson, *Life After Death: Widows in Pennsylvania, 1750–1850* (Philadelphia, 1992).

Architecture and Material Culture

Reinier Baarsen, Gervase Jackson-Stops, Philip M. Johnston, and Elaine Evans Dee, *Courts and Colonies: The William and Mary Style in Holland, England, and America* (New York, 1989).

Richard L. Bushman, *The Refinement of America: Persons, Houses, Cities* (New York, 1992).

Jon Butler, *Becoming America: The Revolution Before 1776* (Cambridge, Mass., 2000).

Cary Carson et al., "Impermanent Architecture in the Southern American Colonies," *Winterthur Portfolio: A Journal of Material Culture*, 16 (1981), 135–96.

Abbott Lowell Cummings, *The Framed Houses of Massachusetts Bay, 1625–1725* (Cambridge, Mass., 1979).

James Deetz, *In Small Things Forgotten: The Archeology of Early American Life* (New York, 1977).

David Hackett Fischer, *Albion's Seed: Four British Folkways in America* (New York, 1989).

John T. Kirk, *American Furniture and the British Tradition to 1830* (New York, 1982).

William H. Pierson, Jr., *American Buildings and Their Architects*, Vol. 1: *The Colonial and Neoclassical Styles* (New York, 1970).

Daniel D. Reiff, *Small Georgian Houses in England and Virginia: Origins and Development through the 1750s* (Newark, Del., 1986).

Robert Blair St. George, ed., *Material Life in America, 1600–1860* (Boston, 1988).

Barbara Wells Sarudy, *Gardens and Gardening in the Chesapeake, 1700–1805* (Baltimore, 1998).

Carole Shammas, "The Housing Stock of the Early United States: Refinement Meets Migration," *William and Mary Quarterly*, 64 (2007), 549–90.

Laurel Thatcher Ulrich, *The Age of Homespun: Objects and Stories in the Creation of an American Myth* (New York, 2001).

CHAPTER 13   BRITISH NORTH AMERICAN RELIGION, EDUCATION, AND CULTURE, 1689–1760

General

Jon Butler, *Becoming America: The Revolution Before 1776* (Cambridge, Mass., 2000).
Jack P. Greene, *Pursuits of Happiness: The Social Development of Early Modern British Colonies and the Formation of American Culture* (Chapel Hill, 1988).
Ned C. Landsman, *From Colonials to Provincials: American Thought and Culture, 1680–1760* (New York, 1997).
Henry F. May, *The Enlightenment in America* (New York, 1976).
Edmund S. Morgan, *Benjamin Franklin* (New Haven, 2002).
Robert Olwell and Alan Tully, *Cultures and Identities in Colonial British America* (Baltimore, 2006).
Esmond Wright, ed., *Benjamin Franklin: His Life as He Wrote It* (Cambridge, Mass., 1990).
Esmond Wright, *Franklin of Philadelphia* (Cambridge, Mass., 1986).

Religion

Sidney E. Ahlstrom, *A Religious History of the American People*, 2 vols (New Haven, 1972).
Randall H. Balmer, *A Perfect Babel of Confusion: Dutch Religion and English Culture in the Middle Colonies* (New York, 1989).
James Bell, *The Imperial Origins of the King's Church in Early America, 1607–1783* (New York, 2004).
James Bell, *A War of Religion: Dissenters, Anglicans, and the American Revolution* (Basingstoke, 2008).
Ruth H. Bloch, *Visionary Republic: Millennial Themes in American Thought, 1756–1800* (New York, 1985).
S. Charles Bolton, *Southern Anglicanism: The Church of England in Colonial South Carolina* (Westport, 1982).
Patricia U. Bonomi, *Under the Cope of Heaven: Religion, Society, and Politics in Colonial America* (New York, 1986).
Patricia U. Bonomi and Peter R. Eisenstadt, "Church Adherence in the Eighteenth-Century British American Colonies," *William and Mary Quarterly*, 39 (1982), 245–86.
Richard L. Bushman, ed., *The Great Awakening: Documents on the Revival of Religion, 1740–1745* (Chapel Hill, 1989).
Jon Butler, *Awash in a Sea of Faith: Christianizing the American People* (Cambridge, Mass., 1990).
Jon Butler, "Enthusiasm Described and Decried: The Great Awakening as Interpretative Fiction," *Journal of American History*, 69 (1982), 305–25.
Milton J. Coalter, *Gilbert Tennent, Son of Thunder* (Westport, 1986).
Ralph J. Coffman, *Solomon Stoddard* (Boston, 1978).
James F. Cooper, Jr., *Tenacious of Their Liberties: The Congregationalists in Colonial Massachusetts* (New York, 1999).
Norman Fiering, *Jonathan Edwards's Moral Thought and Its British Context* (Chapel Hill, 1981).
Christopher Grasso, *A Speaking Aristocracy: Transforming Public Discourse in Eighteenth-Century Connecticut* (Chapel Hill, 2000).
Keith L. Griffin, *Revolution and Religion: American Revolutionary War and the Reformed Clergy* (New York, 1994).

Philip F. Gura, "Going Mr Stoddard's Way: William Williams on Church Privileges, 1693," *William and Mary Quarterly*, 45 (1988), 489–98.

Timothy D. Hall, *Contested Boundaries: Itinerancy and the Reshaping of the Colonial American Religious World* (Durham, NC, 1994).

Nathan O. Hatch, *The Sacred Cause of Liberty: Republican Thought and the Millennium in Revolutionary New England* (New Haven, 1977).

Nathan O. Hatch and Harry S. Stout, *Jonathan Edwards and the American Experience* (New York, 1988).

Alan Heimert, *Religion and the American Mind from the Great Awakening to the Revolution* (Cambridge, Mass., 1966).

E. Brooks Hollifield, *Theology in America: Christian Thought from the Age of the Puritans to the Civil War* (New Haven, 2003).

Rhys Isaac, "Evangelical Revolt: The Nature of the Baptists' Challenge to the Traditional Order in Virginia, 1765–1775," *William and Mary Quarterly*, 31 (1974), 345–66.

Rhys Isaac, "Religion and Authority: Problems of the Anglican Establishment in Virginia in the Era of the Great Awakening and the Parsons' Cause," *William and Mary Quarterly*, 30 (1973), 3–36.

Alessa Johns, ed., *Dreadful Visitations: Confronting Natural Catastrophe in the Age of the Enlightenment* (New York, 1999).

James W. Jones, *The Shattered Synthesis: New England Puritanism Before the Great Awakening* (New Haven, 1973).

Thomas Kidd, *The Great Awakening: The Roots of Evangelical Culture in Colonial America* (New Haven, 2007).

Frank Lambert, *Inventing the "Great Awakening"* (Princeton, 1999).

Frank Lambert, *"Pedlar in Divinity": George Whitefield and the Transatlantic Revivals* (Princeton, 1994).

Brian F. LeBeau, *Jonathan Dickinson and the Formative Years of American Presbyterianism* (Lexington, Ky., 1997).

Janet Moore Lindman, "Acting the Manly Christian: White Evangelical Masculinity in Revolutionary Virginia," *William and Mary Quarterly*, 57 (2000), 393–416.

Stephen L. Longenecker, *Piety and Tolerance: Pennsylvania German Religion, 1700–1850* (Metuchen, 1994).

David S. Lovejoy, *Religious Enthusiasm in the New World: Heresy to Revolution* (Cambridge, Mass., 1985).

Richard F. Lovelace, *The American Pietism of Cotton Mather: Origins of American Evangelicalism* (Grand Rapids, 1979).

Paul R. Lucas, "'An Appeal to the Learned': The Mind of Solomon Stoddard," *William and Mary Quarterly*, 30 (1973), 257–92.

Paul R. Lucas, *Valley of Discord: Church and Society along the Connecticut River, 1636–1725* (Hanover, NH, 1976).

William G. McLoughlin, *New England Dissent, 1630–1833: The Baptists and the Separation of Church and State* (Cambridge, Mass., 1971).

William G. McLoughlin, *Soul Liberty: The Baptists' Struggle in New England, 1630–1833* (Hanover, NH, 1991).

Jack D. Marietta, *The Reformation of American Quakerism, 1748–1783* (Philadelphia, 1984).

George Marsden, *Jonathan Edwards: A Life* (New Haven, 2003).

Perry Miller, "Preparation for Salvation in Seventeenth-Century New England," in *Nature's Nation* (Cambridge, Mass., 1967).

Iain H. Murray, *Jonathan Edwards: A New Biography* (Edinburgh, 1987).

Mark Noll, *America's God: From Jonathan Edwards to Abraham Lincoln* (New York, 2002).

Peter S. Onuf, "New Lights in New London: A Group Portrait of the Separatists, 1740–1745," *William and Mary Quarterly*, 37 (1980), 627–44.

Richard W. Pointer, *Protestant Pluralism and the New York Experience: A Study of Eighteenth-Century Religious Diversity* (Bloomington, 1988).

Sally Schwartz, *A Mixed Multitude: The Struggle for Toleration in Colonial Pennsylvania* (New York, 1987).

Kenneth Silverman, *The Life and Times of Cotton Mather* (New York, 1984).

Thomas Slaughter, *The Beautiful Soul of John Woolman: Apostle of Abolition* (New York, 2008).

Bruce E. Steiner, "Anglican Officeholding in Pre-Revolutionary Connecticut: The Parameters of New England Community," *William and Mary Quarterly*, 31 (1974), 369–406.

Harry S. Stout, *The New England Soul: Preaching and Religious Culture in Colonial New England* (New York, 1986).

Harry S. Stout, "Religion, Communications, and the Ideological Origins of the American Revolution," *William and Mary Quarterly*, 34 (1977), 519–41.

Patricia J. Tracy, *Jonathan Edwards, Pastor: Religion and Society in Eighteenth-Century Northampton* (New York, 1980).

Mark Valeri, *Law and Providence in Joseph Bellamy's New England: The Origins of the New Divinity in Revolutionary America* (New York, 1994).

Marilyn J. Westerkamp, *Triumph of the Laity: Scots-Irish Piety and the Great Awakening, 1625–1760* (New York, 1988).

Michael P. Winship, *Seers of God: Puritan Providentialism in the Restoration and Early Enlightenment* (Baltimore, 1996).

John Frederick Woolverton, *Colonial Anglicanism in North America* (Detroit, 1984).

Arthur J. Worrall, *Quakers in the Colonial Northeast* (Hanover, NH, 1980).

J. William T. Youngs, Jr., *God's Messengers: Religious Leadership in Colonial New England, 1700–1750* (Baltimore, 1976).

Avihus Zahai, *Jonathan Edwards' Philosophy of History: The Reenchantment of the World in the Age of Enlightenment* (Princeton, 2003).

Education and Literacy

James Axtell, *The School upon a Hill: Education and Society in Colonial New England* (New Haven, 1974).

Bernard Bailyn, *Education in the Forming of American Society: Needs and Opportunities for Study* (Chapel Hill, 1960).

Whitfield J. Bell, Jr., *The Colonial Physician and Other Essays* (New York, 1975).

Stephen Botein, "The Legal Profession in Colonial North America," in Wilfred Prest, ed., *Lawyers in Early Modern Europe and America* (New York, 1981).

Gillian Brown, *The Consent of the Governed: The Lockean Legacy in Early American Culture* (Cambridge, Mass., 2001).

Richard D. Brown, *Knowledge is Power: The Diffusion of Information in Early America, 1700–1865* (New York, 1989).

Richard D. Brown, *The Strength of a People: The Idea of an Informed Citizenry in America, 1650–1870* (Chapel Hill, 1996).

Patricia Cline Cohen, *A Calculating People: The Spread of Numeracy in Early America* (Chicago, 1983).

Patricia Crain, *Story of A: The Alphabetization of America from the New England Primer to the Scarlet Letter* (Stanford, 2000).

Lawrence A. Cremin, *American Education: The Colonial Experience, 1607–1783* (New York, 1970).

Alan F. Day, *A Social Study of Lawyers in Maryland, 1660–1775* (New York, 1989).

Sandra M. Gustafson, *Eloquence is Power: Oratory and Performance in Early America* (Chapel Hill, 2000).

Peter Charles Hoffer, *Law and People in Colonial America* (Baltimore, 1992).

Kenneth A. Lockridge, *Literacy in Colonial New England: An Enquiry into the Social Context of Literacy in the Early Modern West* (New York, 1974).

E. Jennifer Monaghan, *Learning to Read and Write in Colonial America* (Amherst, 2005).

Howard Miller, *The Revolutionary College: American Presbyterian Higher Education, 1707–1837* (New York, 1976).

Lamar Riley Murphy, *Enter the Physician: The Transformation of Domestic Medicine, 1760–1860* (Tuscaloosa, 1991).

John M. Murrin, "The Legal Transformation: The Bench and Bar of Eighteenth-Century Massachusetts," in Stanley N. Katz, ed., *Colonial America: Essays in Politics and Social Development* (Boston, 1971).

Margaret Connell Szasz, *Indian Education in the American Colonies* (Albuquerque, 1988).

Margaret Connell Szasz, *Scottish Highlanders and Native Americans: Indigenous Education in the Eighteenth-Century Atlantic World* (Norman, 2007).

Tamara Plakins Thornton, *Handwriting in America: A Cultural History* (New Haven, 1996).

Richard Warch, *School of the Prophets: Yale College, 1701–1740* (New Haven, 1973).

Letter-Writing and Communication

Eve Tabor Bannet, *Empire of Letters: Letter Manuals and Transatlantic Correspondence, 1680–1820* (Cambridge, 2005).

Konstantin Dierks, *In My Power: Letter Writing and Communications in Early America* (Philadelphia, 2009).

Richard Johns, *Spreading the News: The American Postal System from Franklin to Morse* (Cambridge, Mass., 1995).

Anglicization, Manners, and Sensibility

T. H. Breen, "An Empire of Goods: The Anglicization of Colonial America, 1690–1776," *Journal of British Studies*, 25 (1986), 467–99.

T. H. Breen, *The Marketplace of Revolution: How Consumer Politics Shaped American Independence* (New York, 2004).

Richard L. Bushman, *The Refinement of America: Persons, Houses, Cities* (New York, 1992).

Nicole Eustace, *Passion is the Gale: Emotion, Power, and the Coming of the American Revolution* (Chapel Hill, 2008).

Jack P. Greene, *Imperatives, Behaviors, and Identities: Essays in Early American Cultural History* (Charlottesville, 1992).

Dallett Hemphill, *Bowing to Necessities: A History of Manners in America, 1620–1860* (New York, 1999).

Dallett Hemphill, "Manners and Class in the Revolutionary Era: A Transatlantic Comparison," *William and Mary Quarterly*, 63 (2006), 345–72.

Phyllis Whitman Hunter, *Purchasing Identity in the Atlantic World: Massachusetts Merchants, 1670–1780* (Ithaca, 2001).

Sarah Knott, *Sensibility and the American Revolution* (Chapel Hill, 2009).

John M. Murrin, Anglicizing an American Colony: The Transformation of Provincial Massachusetts (unpublished PhD thesis, Yale University, 1966).

Michal J. Rozbicki, *The Complete Gentleman: Cultural Legitimacy in Plantation America* (Charlottesville, 1998).

Robert Blair St. George, *Conversing by Signs: Poetics of Implication in Colonial New England Culture* (Chapel Hill, 1998).

Libraries, Literature, and the Press

Charles E. Clark, *The Public Print: The Newspaper in Anglo-American Culture, 1665–1740* (New York, 1994).

David A. Copeland, *Colonial American Newspapers: Character and Content* (Newark, Del., 1997).

Richard Beale Davis, *A Colonial Southern Bookshelf: Reading in the Eighteenth Century* (Athens, Ga., 1979).

Thomas M. Davis, *A Reading of Edward Taylor* (Newark, Del., 1992).

Norman Fiering, "The Transatlantic Republic of Letters: A Note on the Circulation of Learned Periodicals to Early Eighteenth-Century America," *William and Mary Quarterly*, 33 (1976), 642–60.

David D. Hall and John B. Hench, eds, *Needs and Opportunities in the History of the Book: America, 1639–1876* (Worcester, Mass., 1987).

William L. Joyce et al., eds, *Printing and Society in Early America* (Worcester, Mass., 1983).

Leonard W. Levy, *The Emergence of a Free Press* (New York, 1985).

William Pencak and Wythe W. Holt, Jr., *The Law in America, 1607–1861* (New York, 1989).

William David Sloan and Julie Hedgepeth Williams, *The Early American Press, 1690–1783* (Westport, 1994).

Jeffrey A. Smith, *Printers and Press Freedom: The Ideology of Early American Journalism* (New York, 1988).

John Tebbel, *A History of Book Publishing in the United States*, Vol. 1: *The Creation of an Industry, 1630–1865* (New York, 1972).

Julie Hedgepeth Williams, *The Significance of the Printed Word in Early America: Colonists' Thoughts on the Role of the Press* (Greenwood, 1999).

Edwin Wolf, *The Library of James Logan of Philadelphia, 1674–1751* (Philadelphia, 1974).

Science

Silvio A. Bedini, *Thinkers and Tinkers: Early American Men of Science* (New York, 1975).

Whitfield J. Bell, Jr., *The Colonial Physician and Other Essays* (New York, 1975).

I. Bernard Cohen, *Benjamin Franklin's Science* (Cambridge, Mass., 1990).

Colonial Society of Massachusetts, *Medicine in Colonial Massachusetts, 1620–1820* (Boston, 1980).

James Delbourgo, *A Most Amazing Scene of Wonders: Electricity and Enlightenment in Early America* (New Haven, 2007).

Sara Gronim, *Everyday Nature: Knowledge of the Natural World in Colonial New York* (New Brunswick, 2007).

Brooke Hindle, ed., *America's Wooden Age: Aspects of Its Early Technology* (Tarrytown, 1975).
Randolph Sidney Klein, ed., *Science and Society in Early America: Essays in Honor of Whitfield J. Bell, Jr.* (Philadelphia, 1986).
Ronald Numbers, ed., *Medicine in the New World: New Spain, New France, and New England* (Knoxville, 1987).
Susan Scott Parrish, *American Curiosity: Cultures of Natural History in the Colonial British Atlantic World* (Chapel Hill, 2006).
Raymond Phineas Stearns, *Science in the British Colonies of America* (Urbana, 1970).

The Arts

Owen Aldridge, *Early American Literature: A Comparatist Approach* (Princeton, 1982).
Ralph Bauer, *The Cultural Geography of Colonial American Literatures: Empire, Travel, Modernity* (Cambridge, 2003).
Wendy Cooper, *In Praise of America: American Decorative Arts, 1650–1830* (New York, 1980).
Wayne Craven, *Colonial American Portraiture: The Economic, Religious, Social, Cultural, Philosophical, Scientific, and Aesthetic Foundations* (New York, 1986).
Richard Beale Davis, *Literature and Society in Early Virginia, 1608–1840* (Baton Rouge, 1973).
Emory Elliott, *Revolutionary Writers: Literature and Authority in the New Republic, 1725–1810* (New York, 1982).
Jonathan L. Fairbanks and Robert F. Trent, *New England Begins: The Seventeenth Century* (Boston, 1982).
Norman S. Grabo, *Edward Taylor*, rev. edn (Boston, 1988).
Philip F. Gura, "The Study of Colonial American Literature, 1966–1987: A Vade Mecum," *William and Mary Quarterly*, 45 (1988), 305–41.
Sharon M. Harris, ed., *American Women Writers to 1800* (New York, 1996).
Graham Hood, *Charles Bridges and William Dering: Two Virginia Painters, 1735–1750* (Williamsburg, 1978).
Odai Johnson, *Absence and Memory in Colonial American Theatre: Fiorelli's Plaster* (New York, 2006).
J. A. Leo Lemay, ed., *Essays in Early Virginia Literature Honoring Richard Beale Davis* (New York, 1977).
Richard H. Saunders and Ellen G. Miles, *American Colonial Portraits, 1700–1776* (Washington, DC, 1987).
Jason Shaffer, *Performing Patriotism: National Identity in the Colonial and Revolutionary American Theater* (Philadelphia, 2007).
David S. Shields, *Civil Tongues and Polite Letters in British America* (Chapel Hill, 1997).
David S. Shields, *Oracles of Empire: Poetry, Politics, and Commerce in British America, 1690–1750* (Chicago, 1990).
Kenneth Silverman, *A Cultural History of the American Revolution* (New York, 1986).
Louis B. Wright et al., *The Arts in America: The Colonial Period* (New York, 1966).

Popular Culture

Elaine Breslaw, *Dr. Alexander Hamilton and Provincial America: Expanding the Orbit of Scottish Culture* (Baton Rouge, 2008).

T. H. Breen, "Horses and Gentlemen: The Cultural Significance of Gambling among the Gentry of Virginia," *William and Mary Quarterly*, 34 (1977), 239–57.

Steven C. Bullock, *Revolutionary Brotherhood: Freemasonry and the Transformation of the American Social Order, 1730–1840* (Chapel Hill, 1996).

Linda Colley, *Britons: Forging the Nation, 1707–1837* (New Haven, 1992).

David W. Conroy, *In Public Houses: Drink and the Revolution of Authority in Colonial Massachusetts* (Chapel Hill, 1995).

Bruce C. Daniels, *Puritans at Play: Leisure and Recreation in Colonial New England* (New York, 1995).

Peter Charles Hoffer, *Sensory Worlds in Early America* (Baltimore, 2003).

Daniel Walker Howe, *Making the American Self: Jonathan Edwards to Abraham Lincoln* (Cambridge, Mass., 1997).

Brendan McConville, *The King's Three Faces: The Rise and Fall of Royal America, 1688–1776* (Chapel Hill, 2006).

Richard Cullen Roth, *How Early America Sounded* (Ithaca, 2003).

Sharon Salinger, *Taverns and Drinking in Early America* (Baltimore, 2002).

Nancy L. Struna, *People of Prowess: Sport, Leisure, and Labor in Early Anglo-America* (Urbana, 1996).

Peter Thompson, *Rum Punch and Revolution: Taverngoing and Public Life in Eighteenth-Century Philadelphia* (Philadelphia, 1999).

CHAPTER 14   SLAVERY AND THE AFRICAN AMERICAN EXPERIENCE, 1689–1760

Overviews

Theodore W. Allen, *The Invention of the White Race*, Vol. 1: *Racial Oppression and Social Control*; Vol. 2: *The Origins of Racial Oppression in Anglo-America* (New York, 1994, 1997).

Ira Berlin, "From Creole to African: Atlantic Creoles and the Origins of African-American Society in Mainland North America," *William and Mary Quarterly*, 53 (1996), 251–88.

Ira Berlin, *Many Thousands Gone: The First Two Centuries of Slavery in North America* (Cambridge, Mass., 1998).

Robin Blackburn, *The Making of New World Slavery: From the Baroque to the Modern, 1492–1899* (New York, 1997).

David Eltis, *The Rise of African Slavery in the Americas* (New York, 2000).

Philip S. Foner, *History of Black Americans from Africa to the Emergence of the Cotton Kingdom* (Westport, 1975).

Philip D. Morgan, *Slave Counterpoint: Black Culture in the Eighteenth-Century Chesapeake and Lowcountry* (Chapel Hill, 1998).

Stephan Palmié, *Slave Cultures and the Cultures of Slavery* (Knoxville, 1995).

John Thornton, *Africa and Africans in the Making of the Atlantic World, 1400–1680* (New York, 1992; 2nd edn, *Africa and Africans in the Making of the Atlantic World, 1400–1800*, 1998).

James Walvin, *Black Ivory: A History of British Slavery* (New York, 1992).

Betty Wood, *The Origins of American Slavery: Freedom and Bondage in the English Colonies* (New York, 1997).

Peter H. Wood, "'I Did the Best I Could for My Day': The Study of Early Black History during the Second Reconstruction, 1960–1976," *William and Mary Quarterly*, 35 (1978), 185–225.

Donald R. Wright, *African Americans in the Colonial Era: From African Origins through the American Revolution* (Arlington Heights, 1990).

The Slave Trade and African Background

Philip D. Curtin, *The Atlantic Slave Trade: A Census* (Madison, Wis., 1969).
K. G. Davies, *The Royal African Company* (London, 1957).
David Eltis and David Richardson, *Routes to Slavery: Direction, Ethnicity, and Mortality in the Transatlantic Slave Trade* (London, 1997).
J. C. Fage, "Slaves and Society in Western Africa, c.1440–c.1700," *Journal of African History*, 21 (1981), 289–310.
Linda Heywood, ed., *Central Africans: Cultural Transformations in the American Diaspora* (New York, 2002).
Herbert S. Klein, *The Middle Passage: Comparative Studies in the Atlantic Slave Trade* (Princeton, 1978).
Herbert Klein, "Slaves and Shipping in Eighteenth-Century Virginia", *Journal of Interdisciplinary History*, 5 (1975), 383–412.
Robin Law, "Ethnicity and the Slave Trade: 'Lucumi' and 'Nago' as Ethnonyms in West Africa," *History in Africa*, 24 (1997), 205–19.
Daniel C. Littlefield, *Rice and Slaves: Ethnicity and the Slave Trade in Colonial South Carolina* (Baton Rouge, 1981).
Paul E. Lovejoy, *Transformations in Slavery: A History of Slavery in Africa* (Cambridge, 1983).
Paul E. Lovejoy, "The Volume of the Atlantic Slave Trade: A Synthesis," *Journal of African History*, 23 (1982), 483–7.
Patrick Manning, *Slavery and African Life: Occidental, Oriental, and African Slave Trades* (New York, 1990).
G. Ugo Nwokeji, "African Conceptions of Gender and the Slave Traffic," *William and Mary Quarterly*, 58 (2001), 47–67.
James A. Rawley, *The Transatlantic Slave Trade: A History* (New York, 1981).
Marcus Rediker, *The Slave Ship: A Human History*, 3rd edn (New York, 2007).
Stephanie Smallwood, *Saltwater Slavery: A Middle Passage from Africa to American Diaspora* (Cambridge, Mass., 2007).
Barbara L. Solow, *Slavery and the Rise of the Atlantic System* (Cambridge, 1991).
Hugh Thomas, *The Slave Trade: The Story of the Atlantic Slave Trade, 1440–1870* (New York, 1997).
U. B. Thompson, *The Making of the African Diaspora in the Americas, 1441–1900* (London, 1988).
John Thornton, "The African Experience of the '20 and Odd Negroes' Arriving in Virginia in 1619," *William and Mary Quarterly*, 55 (1998), 421–34.
Susan Westbury, "Slaves of Colonial Virginia: Where They Came From," *William and Mary Quarterly*, 42 (1985), 228–37.

African American Women, Family, Work, and Culture in the British North American Colonies

Ira Berlin, "Time, Space, and the Evolution of Afro-American Society on British Mainland North America," *American Historical Review*, 85 (1980), 44–78.

Ira Berlin and Philip D. Morgan, eds, *Cultivation and Culture: Labor and the Shaping of Slave Life in the Americas* (Charlottesville, 1993).

David Cecelski, *The Waterman's Song: Slavery and Freedom in Maritime North Carolina* (Chapel Hill, 2001).

Margaret Washington Creel, *"A Peculiar People": Slave Religion and Community-Culture among the Gullahs* (New York, 1988).

Sylviane Diouf, *Servants of Allah: African Muslims Enslaved in the Americas* (New York, 1998).

Dena J. Epstein, *Sinful Tunes and Spirituals: Black Folk Music to the Civil War* (Urbana, 1977).

Leland Ferguson, *Uncommon Ground: Archaeology and Early African America, 1650–1800* (Washington, DC, 1992).

Sylvia Frey and Betty Wood, *Come Shouting to Zion: African American Protestantism in the American South and British Caribbean to 1830* (Chapel Hill, 1998).

Michael A. Gomez, *Exchanging our Country Marks: The Transformation of African Identities in the Colonial and Antebellum South* (Chapel Hill, 1998).

Michael A. Gomez, "Muslims in Early America," *Journal of Southern History*, 60 (1994), 671–710.

Lorenzo J. Greene, *The Negro in Colonial New England, 1620–1776* (New York, 1942).

Joan Gunderson, "The Double Bonds of Race and Sex: Black and White Women in a Colonial Virginia Parish," *Journal of Southern History*, 52 (1986), 351–72.

Herbert G. Gutman, *The Black Family in Slavery and Freedom, 1750–1925* (New York, 1976).

Gwendolyn Midlo Hall, *Slavery and African Ethnicities in the Americas: Restoring the Links* (Chapel Hill, 2005).

Jacqueline Jones, "Race, Sex, and Self-Evident Truths: The Status of Slave Women during the Era of the American Revolution," in Ronald Hoffman and Peter J. Albert, eds, *Women in the Age of the American Revolution* (Charlottesville, 1989), 293–337.

Allan Kulikoff, "The Beginnings of the Afro-American Family in Maryland," in Aubrey C. Land, Lois Green Carr, and Edward C. Papenfuse, eds, *Law, Society, and Politics in Early Maryland* (Baltimore, 1977).

Allan Kulikoff, "The Origins of Afro-American Society in Tidewater Maryland and Virginia, 1700–1790," *William and Mary Quarterly*, 35 (1978), 226–50.

Allan Kulikoff, "'A Prolifick People': Black Population Growth in the Chesapeake Colonies, 1700–1790," *Southern Studies*, 16 (1977), 391–428.

Allan Kulikoff, *Tobacco and Slaves: The Development of Southern Cultures in the Chesapeake, 1680–1800* (Chapel Hill, 1986).

Jean Butenhoff Lee, "The Problem of Slave Community in the Eighteenth-Century Chesapeake," *William and Mary Quarterly*, 43 (1986), 333–61.

Russell R. Menard, "The Maryland Slave Population, 1658 to 1730: A Demographic Profile of Blacks in Four Counties," *William and Mary Quarterly*, 32 (1975), 29–54.

Jennifer Morgan, *Laboring Women: Reproduction and Gender in New World Slavery* (Philadelphia, 2004).

Philip D. Morgan, *Slave Counterpoint: Black Culture in the Eighteenth-Century Chesapeake and Lowcountry* (Chapel Hill, 1998).

Philip D. Morgan, "Slave Life in Piedmont Virginia, 1720–1800," in Lois Green Carr, Philip D. Morgan, and Jean Russo, eds, *Colonial Chesapeake Society* (Chapel Hill, 1989), 433–84.

Philip D. Morgan, "Work and Culture: The Task System and the World of Lowcountry Blacks, 1700–1800," *William and Mary Quarterly*, 39 (1982), 563–99.

Philip D. Morgan and Michael L. Nicholls, "Slaves in Piedmont Virginia, 1720–1790," *William and Mary Quarterly*, 46 (1989), 211–51.

Patricia Morton, ed., *Discovering the Women in Slavery* (Athens, Ga., 1995).

Michael Mullin, *Africa in America: Slave Acculturation and Resistance in the American South and the British Caribbean, 1736–1831* (Urbana, 1992).

Patricia Samford, "The Archaeology of African-American Slavery and Material Culture," *William and Mary Quarterly*, 53 (1996), 87–114.

Erik R. Seeman, "'Justice Must Take Plase': Three African Americans Speak of Religion in Eighteenth-Century New England," *William and Mary Quarterly*, 56 (1999), 393–414.

John F. Sensbach, *A Separate Canaan: The Making of an Afro-Moravian World in North Carolina, 1763–1840* (Chapel Hill, 1997).

James Sidbury, *Becoming African in America: Race and Nation in the Early Black Atlantic* (New York, 2007).

Mechal Sobel, *Trabelin' On: The Slave Journey to an Afro-Baptist Faith* (Princeton, 1979).

Mechal Sobel, *The World They Made Together: Black and White Values in Eighteenth-Century Virginia* (Princeton, 1987).

John Thornton, *Africa and Africans in the Making of the Atlantic World, 1400–1800*, 2nd edn (Cambridge, 1998).

Lorena S. Walsh, *From Calabar to Carter's Grove: The History of a Virginia Slave Community* (Charlottesville, 1997).

Lorena S. Walsh, "Slave Life, Slave Society, and Tobacco Production in the Tidewater Chesapeake, 1620–1820", in Ira Berlin and Philip D. Morgan, eds, *Cultivation and Culture: Labor and the Shaping of Slave Life in the Americas* (Charlottesville, 1993).

Betty Wood, *Slavery in Colonial Georgia, 1730–1775* (Athens, Ga., 1984).

Peter H. Wood, *Black Majority: Negroes in Colonial South Carolina from 1670 through the Stono Rebellion* (New York, 1974).

Anne Elizabeth Yentsch, *A Chesapeake Family and Their Slaves* (Cambridge, 1994).

Status, Power, and Resistance in British North America

Thomas J. Davis, *A Rumour of Revolt: The "Great Negro Plot" in Colonial New York* (New York, 1985).

Sylvia Frey, *Like Water from the Rock: Black Resistance in a Revolutionary Age* (Princeton, 1991).

A. Leon Higginbotham, Jr., *In the Matter of Color: Race and the American Legal Process in the Colonial Period* (New York, 1978).

Graham Russell Hodges, *Root and Branch: African Americans in New York and East New Jersey, 1613–1863* (Chapel Hill, 1999).

Graham Russell Hodges, *Slavery and Freedom in the Rural North: African Americans in Monmouth County, New Jersey, 1665–1865* (Madison, Wis., 1997).

Peter Hoffer, *The Great New York Conspiracy of 1741: Slavery, Crime, and Colonial Law* (Lawrence, 2003).

Marvin L. Michael Kay and Lorin Lee Cary, *Slavery in North Carolina, 1748–1775* (Chapel Hill, 1995).

Jill Lepore, *New York Burning: Liberty, Slavery, and Conspiracy in Eighteenth-Century Manhattan* (New York, 2005).

Edward J. McManus, *Black Bondage in the North* (Syracuse, 1973).

Kenneth P. Minkema, "Jonathan Edwards on Slavery and the Slave Trade," *William and Mary Quarterly*, 54 (1997), 823–34.

Edmund S. Morgan, *American Slavery, American Freedom: The Ordeal of Colonial Virginia* (New York, 1975).

Gerald W. Mullin, *Flight and Rebellion: Slave Resistance in Eighteenth-Century Virginia* (New York, 1972).

Robert Olwell, *Masters, Slaves, and Subjects: The Culture of Power in the South Carolina Low Country, 1740–1790* (Ithaca, 1998).

Philip J. Schwartz, *Twice Condemned: Slaves and the Criminal Laws of Virginia, 1705–1865* (Baton Rouge, 1988).

Jean R. Soderland, *Quakers and Slavery: A Divided Spirit* (Princeton, 1985).

John Thornton, "The African Dimensions of the Stono Rebellion," *American Historical Review*, 96 (1991), 1101–13.

Larry E. Tise, *Proslavery: A History of the Defense of Slavery in America, 1701–1840* (Athens, Ga., 1987).

David Waldstreicher, "Reading the Runaways: Self-fashioning, Print Culture, and Confidence in Slavery in the Eighteenth-Century Mid-Atlantic," *William and Mary Quarterly*, 56 (1999), 243–72.

William M. Wiecek, "The Statutory Law of Slavery and Race in the Thirteen Mainland Colonies of British America," *William and Mary Quarterly*, 34 (1977), 258–80.

Free African Americans

Ira Berlin, *Slaves without Masters: The Free Negro in the Antebellum South* (New York, 1974).

Mariana Dantas, *Black Townsmen: Urban Slavery and Freedom in the Eighteenth-Century Americas* (New York, 2008).

Jane Landers, "Gracia Real de Santa Teresa de Mose: A Free Black Town in Spanish Colonial Florida," *American Historical Review*, 95 (1990), 9–30.

William D. Piersen, *Black Yankees: The Development of an Afro-American Subculture in Eighteenth-Century New England* (Amherst, 1988).

Slavery in the Caribbean

Vincent Brown, *The Reaper's Garden: Death and Power in the World of Atlantic Slavery* (Cambridge, Mass., 2008).

Trevor Burnard, *Mastery, Tyranny, and Desire: Thomas Thistlewood and His Slaves in the Anglo-Jamaican World* (Chapel Hill, 2004).

Barbara Bush, *Slave Women in Caribbean Society, 1650–1838* (Bloomington, 1990)

Richard B. Sheridan, "The Formation of Caribbean Plantation Society, 1689–1748," in *The Oxford History of the British Empire*, Vol. 2: *The Eighteenth Century*, ed. P. J. Marshall (New York, 1998), 393–414.

Richard B. Sheridan, *Sugar and Slavery: An Economic History of the British West Indies, 1623–1775* (Baltimore, 1974).

The Development of Racial Thought and Racism

Anthony L. Barker, *The African Link: British Attitudes to the Negro in the Era of the Atlantic Slave Trade, 1550–1807* (London, 1978).

Emily C. Bartels, "*Othello* and Africa: Postcolonialism Reconsidered," *William and Mary Quarterly*, 54 (1997), 45–64.

George Boulikos, *The Grateful Slave: The Emergence of Race in Eighteenth-Century British and American Culture* (Cambridge, 2008).

David Brion Davis, *The Problem of Slavery in Western Culture* (Ithaca, 1975).

Winthrop D. Jordan, *White Over Black: American Attitudes toward the Negro, 1550–1812* (Chapel Hill, 1968).

Michael McGiffert, ed., "Constructing Race: Differentiating Peoples in the Early Modern World," *William and Mary Quarterly*, 54 (1997), 3–6.

John Sweet, *Bodies Politic: Negotiating Race in the American North, 1730–1830* (Baltimore, 2003).

Alden T. Vaughan and Virginia Mason Vaughan, "Before *Othello*: Elizabethan Representations of Sub-Saharan Africans," *William and Mary Quarterly*, 54 (1997), 19–44.

CHAPTER 15   EXPANDING SPANISH AND FRENCH EMPIRES IN NORTH AMERICA

General Histories and the Borderlands

John Francis Bannon, *The Spanish Borderlands Frontier, 1513–1821* (New York, 1970).

Leslie Bethell, ed., *Colonial Latin America: The Cambridge History of Latin America*, 2 vols (Cambridge, 1984).

Stanley J. Palmer and Dennis Reinhartz, eds, *Essays on the History of North American Discovery and Exploration* (College Station, 1988).

Carl O. Sauer, *Seventeenth-Century North America: The Land and the People as Seen by Europeans* (Berkeley, 1971).

David Hurst Thomas, ed., Columbian Consequences, Vol. 1: *Archaeological and Historical Perspectives on the Spanish Borderlands West* (Washington, DC, 1989).

David J. Weber, *The Spanish Frontier in North America* (New Haven, 1992).

David J. Weber, "Turner, the Boltonians, and the Borderlands," *American Historical Review*, 91 (1986), 66–81.

J. Leitch Wright, Jr., *Anglo-Spanish Rivalry in North America* (Athens, Ga., 1971).

Florida

Mark F. Boyd et al., *Here They Once Stood: The Tragic End of the Apalachee Missions* (1951; reprinted Gainesville, 1999).

Amy Turner Bushnell, *Situado and Sabana: Spain's Support System for the Presidio and Mission Provinces of Florida* (Athens, Ga., 1994).

Kathleen A. Deagan, ed., *Spanish St. Augustine: The Archeology of a Colonial Creole Community* (New York, 1983).

Ernest F. Dibble and Earle W. Newton, *Spain and Her Rivals on the Gulf Coast* (Pensacola, 1971).

John H. Hann, *Apalachee: The Land between the Rivers* (Gainesville, 1998).

John H. Hann, *A History of the Timucua Indians and Missions* (Gainesville, 1996).

John H. Hann and Bonnie G. McEwan, *The Apalachee Indians and Mission San Luis* (Gainesville, 1998).

Paul E. Hoffman, *Florida's Frontiers* (Bloomington, 2002).

Paul E. Hoffman, *A New Andalucia and a Way to the Orient: The American Southeast during the Sixteenth Century* (Baton Rouge, 1990).

Charles Hudson and Carmen Chaves Tesser, *The Forgotten Centuries: Indians and Europeans in the American South, 1521–1704* (Athens, Ga., 1994).

Jane Landers, "Spanish Sanctuary: Fugitives in Florida, 1687–1790," *Florida Historical Quarterly*, 62 (1984), 296–313.

Eugene Lyon, *The Enterprise of Florida: Pedro Menéndez de Avilés and the Spanish Conquest of 1565–1568* (Gainesville, 1976).

Bonnie G. McEwan, ed., *The Spanish Missions of "La Florida"* (Gainesville, 1993).

Robert Allen Matter, "Missions in the Defense of Spanish Florida, 1566–1710," *Florida Historical Quarterly*, 54 (1975), 18–38.

Robert Allen Matter, *Pre-Seminole Florida: Spanish Soldiers, Friars, and Indian Missions, 1513–1763* (New York, 1990).

Jerald T. Milanich, *The Timucua* (Oxford, 1996).

Jean Parker Waterbury, ed., *The Oldest City: St. Augustine, Saga of Survival* (St. Augustine, 1983).

Randolph J. Widmer, *The Evolution of the Calusa: A Nonagricultural Chiefdom on the Southwest Florida Coast* (Tuscaloosa, 1988).

New Mexico

James Brooks, *Captives and Cousins: Slavery, Kinship, and Community in the Southwest Borderlands* (Chapel Hill, 2002).

Ramón A. Gutiérrez, *When Jesus Came, the Corn Mothers Went Away: Marriage, Sexuality, and Power in New Mexico, 1500–1846* (Stanford, 1991).

Elizabeth A. H. John, *Storms Brewed in Other Men's Worlds: The Confrontation of Indians, Spanish, and French in the Southwest, 1540–1795* (College Station, 1975).

Oakah L. Jones, *Los Paisanos: Spanish Settlers on the Northern Frontier of New Spain* (Norman, 1979).

Oakah L. Jones, *Nueva Vizcaya: Heartland of the Spanish Frontier* (Albuquerque, 1988).

Caroll L. Riley, *Rio del Norte: People of the Upper Rio Grande from Earliest Times to the Pueblo Revolt* (Salt Lake City, 1995).

Marc Simmons, *Albuquerque: A Narrative History* (Albuquerque, 1982).

W. H. Timmons, *El Paso: A Borderlands History* (El Paso, 1990).

David J. Weber, *Myth and the History of the Hispanic Southwest: Essays* (Albuquerque, 1988).

David J. Weber, ed., *Foreigners in Their Native Land: Historical Roots of the Mexican Americans* (Albuquerque, 1973).

David J. Weber, ed., *New Spain's Far Northern Frontier: Essays on Spain in the American West* (Albuquerque, 1979).

Texas

Juliana Barr, *Peace Came in the Form of a Woman: Indians and Spaniards in the Texas Borderlands* (Chapel Hill, 2007).

Herbert E. Bolton, *Texas in the Middle Eighteenth Century: Studies in Spanish Colonial History and Administration* (1915; reprinted Austin, 1970).

William C. Foster, *Spanish Expeditions in Texas, 1689–1768* (Austin, 1995).

Jack Jackson, *Los Mestenos: Spanish Ranching in Texas, 1721–1821* (College Station, 1986).

Gerald E. Poyo and Gilbert M. Hinojosa, "Spanish Texas and Borderlands Historiography in Transition: Implications for United States History," *Journal of American History*, 75 (1988–9), 393–416.

California

Stephen Hackel, *Children of Coyote, Missionaries of St. Francis: Indian Spanish Relations in Colonial California, 1769–1850* (Chapel Hill, 2005).
Robert Jackson and Edward Castillo, *Indians, Franciscans, and Spanish Colonization: The Impact of the Mission System on California Indians* (Albuquerque, 1996).
James Sandos, *Converting California: Indians and Franciscans in the Missions* (New Haven, 2008).

New France and the Pays d'en Haut

Denys Delage, "L'alliance franco-amerindienne, 1660–1701" [The French–Indian Alliance, 1660–1701], *Recherches amerindiennes au Québec*, 19 (1989), 3–15.
W. J. Eccles, *The Canadian Frontier, 1534–1760*, rev. edn (Albuquerque, 1983).
W. J. Eccles, *The French in North America, 1500–1763* (East Lansing, 1998).
Allan Greer, *Mohawk Saint: Catherine Tekakwitha and the Jesuits* (Oxford, 2005).
Allan Greer, *Peasant, Lord, and Merchant: Rural Society in Three Quebec Parishes, 1740–1840* (Toronto, 1985).
Allan Greer, *The People of New France* (Toronto, 1997).
Gilles Havard, *The Great Peace of Montreal of 1701: French–Native Diplomacy in the Seventeenth Century* (Montréal, 2001).
Peter Moogk, *La Nouvelle France: The Making of French Canada: A Cultural History* (East Lansing, 2000).
Susan Sleeper-Smith, *Indian Women and French Men: Rethinking Cultural Encounter in the Western Great Lakes* (Amherst, 2001).
Richard White, *The Middle Ground: Indians, Empires, and Republics in the Great Lakes Region, 1650–1815* (New York, 1991).

Louisiana

Ira Berlin, *Many Thousands Gone: The First Two Centuries of Slavery in North America* (Cambridge, Mass., 1998).
Bradley Bond, ed., *French Colonial Louisiana and the Atlantic World* (Baton Rouge, 2005).
James Taylor Carson, *Searching for the Bright Path: The Mississippi Choctaws from Prehistory to Removal* (Lincoln, Nebr., 1999).
Emily Clark, "'By All the Conduct of their Lives': A Laywomen's Confraternity in New Orleans, 1730–1744," *William and Mary Quarterly*, 54 (1997), 769–94.
John G. Clark, *New Orleans, 1718–1812: An Economic History* (Baton Rouge, 1970).
Carl J. Ekberg, *French Roots in the Illinois Country: The Mississippi Frontier in Colonial Times* (Urbana, 1998).
Patricia K. Galloway, "Choctaw Factionalism and Civil War, 1746–1750," *Journal of Mississippi History*, 44 (1982), 289–327.
Patricia K. Galloway, ed., *La Salle and His Legacy: Frenchmen and Indians in the Lower Mississippi Valley* (Jackson, Miss., 1982).
Gwendolyn Midlo Hall, *Africans in Colonial Louisiana: The Development of Afro-Creole Culture in the Eighteenth Century* (Baton Rouge, 1992).
Thomas N. Ingersoll, *Mammon and Manon in Early New Orleans: The First Slave Society in the Deep South, 1718–1819* (Knoxville, 1999).
Joe Gray Taylor, *Louisiana: A Bicentennial History* (New York, 1976).

Tanis C. Thorne, *The Many Hands of My Relations: French and Indians on the Lower Missouri* (Columbia, 1996).

Daniel H. Usner, Jr., *American Indians in the Lower Mississippi Valley: Social and Economic Histories* (Lincoln, Nebr., 1998).

Daniel H. Usner, Jr., "From African Captivity to American Slavery: The Introduction of Black Laborers to Colonial Louisiana," *Louisiana History*, 20 (1979), 25–48.

Daniel H. Usner, Jr., *Indians, Settlers and Slaves in a Frontier Exchange Economy: The Lower Mississippi Valley Before 1783* (Chapel Hill, 1992).

John A. Walthall and Thomas E. Emerson, *Calumet and Fleur-de-Lys: Archaeology of Indian and French Contact in the Midcontinent* (Washington, DC, 1992).

Robert S. Weddle, *The French Thorn: Rival Explorers in the Spanish Sea, 1682–1762* (College Station, 1991).

Richard White, *The Roots of Dependency: Subsistence, Environment, and Social Change among the Choctaws, Pawnees, and Navajos* (Lincoln, Nebr., 1983).

Patricia D. Woods, *French–Indian Relations on the Southern Frontier, 1699–1762* (Ann Arbor, 1980).

The West beyond European Hegemony

Ned Blackhawk, *Violence over the Land: Indians and Empires in the Early American West* (Cambridge, Mass., 2006).

Colin G. Calloway, *One Vast Winter Count: The Native American West Before Lewis and Clark* (Lincoln, Nebr., 2003)

Kathleen DuVal, *The Native Ground: Indians and Colonists in the Heart of the Continent* (Philadelphia, 2006).

Pekka Hamalainen, *The Comanche Empire* (New Haven, 2009).

Paul W. Mapp, *The Elusive West and the Contest for Empire, 1713–1763* (Chapel Hill, 2011).

CHAPTER 16   NATIVE AMERICAN SOCIETIES AND CULTURES, 1689–1760

General

James Axtell, *The European and the Indian: Essays in the Ethnohistory of Colonial North America* (New York, 1981).

James Axtell, "The White Indians of Colonial America," *William and Mary Quarterly*, 32 (1975), 55–88.

James Axtell and William C. Sturtevant, "The Unkindest Cut, or, Who Invented Scalping," *William and Mary Quarterly*, 37 (1980), 451–72.

Colin Calloway, *New Worlds for All: Indians, Europeans, and the Remaking of Early America* (Baltimore, 1998).

Andrew R. L. Cayton and Fredrika J. Teute, *Contact Points: American Frontiers from the Mohawk Valley to the Mississippi, 1750–1830* (Chapel Hill, 1998).

Gregory Evans Dowd, *A Spirited Resistance: The North American Indian Struggle for Unity, 1745–1815* (Baltimore, 1992).

W. J. Eccles, "The Fur Trade and Eighteenth-Century Imperialism," *William and Mary Quarterly*, 40 (1983), 341–62.

Robert S. Grumet, *Historic Contact: Indian Peoples and Colonists in Today's Northeastern United States in the Sixteenth through Eighteenth Centuries* (Norman, 1995).

Shepard Krech III, ed., *Indians, Animals, and the Fur Trade: A Critique of "Keepers of the Game"* (Athens, Ga., 1981).

Calvin Martin, *Keepers of the Game: Indian–Animal Relationships and the Fur Trade* (Berkeley, 1978).

Calvin Martin, ed., *The American Indian and the Problem of History* (New York, 1987).

James H. Merrell, "Some Thoughts on Colonial Historians and American Indians," *William and Mary Quarterly*, 46 (1989), 94–119.

Christopher L. Miller and George R. Hamell, "A New Perspective on Indian–White Contact: Cultural Symbols and Colonial Trade," *Journal of American History*, 73 (1986–7), 311–28.

Daniel Richter, *Facing East from Indian Country: A Native History of Early America* (Cambridge, Mass., 2001).

Nancy Shoemaker, *A Strange Likeness: Becoming Red and White in Eighteenth-Century North America* (New York, 2004).

Armstrong Starkey, *European and Native American Warfare, 1675–1815* (Norman, 1998).

Helen Hornbeck Tanner and Adele Haste, *Atlas of Great Lakes Indian History* (Norman, 1987).

Bruce C. Trigger, ed., *Handbook of North American Indians*, Vol. 15: *The Northeast* (Washington, DC, 1978).

A. T. Vaughan, "From White Man to Red Skin: Changing Anglo-American Perceptions of the American Indian," *American Historical Review*, 87 (1982), 917–53.

Wilcomb E. Washburn, *The Indian in America* (New York, 1975).

The Coastal Peoples

Colin G. Calloway, ed., *After King Philip's War: Presence and Persistence in Indian New England* (Hanover, NH, 1997).

William Cronon, *Changes in the Land: Indians, Colonists, and the Ecology of New England* (New York, 1983).

Patrick Frazier, *The Mohicans of Stockbridge* (Lincoln, Nebr., 1992).

Yasuhide Kawashima, *Puritan Justice and the Indian: White Man's Law in Massachusetts, 1630–1763* (Middletown, 1986).

Daniel R. Mandell, *Behind the Frontier: Indians in Eighteenth-Century Eastern Massachusetts* (Lincoln, Nebr., 1996).

Daniel R. Mandell, "Shifting Boundaries of Race and Ethnicity: Indian–Black Intermarriage in Southern New England, 1760–1880," *Journal of American History*, 85 (1998), 466–501.

James H. Merrell, "Cultural Continuity among the Piscataway Indians of Colonial Maryland," *William and Mary Quarterly*, 36 (1979), 548–71.

Jean M. O'Brien, *Dispossession by Degrees: Indian Land and Identity in Natick, Massachusetts, 1650–1790* (Cambridge, 1997).

Ann Marie Plane, *Colonial Intimacies: Indian Marriage in Early New England* (Ithaca, 2000).

James P. Ronda, "Generations of Faith: The Christian Indians of Martha's Vineyard," *William and Mary Quarterly*, 38 (1981), 369–94.

David Silverman, *Faith and Boundaries: Colonists, Christianity, and Community among the Wampanoag Indians of Martha's Vineyard, 1600–1871* (New York, 2005).

Alden T. Vaughan, *New England Encounters: Indians and Euro-Americans, ca. 1600–1850* (Boston, 2000).

Rachel Wheeler, *To Live Upon Hope: Mohicans and Missionaries in the Eighteenth-Century Northeast* (Ithaca, 2008).

The Iroquois

Richard Aquila, *The Iroquois Restoration: Iroquois Diplomacy on the Colonial Frontier, 1701–1754* (Detroit, 1983).

James W. Bradley, *Evolution of the Onondaga Iroquois: Accommodating Change, 1500–1655* (Syracuse, 1987).

Jack Campisi and Laurence Hauptman, eds, *The Oneida Indian Experience: Two Perspectives* (Syracuse, 1988).

Matthew Dennis, *Cultivating a Landscape of Peace: Iroquois–European Encounters in Seventeenth-Century America* (Ithaca, 1993).

William N. Fenton, *The False Faces of the Iroquois* (Norman, 1987).

William N. Fenton, *The Great Law and the Longhouse: A Political History of the Iroquois Confederacy* (Norman, 1998).

Michael K. Foster, Jack Campisi, and Marianne Mithun, eds, *Extending the Rafters: Interdisciplinary Approaches to Iroquoian Studies* (Albany, 1984).

Francis Jennings, *The Ambiguous Iroquois: The Covenant Chain Confederation of Indian Tribes with English Colonies from its Beginnings to the Lancaster Treaty of 1744* (New York, 1984).

Francis Jennings et al., eds, *The History and Culture of Iroquois Diplomacy: An Interdisciplinary Guide to the Treaties of the Six Nations and their League* (Syracuse, 1985).

James T. Moore, *Indian and Jesuit: A Seventeenth-Century Encounter* (Chicago, 1982).

Thomas Elliot Norton, *The Fur Trade in Colonial New York, 1686–1776* (Madison, Wis., 1974).

Daniel K. Richter, *The Ordeal of the Longhouse: The Peoples of the Iroquois League in the Era of European Colonization* (Chapel Hill, 1992).

Daniel K. Richter, "War and Culture: The Iroquois Experience," *William and Mary Quarterly*, 40 (1983), 528–59.

Daniel K. Richter and James H. Merrell, eds, *Beyond the Covenant Chain: The Iroquois and Their Neighbors in Indian North America, 1600–1800* (Syracuse, 1987).

Anthony F. C. Wallace, *The Death and Rebirth of the Seneca* (New York, 1969).

The Micmacs and Abenakis

Colin G. Calloway, *The Western Abenakis of Vermont, 1600–1800: War, Migration and the Survival of an Indian People* (Norman, 1990).

Kenneth M. Morrison, *The Embattled Northeast: The Elusive Ideal of Alliance in Abenaki–Euramerican Relations* (Berkeley, 1984).

Alice Nash, *The Abiding Frontier: Family, Gender, and Religion in Wabanaki History* (Amherst, forthcoming).

L. F. S. Upton, *Micmacs and Colonists: Indian–White Relations in the Maritimes, 1713–1867* (Vancouver, 1980).

Native Peoples of Pennsylvania

Barry C. Kent, *Susquehanna's Indians* (Harrisburg, 1984).

Herbert C. Kraft, *The Lenape: Archeology, History and Ethnography* (Newark, Del., 1986).
C. A. Weslager, *The Delaware Indian Westward Migration* (Wallingford, 1978).

The Peoples of the Southern Frontier

James Axtell, *The Indians' New South: Cultural Change in the Colonial Southeast* (Baton Rouge, 1997).
Kathryn E. Holland Braund, *Deerskins and Duffels: Creek Indian Trade with Anglo-America, 1685–1815* (Lincoln, Nebr., 1993).
David H. Corkran, *The Cherokee Frontier: Conflict and Survival, 1740–1762* (Norman, 1966).
David H. Corkran, *The Creek Frontier, 1540–1783* (Norman, 1967).
Gary Goodwin, *Cherokees in Transition: A Study of Changing Culture and Environment Prior to 1775* (Chicago, 1977).
Tom Hatley, *The Dividing Paths: Cherokees and South Carolinians through the Era of Revolution* (New York, 1993).
Sarah H. Hill, "Weaving History: Cherokee Baskets from the Springplace Mission," *William and Mary Quarterly*, 53 (1996), 115–36.
Charles Hudson, *The Southeastern Indians* (Knoxville, 1976).
James H. Merrell, *The Indians' New World: Catawbas and Their Neighbors from European Contact through the Era of Removal* (Chapel Hill, 1989).
Michael P. Morris, *Trade and the Indians of the Southeast, 1700–1783* (Westport, 1999).
Theda Perdue, *Cherokee Women: Gender and Culture Change, 1700–1835* (Lincoln, Nebr., 1998).
Theda Perdue, *"Mixed Blood" Indians: Racial Construction in the Early South* (Athens, Ga., 2003).
Theda Perdue, *Slavery and the Evolution of Cherokee Society, 1540–1866* (Knoxville, 1979).
John P. Reid, *A Better Kind of Hatchet: Law, Trade and Diplomacy in the Cherokee Nation during the Early Years of European Contact* (University Park, 1976).
John P. Reid, *A Law of Blood: The Primitive Law of the Cherokee Nation* (New York, 1970).
W. Stitt Robinson, *The Southern Colonial Frontier, 1607–1763* (Albuquerque, 1979).
Claudio Saunt, *A New Order of Things: Property, Power, and the Transformation of the Creek Indians, 1733–1816* (New York, 1999).
Richard White, *The Roots of Dependency: Subsistence, Environment, and Change among the Choctaws, Pawnees, and Navajos* (Lincoln, Nebr., 1983).
Peter H. Wood, Gregory A. Waselkov, and M. Thomas Hatley, *Powhatan's Mantle: Indians in the Colonial Southeast* (Lincoln, Nebr., 1989).
J. Leitch Wright, Jr., *Creeks and Seminoles: The Destruction and Regeneration of the Muscogulge People* (Lincoln, Nebr., 1986).
J. Leitch Wright, Jr., *The Only Land They Knew: The Tragic Story of the American Indians in the Old South* (New York, 1981).

CHAPTER 17   IMMIGRATION AND EXPANSION IN BRITISH NORTH AMERICA, 1714–1750

Immigrant Groups: Germans, Scots-Irish, Jews

Bernard Bailyn, *The Peopling of British North America: An Introduction* (New York, 1986).

Bernard Bailyn and Philip D. Morgan, *Strangers within the Realm: Cultural Margins of the First British Empire* (Chapel Hill, 1991).

H. Tyler Blethen and Curtis W. Wood, Jr., *Ulster and North America: Transatlantic Perspectives on the Scotch-Irish* (Tuscaloosa, 1997).

Jon Butler, *The Huguenots in America: A Refugee People in New World Society* (Cambridge, Mass., 1983).

Nicholas Canny, ed., *Europeans on the Move: Studies on European Migration, 1500–1800* (Oxford, 1994).

R. J. Dickson, *Ulster Emigration to Colonial America, 1718–1775* (London, 1966).

David Dobson, *The Original Scots Colonists of Early America, 1612–1783* (Baltimore, 1989).

David Dobson, *Scottish Emigration to Colonial America, 1607–1785* (Athens, Ga., 1994).

A. Roger Ekirch, *Bound for America: The Transportation of British Convicts to the Colonies, 1718–1775* (Oxford, 1987).

Eli Faber, *A Time for Planting: The First Migration, 1654–1820.* The Jewish People in America, 1 (Baltimore, 1992).

Rory Fitzpatrick, *God's Frontiersmen: The Epic of the Scots-Irish* (London, 1989).

Aaron Spencer Fogleman, "From Slaves, Convicts, and Servants to Free Passengers: The Transformation of Immigration in the Era of the American Revolution," *Journal of American History*, 85 (1998–9), 43–76.

Aaron Spencer Fogleman, *Hopeful Journeys: German Immigration, Settlements, and Political Culture in Colonial America, 1717–1775* (Philadelphia, 1996).

Aaron Spencer Fogleman, *Jesus is Female: Moravians and the Challenge of Radical Religion in Early America* (Philadelphia, 2007).

Patrick Griffin, *The People with No Name: Ireland's Ulster Scots, America's Scots Irish, and the Creation of a British Atlantic World, 1689–1764* (Princeton, 2001).

Mark Haberlein, "German Migrants in Colonial Pennsylvania: Resources, Opportunities and Experience," *William and Mary Quarterly*, 50 (1993), 555–74.

Ned C. Landsman, *Scotland and Its First American Colony, 1683–1765* (Princeton, 1985).

Hartmut Lehmann et al., *In Search of Peace and Prosperity: New Settlements in Eighteenth-Century Europe and North America* (University Park, 2000).

W. C. Lehmann, *Scottish and Scotch-Irish Contributions to Early American Life and Culture* (Port Washington, 1978).

Audrey Lockhart, *Some Aspects of Emigration from Ireland to the North American Colonies between 1660 and 1775* (New York, 1976).

Jacob R. Marcus, *The Colonial American Jew, 1492–1776*, 3 vols (Detroit, 1970).

Gwenda Morgan and Peter Rushton, *Eighteenth-Century Criminal Transportation: The Formation of the Criminal Atlantic* (New York, 2004).

Philip Otterness, *Becoming German: The 1709 Palatine Migration to New York* (Ithaca, 2004).

James C. Riley, "Mortality on Long-Distance Voyages in the Eighteenth Century," *Journal of Economic History*, 41 (1981), 651–6.

A. G. Roeber, "In German Ways? Problems and Potentials of Eighteenth-Century German Social and Emigration History," *William and Mary Quarterly*, 44 (1987), 750–74.

A. G. Roeber, *Palatines, Liberty, and Property: German Lutherans in Colonial British America* (Baltimore, 1993).

Daniel B. Thorp, *The Moravian Community in Colonial North Carolina: Pluralism on the Southern Frontier* (Knoxville, 1989).

Barry Aron Vann, *In Search of Ulster-Scots Land: The Birth and Geotheological Imaginings of a Transatlantic People, 1603–1703* (Columbia, 2008).

Lorena S. Walsh, "Staying Put or Getting Out: Findings for Charles County, 1650–1720," *William and Mary Quarterly*, 44 (1987), 89–103.

Robert V. Wells, *The Population of the British Colonies in America Before 1776: A Survey of Census Data* (Princeton, 1975).

Marianne Wokeck, "The Dynamics of German Speaking Emigration to British North America, 1683–1783," in Ida Altman and James Horn, eds, *"To Make America": European Emigration in the Early Modern Period* (Berkeley, 1991).

Stephanie Grauman Wolf, *Urban Village: Population, Community, and Family Structure in Germantown, Pennsylvania, 1683–1800* (Princeton, 1976).

The Backcountry or Frontier Region

Craig Atwood, *Community of the Cross: Moravian Piety in Colonial Bethlehem* (University Park, 2004).

David Colin Crass, ed., *The Southern Colonial Backcountry: Interdisciplinary Perspectives on Frontier Communities* (Knoxville, 1998).

Eric Hinderaker and Peter Mancall, *At the Edge of Empire: The Backcountry in British North America* (Baltimore, 2003).

Warren R. Hofstra, "'The Extention of His Majesties Dominions': The Virginia Backcountry and the Reconfiguration of Imperial Frontiers," *Journal of American History*, 84 (1997–8), 1281–312.

Warren R. Hofstra, *The Planting of New Virginia: Settlement and Landscape in the Shenandoah Valley* (Baltimore, 2004).

George Lloyd Johnson, Jr., *The Frontier in the Colonial South: South Carolina Backcountry, 1736–1800* (Greenwood, 1997).

Terry G. Jordan and Matti Kaups, *The American Backwoods Frontier: An Ethnic and Ecological Interpretation* (Baltimore, 1989).

Peter Mancall, *Valley of Opportunity: Economic Culture along the Upper Susquehanna* (Ithaca, 1991).

James Merrell, *Into the American Woods: Negotiations on the Pennsylvania Frontier* (New York, 2000).

Jane Merritt, *At the Crossroads: Indians and Empires on a Mid-Atlantic Frontier* (Chapel Hill, 2003).

Robert D. Mitchell, *Commercialism and Frontier: Perspectives on the Early Shenandoah Valley* (Charlottesville, 1977).

Gregory H. Nobles, "Breaking into the Backcountry: New Approaches to the Early American Frontier, 1750–1880," *William and Mary Quarterly*, 46 (1989), 641–70.

Michael J. Puglisi, ed., *Diversity and Accommodation: Essays on the Cultural Composition of the Virginia Frontier* (Knoxville, 1997).

Peter Silver, *Our Savage Neighbors: How Indian War Transformed Early America* (New York, 2008).

Richard Slotkin, *Regeneration through Violence: The Mythology of the American Frontier, 1600–1860* (Middletown, 1973).

Georgia

Kenneth Coleman, *Colonial Georgia: A History* (New York, 1976).

Kenneth Coleman, ed., *A History of Georgia* (Athens, Ga., 1977).

Harold E. Davis, *The Fledgling Province: Social and Cultural Life in Colonial Georgia, 1733–1776* (Chapel Hill, 1976).

Alan Gallay, *The Formation of a Planter Elite: Jonathan Bryan and the Southern Colonial Frontier* (Athens, Ga., 1989).

Alan Gallay, "Jonathan Bryan's Plantation Empire: Land, Politics, and the Formation of a Ruling Class in Colonial Georgia," *William and Mary Quarterly*, 45 (1988), 253–79.

Harvey H. Jackson and Phinizy Spalding, eds, *Forty Years of Diversity: Essays on Colonial Georgia* (Athens, Ga., 1984).

Anthony W. Parker, *Scottish Highlanders in Colonial Georgia: The Recruitment, Emigration and Settlement at Darien, 1735–1748* (Athens, Ga., 1997).

Phinizy Spalding, *Oglethorpe in America* (Chicago, 1977).

Phinizy Spalding and Harvey H. Jackson, *Oglethorpe in Perspective: Georgia's Founder after Two Hundred Years* (Tuscaloosa, 1989).

Paul S. Taylor, *Georgia Plan: 1732–1752* (Berkeley, 1972).

Clarence L. Ver Steeg, *Origins of a Southern Mosaic: Studies of Early Carolina and Georgia* (Athens, Ga., 1975).

Betty Wood, *Slavery in Colonial Georgia, 1730–1755* (Athens, Ga., 1984).

Betty Wood, *Women's Work, Men's Work: The Informal Slave Economies of Lowcountry Georgia* (Athens, Ga., 1995).

The Colonial Town

Carl Bridenbaugh, *Cities in Revolt: Urban Life in America, 1743–1776* (New York, 1955).

Carl Bridenbaugh, *Cities in the Wilderness: The First Century of Urban Life in America, 1625–1742* (New York, 1938).

Bruce C. Daniels, *Town and County: Essays on the Structure of Local Government in the American Colonies* (Middletown, 1978).

Carville V. Earle and Ronald Hoffman, "Urban Development in the Eighteenth-Century South," *Perspectives in American History*, 10 (1976), 7–78.

Joseph A. Ernst and H. Roy Merrens, "'Camden's Turrets Pierce the Skies!': The Urban Process in the Southern Colonies during the Eighteenth Century," *William and Mary Quarterly*, 30 (1973), 549–74.

Douglas Greenberg, *Crime and Law Enforcement in the Colony of New York, 1691–1776* (Ithaca, 1976).

Douglas Lamar Jones, *Village and Seaport: Migration and Society in Eighteenth-Century Massachusetts* (Hanover, NH, 1981).

Susan E. Klepp, *Philadelphia in Transition: A Demographic History of the City and Its Occupational Groups, 1720–1830* (New York, 1989).

Gary B. Nash, *The Urban Crucible: Social Change, Political Consciousness, and the Origins of the American Revolution* (Cambridge, Mass., 1979).

G. B. Warden, *Boston, 1689–1776* (Boston, 1970).

Hermann Wellenreuther, "Urbanization in the Colonial South: A Critique," *William and Mary Quarterly*, 31 (1974), 653–68.

Lynne Withey, *Urban Growth in Colonial Rhode Island: Newport and Providence in the Eighteenth Century* (Albany, 1984).

Jerome H. Wood, Jr., *Conestoga Crossroads: Lancaster, Pennsylvania, 1730–1790* (Harrisburg, 1979).

CHAPTER 18 BRITISH NORTH AMERICAN INSTITUTIONS OF GOVERNMENT

Royal Government

Mary Sarah Bilder, *The Transatlantic Constitution: Colonial Legal Culture and the Empire* (Cambridge, Mass., 2004).

H. V. Bowen, *Elites, Enterprise and the Making of the British Overseas Empire, 1688–1775* (Basingstoke, 1996).

Jack P. Greene, *Negotiated Authorities: Essays on Colonial Political and Constitutional History* (Charlottesville, 1994).

Jack P. Greene, *Peripheries and Center: Constitutional Development in the Extended Politics of the British Empire and the United States, 1607–1788* (Athens, Ga., 1986).

James A. Henretta, *"Salutary Neglect": Colonial Administration under the Duke of Newcastle* (Princeton, 1972).

Michael G. Kammen, *Empire and Interest: The American Colonies and the Politics of Mercantilism* (Philadelphia, 1970).

P. J. Marshall, *The Making and Unmaking of Empires: Britain, India, and America, 1750–1783* (Oxford, 2005).

Richard Middleton, "The Duke of Newcastle and the Conduct of Patronage during the Seven Years' War, 1757–1762," *British Journal for Eighteenth-Century Studies*, 12 (1989), 175–86.

Alison Gilbert Olson, *Making the Empire Work: London and American Interest Groups, 1690–1790* (Cambridge, Mass., 1992).

Steven Sarson, *British America, 1500–1800: Creating Colonies, Imagining an Empire* (London, 2005).

Local Government: Town and County

David Grayson Allen, "The Zuckerman Thesis and the Process of Legal Rationalization in Provincial Massachusetts," with a rebuttal by Michael Zuckerman, *William and Mary Quarterly*, 29 (1972), 443–68.

Richard R. Beeman, *The Evolution of the Southern Backcountry: A Case Study of Lunenburg County, Virginia, 1746–1832* (Philadelphia, 1984).

Richard R. Beeman, "Social Change and Cultural Conflict in Virginia: Lunenburg County, 1746–1774, *William and Mary Quarterly*, 35 (1978), 455–76.

Edward Byers, *The Nation of Nantucket: Society and Politics in an Early American Commercial Center, 1660–1820* (Boston, 1986).

Edward M. Cook, Jr., *The Fathers of the Towns: Leadership and Community Structure in Eighteenth-Century New England* (Baltimore, 1976).

Edward M. Cook, Jr., "Social Behavior and Changing Values in Dedham, Massachusetts, 1700–1775," *William and Mary Quarterly*, 27 (1970), 546–80.

Bruce C. Daniels, *The Connecticut Town: Growth and Development, 1635–1790* (Middletown, 1979).

Bruce C. Daniels, *The Fragmentation of New England: Comparative Perspectives on Economic, Political, and Social Divisions in the Eighteenth Century* (Westport, 1988).

Bruce C. Daniels, *Town and County: Essays on the Structure of Local Government in the American Colonies* (Middletown, 1978).

Carville V. Earle, *The Evolution of a Tidewater Settlement System: All Hallow's Parish, Maryland, 1650–1783* (Chicago, 1975).

George W. Franz, *Paxton: A Study of Community Structure and Mobility in the Colonial Pennsylvania Backcountry* (New York, 1989).

Christine Leigh Heyrman, *Commerce and Culture: The Maritime Communities of Colonial Massachusetts, 1690–1750* (New York, 1984).

Richard Holmes, *Communities in Transition: Bedford and Lincoln, Massachusetts, 1729–1850* (Ann Arbor, 1980).

Jessica Kross, *The Evolution of an American Town: Newtown, New York, 1624–1775* (Philadelphia, 1983).

Barry Levy, *Town Born: The Political Economy of New England from Its Founding to the Revolution* (Philadelphia, 2009).

Kenneth A. Lockridge, *A New England Town: The First Hundred Years, Dedham, Massachusetts, 1636–1736* (New York, 1970).

Gwenda Morgan, *The Hegemony of the Law: Richmond County, Virginia, 1692–1776* (New York, 1989).

Gregory H. Nobles, *Divisions throughout the Whole: Politics and Society in Hampshire County, Massachusetts, 1740–1775* (New York, 1983).

A. G. Roeber, "Authority, Law, and Custom: The Rituals of Court Day in Tidewater Virginia, 1720–1750," *William and Mary Quarterly*, 37 (1980), 29–52.

Darrett B. Rutman, "Assessing the Little Communities of Early America," *William and Mary Quarterly*, 43 (1986), 163–78.

Darrett B. Rutman and Anita H. Rutman, *A Place in Time: Middlesex County, Virginia 1650–1750* (New York, 1984).

Stephanie G. Wolf, *Urban Village: Population, Community, and Family Structure in Germantown, Pennsylvania, 1683–1800* (Princeton, 1976).

Michael Zuckerman, *Peaceable Kingdoms: New England Towns in the Eighteenth Century* (New York, 1970).

The Provincial Assembly: Crown versus People

Michael Batinski, *Jonathan Belcher, Colonial Governor* (Lexington, Ky., 1996).

Richard L. Bushman, *King and People in Provincial Massachusetts* (Chapel Hill, 1985).

Robert J. Dinkin, *Voting in Provincial America: A Study of Elections in the Thirteen Colonies, 1689–1776* (Westport, 1977).

Jack P. Greene, "The Growth of Political Stability: An Interpretation of Political Development in the Anglo-American Colonies, 1660–1760," in John Parker and Carol Urness, eds, *The American Revolution: A Heritage of Change* (Minneapolis, 1975).

Jack P. Greene, "Legislative Turnover in British America, 1696–1775: A Quantitative Analysis," *William and Mary Quarterly*, 38 (1981), 442–63.

Jack P. Greene, "Political Mimesis: A Consideration of the Historical and Cultural Roots of Legislative Behavior in the British Colonies in the Eighteenth Century," with a reply by Bernard Bailyn, *American Historical Review*, 75 (1969–70), 337–67.

Jack P. Greene, *The Quest for Power: The Lower Houses of Assembly in the Southern Royal Colonies, 1689–1776* (Chapel Hill, 1963).

Daniel Hulsebosch, *Constituting Empire: New York and the Transformation of Constitutionalism in the Atlantic World, 1664–1830* (Chapel Hill, 2005).

James H. Hutson, *Pennsylvania Politics, 1746–1770: The Movement for Royal Government and Its Consequences* (Princeton, 1972).

Michael Kammen, *A Rope of Sand: The Colonial Agents, British Politics, and the American Revolution* (Ithaca, 1968).

Stanley N. Katz, "Between Scylla and Charybdis: James DeLancey and Anglo-American Politics in Early Eighteenth-Century New York," in Alison G. Olson and Richard M. Brown, eds, *Anglo-American Political Relations, 1675–1775* (New Brunswick, 1970).

Mary Lou Lustig, *Robert Hunter, 1666–1734: New York's Augustan Statesman* (Syracuse, 1983).

Edmund S. Morgan, *Inventing the People: The Rise of Popular Sovereignty in England and America* (New York, 1988).

J. R. Pole, *Political Representation in England and the Origins of the American Republic* (New York, 1966).

Thomas L. Purvis, "'High Born, Long Recorded Families': Social Origins of New Jersey Assemblymen, 1703–1776," *William and Mary Quarterly*, 37 (1980), 592–615.

Thomas L. Purvis, *Proprietors, Patronage, and Paper Money: Legislative Politics in New Jersey, 1703–1776* (New Brunswick, 1986).

Eugene R. Sheridan, *Lewis Morris, 1671–1746: A Study in Early American Politics* (Syracuse, 1981).

Bruce P. Stark, "'A Factious Spirit': Constitutional Theory and Political Practice in Connecticut, 1740," *William and Mary Quarterly*, 47 (1990), 391–410.

Alan Tully, *William Penn's Legacy: Politics and Social Structure in Provincial Pennsylvania, 1726–1755* (Baltimore, 1977).

Political Practices in the Age of Walpole

Bernard Bailyn, *The Origins of American Politics* (New York, 1968).

Richard R. Beeman, *The Varieties of Political Experience in Eighteenth-Century America* (Philadelphia, 2004).

Patricia U. Bonomi, *A Factious People: Politics and Society in Colonial New York* (New York, 1971).

Bruce C. Daniels, ed., *Power and Status: Officeholding in Colonial America* (Middletown, 1986).

Marc Egnal, *A Mighty Empire: The Origins of the American Revolution* (Ithaca, 1988).

A. Roger Ekirch, *"Poor Carolina": Politics and Society in Colonial North Carolina, 1729–1776* (Chapel Hill, 1981).

Joy B. Gilsdorf and Robert R. Gilsdorf, "Elites and Electorates: Some Plain Truths for Historians of Colonial America," in David D. Hall, John M. Murrin, and Thad W. Tate, eds, *Saints and Revolutionaries: Essays on Early American History* (New York, 1984).

Stanley Nider Katz, *Newcastle's New York: Anglo-American Politics, 1732–1753* (Cambridge, Mass., 1968).

John Gilman Kolp, "The Dynamics of Electoral Competition in Pre-Revolutionary Virginia," *William and Mary Quarterly*, 49 (1992), 652–74.

John Gilman Kolp, *Gentlemen and Freeholders: Electoral Politics in Colonial Virginia* (Baltimore, 1998).

Kenneth A. Lockridge, *Settlement and Unsettlement in Early America: Political Legitimacy Before the Revolution* (Cambridge, 1981).

Brendan McConville, *These Daring Disturbers of the Public Peace: The Struggle for Property and Power in Early New Jersey* (Ithaca, 1999).

John McCurdy, *Citizen Bachelors: Manhood and the Creation of the United States* (Ithaca, 2009).

Simon Middleton, *From Privileges to Rights: Work and Politics in Colonial New York City* (Philadelphia, 2006).

Benjamin H. Newcomb, *Political Partisanship in the American Middle Colonies, 1700–1776* (Baton Rouge, 1995).

Gregory Nobles, *Divisions throughout the Whole: Politics and Society in Hampshire County, Massachusetts, 1740–1775* (New York, 1983).

Alison Gilbert Olson, *Anglo-American Politics, 1660–1775: The Relationship between Parties in England and Colonial America* (New York, 1973).

Thomas L. Purvis, "'High Born, Long Recorded Families': Social Origins of New Jersey Assemblymen, 1703–1776," *William and Mary Quarterly*, 37 (1980), 592–615.

Thomas L. Purvis, "Origins and Patterns of Agrarian Unrest in New Jersey, 1735–1754," *William and Mary Quarterly*, 39 (1982), 600–27.

I. K. Steele, "The Empire and Provincial Elites: An Interpretation of Some Recent Writings on the English Atlantic, 1675–1740," *Journal of Imperial and Commonwealth History*, 8 (1980), 2–32.

Albert H. Tillson, Jr., *Gentry and Common Folk: Political Culture on a Virginia Frontier, 1740–1789* (Lexington, Ky., 1991).

Alan Tully, *Forming American Politics: Ideals, Interests, and Institutions in Colonial New York and Pennsylvania* (Baltimore, 1994).

Robert M. Weir, "'The Harmony We Were Famous For': An Interpretation of Pre-Revolutionary South Carolina Politics," *William and Mary Quarterly*, 26 (1969), 473–501.

Robert M. Weir, *The Last American Freeman: Studies in the Political Culture of the Colonial and Revolutionary South* (Macon, Ga., 1986).

Robert Zemsky, *Merchants, Farmers, and River Gods: An Essay on Eighteenth-Century American Politics* (Boston, 1971).

Political Ideology

Bernard Bailyn, *The Ideological Origins of the American Revolution* (Cambridge, Mass., 1967).

Richard Beeman, "Deference, Republicanism, and the Emergence of Popular Politics in Eighteenth-Century America," *William and Mary Quarterly*, 49 (1992), 401–30.

T. H. Breen, "Ideology and Nationalism on the Eve of the American Revolution: Revisions Once More in Need of Revising," *Journal of American History*, 84 (1997), 14–35.

Holly Brewer, *By Birth or Consent: Children, Law, and the Anglo-American Revolution in Authority* (Chapel Hill, 2005).

J. M. Bumsted, "'Things in the Womb of Time': Ideas of American Independence, 1633–1763," *William and Mary Quarterly*, 31 (1974), 533–64.

Richard L. Bushman, *King and People in Provincial Massachusetts* (Chapel Hill, 1985).

Robert M. Calhoon, *Dominion and Liberty: Ideology in the Anglo-American World, 1660–1801* (Arlington Heights, 1994).

H. Trevor Colbourn, *The Lamp of Experience: Whig History and the Intellectual Origins of the American Revolution* (Chapel Hill, 1965).

H. T. Dickinson, *Liberty and Property: Political Ideology in Eighteenth-Century Britain* (New York, 1978).

Eliga H. Gould, *The Persistence of Empire: British Political Culture in the Age of the American Revolution* (Chapel Hill, 2000).

Brendan McConville, *The King's Three Faces: The Rise and Fall of Royal America, 1688–1776* (Chapel Hill, 2006).

Richard K. Matthews. *Virtue, Corruption, and Self-Interest: Political Values in the Eighteenth Century* (Bethlehem, Pa., 1994).

Edmund S. Morgan, *Inventing the People: The Rise of Popular Sovereignty in England and America* (New York, 1988).

J. G. A. Pocock, *The Machiavellian Moment: Florentine Political Thought and the Atlantic Republican Tradition* (Princeton, 1975).

J. G. A. Pocock, *Virtue, Commerce, and History: Essays on Political Thought and History, Chiefly in the Eighteenth Century* (New York, 1985).

J. R. Pole, *The Gift of Government: Political Responsibility from the English Restoration to American Independence* (Athens, Ga., 1983).

Caroline Robbins, *The Eighteenth-Century Commonwealthman: Studies in the Transmission, Development, and Circumstance of English Liberal Thought from the Restoration of Charles II until the War with the Thirteen Colonies* (Cambridge, Mass., 1959).

Lee Ward, *The Politics of Liberty in England and Revolutionary America* (Cambridge, 2004).

CHAPTER 19   BRITAIN, FRANCE, AND SPAIN: THE IMPERIAL CONTEST, 1739–1763

General and the War of Jenkins' Ear

Fred Anderson and Andrew Cayton, *The Dominion of War: Empire and Liberty in North America, 1500–2000* (New York, 2005).

Guy Chet, *Conquering the American Wilderness: The Triumph of European Warfare in the Colonial Northeast* (Amherst, 2003).

Lawrence Delbert Cress, *Citizens in Arms: The Army and the Militia in American Society to the War of 1812* (Chapel Hill, 1982).

W. J. Eccles, *The Canadian Frontier, 1534–1760* (New York, 1969; rev. edn, Albuquerque, 1983).

W. J. Eccles, *Essays on New France* (Toronto, 1987).

W. J. Eccles, "The Fur Trade and Eighteenth-Century Imperialism," *William and Mary Quarterly*, 40 (1983), 341–62.

John Mack Faragher, *A Great and Noble Scheme: The Tragic Story of the Expulsion of the French Acadians from Their American Homeland* (New York, 2005).

John Ferling, *Struggle for a Continent: The Wars of Early America* (Arlington Heights, 1993).

John E. Ferling, *A Wilderness of Miseries: War and Warriors in Early America* (Westport, 1980).

Sylvia R. Frey, *The British Soldier in America: A Social History of Military Life in the Colonial Period* (Austin, 1981).

Don Higginbotham, "The Early American Way of War: Reconnaissance and Appraisal," *William and Mary Quarterly*, 44 (1987), 230–73.

Cornelius J. Jaenen, *The French Relationship with the Native Peoples of New France and Acadia* (Ottawa, 1984).

Douglas Edward Leach, *Arms for Empire: A Military History of the British Colonies in North America, 1607–1763* (New York, 1973).

Douglas Edward Leach, *Roots of Conflict: British Armed Forces and Colonial Americans, 1677–1763* (Chapel Hill, 1986).

Paul Mapp, *The Elusive West and the Contest for Empire, 1713–1763* (Chapel Hill, 2011).

George F. G. Stanley, *New France: The Last Phase, 1744–1760* (Toronto, 1968).

Thomas Truxes, *Defying Empire: Trading with the Enemy in Colonial New York* (New Haven, 2008).

The Struggle for the Ohio

John R. Alden, *George Washington: A Biography* (Baton Rouge, 1984).

Daniel J. Beattie, "The Adaptation of the British Army to Wilderness Warfare, 1755–1763," in Maarten Ultee, ed., *Adapting to Conditions: War and Society in the Eighteenth Century* (University, Ala., 1986).

Andrew R. L. Cayton and Fredrika J. Teute, *Contact Points: The American Frontier from the Mohawk Valley to the Mississippi, 1750–1830* (Chapel Hill, 1998).

Milton W. Hamilton, *Sir William Johnson: Colonial American, 1715–1763* (Port Washington, 1976).

Eric Hinderaker, *Elusive Empires: Constructing Colonialism in the Ohio Valley, 1673–1800* (New York, 1997).

Eric Hinderaker and Peter Mancall, *At the Edge of Empire: The Backcountry in British North America* (Baltimore, 2003).

Alfred P. James, *The Ohio Company: Its Inner History* (Pittsburgh, 1959).

Francis Jennings, *Empire of Fortune: Crowns, Colonies, and Tribes in the Seven Years' War in America* (New York, 1988).

P. E. Kopperman, *Braddock at the Monongahela* (Pittsburgh, 1977).

Lee S. McCardell, *Ill-Starred General: Braddock of the Coldstream Guards* (Pittsburgh, 1986).

Michael N. McConnell, *A Country Between: The Upper Ohio Valley and Its Peoples, 1724–1774* (Lincoln, Nebr., 1992).

James Merrell, *Into the American Woods: Negotiators on the Pennsylvania Frontier* (New York, 1999).

Peter E. Russell, "Redcoats in the Wilderness: British Officers and Irregular Warfare in Europe and America, 1740–1760," *William and Mary Quarterly*, 35 (1978), 629–52.

Timothy J. Shannon, *Indians and Colonists at the Crossroads of Empire: The Albany Congress of 1754* (Ithaca, 2000).

James Titus, *The Old Dominion at War: Society, Politics, and Warfare in Late Colonial Virginia* (Columbia, 1991).

Anthony F. C. Wallace, *King of the Delawares: Teedyuscung, 1700–1763* (Syracuse, 1990).

The Conquest of Canada

F. W. Anderson, "Why did Colonial New Englanders Make Bad Soldiers? Contractual Principles and Military Conduct during the Seven Years' War," *William and Mary Quarterly*, 38 (1981), 395–417.

Fred Anderson, *Crucible of War: The Seven Years' War and the Fate of Empire in British North America, 1754–1766* (New York, 2000).

Fred Anderson, *A People's Army: Massachusetts Soldiers and Society in the Seven Years' War* (Chapel Hill, 1984).

Fred Anderson, "A People's Army: Provincial Military Service in Massachusetts during the Seven Years' War," *William and Mary Quarterly*, 40 (1983), 499–527.

Fred Anderson, *The War that Made America: A Short History of the French and Indian War* (New York, 2005).

Colin Calloway, *The Scratch of a Pen: 1763 and the Transformation of North America* (New York, 2006).

James T. Flexner, *Mohawk Baronet: A Biography of Sir William Johnson* (Syracuse, 1990).

J. Fortier, *Fortress of Louisburg* (Toronto, 1979).

Guy Fregault, *Canada: The War of the Conquest* (Toronto, 1969).

Sylvia R. Frey, *The British Soldier in America: A Social History of Military Life in the Colonial Period* (Austin, 1981).

Richard Middleton, *The Bells of Victory: The Pitt–Newcastle Ministry and the Conduct of the Seven Years' War, 1757–1762* (Cambridge, 1985).

Alan Rogers, *Empire and Liberty: American Resistance to British Authority, 1755–1763* (Berkeley, 1974).

Harold E. Selesky, *War and Society in Colonial Connecticut* (New Haven, 1989).

Ian K. Steele, *Betrayals: Fort William Henry and the "Massacre"* (New York, 1990).

Matthew Ward, *Breaking the Backcountry: The Seven Years' War in Virginia and Pennsylvania, 1754–1765* (Pittsburgh, 2003).

The Cherokee War

David H. Corkran, *The Cherokee Frontier: Conflict and Survival, 1740–1762* (Norman, 1966).

Tom Hatley, *The Dividing Paths: Cherokees and South Carolinians through the Revolutionary Era* (New York, 1995).

John Oliphant, *Peace and War on the Anglo-Cherokee Frontier, 1756–1763* (Baton Rouge, 2001).

Pontiac's War

David Dixon, *Never Come to Peace Again: Pontiac's Uprising and the Fate of the British Empire in North America* (Norman, 2005).

Gregory Evans Dowd, *A Spirited Resistance: The North American Struggle for Unity, 1745–1815* (Baltimore, 1992).

Gregory Evans Dowd, *War under Heaven: Pontiac, the Indian Nations, and the British Empire* (Baltimore, 2002).

Richard Middleton, *Pontiac's War: Its Causes, Course, and Consequences* (New York, 2007).

Jon Parmenter, "Pontiac's War: Forging New Links in the Anglo-Iroquois Covenant Chain, 1758–1766," *Ethnohistory*, 44 (1997), 617–54.

The Emergence of Racial Identities and the Paxton Riots

Kevin Kenny, *Peaceable Kingdom Lost: The Paxton Boys and the Destruction of William Penn's Holy Experiment* (New York, 2009).

Jane Merritt, *At the Crossroads: Indians and Empires on a Mid-Atlantic Frontier* (Chapel Hill, 2003).

William Pencak and Daniel Richter, eds, *Friends and Enemies in Penn's Woods: Indians, Colonists, and the Racial Construction of Pennsylvania* (University Park, 2004).

Nancy Shoemaker, *A Strange Likeness: Becoming Red and White in Eighteenth-Century North America* (New York, 2004).

Peter Silver, *Our Savage Neighbors: How Indian War Transformed Early America* (New York, 2008).

Alden Vaughan, "Frontier Banditti and the Indians: The Paxton Boys' Legacy, 1763–1775," *Pennsylvania History*, 51 (1984), 1–29.

Index

Page numbers referring to maps and figures are in italics; subentries are listed chronologically and thematically rather than alphabetically.

Congarees, 417
Congregationalists, 156, 310, 311, 313, 315
Connecticut: establishment, 97–9, 100;
    border disputes with Dutch, 119, 120;
    charter confirmed, 134, 136; reaction to
    and effect of Restoration, 135–6; and Long
    Island, 141; duke of York tries to take over
    western, 145; conflict with James II, 181,
    184; joins Dominion of New
    England, 186; Glorious Revolution
    settlement restores charter, 189; abortive
    invasion of New France, 192; witchcraft
    trials, 204; Bellomont made commander of
    militia, 215; and War of the Spanish
    Succession, 216–17; silver industry, 245;
    paper money, 253; land ownership, 259;
    local elites, 280; churches adopt Saybrook
    Platform, 308, 310; other religious
    changes in eighteenth century, 308, 311,
    313, 316; free African Americans, 360;
    population growth in eighteenth
    century, 435; politics after 1690, 449,
    463, 465; suspending clauses, 462;
    intercolonial conflicts, 466; factional
    fighting, 467; joins attack on Louisburg,
    475–7; attends Albany Congress, 480; and
    French and Indian War, 493
Connecticut River Valley, 78, 97, 171, 204,
    241–2, 467
Conoys, 224, 405, 413
consumerism, 231, 256–7, 299–300, 303–4,
    325, 424; moral critique, 304
contraception, 260, 266
Conventicle Act (1664), 136
convicts: use as labor, 238
Coode, John, 195–6
Cooke, Elisha, Jr., 456, 467
Cooper, Anthony Ashley *see* Shaftesbury,
    Anthony Ashley, earl of
Copley, John Singleton, 331; portraits by, *302*
Corey, Giles, 208
Corey, Martha, 205, 208, 210
corn, 240, 242, 381
Cornbury, Lord, 447, 457, 459, 461
Coronado, Francisco Vázquez de, 38, 375
Corporation Act (1661), 136
Cortés, Hernando, 27, 36
Cosby, William, 447, 459, 468
cotton, 236

Cotton, John, 91, 93, 94, 95, 100, 102
Council for New England (formerly Plymouth
    Company), 80, 84, 97, 99, 101, 121
councils, provincial, 458, 463
county courts, 450, 451, 453
Covenant Chain of Friendship, 134, 145–6,
    397, 403; broken, 473, 479–80
crafts *see* applied arts and crafts
Craven, earl of, 149
Creeks: in Carolinas, 149; involvement in
    imperial wars, 219, 374; attitude to
    European alliances, 221; attack Spanish
    missions, 373, 374; in Louisiana, 390,
    391, 393; in Georgia, 416, 440, 441;
    after 1700, 421–4, *422–3*; and
    liquor, 441; *see also* Apalachicolas (Lower
    Creeks); Upper Creeks
Creoles, 337, 359
Crèvecoeur, J. Hector St. John, 279n, 437
crime and punishment: Native American
    attitude to killing, 17–18; Native American
    execution method, 18; Jamestown, 62,
    69; New England, 91, 92;
    Maryland, 122–3; slaves in West
    Indies, 132–3; New York, 141, 143, 147;
    Crown makes changes to system in
    Dominion of New England, 185;
    punishments for fornication, 293;
    slaves, 132–3, 339–40, 365–6; protection
    for slave owners, 340; treason, 365n;
    contrast between French and Algonquian
    systems, 387; urban crime, 446; *see also*
    judiciary and justice system; laws
Croghan, George, 437, 478, 484, 504
Cromwell, Oliver, 120, 125, 134, 135
Cromwell, Richard, 135
Crown Point, 484, 495, 496
Crozat, Antoine, 392
Cuba, 36, 37, 475, 498, 501
Culpepper, John, 134, 155
Culpepper, Lord, 156, 160, 165
Culpepper's Rising (1677), 134, 155
culture, 308, 309, 326–34;
    Anglicization, 324–6; popular, 332–4;
    African American, 355–9
Cumberland, duke of, 489
Cusabos, 153
customs duties *see* taxes and customs duties
Cutler, Timothy, 311

Wheelwright, Reverend John, 94, 99
Whigs: beliefs, 182
White, John: drawings by, *12*, 13, *14, 15, 44, 57*; on Native Americans, 12, 21, 43; botanical work, 43; plans for City of Raleigh, 44; Roanoke relief expedition, 45
White Oaks, 462
Whitefield, George, 308, 314–15, 318, 357, 366, 441
Whitney, Eli, 236
Willard, Parson Samuel, 208
William III, king of Great Britain and Ireland: ascends throne, 181, 187; colonial reaction, 188, 190–2, 197; colonial policy, 201–2, 215; and Pennsylvania, 223
William of Orange, 144
Williams, Abigail, 204
Williams, Eunice, 216
Williams, Reverend John, 216
Williams, Roger, 78, 93, 96, 104, 211
Williamsburg, 284, 332, 360, 362
Wingfield, Edward, 57
Wingina, Chief, 43
Winnebagos, 386
Winslow, John, 489
Winslow, Josiah, 171
Winthrop, Fitz-John, 184, 192, 214
Winthrop, John, *87*; background, 87–8; voyage to America, 88; landholdings, 89; as governor, 91, 92, 93; and Hutchinson, 94, 95; on Cotton's law code, 102; on equality, 279; death, 78
Winthrop, John, IV, 330
Winthrop, John, Jr., 141, 167–8, 245
Winthrop, Wait, 184
Wisconsin River, 384
Wise, John, 313
witchcraft trials, 200, 202, 203–12, *206*, 284
Wolfe, General James, 473, 495, *496*
women: Native American jobs and roles, 11–12, 13; Native American relationship with men, 15–16; Native American political role, 19; western European jobs and roles, 29; western European relationship with men, 29; Puritan role and status, 94; encouraged to emigrate to New France, 112; in

Maryland, 127–8; Englishwomen's property rights compared with Dutch women's, 144; rights in New York, 148; shortage in Virginia, 157; Salem witchcraft trials as reflections of gender repression and gendered power, 210–11; Quaker treatment, 225, 270; and childrearing, 268; education, 268–9, 288, 299; and patriarchal authority, 272–8; in colonial society, 284–307; gender ideology, 285, 286–7; domestic skills, 288; life expectancy, 291, 293; notable businesswomen, 301–3; in eighteenth century, 296–307; and spending, 304; threat of consumerism to gender ideology, 304; literacy, 320–1; slave women experiences, 350–1, 353–5; treatment in New France, 382; consumer revolution leads to lowering in status of Native American women, 424–5; and voting rights, 454–5; consequences of French and Indian War, 500; *see also* families
Woodward, Dr Henry, 373
woolen industry, 229, 241, 245, 250, 251
Woolman, John, 366
Worcester, 432
writing: Mayan system, 6–7
Wyandots, 385, 415, 477, 484
Wyatt, Sir Francis, 72, 73

Yacomicos, 122
Yale, 308, 311, 321, 373
Yamacraws, 440
Yamasee War (1715), 200, 220–1, 361, 420, 421
Yamasees: background, 149, 416; attack Florida, 200, 219, 374; migrate to Florida after Yamasee War, 397, 417, 440
Yeamans, Sir John, 151, 152, 153
Yeardley, George, 68–9, 76
York, Maine, 99, 203

Zacatecas, 375
Zenger, John Peter, 447, 459, 468, 471
Zheng He, 33